JACKIE
ETHEL
JOAN

JACKIE ETHEL JOAN

WOMEN OF CAMELOT

J. RANDY TARABORRELLI

WARNER BOOKS

A Time Warner Company

Warner Books, Inc., 1271 Avenue of the Americas,
New York, NY 10020

Visit our Web site at www.twbookmark.com

 A Time Warner Company

Printed in the United States of America
First Warner Books Printing: February 2000
10 9 8 7 6 5 4 3 2

Library of Congress Cataloging-in-Publication Data

Taraborrelli, J. Randy
    Jackie, Ethel, Joan : women of Camelot / J. Randy Taraborrelli.
        p.   cm.
    ISBN 0-446-52426-3
    1. Onassis, Jacqueline Kennedy, 1929– 2. Kennedy, Ethel,
1928– 3. Kennedy, Joan Bennett. 4. Presidents' spouses—United
States—Biography. 5. Legislators' spouses—United States—
Biography. I. Title.

E843.K4 T35 2000
973.922'0922—dc21
[B]
                                                        99-051800

As always, for
Rose Marie Taraborrelli

A Note from the Author

Considering the many hundreds of books published about members of the Kennedy family over the last forty years, it's surprising that no author before me has attempted an in-depth examination of the relationships among the sisters-in-law, Jackie Bouvier Kennedy, Ethel Skakel Kennedy, and Joan Bennett Kennedy. While it had been long assumed by some observers that no connection existed among the three women, I always believed that their lives—as well as those of their families—were so completely transformed by marrying three of Joseph P. Kennedy's sons that there would at least be some interesting interplay among them. And if there were no relationship at all, I decided, then the reasons for such estrangement could also prove to be interesting. As it turned out, much to my fascination, they related to one another very much like sisters—sometimes lovingly, sometimes contentiously.

The concept behind this book has been an interest of mine for many years, dating back to January 1980 when, as a Los Angeles magazine reporter specializing in African-American pop culture, I was given the unusual assignment to write a series of articles about the Kennedy family's relationship with that of Martin Luther King Jr.'s for a magazine called *Soul* (which I would later edit and publish). As part of my research, I not only interviewed King's widow, Coretta Scott-King (excerpts of which are included in this text), I also conducted a number of personal interviews and had many conversations with long-time Kennedy family friend and unofficial historian Kirk LeMoyne "Lem" Billings. At first I found Lem to be a difficult and conflicted person, but I later learned that his complexities were the result of his loving but often ambivalent relationship with the powerful Kennedy family. As a college roommate of John Kennedy's and constant companion to many family members, he was a fountain of information for me and—as I found out after conducting hundreds of interviews with others—he was accurate in just about every observation he ever made about any of the Kennedys.

He told me one story that I didn't use in the text of this book, but it illustrates the kind of relationship he had with Jack and Jackie.

Lem was a big fan of Greta Garbo's, whom he had once met at the Cannes Film Festival. "I was obsessed with her," he told me, "and couldn't stop talking about her for quite some time. Jackie told me she was sick of hearing about her. I couldn't blame her."

The President and First Lady decided to play a practical joke on Lem. They invited Greta Garbo to the White House for a private dinner. They also invited Lem. When he showed up, he found his idol, Garbo, casually sitting with Jack and Jackie, talking and laughing as if they were old friends (which they weren't). Lem was astonished. "Why, Greta! Oh my gosh. How are you?" he said excitedly. After the actress had sized Lem up from head to toe as only Greta Garbo could, she turned to Jackie and, in her most imperious tone, said, "Who *is* this man?" (Many years later, in the 1980s, Jackie would tell her secretary and close friend Nancy Tuckerman that she herself was fascinated by Garbo, so much so that she once followed her through the streets of New York for ten blocks "before she finally lost me.")

When Lem died of a heart attack at the age of sixty-five in May 1981, the Kennedys paid tribute to him at his funeral. "Yesterday was Jack's birthday," Eunice Kennedy Shriver said in her moving eulogy. "Jack's best friend was Lem, and he would want me to remind everyone of that today. I am sure the good Lord knows that heaven is Jesus and Lem and Jack and Bobby loving one another." At the time of our interviews, though, it seemed that Lem Billings's status in the family was in jeopardy as a result of personal disagreements. "I think they hate me now" is how the emotionally charged Billings put it to me. "I doubt they ever appreciated me. To the Kennedys, the line between love and hate is not only thin, it's blurred. But love knows many paths," he concluded, "and always finds its way back to the right heart."

I was deeply touched by Lem Billings's devotion to the Kennedys, troubled by his strained relationship with them, and also inspired by his optimism that somehow it would all work out for the best. I quickly became intrigued by his recollections that—politics aside—the Kennedy family was like most large families, in that loving relationships often gave way to conflict and then usually—or at least hope-fully—to reconciliation.

I decided to research and then write an in-depth article about Jackie, Ethel, and Joan. My intention was that the resulting feature would be candid enough to relay the kinds of stories that would be identifiable to anyone who has ever watched as his or her own family, regardless of wealth or status, grew and its members interacted with one another during difficult times. After just a few interviews with key people in the Kennedy circle, the story of the three sisters-in-law quickly began to emerge.

My career as a reporter took a different turn when, in 1984, I signed with Doubleday and Company to write my first book, a biography of Diana Ross. Throughout the years, as I wrote a number of other books, I continued developing the story of Jackie, Ethel, and Joan Kennedy, hoping to one day find a publisher for the work. Like most things having to do with the publishing business, the timing had to be right, the research completed, and the publisher willing—all of which finally occurred after my eighth book, *Sinatra: A Complete Life*, was published in 1997. It was then that Warner Books publisher Maureen Mahon Egen agreed with my ICM agent, Mitch Douglas, that it was time to publish this work, which was originally titled *The Kennedy Wives*. Over a two-year period, Ms. Egen masterfully helped me shape the manuscript into the book you are now holding in your hands, *Jackie, Ethel, Joan: Women of Camelot*.

Jackie Bouvier Kennedy, Ethel Skakel Kennedy, and Joan Bennett Kennedy were strong and courageous women who, despite the many challenges presented them, still managed to lead full, joyous lives. Over the years that I dedicated myself to this work, I found their stories to be heartwarming and moving. This was truly a labor of love for me; I became personally attached to these women in a way perhaps only another biographer can relate to. It is now my hope that the reader will recognize just a bit of his or her own familial experience in the complex relationships among the Kennedy sisters-in-law because, power, politics, and money aside, people are still people, families are families . . . and most of us, at one time or another, have to work to get along with those we dearly love. In the end, at least in my view, it's always worth it.

Contents

JACKIE
ETHEL
JOAN

"Even though people may be well known, they hold in their hearts the emotions of a simple person for the moments that are the most important of those we know on earth: birth, marriage, and death."

—Jackie Kennedy
October 1968

Prologue:
Long Live the Queen

It was a somber Monday morning in May 1994, when the friends and family of Jacqueline Bouvier Kennedy Onassis gathered at St. Ignatius Loyola Roman Catholic Church in New York City for a final farewell to her. It wasn't easy for anyone to say good-bye to this remarkable woman—those who knew her well, those who loved her dearly, and the rest of the world, fans and skeptics alike, who had watched her extraordinary life unfold over the years.

Though she was an accomplished woman with a wide scope of personal experiences, her friends realized that Jackie's greatest source of pride was the way she had raised her two children, John and Caroline. When they were grown, she then found satisfaction as a book editor for two major publishing companies, Viking and then Doubleday: simply another working woman fetching her own coffee rather than troubling her assistant with such a task.

In truth, she must have known that she was much more than just another nine-to-five member of the Manhattan workforce. After all, she had been married to a president. She had been the First Lady. She had traveled the world in grand style, met with kings and queens, lived in luxury and wealth, never wanted for much (at least in terms of the material), and experienced the intense love and unabashed adoration—and, of course, criticism—of millions of people, just for being who she was: Jackie. Though her last name was now Onassis, she was still Jackie Kennedy to everyone who remembered a certain time . . . a certain place.

Once, long ago, though it seemed like just yesterday, Jackie had been the queen of what was the brightest and best of Camelot: the mythical kingdom she took as an emblem of the Kennedy years when she spoke to a journalist in the days after her husband, John Fitzgerald

Kennedy, was brutally cut down in his prime, shot to death as he sat next to her in an automobile in Dallas in 1963. As First Lady, and even beyond her classic reign over this so-called Camelot, she was a woman whose style, personality, and refinement had made such an indelible imprint on our culture that she actually seemed immortal—which was why her death was such a shock. If it was sometimes difficult to remember that she was a woman—flesh and blood like the rest of us—her mortality, the result of the very human and unforgiving disease, cancer, was an all-too-cruel reminder.

Hundreds of mourners—friends, politicians, socialites, writers, artists, entertainment figures—as well as the many members of the Kennedy family came to bid a tearful adieu to Jackie and to remember their experiences with her. It was a funeral of deeply felt prayers, music, poetry, and warm feelings in the same great marble New York church in which the former First Lady had been baptized and confirmed.

"It was a service that Jackie would have loved," said Joan Kennedy afterward, "full of meaning, full of genuine emotion. If you knew Jackie, you knew that there was nothing insincere about her."

Perhaps no one understood Jackie better than her Kennedy sisters-in-law, Ethel and Joan, for the three of them shared the special burden of having married into a powerful, ambitious, and often confounding family. Like sisters, they would reach out to one another over the years to comfort and console during times of immeasurable disappointment and pain. And, like sisters, they were also known to accuse and attack one another. However, throughout the Camelot years of the 1960s they would forge a sisterhood, sometimes against great odds.

Ethel and Joan likely would never forget what Jackie had meant to them. As Ted Kennedy delivered the eulogy, his ex-wife, Joan, must have been reminded of Jackie's patience and kindness to her during the many challenges presented by a life sometimes gone awry. "She was a blessing to us, and to the nation, and a lesson to the world on how to do things right," said the senior senator from Massachusetts. Joan had been able to depend on her older sister-in-law for a sympathetic ear and sensible advice. Now, with the finality of Jackie's death, Joan might find it difficult to reconcile the fleeting passage of years.

Sitting with her large family, Ethel seemed contemplative and understandably saddened this morning. Through the years, her relationship with her sister-in-law had been complex, a mixture of admiration, respect, and understanding, as well as envy and the inevitable contentiousness that arises from vast differences in temperament. As often happens in life, the two sisters-in-law allowed a personal disagreement to come between them. With the passing of time, their difficult estrangement became the natural order of things, almost a habit. Still, inextricably bound to Jackie by tradition and history, a visibly shaken Ethel Kennedy was present at her sister-in-law's bedside in New York the day that non-Hodgkins lymphoma took her from this world.

At just sixty-four years old, Jackie most certainly was gone too soon—"too young to be a widow in 1963, and too young to die now," as Ted Kennedy put it in his stirring eulogy. Just as she had requested, she was laid to rest on a verdant hillside in Arlington National Cemetery beside the eternal flame she herself had lit thirty-one years earlier for her husband. As their mother's mahogany casket, covered with ferns and a cross of white lilies, was placed next to the final resting place of their father, Caroline and John Jr. knelt at the graveside and fought back tears in the stoic manner known to all Kennedys. On either side were buried Jackie's stillborn daughter, Arabella, and infant son, Patrick.

"God gave her very good gifts," intoned President Bill Clinton at the graveside, "and imposed upon her great burdens. She bore them all with dignity and grace and uncommon common sense. . . . May the flame she lit so long ago burn ever brighter here and always brighter in our hearts." The President concluded, "God bless you, friend, and farewell."

For Jackie Kennedy Onassis it had been a life of joy, laughter, and fairy-tale endings, as well as despair, sadness, and tragedy—much of it shared in common experience with her sisters-in-law, Ethel Skakel Kennedy and Joan Bennett Kennedy.

There is much to remember of a time that was like no other. Indeed, even after all these years, we still look back with wonder.

PART ONE

Joan . . .

Young Joan Bennett Kennedy gazed out upon a cold but clear Cape Cod morning from the veranda of the large three-story clapboard house owned by her in-laws, Rose and Joseph P. Kennedy. Ignoring the many friends, family members, photographers, and Secret Service agents coming and going, rushing in and out of the house and slamming the screen door behind them, she quietly slipped into a knee-length wool coat before wrapping a silk scarf around her head. As she walked down the porch's few wooden steps, she tied the scarf below her chin to keep her blonde hair from being mussed by unpredictable ocean breezes. After a stroll across an expansive, well-manicured lawn, and then down a wood-chipped pathway, she found herself on the sandy coves where the Kennedys went to seek rare moments of privacy and reflection. Joan walked along the shore of wild dune grass and sand, and slowly headed for the breakwater.

It was November 9, 1960. In what would turn out to be the closest election race in American history once all the votes were tabulated, Joan's brother-in-law John Fitzgerald Kennedy had been elected thirty-fifth President of the United States. In fact, he had received only about 100,000 more popular votes than Richard M. Nixon, out of some 103 million cast, the equivalent of about one vote per precinct. This close call would find Jack ensconced in the most powerful office in the world—a lot to take in for any member of Kennedy's close-knit family but especially for Joan, the least politically inclined of them all.

As Joan walked along the beach, other family members celebrated Jack's victory in a fashion so typical of the Kennedys: by playing a raucous game of touch football in Rose and Joseph's sprawling, beachfront yard. William Walton, an old friend of the family who had assisted Jack in the campaign and who was now his and Jackie's house guest, was on one of the teams. He recalled, "That family had the meanest football players ever put together. The girls were worse than the men; they'd claw, scratch, and bite when they played touch football. Playing to win was a family characteristic. Jack, Bobby, Teddy, Peter Lawford, Eunice and Ethel . . . tough players, all."

"That's my brother Jack," Bobby said with a laugh as the new President fumbled the ball. "All guts, no brains." The President-elect, dressed in a heavy sweater over a sport shirt, tan slacks, and loafers, took a tumble. As he raised himself from the soft ground, his shock of auburn hair mussed and his blue eyes twinkling, he looked more like a high school student than the next leader of the Free World. The only reminder of his age—forty-three—and his aching back was the groan he let out as he got to his feet.

Joan, the youngest Kennedy wife at twenty-four, had arrived the night before from her home in Boston, without her boyishly handsome husband, Ted. He showed up in the morning by plane from the West Coast where, as the campaign's Rocky Mountain coordinator, he had been given charge of thirteen states—ten of which had been lost, including the most important, California. Joan had been up late. At midnight, she was still at Ethel and Bobby's with the rest of the family, monitoring election results. Exhausted, Jackie and Jack had already retired to their own home, though Jack kept popping over to his brother's throughout the early morning hours to get updates. When it looked as though a win was probable for her brother-in-law, Joan became caught up in the excitement and started calling Republican friends on the telephone to collect election bets. "Pay up," she told one chum in Boston. "I told you he'd win." (Later that morning it wouldn't look quite as promising for the Kennedys when Jack's lead began to dwindle, but eventually the slim margin would be decided in his favor.)

Joan and Ted were parents of a baby daughter, Kara, born in February of that year. They had been married for a little over two years and were about to move from their first home—a modest town house in Louisburg Square, the most exclusive part of Beacon Hill—into a three-story, ivy-covered, redbrick house, one of fifteen others in a horseshoe-shaped enclave in nearby Charles River Square. Ted had actually wanted to move to California to get out of his brothers' shadow and away from the overwhelming Kennedy family influence. In fact, when he and Joan went there to look for a home, Joan enjoyed the West Coast so much she began to anticipate a contented life there, with the large family she hoped to one day raise in year-round California sunshine. However, much to her dismay, the Kennedy patriarch, Joseph, wouldn't hear of such a move. He suggested—insisted, actually—that the newlyweds return to the Washington area. As Joan would tell it, "And that was the end of *that*." She expressed amazement at Ted's compliance and the way he changed their plans without another word being spoken about it, even to his own wife.

A year and a half earlier, the family and its advisers sat down at Joseph Kennedy's dining-room table in his Palm Beach estate and, over a lunch of roast turkey and stuffing, decided that Jack would run for highest office. (Joan, who had just one sibling, once wondered aloud, "Why is it that large families always make big decisions while eating lots of food?") It was then that Ted abandoned any long-range goals for himself, at least for the foreseeable future. Though he had graduated from Harvard, had received his law degree from the University of Virginia Law School, and had been admitted to the Massachusetts bar, he and his father decided that he would not practice law. Rather, he would devote himself to active political work on behalf of his brother's presidential campaign. A month after their daughter Kara was born, a still-weak Joan joined Ted on the campaign trail, probably not because she wanted to but because she had no choice. Still recovering from a difficult pregnancy, she couldn't possibly have found the idea of dragging herself and her infant from one state to the next the least bit appealing. In fact, she would confide to certain friends of hers that she thought it was "unfair of the family to expect me to go." Joan didn't last very long on the campaign trail with Ted—and then, later, with Ethel—but certainly not for lack of trying.

The election of John Kennedy was an exciting milestone for the family, and of course, Joan joined in their enthusiasm. However, she must have had certain reservations. From the day she became engaged to Ted, her life was not her own. He and his family had overpowered her, from dictating the kind of wedding she would have to deciding where she would live—and that was before Jack had become President. Now that he had won the election and the family was even more influential, the Kennedys had more ambitious plans for Ted. So what would the future hold for her and her family? As she later put it, "I wondered if I would ever be who I really wanted to be, who I was inside, or would I have to conform in some unnatural way. With that family, I found out fast that if you didn't join in . . . you were just left out."

————————————

Jackie . . .

Out in the distant vista of space and sea, Joan saw a slender female figure standing on the beach, facing the rolling ocean. Long arms wrapped around herself and slim shoulders hunched forward, she appeared to be trying to keep the Nantucket Sound chill at bay. It was Joan's thirty-one-year-old sister-in-law, Jacqueline Bouvier Kennedy.

Wearing a beige raincoat, flat-heeled walking shoes, and a scarf around her hair, Jackie, too, had slipped away while the others played touch football. She rarely, if ever, participated in such family rough-housing. Luckily for her, she was nearly eight months pregnant and not expected to play sports, even by the always competitive, game-loving Kennedys. "She seemed completely dazed as people kept coming over to her to congratulate her, to talk about what had happened, to just share in the joy of it all," recalls Jacques Lowe, the family's photographer, who documented official as well as candid moments on that day. "It was too much to take. She needed to get away."

Jackie Kennedy was the kind of woman who lived her life fully, getting as much from each day's experiences as possible and savoring every moment along the way. While being the wife of a senator had obviously afforded her a certain amount of respect and prestige in which she had delighted, becoming the country's First Lady promised an even headier adventure. However, Jackie was known for her paradoxical personality. As would later become well known, she enjoyed recognition yet abhorred publicity. While she savored her celebrity, she expected her privacy and that of her family to be respected. True, she enjoyed money, power, and status, but she placed equal importance on practical female concerns of the day, such as raising her family and being a good wife.

By this time, November 1960, Jackie had one child, two-year-old Caroline. That morning, she prompted the tot to greet her father at breakfast by saying "Good morning, Mr. President." In seventeen days, Jackie would give premature birth to a boy at Georgetown University Hospital, John Fitzgerald Kennedy, Jr., nicknamed "John-John" by the press. The baby would be so sickly at birth, it would be thought that he wouldn't survive. However, in time, he would grow to be strong and healthy, like most Kennedy stock. Just after his birth, Jackie would move from her home in Georgetown to a new one in Washington, the White House.

Jackie's greatest concern about becoming First Lady had to do with the scrutiny her new position was sure to guarantee her and her family. She had become aware of her duty to be accessible to the press— or at least appear to be that way—early on in her husband's campaign. When she watched Jack's historic debate against his opponent, Richard Nixon, on television in her Hyannis Port living room, she was joined by twenty-five reporters and photographers. They sat with her and took note of her every "oooh" and "aaah," in the hope of divining her opinion of his performance. "It was so dreary," she later recalled, using a favorite phrase.

Meeting with some of the female members of the Washington press corps in her Georgetown home was undoubtedly another memorable event for Jackie. A few had intimated that if she didn't invite them to her home, they might not be kind to Jack in their reporting. Jackie probably knew that once they had a chance to become more familiar with her, they would become allies. However, the prospect of their trooping through her private residence must have been repugnant to her. Like her sister-in-law, Joan, Jackie was obviously not happy doing things she didn't want to do, just to benefit her husband's political future, but for Jack and his family she would often be asked to subordinate her own desires. So Jackie had some of the more important female reporters over for tea and, true to form, proceeded to dazzle each one of them.

The media's euphoria about Jackie would not last long. Soon the press would be criticizing everything she did, from how much money she spent on clothing to how much time she spent away from the White House. Throughout her life she would engage in a love-hate relationship with the press, seemingly reveling in the fact that everywhere she went she was recognized and photographed, yet also acting as if she detested the attention, never revealing more of herself than absolutely necessary. After Jack was elected, Bess Truman said of Jackie, "I think she will be a perfect First Lady. But she drops a curtain in front of you. No one will ever get to know her." When Jackie brought her new German Shepherd puppy, Clipper, on a flight from Hyannis Port to Washington, a journalist sent her a note asking what she intended to feed the dog. She responded with one word: "Reporters."

The salty air and crisp breeze of the southern Cape had always seemed to invigorate Jackie Kennedy on her solitary walks along the beach during times of confusion. It was one of the few things she had in common with the other Kennedys—and one other Kennedy wife. Joan finally caught up with her sister-in-law. Sharing a smile, the two women walked together along the shore.

Ethel . . .

Bobby Kennedy cocked back his arm and sent a pass sailing off to his athletic wife, Ethel. "I've got it. I've got it," she hollered as she positioned herself right under the dropping football. Ethel's prowess in sports had always been a marvel. After catching the ball gracefully, she let out a loud "Yes sir, kiddo!" and then spiked it to the sand. She began jumping about, arms raised to the sky, hands shaking in the air, in her own victory dance. Certainly few were filled with more joy on this chilly November election day than Ethel Kennedy. If she had a care in the world, it wasn't obvious.

Not really a contemplative woman, Ethel Skakel Kennedy seemed always eager to meet her destiny head-on. She experienced life for all it was worth, much like Jackie. However, whereas Jackie (and, to a certain extent, Joan) needed meditative moments to analyze her problems, sort out inner turmoil, and then determine productive courses of action, Ethel surrendered all responsibility for her life to God. It was easier for her to handle unexpected circumstances that way, she had said, and it worked for her.

Thirty-one-year-old Ethel's brood already numbered seven: Kathleen Hartington, Joseph Patrick, Robert Francis, Jr., David Anthony, Mary Courtney, Michael LeMoyne, and Mary Kerry (two girls named Mary!), all born in the last eight years.

Ethel and Bobby lived in a rambling two-story home in a McLean, Virginia, estate known as Hickory Hill. The white-brick Georgian manor—which was once the Civil War headquarters of Union General George B. McClellan and now included stables, orchards, and a swimming pool—was always filled with children, friends, family, business associates, and anyone else who happened by. Ethel loved to entertain. Jackie and Jack had lived at Hickory Hill first; it was rumored that Joseph had given the six-acre estate to them as a gift, but Jack had actually purchased it himself. Jackie had planned to raise her children there; however, when she had a stillbirth in 1956, she no longer wanted anything to do with Hickory Hill. So after Jack lost a bid for the vice-presidential nomination in 1956, the couple moved back to Georgetown. Meanwhile, Ethel and Bobby bought Hickory Hill.

Ethel was complex. She could be as critical as she could be accepting, as heartless as she could be generous, as wicked as she could be loving. Moreover, even though the Kennedys were known to be competitive (and not only with outsiders but also against each other), her aggressive nature was a source of amazement even to family members. Jackie liked to say, "Ethel loves politics so much, I think she could be the first female president, and then, God help us all."

Whereas Jackie and Joan worried about the encroachment into their personal lives that would result from Jack's election—not only from outsiders, but also from the family itself—Ethel had no such concerns. She actually seemed to enjoy the intrusion. The more chaos in her life, the better; it seemed to make her feel involved, a part of important things. She would do whatever she had to do in the name of "Kennedy" because family loyalty was paramount to her. Hers was no ordinary family, either. The Kennedys held an important station in life, were influential in government, and had, as they say, "friends in high places." She once explained, "Whatever my problems were, they didn't matter. In the bigger picture, we were doing great things for the nation. How dare I complain about a lack of privacy?"

If she had to host reporters for lunch, Ethel would lie awake the night before—not fretting the occasion, as Jackie or Joan would have done, but anticipating every moment, anxious to do her best to represent her husband and his family in the best possible light. She would be sure to know the right meal to serve, the perfect outfit to wear, the appropriate thing to say. In the end, the success of the event would be not only a victory for the family but a personal one as well, giving her a sense of purpose and accomplishment.

In fact, the preceding evening, at just before midnight, Ethel Kennedy was in her bedroom, dressed in brightly patterned wool slacks, holding an impromptu press conference with reporters from *Time* and *Life* magazines. The journalists had been staying in Rose and Joseph's servants' quarters for the last couple of nights.

"Are you happy, Ethel?" one writer asked her.

"Oh, I sure am," she answered enthusiastically. "It's terrific. This is the day we've been waiting for, the happiest day of our lives." After a few more questions, Ethel told the press to "go on downstairs and get some food. Go ahead, help yourself." She loved the press, and in return, the reporters loved her.

As far as her father-in-law's dictates were concerned, Ethel would gladly live where he wanted her to live, say what he wanted her to say, and do what he wanted her to do—not grudgingly, but willingly. It all seemed a joy to Ethel. It wasn't that she lacked an identity; she was a Kennedy wife, she was proud of it, and that was her identity. Though she had been up late the night before with the family, that didn't stop her from doing her duty and rising at 6:30 A.M. to fix a breakfast of ham and eggs, rolls, and coffee for the eleven guests staying at her home. "The maids are all out," she explained, as her visitors devoured the meal. "So I did the best I could."

"You know, in November [1962], I think Bobby may run for governor of Massachusetts," Ethel had told Jackie a couple of weeks earlier at a family dinner. "If he does, he's bound to win. Then after that, it'll be one step at a time, until *we're* in the White House."

"Does Bobby know of these plans?" Jackie asked her sister-in-law. Jackie had been given to understand that he would become Jack's Attorney General. After all, Bobby had devoted the better part of recent years to his brother's campaigns and had been the skilled manager of his presidential run. A tireless worker, he gave uninterrupted eighteen-hour days to Jack's race, so much so that Ethel was concerned he would have a breakdown. Throughout the night before, Bobby sat in front of the television screen, his eyes red-rimmed and

hollow, monitoring the returns, while everyone else—even Jack—-
went to bed.

Ethel answered Jackie's question: "Bobby and I discuss everything,"
she said. "You see, *we* happen to be close that way. It's nice, that kind
of closeness in a relationship."

Ethel's probable implication was that Jackie had no influence over
her husband's plans, whereas Ethel mapped out every one of Bobby's
career moves in tandem with him. "Well," Jackie responded, "hopefully you will also discuss any plans with Grandpa [Joseph]. Because, as
you and I both know, he's the one who will have his way in the end.
Not you. Not Bobby. Grandpa."

. . . and the Secret Service

Like all of those in the Kennedy family, Jackie, Joan, and even, to a
certain extent, Ethel treasured the privacy of their family lives—what
little privacy they had while living in the public eye. However, the entire family realized that the spotlight was about to intensify, now that
their beloved Jack was the nation's Chief Executive.

Already the family compound of homes was surrounded by not
only reporters but also the Secret Service agents responsible for John
Kennedy's security and for that of his family. Sixteen of these dark-
suited, officious-looking men had arrived at seven that morning with
full knowledge of the backgrounds of not only family members but
their employees as well. Each agent walked about the compound
greeting people as if already having made their acquaintance when
actually—at least in most cases—no introductions had been made
before this day.

Like all First Ladies, Jackie would be assigned her own Secret Service agent, Clinton (Clint) J. Hill, who would be at her side whenever
she ventured forth, whether in this country or abroad. In time, just by
virtue of their constant association, "Dazzle" (his Secret Service code
name) would come to share a special friendship with "Lace" (Jackie's
code name). Still, it was typical of Jackie's sense of formality that she

would always refer to him as "Mr. Hill." She also made certain that her children addressed the agents responsible for their well-being in the same fashion.

Clint Hill recalls, "When you're with the wife of the President, you're pretty much on your own, without a lot of other Secret Service support. You become close, as Mrs. Kennedy and I did. It was really an invasion of privacy for her. She lost her freedom. If a woman hasn't been in a position that required great security prior, which she had not, it's something that is very new and causes problems for her. She hated it."

As Jackie and Joan continued their walk along the sandy Cape Cod shore, according to what Joan later told friends, they talked about the future. "I wonder what will happen to us now," Jackie said. "What will happen to our children? Will we ever have any privacy again?"

Just as Jackie was posing her question regarding privacy, Joan turned around to find three Secret Service agents running toward her. In seconds, one of the men caught up to her and Jackie. Wearing a dark business suit, thin black tie, and black hat, he must have looked out of place on the beach with his walkie-talkie. "Maybe you should both go back to the Big House," he suggested, using the family's name for Rose and Joseph's home. Clearly, he didn't like idea of the two of them walking along the beach alone. "You do have a press conference soon. Just a reminder . . ."

"Well, there you have it," Joan said to Jackie. "Does that answer your question?"

"Oh, how dreary," Jackie responded. "I'll tell you one thing: I will not be followed by these men for the next four years. I refuse to allow it."

Jackie turned to face Clint Hill. "I *refuse*," she repeated.

Ignoring the agent's request, the two young women continued their walk in the bracing, sea-charged air—with the three identically dressed Secret Service men trailing close enough behind to hear their conversation.

"So what do you think about Ted's plans?" Jackie asked Joan.

Unlike Ethel, Joan barely had a clue what her husband—and his father—had in mind for the future. She knew that Ted was being groomed to run for Jack's senatorial seat in 1962, but she could provide no details. He mentioned something about leaving for Europe soon for a six-week fact-finding tour with a Senate Foreign Relations Committee unit. However, all Joan knew about that trip was that she would not be accompanying him. (Upon his return, Ted would end up taking a job as a dollar-a-year assistant district attorney of Suffolk County in Massachusetts while he prepared for his senatorial campaign.) There would always be a marked difference between the wives in terms of how they related to their husbands, and nowhere was it more evident than in Joan's ignorance of her husband's plans. Contrary to what Ethel liked to believe, Jack always discussed his future intentions with Jackie, just as much as his brother, Bobby, did with Ethel. Not so with Joan and Ted.

"Ted doesn't tell me anything," Joan said as she and Jackie walked along. "Usually I get my information through the grapevine. And when I ask him about it, he treats me as if I wouldn't understand what he was talking about." Jackie merely shook her head. If Joan had asked for advice, Jackie would perhaps have given her some. She didn't ask, however, so Jackie didn't offer.

"Well, at least we have some good parties coming up," the incoming First Lady offered, changing the subject. Jackie, who always enjoyed social gatherings, was referring to the balls, receptions, and other inaugural festivities that would usher in the new administration. When one considers that this was 1960 America, with all that that involved—the Cold War, growing tensions in Cuba, a communist regime sixty miles off the coast, the Civil Rights movement, a supposed missile and arms gap, nuclear proliferation, and the expansion of the Soviet sphere of influence—Jackie's observation appears in a strange light. Above all else, at the outset of this administration the new First Lady seemed to be looking forward to balls and parties. Even the Secret Service agents thought this was odd, though they weren't supposed to be listening.

Joan stopped walking. "Oh, my God," she exclaimed. "I have nothing to wear. What will I wear?"

"Oh, the ever-so-important details," Jackie said with a laugh. She had already started planning her wardrobe with her couturier, Oleg Cassini.

"So how's it shaping up?" Joan asked.

"Why, it's wonderful," Jackie said. "In fact, I'm completely overwhelmed by my own good taste."

The two sisters-in-law dissolved into laughter. Jackie hooked her arm around Joan's. Then, as the good friends turned and began to walk back to the Big House, Jackie nestled her head on Joan's shoulder.

Jack Defeats Nixon

The so-called Kennedy compound, where the family had congregated to await the results of the 1960 election, was actually a triangle of large Cape Cod–style houses separated by a common, meticulously kept lawn. At one corner of the triangle was the Big House on Scudder Avenue, a large seventeen-room home with green shutters, facing Nantucket Sound, which had belonged to Joseph and his wife Rose since 1926. Their eldest living son, Jack, and his wife Jackie owned a smaller home a hundred yards away on Irving Avenue, surrounded by hedges. Another hundred yards across Jack's back lawn was the middle son Bobby's home. The youngest male sibling, Ted, and his wife Joan would purchase a home on Squaw Island, a peninsula about a mile from the compound, in March 1961. These were all summer homes—typical white-clapboard New England structures that looked like large oceanfront hotels, which were usually closed up after the Christmas holidays. For election day, Bobby's house had been utilized as a makeshift campaign post, complete with telephones linked to Democratic headquarters all across the nation, televisions, Teletype machines, fourteen secretaries, and a vote-tabulating machine, all set up in Ethel's dining room.

On the afternoon of the presidential victory, the entire Kennedy family was scheduled to go by motorcade to the Hyannis Armory, which had been converted into a pressroom. There, about four hundred television, radio, and print reporters from around the world had been waiting for hours for an opportunity to share in the family's victory and to hear the new President and First Lady speak. "There were so many of them and they were all so charismatic, it seemed even more newsworthy," recalls Helen Thomas, who has been UPI's White House bureau chief since 1961 and the first woman to be elected an officer of the National Press Club. "People were fascinated by them. It wasn't just as if we had elected a man into office. In some odd way, it was as if we had given national approval to a new dynasty."

Before the press conference, the family gathered at Rose's for a lunch of tuna-, lobster-, chicken-, and egg-salad sandwiches; the kinds of "simple foods" they most often favored for lunches on the Cape, all leftovers from the night before when the Mayflower Catering Service had provided a buffet at Ethel's for campaign workers. For dessert, they enjoyed a nice assortment of petits fours, eclairs, and turnovers. Afterward, the casually dressed Kennedys would need to change clothing quickly for the media.

With his eye on the historical value of having the family together on such an important day, young Jacques Lowe—who had been Jack Kennedy's official and personal photographer since his reelection to the Senate in 1958—wanted nothing more than to take a family photograph for posterity. "I knew that if I wanted to do it, though, I'd have to do it rather quickly," he recalls some thirty-five years later. "You couldn't get them all in the same room at the same time, let alone have them pose for a picture. It was all just that hectic. As they raced about, I asked this family member and that one whether we could all get together for a picture, and everyone kept saying 'Later, Jacques, later.' Finally, I spoke to Joe, and he agreed with me. A photo should be taken." Joseph then ordered everyone to be suitably attired for posterity and to meet in the library.

Half an hour later, the family drifted in, the men (except for Peter Lawford, Jack's sister Pat's husband) in dark business suits with the requisite amount of white handkerchief showing in the breast pocket. The women had their own version of the uniform. Jewelry consisted of pearls, either one or two strands, and/or a tasteful gold pin worn close to the right shoulder. Earrings should be inconspicuous enough to be barely noticed. All the ladies wore black or gray long-sleeved dresses or suits, with two notable exceptions: Rose and Ethel. Rose wore a bright red short-sleeved sheath dress, which highlighted her still slim figure; it would be sure to stand out against all the dark clothes everyone else was wearing. Ethel appeared in a bright pink dress with matching sweater. Not only did the color clash with her mother-in-law's outfit, but she also wore a shade of pink that Rose occasionally claimed as her own because it matched her name. (Rose was probably too excited by the importance of the occasion to make mention of it to Ethel, however.)

Everyone was there but Jackie. "Jackie was always late," says

Jacques Lowe, laughing. Because she had gone for another walk along the beach, she was delayed in getting ready for the photo session. But the wait was worth it when she finally appeared at the door, stunning in a sleeveless maternity dress in a shade that just matched her mother-in-law's and made her look radiant, with two strands of pearls and a pin. "Oh, my, is everyone here already?" she said.

Jack, magnificently tanned and looking fit in his dark suit, stood up and walked to the entryway to meet his wife. Taking her by the arm, he escorted her into the room, beaming with pride. As if on unspoken cue, the elderly Joseph stood up and began to applaud. Rose joined her husband, standing and applauding, then Bobby and Teddy followed suit. Soon the library was filled with cheers and whistles as the entire family gave Jackie Kennedy a rousing standing ovation, a heartfelt demonstration of their respect for her new position as the nation's First Lady.

"Oh," Jackie exclaimed, visibly moved by the overwhelming reception. "How absolutely wonderful."

As everyone applauded, Jackie stood in the center of the room, looking from person to person, making brief eye contact with each cheerful Kennedy face. All the while she grinned broadly, shaking her head in disbelief. She went to Rose and embraced her, then to Joseph. When she found Joan, who was clapping while standing alone in a corner, Jackie walked directly to her and kissed her on the check. After whispering something in her ear, the two women hugged each other.

Then, as the applause continued, Jackie worked her way to the other side of the library, embracing the Kennedy sisters, Eunice, Pat, and then Jean.

During the long campaign, the women born into the Kennedy family had become impatient with Jackie's stubborn reluctance to do press interviews and become chatty with reporters, feeling that she was shirking her responsibility as the wife of the candidate. The Kennedy sisters would do almost anything to get their pictures in the paper for, as far as they were concerned, every published article about them was helpful to their brother's cause and served to inch him—and them—just that much closer to the White House. They took after their mother, the family's matriarch, Rose, who, even at the age of seventy, never stopped touring the country, posing, speaking, shaking hands, and doing what was expected of all Kennedy women when their men were running for office. Rose had been the one to define the duties of the female members of the family by virtue of the fact that her experience as a campaigner went all the way back to her youth, when her father, the legendary "Honey Fitz," ran for mayor of Boston. Campaigning had always been an important part of the lives of these Kennedy women, and they expected Jackie to be just as excited about the traveling, the speeches (which were usually short and inconsequential), the photos—all of it.

"Those girls all looked and sounded like their brother Jack," recalls Liz Carpenter, Lady Bird Johnson's press secretary, who campaigned with Lady Bird and some of the Kennedy women, including Ethel, in six cities through Texas. "They all made speeches, used the word 'terrific' a lot. Everything was 'just terrific, kiddo.' They threw themselves into it, the Kennedy sisters, and Ethel fit right in, with high energy. In August of 1960, this Kennedy enthusiasm—all those bucked teeth and talk of 'vig-ah'—completely captivated Texas. In fact, we ended up carrying the state. Jackie wasn't there, though. So all you heard was, 'Where's Jackie? Where's Jackie?'"

The one Kennedy woman people seemed to care most about was the one who seemed the least interested: Jackie. This fact served only to exasperate further the rest of them. Poor Eunice, so politically savvy that her father Joe once said she could have been President herself if she'd only been "born with a set of balls," found herself at political tea parties answering inane questions about her sister-in-law's ever-changing hairstyles. "Well, she does change it a lot, doesn't she?" Eunice patiently agreed with one socialite. "However, I don't think she does it for any kind of effect, but rather because, well, she just likes her hair to be in different styles from time to time. I'm sure you understand." When the satisfied voter walked away, Eunice rolled her eyes.

Campaigning was difficult for Jackie, especially when she had to be in front of an audience. For instance, she had been asked to warm up the crowd before her husband made an appearance in Kenosha, Wisconsin. Completely unprepared to render a speech, she didn't know what to do, only that she would have to do something, and do it quickly. "Just get 'em singing," a campaign worker said to her as she walked nervously onto the stage.

Jackie Kennedy stood in the spotlight and, with her characteristic whisper, said, "Now come on, everybody, join me in this wonderful song." She then began singing a weak, tin-eared, *a cappella* version of "Southie Is My Old Hometown." This tune, apparently, was a popular one in Boston but nowhere else and, judging from the audience's reaction, definitely not in Kenosha. As Jackie sang, the crowd of potential voters sat before her slack-jawed and bewildered.

After Jackie was finished, she acknowledged a smattering of polite applause and hastily brought out her husband, the candidate, to wild cheers. "It was the most embarrassing moment of my life," Jackie cried afterward. "Well, I don't know about that," Jack said with a grin. "I thought you sounded rather tuneful." The next day, newspaper reporters made unkind jokes about Jackie's "unusual concert performance."

Luckily, because Jackie was pregnant, she was able to sit out the last few months of the campaign.

As frustrated as the Kennedy women were about Jackie, they were even more aggravated by Joan. Whereas Jackie was fully capable of doing what was expected of her but just didn't want to, Joan seemed emotionally unprepared to handle the rigors of campaigning. Despite her great beauty and vivacious personality, she was too shy and self-conscious to be an effective stumper.

In September, Joan and Ethel embarked on a trip to Chicago, where they spent three days attending rallies and meetings with female voters. Ethel was in her element and found it all exhilarating: meeting the voters, answering questions, talking about Jack, Bobby, and the family. A public relations strategist by instinct, Ethel fairly dragged Joan from meeting to meeting, prompting her in her answers, coaching and cajoling her every step of the way. By the time they left Chicago, Ethel was more exhausted by her tutoring of Joan than she was by the purpose of the trip itself.

When Joan was asked to appear on a television show with Lady Bird Johnson, she declined the invitation, explaining that she wouldn't know what to say. Ted was embarrassed by her lack of confidence and later chided her for it, which only added to her humiliation. He wanted her to satisfy his family's criteria for the perfect Kennedy woman, which meant that she should be able to handle herself in front of people, be charismatic and personable, and, if called upon to do so, appear on television and make it look like second nature.

In San Francisco, Joan joined her sister-in-law Pat at rallies and meetings, looking like a frightened child on the first day of grade school, while Pat displayed the kind of exuberance and public relations savvy for which the Kennedy women were well known.

Jean had just given birth in September to her second son, William Kennedy Smith, but that didn't stop her from replacing Joan at Ethel's side in Florida during the month of October. "Ethel and I are a great team," she told one packed audience, "because we have the same goal: to see John Fitzgerald Kennedy elected as President." As Ethel followed Jean on the podium, she smiled appreciatively at her, probably relieved to be paired finally with someone who could make an impact on voters. "Believe me when I tell you that the difference between Joan and Jean is a lot more than just a letter," she said later.

The impromptu standing ovation the Kennedy women gave Jackie in the library on the day Jack was elected was a clear acknowledgment that whatever their frustrations about her, they now recognized that she was the First Lady and thus deserved their respect. Also, the brief and personal moment Jackie shared with each of them was, in a sense, her recognition of the role they had played in her husband's successful campaign. After kissing Joan, Eunice, Pat, and Jean, Jackie finally reached Ethel. By the time she got to her, the applause had died down.

Jackie reached for Ethel. However, rather than melt into an embrace with Jackie, as had the other women, Ethel took a step backward and then held out her hand, palm down. After Jackie took it in hers, the two sisters-in-law shared an uncomfortable and brief moment, one that said a great deal about their uneasy relationship. Later that evening, in the presence of photographer Stanley Tretick at a photo session for the Kennedy women, Ethel would be overheard expressing concern that perhaps the family had afforded Jackie more preferential treatment than necessary by giving her such an ovation.

"Okay now," Jackie finally said, turning from Ethel, "let's take those pictures now, shall we?"

"Show us how they do it in Hollywood," Eunice joked to Peter Lawford, who crossed his eyes and made a face. Everyone laughed.

As the motorcade that would take the Kennedys to the Armory for the press conference began to form in front of the Big House, the family members inside busied themselves deciding who would sit where for the photograph. Two more photographers, Paul Schutzer of *Life* and Stanley Tretick of UPI, were invited to join Jacques Lowe in his work. "It was sheer bedlam, with all three of us shouting at the Kennedys," Lowe recalls. "'Look this way, Mr. Kennedy. Over here, Mrs. Kennedy.' It was just madness. Everyone was laughing, trying to figure out what to do, where to look. It was a wonderful, joyous time."

In the several photos taken that afternoon in the library, the entire Kennedy family—Rose and Joe, Jack and Jackie, Bobby and Ethel, Ted and Joan, Pat and her husband Peter Lawford, Eunice and Sargent Shriver, and Jean and Stephen Smith—look to the future with confidence, their faces frozen in bright smiles.

The Pre-Inaugural Gala

January 19, 1961, was the date on Jackie Kennedy's calendar that marked the Pre-Inaugural Gala at the National Guard Armory in Washington. Calling upon her "overwhelming good taste," the new First Lady had decided that she wanted to wear the color white for the occasion, and so, following her explicit instructions, Oleg Cassini designed a white, double-satin gown with elbow-length sleeves, princess-shaped bodice, and a two-part bell-shaped skirt. World-renowned hairdresser "Mr. Kenneth" (whose full name is Kenneth Battelle) was flown in from New York to create a hairstyle that he hoped would be dazzling with the dress.

It would be a new era of elegance in the White House; clearly, Jackie had already decided as much. The dowdy and dreadfully conservative Eisenhowers were "out." After eight years of that stuffy old guard, it was now time for youth, elegance, and glamour in Washington. All of Jackie's fashions would be original creations, she insisted to Cassini. "Make sure no one else wears exactly the same dress I do," she would write to him, adding that she did not want to see any "fat little women hopping around in the same dress."

This was a Big Night, and Jackie had always savored Big Nights. However, she was ill and weak after the recent cesarean section necessary for the arrival of John Jr. and not feeling at all well. Was she up to the task of re-creating herself, of masking any appearance of poor health and of radiating nothing but youthful, blooming vigor? As a public person, she believed it to be her responsibility to always be cordial, look her best, and pretend she felt that way even if she didn't. "You shake hundreds of hands in the afternoon and hundreds more at night," she said. "You get so tired, you catch yourself laughing and crying at the same time. But you pace yourself, and you get through it."

Oleg Cassini's shimmering winter-white satin gown turned out to be another lucky choice in the life of Jackie Kennedy, for the night of the Pre-Inaugural Presidential Gala (organized by Frank Sinatra and actor Peter Lawford) marked one of the biggest blizzards in Washington's history. In some ways, Jackie's superbly cut gown transformed the unfortunate snowstorm into a magical backdrop for a modern-day snow queen. By the time the Kennedys left for the gala, huge snowdrifts had brought the city to a standstill, but that didn't prevent hundreds of spectators from lining the streets, all straining to catch a glimpse of the glamorous First Couple as their limousine crept by at ten miles per hour.

When Sinatra heard that the Kennedy car was at last pulling up to the door, he rushed into the swirling snow to personally escort them inside. Jackie, her hair heavily lacquered to withstand the fiercest gusts, extended her white-gloved hand and Sinatra led her into the building.

At this time, it was no secret that Jackie disliked Frank Sinatra. She found the singer's personal style and behavior unseemly. On this point, she and Bobby were in wholehearted agreement. About three weeks after the Pre-Inaugural Gala, when Jack mentioned that he and Jackie should buy Sinatra a gift to thank him for his work on the campaign, Jackie would suggest a book of etiquette—"not that he would ever actually read such a thing."

However, this was such an important night—the kickoff to what would be her career as First Lady—that Jackie transcended her dislike for Sinatra. While flashbulbs popped all around her, the glamorous Mrs. Kennedy just smiled broadly as the handsome crooner led her to the raised presidential box.

Sinatra's friend Jim Whiting, who was a part of the singer's circle for years, recalls that "Sinatra once told me that when he was escorting her to the box, she may have been all smiles, but she was very tense. She was gripping his hand so tightly he didn't know whether she was angry at him or just nervous."

According to Whiting, when Sinatra whispered words of comfort in Jackie's ear, she poked him in the ribs with her elbow and, still maintaining a happy face for the photographers, hissed at him under her breath, "Look, Frank. Just smile. That's all you have to do, okay? Just smile."

"Frank said that she was very rude," recalled Whiting. "He said she was pissed off, at the weather, at him, and who knows at what else. Frank was annoyed at her as well, because as he said, 'If it wasn't for me, the whole goddamn event wouldn't have taken place.' He set it all up, every second of the entertainment, anyway."

During the show, Sinatra sang a special rendition of "That Old Black Magic" (changing the lyrics to "That old Jack magic has me in its spell"), while a white spotlight fell on the President and First Lady, bathing them in an ethereal glow. Later Sinatra sang the title song from his 1945 Oscar-awarded short film on racial tolerance, "The House I Live In," which reduced even the chilly Jackie to sentimental tears. "She was dabbing at her eyes like some little bobbysoxer," Whiting said. "In the end, I guess even she couldn't resist him."

The next day, January 20, was a bitterly cold Inauguration Day, but the always distinctive Jackie would be the only woman on the President's platform not covered in mink. Her refusal to wear a fur coat had inspired Cassini to design a simple, fawn-colored suit with a trim of sable and a matching muff. On her head she wore what would soon become a trademark of hers—a pillbox hat—this time in matching beige, by Halston.

At twelve o'clock, Jackie stood in the freezing cold between Mamie Eisenhower and Lady Bird Johnson in the stands and watched the historic moment as her husband was sworn in as the thirty-fifth President of the United States, taking his oath on the Bible that had belonged to his maternal grandfather, "Honey Fitz" Fitzgerald. Along with her sense of style and fashion, Jackie's other touches were already imprinting a sense of culture and beauty on the Kennedy administration. It was she who had suggested that Robert Frost recite a poem at the ceremony. The eighty-six-year-old poet, blinded by the sun and continually interrupted by the fierce winds blowing at his pages, gave up trying to read what he had written especially for the occasion and instead recited a poem from memory. It was Jackie's idea also for black opera singer Marian Anderson to sing "The Star-Spangled Banner," making a statement about civil rights right from the beginning of her husband's administration.

Ethel, Joan, and the other Kennedy women—the sisters, Eunice, Pat, and Jean, and mother, Rose—watched with misty-eyed reverence.

"We all knew that Jack had reached a new plateau," Ethel would later recall, "and that nothing would ever again be the same, for any of us."

Probably because so much attention was focused on Jackie, there was some discussion among reporters about the fact that her relationship with Jack seemed remote, even on this important day. For instance, after the swearing-in ceremony, he didn't follow tradition and kiss his wife, as his predecessors had done. Because she was regarded as having been so loving and supportive through the years, the fact that Jack seemed to ignore her did trouble some female observers. (He hadn't mentioned her name when he accepted the nomination of his party in Los Angeles, either.)

"Why didn't he kiss her? That was what a lot of women wanted to know," recalls Helen Thomas. "Actually, he didn't really pay any attention to her at all. It made some women in the country a bit uncomfortable. However, Jack also fairly ignored his own mother, Rose, that day. His was considered a male victory by the men in the family, and the hugs and handshakes between Jack and his father and brothers made that fact clear not only to Jackie, but also to Eunice, Pat, and Jean, as well as Ethel and Joan."

For her part, Jackie did not attempt to kiss her husband when she saw him at the Capitol rotunda following his speech, not so much as a matter of taste but rather because she was just feeling so unwell. "Everyone noticed how detached she looked during the ceremonies," recalls John Davis, Jackie's first cousin, who was present, "and how she and Jack never seemed to exchange even so much as a glance during the speeches and recitations. Grimly, she hung in there, trying to look enthusiastic in the freezing cold."

Jack

John Fitzgerald Kennedy, known to his friends and family as "Jack," was born on May 29, 1917, in the Massachusetts suburb of Brookline, the second of nine children. Descended from Irish forebears who had immigrated to Boston, his paternal grandfather, Patrick J. Kennedy, was a saloonkeeper who went on to became a Boston political leader. Jack's father, Joseph Patrick Kennedy, a Harvard graduate, was a bank president at twenty-five before marrying Rose Fitzgerald, the daughter of John Francis "Honey Fitz" Fitzgerald, mayor of Boston.

As an infant, Jack lived in a comfortable but modest home in Brookline, but as the family grew and Joseph made more money in the stock market, the Kennedys moved to larger, impressive estates, first in Brookline, then in the suburbs of New York City. Jack's childhood was a happy one, full of the family games and sports that would characterize the Kennedys' competitive nature. He attended private, but not Catholic, elementary schools. He later spent a year at Canterbury School in New Milford, Connecticut, where he was taught by Roman Catholic laymen, and four years at the exclusive Choate School in Wallingford, Connecticut. Jack grew up in the shadow of his older brother, Joseph, who dominated family competitions and was a better student. However, after young Joseph was killed when his plane exploded in midair over England during World War II, father Joseph focused on Jack as the family's entrée into political prominence.

Of the three remaining brothers, Jack was the first to enter the political arena, running for Congress from Massachusetts' Eleventh District in 1946, which he won by a large majority. He stayed in the House of Representatives until 1953, when he was elected senator. Every step along the way, Jack was encouraged, prodded, coaxed, and bullied by his father to run for President. However, during the 1960 Presidential campaign, Joseph kept a low profile. Even though he was constantly advising Jack and Bobby, he stayed away from crowds and photographers, giving rise to the then-popular chant: "Jack and Bobby will run the show, while Ted's in charge of hiding Joe." Joseph realized that coming out in support of his son would not enhance the candidate's progressive image. It was good that he stayed out of sight because, politically, Joseph was poison. He had completely destroyed his own political career and reputation by making negative comments about FDR and seeming to endorse some of Hitler's policies, so suppressing his inflammatory nature was the best thing he could do at this time. The less said by him during his son's campaign, the better.

Jack was an urbane, Harvard-educated, good-looking, Northeastern Irish Catholic—the first President of that faith in a country that was, at the time, only 26 percent Catholic. Brimming with ideals and youthful vigor—or *vig-ah*, as the Kennedys pronounced it in their Boston accents—he would usher in a new era in history, not just for this country but for the world at large. At forty-three years of age, he was the youngest President ever elected.

During his short Presidency—the New Frontier, as it was called—JFK would be best remembered for the deep sense of idealism he would rekindle in millions at the dawn of the sixties. He was a President who made Americans feel that anything was possible. His optimism and eloquence, his ability to communicate to all Americans the possibility of a better life, made him unique in every way as he challenged Americans to look beyond the selfishness of their daily lives and focus attention on their communities, their nation, their world. Many young people would enter politics because of Kennedy's influence. On a larger scale, Kennedy's attempt to communicate a giving, open spirit caused many to join the Peace Corps or begin careers as teachers, nurses, and other public servants. Kennedy's Inaugural Address that wintry day in 1961 would be widely acclaimed as the most memorable and unifying symbol of the modern political age: "Ask not what your country can do for you, ask what you can do for your country."

Perhaps the late Laura Bergquist Knebel, who covered the Kennedys for *Look* magazine and wrote many insightful pieces about the family, said it best when, at the age of forty-five in 1963, she observed, "For the first time in my life, the President of the United States was not an Olympian-remote, grandfatherly figure, but a contemporary—brighter, wittier, more sure of his destiny and more disciplined than any of us, but still a superior equal who talked your language, read the books you read, knew the inside jokes. In a world run by old men, he was a leader born in the twentieth century, and when they said a new generation had taken over, you realized it was your own."

The Five Inaugural Balls

Five official Inaugural Balls were held to celebrate the incoming administration. For the first one, at the Mayflower Hotel in Washington, D.C., Jackie was spectacularly gowned in a white chiffon sheath with a bodice embroidered in silver thread, over which she wore a billowing, floor-length, white silk cape. She accessorized with long white opera gloves and dazzling diamonds borrowed from Tiffany's. With an afternoon's rest, her troop of beauty experts, and the aid of the Dexedrine flowing in her veins administered by her husband's doctor, Janet Travell, an exhausted Jackie managed once again to rise from the ashes like a glittering white phoenix.

Joan and Ethel were, of course, also dressed in elegant evening gowns. Ethel's was white with straps and matching gloves; Joan's was white too, but with a black-sequined strapless bodice. Ethel had been concerned earlier because her gowns for the day's and evening's events had been stuck in the trunk of her dressmaker's car, which was buried under heaps of snow. She was relieved to find that, once the snow was shoveled off the automobile, her expensive gowns were unharmed.

But the crowds really weren't that interested in Joan or Ethel anyway, nor in Rose, the Kennedy sisters, or any other woman at the ball. At least in terms of exquisite glamour, this evening was all about Jackie, for she was the greatest symbol of the new Kennedy era. Or as Ethel put it to Bobby, "Jeez. They just want to touch her, don't they? It's like being at a wedding with the most popular bride in the world."

Even Ethel, who was rarely impressed by Jackie, appeared awestruck by her sister-in-law's charisma and beauty. In fact, there were times when she was caught staring at Jackie, a curious expression on her face. During these moments, she would watch the new First Lady's every movement: the lively way she greeted boring dignitaries, as if she had found a long-lost friend; the casual way she tilted her head back when she laughed at jokes she must have known were not funny; the frosty way she stared at anyone who approached her before first greeting her husband, the President. It was as if Ethel were studying her sister-in-law in the hope that she might learn a little something—a new trick, perhaps—about the simple but not easy art of high elegance. At one ball, a Secret Service agent noticed Ethel watching intently as Jackie stood alone, doing nothing at all. Just being Jackie.

For Joan's part, whenever she got near Jackie, she could only gaze at her and become tongue-tied whenever she tried to speak. To Joan, it was as if her sister-in-law had undergone some magical transformation. No longer was she the worried, pregnant Jackie who needed an understanding ear while walking along the beach a couple of months earlier. Now she was a completely different woman, someone who possessed so much self-confidence that it was difficult to believe she had ever experienced a confused or vulnerable moment. This new Jackie was not to be touched, certainly not to be comforted, but rather to be just looked at and adored from afar as if she were a portrait in oil crafted by a European master. As happy as she surely was for Jackie, Joan must have felt a great divide between herself and this rare work of art.

Ethel felt it as well. "Jackie completely ignored me the whole night," Ethel would later complain to Eunice, who had sprained her ankle earlier in the week and was limping about throughout the festivities. "I would walk over to her, wanting to introduce someone, and she would look right through me. It was humiliating. At one point, I waved my hand in front of her face and said, 'Hello? Is anyone there?' And she just stared at me. I'm telling you," Ethel decided, "that girl was on drugs or something."

"Of course she was," Eunice said. "She was sick because of the baby. And Ethie [the family's nickname for her], do you have any idea how much pressure she was under? She was dazed the whole time."

But as far as Ethel was concerned, Jackie was not the only one with overwhelming responsibilities that evening. "We were *all* under pressure," she told her sister-in-law. "But *I* was friendly to everyone, just as I always am. And you know I always am!" Ethel was obviously disgruntled. "You would have thought she would be the happiest woman in the world," Ethel continued, according to a Kennedy intimate. "But no, not Jackie Kennedy. To tell you the truth, I felt like going over to her, shaking her, and saying, 'Would you please smile? You're the First Lady, for goodness' sake!'"

By the time the Kennedy contingent reached the third ball at the Armory, Jackie's Dexedrine was wearing off. The crowd of one thousand people gave the First Couple a twenty-minute standing ovation, which, as Rose Kennedy later observed, "engulfed the President and First Lady with a tide of love and admiration." As Jack and Jackie waved from their silk-draped presidential box on the balcony, a spotlight shone on the new President and the band played "Hail to the Chief." It was a thrilling experience, but not enough to keep Jackie afloat. The blinding glare of the searchlights that had been trained on her and Jack had given her an intense headache, even though one would never know it from the wide smile on her face for the benefit of cameras.

Right behind Jackie sat her young and completely awed sister-in-law Joan, her eyes wide with astonishment at all the pomp and circumstance. She had never seen so many people, all packed shoulder to shoulder below her, gazing up at the presidential box. "It was like we were somehow different from them," she would later recall. "A very strange feeling to be stared at and cheered by so many people."

The Kennedys were used to pageantry—though perhaps not of this magnitude—having been in politics for years, winning elections, dealing with people, being respected and the subject of great attention and even adoration. While Ethel had already seen a number of campaigns through to their conclusion, this one had been a new experience for Joan. The inaugural proceedings had the younger sister-in-law captivated. As her sister Candy put it, Joan was "like Dorothy in Oz, it was all new and exciting. But more than that, it was surreal. Joan said she spent most of the time walking around with stars in her eyes, spellbound."

Joan was supposed to be seated next to Jackie's stepfather, Hugh "Hughdie" Auchincloss, with Ted to her left. However, because Hughdie didn't show up—though no one seemed to know why—there was an empty seat between Joan and Jackie's mother, the socialite Janet Auchincloss. Throughout the proceedings, Joan seemed preoccupied. Should she remain with her husband, or should she move over and sit next to the dour-looking Janet? Or was the presence of Janet's stepson, Hugh "Yusha" Auchincloss, Jr., to Janet's right, enough to keep the older woman from looking so alone on television? For Joan, this was a predicament.

Joan glanced at Janet and then motioned to the vacant seat. With all of the noise and lights, perhaps Janet misunderstood Joan's intentions and thought she was indicating that she (Janet) should move over and sit next to her. Or maybe Janet simply didn't want Joan filling the empty seat. Whatever the case, she shot Joan a cross look so uninviting that it visibly startled the Kennedy wife. Joan quickly averted her eyes, probably hoping nobody had noticed the exchange.

Ethel, however, seated to the left of Ted, had observed exactly what had occurred between Joan and Janet. The next day she commented, "Jackie's mother gave Joan a look that took the poor dear's breath away. Now, if it were me and she had ever dared to look at me that way, I would've hit the old bag right over the head with my purse."

After this ball was over, Jackie made her apologies and told Jack to go to the rest of the functions without her. She would regret it later, saying, "I was just in physical and nervous exhaustion because the month after the baby's birth had been the opposite of recuperation. I missed all the gala things. . . . I always wished I could have participated more in those first shining hours with him [her husband], but at least I thought I had given him the son he longed for. It was not the happy time in my life that it looks like in all the pictures. You know, you just sort of collapse. He [John Jr.] was born prematurely because of all the excitement. He was sick. I was sick."

Ethel also begged off early, as did Joan and Ted. "I was so exhausted by the whole thing," Joan recalled, "that my knees were weak. I felt every emotion. You were sorry it was over and glad it was over at the same time. I also wondered: What now? What next?"

Bobby and Jack continued on to two more balls before ending the evening after midnight by stopping at columnist Joseph Alsop's home for a nightcap and some hastily warmed-over terrapin (turtle) soup.

Meanwhile, Ethel slept alone at Hickory Hill, perhaps dreaming of bigger and better things for herself and her husband.

And Jackie slept at the White House. The elegant toast of the nation was now alone with her thoughts, her pounding headache, and her sore lower back, which she treated with a heating pad. Perhaps appropriately enough, while her bedroom was being remodeled, she had taken the Queen's Room, a guest bedroom on the second floor that was usually reserved for royal visitors—no fewer than five reigning queens had slept there at one time or another—and not ordinarily occupied by First Ladies. She was so physically and emotionally drained that she would stay in bed for the next few days, seeming almost paralyzed by the magnitude of the life change she was about to experience.

Bobby

One of the first controversies of the Kennedy administration occurred just after Jack was elected, and it had to do with his decision to name his thirty-five-year-old brother, Bobby, to the post of Attorney General. Jack was adamant that Bobby deserved the position in that he had devoted the last ten years to getting Jack into the White House. However, Bobby wasn't so sure he wanted the job. "I had been chasing bad men [criminals] for three years," he once said, "and I didn't want to spend the rest of my life doing that." Bobby also knew he was a hothead. As Attorney General under Jack, he might become embroiled in controversies that could reflect poorly on his brother.

Critics in the media, such as the political analysts at the *New York Times*, cited nepotism as the major reason Bobby should not be appointed to such an important post. Privately, even Lyndon Johnson joined the group of naysayers, calling Bobby "a little fart." But Jack announced that he wanted Bobby to take the job—though he did not explain that his father, Joseph, had been so insistent that there was no talking him out of the notion.

"Poor Ethel wasn't happy about it at all," the late Kirk LeMoyne "Lem" Billings, a close friend of the family's, once said.* "She wanted Bobby to break away from Jack. She had her heart set on him running for governor, that was her plan. She was afraid he would always be connected to his brother's achievements. She was also afraid she would always be in Jackie's shadow, a prospect that sent chills down her spine." Once the offer was officially extended, however, and the critics began to descend upon the Kennedys, Ethel adopted a different stance. "He's the man for the job," she said in 1961, "and he should have it. I don't care what anyone says."

---

*Billings and Jack Kennedy had been roommates during Jack's sophomore year at Choate and then at Princeton, until Jack transferred to Harvard to be near Boston doctors for health reasons. Although Billings never served the President in an official capacity, he was a frequent guest at the White House and remained a close friend of the family until his death at the age of sixty-five in May 1981.

Bobby brought out Ethel's most competitive streak. No one could say a word to her, or in her presence, against Bobby. Bobby was not like Jack, a man who could turn away wrath with wit and a smile. Especially during his early days in politics, Bobby was much more like his father, Joseph: a temperamental person compelled to speak his mind, and often without forethought, when someone had an opposing point of view. As a result, Bobby would make more than a few enemies during his short lifetime. In turn, Ethel would make each of them *her* enemy; and although at times she may have appeared to have forgotten their transgressions, she rarely, if ever, forgave them.

"Ethel Kennedy adored Bobby," recalls Helen Thomas, "and, I would have to say, to the exclusion of everything else. Whereas Jackie made certain that she had a life separate and apart from her husband's, Ethel had no such desire. From the beginning," she concludes, "Bobby was the center of her universe. While it's a cliché to say that 'he was her life,' if ever a cliché rang true, it would be this one."

When Bobby finally went before the Senate Judiciary Committee for his confirmation hearings on January 13, 1961, with Ethel and his sister Jean watching, only a few Republicans noted his lack of experience as an attorney (he had graduated from law school ten years earlier but had never tried a case), concerns about his finances, and whether any of his holdings would conflict with his job. In the end, after two hours of questioning, all fourteen of the committee members voted to approve Bobby's nomination as Attorney General. Ethel was so excited that she went out and bought Bobby a six-foot mahogany desk that had belonged to Amos T. Ackerman, U.S. Grant's second Attorney General and the first to head the newly created Justice Department in 1870.

As the nation's top law official, Bobby would wield a great deal of power. "And along with that power, came those perks that Kennedy men loved more than life itself," says Kennedy friend George Smathers (a senator from Florida from 1950 to 1968). "Women, women, women."

Some have speculated that Bobby's womanizing was a way of competing with his older brother. Bobby was smaller and more wiry than Jack. He was also shy and withdrawn, while Jack was bold and gregarious. Bobby often appeared unruly—his hair always looked as though he had just driven a fast sports car with the top down—

whereas Jack was meticulously groomed. In the past, Bobby had certainly seemed determined to assume those facets of Jack's personality he admired, and perhaps he even appreciated Jack's way with women.

In 1961, just after Jack moved into the White House, Ethel all but ignored Bobby's brief affair with blonde actress Lee Remick, ten years his junior and remembered today for her roles in *Anatomy of a Murder* and *Days of Wine and Roses*. "Bobby Kennedy gave such eloquent expression to his passion for me," the late Remick told Marilyn Kind, once a close friend of hers.

According to Kind, Lee telephoned Ethel Kennedy one evening to inform her of the affair. "You're on your way out," Lee coolly informed Ethel.

As Lee remembered it, Ethel was understandably angry. Before hanging up, she told Lee that Bobby was sleeping right next to her and warned her to never call again.

Bobby was, indeed, sound asleep. But in Lee's bed.

Whenever a friend or even a Kennedy family member informed Ethel of one of Bobby's indiscretions, she often chose not to believe them. "It's not true," she once said. "I have asked Bobby if he ever cheats on me, and he assures me that he does not. And that is the end of that."

Though Ethel usually ignored stories about her husband and other women, there were times when her curiosity seemed to get the best of her, especially if people close to her were whispering about certain liaisons or if she kept reading about them in the fan magazines she so enjoyed. On rare occasions, she would go to Jackie and ask if she had personal knowledge of a particular rumor regarding Bobby and another woman. However, Jackie always seemed uncomfortable discussing Bobby's personal life, perhaps afraid that she would become involved in a dispute between her in-laws that was really none of her business.

By 1961, the dawn of the Camelot years, Ethel and Bobby already had seven children, with four more to come. Many aspects of their life together were favorable; Ethel's marriage was not a complete sham, Bobby's infidelities aside. He was tender and loving to his young wife, though not in an overt, obviously passionate manner. He fascinated her with his intelligence, his drive, his passion and ideals. They had common goals and ambitions, and their life together at 1147 Chain Bridge Road—Hickory Hill—in McLean seemed to be a happy one, at least to outsiders. The Kennedy family photographer, Jacques Lowe, recalled the first time he visited Hickory Hill:

"Oh, it was a gorgeous experience entering the Robert Kennedy home for the first time. I remember the first night coming to dinner, having spent the day with Robert on Capitol Hill. They had five children then and had recently bought Hickory Hill. I had known Robert for some time in my role as a magazine photographer covering the up-and-coming investigator. He had been sober and serious, revealing sudden flashes of humor and sometimes anger; but I was not prepared for the man I met on coming to the house late that night. All of his reserve seemed to melt in the glory of his family, and the long, difficult day was forgotten in the warmth of love of a father for his children and vice versa. It was chaos, with all the children talking at once and Bobby answering each of them with humor and sometimes trying to be stern, at which he didn't fully succeed. Ethel instantly accepted this stranger [Lowe] into the house, and later on I had to go upstairs to say the evening prayers with the children, which took place after a family pillow fight."

It seemed the picture-perfect, happily married lifestyle; maybe for Ethel Kennedy it was and perhaps she sensed that it would remain that way as long as she refused to accept that Bobby had a secret life. As long as he was there for her when she needed him and for his children—and he always was—she seemed content.

The Skakels

Ethel Skakel was born on April 11, 1928, at Chicago's Lying-In Hospital, the sixth child to be born in the Skakel home in ten years; three brothers, two sisters, and a younger sister born five years later completed the family. Ethel's mother, Ann, was a large woman, taller and heavier than her husband, who kept the weight she gained with every child and eventually tipped the scale at close to two hundred pounds. Nicknamed "Big Ann" by friends and family members, she was a formidable woman both in stature and determination.

Big Ann was married to the ambitious and distant George Skakel, owner of Great Lakes Coal and Coke Corporation, which was well on its way to becoming one of the largest privately held corporations in America. The family was prosperous and never wanted for anything material, even when the Great Depression of 1929 hit. Though Great Lakes Coal and Coke foundered at that time, the Skakels curtailed some of their extravagances, though not many. In fact, against all odds, now sole owner George Skakel became a millionaire *during* that economic hardship. When the aluminum industry recovered, the fortunes of the Skakels soared.

Because George conducted so much of his business on the East Coast, the family moved to a rented mansion set on twelve acres in Larchmont, New York, in 1933. Whenever George utilized the house for business entertaining, Ann assisted in grand style. The parties were always impressive, with a hired staff to serve the finest foods and liquors—especially liquor. George had apparently inherited a tendency toward alcoholism from his father and soon became afflicted with the disease. (With such an abundance of liquor always available, some of the Skakel offspring would experiment by drinking whatever was left in the guests' glasses after parties. Unfortunately, Georgeann, the oldest, was an alcoholic at fifteen.)

A year later, the family moved from Larchmont to a furnished thirty-room mansion on Lake Avenue in Greenwich, Connecticut, complete with parklike grounds, a guest house, servants' quarters, stables, and six-car garage. George was proud that he had purchased it at a bargain price in the midst of the Depression.

Ethel's relationship with both parents was strained and distant. She was closer to her brothers and sisters, always in trouble with them and joining them in antagonism against Ann and George. As a youngster, Ethel was enrolled in Greenwich Academy, one of the leading Northeast day schools, where the girls wore uniforms and discipline was strict. She had no respect for authority, however, which may have enhanced her status with her classmates but completely dismayed her instructors. She was in trouble so often it was a wonder that she was not expelled.

The behavior of the other Skakel children was also troubling. Because George was a hunting enthusiast, there were always guns lying around in the Lake Avenue home. The Skakel boys would shoot the firearms from the windows of their cars, using the .45 caliber weapons to destroy mailboxes and streetlights.

Once old enough to drive, every Skakel child had his or her own automobile, which he or she drove at high speed; the Skakel boys, particularly Jim and George Jr., were such notorious drivers that most Greenwich mothers forbade their daughters to ride with them. Skakel cars were wrecked on a regular basis, and brand-new automobiles would be abandoned in ditches, ponds, and swimming pools. Ethel had a red convertible, which she often drove as recklessly as her brothers.

When Ethel was fifteen, she enrolled in the Convent of the Sacred Heart, Maplehurst, in the Bronx, New York. There, as at Greenwich Academy, Ethel excelled at sports but was a mediocre student. Despite her rowdy, trouble-making nature, she had always felt a strong emotional connection to God, and at Maplehurst she showed the greatest interest in religion classes. She embraced those studies with a zeal that made her mother proud. After graduating from the convent in the spring of 1945, she followed her older sister by enrolling in Manhattanville College in New York City in the fall.

At Manhattanville, Ethel's best friend and roommate was the shy Jean Kennedy, next-to-last child in the large and wealthy Kennedy family. The first time Jean took Ethel home to Hyannis Port to visit her family, Ethel was immediately struck by how different the Kennedy lifestyle was from her own. She saw discipline; she saw order; she saw caring.

Early in their friendship, Jean introduced Ethel to her brother Bobby on a ski weekend, certain they would hit it off. However, Ethel was interested in the much more debonair Jack, who was also present during that particular vacation break. If Jack noticed her at all, though, he would probably have seen her as a skinny tomboy—the way most young men viewed her, which did not bother her in the least. She was always completely comfortable with who she was, or at least she appeared that way. With Ethel clearly interested in Jack, Bobby became attracted to Ethel's sister Pat. Still, for the next two years, Bobby and Ethel dated occasionally.

After dating Pat—and a few others—Bobby finally turned to Ethel in a more serious manner. Friends would observe that the relationship seemed to lack romance, noting that Bobby and Ethel were more like close siblings than boyfriend and girlfriend, but after two years he proposed marriage.

At the time that Bobby proposed, Ethel was seriously considering becoming a nun. Her family's spiritual zeal had always been clearly in evidence in the Skakel home when Ethel was growing up. Crucifixes and other religious objects hung on the walls; shelves in the large library were filled with Catholic books, some of them rare manuscripts. Her mother often played host to the most pious of nuns and priests. So zealously did mother and daughter proselytize that some of Ethel's friends were actually forbidden by their parents to play at the Skakel home.

"How can I fight God?" Bobby asked his sister Jean when he learned that he was competing with the Lord for Ethel's devotion. Ethel was unsure whether she wished to marry any man. She didn't feel the passion for Bobby she had read about in the fan magazines and seen on the screen in movie theaters. Her friends from school shared with her stories about their romances, and even though they were Catholic girls, well aware of certain limitations in a relationship, their experiences may have seemed more intense, more romantic, more loving than Ethel had known in her time with Bobby—or with any man, for that matter. "She thought, 'Maybe I'm just not cut out to be married, to be anyone's wife,'" recalled a friend of hers from Manhattanville. "She was confused, but back then we didn't address such confusion as we would today. In our circle, you either got married, or you became a nun. Those were your choices." In the end, Ethel opted for marriage to Bobby.

Once Bobby and Ethel became engaged, Ethel couldn't wait to get out of Manhattanville. With her major in English and her minor in history, she was only an average student when she graduated in June 1949.

Soon afterward, a tray holding a wide variety of diamonds from which Ethel would choose arrived at the Skakel home, sent by Bobby (an unusually generous gesture for a member of the thrifty Kennedy clan). Ethel chose an exquisite, large-sized, marquis diamond. Unlike most grooms-to-be, Bobby was not with Ethel when she made her selection. (At least Ethel had the opportunity to select her own ring. Future father-in-law Joseph would select Jackie's engagement ring, as well as Joan's!)

Big Ann was delighted with her daughter's decision to marry Bobby. She realized that Ethel's marriage into the rich and famous Kennedy clan could raise the Skakels to the top of Catholic society. From the time the engagement was announced, Ann took charge of planning the various pre-wedding parties and other family gatherings. Ann sent out twelve hundred invitations, forcing employees at the small Greenwich post office into overtime work.

The day of the wedding started in typical madcap Skakel fashion. Years before, Big Ann had equipped her home with a beauty salon, believing that it would be cost-effective and convenient to have one in a household inhabited by so many females. The room was fully appointed with chairs, hair dryers, sinks, and an array of beauty products. On the day of the wedding, the bridesmaids had their hair and makeup done in the home salon by hairdressers brought in especially for the occasion. After their hair was perfectly coiffed, the young ladies went out on the grounds to mix with the male members of the bridal party, many of them Bobby's hulking football-playing chums from Harvard. As unexpected high jinx got into full swing, several maidens ended up in the pool, their hairstyles ruined. "So typical of a Big Ann wedding," one guest remarked to the press later.

On June 17, 1950, twenty-two-year-old Ethel Skakel stood in the rear of St. Mary's Roman Catholic Church in Greenwich on the arm of her father, George Skakel, about to marry Bobby Kennedy and forever join the ranks of the elite Kennedy family. In this well-planned and tastefully executed affair, she would be the first woman since Rose to take a Kennedy husband. All of Ethel's attendants wore white lace over taffeta dresses with wide-brimmed, eggshell-white hats delicately trimmed with pink and white flowers. Ethel looked lovely in a white satin wide-neck gown with pearl-embroidered lace overskirt. The same lace held her fingertip-length tulle veil. Around her neck she wore a tasteful single-strand pearl necklace. In her arms she held a bouquet of lilies, stephanotis, and lilies of the valley, matching the white peonies and lilies that decorated the church. Also waiting to make its entrance was the Skakel-Kennedy bridal party, filled with young and promising relatives and friends, including Ethel's and Bobby's siblings.

At the altar stood the handsome twenty-four-year-old groom, Bobby. Next to him was his best man, older brother John

As the two thousand guests, hundreds of whom were uninvited, crammed into the church, waiting for the ceremony to begin, the pipe-organ music began. In the pews, waiting amidst the gorgeous floral arrangements for the bride's entrance, sat the well-heeled, well-known guests, including diplomats, politicians, entertainers, and socialites. The bridesmaids entered, followed by Ethel, who appeared to be an ethereal cloud of white in her beautiful wedding finery. It was a memorable ceremony.

"What I want for you is to have a life with Bobby as happy as the one I have had with his father," Rose told Ethel afterward as she embraced her new daughter-in-law during the lavish reception at the Skakels' Lake Avenue mansion. "Lots of children, Ethel. Have lots and lots of children. They'll keep your marriage strong, as strong as mine."

From the start, Ethel and Bobby were devoted to one another. Neither would ever seem to regret their decision to wed; the differences in their personalities meshed together to create what many of their peers considered to be the perfect couple. "The best thing I ever did was marry Ethel," Bobby would later comment of the woman who was his partner, his supporter, his friend.

"Whatever they did, they put their whole hearts and souls into it," observes Mary Francis "Sancy" Newman, a neighbor of the Kennedys in Hyannis Port. "They were ideal in that way and seemed to have the kind of marriage most people of that time wanted. You could see in the way they looked at one another that they adored each other."

As she would later tell friends, Ethel was a virgin when she met Bobby—not a surprise, considering her strict Catholic upbringing and education. In fact, the word "sex" was never uttered in the Skakel home because Big Ann was so puritanical. Women weren't even allowed to wear pants in the Lake Avenue home, because Big Ann found them amoral. Short tennis dresses were deemed acceptable for sports activities, but a woman had to change into something more appropriate as soon as she got off the court. Bobby later told friends that he didn't know Ethel was a virgin until their wedding night, though he certainly must have suspected as much. He didn't dare ask, and she wouldn't think to tell him.

Years later, at a Hyannis Port luncheon with Jackie, Joan, Jean, Eunice, and some close friends, Ethel admitted that her wedding night had been "a disaster." She said that her inexperience had been obvious, and that she had been intimidated by Bobby. "It was just terrible," she said. "I think Bobby was finished before I got into the room . . . or at least that's how it felt to me."

Joan laughed. "Well, really, whose honeymoon has ever been anything but terrible?" she asked.

At that moment Rose walked into the room. Immediately, the women stopped talking. Discussing such matters in front of the family matriarch was considered inappropriate. Ethel instinctively put a hand over her mouth.

"Now, just what are you ladies talking about?" Rose asked.

"Oh, we were just saying how well Bobby sleeps at night," Jackie said quickly.

"That he does, dear heart," Rose said. "That he does." Then she added, "He gets that from me, you know."

After honeymooning in Hawaii and a drive back east in Pat Kennedy's convertible, which the newlyweds picked up in Los Angeles, Bobby went back to his final year of law studies at the University of Virginia in Charlottesville, while Ethel began her life as a Kennedy wife. The couple settled into a small one-and-a-half story colonial home—much simpler surroundings than Ethel was accustomed to, but it was an environment in which she seemed content. Ethel surrounded herself with friends who knew how to cook—because she didn't—and domestics who knew how to clean—because she didn't. "A girl has to have *some* help, after all," Ethel explained to Rose, who was already harping on her daughter-in-law to cut back on her spending, a running theme throughout their relationship.

For the next year, Ethel focused her attention on getting to know her husband's personality. He could be explosive at times but was for the most part gentle and retiring. She assisted him with his studies in any way she could and, as she would later recall, she set about "doing what newlyweds do, try to learn all you can about your spouse before the children come along and completely ruin any time you may have with him."

On spring and summer weekends the couple would fly to Hyannis Port to be with Bobby's parents and in fall and winter they flew to Palm Beach, Florida, for the same purpose. Ethel spent much time poring over books, encyclopedias, and almanacs, in an effort to learn as much as possible about every subject so that she could, as she put it, "keep up with those Kennedys." Parlor games such as Twenty Questions were especially popular in the Kennedy household, and competitive Ethel wanted to be certain she was not embarrassed by all of those erudite Kennedy offspring.

Dorothy Tubridy, a friend of the family's from Ireland, understood Ethel's predicament. In an oral history for the Kennedy Library, she once recalled, "They all read the newspapers every day, and at dinnertime somebody might come out with a name, or something that happened that had been written about, and if you didn't contribute to the conversation, you'd be immediately pounced on and asked why you haven't read one of the twelve newspapers! It was frightening. I would feel so stupid if I couldn't follow the conversation."

In 1951, three years after Bobby had graduated from Harvard, he was admitted to the Massachusetts bar. He and Ethel departed for the Skakel estate in Greenwich to await the arrival of their first child, Kathleen (named after Bobby's late sister), who was born on Independence Day.

"It was a difficult pregnancy," recalls the Kennedy family nurse, Luella Hennessey, who tended to Ethel at Greenwich Hospital. "Ethel was depressed, upset. She was too small to have a baby as large as Kathleen, and it caused her to have certain female problems, very severe internal problems. [Her perineum was damaged during the birth.]

"She was embarrassed about it. She told me that none of the men in the family should ever know. For her to not have an easy pregnancy was a sort of defeat. She hated to be defeated. I don't think Bobby ever really knew how much pain she was in, how she suffered. When he would walk into the hospital room, she would have a full face of makeup on and a smile on her face. Then when he would leave, she would absolutely collapse in tears. Already, she had that Kennedy stiff upper lip in a time of great stress." Luella concluded that "Ethel was hand made for the Kennedy family."

"I won't be having any more children," a choked-up Ethel told Luella as she held her newborn in her arms.

"Oh, yes you will, honey," said the nurse, trying to comfort her. "You'll forget the pain. All women do. I promise."

"Oh no I won't," Ethel countered. "A smart woman would never forget this kind of pain."

After the baby's birth, Ethel and Bobby moved into one of the Skakel family guest houses, and in less than six months Ethel was pregnant again—just in time to start stumping for Jack's senatorial campaign (of which Bobby was campaign manager) in Massachusetts. Though she was afraid of the pregnancy because of how difficult her first one had been, Ethel was expected to help campaign for Jack's election through the summer of 1952, just as all of the Kennedy women did: Rose, Jean, Pat, and Eunice. "They expect a lot of you in this family," she told one friend. "And I can't let them see me as weak. That would be the worst thing possible."

On September 24, Ethel gave birth to a boy, Joseph Patrick (Joseph after Bobby's deceased brother). Two months later, in November, Jack won his senatorial campaign.

In January 1953, Ethel and Bobby moved their small family to Washington, D.C., where Bobby had just taken a job working for the Permanent Subcommittee on Investigations of the Senate Government Operations Committee, known as the McCarthy Committee for its chairman, Senator Joseph McCarthy of Wisconsin. Ethel found a modest four-bedroom home in Georgetown, which the couple would rent. While the surroundings in their new home weren't opulent, Ethel couldn't help but hire a staff of servants, who wore different color uniforms every day to work. It was a happy time for Ethel, Bobby, and their small family. Their life together was just beginning, and although they didn't know it at the time, they would soon devote themselves to the most important of all family goals: getting a Kennedy elected to the White House.

Not One to Feel
Sorry for Herself

On a blustery Sunday in January, three days after JFK's inauguration, Bobby Kennedy was sitting behind blonde movie star Kim Novak, his arms crossed in front of her. After somebody gave them a shove, the toboggan on which they were sitting went sliding down a snow-covered hill. Kim squealed in delight as Ethel Kennedy, who was leaning against a nearby tree, watched with an unhappy expression on her face. She had heard rumors of an affair between her husband and Kim, and—from what she told friends—she didn't believe the stories, yet found them troubling just the same.

Bobby had invited a group of friends, including Dave Hackett and Samuel Adams, chums from the Milton Academy he had attended as a youth, to Hickory Hill for a day of tobogganing. Four inches of snow remained on the ground from a recent blizzard, the air was cold and crisp, and Bobby was relaxing for the first time in a long while. Among the invitees was the actress Novak, who had been at the Sinatra party on the night of the inauguration.

Bobby and Kim walked back to the top of the hill, giggling and laughing all the way, before getting back on their toboggan.

"Bobby, don't you want to play football?" Ethel hollered out at him.

"Not now, Ethel," he answered, as he and Kim positioned themselves on the sled for another trip down the hill.

Ethel finally went back into the house alone.

About an hour later, Ethel's assistant, Leah Mason, found her employer in the kitchen with Pat Kennedy Lawford. (The divorced Mason, who lived near Hickory Hill and now lives in Europe, would work for Ethel on and off for many years; she says that she was dismissed and rehired "at least a dozen times" over a ten-year period.) As soon as Leah walked into the room, Ethel snapped at her about something. She seemed upset. It was Leah's feeling that the presence of Kim Novak in her home had made Ethel very uncomfortable.

"Don't be mad, Ethie," Pat said.

"I don't know what you're talking about," Ethel responded, as she put dishes into a cabinet. "Everything is fine. Bobby's just having fun."

Just then Ethel dropped a plate onto the floor. It shattered into pieces. "Oh, no! That was one of my mother's best dishes." Ethel crumpled into a chair. "And now it's broken. Oh, my God."

When he heard the dish break, Bobby and some of the other guests ran into the kitchen, to find Ethel sobbing. Bobby got on his knees in front of her and asked her to tell him what was wrong. Tearfully, Ethel said that she was distraught, that the campaign, the inauguration, and the many before- and after-parties had completely worn her down.

"I know," Bobby said, patting her on the back softly. "I know."

Ethel looked up at the ceiling. "Oh, dear Lord," she said, as Bobby continued to comfort her. Then, after about five minutes, she composed herself, perhaps feeling self-conscious about her outburst. "Well, enough of that." She stood up and began wiping away her tears. "I'm not one to sit here and feel sorry for myself. You know me, Bobby," she added. "I have all the energy in the world."

Bobby grinned at her as he got up off his knees. "That's my Ethel," he said to the others in the room. "Never one to let anything get her down." Everyone agreed. Then, as Bobby, Leah, Pat, and the others left the room, Ethel hollered after them, "We're going to have dinner soon . . . so don't think you're gonna be stayin' out there too long."

White House Infidelities

During the Camelot years, the Kennedys' home and family were unlike most others. Because of their power, money, and influence, Jackie, Ethel, and Joan had different concerns and pressures from most young women. While family values were important to them, power, prestige, and money were also meaningful to Jackie and Ethel. Joan was much less interested in being powerful or famous.

Just by virtue of their prominence in society, the Kennedys and others of their class lived by different rules. In Washington and especially in its tony Georgetown section, they lived in a world in which one code of behavior applied to the middle class and another to the wealthy upper class. Infidelity was an accepted transgression if the players had wealth and status. Perhaps it was thought that these privileged philanderers were better equipped—just by virtue of their worldly experience—to handle emotional ambiguities than were everyday married couples living in the heartland.

"In the Kennedy world, infidelity wasn't supposed to matter," noted the prolific author Gore Vidal, who was obliquely related to Jackie through marriage (his mother had been married to Hugh Auchincloss before he married Jackie's mother, Janet). "In the rest of the world, yes, heterosexuality, marriage, and children were—are—ideals. But the Kennedys moved in a world of money and power. Women who cared about money and power knew how to strike a balance between what they had and what they didn't have. Someone like Joan Kennedy, I can understand why she never fit in. If she wasn't interested in money and power, what was she doing in that family, anyway?"

Divorce was a complex matter in the fifties and sixties, especially among Irish-Catholics like the Kennedys. To say that it was "frowned upon" would be an understatement. It was unacceptable. "You just had to live with it," is the way Joan once put it.

Some of the Secret Service agents who protected Jackie during her White House years recall a marriage that, at times, seemed ideal. "From the way it appeared on the outside, it seemed to be an excellent relationship," says Anthony Sherman, who served two years on presidential detail. "I was with them a lot, and I saw what seemed like a genuine love there. I never heard any yelling or anger between them. I was with them many times where they had the children at the beach, or they would go to get ice cream at the local parlor in Hyannis Port, holding hands, being loving. I think that they were best together when they were with the children."

President Kennedy's risk-taking and infidelities have been well documented over the last three decades by everyone from mainstream journalists and academic historians to muckrakers and tabloid reporters. Even his friend and Kennedy loyalist Arthur Schlesinger now says, "His sexual waywardness does not constitute John Kennedy's finest hour." (He hastens to add, "But exaggeration is possible.") As George Smathers put it, "I've shaken hands with eleven presidents in my lifetime, and the only two who were one hundred percent totally faithful to their wives were Harry Truman and Richard Nixon. Those were the only two. The rest, at some point or another, slipped."

It would seem that once John F. Kennedy got into office, with an army of Secret Service men to protect his privacy, he more than just "slipped." Joseph Paolella, an agent who worked at the White House from 1960 to 1964, recalls, "His womanizing was one of those things you didn't talk about to anyone except other agents. You just accepted it as a part of the job." Paolella notes that an important part of his job during the Kennedy administration was to prevent Jackie from stumbling upon the President's indiscretions—not because she didn't know about them but, rather, to save the couple from an embarrassing situation.

"Jackie was full of love, and full of hurt," said Lindy Boggs, who succeeded her husband, Hale Boggs, as a Louisiana congresswoman. "When she really loved something, she gave herself completely. But I don't think he could love anyone too deeply. They were two private people, two cocoons married to each other, trying to reach each other. I think she felt that since he was so much older than she was, that it was up to him to reach more than she did. But he couldn't."

Jackie was a smart woman who had made a choice to remain with an unfaithful husband. She was not only standing by her man, she was standing by her political party, her job as First Lady, her country, and, of course, her children. Try as she might to ignore it, though, her husband's unfaithfulness had to hurt. Her cousin John Davis referred to it as "Jacqueline's festering wound, one which remained for a lifetime." Her longtime friend Joan Braden, the wife of columnist Tom Braden and a close friend of all of the Kennedys since having worked as an aide to Jack in the 1960 campaign, called it "the cross she didn't have to, but chose to, bear."

Even though she had decided to accept it, Jackie sometimes lashed out at Jack for his behavior, especially if he seemed to be flaunting his unfaithfulness. A source close to the Kennedy administration tells this story: One afternoon while taking inventory of White House furnishings, Jackie walked into the Lincoln Room, where Abraham Lincoln held many cabinet meetings and where his large bed was now kept. There she found her husband and a secretary—not in a compromising position, but suspiciously alone just the same. Jackie discreetly closed the door. When Jack emerged from the room, he found his wife's clipboard on the floor, propped up against the opposite wall. On a blank page was written in Jackie's handwriting two words: "See Me."

Later, Jackie confronted Jack in an argument loud enough for some of the Kennedy staff to overhear, which was very uncharacteristic of the First Couple. Jack denied that anything inappropriate had transpired in the Lincoln Room and explained that he was merely showing it to a new secretary who had never seen it. Jackie, exasperated by his feeble excuse, demanded to know if he was "some [expletive deleted] little tour guide or the [expletive deleted] President of the United States." It would seem that she could live with his unfaithfulness, but she could not accept it when he treated her as if she was completely naïve.

That same week, Jackie and George Smathers were dancing together at a White House gathering. "I know you and Jack get so tired of this sort of stuffy function," Smathers recalls her saying to him. "I know that you'd much rather be sailing with Jack down the Potomac on *The Honey Fitz* with some pretty girls, like Marilyn [presumably Monroe]." When Smathers protested, Jackie said, "Oh, please, George. Don't give me that. I've watched you guys too long. I know what's going on, and I'm not fooled by any of it. When are you two going to grow up?"

George Smathers didn't have an answer to her question.

"That's what I thought," Jackie said as she broke free of his hold.

Jackie, Ethel, and Joan each felt the sting of a cheating husband, and their shared experiences caused them to unite in a special sisterhood. Shortly after the incident in the Lincoln Room, Jackie hosted one of her small dinner parties at the White House. The sisters-in-law sat with their husbands, Jack, Bobby, and Ted, and a few other friends. After dinner in the White House dining room, beautifully refurbished in an American Federal motif, they adjourned to the Treaty Room for cigars, coffee, and liquor. Once used as a cabinet room by President Andrew Johnson, it had been transformed by Jackie into the Treaty Room, with Grant furniture and framed facsimiles of all the treaties that had been signed in it through the years. (Always with an eye toward history, she would ask Jack, when the time came, to sign the U.S.–Soviet Nuclear Test Ban Treaty in this room, which he did.) There was no personal covenant in the Treaty Room this evening, however, as a brief and heated exchange occurred between Ted and Joan. According to a witness who worked as a social secretary to Ethel at the time, all were eating their *soufflé au chocolat* when Ted and Joan began discussing a young secretary who worked for Ted. Joan hinted that she felt Ted was becoming "just a little too close" to the woman.

"This is not the place to discuss it," Ted said angrily. Joan opened her mouth to protest, but Ted silenced her with a stern look. After an uncomfortable moment, he popped open a bottle of 1959 Dom Perignon, poured the bubbly into a glass, and handed it to Joan.

"She feels better after she's had a little drink," he told the others with a chuckle.

"Don't we all," Ethel said, wryly.

Humiliated, Joan put the drink down and ran from the room. Jackie, who was drinking a daiquiri, handed it to Jack without a word, got up, and followed Joan. After a beat, Ethel rose and followed her sisters-in-law.

The Bouviers

Why would an intelligent, beautiful, and graceful woman such as America's youngest First Lady, Jackie Kennedy, put up with such flagrant infidelity from her husband? The answer is as complex as the woman herself. Part of solving the puzzle is in understanding the qualities and feelings Jackie developed through her relationships with her parents.

While there were a number of superficial similarities between the backgrounds of Ethel Skakel and Jacqueline Bouvier, there were also important distinctions. Though both women came from wealth, the manners by which they were raised couldn't have been more different. Ethel was raised in a home full of pistol-shooting, car-wrecking juvenile delinquents, and she enjoyed every second of it. That kind of lifestyle would have appalled Jackie, who had enjoyed a genteel, elegant upbringing.

John Vernou "Black Jack" Bouvier, Jackie's father, was a personable and self-confident man, a world-class rogue who had always exuded a sensual charisma. Devilishly handsome, with dark, slicked-back hair and a Clark Gable mustache, Black Jack earned his nickname because of his potent sex appeal and his legendary womanizing, not to mention his year-round suntan. Although his father, known as The Major, was a much-admired lawyer, and Jack himself had a seat on the stock exchange, he was not an erudite, serious person. A man who insisted on living his life recklessly, he gambled compulsively, drank to excess, squandered his money, and borrowed from nearly everyone he knew in order to maintain his lavish lifestyle. His charm was so great, though, that both men and women tended to forgive him his excesses—as well as his debts.

Jackie's mother, Janet Lee Bouvier, was a sometimes confounding woman whose love for money and status practically ruled her life. Janet had created a fanciful story about her family tree, saying she was of French aristocratic background, and then handed the myth down to Jackie. For Jackie, just as it was for her mother, even in the early days image was everything. Janet had even managed to put together a phony genealogy to prove her heritage to skeptics. She was actually just following the lead of her father, James T. Lee, who had claimed he was the son of a high-ranking Confederate officer in the Civil War, and also that he was born in New York City. Neither assertion was true.

Janet passed down to both her daughters the imperative to improve their social standings and acquire wealth. Her own father had risen from the slums of Manhattan's Lower East Side and made a fortune in real estate development. Merely having money, however, wasn't enough for Janet; she yearned to be a part of high society. So she overlooked Black Jack's shady reputation and accepted an offer of marriage from him, mostly because of the reputation of his father and the prestige he held in social circles. Marrying into the Bouvier family was likely to improve her station in life. Ironically, while she married him because of his family's pedigree, he married her for her family's money: Sometimes he had his own, sometimes he did not, so it was a good idea for him to marry into wealth. Janet didn't let on to Black Jack that her family's wealth was also overstated. Still, she and her new husband managed to settle in the wealthy resort town of Southampton, on the eastern end of Long Island, New York.

John and Janet would have two daughters: Jacqueline, born on July 29, 1929, just months before the stock market crash decimated the fortunes of so many Wall Street financiers; and Caroline Lee (known as Lee), born three and a half years later.

From all accounts, Jackie was a headstrong, precocious child. Her mother imparted her own love of riding to Jackie, and both mother and daughter rode in horse shows together. Jackie started competing at five years of age and was as competitive as any Kennedy when it came to winning blue ribbons.

Even as a child, Jackie learned out of necessity not to reveal her feelings. In September 1936, Janet insisted on a six-month separation from Black Jack that later resulted in divorce. In those days divorce was not the common occurrence it is today, and Janet made it appear even more lurid by leaking a story to the newspapers that she was divorcing her husband because of adultery; she even identified his mistresses by name. Jackie, who quickly became the object of much schoolgirl gossip, immersed herself in her studies and spent more time than usual on her riding lessons, as though nothing unusual was happening.

In 1940, when Jackie was eleven, her parents divorced. Janet soon bettered her social position by marrying an even wealthier man, Hugh Dudley "Hughdie" Auchincloss, an investment banking attorney whose fortune was seemingly secure. Auchincloss had three children from his previous marriages and would have two more with Janet.

In her new life with her stepfather, Jackie would experience a lifestyle even more lavish than the one to which she had grown accustomed, and she would take full advantage of the resources her privileged world afforded her. Attending the best schools available, she excelled in her studies. Because she was able to travel, she mastered four languages and acquired a vast knowledge of foreign cultures. Surrounded by the finest things in life, she developed impeccable taste and an appreciation for art, music, literature, and architecture.

The Auchinclosses divided their time between two estates. The first was Hammersmith Farm, overlooking Narragansett Bay in Newport, Rhode Island. This was a sprawling, twenty-eight-room mansion with thirteen fireplaces and a working farm that supplied the Newport naval base with eggs and milk. Because so many of the local farmhands had gone to war, all of the children were put to work; Jackie was responsible for feeding two thousand chickens each day. The other Auchincloss home was Merrywood, located on forty-six acres and

fronting the Potomac River in Virginia. The property included an indoor badminton court, stables, an Olympic-size pool, and a kitchen
with enough facilities to serve three hundred people. Yet the opulence
was all a charade. Just as Black Jack could never hang on to his money
and was always in debt, Auchincloss had similar financial problems
due to bad investments and poor management. Whether the family
had enough money to support its lifestyle was always a big concern,
and Jackie learned to live with it. If she was going to marry for wealth,
she would be sure that the gentleman she was marrying truly *was*
wealthy and not just *acting* wealthy.

Although there was a rancorous tug-of-war between Jackie's
mother and father for the beautiful, dark-eyed child's affections, Jackie
and her natural father shared an almost obsessive love for one another.
When she went to Vassar College (making the Dean's List in her first
year), she kept photos of her father in her room and spoke of him constantly. For his part, Black Jack's New York apartment was filled with
many stunning pictures and expensive oil paintings, some of Lee, but
many more of Jackie. John Davis recalls, "Jackie so loved being with
her father, it was as if she just bathed in his compliments of her. Janet
would notice this, and it would drive her completely up the wall. She
was very jealous of the way Jackie idolized her father."

The love Jackie had for her father, along with the social ambition
inspired by her mother and the penchant she had for the finer things
in life, all came together to form the model of what she wanted in a
mate. Unlike her mother, Jackie would not marry only to improve her
status, though that was a consideration. Instead, she would wait until
she met a man with whom she could actually fall in love and who also
happened to embody the qualities she was looking for: a wealthy person who would match her in intelligence and ambition, yet someone
who also had the swagger and panache of her adored father. She had
dated a number of men and was even briefly engaged to one—John
Husted, a handsome investment banker—before settling on a young
senator from Massachusetts, John F. Kennedy. The two met in May
1951 at a party hosted by newsman and Kennedy family friend Charles
Bartlett and his wife, Martha. Although Jackie was still in college, she
had enough poise to interest Jack, twelve years older and a man who
reminded her very much of her own father. "Jackie, who was a college
senior at the time, couldn't have been attracted to a man unless he was

dangerous, like her father," Lem Billings once observed. "It was Freudian. Jack knew about her attraction to Black Jack and even discussed it with her. She didn't deny it." They were immediately drawn to one another, and thus the storybook tale began.

Jack conducted an unromantic courtship: He was undemonstrative in public, did not send flowers, gifts, or love letters, and, like his brothers, barely made it clear that he was interested. Notorious for not carrying money with him, he expected whomever he was with to pick up the tab for taxis and meals. So when they dated, this chore fell to Jackie. Still, she knew a good thing when she saw it, and she saw it in Jack: She was swept away by him.

The package that Jackie presented to her beau was certainly an appealing one to the politically ambitious John Kennedy and his family. Joseph Kennedy's lifelong obsession was to have a son in the White House. After his first son, Joseph Jr., was killed in an air mishap during World War II, the elder Kennedy put all his attentions into the next in line, Jack, whom he began grooming for the Presidency. When thirty-five-year-old Jack won a congressional seat in November 1952 by defeating three-term Massachusetts senator Henry Cabot Lodge, he was encouraged by his father to change his playboy image and find a wife, a partner for public relations purposes as well as for mating, a potential First Lady.

There were many women in Jack's life, some of them famous actresses such as Lee Remick, Zsa Zsa Gabor, and Sophia Loren, and some of them not as well known, like Ruta Lee; but they were always sexy, young, and ready to follow him anywhere. Entire books have been written about his life and times before he knew Jackie.

Because Jackie had the sophistication and class that wives of heads of state were supposed to project, along with beauty and glamour equal to the movie stars to whom father and son had always been attracted, she soon became a front-runner in the marital race. Also in her favor was the fact that she had a "proper" upbringing and her reputation was untarnished, which was expected of political wives at the time; for the most part, Jack's other girlfriends were anything but demure. Jack had also said in one interview that what he was looking for in a spouse was someone "intelligent but not too brainy." As insulting as that comment may have been, Jackie, a woman of her times, understood it. "No man wants a woman who's smarter than he is," she said, so typically 1950s in her attitude about male-female relationships.

"She was also funny. People always tend to forget her wicked sense of humor," said Sancy Newman, a neighbor of the Kennedys in Hyannis Port who knew Jack and all of the Kennedys as children. "She was completely different from anyone he had ever dated, not your average pretty girl. She had great wit and could give it right back to him just as quickly as he could throw it at her."

Stephen Smith, Jean's husband and Jackie's future brother-in-law, once recalled, "Jack always said how smart Jackie was, and she really was. What they had going between them was this sense of humor. And she could cut him down, and did—no question about it. When she felt strongly about something, she let him know it and let everyone else know it, too."

"She's the one," Joseph told his son. "I have a good feeling about this girl, Jacqueline. Trust me. She's the one."

While Jack and Jackie were dating, John Davis met with his cousin for lunch at the Mayflower Hotel in Washington. Jackie was working at the time for the *Times-Herald* newspaper as "The Inquiring Photographer," a job that found her snapping pictures of people after asking them questions about current events. She would then combine photos and text for a column.

He recalls, "Jackie thought that Jack was rather vain. She talked about how he had to have his hair done all the time, how he had to always look just right. I laughed to myself because, certainly, she was very much the same way. She said that he would sulk for hours if he was at a party and hadn't been recognized. Again, I laughed to myself. That, too, was very much like Jackie. Then she said to me, 'Really, John, I think the Kennedys are terribly, terribly bourgeois.' I laughed to myself, again . . . for obvious reasons."

Jackie began devoting time and energy to Jack's work by helping him edit and write senatorial position papers on Southeast Asia, and even translating several books for him, including the work of French writer Paul Mus, who was an expert on France's involvement in Vietnam. (Fluent in French, Jackie had attended the Sorbonne after her two years at Vassar.)

"Whenever he came across something in French, the senator would think, 'My wife could translate the research material,' " recalls Kennedy friend and speechwriter Ted Sorenson. "I don't think she herself regarded herself as a political savant or counselor. She had judgments of political figures as people, as individuals, but usually not related to their political positions—except that she loved Jack and people who liked him, and who he liked, she liked. People who were mean to him, she didn't like. There was something there between them, and it was good."

Others perceived Jack and Jackie differently. "I could see Jack behaving very badly with Jackie very early on, at the beginning of their engagement," recalls Betty Beale, who was a columnist for the *Washington Evening Star*. "I talked to Jackie on the phone shortly after they announced the engagement so that I could write about it. She told me in an offhand way that he was going to Eden Roc [with his friend Torby McDonald and father, Joseph] for a vacation on the French Riviera without her. The men had chartered a boat, and off they went for a wild time. You'd think that an engaged man would be lusting after his fiancée and want to be with her. She didn't express any concern or annoyance about him going, however, she just told me matter-of-factly, 'Jack is going away. He's gone every year, and he's going back.' She minimized its significance."

Jackie's First Meeting with Ethel

By the time Jackie Kennedy got into the White House in January 1961, she and Ethel Kennedy had known each other for about six years "for better or worse," as Jackie once referred to their often contentious relationship. Sweetness and light weren't always possible in a family like the Kennedys, whose members had widely differing temperaments, and probably no two of them were more at odds over the years than Jackie and Ethel. Once she became First Lady, Jackie was the embodiment of everything Ethel wanted to be: a powerful, intelligent, and attractive woman who commanded the world's attention and respect just for being herself. Ethel felt that, if her life worked out as she planned, Bobby would one day be President and she would have the status she so craved. Meanwhile, she just had to tolerate the fact that Jackie had it and she didn't—at least for the time being.

From the first time they met, though, Jackie presented herself as a princess, even on Ethel's own, royal, home turf.

In March 1953, when Ethel Kennedy settled into her new Georgetown home, she longed to meet Bobby's new friends in government. She hoped to demonstrate her ability as a hostess to the Kennedy family, especially after Jean had told her, "You can't be in this family unless you know how to entertain." Ethel had certainly come from a clan who knew how to throw a good party, and she was anxious to show Bobby's side of the family that she was worthy of her distinction as the only Kennedy wife so far (other than the matriarch, Rose). So she decided to host a get-together at her home in honor of St. Patrick's Day—an affair of about thirty people, mostly family but with some important business associates of Bobby's as well. When Bobby's brother Jack heard about Ethel's plans, he called to ask if she could invite his new girlfriend, Jacqueline Bouvier. Ethel readily agreed. She liked the senator a great deal and would do anything to please him.

Two days later, Ethel telephoned Jackie to invite her to the party and inform her of the unusual theme: All of the guests were to wear black, which seemed particularly strange for a St. Patrick's Day party.

On the night of the party, Jack showed up first, on crutches and slippers, his chronic back troubles causing him great discomfort. "I'm dying here," he said. "This damn back is killing me." Jim Buckley, brother of magazine publisher William F. Buckley and who would go on to become a New York senator and one day marry Ethel's college friend Ann Cooley, asked Jack about his date. "Oh, she's a looker," Jack said. "Wait until you get a load of her. She's my new dance partner," he added with a grin.

Anxious to make an entrance befitting a Bouvier—and perhaps hoping to impress her new beau and his friends—Jackie was the last to arrive. Whereas everyone else had either driven his or her own car or took a cab to Bobby and Ethel's, Jackie showed up in a chauffeur-driven black Rolls Royce. She did wear black, though, as did all of the guests. Jackie wore an elegant dark cocktail dress embroidered with silver threads in medallion shapes, along with white pearls and matching earrings. A black fur coat was the perfect wintry touch.

As if on cue, shortly after Jackie's arrival, Ethel came swooping down the staircase from the second floor. "Here I am, everybody. *How are you all?*" Her smile was dazzling as she walked about the room, meeting and greeting her guests, all of whom looked at her with expressions of astonishment. Ethel was wearing a stunning green diaphanous gown—and not just one shade, but layer upon layer of different hues of green. The center of attention, Ethel graciously spent time with each guest and began to acquit herself well as the ideal hostess.

Jackie stood in a corner and watched Ethel with an inscrutable expression. Lem Billings, who attended the party, remembered, "About an hour into the party, she came over to me and said, 'Interesting woman, that Ethel.' I told her, 'Once you get to know her, I think you'll like her.'"

Billings asked Jackie, "Now, does it upset you, the way she set this up?"

"Oh, no. Not in the least," Jackie said with a chuckle. "After all, it *is* her party. As hostess, she can do whatever she likes, don't you agree? Now, personally, I would never do anything like that. But how utterly clever of her."

To another guest, Jackie said, "How refreshing it will be to know someone who has no interest whatsoever in impressing anyone with her fashion taste."

When Jackie and Ethel finally met for the first time, their exchange was unmemorable, chilly and brief. Jackie stayed to herself for the rest of the evening, not mingling but rather seeming to pose regally in front of the roaring fireplace—a perfect picture. The way she had positioned herself she had everyone's attention, and so for the next hour Jack fetched his senatorial friends and brought them over to make her acquaintance. All the while, Ethel eyed Jackie, muttering to Bobby that the Bouvier interloper was trying to pull the room's focus to her. "It's *not* my imagination," she was overheard saying angrily. Finally, long before any of the other invitees, Jackie walked over to Ethel and Bobby and told them that she had to go.

"Before dinner?" Ethel was flabbergasted. "But we have a wonderful meal prepared."

Jack was already helping Jackie with her fur as she apologized and said that she had "the most dreadful headache ever." As much as she wanted to stay, she said, she couldn't.

Jackie then walked through the small crowd, shaking hands and kissing cheeks as if she were royalty. After she had bid adieu to everyone, Jack escorted her to the front door and to her waiting Rolls. Some of Ethel's guests peered through the front windows to watch with mesmerized expressions as the uniformed chauffeur popped out of the driver's side of the car, whipped around to the other side, and opened the door for Jackie. After she had gotten into the automobile, he closed the door and ran back to the driver's seat. As the car started to pull away, Jackie rolled down the window and grandly waved farewell to her fans in Ethel's living room.

"Well, I never . . ." Ethel said, not bothering to hide her fury.

"Clearly," Bobby said, his eye twinkling. He was taken with Jack's new girlfriend and liked her from the start.

Later, over dinner, Ethel still couldn't get over what had occurred with Jackie. "Jack-leen," she observed as she and her guests discussed Jack's new girlfriend. "Rhymes with 'queen,' doesn't it?" It was a stolen quip, actually; Eunice had already said it after meeting Jackie for the first time.

Still, Jack was amused by the observation. "Seems rather appropriate, doesn't it?" he said.

The next day, Jackie sent Ethel a letter. "I had such a wonderful time," she wrote in her difficult-to-read backhand. "So many fascinating people, so much wonderful conversation. And you, Ethel, were the most perfect hostess, so lovley [sic], and so beautiful in your greenery. I thank you so much for inviting me, and I feel absolutely dreadful that I had to leave in such a completely inappropriate rush."

Upon receipt of the note, Ethel found herself confused about "Jackleen." Anyone who complimented her on one of her parties was definitely a person Ethel appreciated and wanted in her circle. However, because Jackie had also proved herself to be a scene-stealer, Ethel didn't know whether to love her or loathe her. Of course, in years to come, Ethel's predicament would be one in which many people would find themselves when it came to Jackie.

Despite the letter Ethel had received—which, because it was so confounding to her, she shared with anyone—most of her friends were appalled by Jackie's behavior at the gathering. However Ethel, never one to conform, decided to take an opposing point of view. "You know what? I like her," she said approvingly. "I really do. I like her nerve. My mother would get a kick out of her, too."

A week later, as Ethel and Jackie enjoyed lunch together in a

Washington restaurant, Jackie gifted her with a pin: a delicate green four-leaf clover with a small diamond in the center of each leaf. Jackie further ingratiated herself by sharing a confidence with Ethel: The reason she had to leave the party in such a rush was that she was suffering from premenstrual cramps. According to what Ethel would later recall, Jackie said that her illness made it unbearable for her to have to meet all of the people Jack kept bringing over to her. Also, she said she was "absolutely freezing," which was the reason she was standing in front of the fireplace during most of the party.

Ethel explained that the reason the temperature was so frigid in her home was that Rose Kennedy was angry at her and Bobby for their spending habits, "and Bobby said I could only have the party if I didn't use any heat. He said, 'It's either heat or a party. You choose.' So, naturally, I chose the party."

"Well, naturally," Jackie agreed.

After the two women shared a hearty laugh, Jackie asked Ethel to keep sacred the secret of her premenstrual cramps. Ethel promised to tell "not a soul."

But how could she resist? In weeks to come, Ethel would tell just about everyone she knew all of the details of her lunch with Jackie, including her little secret. Ethel also proved herself to be a perceptive woman because, after just one luncheon with Jackie, she seemed to understand something about her that it usually took others much longer to discern. "She asks a lot of questions, on and on and on with the questions," Ethel said. "And I'm sitting there answering all of these questions when it suddenly hit me: As long as she keeps me busy talking, she doesn't have to give me any information about herself."

Jack Proposes Marriage

In the months after their first meeting, Ethel Kennedy and Jackie Bouvier got to know each other on weekend Kennedy outings. Football games at the Georgetown Recreation Center were particularly amusing. Ethel fit right in with the Kennedy brothers—and even their sisters, who played a raucous and sometimes even violent game. Jackie, of course, hated these kinds of sports. The first time she got out on the field, she somehow managed to catch a ball hurled at her by Jack. Stunned at her good luck, she stood in the middle of the field, dazed, and said, "Now, which way do I run, exactly?"

"Aw, get that debutante off the field," Ethel said, annoyed. "You gotta be kidding me!" (Ethel had never gotten over her astonishment when Bobby told her that Jackie had once been given the title "Queen Deb of the Year" by New York society reporter Cholly Knicker-bocker—a.k.a. Igor Cassini, brother of designer Oleg. "And she was actually proud of that?" Ethel wanted to know.)

Trying to fit in, Jackie continued to play football every time a game was organized, until one weekend she sprained her ankle. (Some say she broke it.) As she sat in the middle of the field, sobbing and hold-ing her foot, Jack, Bobby, and the other Kennedys stared at her in dis-belief. Kennedys don't cry, after all—or at least that had always been the family myth. It was Ethel who ran over to the "debutante," her mothering instincts surfacing. "Oh, you poor dear," she said as she helped Jackie hobble to the sidelines. "Now, you have to go straight home and get some ice and put it in a towel, then use it on your ankle. Otherwise it will swell." Then she turned to the others, who were by now laughing, and screamed at them, "Don't laugh at her. Don't be so mean. She's getting better at the game."

After that incident, however, Jackie decided that she would never play football with the Kennedys again.

For years, it has been said that Jackie and Ethel were not, and could never be, friends. That was not the case. In fact, Jackie and Ethel treaded warily into a friendship and developed a deep, profound un-derstanding that would last for decades. At the beginning they set cer-tain boundaries.

For instance, Jackie loved to talk about her father's sexual exploits, shocking Ethel with her frank discussions. Because Ethel, who never liked talking about sex, was clearly uncomfortable hearing about Black Jack's private life, he soon became a subject the two women rarely dis-cussed. Jackie's parents were divorced, and Jackie had no problem with divorce at all. Ethel didn't believe in divorce, however, and was vocal about her disapproval. Once, at a family picnic, the two women engaged in a heated discussion about whether or not Jackie was a true Catholic because, as Ethel put it, "If you were, you wouldn't approve of divorce."

"Well, if you were, you wouldn't be so judgmental about what I do and do not approve of," Jackie shot back.

"Oh yeah? Well, I . . . I . . . I don't even know what you're talkin' about," Ethel said.

In time, the two women learned not to broach the subject of divorce, though they did have many more discussions about the pros and cons of Roman Catholicism. (Jackie was fairly religious, actually, but few could match Ethel's devotion.)

Nevertheless, Ethel did continue to give Jackie a hard time for many years to come. "Ethel was more Kennedy than the Kennedys," says John Davis. "She made Jackie prove herself, yes. She could try a saint's patience, and even though my cousin [Jackie] was not a saint, she was pretty close just by virtue of the fact that she never went to blows with Ethel, at least not to my knowledge."

"Jackie was put through her paces by the whole family," says family friend Dinah Bridge. "And she stood up extremely well to the Kennedy barrage of questions, and that was quite a barrage. You had to know the form to keep up, you know, because the jokes went so fast, and the chitter-chat."

It's often been reported over the years that Jackie worked hard to win the Kennedys' acceptance, that she longed for their approval; yet this was an inaccurate assessment. While she did want to make Jack happy, and hoped his family would accept her, Jackie had the self-confidence to know that they would have no choice. "She already had Jack," says Lem Billings. "She didn't need the rest of them. That was her attitude. If they like me, great. If not, the hell with them. I am who I am. They're lucky to have me in the family at all."

At one Kennedy outing on one of their yachts, Eunice opened the picnic basket she always packed for the family and began handing out thick peanut-butter and jelly sandwiches to all aboard.

"I put extra strawberry jam on this one for you," Eunice said as she handed Jackie a sandwich, the messy jelly dripping out of its sides and down her hands.

"Oh my God, no," Jackie said, looking at the offering with disgust. She hated jelly. "I brought my own lunch." She opened her own wicker picnic basket and pulled from it a plate of *pâté*, a vegetable quiche, and a bottle of white wine. "Anyone care for some?" she offered, as family members around her shared not-so-secret looks of exasperation.

"*Pâté?* Hell, yeah," Joseph said enthusiastically. "I'd love some." From the start, Joseph liked Jackie and appreciated her individuality and sense of flair. "Who else do we know who speaks French, Spanish, and Italian?" he would say. "That's going to come in handy for Jack, believe me." For her part, Jackie would say of Joseph, "When I first met him, I did not realize that I was supposed to be scared of him—so I wasn't. That may have been *lèse-majesté*—but it was a wonderful way to start."

By the summer of 1953, Jackie had won over the rest of the Kennedys. "I'm so glad we'll be sisters-in-law," she told Ethel one afternoon at a pre-wedding party at Joseph and Rose's. After Bobby proposed a toast to the soon-to-be-newlyweds, Jackie gave a small speech to those present at the table: Rose and Joseph, Bobby and Ethel, Ted, Eunice, Pat, Lem Billings, and a few others. She loathed the idea of getting up and speaking, but it was a Kennedy tradition that everyone had to give a toast, whether he or she liked it or not.

"Ethel and I couldn't be more different," Jackie said, her toast directed to her future sister-in-law. She continued to say that if all of the family members were of the same disposition, "we'd be a very prosaic bunch, now wouldn't we?" In conclusion, she added that in the short time she had known the family, she'd come to realize that the Kennedys "are nothing if not the most exciting family, perhaps in the world."

"Hear, hear!" Joseph said, laughing. "That's the truth, isn't it, Rose?"

"Hear, hear!" Rose repeated, smiling approvingly.

She sat back down next to Jack, who smiled warmly at his fiancée, who had once again dazzled his entire family.

"Okay then. Here's to Jack and Jackie," Ethel said, raising her glass and seizing some attention for herself in the process. "Long may they be happy."

"Long may they be happy," everyone repeated as they clicked glasses.

In time, Jackie began to reveal concerns about her future husband's philandering. Estelle Parker, the fashion designer who fitted Jackie for her trousseau, recalls Jackie asking her for her opinion about men who cheat on their wives. "She seemed confused, undecided," said Parker. "She also realized that if she married into that family she would be expected to cater to their every whim. Kennedy women were treated like second-class citizens. Jackie wasn't prepared to tolerate that sort of treatment."

However, Jackie dismissed her apprehension and decided she could handle any problems she might encounter with her husband and his family. She was the type of woman who could look at a problem from all sides, make a decision about its solution, and then follow through with it. "I'll find my own place in this family," she told Lem Billings. "Don't worry about me."

So the wedding was on. "I'll never forget when I got a letter from Jack asking me to be an usher," recalled his good friend Paul "Red" Fay. "It said, 'I guess this is the end of a promising career in politics, which has been mostly based on sex appeal.'"

On September 12, 1953, in a lavish ceremony at St. Mary's in Newport, Jacqueline Bouvier and John Fitzgerald Kennedy were wed. No one was happier than Jack's father, Joseph. Not only did his son have a beautiful new wife who would one day make the perfect First Lady, but the media coverage was all that the publicity-hungry Kennedy patriarch could hope for.

While Janet Auchincloss had hoped for a small, elegant wedding, Joseph wanted it large and showy. For Joseph, this ceremony was not just a social event, it was part of a political campaign. In the end, Janet gave in. It was important to her that her daughter marry well. If the Kennedys weren't as aristocratic as she would have liked (she had hoped that Jackie would marry a French nobleman, or at least a Rockefeller), they did have money, and right now she didn't. Her husband was cash-poor, even though he and his wife were still somehow living like royalty.

Bobby was the best man, and Ethel was one of the bridesmaids. Jackie's sister, Lee, was matron of honor. Among the six hundred invited guests were prominent politicians and influential newspaper and magazine writers. Boston Archbishop Richard Cushing celebrated the nuptial mass, assisted by four other prominent Catholic clergymen. As an added bonus, Cushing read a telegram from Pope Pius XII, who also approved of the marriage. The church was decorated with pink gladioli and white chrysanthemums, and three thousand spectators converged upon it to get a glimpse of the thirty-six-year-old groom and his twenty-four-year-old bride.

"It was a beautiful, fairy tale of a wedding," recalls Sancy Newman, who attended all three of the brothers' weddings. "Everyone said the most perfect things, wore the most perfect clothes, and had the most perfect manners. It was picture perfect."

After the ceremony, Jack and Jackie spent their wedding night at the Waldorf-Astoria in New York before departing for a honeymoon in Acapulco and then, on the way back, at the bucolic San Ysidro Ranch outside Santa Barbara, California.

Upon their return, the newlyweds rented a two-bedroom home in Georgetown, a short distance from where Ethel and Bobby lived. Ethel loaned drapes and slipcovers to Jackie for the new house, and even though their tastes were completely different, Jackie still appreciated Ethel's thoughtfulness.

As Kennedy intimate Chuck Spalding recalled, "People have always said how different they were, and in terms of their personalities, yes, that was true. But as wives, they had a lot in common. For instance, it's been thought for years that Ethel was the greatest housewife in the world. Untrue. That was a myth created, I think, because of all the children. She was a mess, though, a sloppy mess. She had a lot of help around the house, maids and servants, whom she treated very poorly but who were there just the same, picking up after her and her kids. Jackie was just as bad. She was a woman who had never scrubbed a floor a day in her life. And as a cook? Forget it! Women of her class never cooked their own meals anyway."

One morning, according to Spalding, newlywed Jackie pulled sister-in-law Ethel aside at a family gathering to ask a question. "Now, just how do you make that delicious fried chicken of yours?" she wanted to know.

"Whoever said I made delicious fried chicken?" Ethel asked.

"Well, Jack says you make the best fried chicken in the world."

Ethel laughed. "No, it's his sister Eunice. She's the one who makes fried chicken. All I did was get the recipe from her and give it to my cook. And now *she* makes the best fried chicken in the world, too. I can lend it to you if you like."

Jackie thought it over, then asked, "Do you think you could lend me your cook instead?"

All of This, and More

Just a little over a year into their marriage, the newlywed Kennedys were faced with their first major challenge as they dealt with Jack's serious health problems. Ten years earlier, in 1944, Jack had undergone spinal surgery, partly because of injuries he had sustained when the PT boat (the famous PT-109) that he commanded during the war was rammed and split by a Japanese destroyer. After a night in the water, and with his back crippled by the crash, the heroic JFK swam five hours to land, towing the boat's badly burned engineer behind him. Kennedy had already suffered from back problems even before 1944, however, dating from a football injury at Harvard.

In October 1954, Jack was admitted to the Hospital for Special Surgery at Cornell University Medical Center in New York City for more spinal surgery. At that time, doctors performed a double-fusion operation on his spine, in hopes of strengthening his back. It didn't go well, and for the next three days he would be on the critical list.

Lem Billings recalled, "Jackie was usually the type to never show fear, but she was scared, very much so, about all of Jack's illnesses. Not only did he have Addison's disease [caused by underactive adrenal glands], he had a variety of back problems. He was on different drugs and medications, so many you couldn't keep track of them all, including cortisone shots to treat the Addison's. [One of the side effects of cortisone is an increase in libido, which likely exacerbated an already existing problem of hypersexual activity for JFK.] He had muscle spasms, and was being shot up with Novocain all the time. He was always very sick.

"After that first operation, he was in bad shape, critical condition for, I think, three weeks. They had to give him the Last Rites while Jackie stood there. His face was pale and swollen, his breathing heavy and irregular. I remember Jackie placing her hand on his forehead and saying, 'Help him, Mother of God. Oh, help him.'"

So frightened was she that while she stood at her husband's side, Jackie barely heard the priest as he intoned the Last Rites, "*Libera me, Domine, de morte aeterna . . .*" Afterward, slumping into a plastic chair in the hospital corridor, she said to Lem Billings, "What if Jack can't take all of this? What if we lose him?"

Billings put his hand on her shoulder. "Listen, he's too goddamn stubborn, Jackie," he told her with a smile. "I've known him too long to think otherwise. He's not going anywhere. I promise you that."

Jackie looked up at her husband's good friend with tears in her eyes. "If I ever lose him, Lem, I'll die," she said, and she seemed to really mean it.

Later that day, after news had gotten out that the senator was on his deathbed, reporters began to congregate at the hospital. Most were contained in the lobby, but one managed to sneak up to Jack's floor. He confronted Jackie as she was fretting to Ted about her husband's condition. "Mrs. Kennedy, is it true that your husband is dying?" he asked. Jackie was stunned by the question. Ted turned and, with tears in his eyes, snapped at the reporter, "Look, my brother's darn sick, that's all. But he's going to pull through, you wait and see. His name is Jack Kennedy—*Kennedy*—and he's going to pull through. You got that?" Then Ted took Jackie's hand and led her away. Edward DeBlasio, a writer who tells this story, adds: "The expression in her eyes was one of pure love, for what Ted had said, for what he had done, for how he had helped her in this, her most trying hour."

"When Jack began to recover, Jackie was at his side every moment," recalls Kennedy friend Charles Bartlett. "She really rose to the occasion, spending every second trying to entertain him, calm him, show him her love for him. Playing games, checkers, Twenty Questions, whatever it took to keep his mind off his pain. The family was very impressed with the way she hung in there. She even brought Grace Kelly to his bedside, for goodness' sake."

Grace Kelly, in an oral history she gave for the JFK Library in June 1965, recalled, "I had been to a dinner party where I met Mrs. Kennedy and her sister for the first time. They asked me to go to the hospital with them to pay a visit and help cheer him [Jack] up. They wanted me to go to his room and say I was his new night nurse. Well, I hesitated. I was terribly embarrassed. Eventually, I was just sort of pushed into the room by the two of them. I introduced myself and he had recognized me at once, and he couldn't have been sweeter or more quick to put me at ease."

A few days after Jack's surgery, Jackie arrived to find a poster of a movie star taped above Jack's bed. It was Marilyn Monroe, in shorts and a tight sweater.

"Now, what is that doing up there?" Jackie wanted to know.

"I like her," Jack said with a grin. "I find her rather attractive, don't you?"

Two doctors would later say they noted an uncomfortable silence in the room, after which Jackie said, "You know, I have the exact same outfit. Why not take that down and I'll have a similar photo made of myself for the same space?"

"A capital idea," Jack exclaimed. However, the poster of Marilyn remained until the day he checked out of the hospital. In fact, he had it turned upside down, so that her legs were in the air.

For the next few months, Jack would suffer immeasurable pain, and would have to endure another operation as a result of an infection caused by a metal plate implanted during the first surgery. In one of her oral histories filed at the JFK Library, Jack's primary physician, Dr. Janet Travell, recalled a conversation between Jackie and Ethel at the Hospital for Special Surgery.

"Mrs. Kennedy [Jackie] was the most patient, understanding, and brave woman," said Travell. "At one point, she learned that she had to change the senator's dressing. This wasn't easy. It was a substantial wound, a gaping wound, very difficult for a layperson to deal with. Mrs. Kennedy would be the one who would have to change the dressing when he would be released from the hospital, and she did it, and valiantly." In truth, Jackie did not have to be the one to change the dressings, therefore she must have wanted to. Certainly she must have felt it was her duty as Jack's wife, and perhaps she also didn't want anyone else to see his pain.

George Taylor had been Jack's valet and chauffeur up until 1946, when Jack had become a congressman. Even after that time, he remained friends with him, and visited him at the hospital. He once recalled, "I remember the day Ethel came to visit, and she found out that Jackie was going to be changing these dressings and caring for Jack. She didn't understand it at all. 'How can you do it?' she asked her. 'How can you bear to see him that way? I could never do it.'

"'When you love someone,' Jackie told her, 'you do all of this and more, Ethel. All of this and more.'"

*   *   *

By 1955, Ethel Kennedy had given birth to a third child, Robert F. Kennedy, Jr. The next baby, David Anthony, would be born a year later. (In the course of the 1950s, Ethel and Bobby would have three more children: Mary Courtney, Michael LeMoyne, and Mary Kerry, in 1956, 1958, and 1959, respectively.)

A year earlier, Bobby had resigned his post on the McCarthy Committee after only seven months, following a dispute with committee Republican majority counsel member Roy Cohn. He then went to work with his father, Joseph, as his assistant on the Commission on Reorganization of the Executive Branch (also known as the Hoover Commission, since it was headed by former President Herbert Hoover). Bored, Bobby didn't keep that job for long and ended up back on the McCarthy Committee, this time as counsel to the committee's three-member Democratic minority. Bobby joined just in time for the historic nationally televised Army–McCarthy hearings from April 22 to June 16, 1954, which focused on allegations that the U.S. Army was harboring communists; the Army countercharged that Roy Cohn had sought preferential treatment for Private G. David Schine, Cohn's best friend and a recent Army draftee. (The question of Cohn's possible homosexual relationship with Schine was also raised in private quarters.)

As the fifties progressed, Bobby would become known for his racket-busting stance, especially as Chief Counsel to the Senate Permanent Subcommittee on Investigations (known as the Senate Rackets Committee).* By going up against thugs and mobsters as well as assorted blue-collar criminals in the Capitol's hearing rooms, Bobby acquired his reputation as the shrewdest, most hotheaded of the Kennedy clan. Because Jack was one of the thirty-six senators on the committee, Ethel and Jackie would spend much of the next two years attending the hearings. They were proud of their husbands' work, and the time they spent together—and with the Kennedy sisters—strengthened their relationship.

It was at around this time that Ethel and Bobby moved into Hickory Hill. Ethel modeled her Hickory Hill lifestyle after Big

*Estes Kefauver, a Democrat from Tennessee, chaired the committee's hearings into organized crime, which set the stage for his selection, over Jack Kennedy, as Adlai Stevenson's presidential running mate in 1956.

Ann's hectic Lake Avenue estate, and the same kind of mad, hysterical goings-on would come to characterize Ethel and Bobby's home life.

On October 4, 1955, Ethel Kennedy received terrible news: Her parents, George and Big Ann, had been killed in a fiery plane crash near Oklahoma City. They had been on a business trip and George, an experienced aviator, was behind the controls. Three days later, Ethel joined her brothers, sisters, and family friends for the solemn requiem High Mass at St. Mary's in Greenwich.

In the same way that she would take on most of the ordeals of her life—including when her brother George died in another plane crash in 1966, or when, a few months later, George's widow, Patricia, choked to death on a piece of meat—Ethel handled the tragic loss of her parents stoically and with a deep sense of the Divine. After Ethel had married Bobby, a distance had developed between her and her family, who did not approve of what they viewed as the Kennedys' amoral ways, not only with women (Ann was particularly infuriated at reports of Joseph's philandering), but also with some of the family's politics as well as their religious convictions—or lack thereof. "Ann thought they were hypocrites," said Skakel family friend Lawrence Alexander. "And Ethel had to choose a lot of the time. She always chose Bobby and his family. Always."

About two weeks after Ethel returned from the funeral, Jack and Jackie paid her and Bobby a visit. Remembered Lem Billings, "Ethel was her old self, as if absolutely nothing had occurred. Later, Jack told me that Jackie had expected to find her to be very upset, visibly grieving. Jackie arrived wearing all black, in recognition of what had occurred. Ethel wore pink. Jackie's expression was so pitiful that it would have made anyone feel badly. Ethel was all smiles."

Billings says that Jackie found Ethel's attitude completely perplexing. It is more likely, however, that Jackie fully understood the manner in which Ethel concealed her feelings because, in fact, Jackie would often do the same thing. Most people never really knew what Jackie was thinking either.

"They were there for over an hour and not one single word was said about the tragedy that had occurred. In the Kennedy family, you never addressed tragedy, and the Skakels were exactly the same way," said Billings.

As they were getting ready to leave, Jackie approached Ethel.

"I just want to tell you how very, very sorry I am," Jackie said.

"About what?" Ethel asked. The two women studied each other for a moment. Suddenly Ethel's eyes began to fill with tears, her deep pain evident. She turned away, embarrassed.

Two years later, Jackie's beloved father would pass away. In his last few years, because he had become a resentful old man who felt that life had treated him unfairly, it had become difficult for Jackie to continue to have Black Jack in her life. His well-regarded charm had begun to wear as he aged, and friends were no longer as eager to bail him out of his financial woes. Jack had never expected to end up with no money, yet that's exactly what happened to him.

Whenever Jackie visited her father during his latter years, she always left with a deep sense of regret that he was nothing like the man she had so idolized. He was perpetually angry and expressed bitterness at having been "abandoned" by both of his daughters. In the summer of 1957, when Black Jack became ill and was hospitalized in New York, Jackie rushed to be by his side. She had arrived too late, however. His last word, according to a nurse, had been "Jackie."

Not allowing her grief to get in the way of practicality, Jackie managed to arrange all of the details for the funeral service at St. Patrick's Cathedral, notifying only immediate family members and just a few of Black Jack's business associates. Before she closed the coffin, Jackie took off a bracelet her father had given her as a gift and placed it in his hand.

Jackie's cousin Edie Beale recalls, "I remember that about a dozen of Jack's old beaus [sic] showed up at the funeral, much to Jackie's consternation. They just showed up, all dressed in black. And there they sat, like a fan club of Black Jack's.

"Jackie didn't cry at the funeral, not a drop. And when they buried him in East Hampton, no tears. Not a drop."

After the service, Ethel and Bobby paid Jack and Jackie the requisite post-funeral visit. Mirroring Ethel's reaction to her parents' sudden death, Jackie acted as if nothing tragic had occurred in her life as she and her sister-in-law ate the stuffed baked peaches that had been prepared by Ethel's cook. Before leaving, Ethel presented Jackie with a Bible.

"Hopefully, we won't have too much more grief in our lives, Ethel,"

Jackie said as she embraced her sister-in-law. Little did the two know what lay ahead for both of them. In just a few years—the Camelot years—they would know the kind of heartbreaking sorrow most people could never imagine. One of them would somehow weather the storm and continue with her life in a fulfilling way despite the tragedies. The other—her dreams shattered, her ambition scuttled—would never be the same.

Joseph and Jackie's Deal

Always ambitious and status-conscious, Jackie Kennedy, it would seem, made a bargain with herself early in her marriage: Any unhappiness she felt as a result of her marriage would be a tradeoff for her position in the formidable, almighty Kennedy clan. Also, those who knew her well realized that she was committed to the notion of family values where her children were concerned; she didn't want John Jr. and Caroline to come from a broken home.

Jackie hadn't always felt this way, though. Back in 1957, after the Democratic convention, she was unhappy in her marriage and distressed that her husband chose not to be at her side when she had a stillborn child, a girl she had named Arabella. Instead, he was on a Caribbean vacation.

Ethel and Jackie had lunch a month after the tragic pregnancy. Ethel later discussed details of the luncheon with a Georgetown friend, Mary Fonteyn.

"I don't want to be married to a man who is so selfish," Jackie said bitterly. "I am so miserable being married to this . . . this . . . *person.*"

Ethel was astonished. "Well, Grandpa will never let you out of that marriage, Jackie."

"Oh?" Jackie asked serenely. "Well, we'll just see about that."

According to what Ethel remembered, she left the luncheon feeling very uneasy. For the next couple of months, the Kennedys whispered among themselves that Jack's marriage was in trouble. When Washington columnist Drew Pearson printed rumors of marital discord, his story was picked up and expanded upon by *Time* magazine. After reading it, Joseph asked his son about the state of his marriage, and Jack said all was well.

Ethel, perhaps thinking she could win some points with the Kennedy patriarch, decided to betray her sister-in-law's confidence. She would later say she was doing it to "help" Jackie, though how she thought she was helping was unclear. She called Joseph and told him of her lunch with her sister-in-law and of Jackie's contemplation of divorce. Joseph thanked Ethel, probably for being such a good little Kennedy, then he sprang into action.

Sixty-eight-year-old Joseph Kennedy, who had recently undergone surgery to have his prostate removed, arranged to have a luncheon meeting with Jackie at Le Pavillon, an elegant French restaurant on East 57th Street in New York. Though he was still in a weakened state from the surgery, he wasted little time getting to business after he and Jackie sat down under bright crystal chandeliers in plush surroundings.

Because of the damage it would do to Jack's political future, divorce was not a possibility for her, Jackie was told as she picked at her chicken *polonaise*. Something would have to be negotiated, Joseph offered, a way to make her happy in a marriage that was no longer working for her.

According to a lawyer who worked for the Kennedys from 1957 to 1961 and who wishes to remain anonymous, Joseph and Jackie actually agreed upon a trust fund in the amount of one million dollars for any children she might have in the future. Perhaps Joseph was hoping to give her an incentive to try once again to have a baby. As far as he was concerned, even giving birth was a political act, for each new child demonstrated the Kennedys' commitment to family values. However, according to the lawyer, it was also agreed that if Jackie didn't have any children within five years, the million dollars would revert to her. Also—this not from the lawyer but from family friend Lem Billings—Jackie told Joseph, "The price goes up to twenty million if Jack brings home any venereal diseases from any of his sluts." Billings says that Joseph agreed, saying, "If that happens, Jackie, name your price."

According to Ethel's good friend Mary Fonteyn, Joseph agreed that Jackie could distance herself from the Kennedys and she would not be expected to see them as much or attend as many of their clique-ish social functions. She wasn't interested in politics, she said, and wanted to now devote her time and attention to literature and art. She wanted more freedom from the family, with only occasional dinners when at Hyannis Port.

"You should have the space you need," Joseph told his daughter-in-law.

"I'm so happy that you can see this from my perspective," Jackie said. The relationship these two shared had always been strong, and this meeting would only add to their deep understanding of one another.

When Ethel heard through the family grapevine that Joseph had given Jackie a million dollars to stay married to his son, she demanded to know if there was any truth to it. Ethel first asked Bobby, who said he believed it to be false. Unconvinced, she went to Rose who, in the company of Eunice and several Kennedy intimates, casually told her the truth: that Joseph had set up a trust fund for Jackie's children, should she have any.

"What?" Ethel said, immediately outraged. The women had been sitting on the porch at Rose's home in Hyannis Port. Ethel jumped from the chair. "Why would Grandpa set up a million-dollar trust fund for Jackie's children when she doesn't even have any?" Ethel wanted to know. "I have five babies right now, and there's no trust fund for them. A million dollars!" she said incredulously.

"Dear heart, you know I don't have an answer for you about that," Rose said calmly, as everyone else on the porch froze in anticipation of how this scene would be played out.

Ethel shook her head angrily. "Well, why can't Bobby and I have a million dollars, too?" she asked. "That seems only fair."

"I'm sorry, but you'll have to talk to Mr. Kennedy about this matter," Rose said formally, then she got up and walked away.

Ethel picked up a pillow from a *chaise longue* with her left hand, shot it into the air, and punched it. "A million dollars!" she repeated.

"Ethel didn't have the nerve to talk to Joseph, I guess, because, from my understanding of it, she wanted Bobby to take up the matter with his father," Mary Fonteyn said. "Ethel and Bobby fought for weeks about the matter until, finally, Bobby went to Joseph and explained the problem to him. Annoyed at the whole matter, Joseph set up a trust fund for each of Bobby and Ethel's five children,

$100,000 for each child, which each would receive at the age of twenty-one."

Despite Joseph's efforts, Ethel was still unhappy. She wanted an even million, just as Jackie had. Finally, Bobby told Ethel that if she pushed his father any further, Joseph would probably rescind the original offer. So Ethel let it go, but she wasn't happy about it.

It is not known if Jackie ever learned who had betrayed her by telling Joe of her discontent, but one might presume that had she known it was Ethel, she would have been angry with her. In fact, such a breach could have caused a serious rift between them, one that might never have been smoothed over. "Or maybe not," offers Mary Fonteyn, who remained friendly with Ethel until 1960, when the two had a falling out over Mary's refusal to loan Ethel money. ("She didn't need it," says Fonteyn. "She just wanted to see if I would do it, to test me. And I refused to play her game.") Says Fonteyn, "Jackie was the kind of woman who would weigh the pros and cons of every situation and then decide how she felt about the outcome. True, she would have been angry with Ethel, but since Ethel's lack of loyalty resulted in money for Jackie's children, it's likely she decided it was worth it."

Sisterly Advice

For each of the Kennedy wives, the Camelot years would provide entirely different life experiences. For Jackie, these were the years she was granted power and prestige as First Lady of the land, the most famous, revered woman in the country. These were her glory years, and she enjoyed them to the hilt. However, there was a price to pay for them. She had no treasured privacy, she was sick much of the time, worn down by physical exhaustion, and she was in a marriage that was less than satisfying. Still, she was a Kennedy—in fact, with the exception of her husband, she was *the* Kennedy—and she enjoyed her life to the fullest.

These were years of frustration for Ethel, however. She was never able to fully enjoy her role as a Kennedy wife because it vexed her so that she wasn't *the* Kennedy wife—the role played by Jackie. She was proud of her husband, the Attorney General, however, and lived with a great sense of anticipation about his future. Everyone in the family anticipated—either openly or secretly—that Bobby would probably be sitting in the Oval Office one day himself.

For Joan, the Camelot years were the most confusing of her life in that she found herself thrust into a world for which she was completely unprepared. She enjoyed very little of it. Married to Ted in 1958, she quickly became painfully aware that he was like his brothers when it came to the notion of being faithful to their wives: He didn't believe in it.

While Jackie and Ethel had plenty of experience with marital infidelity—all of Ethel's siblings had their own problems with fidelity, as did many of her relatives—Joan had none. At least to her knowledge, her father, Harry Bennett, had always been faithful to her mother, Ginny. Joan had not grown up in a world where husbands cheated on their wives and got away with it. "Joan had not been bred to accept infidelity," observed her former assistant, Marcia Chellis. "She was not a saint, like Rose. Nor was she a very good actress."

"She came in as sweet as can be," observed Secret Service agent Larry Newman, "the kind of girl anyone would want to date, the kind who would never take a drink, never be anything but cheerful and sunny. We'd be on post and see her and Ted and say, 'What a lucky bastard he is, to have a girl like that, so perfect.' Then, of course, as time went on . . . she got ripped to pieces."

By 1961, Ted had grown accustomed to being unfaithful to his twenty-four-year-old wife, even bringing his current girlfriends to the White House for a swim and lovemaking after his brother was elected into office. He was often not discreet.

For instance, at one dinner-dance party Ted and Joan hosted at a Washington hall, Ted became fixated on the married blonde daughter of one of the country's most famous industrialists. Before long, the two were engaged in an erotic slow shuffle on the dance floor. Joan, who had positioned herself so that her back was to her husband and his dance partner, carried on a lively conversation with friends, none of whom could help but stare over her shoulder and watch in dismay as Ted nibbled on the ear of his consort. When he was finished dancing,

Ted walked over to his wife. "Drink, darling?" Joan asked, as she held a martini out to him. "On second thought," she said, and then quickly downed it herself. "As you know, I always feel so much better after I've had a drink," she concluded, spitting the words out at him. Then she rose and walked away.

Joan would later explain that she blamed herself for Ted's infidelities. "When one grows up feeling that maybe one is sort of special and hoping that one's husband thinks so, and then suddenly thinking maybe he doesn't," Joan once told an interviewer, "well, I didn't lose my self-esteem altogether, but it was difficult to hear all the rumors. And I began thinking, well, maybe I'm just not attractive enough."

Joan's view of herself as being inadequate was completely different from the way her sister-in-law Jackie felt about herself. Jackie believed that she had no inadequacies to speak of and never took the blame for anything for which she wasn't completely responsible. Inadequate? "Perish the thought," she might have said.

Because Ethel wasn't a reflective person, she seemed never to give much thought to whether or not she deserved to be a part of the Kennedy family. A pragmatic as well as spiritual woman, she seemed to believe she was in her rightful place, "or God wouldn't have put me here." And as for Bobby's cheating, she probably never thought much about the reasons for that either. She didn't want to face it as a reality in her life, let alone spend meditative moments dwelling on the subject. Also, she was an extremely busy mother. "Look, I have too many kids. I can't afford the luxury of sitting around thinking about how I feel about things," she would say. However, when she did ponder Bobby's behavior, she usually blamed his father for having handed down the legacy of infidelity. She didn't blame herself. "He's like Grandpa," she very astutely observed to one of Bobby's sisters, "in that he thinks the only way he can be powerful is to prove he can have any woman he wants. I just ignore it."

Jackie's and Ethel's kind of thinking broke a long-standing Kennedy tradition, one by which women were blamed—and accepted blame—for everything that ever went wrong in the household, be it a child having trouble in school or a husband who was being unfaithful. Jackie, and to a great extent Ethel, wouldn't play that game. Joan, though, perfectly fit the Kennedy mold. She not only accepted blame when it was being doled out, she'd offer to take more if it made everyone else feel good about themselves.

As beautiful as she was on the outside, Joan Kennedy was just as lovely on the inside. Sweet and sincere, she found herself swept into the formidable Kennedy family without much preparation.

"She often cried when telling me how much she loved Jacqueline as a sister," recalls John Davis. "She admired Jacqueline so much because—well of course they had much in common in terms of their love for art and music. But also, Jackie had qualities Joan wished she had: strength, courage, determination. Living under the pressure cooker of the Kennedy household was so unbearable it almost drove Joan to madness at times. I'd never seen such a sad woman, and neither had Jackie."

One of Jackie's Secret Service men recalls hearing a conversation between Jackie and Joan while at a reception at Jackie's favorite restaurant, La Salle du Bois, on M Street in Washington.

Whenever she was feeling insecure, Joan fell back on her looks and sense of glamour, and tried to be as stylish, beautiful, and desirable as possible. For this luncheon, she wore a short, hot-pink skirt two inches above the knee with matching stockings and white high heels. She looked as willowy as a fashion model, her blonde hair flowing to her shoulders in silky waves. For her part, Jackie was in virginal white: shoes, stockings, simple shift dress, and—unusual for her—a touch of typically sixties white eye shadow.

As the two glamorous sisters-in-law ate chilled mangos as appetizers, Joan asked Jackie about her perfume.

Jackie smiled. "I never tell anyone what perfume I wear," she said with a wink. "I can't take the competition."

After about thirty minutes of pleasantries, Joan began to confide in Jackie about a problem: She had found a gold necklace in her bedsheets that was not hers.

Once Jackie had heard the entire story, she said that there was really nothing Joan could do about it. She advised her to "build your own life within this Kennedy world. Find those things you do best and do them."

"But what about Teddy?" asked Joan, still an insulated and isolated Bronxville girl at heart.

"Oh, forget it! He'll never change," Jackie said. He was very much like his brothers, Jackie explained, each of whom had to conquer every attractive woman in his path, all in a hopeless effort to prove his masculinity. Somehow, maybe instinctively, Jackie had always been able to see right through the mystique of masculine, sexual conquest that was such a part of the Kennedy ethos. As she told Joan, "No woman is ever enough for a guy in that family."

"And you just live with it?" Joan asked.

Jackie dragged on her Merit cigarette, one out of her three-pack-a-day habit. "Frankly, their behavior makes me sick to my stomach," she told her young sister-in-law. "And I've been around it all my life." It was true that for years Jackie had lived in the world in which the rich and powerful move. She was not at all shocked by the kinds of casual relationships that flourished on Capitol Hill. Moreover, her own father had flaunted his affairs in front of her, often talking to her about his girlfriends and making light of his conquests. If she could accept that kind of behavior from him, she certainly could of Jack, even if it did make her "sick to her stomach."

Joan said nothing. Perhaps she felt that if a woman like Jackie, the First Lady, was powerless to stop her husband from cheating, she was helpless to do anything to stop hers.

"I say focus on yourself, Joan," Jackie continued. "And your kids. Forget Teddy."

Joan nodded. "Focus on me," she repeated, as if the thought had never occurred to her before. "Focus on me," she said again, as if it were a new mantra.

The Secret Service agent says, "I felt bad for Joan but had great admiration for Jackie. She was an amazingly strong and resilient woman, determined to have her own life, and not be dependent in any way on her husband. I was standing right next to her, and she looked at me as if she wanted me to hear what she was saying. Maybe she wanted me to spread the word to the other agents that she wasn't a naïve little fool, which I later did."

Before she got up to mingle with some friends, Jackie asked Joan to call her later in the week just to keep her informed of what was going on with Ted. Jackie also told her sister-in-law that perhaps she would find something for her to do at the White House. "That'll keep you busy," Jackie said with a laugh. "Creative satisfaction is where you find it. If you're busy enough, believe me, you won't give Teddy a second thought."

Before she walked away, Jackie added one last thought that the agent who overheard this conversation would never forget: "Make sure Ted knows you found that necklace."

And with that bit of advice, Jackie departed. Joan remained at the table to mull over her lesson, absentmindedly flipping through the pages of a *Paris Match* magazine left by her sister-in-law.

The Bennetts

Those who knew Joan Kennedy best during her Camelot years have said that she was the family's emotional heart, its conscience. One could always rely on Joan to be the understanding, compassionate Kennedy during times of crisis. Though it appeared that she didn't know how to handle her own life, she was known for a clear-eyed assessment whenever asked for an opinion about someone else's complex issue. Whereas Jackie was known for her practical advice, and Ethel for her religious point of view, Joan's perspective was more reasonable and heartfelt.

Because she seemed so victimized by Ted, it often appeared that she was a weak person who—unlike her sisters-in-law and other women in the family—did not know how to reconcile herself to her husband's unfaithfulness. Ted's philandering was unacceptable to her, even abhorrent. She couldn't fathom why she should accept it, and never really understood how Jackie and Ethel allowed it. Joan felt that fidelity was paramount in a marriage, whereas her sisters-in-law and many others in her circle believed that there were other concerns, such as power, prestige, money, and even children.

Of course, Joan was stuck in the wrong time and place to do anything about her marital frustrations, other than to complain about them to Jackie and let it all crush her emotionally.

Virginia Joan Bennett was born in the early-morning hours of September 2, 1936, at Mother Cabrini Hospital in Riverdale, New York, daughter of Harry Wiggins Bennett and the former Virginia Joan Stead, after whom she was named. Her father was Protestant, but Joan was raised a Catholic, like her mother. A successful advertising executive, Harry provided well for his family, which also included a sister, Candy, two years Joan's junior. The family first lived in an upper-middle-class neighborhood in Bronxville, New York, in a four-room apartment in a complex called Midland Gardens.

Harry Wiggins Bennett was a strikingly handsome and amiable Cornell graduate, nothing at all like carefree Black Jack Bouvier or the tough-minded George Skakel. Easygoing, congenial, and fair-minded, he was "a nice, nice person and hard worker," as Joan put it. A little bit over six feet tall, gregarious, charismatic, with a deep, resonant voice, Harry enjoyed acting in neighborhood theatrical productions as a hobby. Joan was, as she recalled it, "the apple of his eye," always trying to please her father, who believed that life was good and fair, so there was no sense in complaining about it—no matter what happened.

"I was always told to smile, always smile—and never complain. It was the same thing in my marriage," she would observe.

Joan's mother, Ginny, was a small-boned, attractive woman with a round, clear-complexioned face and contagious smile. An amateur seamstress, she made most of her daughters' clothing when they were in school. Ginny was also the household disciplinarian, doling out occasional whacks, when she felt it necessary, with a hairbrush that she kept hanging in sight with a bright pink ribbon. She also enjoyed playing the piano and began giving Joan lessons when the girl turned four, rewarding her daughter with gold stars when the child made progress.

It would seem, at least on the surface, that Joan's upbringing was anything but eventful. While her sister Candy was outgoing and social, Joan was a shy, completely unathletic, retiring yet bright student who never expected much of herself or anyone else except, as she said, "to be treated fairly, nicely." A thoughtful, introspective person, she would spend hours alone in her own world which was filled with the arts and her music.

There were cracks in the veneer of the Bennetts' idyllic middle-class life, however, and they were apparent to anyone who knew the family.

"It struck me as odd that the girls never referred to their parents as

'Mom' and 'Dad,' it was always 'Harry' and 'Ginny,'" said Joseph Livingston, who was a childhood friend of Candy's and who spent time with Joan. "There were problems, but I think they were never looked at or analyzed. Both parents were drinkers, though no one ever mentioned it, ever. It was as if it didn't exist, which is the way it is in many alcoholic families. It doesn't exist."

Like Jackie, Joan was the eldest of two daughters and closest to her father; she idolized him, and he felt the same about her. And like Jackie's mother, Joan's mother was a difficult woman to please or understand. She was never completely satisfied with herself or her daughters. Ginny thought Candy was too much the party girl, while, on the flip side, she thought that Joan was too complacent. She urged her teachers to make the girl work harder. She expected a lot from her children. Recalled Livingston, "She used to say, 'I just want things to be *right*.' But nothing was ever right where she was concerned. As a kid, I remember staying out of her way because if I didn't, she would pull me to the side and start straightening my tie or rearranging my hair, saying, 'It's just not right, Joseph. It's not *right*.'"

As her father made more money, Joan's family became upwardly mobile, moving into a four-bedroom Mediterranean-style home on a quarter-acre plot in Bronxville and enjoying a thoroughly uneventful lifestyle. Unlike Jackie and Ethel, Joan had no cooks, nannies, housekeepers, or other servants as a child. "We did for ourselves," Joan says.

As a teenager, Joan's beauty blossomed, but she still had trouble making friends, especially in high school, where she remained reclusive. Her sister Candy was more popular. "She was a cheerleader and went out on dates while I went to the library," Joan recalls.

On a visit to Bronxville, a researcher would be hard pressed to locate people who remember Joan Bennett; she apparently made little impression in high school. Even fellow students are surprised to learn that she was actually in their class. "I went to school with her?" said one woman who had been in her twelfth-grade history class. "You must be joking!"

"She stayed to herself," said Ted Livingston, Joseph's brother, who dated Joan when both were in the eleventh grade. "But then I got a load of her mother one day when I went to pick Joan up for a date. And I knew why.

"The mother made me nervous; just her presence in the room made everyone a little uneasy. Joan came downstairs all smiles, beautiful, and wearing a blue knee-length dress and white sweater. Mom followed, also smiling. She seemed jittery, but trying very hard to act casually. Then, just before we left, Ginny said to Joan, 'I'm still not sure that that dress is the right color for you, Joan. I think it makes you look, oh I don't know, pale, I guess. You just don't look right.' You could just see Joan's happiness just sort of evaporate. She deflated right in front of me. I felt terrible for her."

Joan's former assistant, Marcia Chellis, recalls, "Joan talked occasionally about her father but she rarely spoke of her mother, and I sensed that there were unhappy memories she did not care to recall.

"For Joan's mother, little or no help would have been available to her for a condition [alcoholism] that was then considered to be a social stigma, a shameful secret, and a sign of personal weakness, especially for a woman. Joan may have been deprived of the warm, secure mother-daughter relationship that provides the basis for self-esteem."

In June 1954, Joan graduated from high school and enrolled in Manhattanville College of the Sacred Heart, a Catholic women's college which had just recently moved from Morningside Heights in New York City to a new fifteen-acre campus in Purchase, forty-five minutes north of Manhattan. The young women who attended Manhattanville were taught by nuns. It was an organized environment in which Joan—whose major was in English and minor was in music—seemed to fit, especially as she immersed herself in the study of classical liturgical music, to which she was exposed by attending daily Mass and High Mass on Sundays.

While in college, Joan emerged; her personality and beauty began to shine. "Thank God, my wallflower days were over," she recalls. She became a New York "debutante" twice: first at the Fifth Annual Gotham Ball and then, a few weeks later, at the Nineteenth Debutante Cotillion and Christmas Ball. She then began competing in a number of beauty contests and in March 1956 was picked as "Queen" by the Bermuda Chamber of Commerce for its annual floral pageant.

In 1957, twenty-one-year-old Joan met her future husband, Ted, during her senior year at Manhattanville. That was the year the Kennedy Physical Education Building, located on campus and financed by Joseph Kennedy, was completed. Because mother Rose,

daughters Eunice and Jean, and daughter-in-law Ethel had all attended Manhattanville, the dedication of the new building was a big
family moment. Many of the Kennedys showed up for the ceremonies,
including Rose and Joseph, Bobby, Jack, and Ted, as well as Ethel and
Jackie.

The day of the ceremonies, Joan would later recall, "the place was
buzzing with anticipation because of the distinguished guests, but I
locked myself in my room to write my [school] papers. I was probably
the only one of the seven hundred students who was absent from the
dedication of the gymnasium. I missed Ted's dedication speech entirely." Joan did attend a tea that followed the ceremony, which was
also attended by the rest of the school's seniors and the Kennedy family. There, Joan saw Jean Kennedy Smith, whom she had met a few
months earlier at a party at George Skakel's home in Greenwich. Jean
mentioned that she wanted Joan to meet her "little brother." Joan recalled, "I looked up and saw Ted's six feet two inches towering over
me. At first, I was flabbergasted and surprised, and then when Jean
drifted away, I knew, somehow, this was the man I would marry."

Twenty-five-year-old Ted was a third-year law student attending
school at the University of Virginia in Charlottesville. He was the
only Kennedy sibling, other than the disabled Rosemary, yet unmarried. At six feet two inches and two hundred pounds, Ted was a
better athlete than student. He'd been a rabble-rouser in college—
"Cadillac Eddie," they called him—known for his heavy drinking
and reckless driving habits. Rose had asked him to speak at the dedication—it would be his first important public address—and he had
agreed to do so.

"I had never heard of the Kennedys," Joan recalls. "Never heard of
them! I just took no interest in current events. I didn't know what was
going on in the real world."

Jean, who had a fairly good track record as a matchmaker (she had
already introduced Ethel into the family), seemed to have another
success. Ted and Joan hit it off immediately and began to date soon afterward. "He [Ted] liked her a lot," said Kennedy family friend Lem
Billings. "He said to me, 'She's so relentlessly cheery, nothing gets her
down.' 'Nothing?' I asked. 'Nothing,' he answered. 'She's perfect for
my family.'"

Naïve though she may have been, Joan did detect problems in Ted's character from the very beginning. She had heard about his "Cadillac Eddie" reputation but didn't want to know anything about it. Nothing negative or controversial was allowed to exist in her life. "It was her reaction, I think, to her mother's determination that she be the perfect little girl," observed Theresa Carpenter, who attended Manhattanville with Joan, "and to the fact that her mother was far from perfect herself and never really tried to hide that from her children."

Though Joan continued dating other men, she saw Ted a few more times during the next seven months. A devout Catholic, she, like Ethel, was still a virgin when she married.

After Joan's June 1958 graduation—sixty-eighth in her class of 108—she accepted Ted's invitation to spend the weekend with him in Hyannis Port, where he wanted her to meet his mother, Rose. "My earliest memory of Joan was meeting her at the airport in Hyannis," recalls Ted's cousin and best friend, Joe Gargan, who had been sent to pick up the young Miss Bennett. "You couldn't help but notice how pretty she was—really beautiful, and just as nice."

Bringing Joan home to meet mother was a big move. Ted knew how eager Rose was for him to marry "the right girl of the right faith," and Rose had made it clear that if he married the "wrong kind of girl, we'll all suffer." In fact, Rose had been saying a nightly rosary that Ted would do the family proud and bring home the perfect Kennedy wife.

The way Ted had described Joan didn't impress Rose. Joan didn't come from a family Rose had ever heard of, and she was afraid that the Bennetts weren't very wealthy.

"Oh well, if Ted is interested in her, what can I say?" she told Ethel when the two discussed Ted's plans in front of an acquaintance.

"I don't know if this girl has much class," Ethel said. "I've met her and she seems so . . . normal."

Rose agreed.

"Oh well," Ethel decided. "Good-bye wine and cheese. Hello macaroni and cheese."

However, much to Rose's relief, Joan made a good impression on her. She was beautiful, had a good upbringing, seemed well educated, and was properly respectful. The facts that she was Catholic and had attended Manhattanville were most important to Rose.

"She asked me about Bronxville, Manhattanville, the nuns," Joan recalls, "but mostly we talked about music. [Rose] played the piano very well, and she asked me to play. I had to give a big recital in order to graduate, and I played some of that music, some Brahms. She played a Chopin étude for me. There was something that first week I met her that really connected. There was so much in common."

After Joan's visit, Rose was on a cloud. Joan may not have been as well bred as Jackie or as wealthy as Ethel, but she was beautiful, charming . . . and Catholic. "I can't believe our luck," she told her daughter Eunice. Still, just to be sure, Rose called Mother Elizabeth O'Bryne, the president of Manhattanville, to verify that Joan was the kind of woman she had presented herself as being. "Oh yes," Mother Elizabeth told mother Rose. "Joan Bennett is an outstanding young woman. Ted is fortunate to know her."

If Joan had any problems in her life, she didn't reveal them to Rose, which was precisely the right thing for her to do. Rose was convinced that *everyone* had problems. "She's not a whiner," Rose would say later. Rose realized that Joan would see only what she wanted to see: a necessary trait, in Rose's view, for being a Kennedy wife.

Joan would spend three more weekends at Hyannis Port before September was over. During her last visit of the month, Ted proposed marriage.

As a law student in Virginia and nominal head of Jack's reelection campaign to the Senate, Ted Kennedy was a busy man at this time. "I was young and naïve then," Joan has recalled, "but looking back, there were warning signals. We didn't see each other from the time of his proposal until the engagement party."

As the November wedding date approached, Joan became concerned. "You would be amazed what you learn about a man after you decide to marry him," she would say later. "That's because you start sizing him up for the first time, not as a date but as a potential husband." Joan didn't like what she was seeing in Ted. He seemed uninterested in her, and she suspected he was still dating other women. Friends told her that they'd spotted him with different women and in compromising situations. He seemed not to want marriage, and it looked to Joan as though he was being pushed into it by his family.

Just as would be the case in years to come, Joan felt that she could not speak to Ted about her concerns. Instead, Joan spoke to her father about her worries. Then the men—Harry Bennett, Ted, and Joseph Kennedy—had a conference in Hyannis Port to determine Joan's future. When Harry told Joseph that Joan had misgivings about the marriage, the Kennedy patriarch exploded. The engagement had already been announced, he argued. "He said they're not going to put in the papers that my son is being tossed over," according to Mary Lou McCarthy. "He forced this issue. He was God. The wedding was going to happen whether Ted or Joan like it or not. I told Joan, 'You can't cure the addicted woman-chaser.' And she said, 'I have no choice but to try, do I? What else can I do?' From the beginning, she was in trouble, and she seemed to know."

So the marriage was on. Ted was late for his own engagement party in Bronxville, where Joan was living with her parents in between the ceremonies of graduation and marriage, and he didn't even think to give Joan a ring until the night of that party, when he presented her with a box. Inside was a ring he had never even seen; it had been purchased by his father. When Joan expressed her fears to her mother, Ginny, the older woman asked a litany of questions: Had Joan done something to make Ted dissatisfied with her? Had she taken Ted for granted in some way? Had she grown careless about her appearance? Joan decided that she had done all of those things and that she would try harder to be the perfect mate for Ted. Ginny's words echoed in her head: "He may be a little raw, but Ted can finance a marriage, and a girl needs a man who can do just that. And he likes children, Joan. And you want children, don't you? Keep him happy whatever you do." Ginny's final words of advice were to "get the ring," as if it had some magical property.

As with Jackie's big day, decisions on how Joan's wedding day was to look would be made by Rose and Joseph. Joan had hoped to be married by Father John Cavanaugh, the president of Notre Dame University. But Joseph had other ideas; he wanted Francis Cardinal Spellman of New York to perform the ceremony. While Joan kept her mouth shut, Ginny mentioned to Rose that her daughter had her heart set on Father Cavanaugh. "Oh, well, I'm sure he's a good priest," said Rose. "But he's not a Cardinal now, is he, dear?"

"I had no idea what I was getting into," Joan would later say. "I was just a nice young girl marrying a nice young man. I was to go abruptly from a private, eminently predictable life of contemplation in a windowless cubicle [at Manhattanville] to the rough-and-tumble arena of national politics."

Joan became Mrs. Edward Kennedy on November 29, 1958, at St. Joseph's Roman Catholic Church in Bronxville in front of just a few hundred guests, including Jackie and Ethel (and five of the six children Ethel already had at that time), Jack and Bobby, and the rest of the extended Kennedy family. Whereas Jackie's and Ethel's weddings were attended by more than fifteen hundred people, Joan's seemed oddly downsized by Kennedy standards. Joan's father, Harry, had decided that he wanted the ceremony committed to film for posterity. However, no simple handheld camera work would do. He had the church lit like a Hollywood movie, with floodlights all about. Ted and Joan also had microphones hidden in their outfits so that they could be heard on film as they said their vows.

Joan was a beautiful bride, wearing an ivory satin full-skirted gown with fitted bodice and long sleeves. Jean Kennedy was one of Joan's four maids of honor, along with Joan's sister Candy. In what Joe Gargan remembers as "a joyous occasion enjoyed by all," Bobby Kennedy was one of the ushers; Jack was Ted's best man. The next day Joan found her and Ted's picture on the front page of the New York *Daily News*.

During their honeymoon, Ted found that his new wife had not been fibbing: She really was a virgin. "Perfect and untouched in any way," is how Joan put it later. She delighted in telling her assistant Marcia Chellis that she was the one who had "caught" Ted. "The only reason he wanted to marry me," she said, "was because he couldn't get me any other way." After a three-day honeymoon, Ted went back to his law studies and Joan began her life as a Kennedy wife.

PART TWO

A Legacy of Infidelity

The story of the family into which Jackie, Ethel, and Joan married is one of the great political tales of our time, of a dynasty that brought forth three of the most politically savvy—and arguably most self-destructive—men of the twentieth century. It is the story of dreams finally realized and of dreams in ruin.

When people think of Jack, Bobby, and Ted Kennedy, they often think of them as a unit—the three politician brothers. Yet each was his own kind of person. Jack, the golden boy, wore the mantle of leadership with wit and grace. Bobby, fiercely loyal, was scrappy to the point of being pugnacious. Ted, "the kid" well into his later years, was fun-loving but often unwilling to take responsibility for his actions, and his infractions had to be covered up by the family name and the money that stood behind it.

Whether or not one needs to be a great man in order to be a great leader has always been a hotly debated question, especially in recent times. Arthur Schlesinger makes this point: "History shows no connection between private morality and public conduct. Martin Luther King, Jr., for example, had wayward sexual habits but was all the same a tremendous moral force for his people and his nation. On the other hand, Pol Pot of Cambodia was a faithful family man. All he did was murder hundreds of thousands of his countrymen."

While the story of each important American politician is unique, how his personality and morality were shaped and molded can often be traced to his family's background—and to his parents' example.

The Kennedy family lived in a rarefied world, one in which patriarch Joseph had endowed each of his children with ten million dollars in trust just so that they would never have to work. Throughout their political careers, Jack, Bobby, and Ted would have a difficult time understanding poverty. Similarly, Joseph endowed each of his sons with a distinct impression of a woman's allotted roles. His sons were brought up neither to understand, nor to be considerate of, women.

The standard for the way Kennedy husbands treated Kennedy wives was set years earlier by Joseph Kennedy, who started the legacy of rampant infidelity among the men of the family. A Harvard graduate obsessed by his pursuit of wealth and power, the dynamic Kennedy used his skill in manipulating the stock market in the early 1900s to build—or in any case preserve—his empire when the market collapsed. There have also been persistent stories that, during Prohibition, Kennedy made money as a bootlegger. Inspired by Franklin Delano Roosevelt, for whom Joseph would aggressively campaign, his ambition would move him from the world of high finance into politics. Joseph viewed politics as a ladder of social mobility and finance, not an instrument of social change.

In marrying Rose Fitzgerald, the beloved oldest daughter of John F. "Honey Fitz" Fitzgerald, the mayor of Boston, Joseph found the ideal wife. A devout Catholic, Rose was silent, devoted to the family name, and fiercely loyal. Just as Joseph would set the stage for his sons' future behavior, it was Rose who would act as an example of how Jackie, Ethel, and Joan were supposed to behave.

As soon as he and Rose were married, Joseph started seeing other women, and in spite of his own Catholic background, he flaunted his affairs in front of his entire family. Rose immediately started having babies—almost one after the other. A stoic woman, she believed in strict discipline for her children and ran her household as if it were an army barracks. She would have only limited contact with her children, however. Each time a new child was born, Rose would hire another nanny.

Rose, who went to church every morning and allowed sexual relations with her husband only for childbearing purposes, at first tried to curb Joseph's unfaithfulness. Early in their marriage, she became dismayed by her husband's philandering and returned to the open arms of her parents (leaving her three children with their nannies). Eventually, though, she went back to Joseph and learned to ignore as best she could his indiscretions.

As Mrs. Joseph Patrick Kennedy, Rose had problems other than her husband's unfaithfulness, such as the deaths of two of her children and the mental retardation of another. Twenty-nine-year-old Joseph

Patrick Jr. died when his plane exploded during war maneuvers in 1944. Twenty-eight-year-old Kathleen (nicknamed "Kick"), widow of the Marquis of Hartington who, after her husband was killed in action and over her mother's heated objections, began an affair with the Protestant and already-married British Earl Peter Fitzwilliam, died with him in yet another plane mishap in 1948.

Rose and Joseph's oldest daughter, Rose Marie, known as "Rosemary," had been born retarded, perhaps as a result of a lack of oxygen. For years, Rose denied anything was wrong. When she finally had her daughter tested, she learned that Rosemary had the mental capacity of a seven- to nine-year-old. In 1949, after doctors performed a lobotomy on her, Rosemary was institutionalized. At the time of this writing, she is eighty-one years old.

Joseph's womanizing gradually became more brazen. In 1928 he began an almost public affair with screen actress Gloria Swanson. Rose knew what was going on between them, yet she chose to convey to the world that she believed the beautiful actress was an important business associate of her loving and entrepreneurial husband. Later, Gloria would say that Rose was either "a fool or a saint."

Rose's *modus operandi* throughout her marriage was simple: If one doesn't see it, one doesn't have to deal with it. Her way of coping with a humiliating situation was to pretend that it was not occurring, or to blame the press for writing about it.

"[I] began to accept the idea that gossip and slander and denunciation and even vilification are part of the price one pays for being in public life," she said in her memoir, A *Time to Remember*, which was actually written by Robert Coughlin with her approval. "But neither Ethel nor Jackie nor Joan had been brought up in a political atmosphere. I made sure to warn them in advance what they were in for: that they might be hearing and reading all sorts of scandalous gossip and accusations about members of our family, about their husbands, and for that matter about themselves, and eventually even about their children; that they should understand this and be prepared from the very beginning, otherwise, they might be very unhappy."

It is said that the Kennedy sons admired the way their mother turned a blind eye to her husband's infidelities. The sons viewed their mother's determination to keep her marriage together as a confirma-

tion of her great strength and resolve, and also as her way of respecting her husband's desire to do just as he pleased.

Jack's Affair with Marilyn

Jackie Kennedy may not have felt threatened by most of the women
with whom her husband became involved, but Marilyn Monroe was
another matter. In terms of her private life, at least based on the best
evidence we have, nothing bothered Jackie more than her husband's
assignations with Marilyn.

Even today, no one seems sure when Jack's affair with Marilyn
began. Some have said that he had been introduced to her by his sister Pat and her husband, Peter Lawford, in 1955, and the affair commenced immediately. Others insist the two met a year earlier.

At the time, Marilyn Monroe was a personality as famous and, in her
own way, as prominent as John F. Kennedy. In the show business world
there was as much public interest and scrutiny about the life of the
blonde movie star as there was in the political arena about the
Kennedys. As a result there was a very real possibility that the affair
could become public knowledge and that the scandal could destroy the
careers of everyone involved. "Yes, there was concern," says Peter Summers, one of Kennedy's political advisers with the job of handling relations with the TV networks during the 1960 campaign. "And Marilyn
was spoken to very frankly about it. The President was spoken to very
frankly about it."

"There were actually some good times with Marilyn," recalls
George Smathers. "Jack, Marilyn, I, and other friends would all get
aboard the *Honey Fitz* and go sailing down the Potomac, and then turn
around and come back. That would get you back at around eleven-
thirty at night, just in time to get Jack to bed. This kind of thing went
on frequently. Marilyn felt a part of the family, I think."

In the summer of 1961, Marilyn apparently thought it would be interesting to wangle a formal White House invitation. Jackie was in the
midst of planning a state dinner to be held in honor of Pakistan's Presi-

dent Mohammed Ayub Khan at George Washington's Virginia estate, Mount Vernon, just outside of the capital. Marilyn called Jack to tell him she wanted to attend, but he did not return her telephone call. Bobby, who didn't really know Marilyn at this particular time, intercepted a message from her. When he mentioned it to Ethel, Ethel alerted Jackie. Jackie pondered the notion of inviting Marilyn, wondering aloud if perhaps Jack "should be forced to face his little mistakes." In the end, however, it was decided not to extend an invitation to the actress.

Jackie had an eye toward history that seemed to overshadow any personal matters. According to those who knew her best, she was concerned—for her husband, her children, and herself—that Jack's relationship with Marilyn might be a political liability. "What would happen if news of the affair leaked out before the presidential election in 1964?" asked George Smathers rhetorically. "Sure, she was bothered by the prospect." Apparently, Jackie actually felt great pity for Marilyn and thought her husband was acting irresponsibly by engaging in an affair with a woman who clearly could not control herself. "She's a suicide waiting to happen," Jackie said of Marilyn.

One woman who worked for Jackie throughout her time at the White House and for many years afterward (and who does not wish to be identified) overheard a conversation between Jack and Jackie regarding Marilyn Monroe. She recalls, "I was walking through the East Wing, and the two of them were having a discussion. I overheard just a piece of it, but enough to let me know there was trouble."

She reports that Jackie said to Jack, "I want you to stop it. I don't like it one bit, Jack. This one is different. This one worries me. She's trouble." She adds that Jackie used graphic language, which she never used unless she was upset. "She wanted Jack to knock it off with Marilyn," says the source, "leave her alone, have some pity on her."

Jack denied being anything more than Marilyn's friend. "Sure," he told his wife. "If you want me to stop being friends with her, that's no problem."

In the era of the late 1950s and 1960s the public was completely unaware of what was going on with the President and the movie star. Today, Jack would never get away with such an affair, nor with his other womanizing. The impeachment of President Bill Clinton and the publicity surrounding his personal affairs illustrates that it's a different America today, and the media is different as well. These days, the public consequences of illicit behavior in the White House can be grave. As Jack's own son, the late John Kennedy, Jr., said in 1998, "Hellish torment awaits those who mix an undisciplined libido with a political career."

Recalls Helen Thomas, "In the sixties, it was a different time, and you had certain unspoken agreements. It wasn't like today. . . . The media is different, more invasive now. JFK and Marilyn would be in all the papers today, on all the tabloid shows. The affair would be huge news. But back then, we were more polite."

Michael Selsman, Marilyn's press agent at the time through the Arthur Jacobs Agency, recalls a time when members of the press had a covenant not only with the White House but with publicists and one another to protect the highest office in the land. Selsman says, "Reporters knew where to draw the line, and it was a matter of doing business. What I would do, as a publicist, was trade 'exclusives' about my other clients in order to keep the Marilyn-JFK stories quiet and everyone in the press happy. No one in the media ever caused a problem. You really didn't attack a sitting president back then with his personal life, only his politics."

"We were respectful of the First Lady," concludes James Bacon, a veteran reporter working in Hollywood at the time and a good friend of the Kennedys and Monroe. "You wouldn't have written about such a thing just out of respect for Jackie, never mind what he was doing."

Jackie's Expensive Diversion

"Okay, now how many more pieces are we looking at?" Jackie Kennedy asked a young White House curator, Jim Ketchum. America's glamorous First Lady was sitting cross-legged on top of a two-drawer file cabinet, a clipboard in one hand, a pen in the other. In tight blue jeans and a white sweatshirt, her dark hair pulled back into a ponytail with a white bow, she was the picture of wholesome perfection—including the giant ink blotch on her left cheek. She and Ketchum were in the Broadcast Room of the White House, which was used for storage those days. They were keeping track of some invaluable antiques being returned to the White House after an exhibition in New Jersey.

"There's a lot left, Mrs. Kennedy," Ketchum answered, as he too checked the inventory sheet. "Looks like we're going to be here for a while."

"Really?" Jackie said, looking up from her list, a surprised expression on her face. "Well, I have things to do. I have a state dinner to plan. Come with me. We don't have all day."

"She then jumped down off the cabinet, walked out to the truck, and for the next hour, helped six rather amazed movers carry valuable pieces of furniture into the White House storage area," recalls Ketchum, a smile on his face at the memory even now, so many decades later. "Later one of the guys asked me, 'Who was that lady?' When I said, 'The *First* Lady,' his jaw slackened. I don't think we who were involved in White House restoration ever saw her as the symbol of pristine elegance that the rest of the country saw," he concluded. "To us, she was Mrs. Kennedy, the go-getter. Jackie, the kid."

Ketchum recalls, "That wasn't the only time she ever went out there and unloaded a truck with the boys. It was a regular routine for Jackie, who was the most energetic and smartest person I have ever worked for. And holding it all together was a wild sense of humor which played a vital role, I think, in her surviving some of the slings and arrows that she had to suffer during the White House years. I remember that she had dictated a letter saying that she wanted to help the tourists understand the significance of some of the pieces in the state rooms. So to achieve that, she said in her memo, she wanted to place 'tastefully designed vitrines' in the East Wing, which would hold pamphlets and that sort of thing. Her handwriting was sometimes hard to read, and the architect wrote her back saying that he was confused. Did she really want him to come up with 'tastefully designed latrines' for the East Wing? Jackie couldn't stop laughing when she got that letter. She showed it to everyone she came in contact with for days.

"She loved her work," Ketchum adds, "and didn't take herself that seriously, and loved it if you didn't take yourself that seriously, either. Whatever was going on in her personal life—and I have no idea what that was because she never, ever presented it to me—she lived her own life in the White House, and in a fulfilling way."

She realized early on that she owed it to herself to not compromise

her goals, and to tend her own needs as well as those of her children.
So, even though in the public consciousness she and Jack were insep-
arable, she actually built a life for herself separate and apart from her
husband's. Bobby Kennedy, who always seemed to have a bit of a crush
on his sister-in-law, recognized as much when, in 1961, he said to
writer Laura Bergquist Knebel, "Jackie has always kept her own identity. That's important in a woman. She's poetic, whimsical, provocative, independent, and yet very feminine. What husband wants to
come home at night and talk to another version of himself? Jack
knows she'll never greet him with 'What's new in Laos?'"

Larry Newman, who joined the Secret Service in 1960 and in the
fall of 1961 was promoted to presidential detail, was assigned to Jackie
along with Clint Hill. Because the essence of his job had to do with
observing Jackie's activities, he can say with authority, "The way she
was validated my wanting to protect her. . . . There was a sadness
there . . . but she made it work somehow. She definitely channeled her
energy and any frustration she had into special projects."

"She survived because of the interests she had," observed Dorothy
Tubridy, a Kennedy family friend from Ireland, "in ballet and art and
those kinds of things that the Kennedy sisters weren't particularly interested in. She had her own life, she made her own interests, and she
created this atmosphere about herself. I think it helped."

One of the accomplishments for which Jackie Kennedy will always
be highly regarded was her restoration and refurbishing of the White
House. The well-traveled Jackie had always considered European culture the most artistic in terms of style and aesthetics, but as First Lady
she refocused her devotion for "the finer things" in her native land. In
the process of refurbishing the White House, she would learn a great
deal about American history and art, and she passed that knowledge
on to millions of citizens. Comments Jackie made to her sister-in-law
Joan during a luncheon in Washington, when Joan complained about
Ted's philandering, would seem to indicate that Jackie had other motives for her work at the White House. She told Joan that she would
"find something for you to do at the White House. That'll keep you
busy. You won't give Teddy a second thought."

"I think Jackie wanted to make her mark, keep herself busy," said
Mary Barelli Gallagher, who was Jackie's personal secretary. "Any woman

in her circumstances would understand. I think she needed an outlet for whatever that natural female instinct is to put her stamp on things."

As has been widely reported, Jackie's first reaction, when Mamie Eisenhower took her on a tour, to the presidential quarters had been one of utter disbelief. She could not understand why the most important family in the country should have to reside in such a cold and dreary place.

With her newfound position, Jackie had the power to make changes happen, and happen quickly. There were 132 rooms in the White House at this time, and during Jack and Jackie's stay there, their second-floor living quarters consisted of a living room, kitchen, dining area, and five bedrooms. The Secret Service was not permitted in the family's quarters so as not to intrude upon their privacy, and also so that the living area would not look like an official governmental office but like a home.

First, Jackie persuaded Congress to designate the White House a national museum, thus guaranteeing the necessary funding to do whatever she wanted to do with it and also to ensure that her work there would be preserved for future generations. Of course, her purpose would prove to be twofold: She would not only be able to indulge her expensive tastes in antiques and other furnishings, she would also be doing something historically relevant for the White House. By refurbishing the presidential quarters, she would be redesigning her own personal space in a tasteful, elegant way that she and her family could enjoy for years to come.

With typical determination and zeal, Jackie thrust herself full-speed into the project. She used her time while she was recovering from John's birth to study the history of the White House and its decor. Then she set her plan into action. "Everything in the White House must have a reason for being there," Jackie declared. "It would be sacrilege merely to *redecorate*—a word I hate. It must be *restored*. And that has nothing to do with decoration. That is a question of scholarship."

Since some of the rooms cost as much as $250,000 to restore, Jackie had to rely on the generosity of the multimillionaire members of her restoration committee to underwrite the costs. She became an expert at charming the heads of corporations into donating things she wanted for the White House: carpets, fabrics, chairs. While the donor got the honor of supplying a small piece of history to the Kennedy White House, Jackie got those antique wing chairs she wanted so badly.

Using her charm, Jackie managed to coax some of her many socialite friends into donating valuable art to the White House collection. She secured over 160 new paintings to adorn the White House walls.

Along with soliciting treasures from outside sources, Jackie also thoroughly explored the White House basement and storage facilities. Her treasure hunts uncovered Lincoln's china, a Bellange pier table, and President Monroe's gold and silver flatware. So focused was she on her work that she once completely ignored Martin Luther King, Jr., in an elevator because she had just learned of the existence of a certain antique chair in the White House basement.

While it may seem to minimize the importance of Jackie's work, the fact—at least according to those who knew her best—is that shopping and buying had always been a great ego fortifier for Jackie Kennedy. Even Jackie herself said, "I think that shopping to give yourself a lift is a valuable form of do-it-yourself therapy."

"Like a lot of women, she felt better about things—and about her marriage, I would venture to say—when she was busy," concluded her longtime friend Joan Braden. "She stayed busy, a lot," Braden said with a laugh. "I'd never known anyone so busy."

Jackie's White House labor was definitely a great success as far as the country was concerned, and it was historically relevant as well. Her specific ideas on how to use the presidential home to preserve the history of the country made her a pioneer in the historical preservation movement, which was sorely needed nationally. Jackie's work would also directly inspire President Lyndon Johnson to promote successful legislation for establishing the National Endowment for the Humanities as well as the National Endowment for the Arts.

Madcap Ethel during the Kennedy Presidency

Ethel Kennedy, taking full advantage of the Kennedy craze, was determined to let her own inimitable personality leave an imprint on the Kennedy years, but in a very different way from her sister-in-law the

First Lady. While Jackie was usually serious, refined, and dignified, Ethel was madcap, boisterous, and fun-loving.

Jackie's soirees at the White House were written up and much discussed for their careful elegance and sophistication. Under the First Lady's discerning eye, once-stodgy state dinners became more relaxed and enjoyable, although they were as carefully choreographed as ever. One of her innovative changes was to have smaller tables at dinner parties so that the guests at each table could more easily interact with each other. She mixed artists, musicians, writers, and entertainers with heads of state. "Jackie's style was unique," says etiquette expert Letitia Baldrige, who was Jackie's social secretary. "She knew everything about every person on the guest list."

During their shortened term in office, the Kennedys would host sixty-six state dinners, not to mention the dozens of private parties for friends, politicians, and other associates. "She wanted everything that was the finest in music, drama, ballet, opera, poetry," recalls the president's press secretary Pierre Salinger, "and set a tone that would encourage culture around the country."

"Suddenly, this inbred, old-style society that was utterly foreign to the rest of the country was on the stage," said former White House *Time* magazine correspondent Hugh Sidey. "Washington was visible all over the world. They were young people who liked a good time."

"The French know this," Jackie once noted. "Anybody knows this: If you put busy men in an attractive atmosphere where the surroundings are comfortable, the food is good, you relax, you unwind, there's some stimulating conversation. You know, sometimes quite a lot can happen. Contacts can be made, you might discuss something . . . you might have different foreigners there and then say . . . 'Maybe we ought to see each other next week on that,' or . . . it can be very valuable that way. . . . Social life, when it's used, is part of the art of living in Washington."

Jackie did it one way; Ethel did it another way entirely.

Betty Beale, a society columnist for the *Washington Evening Star* who covered eight presidents and their wives at glamorous White House functions from Truman through Reagan, observes, "Ethel never pretended to be chic. She was a terribly active frequent mother, who had a busy home life with all of those children, but somehow ended up finding herself the second most prominent hostess in the nation—

Jackie being the first—all as a result of her brother-in-law becoming president. But their styles, from dress to entertaining, were entirely different. She had clearly decided that if she had to do it, she would be as different from Jackie Kennedy doing it as was humanly possible."

Ethel prided herself on the inelegant, comical touches that set her parties apart and were very much an extension of her own outlandish persona. As a result she became one of the most talked-about party-givers in the country. For example, at a formal St. Patrick's Day dinner party, Ethel brought the traditional green motif to new extremes. Men in dressy black tie and ladies in formal evening gowns—all with green accessories—were dumbfounded when they discovered, among the green centerpieces, the largest live bullfrogs Ethel could find. Decorative bullfrogs as a living centerpiece were a touch that only Ethel would think of. "At another party, she turned the lights down low," recalls Betty Beale, "and put a live chicken in the middle of the table, for fun. She really wanted people to be happy. She set a tone for things, and wanted to surround herself and Bobby with a sense of gaiety. She was fun."

Guests arriving for a dinner party in honor of General Maxwell Taylor, a family friend for whom her youngest son was named, were surprised to drive up to Hickory Hill only to find a man dangling from a tree by parachute. Ethel had hung a dummy from a limb to pay homage to Taylor, who had parachuted into Normandy on D-Day.

Stories about Ethel's party antics are often recounted with good humor by family members at Hyannis Port gatherings. When she threw a party for the veteran diplomat and statesman Averell Harriman on his seventy-fifth birthday, Ethel decorated Hickory Hill with hundreds of photos of Harriman taken with world-famous figures through the years, adding an outlandish caption to each photo. And when the much respected poet Robert Frost came to dinner, madcap Ethel handed each guest a pad and pencil and announced a poetry-writing contest. Then there was the time Ethel playfully sprayed the shirt of a young member of a visiting European family with shaving cream.

C. Wyatt Dickerson, married to the late newscaster Nancy Dickerson, attended many parties at Ethel's home and recalls her as "a spectacular hostess, with all of the Kennedy polish and charm but a dash of madness. At one party, Arthur Schlesinger was pushed into the pool. Peter Lawford and I were hiding in the bushes hoping that we wouldn't be next."

Guests in full dress being tossed into the Kennedy swimming pool—or "dunking," as it came to be called in political circles—became another of Ethel Kennedy's trademarks. In fact, taking an unexpected dip at a formal party at Hickory Hill became a sort of initiation into the Kennedy family's good favor. One knew he was a beloved friend of Mr. and Mrs. Bobby Kennedy when he was dunked by Ethel during one of her gatherings. Senator Kenneth Keating of New York once sent Ethel a letter saying, "I hope the mad rumor isn't true—that you're changing the name of Hickory Hill to Drip-Dry Manor." Even some of the most respected newspapers of the day, like the *New York Times*, reported on who was dunked at the latest Kennedy bash.

Sometimes Ethel's eccentric behavior affected the seating arrangements. When she threw herself a birthday party, for instance, she seated the twenty-four women guests at one table, while their male companions found themselves seated at another.

Much of what Ethel did with her life, though, was not considered traditional behavior, especially by the family's matriarch, Rose.

"Rose Kennedy thought Ethel's parties were outrageously overdone," says Barbara Gibson, who was Rose's secretary. "After attending one, she made a comment to me about it that was typical of the way she felt about Ethel: 'Oh my, now aren't *we* rich.'

"Rose disapproved of Ethel, mostly. She didn't approve of the way she kept Hickory Hill, the way she raised her children. There were always plates of food lying around all over the place. Whenever anybody finished a meal or a snack, that's where the dish was left. The kids ran wild. The place was a wreck.

"Ethel used to go through cooks like water. The cooking school would send her chefs just for the experience, but they wouldn't last long. She could be completely unreasonable. She must have had twenty-five secretaries in a five-year period, she was that difficult. Her spending habits also annoyed Mrs. Kennedy," continues Barbara Gibson. "For instance, she would go shopping and see something she liked, then buy it in every color. If she saw a belt she liked at Saks Fifth Avenue, she would order six of them. Mrs. Kennedy thoroughly disapproved of this kind of spending. Ethel would buy expensive perfumes in decorator bottles, and when Rose would go into the bedroom and see those big bottles on the dresser, she would become absolutely distraught."

Joan's Social Impasse

While Jackie and Ethel were considered exemplary hostesses by their friends and by others in Washington and Georgetown political circles, Joan Kennedy didn't fare as well in that regard in the beginning of the Camelot years. In time, she would be regarded as one of the city's most successful hostesses—but it wasn't always that way.

Kennedy intimates still recall what happened when twenty-nine-year-old Joan hosted a fifteenth-anniversary party for Ethel and Bobby at her and Ted's Georgetown home on June 25, 1965. For Joan, who rarely entertained, this was an important evening. "We've never given a big party in Washington," she said excitedly, "and we want it be the best ever." Always insecure in her role as a Kennedy wife, Joan set out to make her sister- and brother-in-law's party the social event of the season.

Unfortunately, once Joan's planning was well under way, she discovered that Washington socialite Mrs. Perle Mesta*—well known for her ultraglamorous, ultraextravagant parties—was hosting a bash honoring Senate Majority leader Mike Mansfield of Montana on the same night. Perle had invited to her splendid Northwest Washington penthouse many of the same guests Joan had invited to her event. After some quick checking, Joan was horrified to learn that most guests had accepted invitations to both parties.

Calling it "a ghastly social impasse," the *New York Times* facetiously reported the story in a four-column headline: "Crisis in Capital; Two Parties on the Same Night."

Since Perle was having a dinner party and Joan's was an "after-

---

*Mesta, appointed Ambassador to Luxembourg by Harry Truman, was immortalized by composer Irving Berlin in the hit Broadway musical *Call Me Madam*, starring Ethel Merman.

dinner dance," there was some hope that it might work out, with guests having dinner at the Mestas' and then driving over to the Kennedys' for dancing and entertainment. Joan was doubtful, but she had no choice but to forge ahead with her big night.

"She's having filet of sole and guinea hen," Joan wailed. "How can I compete with *that?*" Doing her best to try, Joan booked Lester Lanin's orchestra, as well as a group of flamenco dancers from the Spanish Pavilion of the New York World's Fair.

Perle retaliated by announcing that she had decided to host drinks and dancing *after* her party, hoping that would hold the guests at her place. Now there was an out-and-out social war between the two Washington hostesses.

As it turned out, however, there were no winners in this particular battle. Kennedy historian Lester David, who attended Joan's party, painted the scene: "Joan ordered a huge tent set up in her garden, a dance floor placed over the grass, pretty little pink-covered tables with gilt chairs, and chairs of wrought iron painted white for the shrubbed patio. A fountain, with lights playing upon the spraying water, would splash prettily atop a stepped-up terrace in the rear."

Yet in spite of Joan's extravagance, of the one hundred senators invited, only sixteen showed up. She also got a couple of cabinet members and the wife of the French ambassador. It was a disappointing turnout.

"With parties like this one, who needs wakes?" Ethel deadpanned, looking around at the sparse crowd. "There are more flamenco dancers here than there are guests!"

For all her planning, Perle didn't fare much better, with fifty guests in all—a few more than Joan, but nothing near the number that had been expected. Not wanting to snub either hostess, people had decided to play it safe by staying home.

"I think it was so mean of Perle to do that," Joan lamented later to her friend Joan Braden. "How many parties do I give? Why couldn't she let me shine, just once!"

Trying to Understand Each Other

"It's not always easy," Joan Kennedy once said when discussing the Kennedy women, "because we are so different. We really have had to work to try to understand each other. None of it has ever come easily. We have our own personalities, even though the public thinks we're all the same, just one big Kennedy wife."

Yet the three wives had very different personalities: Jackie was strong and independent, Ethel was difficult and ambitious, and Joan was insecure, sensitive, and long-suffering.

Like Jackie, Joan could not compete with the Kennedy sisters or Ethel in sports such as sailing, waterskiing, and football. However, whereas Jackie adopted the attitude that she was above those silly sports and wanted nothing to do with them anyway, Joan felt she was inferior.

"I'm just a flop," she told family nurse Luella Hennessey after an unsuccessful day on water skis. "They all do it so well."

Luella Hennessey, who had known the family since the 1930s, recalled, "She admired the Kennedys so—their self-confidence, their poise, their physical strength. She knew she didn't have their stamina, that she hadn't been brought up for this kind of competition, but to please her family, especially her husband, she wanted with all her heart to be as good as the others. When she found again and again that she wasn't, she was terribly disheartened."

"I always said that Ted should have married my younger sister, Candy," Joan recalls. "She was always the female athlete. She plays tennis and golf and rides beautifully, where I'm allergic to horses."

At Hyannis Port, the nonathletic Kennedy wives, Joan and Jackie, would take long walks and discuss books, music, and cooking recipes, while Ethel and the Kennedy brood, including Eunice, Jean, and Pat—whom Jackie called "The Rah Rah Girls"—engaged in sports.

"You know, when they have nothing better to do, they run in place, or they jump all over each other like wild gorillas," Jackie once told Joan.

Whereas Jackie had wit and sarcasm, Joan was just *nice*. She rarely said anything unkind or critical about anyone, even in jest. "If someone opened the door for me, I would send them a thank-you note," she once recalled.

As sisters will often do, Jackie, Ethel, and Joan sometimes crossed the fine line between teasing and hurtfulness. Once the Kennedy women were sitting on Joseph and Rose's porch telling one another about their secret fantasies.

"Oh, my," Jackie said dreamily. "I so wanted to be a ballerina. That was always my dream, my most secret fantasy of all."

"What?" Ethel screamed out. "You must be joking! With those clodhoppers?" She pointed at Jackie's size elevens. "You'd be a lot better off going out for soccer!"

Everyone laughed heartily, including Jackie. She could dish it out, as well as take it. Jackie would snipe at Ethel and rib her about "bucked teeth" or the disorganized way she kept house: "like a war zone," Jackie would say of Ethel's household, "a complete war zone!" She also did a mean impression of Ethel. She'd buck out her front teeth, pop her eyes, extend her hand, and say, "Hiya, Keed." Ethel would be annoyed every time Jackie did it for friends.

Joan could not be teased about any of her shortcomings by anyone, let alone her sisters-in-law, who so intimidated her. Jackie liked Joan immediately and instinctively knew that she was too sensitive to rib. However, Ethel couldn't resist mocking Joan from time to time.

"As a sister [-in-law], she's an easy mark," Ethel would say with a grin. "How can you *not* enjoy watching Joan Kennedy squirm."

One well-known story among Kennedy intimates shows Ethel in a poor light, criticizing Joan's fashion taste. For a Hyannis Port boating excursion, Joan showed up wearing a stylish, leopard-print swimsuit with matching hat and scarf. She looked stunning, even if her choice of clothing may have been inappropriate for a rugged day of boating. As soon as Ethel saw Joan, she began to mock her. "What did you think, that there would be photographers here?" she asked. "Is that what you thought? That this was a *Look* magazine cover story? Maybe I should have dressed up like a model, too."

Realizing that Joan was at a loss for words, Ethel smiled cheerily and said, "Oh, forget it, Joan. Why don't you go on over there and get yourself some fried chicken. Eunice really made a good batch this time."

For the rest of the day, Joan said little. It was as if she couldn't wait for the day—which had started out on such a promising note—to just end.

"Why did Ethel have to do that?" Eunice asked. "I just don't understand that woman. We're all sisters, after all."

True to Ethel Kennedy's contradictory nature, though, there were also times when she would come to Joan's rescue. Kennedy intimates remember one of those moments well because it was under such unusual circumstances.

It happened on January 29, 1961, the evening Jackie and Jack opened the White House for its first public party. The invitees included Cabinet officers, congressional leaders, new Cabinet appointees, as well as campaign workers and family members. Also, certain members of the press were invited. A bar had been set up in the family dining room, and another in the East Wing, which was unusual. The previous administration had not served hard liquor at large parties. Rather, the Eisenhowers just spiked the fruit punch and hoped for the best. The Kennedys, however, believed that in order to entertain well a full bar was mandatory.

"Ted seemed to have spent an awful lot of time at the East Wing bar," recalled one reporter present at the festivities. "So much so that his wife was becoming annoyed."

Joan looked elegant in a streamlined pink, asymmetrical evening gown, her blonde hair pulled back in a simple chignon. When Jackie saw her, she rushed over and complimented her. "Oh my God, Joan! Just look at you," she exclaimed, her brown eyes wide with enthusiasm. "You look fantastic in that color. That's your color, Joan. Pink. Always wear pink."

Joan smiled graciously, letting the First Lady's compliment sink in.

"Oh yeah? Well you shoulda seen her when she woke up this morning," cracked a male voice behind her.

"It was Ted," remembered the reporter, "just a little drunk, and a lot mean. He was holding his dessert in one hand [*Frambois a la crème Chantilly*: raspberries topped with whipped cream], and spooning it out with the other. He had a smug look on his face."

Jackie stared at her brother-in-law for a moment, her lips pressed together, a hard look in her eyes. She started to speak but checked herself. Instead, she walked away, shaking her head in disgust.

Ten minutes later, a campaign worker came over to Joan and paid her a compliment about her hairstyle. "Why, thank you," Joan said, her smile bright. "I just thought I'd try something a little different, you know?"

"You wanna see different?" Ted asked, cutting in. He had walked away, but suddenly he was back. "You oughta see her hair when she wakes up in the morning," he said with a chuckle. "It's not so pretty."

As the staffer walked off, muttering to herself, the expression on Joan's face was of complete bewilderment. Quick tears came to her eyes; she blinked rapidly.

Ethel Kennedy happened to have overheard the exchange. She grabbed Ted by the arm. "What's the matter with you?" she demanded. "This is your wife. How dare you insult her here, of all places? Now leave her alone, you big brute." Then Ethel grabbed Joan's hand. "Come on," she said to her stunned sister-in-law, "I have someone I want you to meet." The two women headed for the other side of the room, leaving Ted staring into his empty dessert bowl. As they left, Joan, with an aching expression on her face, looked over her shoulder at her embarrassed husband. For just a moment, it was evident that there was a richness of understanding between Ethel and Joan.

Jackie's Documentary: A Tour of the White House

It was February 14, 1962, when the public got its longest and closest look at Jackie Kennedy in a remarkable hour-long documentary, *A Tour of the White House with Mrs. John F. Kennedy*. During the program, television cameras followed the First Lady and news correspondent Charles Collingwood from room to room as she answered questions about the recent renovations she and her committee had made to the presidential quarters. In truth, Jackie's television special was as much a political exercise as it was an opportunity to show off her work, for as First Lady she represented her husband in everything she did.

Politics being the essence of the Kennedy men's world, much was expected of the Kennedy women whenever campaign time rolled around, and they did their part, usually with great success. TV appearances, though, were a bit more challenging.

In 1958 during Jack's senatorial campaign, a television special was broadcast to Massachusetts viewers titled *At Home with the Kennedys*, featuring Rose, Jackie, Eunice, and Jean, who had her baby, one-year-old Steve Jr., on her lap. Sitting up as straight as rods, their hands clasped in their laps, they looked like robots. "You have the Sacred Heart way of sitting," explained Joan, who, though she wasn't present for this television appearance, was well aware of the importance of posture in the Kennedy family. "Rose showed us all how to sit on stage, poised. You don't have your legs crossed. They're together, maybe crossed at the ankle. From the beginning, she was after me about my poor posture. I was five feet eight when I was twelve, one of those tall girls who are always scrunched over. And she would say, 'Stand up straight. You have a beautiful figure. Stand up and show it.'"

During the television special Rose, in a sensible dress suit with pearls, wondered aloud at her son Jack's good fortune in finding a wife so fond of campaigning. Jackie, the rhythm of her speech robotic and her demeanor stiff, replied, "I've always enjoyed campaigning so much, Mrs. Kennedy." She pronounced each syllable slowly, deliberately, and unnaturally, in an odd, upper-class tone. "Since September 15, Jack and I have been traveling through the state trying to meet as many people as we can. Your son Teddy, who as you know is a campaign manager, set up the schedule for us last summer. We visited 184 communities."

"Well, congratulations, Jackie," Rose said, as if giving her a royal blessing, "and congratulations to Jack for having found a wife who is so enjoying the campaign."

This television show—which also featured home movies narrated by Eunice and Jackie—is actually credited with being helpful to Jack's victory. Apparently, the public was fascinated by the Kennedys whatever way it could get them.

Joan, praised for her blonde beauty, did not giver herself credit for the attributes she had, so her lack of confidence was easily noticeable on camera whenever she had to give a televised speech, usually at a press conference.

Ethel carried her "rah-rah" spirit into the political arena, but politics exhausted her and television was her greatest enemy. She too appeared wooden and unnatural whenever she was interviewed, and, worse, she never really looked as attractive on television as she did in life. Her features were somehow hardened by the camera's lens, and she knew it.

"I am just not that ugly," she once said after seeing herself being interviewed on a late-night talk show. "I refuse to accept it."

The nation got a real surprise when *A Tour of the White House* was broadcast in February 1962. One of the reasons this special was groundbreaking is that cameras had never before been allowed in the upstairs residence of the White House. The most startling revelation to the forty-six million viewers, however, was not Jackie's work on the White House but Jackie herself. She seemed knowledgeable enough about the furniture and heirlooms she had used to decorate the rooms, including the Reception Room, State Dining Room, Red Room, Blue Room, and Lincoln Room. She rattled off the names of donors, as well as the history of wallpaper, silverware, china, sofas, desks, lamps, clocks, and portraits. But her delivery was stiff, and she seemed a bit dazed. She appeared to be reading cue cards or, at the very least, to have memorized large blocks of information. She projected an impression almost of slow-wittedness.

It was as if everything Jackie had to say had been so carefully scrutinized in advance and memorized before each take, that there was no possibility she would be able to come up with a single anecdote on her own, nor would she take the chance of doing so. (Later, it was learned that she had made a number of errors and had recorded corrections to be dubbed over the mistakes.)

Jackie Kennedy, who was thirty-three at the time, had so much class, sophistication, and self-confidence; yet throughout the program she seemed self-conscious, as if terrified of making a mistake. Her lack of stage presence was startling, considering her position in the country. Even her walk seemed awkward and unsteady. Her nervousness did have its endearing moments, though. "If you knew her, you would know that she was the last person in the world you would ever have expected to be seen giving a televised tour," says Jim Ketchum. "It was just not in her, or her manner. It must have taken great courage."

It should also be noted that television coverage of public figures was unsophisticated at that time and that events such as Jackie's tour were relatively new. Viewers were not expecting technical wizardry, nor that their public figures be polished and smooth. Today, Jackie would have had to take courses in media training just to live up to the standards of "sound bite" television. It's interesting that people have always said the reason Jackie never gave interviews in her later years was that she was hoping to maintain a sense of mystery about her life. But according to those who knew her best, the actual reason was that she knew she was terrible on television. She made a wooden interview subject, and that she had so little charisma when in front of a camera was her *real* secret.

Also, she never felt that she was articulate, even decades later. When her friend Aileen Mehle (the gossip columnist "Suzy") asked Jackie for an interview, instead of just begging off without explanation, Jackie said, "I couldn't. I just couldn't. I'd feel like such a jackass, like such a fool. My answers are always so asinine."

During her White House tour, though at times she seemed almost unearthly, she really was fascinating to watch. People today watch *A Tour of the White House with Mrs. John F. Kennedy* with as much fascination as did viewers in the sixties.

———————

The Voice

Jackie and Jack hosted a small dinner party at the White House on the night Jackie's television special aired. Their guests were reporter Ben Bradlee, who at that time worked for *Newsweek*, and his lovely wife, Tony; Max Freedman, American correspondent for the Manchester *Guardian*; and New York socialite "Fifi" Fell, a friend of Jackie's. It was nanny Maud Shaw's day off, so Jackie had her hands full with the children as well as with dinner preparations. And to make a woman's life even more complex, a king had visited earlier that day.

King Ibn Saud of Saudi Arabia had come by the White House bearing gifts, including some for little John that confounded his mother: a small jacket that would have sold for about five dollars at any Sears, as well as a few other children's clothes that the King had turned inside out, apparently to prove they had never before been worn. Jack and Jackie, in turn, gave the King a relief map of the United States. As soon as the King took off for Saudi Arabia, the dinner guests arrived.

After a meal of *fettuccini rené* (*fettuccini alfredo*, to which was added chicken stock and sour cream), the party moved to a small sitting area off the Lincoln Room to watch Jackie's show.

They watched the program—which was broadcast on all three networks—in absolute silence, and Ben Bradlee later said they were "impressed with Jackie's knowledge and poise." Oddly, Bradlee's wife, Tony, felt that Jack was actually jealous of the attention Jackie was getting, as all eyes were on her during the "performance." Also, Jack had referred to her as "Jackie" during a brief spot he had on the show, and he now wondered aloud if perhaps he should have called her "Jacqueline," as he usually did in public.

After the show had aired, the phone rang constantly, with friends and family wanting to lodge their opinions. Jackie wasn't interested in their comments, however, perhaps feeling some would be critical. When Eunice telephoned, Jackie vigorously shook her head, indicating that she did not want to speak to her. In front of guests, the moment hung awkwardly and uncomfortably.

Jack winked at his guests and told his sister, "Look, poor Jackie went to bed. She's crying her eyes out. So call back tomorrow." Then he quickly hung up.

Later, and privately, everyone present would agree that the show was "unusual" and that the voice that had come out of Jackie that night on the air was a revelation. She sounded as if she had just learned the English language phonetically. Her voice was so soft and breathy during the filming that producer Perry Wolff, standing less than four feet away, could not hear a word she was saying.

"When she was placed in a formal situation as the center of attention, her voice, and the way she acted, was a retreat from herself," former senator John Glenn observed, "more formal as, perhaps, a defense mechanism. She was careful what she did, careful about every word she said. But in private she sounded different—relaxed, easy."

It would seem that Jackie, ever conscious of trying to be all things to all people—the perfect mother, the perfect wife, the perfect First Lady, and the all-round perfect woman—chose to mimic a voice that in that day was considered demure and feminine. Hairdresser Mickey Song, who had styled Jackie's hair before she became First Lady, recalls, "When I first met her she had a normal voice. I remember seeing her later on TV when she did the tour and thinking, 'I don't remember her sounding like that.'"

"She was such an innocent girl when she first came to the White House in 1961," recalls Robin Duke, wife of the President's chief of protocol, Angier Biddle Duke. "She didn't know how to talk on television. She was so inexperienced that she put on that wispy little baby voice, which none of us had ever heard her use before."

Jim Ketchum observes, "I think she was a bit self-conscious of herself and, yes, put the voice on. When talking to her day to day, you weren't aware of her sounding like that. It was a mode she shifted into when the little red light started flashing on the camera. It was a very different sound from what I heard day in and day out at the White House."

Ethel, never one to pull a punch, summed it up best when, while viewing the special with Bobby and friends, she said, "Oh my God, where'd that voice come from?" Ethel was accustomed to Jackie's "other voice," the one she used privately. It was a deeper, more expressive tone, one that Jackie would use when she was angry at Jack or at one of her staff members—or angry at Ethel.

The day after the broadcast, according to a Kennedy intimate, Ethel telephoned Jackie to render her review. "Look, if you want my opinion, Jackie," she said—even though Jackie did not ask for it—"I think you should act more normally when you do those kinds of things in the future."

In her defense, Jackie said that she *was* acting normally.

"Oh, hogwash," Ethel countered. "I know you, Jackie. And you're not that way at all."

Sister-in-law Joan also telephoned Jackie, but to praise her. "I couldn't have done it," she said later. "I couldn't have gone up there in front of the nation and talked so knowledgeably about all of those old antiques. Jackie has such class, and ease."

Jackie appreciated Joan's support, and she probably would have accepted her criticism as well, knowing that it wasn't malicious in intent. However, she was so stung by Ethel's comments that Kennedy insiders were surprised at her reaction, especially since she was not ordinarily sensitive about her voice. Jim Ketchum remembers an employee at the White House who did an impression of Jackie that, had she been a sensitive person, would have hurt her feelings. "But she would gather us all together and make this woman do the impression at the drop of a hat," he says. "'No one is leaving this room until you do it,' she'd say, and she loved it. 'Do it again!' she'd say, laughing. 'One day I'm going to make you do this at a private party with Jack and the others. Jack would adore it.'"

For whatever reason, and true to her contradictory nature, Jackie did not like Ethel critiquing her performance and acted distantly toward her for the next few weeks. Rather than bring her hurt to the surface, perhaps she was just allowing Ethel to wonder what she was thinking.

"Lots of luck in that regard," Ethel said to reporter Laura Bergquist Knebel, who was writing a cover story on Jackie for *Look* magazine. "The wheels go 'round constantly in her head. You can't pigeonhole her. You have a hard time getting to the bottom of *that* barrel."

Then, as if to take the sting from her observation because she was, after all, talking to a journalist, Ethel quickly added, "Which is great for Jack, who's so inquisitive."

The public didn't seem to mind Jackie's girlish delivery in the least. If anything, her appearance on the television special added to the nation's fascination. "I remember watching and listening to Mrs. Kennedy more than thinking about the White House," Barbara Bush would recall.

College girls across the land began imitating her breathless voice, which was described by one student as sounding "expensive." Plastic surgeons reported clients asking for nose "bobs," to look just like Jackie. She was a movie star without ever having made a movie, and the public was more captivated by her than ever.

Despite the fact that it was poorly directed and edited in an amateurish manner, the documentary went on to win an Emmy and a Peabody Award. "Television at its best," wrote a critic for the *Washington Post*. White House historian Carl Anthony says: "Jackie Kennedy's interest in the restoration of the White House was the first truly public project of a First Lady to be permanently linked in the public's mind with the role of the First Lady."

Jackie's popularity reached beyond the White House walls: Her clothes, hair, and makeup were having a visible impact on 1960s culture. "Everyone copied her and mimicked her," Letitia Baldrige said. "So she had an enormous influence on the American public."

"Secrets Always Come Out"

On March 14, 1962, reporters jammed into Joan Kennedy's small living room at 3 Charles River Square (which she and Ted had moved into in 1961) to hear her husband, Ted, make the formal announcement of his candidacy for the Senate. As the press noisily converged upon the Kennedys, their two-year-old daughter, Kara, began to wail uncontrollably in the nursery off the main hallway, and Joan appeared distracted by Kara's cries. A nurse shut the door quickly to muffle the baby's crying, but Joan still appeared uneasy.

Ted's political career, like those of his brothers, was really the brainchild of the Kennedy patriarch, Joseph. Ted never wanted to be a senator. Knowing that he would always be in competition with his brothers for familial as well as public acceptance in the political arena, he had told Joan that he wanted to get as far away from the confines of the Kennedy dynasty as possible—to the West Coast, in fact.

"His main reason was that in a new state, among new people, he would have to succeed or fail on his own," Joan recalls.

In the early sixties, however, when the young couple went to the West Coast to start looking for a home, Joseph made it clear that not only were they expected to stay in Massachusetts, but that Ted would run for the Senate the following year and take Jack's seat. Joseph always believed that the family had a proprietary claim to that seat. "I paid for it," he said. "It belongs to the family."

Even Jack was against Ted's candidacy, fearing that charges of nepotism would damage his Presidency. He suggested to his father that Ted be allowed to live outside the public eye, that he should be the one brother with a normal family life—an idea that suited Joan just fine.

Joan almost got her wish when it was determined that Ted could not be appointed to Jack's vacant seat because he would not have reached the age of thirty—the minimum age for a senator, as dictated by the Constitution—until February 22, 1962. Someone would have to fill the chair for a year until a new election could be held in 1962 to complete the final two years of Jack's unexpired term. Governor Foster Furcolo was persuaded by the White House to name Benjamin Smith, a former house mate of Jack's at Harvard and a close family friend, who agreed to vacate the seat after the term so that a Kennedy could possibly move into it.

Because the boys usually did what Joseph told them to do, though, there was really no debate. Ted would run for the Senate, even though his legislative experience was nonexistent.

After he finally announced his candidacy for the Senate on March 14, the reaction against was immediate. The *Wall Street Journal* reported: "If a third Kennedy acquires high national office, the rest of us might as well deed the country to the Kennedys." If he lost, the *Journal* warned, "he might find that at the next family dinner he would have to eat in the kitchen." The *Washington Post* paraphrased Winston Churchill, saying Ted was a modest man, "with much to be modest about." Joan was dismayed and felt that the media was "mean-minded and cynical."

It got worse, though, at the end of the month, when a family secret was revealed: Ted had cheated on a Spanish test at Harvard eleven years earlier—he'd had another student take the test for him—and was expelled as a result. The reason he had done so, as he later explained, was that Joseph had been banking on his son passing all his exams, and there was no way he was going to pass Spanish: As a student who always struggled through his classes, Ted had particular trouble with languages. Also, if he didn't pass his Spanish class, he would get kicked off the varsity football team. So he did what he felt he had to do. After nineteen-year-old Ted was expelled from Harvard, he enlisted in the army for two years. Ted was later reinstated at the prestigious college, and after finally graduating from Harvard, he went on to the University of Virginia Law School.

Joan felt that Ted had made an honest mistake and that his father had been indirectly responsible by always putting too much pressure on Ted. Joan believed that it should not be held against her husband. She couldn't fathom why "such a big deal" had been made of the matter when it had happened eleven years earlier. This would be her first inkling of what she would later call "the cruelty of politics."

Jack called to tell Ted that he had met with reporters from the *Boston Globe*, but to no avail; the negative story would run. Joan was so anxious that she called Jackie to see if there was anything she as First Lady could do to put the brakes on this runaway scandal.

On March 26, 1962, Jackie Kennedy was in London at the town house of her sister, Lee Radziwill. She was making a two-day rest stop, recovering from a strenuous and much-publicized fifteen-day tour of India and Pakistan. ("She really broke her ass on that trip," Jack would tell Ben Bradlee.) On March 28, Jackie would dine with Queen Elizabeth II at Buckingham Palace. She would then return to Washington on March 29, a day before the story about Ted was scheduled to hit the stands.

The Radziwills, Lee and her husband Prince Stanislaw, had invited a few friends for an impromptu dinner to honor Jackie on her first night in London. Together they watched the BBC's broadcast of the First Lady's White House tour, which was shown in England at a later date than it had been in America.

Just before the broadcast got under way, the telephone rang: It was Joan Kennedy calling from the United States.

"She was upset," recalls Mari Kumlin, a designer friend of Lee's who was visiting her from Switzerland. "We kept hearing Jackie say things like 'Now calm down, Joan. It's not that bad, Joan. Take it easy, Joan. Don't be ridiculous, Joan.' Apparently, this big scandal was about to break, something to do with Ted having cheated on a Spanish test and getting kicked out of Harvard because of it. Jackie hung up with Joan and placed a call to Jack to see if there was anything he could do. From what I later understood, he apparently told her that he had already tried to stop the story, had met with the newspaper reporters and had even suggested that they run the juicy tidbit as part of a bigger story about Ted, but that the reporters felt that the cheating incident would get buried that way. They wanted to make it a big deal."

As the others watched her flickering image before them on the television set, Jackie preoccupied herself with the matter at hand in

Washington. She called Joan back to tell her that nothing could be done about it.

"Secrets always come out, don't they?" she observed to Joan. "Sometimes it takes years, sometimes not. We're lucky this one took eleven years, I guess."

Joan said something—it's not known what—to which Jackie, in the presence of the others in the room, responded, "Look, if I were you, Joan, I would just forget it. Act like it's not even happening. And just go on with your life and Ted's campaign.

"Trust me. When it comes out, it will be the biggest news in the land," Jackie continued, "and then two days later something else will come along and that will be even bigger news. Who knows?" The First Lady laughed. "Maybe we'll get lucky and someone important will keel over and drop dead."

Before she signed off, she said, "Now go and hug Kara. That will make everything all right."

After Jackie had hung up, she said to the others, "You know, that poor dear is not cut out for this kind of life, she really isn't. She's like a sister, and I worry about her because I'm afraid her troubles have only just begun."

"Teddy cheated on a Spanish test?" Lee asked, ignoring Jackie's opinion of Joan. She knew that Jackie's brother-in-law had been kicked out of Harvard but she didn't know the reason why.

"I guess so," Jackie said, shrugging her shoulders with resignation. "Are you the least bit surprised?"

Jackie didn't mention that when Ted was still an undergraduate at Harvard, he had asked her to write a term paper for him, and she had done it, "but only because I felt sorry for him," she would later explain. "He just could never keep up. Never."

The story about Ted's cheating at Harvard broke, as expected, the day after Jackie returned to Washington. As headlines screamed out his lack of judgment, Ted became dejected. "He feels like he's been kicked in the balls," Jack said privately, "he's really singing the blues."

Jack also noted in a conversation with Ben Bradlee that Ted's cheating "wouldn't go over with the WASPs. They take a very dim view of looking over your shoulder at someone else's exam paper. They go in more for stealing from stockholders and banks."

Jackie's advice to Joan, however, proved to be right on the mark. After Ted had made his apologies to the public, his campaign for his party's nomination to fill JFK's Senate seat against his opponent, Edward McCormack,* rolled on, despite the humiliation. Ted would stump until early June under the slogan "He can do more for Massachusetts." At the Democratic Party Convention in June 1962, he defeated Ed McCormack by a two-to-one margin.

*McCormack is the nephew of the late John W. McCormack, Speaker of the House from 1962 to 1971.

PART THREE

Bobby Meets Marilyn

Bobby and Ethel Kennedy first encountered Marilyn Monroe on February 1, 1962, at a party for Bobby hosted by Peter Lawford and his wife Pat, Bobby's sister, at the Lawfords' twenty-seven-room Malibu mansion. According to family friend Joan Braden, who attended the party, Marilyn was first introduced to Bobby by Pat. He didn't seem impressed until Braden whispered to him that this was "*the* Marilyn Monroe, the genuine article. *That* got his attention," she said, laughing.

In her 1989 memoir, *Just Enough Rope*, Joan Braden wrote, "Bobby turned and I turned and there she was—blond, beautiful, red lips at the ready, clad in a black-lace dress which barely concealed the tips of her perfectly formed breasts and tightly fitted every curve of the body unparalleled. Bobby paid attention. He sat next to her at dinner; around our table of eight were Kim Novak, Angie Dickinson, and me. Who the men between us were, I can't remember. I can only remember the women and the dresses which showed off their bosoms."

Years later, in an interview, Joan added: "They had an instant rapport, not surprising in that they were both charismatic, smart people. Bobby enjoyed talking to intelligent, beautiful women, and Marilyn certainly fit the bill. She was also inquisitive in a childlike way, which I think he found refreshing. I found her to be delightful, and everyone at the party was completely enthralled by her and rather dazzled by her presence."

At the dinner table, Marilyn proceeded to further enchant Bobby. "From her tiny black purse, she extracted a folded piece of paper, and unfolded it to reveal, in bright lipstick, a list of questions," said Braden. "The first was, 'What does an Attorney General do?' There were some giggles from somewhere at the table and the man next to me whispered, 'Don't. She's had a sad and lonely life and she has no self-confidence at all.'" Marilyn read other lipstick-written questions, each of which, Braden recalls, "was as innocent and childlike as the first, totally without guile or pretense except for the medium in which they were written. Bobby was enthralled."

One might question how Bobby could be so openly flirtatious at a party at which his wife was also in attendance. Ethel had grown accustomed to this sort of thing, however, and, although disapproving of it, she kept her mouth shut.

Ethel had actually been excited about meeting Marilyn. She was not immune to the power of the screen star's charisma and personality. In fact, about a year earlier, she had said that she wanted Marilyn to play her in a movie that was being developed by 20th Century-Fox based on Bobby Kennedy's book *The Enemy Within*. (The film was never made.)

Now, a year later, Ethel was in the same room with Marilyn, who seemed to be flirting with her husband. Ethel reportedly said later to Pat Kennedy in the company of two Kennedy aides, "I just think she's a big phony, and if I'm never around her again, that would be fine with me. Women like that make me so mad—trying to seduce a married man. I'm furious about this, I really am."

"Oh, Ethel, Marilyn's harmless," said Pat.

"Harmless, my foot," exclaimed Ethel. "This one is where I draw the line," she said, apparently more adamant about this woman than she was about all the others.

As the evening wore on, Bobby seemed to fall further under Monroe's spell, especially when he started coaching her in the rudiments of the popular dance craze the Twist, all under the suspicious gaze of Ethel. When Marilyn became too drunk to see herself to her Brentwood home, Bobby offered to drive her. Perhaps mindful of Ethel's ever-frozen stare, he asked his press agent, Ed Guthman, to accompany them. Marilyn plopped herself in the front seat next to Bobby, leaving Guthman in the back. Following the short drive to her house, Bobby walked the wobbly Marilyn unsteadily to her door, where she was met by her housekeeper, Eunice Murray.

After this party, Bobby and Marilyn apparently began seeing one another socially whenever he was on the West Coast.

Peter Dye, a frequent guest at the Lawford home, recalls, "I know Marilyn was nuts about him because she told me as much. She was fascinated by him. I also think she was scared to death of him because he gave off an air about himself."

Max Block, a former president of the Meat Cutters Union, says that he and one of Bobby's enemies, Jimmy Hoffa, were told about meetings between Bobby and Marilyn Monroe at the Desert Inn in Las Vegas by the manager of the hotel, Wilbur Clark. "He told me he checked them in every few weeks into a suite of rooms on the seventh floor," says Max Block. "One day I was sitting with him, and Bobby passed by and said, 'Hello, Wilbur.' Clark said, 'Hello, Bobby. This is my friend Max Block.' Kennedy said, 'Oh, I know Block from New York.' And he kept going. I asked where he was going, and Clark said, 'He's going to see Marilyn upstairs.' When I mentioned to Jimmy about Bobby and Marilyn Monroe, he said, 'I know all about that.'"

_____

"Life's Too Short to Worry about Marilyn Monroe"

In the spring of 1962, the President of the United States would celebrate his forty-fifth birthday on May 29. Peter Lawford came up with the idea of having Marilyn sing "Happy Birthday" to Jack at a huge birthday salute being planned at Madison Square Garden. Many other celebrities would be performing at the gala, which was thrown by the Democratic Party to raise money for the next presidential campaign; performers would include singers such as Ella Fitzgerald, Maria Callas, and Peggy Lee. The notion of the sexy movie star serenading the President might have been an example of Lawford's warped sense of humor; friends insist that having Marilyn as the show's finale was his idea of an in-joke.

At this time, Marilyn Monroe was causing problems for her studio, 20th Century-Fox, during production of her latest film, *Something's Got to Give*. Pleading illness, she had missed so many days of principal photography that the movie was behind schedule. Naturally, the studio heads were adamantly opposed to her taking more time off to attend the President's birthday celebration.

On the other hand, Bobby Kennedy was just as determined to have Monroe present. Upon learning that Fox was threatening a lawsuit if she left the set to attend the gala, Bobby personally telephoned studio head Peter Levathes in Hollywood to ask that Monroe be permitted to fly to New York without penalty. He explained that her performance would be "very important to the President of the United States." When Levathes turned him down, Bobby became exasperated.

Bobby then went over Levathes's head to the most powerful man at Fox at the time, financier Milton Gould, to whom he explained that Marilyn's appearance was "of critical importance to the current administration." Gould recalls Bobby as having said, "The President wants it, and I want it." When Gould's answer was emphatically negative, the Attorney General threatened him, telling him that he would be "sorry for this" and reminding him that he was "dealing with the First Family in America."

Bobby Kennedy needn't have worried. With or without the studio's permission, Marilyn Monroe was determined to perform at the event. She announced that she would not be available for work and then made plans to leave for New York. (Her decision would result in an eventual breach-of-contract lawsuit from Fox.)

Famous for her revealing wardrobe, Marilyn had designer Jean Louis create what was probably the most daring gown of her entire career—one made of the sheerest flesh-colored netting. With the fabric covered by hundreds of rhinestones, Marilyn appeared to be wearing nothing but beads speckled over luscious flesh. (In October 1999, at an auction of Marilyn's belongings at Christie's, in New York, this gown commanded more than a million dollars.)

By her own choice, the First Lady would not be present for the Madison Square Garden birthday party. She had heard about Marilyn Monroe's planned performance despite the fact that the chairman of the Democratic Party had called one of the show's organizers, Richard Adler (who wrote the music to *The Pajama Game* and *Damn Yankees*), to demand that Marilyn be removed.

It would seem that Jackie suspected trouble ahead. "I'm not going to sit and watch *that*," she told her Secret Service agent in an unusual moment of candor. "If you ask me, I think this administration is completely out of control with all of this Marilyn business."

When the agent did not respond, Jackie may have realized the inappropriate nature of her comment, because she said, "Forget I ever said that, please."

Nunziata Lisi, a friend of Lee Radziwill's who lived in Italy at the time, says, "According to what Lee told me, Jackie did not have a fight with Jack about the Madison Square Garden matter, or even a discussion about it. Her position, from what I gathered, was that if Jack actually approved of such a thing, knowing full well that she would be unhappy about it—and maybe even humiliated by it—then it wasn't worth a big brouhaha. It was just not worth going. Or, as Lee told me Jackie put it, 'Life's too short to worry about Marilyn Monroe.'"

As she always did when she wanted to get away, Jackie took the kids to Glen Ora, outside Middleburg, Virginia, two hours from Washington. She and Jack rented this four-hundred-acre, seven-bedroom estate as a weekend retreat. Jackie always savored her time there, referring to Middleburg as "home" and Washington as "the White House."

By 1962, Jackie was spending as many as four days a week at Glen Ora with her children, her horses, and other animals, living what she called "a good, clean life"—which, more often than not, did not include Jack. Jack hated Glen Ora. While Jackie had a strong affinity for horses, the President was allergic to them.

While at Glen Ora during this particular May, Jackie participated in the Loudoun Hunt Horse Show, taking a third-place ribbon. "It was very simple there at Glen Ora," Eve Fout, a friend of Jackie's from Middleburg, recalled to First Lady historian Carl Anthony. "The press would poke around, usually when there was a big event going on. Sometimes, someone would call me and tell me more about what we had just done than even I knew. Jackie said, 'Look, if I worried about what people said about me every day, I couldn't get up in the morning. I learned very quickly.'"

Eve Fout further recalled that at Glen Ora, Jackie "lived like everyone else. Wait in line at the store, go right into any of the shops. She always had meals at home. Only four times in all those years did she go out to eat, two times at a restaurant, two times at friends' homes. She said that if that was antisocial, then that is what she was, and should be, at that period in her life."

On May 19, 1962, approximately twenty thousand Democrats celebrated the President's forty-fifth birthday at massive Madison Square Garden (even though Jack's birthday was still ten days away). Jack, Bobby, Ethel, Rose, Pat, and Eunice were all present.

Backstage, Monroe was buckling under the pressure and was jittery at the prospects of such an important appearance. Up close, her ivory face makeup and heavy eyeliner gave her an almost Kabuki-like appearance, adding to her aura of fragility. After all the other performers had done their numbers, Peter Lawford finally brought her onto the stage. A gasp from the audience greeted her as she trotted delicately out like an oriental empress. The $12,000 Jean Louis beaded gown was so tight, she could take only the tiniest of mincing steps at a time. Hugh Sidey of *Time* magazine, who was present at the gala, recalls, "There was a feeling of euphoria mixed with a sense of astonishment that this scene was actually taking place, and that it was for the benefit of the President of the United States, who seemed to go limp. When I say 'limp,' I mean that he was visibly affected. His mouth was wide open, as if he didn't know whether to be shocked, excited, appalled, or what."

After Lawford helped her remove her ermine stole, Marilyn sang her little birthday song to the President and then another number, with special lyrics written for the occasion by Richard Adler, to the tune of "Thanks for the Memories," Bob Hope's theme song. ("Thanks, Mr. President/For all the things you've done/The battles that you've won/The way you deal with U.S. Steel/And our problems by the ton/We thank you so much.") While performing, she seductively ran her hands up her curvaceous body and nearly cupped her breasts. It was an act that might have been more appropriate at a burlesque show than at a political fund-raiser.

After Marilyn had the audience join her in another rousing round of "Happy Birthday," she brought Jack onto the stage. "I can now retire from politics after having had 'Happy Birthday' sung to me in such a wholesome way," he joked from behind a podium emblazoned by the presidential seal.

A friend of Marilyn's, Jeanne Martin—whose husband of twelve years, entertainer Dean Martin, was co-starring with Marilyn in *Something's Got to Give* at this time—can still vividly recall the strong emotions she felt as she sat in the VIP section of the audience more than three decades ago. Of Monroe's stage presence, she says, "That performance was beyond the pale. I squirmed in my seat, tried to look away. . . . It belittled the entire Presidency, as well as Jackie's position as First Lady."

Jeanne, who has remained close to the Kennedys through the years, put the blame on the President himself. "Certainly Marilyn couldn't have done it without Jack's approval," she says. "I never believed it was a complete surprise to the President. Why would he allow her to do that?" (And in fact, Marilyn's performance was not a surprise: Jack had been forewarned by Bobby.)

Beverly Brennan, an investment banker who met Pat Kennedy through Peter Lawford in 1954, recalls that Pat found the performance "hysterical and very good." As for Jackie, Pat said, "She can take a joke. She has such a vicious sense of humor herself." Pat Kennedy also told Beverly Brennan that she had telephoned Jackie at Glen Ora when she heard that the First Lady wasn't going to be present at the celebration, to assure her that the performance would be "just a harmless Marilyn Monroe prank." She assured her that, as Marilyn's close friend, she would never allow the screen star to do anything that would embarrass the First Lady, and she also advised Jackie that her absence would only focus more attention on the spectacle. Apparently, Jackie was not convinced.

The day after the President's birthday party, Jackie, still at Glen Ora, saw a news broadcast of Marilyn's breathless, sultry rendition of "Happy Birthday."

Jackie's right-hand man, Clint Hill, was with her at Glen Ora, as always. Hill, a former football star at Concordia College in North Dakota, was married to his high-school sweetheart, Gwen Brown. Much more than just a Secret Service agent to Jackie, he was now responsible for many aspects of her busy life. "I also dealt with her maid, I dealt with her nanny for the children, and her day-to-day operations," he recalls. "On a lot of things she would deal directly with me instead of going to a social secretary or a press secretary."

Jackie, appearing bewildered and frustrated, paced the living room. When the phone rang, she jumped for it. It was Ethel, calling to express her anger about Monroe's act and the way Jack had responded to it. Ethel apparently felt, as had Jeanne Martin and others, that Marilyn's performance was an insult to Jackie. Ethel said she was calling to make sure Jackie was not too upset, and to discuss with her how she might handle the matter with the President.

As Jackie spoke to Ethel, her voice rose. "My understanding of it is that Bobby was the one who orchestrated the whole goddamn thing," she said, blazing out the words in frustration. "The Attorney General is the troublemaker here, Ethel. Not the President. So it's Bobby I'm angry at, not Jack."

"It's just all so exhausting," a weary Jackie told Ethel. "And what about that poor woman?" she added, referring apparently to Marilyn. "Look at how they are exploiting her."

As the conversation ended, Jackie thanked Ethel for her concern and asked where she could locate Bobby. Told that the Attorney General was in his office, she promptly called him. The two spoke angrily for about five minutes. Jackie's terse, obscenity-laced end of the conversation was completely uncharacteristic of the warm rapport she ordinarily shared with Bobby. However, she was clearly upset. After accusing Bobby of having sanctioned "a sick game" with a movie star, Jackie hung up on him, her hands visibly shaking.

Jackie's Ultimatum to Jack

Angry about the ongoing scandal regarding her husband's relationship with Marilyn Monroe, it now seems—based on the best evidence available—that Jackie Kennedy finally gave the President an ultimatum immediately following the Madison Square Garden celebration: Stop seeing Marilyn, or lose his First Lady.

A Secret Service agent who spent much of his time on White House detail protecting the First Lady and her children—who asked not to be named in connection with the ultimatum since he still maintains a close relationship to the family—explains how Jackie went about it. The agent says that when Jack joined his wife at Glen Ora two days after the Marilyn Monroe performance, she told him that if he didn't end his association with Marilyn "once and for all," she would leave him. It would be done quietly at first, Jackie told him. However, just prior to the 1964 presidential campaign, she threatened, she would officially file for divorce. The agent says, "After that threat, I never heard another word about him and Marilyn Monroe."

Beverly Brennan, Pat Lawford's friend from Los Angeles, further corroborates the story, saying that after the Madison Square Garden show, Pat Lawford told her, "Do you know that Jackie actually threatened to divorce Jack unless he stopped being friends with Marilyn?

And he agreed to such a thing?" Brennan says that Pat was "dumbfounded by the whole thing."

Nunziata Lisi, Lee Radziwill's friend from Italy, says, "Lee told me that with the threat of his crumbling marriage interfering with Jack's possible reelection in 1964, Jackie had finally found her strongest bargaining chip: divorce." Lee told Nunziata that she doubted Jackie would ever have actually given up her position as First Lady, but she applauded her sister's decision to finally force an end to the affair.

"Jackie's sick to death of this whole thing," Jack told his friend George Smathers. "She's all over me about it. So let's end it with her [Monroe] before it's too late."

The President then made swift moves to distance himself from the star. At his request, Smathers contacted a mutual friend of his and the Kennedys, Bill Thompson, and asked him to speak to Marilyn about, as Smathers puts it, "putting a bridle on her mouth and not talking too much because it was getting to be a story around the country."

Meanwhile, Jack simply stopped returning Marilyn's telephone calls. As far as he was concerned, the affair was over.

Bobby's Rumored Affair with Marilyn

By the summer of 1962, the resumption of atmospheric testing of nuclear weapons was causing great alarm among Americans, while heightened tensions with the Soviet Union continued to threaten world peace. Obviously, these matters were of great concern to the Kennedys, as they were to the rest of the country; in Ethel Kennedy's household, however, another troublesome situation seemed to monopolize a great deal of her time: Bobby and, yet again, Marilyn.

Ethel had been infuriated by Bobby's flirtatious behavior with Marilyn at the Madison Square Garden after-party.* The next day she

---

*The party was hosted by the late Arthur Krim and his wife, Dr. Mathilde Krim, who recently revealed that the Secret Service confiscated all of the photographers' film of Marilyn with the Kennedy brothers. Only one photo of the three has somehow managed to survive.

called her sister, Georgeann, and, according to Georgeann's husband, George Terrien, said that she would have liked to have scratched Monroe's eyes out. "But Ethel was a good Kennedy wife," notes Terrien, and "she kept her mouth shut and looked the other way."

The true nature of the relationship between Bobby and Marilyn still stirs controversy among Monroe and Kennedy confidantes and family members.

"Let me just set this straight once and for all," said Chuck Spalding, who was close enough to the Kennedys that he could at least have an opinion about it. "The answer is a flat-out 'no.' Marilyn liked Jack, maybe loved him. She flirted with Bobby, and he flirted back, but that was it. These stories about Bobby and Marilyn are all junk. Maybe Ethel thought they were having an affair, but I am certain that it was nothing more than a flirtation."

"If Marilyn and Bobby were involved, it was very gently orchestrated," said Milt Ebbins. "I was Peter's [Lawford] closest friend. He told me everything—things that will never be revealed. He never told me about Bobby and Marilyn, and he told me things that would have been considered much more confidential than that."

Even though there are dozens of peripheral people in and around the lives of both principals who claim that the two did have a sexual affair, those closest to the two are adamant that the relationship never grew past the flirtation stage. Unfortunately, one important person in Bobby's life believed that he was indeed intimate with Marilyn Monroe, and that person was Ethel Kennedy.

"She most certainly did believe it," says Leah Mason, who worked for Ethel as an assistant off and on for many years at Hickory Hill. "She was sure that an affair was going on. And she was extremely unhappy about it."

Ethel apparently attempted to recruit Frank Sinatra to talk to Monroe about her relationship with Bobby. According to Sinatra's friend Jim Whiting, "Frank didn't really believe that anything serious was going on between them, and he figured if anything was happening, it was probably just Marilyn flirting, pretty much the way she used to flirt with everyone." And yet whenever Frank Sinatra did ask Marilyn Monroe about her relationship with the Kennedys, she was evasive. In the end, neither Sinatra nor anyone else would be much help to Ethel Kennedy.

Joseph's Stroke

By this time the life of Kennedy patriarch Joseph had taken a dramatic and tragic turn. On December 19, 1961, he had suffered a stroke while playing golf at the Palm Beach Country Club that left him severely debilitated. Jack and Jackie had been in Palm Beach at the time. Jack had left for Washington early in the day while Jackie and Caroline stayed behind in Palm Beach. (John Jr. was in Washington with the children's nanny, Maud Shaw.) Apparently, Joe didn't notice any symptoms until he returned to the estate for a swim with Jackie. After going to his room to rest and change, he emerged unable to speak or move his right side. Joe's niece Ann Gargan took him to St. Mary's Hospital in West Palm Beach while Jackie telephoned Jack and Bobby to tell them what had happened.

The prognosis for Joseph was not good. After he'd been on the critical list a few days, he was given Last Rites. If he did live, he would be paralyzed, would probably never walk again, and would not speak. The family was devastated by this tragic turn of events.

"Well, I'm sorry but I just can't believe he won't walk," Jackie told Bobby one afternoon shortly after the stroke. In fact, she refused to shed a tear for Grandpa.

"Why should I cry?" she asked. "I know he will be fine."

Immediately after receiving word of the stroke, all of the Kennedys went to Palm Beach to visit the ailing Joseph and to lend emotional support to Rose. To his children, Joseph was still the family's respected patriarch, the indomitable figure whose vision had been responsible for the historical dynasty that was not only their own proud legacy, but also the birthright of their children. His daughters- and sons-in-law, as well as his own offspring, felt unequivocal respect, love, and admiration for Joseph. Though Joseph was ruthless, ". . . he's the reason we exist at all," Jackie had said. "Without him, without his vision, his dream, his desires for his children, none of us would be who we are. We'd all have done something with our lives, obviously, but not *this*." For his part, Jack had critical differences with his father on certain political issues, but he loved him deeply. This sudden illness was a terrible blow.

While Jackie seemed sure from the outset that Joseph would recover, the rest of the family seemed resigned to their patriarch's paralysis. Even the ever-religious Ethel had little faith in a miracle, saying that it was "God's will" that Joseph not walk again.

The day she first visited Joseph in the hospital in Florida, Jackie went to a department store in Palm Beach and bought a walking cane. She and Ethel were standing in Rose's kitchen in Palm Beach when Jackie pulled the cane from a box. Ethel looked at it with incredulity. "It's useless, you know," she said. "Grandpa will never walk again. Didn't you hear?"

"I just need to get it engraved," Jackie said, ignoring her sister-in-law's words. "Now, let's see where I can have that done." Jackie turned to Dora, the cook. "Where's Frank?" she asked. "He'll know."

Before leaving the kitchen to find Frank Saunders, the Kennedy chauffeur, Jackie turned to Ethel and added, "Oh, and by the way, Ethel, Grandpa will walk again. I can promise you that." Jackie intended to keep the walking cane until she felt that it was time for Joe to use it, then she would give it to him as a gift.

Six months later, Joseph was a patient in Horizon House, a rehabilitation center in New York. Joseph had endured a difficult half-year of recovery at Hyannis Port. Before he was taken to the center, his convalescence was slow and arduous. For Rose, her husband's challenges took on nightmarish proportions. It was as if she could do nothing right for him. "Ya! Ya! Ya!" he would scream at her, swinging his fists in frustration. Rose would run from the room in tears, asking Rita Dallas, "What did I do? What did I do?" Every day a new drama unfolded, whether it had to do with Joseph's refusal to eat or his insistence on getting out of his wheelchair. Once he struck Rita, giving her a black eye. So by the time Joseph was whisked off to Horizon House, it was a welcome relief for Rose and the household staff (a total of ninety-three nurses would work for the Kennedys during the years after the stroke).

Unlike Rose, who could do nothing right for Joseph, it seemed Jackie could do no wrong. Many people wondered how Jackie could feel so much warm emotion towards a man who so blatantly flaunted his infidelities, who so thoroughly manipulated his family's lives, who used his wealth to try to control and contain everyone around him.

But Joseph, like his son Jack, reminded Jackie of her own father, the flamboyant, woman-loving Black Jack.

From the first time she met the Kennedys, Jackie had found a staunch ally in Jack's father. She set out to charm Joseph, and she succeeded. Jackie did not have to be guarded the way she acted with him; she wasn't afraid of Joseph. She genuinely loved him. He felt the same, and he also enjoyed her sense of humor. One of his prized possessions was an original watercolor painting by Jackie of dozens of Kennedys romping on a beach. Overhead, a plane trails a banner: "You can't take it with you. Dad's got it all." Joseph hung the painting in the living room of his Palm Beach mansion.

Another favorite painting of his by Jackie was a watercolor in which protesters march holding picket signs reading: "Put Jackie and Joan back in American clothes"—a spoof of a silly 1960 campaign controversy having to do with Jackie, Ethel, and Joan wearing only French-designed clothing.

Often defensive because his Irish Catholic background kept him from being accepted in society, Joseph appreciated that Jackie could move easily in social circles closed to him, and he recognized that her beauty and her knowledge of art and music had always been valuable assets to Jack's political career. He also admired her independence. While his own children deferred to his wishes, Jackie used to tease him. It was as if Joseph had taken her father's place in her life, especially when Jackie and Joseph would sit poring through photo albums of her wedding. Jackie, with her slender frame and delicate femininity, was just the type of woman that Joseph responded to. They adored each other.

The day after his arrival at Horizon House, as Rita Dallas tried to convince Joseph to take a nap, there was a knock on the door. It opened slowly, and Jackie peeked in. Joseph's face brightened at the sight of her.

Jackie walked into Joseph's room and sat on a footstool at the side of his bed. As Rita Dallas looked on, Jackie took Joseph's deformed hand into her own. She told him that she was praying for him and that she had great faith in a "speedy recovery."

Joseph nodded his head and placed his hand on her cheek. Jackie rested her head on his lap and kissed his hand. Then she stood up to kiss the side of his face that had been paralyzed.

At Horizon House

Joseph worked tirelessly at Horizon House to regain his faculties, with periodic visits from all of his family members lending their support and encouragement—except for Ethel, who said that she could not bear to see her father-in-law in such a weakened state.

Joan would sometimes visit her father-in-law with Ted, and she would often show up at the hospital alone. Nurses remember her sitting and talking to the old man for hours, leaving his side only to break down in tears in the hallway. She so loved Joseph, perhaps because he praised her at every opportunity, even at Jackie's expense.

One story about Joseph that Joan has often told has to do with the time she, Jackie, Ethel, their husbands, and the rest of the Kennedys were at the Big House for Thanksgiving dinner. They were all gathered around Rose's polished fruitwood table in her ivory-and-gold dining room. As it did every year, a centerpiece of gourds, small pumpkins, bananas, apples, and autumn leaves with four silver candlesticks decorated the table, with platters of food placed all about it: hot clam broth; a butter-browned twenty-six-pound turkey on a silver serving dish; homemade cranberry sauce; buttered string beans; creamed onions; mashed orange sweet potatoes with a melted marshmallow topping; corn muffins; and for dessert, apple or pumpkin pie and vanilla ice cream. "Eh, now *this* is living," Ted would say.

Despite their tremendous wealth and the manner in which they relished their lifestyle, the Kennedys were also notoriously thrifty. Rose was known to run around the house scolding the help for leaving lights on; she would loosen bulbs in the closets because "you don't need light in a closet." Joseph and Rose both liked to think they had money problems, though they had millions.

"No one in this family lives within her means, except for Joan," Joseph said as they ate. "She's thrifty, and I like that about her, let me tell you."

Once Ted bought Joan a diamond pin worth many thousands of dollars. Joan decided to wear it to an embassy reception in Tokyo, and to offset its loveliness she wore two strings of pearls that she had purchased for fifteen dollars each at Garfinckel's in Washington. "Everyone thinks they look real," she told a reporter candidly. "But, you know, I don't think I'll buy the real thing. These are good enough, don't you think?" That was the kind of behavior Joseph liked in Joan.

"Now you, young lady," Joseph said, pointing an accusatory finger at Jackie, who was known for shopping binges that involved tens of thousands of dollars spent on antiques, clothes, and jewels. "I see not the slightest indication that you have any idea of how much money you spend. Bills come in from Italy, Paris, Rome, all over the world for your extravagances. It's completely ridiculous to have such disregard for the value of money. You should be more like Joan."

Ethel, sitting next to Joseph, may have feared he might criticize her next. In truth, Ethel was as big a spendthrift as Jackie, with no concept of the value of money. Once when an accountant told her that her checking account was overdrawn, she responded very seriously, "But how can that be? I still have checks left!" Barbara Gibson, who would later become Rose's personal secretary, says, "Ethel was big on fine wines and would order her favorite, *Pouilly Fuissé*, by the case. She would buy designer dresses she liked in a variety of colors. When you went to her home for dinner, it was always luxurious—lobster tails, prime rib. I remember when Rose Kennedy and I went to Ethel's once, and the menu was Alaskan King Crab. Sarcastically, Rose said something like, 'It must be nice to be so very, very rich.' "

If being reprimanded for her spending habits hurt Jackie at all, she knew just how to receive the criticism with good grace, allowing Joan her moment of glory.

"Oh, you are so right, Grandpa," Jackie said, with a pointed look at Ethel. "We should *all* be more like Joan."

Joan enjoyed telling that story, and she told it often. "I love Grandpa and Jackie for that," she said.

Joseph's illness was therefore especially difficult for his youngest daughter-in-law, and the visits were emotionally draining. Ted told her that if visiting his father was so upsetting, perhaps she should stop going. Yet Joan continued to go.

One day Joan showed up with Jackie, and the two sisters-in-law wheeled Joseph up and down the hospital corridors, gossiping and laughing like sisters, as if the old man wasn't even there. One of Joseph's therapists, Patricia Moran, remembers Joseph abruptly stamping his foot on the floor in order to get their attention. "It's as if he was saying, 'Pay attention to me, why don't you.'" Afterwards, she says, they all laughed heartily, Joseph included.

"Gosh, what can we do to get Ethel down here?" Jackie would ask Joan. "When is she going to learn to deal with the real world? It is often not pretty, you know? Maybe Bobby can do something." Even Bobby, however, was unable to convince his wife to visit Joseph.

Despite her reluctance to show up at Horizon House, Ethel had great love, respect, and admiration for her father-in-law, holding him in high esteem and, like Jackie and Joan, seemingly ignoring the fact (or maybe just accepting it and not allowing it to affect her opinion of him) that it was really Joseph who had set the standard for the womanizing that would continue to plague all their marriages. Like Jackie and Joan, Ethel always made certain that her children treated Grandpa with the utmost respect.

"Everything we have, all that we are, we owe to Grandpa," Ethel would tell her offspring just before they visited Joseph. "You see that bike? It's because of Grandpa that you have it," she would say. "You see that swimming pool? It's because of Grandpa that you have it. Now go over there and kiss your Grandpa."

The Walking Cane

Joseph Kennedy made rapid progress during his therapy, though he did not regain his speech and never would; the day soon arrived in the summer of 1962 when he would take his first poststroke steps—a major achievement in the life of any handicapped person and the ultimate goal of months of painstaking therapy. It was a miracle, Rose said, "a true miracle."

With fitted leg brace and a surgical shoe, Joseph was about to rise from his wheelchair when a doctor handed him a hook-handled cane supplied by the hospital. His face became crimson red as he screamed out, "No! No! *No!*" The ordinary cane was offensive; he wasn't just any man and would not use the cane anyone else would be given. He threw the offending stick across the room, narrowly missing a nurse. After a great deal of coaxing, Joseph finally agreed to use the cane, but only after the doctor had promised to buy him a new, more handsome one.

With two attending physicians, several staff doctors, many patients, his business associate Ham Brown, and his nurses Luella Hennessey and Rita Dallas watching—a full audience—Joseph was just rising from the wheelchair again when there was a clattering of heels in the hall. All eyes turned to see Jackie quickly walking down the hallway flanked by two Secret Service agents, one of whom was Clint Hill. "Please, stop!" she implored.

Surprised, Joseph dropped back down into his chair, his mouth agape. Jackie, dressed in a pale yellow and white sleeveless shift with white heels and accessories, rushed to her father-in-law like a beam of light. She bent down and kissed him on the cheek, and soon the entire room was filled with her exuberant energy. Jackie said that she had heard Joe was going to be taking his first steps, and she wanted to be with him when he did so.

Joseph's eyes were brimming with tears as Jackie hugged him warmly. Taking his face in her hands, she continued, "The whole family is so proud of you. Jack told me to give you a big hug." They began to weep. Reaching into her pocketbook, she took out a handkerchief. "Aren't we ridiculous?" she asked with a smile as she wiped his eyes.

Jackie motioned to Clint Hill to come to her side. The agent handed the First Lady a long, wrapped package. Jackie opened the side of the box and pulled from it the expensive black and silver walking stick she had purchased the day she heard Joseph had been stricken and would never again walk. On the band was engraved "To Grandpa, with love, Jackie."

Joseph took the walking stick and rose from his chair; Jackie hooked her arm through his. "Come on," she said. "Let's take a walk."

Life at the Hyannis Port Compound

Despite the controversies surrounding the Kennedy brothers' relationships with Marilyn Monroe, family life at the Hyannis Port compound continued as if nothing was wrong. Keeping the family name unsullied was of prime importance to the Kennedys, even among each other.

In the tradition set by Rose, if family members didn't recognize unpleasant things, then surely they weren't happening. Those who married into the stoical clan had to follow the Kennedy line, no matter what their private opinions. So it was easy for them to celebrate the Fourth of July in 1962 at Hyannis Port as if they didn't have a care in the world.

Cape Cod is where the many Kennedys would congregate during the summer months and for holidays, birthdays, or during times of trouble. Whereas the Palm Beach compound—the winter home—was inhabited by Joseph and Rose, with rented homes nearby for the others, in Hyannis Port everyone was thrown together in close proximity.

In many ways, the beauty and serenity of the Hyannis Port compound made it seem a million miles away from the real world, especially in the summer of 1962, when racial tensions and violence were at an incendiary level in some American cities, particularly in the South. In a couple of months, the situation would escalate into a race riot when James Meredith would attempt to register at the all-white University of Mississippi. That night, Jack would appeal to white Mississippians in a nine-minute televised speech, during which he would plead for racial tolerance.

"Summer picnics were the favorite outings of young and old alike during those wonderful Cape Cod days," recalled Jacques Lowe. "Basket upon basket would be filled with hot dogs and hard-boiled eggs, hamburgers and marshmallows, cokes and beer. All the Kennedy children and their friends and pets would crowd into the *Marlin* [the Kennedy yacht] and motor over to some nearby island such as Great Island. There on the beach, a barbecue would be set up, baseball bats and footballs would come out, and the children and the grown-ups would partake in the simple joy of living."

Jackie would find herself at the Hyannis Port compound often, even in later years, after she was no longer a Kennedy. She enjoyed the peace and serenity there, as well as a sense of security, and though she may not have wanted to admit it for fear that her presence would become obligatory, she actually enjoyed the company of most of the Kennedys. She and Jack rented from Morton Downey another home nearby on Squaw Island, so they had a place to go to when Jackie tired of being so close to the family.

Jackie always disliked celebrities who visited Hyannis Port and expected her to be gracious to them. "Being nice is what I have to do at the White House as part of my job," she explained to one of her secretaries, "but I don't want to have to do it here [at Hyannis]. When I'm here, I'm off."

Judy Garland owned a summer home in the area, near the yacht club, and enjoyed visiting the Kennedys in her free time. As her teenaged children, Liza Minnelli and Lorna Luft, played with Ethel and Bobby's children, a barefoot Judy would wander from one Kennedy home to the other, a martini in one hand and a cream cheese and olive sandwich in the other. Ethel would welcome her with open arms but, according to Frank Saunders, Rose's chauffeur, Jackie thought of her as "that woman who thinks she can just drop in whenever she wants." Once, when Jackie was painting with watercolors on her sunporch, Judy barged in and attempted to engage her in a conversation. As Judy later complained to Rose, Jackie said, "I don't mean to be rude, but you'll have to stop talking. Watch, if you like. But no one talks to me when I'm painting." As a disgruntled Judy rushed off, Jackie hollered after her, "Next time, Miss Garland, please call first."

One weekend soon after Jack was elected to the Oval Office, Frank Sinatra came to visit. Annoyed that her husband would allow the singer access to their private getaway when he was well aware of her feelings about him, Jackie refused to leave her bedroom for the entire weekend. Sinatra had a basket of roses delivered to her home. When he left the compound at the end of the weekend, the basket was still on the sunporch, the roses wilted and the card unopened.

Ethel loved the Hyannis Port way of life and could often be found in Rose's kitchen, cooking or making fresh coffee for her sisters-in-law (though she would bristle when Jackie would ask for hers to be "dusted with just a whisper of cinnamon"). Like Jackie and Jack, Joan and Ted had a home on Squaw Island (though, unlike the First Couple, they did not also have one in the compound), only about five minutes from Rose and Joseph and the other Kennedys. For Joan, never comfortable with her role as a Kennedy wife, being so close to all of those Kennedys was sometimes more than she could bear. In Hyannis Port, she took comfort in knowing that her retreat on Squaw Island was just a short distance away when it all became too much for her.

Joseph and Rose's home on Scudder Avenue was not the big, extravagant mansion expected by many visitors, but rather a simple, white-painted, Cape Cod–style two-floor home with a veranda that wrapped around the front and sides. Furnished simply rather than elegantly, the home boasted a pool and tennis court, which were used by all of the Kennedys. Boats were always docked in front of the main house in time for summer jaunts. Walks on the nearby beach provided not only recreation for the family but also meditation during times of difficulty.

No matter what calamity was going on in the rest of the country— or in the individual Kennedy homes—the Fourth of July was a favorite time for the Kennedy family because it marked the beginning of summer. By July 1962, Joseph Kennedy was home from the rehabilitation center, making the holiday all the more momentous.

The arrival of the President and First Lady was the much-anticipated event that kicked off the holiday festivities. Also present for this Fourth of July celebration—they always seemed to be in recent years— were a number of celebrities, politicians, and, of course, members of the press with cameramen and photographers in tow. On the water in front of the main house were Coast Guard cutters, holding back pleasure boats and sightseers. The *Honey Fitz*, Jack's yacht, and the *Marlin*, the Kennedy family's boat, were both anchored in the Sound, bobbing up and down on calm waters. Early in the afternoon of the Fourth, the entire family—as well as governesses, nurses, gardeners, and other employees—gathered outside of Rose and Joseph's home, waiting for the guests of honor: Jack and Jackie. Ethel and Bobby were there, of course, and Ted and Joan. Also present, as they were for all family functions, were the Kennedy sisters: Eunice, Pat, and Jean, and their husbands, Sargent Shriver, Peter Lawford, and Stephen Smith.

The women of Camelot: Ethel, Joan, and Jackie, the Kennedy sisters-in-law, at Hyannis Port in 1960, just before Jackie became First Lady.
(© JACQUES LOWE)

Ethel Skakel's wedding day, June 17, 1950, to Robert Kennedy. In many ways, Ethel and Bobby were the ideal couple, with the same goals and philosophies—or, as Ethel would say many years later, "When you think of me and Bob, think 'soul mates.'" (PHOTOFEST)

Jackie Bouvier's wedding day, September 12, 1953, to John Fitzgerald Kennedy, at the time a Democratic senator from Massachusetts. Much has been written about their complex union, but on this day there was nothing but great happiness and optimism for the future. (PHOTOFEST)

Joan Bennett's wedding day, November 29, 1958, to Edward Moore Kennedy. Joan later said she "had no idea what I was getting myself into" when she married into the powerful, controversial Kennedy family. Like many brides of her generation, she was young, innocent, a bit naïve . . . and very beautiful. (PARAGON PHOTO VAULT)

Ethel and Jackie were in the audience at the hearing of the Senate labor rackets committee on March 3, 1957. Bobby was the committee's chief counsel, while Jack was a member of the committee. By this time Ethel already had reservations about Jackie—whom she and some of the other Kennedy women called "Jack-leen" (because it rhymed with "Queen"). (UPI/CORBIS-BETTMANN)

Jackie, Ethel, and Joan campaigned for JFK's presidency, even though Jackie and Joan didn't really enjoy politics. The three are seen here in a receiving line in Maryland just before the primary election there in May 1960. (AP/WORLDWIDE PHOTOS)

When Jackie's advanced pregnancy prevented her from safely continuing on the campaign trail, Joan and Ethel carried on, attending many Democratic tea parties—this one in Erie, Pennsylvania, in October 1960—while stumping for their brother-in-law. (UPI/CORBIS-BETTMANN)

The First Family, photographed on Election Day, November 9, 1960. The entire family honored Jackie with a standing ovation just prior to this sitting, much to Ethel's chagrin. Standing, left to right: Ethel Kennedy, Stephen Smith, Jean Kennedy Smith, John Fitzgerald Kennedy, Bobby Kennedy, Pat Kennedy Lawford , Sargent Shriver, Joan Kennedy, and Peter Lawford. In the foreground: Eunice Kennedy Shriver , Rose Kennedy, Joseph P. Kennedy, Jackie Kennedy, and Ted Kennedy. (ARCHIVE PHOTOS)

The Rulers of Camelot at the
Inaugural Ball, January 20,
1961: The King, JFK, with his
queen, Jackie; and her hand-
maidens, Ethel and Joan.
(PARAGON PHOTO VAULT)

Jackie and Jack at the Inaugural Ball at the Mayflower Hotel in
Washington. Though Jackie was ill and weak from the birth of
John Jr., she still managed to dazzle. (PHOTOFEST)

Jackie was proud of her performance when she gave a tour of the White House on February 14, 1962, for an international television audience. However Ethel, who felt that her sister-in-law's appearance seemed "phony," wondered, "Where did that voice come from?" (PHOTOFEST)

Jackie and Lady Bird Johnson, wife of Vice President Lyndon Johnson, always shared a warm relationship; correspondence that spans forty years is testament to a friendship that superseded the political differences between the Kennedys and the Johnsons. Here Lady Bird, wearing a Red Cross aid's uniform, escorts Jackie into a luncheon hosted by the Senate Ladies Red Cross Unit in the Old Supreme Court Chamber in Washington in May 1962. (PHOTOFEST/ICON)

Marilyn Monroe, just before going on stage at Madison Square Garden in 1962 to sing "Happy Birthday" to the President. Knowing that her husband was having an affair with the screen star, Jackie refused to attend the gala, saying "Life's too short to worry about Marilyn Monroe." (PHOTO FILE)

The Kennedys may have had problems with Marilyn Monroe in 1962, but one would never have known it by this photo taken at the Kennedy compound shortly after the Madison Squre Garden birthday party. Singing one of their favorite family songs are (l–r): Joan, Eunice, Jackie, Ethel, Pat, Ted, Bobby, Jack, and Steve Smith (Jean's husband). (JOHN FITZGERALD KENNEDY LIBRARY)

Upset by her husband's relationship with Marilyn Monroe as well as the screen star's sudden death, Jackie took a "private vacation" to Ravello, Italy, in August 1962. "Isn't it tragic enough," she told friends of Monroe's suicide while on a cruise to Capri, "without our gossiping about it under the stars?" (PHOTOFEST)

Upon Jackie's return from Ravello, all seemed back to normal when the entire family posed together for this photo at the Hyannis Port compound. Standing, left to right: Sargent Shriver, Steve Smith, Ethel, Jack, Pat, Rose, Bobby, Eunice, Jean, Ted, and Joan. In front, Jackie and Joseph Sr. (JOHN FITZGERALD KENNEDY LIBRARY)

Joan Kennedy; Jackie's sister, Lee Radziwill; Jackie's mother, Janet Auchincloss; and Jackie watch solemnly as President Kennedy delivers his State of the Union message to Congress in 1963. (UPI/CORBIS-BETTMANN)

Jackie and Jack, with their children, John and Caroline, on November 18, 1963, four days before JFK's murder. At this point Jack and Jackie had gotten closer. As his close friend Senator George Smathers put it, "He was as faithful as he was ever going to be . . . more than Jackie hoped for, but less than what she deserved." (PHOTOFEST)

Jackie and Jack appear at a speech in Fort Worth, Texas. The photo is especially poignant in that Kennedy would be dead, and Jackie's life forever altered, in just a couple of hours. (PARAGON PHOTO VAULT)

A grieving Jackie, escorted by Bobby and Ted, leaves the Capitol for the funeral procession to the church. "Who cares what happens to me now?" she would later ask. (PHOTOFEST)

This photo of Jackie at her husband's funeral in November 1963 says it all: the grief, despair, and sense of hopelessness she felt at this terrible time in her life. Her sisters-in-law were concerned about her, so much so that Ethel suggested she move into her home so that she could keep an eye on her. Jackie declined the offer. (PHOTOFEST)

Bobby shares a parting glance with Jackie after he and Ethel leave her temporary Georgetown home on December 6, 1963, just after Jackie moved out of the White House. In a few months, rumors would begin circulating that Jackie and Bobby were having an affair. While most people did not believe the ridiculous stories, Ethel seemed suspicious just the same. (UPI/CORBIS BETTMANN)

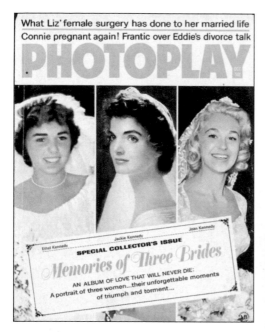

What Liz' female surgery has done to her married life
Connie pregnant again! Frantic over Eddie's divorce talk

PHOTOPLAY

SPECIAL COLLECTOR'S ISSUE
Memories of Three Brides
AN ALBUM OF LOVE THAT WILL NEVER DIE:
A portrait of three women...their unforgettable moments
of triumph and torment...

Priscilla and Linda in Love Battle Over Elvis!
Betty Ford: Her Private Agony—Her Public Courage

modern screen

THREE TORMENTED MOTHERS CRY—
DEAR GOD, NOW THEY'RE AFTER OUR CHILDREN

Fear Drives Jackie Away From Ari

Joan Finds Refuge In Hospital

Ethel Calls White House For Protection

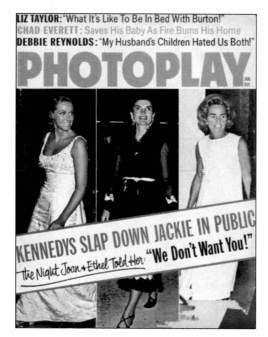

LIZ TAYLOR: "What It's Like To Be In Bed With Burton!"
CHAD EVERETT: Saves His Baby As Fire Burns His Home
DEBBIE REYNOLDS: "My Husband's Children Hated Us Both!"

PHOTOPLAY

KENNEDYS SLAP DOWN JACKIE IN PUBLIC
the Night Joan & Ethel Told Her: "We Don't Want You!"

Even though they weren't movie or television stars, Jackie, Ethel, and Joan became staples of fan magazines that were popular in the 1960s and '70s. Here are just a few of the many publications that featured the women on their covers. Oddly, the three sisters-in-law read the magazines religiously and often believed what they read about each other! (J. RANDY TARABORRELLI COLLECTION)

After the President's death, Jackie sent Joan to Europe to represent the Kennedy family on a touring exhibit of JFK memorabilia, in the hopes of making her finally feel an integral member of the family. Here, Joan poses with the President's rocking chair. (DEUTCHE PRESSE/ARCHIVE PHOTOS)

Joan, Jackie, and Secret Service agent Clint Hill at Northampton's Cooley Dickinson Hospital after Ted's near-fatal plane crash in June 1964. "Maybe it's a curse," Joan told Jackie. "Look at the things that have happened. Can we just chalk it up to coincidence?" (UPI/CORBIS-BETTMANN)

The woman behind the man? Joan campaigned for the injured Ted in 1964, the first Kennedy wife to stump for an incapacitated husband. Joan yearned for his appreciation and respect, but in Ted's view, she was just doing her duty—nothing more, and nothing less. (PARAGON PHOTO VAULT)

When Ted and Bobby were both senators at the same time (from Massachusetts and New York, respectively), they and their wives, Joan and Ethel, often went out on the town together. Ethel loved a public life, whereas Joan was intimidated by it. (GLOBE PHOTOS)

Bobby and Ethel pose with their brood after attending Easter Mass at St. Luke's Catholic Church in McLean, Virginia, just two months before Bobby's murder: Michael, David, Robert Jr., Joseph, Kathleen, Matthew, the senator, Christopher, Ethel, and Mary. (PHOTOFEST)

Ethel is escorted by Ted to their pew in St. Patrick's Cathedral for Bobby's funeral services on June 8, 1968. The bombastic Ethel would never be the same after Bobby's death, choosing to live the rest of her life in the shadow of his memory. (PHOTOFEST)

Ethel, her son Joseph, and Jackie at Bobby's funeral services. For a time the sisters-in-law were bound by the joint tragedies. (GLOBE PHOTOS)

After Bobby's death Ethel gave birth to their eleventh child, Rory Elizabeth Katherine Kennedy. Joan and Ted are seen here escorting her home from the hospital. (GLOBE PHOTOS)

"Have you had enough of your Greek tycoon?" Ethel asked Jackie at lunch one day shortly after this photo was taken in 1968. Though Ethel—along with Joan—attempted to convince Jackie not to marry Aristotle Onassis, they were unsuccessful. For the cameras, the two sisters-in-law looked happy and composed, but behind the scenes raged a war over the shipping magnate. (GLOBE PHOTOS)

On July 22, 1969, Joan went with her husband to the funeral of Mary Jo Kopechne, who drowned in a car Ted was driving on Chappaquiddick Island. (Ethel accompanied them to the services, while Jackie chose to stay behind rather than associate herself to the scandal.) Joan would later say that the death of Mary Jo was the beginning of the end of her marriage to Ted, even though they wouldn't officially announce divorce plans for twelve more years. (PHOTOFEST)

By November 1969 Joan and Ethel had become closer, united by Ted's bumbling actions at Chappaquiddick after Mary Jo Kopechne's drowning. Here one can only wonder what the two women were whispering while Ted offers yet another explanation to the media during a press conference. (UPI/CORBIS-BETTMANN)

The Fourth of July in Hyannis Port, 1962

Seventy-one-year-old Rose Kennedy, attired in her favorite shade of pale rose, waited regally in her bedroom for her son, the President, and his wife, Jackie, to make their grand Fourth of July appearance at the Kennedy compound. On her dress were safety-pinned notes containing suggestions she wished to make to her children during the day's festivities; on some days she would be covered almost head to toe in these notated reminders. As the matriarch of the Kennedy clan, she felt that Jack and Jackie should come to her rather than expect her to come to them—but that was only when they visited her at her own home. When visiting the White House, Rose stayed to herself, treating her son and his wife almost as if they were strangers.

"I never wanted to intrude on his time," she once said, "or the time of my husband. I always thought they had a lot of responsibilities, a lot of things on their minds, and I would keep out of the way and leave them uninterrupted." Rose treated her son very formally after he became Chief Executive, referring to him as "Mr. President" in public, always with an eye toward protocol.

(As she aged, Rose continued to see only what she wished to see. When told that Pat had a drinking problem, her response was "Impossible! Pat doesn't drink." When told that Joan also seemed to be imbibing too often, her reaction was, "Impossible! Joan could never keep that figure of hers if she drank." When told that Bobby was having an affair with Marilyn, she told her secretary, Barbara Gibson, "Impossible! Bobby is much too sanctimonious to have an affair.")

At the appointed time, the eyes of every Kennedy family member and guest scoured the skies until they finally caught the breathtaking sight of the three presidential helicopters. They would land, one by one, on a pad that had been built at the front of Joseph and Rose's lawn, off the cul-de-sac, as people all around cheered with excitement and delight.

The first two helicopters carried governmental aides and chiefs of staff, as well as Secret Service agents. Once landed, the officers quickly exited and then lined up in front of the third helicopter, forming an honor guard. Finally, the President, his full head of hair blowing in the wind, made his spectacular entrance from the third aircraft. He stopped for a moment and waved to the tourists, acknowledging the people waving to him from the boats. Whistles began to blow in a wild salute, and every tourist shouted and cheered. It was clear from the loud reaction that people adored him.

On the porch, Jack's family applauded and the staff stood respectfully at attention. Taking in the scene of adulation before him, Jack eagerly bolted down the steps. Then he turned to await Jackie, Caroline, and the children's nanny, Maud Shaw, who was carrying John. After taking a moment to gather his family around him, he and his small brood walked through the honor guard. Then all of the children—cousins, nieces, and nephews—broke loose from their parents and swooped down across the lawn, screaming, jumping, and cheering for the President.

Flashing his trademark grin, Jack walked straight to his seventy-three-year-old father's wheelchair. He put his hand on his shoulder and kissed the old man on the cheek. Jackie, wearing a navy-blue two-piece dress suit with matching hat and gloves, knelt down in front of Joseph and whispered in his ear with a sly conspirator's smile. He laughed with delight at their private moment. Others began to approach Jackie respectfully, waiting for her to recognize them, then saying just a word or two. However, there seemed to be one dissenter: Ethel, who stood alone in a corner. She must have known that she was expected to greet Jackie, but she did not seem eager to do so. Perhaps it still bothered her that Jackie was accorded such reverence from relatives. She had earlier told Bobby she believed that, when they were all together at the private Hyannis Port retreat, Jackie should be treated like everyone else in the family.

After a receiving line of family members was formed, with Ethel included, the First Couple greeted their relatives in a more organized fashion: Ted and Joan, Sargent and Eunice Shriver, Stephen and Jean Smith, Peter and Pat Lawford. Jack and Jackie shook hands with everyone. Then they reached Bobby and Ethel.

Jack and Bobby shook hands firmly, then Jack embraced Ethel. Jackie greeted Ethel with a warm hug. Ethel, caught up in the moment, responded with a tight sisterly hug of her own. Instead of moving along, as she had done with the rest of the family, the First Lady stopped for a moment and whispered something in Ethel's ear, an honor thus far accorded only to Joseph Kennedy. Ethel's eyes widened at Jackie's comment, then she broke into an ear-to-ear grin. Impulsively, she kissed Jackie on the cheek in appreciation, and then gazed at her devotedly. To everyone present, Ethel's glowing expression indicated that even she could not resist Jackie's charm. Clearly, she was bowled over that Jackie had deemed her worthy of even an extra moment of sisterly chatter.

Joan's Many *Faux Pas*

Jackie and Ethel Kennedy both seemed to enjoy the public eye, and even though they often complained about the constant attention, in truth they thrived on it because they felt in control. Jackie and Ethel both had the kind of relationship with the press in which reporters knew which lines of privacy they could not cross.

"The reporters all loved her," recalls newsman James Brady of Ethel. "She chewed gum and called us 'kiddo,' and helped us get hold of Bobby for a quote when he was closeted with more important people. She also invited us out to the house in Virginia to play football and get thrown in the swimming pool and meet the famous jocks and pretty girls who always seemed to be hanging around. She was lively and unspoiled, suntanned and athletic—no great beauty and no intellectual, but she was everything else the Girl Scout oath requires."

Look magazine's Laura Bergquist Knebel once noted that she would edit her material when writing about Jackie and Ethel so that the two women and their powerful husbands would not be offended by anything that was published. Besides being good business for the magazine, it also prevented Knebel from having to endure the wrath of the two wives should she publish something they felt was too much of an invasion. Jackie, the "letter-writer" of the two, would be the first to make her feelings known in a stinging note.

Joan, however, was such a congenial person that reporters like Bergquist Knebel felt a more casual relationship with her. They could "chat" with her—tape recorder running—and every word she said was on the record, even the ones that could prove embarrassing. She was a private person living a public existence.

"I felt sorry for Joan," says Helen Thomas. "I thought she was so gentle, so beautiful and so fragile, and being thrown into the situation she was in was difficult—not only for her to deal with, but for us to watch her do it, firsthand. She was always very gracious to us and very nice. I think she was really a tragedy. You wanted to protect her, which wasn't always possible under the circumstances."

Jackie and Ethel knew how to censor themselves in interviews. It somehow came naturally to them to say only that which they would not later regret reading. However, when Joan had to give interviews to magazine and newspaper reporters because her husband or one of his handlers asked her to do so, she couldn't help but panic. After being burned by a few embarrassing articles, it was as if every word she uttered had to be so carefully selected that she was almost afraid to speak at all.

For instance, in one interview, she said, "You know, Jackie talked me into wearing a wig. She has three of them, and she wears them a lot, especially for traveling. I tried one, but it just felt silly."

Apparently, Joan wasn't aware of the fact that much of the media had been speculating that Jackie wore wigs from time to time, a speculation that Jackie's spokespeople had said had no validity whatsoever. "The First Lady in a wig?" Letitia Baldrige said, outraged. "Why, never!"

When Joan made her comments, a resounding "Ah-ha!" could practically be heard *en masse* from a suspicious media. One of Jackie's handlers telephoned Joan to tell her that the First Lady would appreciate it if she did not give away any of her grooming secrets in the future. "The First Lady is livid," Joan was told. "She guards her privacy with her very life, and you should know that."

At that time—not only because of Joan's occasional *faux pas* but also because it was a politically correct thing to do—many publications would send completed stories to the Kennedy camp for approval prior to publication. This practice—regarded as unethical by some reporters—assured that cooperative magazines would be on the Kennedys' "approved list" for future stories and that writers from the magazines would have "access" when such cooperation was necessary to complete a feature.

Magazines such as *Time* and *Newsweek* would always publish unauthorized features rather than jeopardize their reputations as unbiased, credible sources of news. But many—in particular the women's magazines, such as *Ladies' Home Journal* and *Good Housekeeping*, which appealed to a large cross section of female voters—would happily send their stories to the Kennedy camp before publication, in order to ingratiate themselves with the family. This practice always proved to be problematic for all three Kennedy wives because whatever they said in interviews for these magazines would be picked apart by their husbands and their husbands' attorneys and publicists prior to publication. As a result, they would often be berated for not having had better judgment in expressing themselves.

An excellent example of the extremes to which the Kennedys went to make certain that the wholesome, spit-and-polish image they wished to feed their constituency remained intact is the way a simple "puff-piece" story about Ted in the women's magazine *Redbook* was handled. Ted had encouraged Joan to consent to an interview for the story, and prior to its publication, the feature was gone over repeatedly by Bobby and Ted, as well as attorneys and publicists and other Kennedy handlers, each word scrutinized for its impact and meaning.

The twenty-eight-page manuscript for *Redbook*, titled "What Makes Teddy Run" and written by William Peters, was submitted to the Kennedy camp by Peters for its approval on December 1, 1961. The feature was sent to Ted's office. Ted then sent a copy of it to Bobby for his approval as well, along with a memo (not dated, but found in the Kennedy Library).

Ted noted in his memo to Bobby that the first half of the article was favorable, but that his greatest concerns included a comment from Joan about her youth in Bronxville in which she was quoted as having said: "The entire community is so highly restricted that I actually never met a Jew as I was growing up." He was also concerned about Joan's description of the amenities found at the Kennedys' Cape Cod compound: "Besides all of the sports equipment—boats, water skis, tennis courts, riding horses, nearby golf courses, and everything else—they have their own projection room for movies. If you want a steam bath, they have that, too!"

Ted also noted Joan's comment that even when the adults are playing "hide-and-seek and kick-the-can with the children, they play as though they were adult games of wits. They play hard, and to win." There were other problems as well, having to do with the writer's references to, as Ted put it, "my emotional detachment and insensitivity" when it came to segregation issues at the University of Virginia, where he attended school.

In response to this memo, Bobby wrote a six-page memorandum to Ted, dated December 14, 1961. In it, he suggested that Ted speak directly to the author, William Peters, about his concerns, rather than go above his head to the magazine's editor.

"You will want to have them eliminate the quote on what Joan said about never meeting a Jew," Bobby wrote. And regarding Joan's enthusiasm for the luxuries found at Cape Cod, Bobby suggested that Ted ask Peters to "leave out the projection room and the steam bath. I would just say to him that you don't think it adds anything and it might appear that it shows our bragging about being more fortunate than others." Bobby also suggested, "Peters should straighten out the fact that you *did* know there had been Negroes at the law school." Bobby pointed out other passages in Peters's article that he wanted to change.

All of the changes that the Kennedys hoped would be made to the *Redbook* story were made before the magazine went on sale.*

Joan would continue to cause problems with her candor. A size eight, she was always a clothes horse, enjoyed fashion, and often wore gowns that had been designed by Oscar de la Renta and Galanos, as well as Zuckerman suits and dresses by Mollie Parnis and Adele Simpson. In 1962, she would tell an interviewer that she appreciated Oleg Cassini's clothes "because he gives me fifty percent off, which I think is terribly nice." Cassini wasn't happy that Joan had announced that she got a discount to wear, and advertise, his creations, and he sent the magazine's editor a letter saying that Joan was "mistaken." ("Why, I don't recall that at all," Oleg Cassini says today. "I know that I didn't design anything for her specifically. But if she ever wore my clothing, I'm sure I was honored.")

"Ted is the favorite uncle," Joan also said to the same reporter when talking about the Kennedy offspring. "He's so big, he can roughhouse with all the children. The President is the same way. But now his back is a problem. He can barely pick up his own son."

The White House was extremely sensitive to reports about Jack's

---

*See the source notes at the back of this volume for detailed correspondence between the Kennedy brothers relating to the *Redbook* story.

bad back, which had become an issue in the 1960 election. Ever since the 1954 spinal surgery, the Kennedy handlers were careful to never mention his back as a problem. Dr. Janet Travell regularly administered Novocain injections just to get Jack through the day because he was so crippled by his back, and the White House did all it could to keep the truth of his condition under wraps. Then, in one interview, Joan blew years of public relations strategy.

"What is wrong with you?" Ted asked Joan after reading the story. "Are you crazy? Look at the mess you've caused."

Joan burst into tears and apologized.

The matter became such a Kennedy camp scandal that Bobby told Ted, "We're going to have to just make sure Joan doesn't say a word about anything to anybody. What else can we do? Tell her to issue a denial. And tell her not to say a single thing about anyone's health ever again."

So, doing her Kennedy duty, Joan issued the required denial, saying, "My remarks were taken completely out of context." The media jumped all over Joan, making her out to be either a liar or an idiot. "Personally, I think she's doing the best she can," Ethel said to a secretary of hers, trying to be charitable. "I mean, we're talking about Joan here, aren't we?"

When Jackie heard about what had been happening, she telephoned Joan to put her mind at ease. According to what Joan later told family friend Joan Braden, Jackie said not to worry about what had occurred. "Look, you're only human," she told Joan. "My goodness, they are overreacting, those guys." Jackie said that it was obviously true that Jack had a back problem, and the fact that he could still run the country despite it should be considered "admirable, not controversial. So don't give it a second thought, Joan," she concluded.

Joan later said that she was so grateful to Jackie for trying to put her mind at ease, "I couldn't stop crying for three days about the whole thing."

Of the three wives, Joan was still the best liked by reporters, despite—or maybe even because of—her blunders with the press. Her brand of thoughtfulness was rare on Capitol Hill. For instance, a fashion reporter from a Washington daily once telephoned her to ask what she intended to wear at a charity fashion show. The writer explained that she wanted to put her "piece to bed" on the day of the show rather than wait until after the show had occurred to write about it. The fashion reporter was unethical, perhaps, but Joan empathized with the woman when she said she wanted to spend some extra time with her children.

"I'll be wearing a lovely white chiffon gown," Joan said, before giving details of the designer and exact description.

However, that night at dinner before the show, Joan spilled red wine on herself. Some of the other senators' wives who were not modeling offered to switch dresses with her, but Joan wouldn't hear of it.

"I promised a writer I'd be wearing this dress, and she already wrote her story," Joan explained as she frantically attempted to remove the stain with seltzer water. "I can't embarrass her. So I'm going to wear this darn dress if it's the last thing I do."

Joan did wear the gown, wine stain and all.

Pat Finds Jackie "So Insecure"

By mid-July 1962, the President had ended his relationship with Marilyn Monroe. In fact, Jack had so quickly distanced himself from Marilyn that, according to close associates, he referred to the actress, his relationship with her, and Jackie's concern about it as "The Monroe Matter." However, Marilyn was still not entirely out of the picture. Jackie was now apparently aware that Bobby also had some involvement with the actress, though she was unsure to what extent. In Jackie's view, Marilyn Monroe was probably like a bad headache that wouldn't go away.

It was Lee Radziwill's idea that Jackie meet her in Italy for a vacation to take some time away from "The Monroe Matter."

Nunziata Lisi, the Italian friend of Lee Radziwill's who lived in the small, picturesque Italian resort village of Ravello, on the southern coast of Italy, now says, "Lee told me that she wanted to take Jackie's mind off a big problem having to do with the President and a famous movie star, whom she did not name.

"She said that Jackie was completely worn out by the whole business and, for some reason, thought that it was all going to come out, be made public, because there was so much carelessness involved in it," says Lisi. "She didn't want to be around for the fallout. She was exhausted. Lee suggested that she spend a couple of weeks in Ravello—where Jackie's stepbrother Gore Vidal would later live—so I made all of the arrangements for her to arrive on August 6. Lee was in France and would be meeting Jackie in Italy. Most of all, I was looking forward to meeting the much-beloved Jackie Kennedy, and was hopeful that she would forget all of her troubles while in the lovely town of Ravello."

Before leaving for Ravello, Jackie had decided to rent her summer home at Hyannis Port to her sisters-in-law, Eunice and Pat. Though she didn't say so at the time, it seemed clear to people that she planned to be gone all summer.

Preparing the house for Eunice and Pat was no easy task. The home was furnished simply but in good taste, with a lot of white-painted rattan furniture and large, stuffed, floral-printed sofas and chairs. Jackie asked her secretary to make certain that recently purchased cushions for the furniture on the porch—where Jackie did many of her watercolors—were stored out of sight in the basement. They were replaced by a much older set, there and also outside on the patio. Not trusting that her nieces and nephews would be as considerate of the furniture as her own children, Jackie ordered old, worn, green chintz slipcovers put on the indoor furniture over the flower-patterned cushions. All of her expensive glass and china was to be stored, and only the cheap pieces left on view. All towels and other linens, including sheets and pillowcases, were to be packed away in the basement. John Jr.'s and Caroline's toys were to be stashed away as well, lest any of their rowdy cousins break one of them. "But you can leave the croquet set," Jackie said. "I don't see how they can break a croquet set."

After the house was ready for them, Jackie met with Pat there to talk about the terms of the rental, according to Beverly Brennan. "As I recall it, the plan was that the two sisters-in-law would rent the place for the months of July, August, and September, at $1,800 per month," said Brennan. "But the problem was that Jackie wanted all of the money up front—$5,400. Pat had a check prepared for only $900 for the first month. Jackie was adamant. Grudgingly, Pat tore up the original check and wrote another for $2,700, telling Jackie she would have to get the rest from Eunice."

At that meeting, according to what Pat Lawford later told Beverly Brennan, Jackie took this opportunity to discuss the Marilyn Monroe problem, and she asked Pat to talk to Marilyn. Jackie may have been just as concerned about Bobby's relationship with Marilyn at this time as she had been about Jack's. It's not known what Jackie asked Pat to say to Marilyn.

Pat, always determined to maintain her privacy, did not discuss many details of her talk with Jackie about Marilyn, but she did later tell Brennan that she thought Jackie was being "ridiculous." She told her, "Jackie is the First Lady. What does Marilyn have that she doesn't have? Why is Jackie so insecure? I don't get it."

"Jackie probably left the meeting feeling that Pat was completely useless to her," said Brennan. "She accepted Pat's money and took off with her Secret Service agent to her home on Squaw Island. Later, I was at a party with Pat and Peter, and Pat said, 'You know, Jackie is still upset about this Marilyn thing. What do you think about that?' And Peter said, 'With all she has to worry about, she's still worried about Marilyn? I think that's absolutely priceless,' to which Pat said, 'I agree. Isn't it?' Then they shared a laugh. It seemed to me that they both rather enjoyed the fact that Jackie was annoyed, as if she was somehow getting her comeuppance for some transgression that I didn't know about."

Marilyn Monroe's Death

Marilyn Monroe's actions during the last day and night of her life have been studied and documented by dozens of biographers and historians in seemingly countless books about the tragic movie star. It is known that on her last day of life Marilyn Monroe was greatly distressed. Dr. Ralph Greenson, who saw her late that afternoon, observed that she seemed "somewhat drugged and depressed" and, as a precaution, asked Marilyn's housekeeper, Eunice Murray, to spend the night with her.

Alone in her bedroom with her pills, Marilyn Monroe took her phone with her, put on a stack of her favorite Frank Sinatra records, and closed the door. She made a series of phone calls to reach out to friends such as Peter Lawford and Sydney Guilaroff, her hairdresser.

She often called people to tell them that she was thinking about committing suicide. In fact, she had tried to kill herself on numerous occasions in the past, and had been saved just in time by the people she had warned of her intentions.

Whether she had actually intended it to happen or whether it was purely an accident, on this evening Marilyn Monroe slipped under the complete control of the many pills she had taken. Some time later in the evening, in the stillness of her locked bedroom, alone, naked, her hand still clutching the phone, she closed her eyes for the final time.

On August 6, Bobby and Ethel were with their San Francisco host John Bates when they heard the news on the radio: Marilyn Monroe was dead. Bates recalls, "To tell you the truth, we didn't treat it that seriously. Bobby said something like, 'Wow. Imagine that. Marilyn's dead.' It was taken lightly by both him and Ethel."

Ed Guthman, Bobby Kennedy's press representative, was also in San Francisco, where Bobby was set to address the American Bar Association. He says that Bobby had a slightly more emotional reaction. "We talked about the terrible tragedy," Guthman said. "He said, 'How terrible. How truly terrible.' That was about it."

"I believe it was Monday morning when I heard from Ethel," says her assistant, Leah Mason. "Bobby was going to give his speech to the lawyers that day, and I believe she said they were headed to Seattle after that for the World's Fair. Then they were going fishing on the Washington coast before camping on the Olympic Peninsula with Justice [William O.] Douglas. She called me at Hickory Hill specifically to tell me that if anyone called to ask about Marilyn's death, they should be told to contact Mr. Kennedy's office. That I shouldn't have any comment. Nobody called, though. I didn't get one call. . . . Mrs. Kennedy sounded upset," says Mason. "She said, 'That poor woman, she actually killed herself. Can you believe it? I'm sure she must have overdosed. How terrible.'"

Ethel knew virtually nothing about Monroe; it appears that she considered reaching out to any survivors Monroe might have had. "I wonder if she has a mother living, or any children," she said to Mason. "I don't know a thing about her. You find out."

Later that day Mason did some research and found out that Marilyn had died childless, that her father was unknown, and that her mother was in a mental hospital somewhere. The next day Ethel called Mason. "I then told her what I learned about Marilyn's family," Mason remembers. "Ethel was quiet for a moment. Then she said, 'How awful,' and hung up the phone without even saying good-bye."

Jackie Kennedy flew to New York from Virginia with four tennis racquets, a golf bag, and eleven suitcases in preparation for her trip to Ravello for the vacation suggested by her sister, Lee Radziwill. The trip had been specifically designed to help Jackie forget her Marilyn-related problems. Ironically, on that same day, while in New York, Jackie heard about the movie star's death from news reports—and almost canceled the vacation.

Nunziata Lisi, who had helped organize and plan the trip and was anxious to meet the First Lady, recalls, "I received a telephone call from Lee telling me that she had just heard from Jackie, and that Jackie wanted to cancel the trip because Marilyn Monroe had died. I was shocked. This was the first I had heard of her death. She said that Jackie was 'bloody distressed' about it."

"Then that's even more reason for her to come," Lisi remembers having told Radziwill.

"That's what I think," Lee told her. "But Jacks [Lee's nickname for her sister] is very distraught, and she wants to go back to Virginia now. She said she's in no mood for a vacation."

"But I don't understand why she cares so much about a death of this movie star," Lisi said. "I know it's terrible, but—*really*!"

Lisi recalls that there was a pause on the line, after which Lee said, "What can I tell you? She had great empathy for this person. I don't know why . . . I don't even know that she's met her."

Two hours after her first conversation with Nunziata, Lee called back.

"Guess what!" she said, brightly. "Jackie's coming after all. I talked her into it. Thank goodness. I think the trip will do her a world of good." Jackie would be accompanied by her daughter, Caroline, Maud Shaw, and three Secret Service agents. Her son, John, would stay behind, sick with the flu.

It would seem that she never openly discussed it, so it's not known exactly why Jackie Kennedy was so upset about Marilyn's death, only that she most certainly felt great anxiety over it. In the end, Jackie's specific feelings about Marilyn Monroe remain as much a mystery as the movie star's death. However, unlike what has been assumed for decades, Jackie most certainly was impacted by Monroe's death, as was made clear to observers before and during her trip to Ravello, which was described by a White House press release as "a private vacation."

As distressed as she was about Marilyn's death privately, in public Jackie remained remote and detached from it. She released a simple statement to the media: "She will go on eternally," the release said. With that impersonal statement, Jackie Kennedy closed the subject of Marilyn Monroe, refusing to ever discuss her again publicly.

Jackie Goes Away to Think

The picturesque clifftop village of Ravello, Italy, some twenty-five miles south of Naples on the Gulf of Salerno, must have seemed to Jackie a million miles away from her marital woes. El Episcopio, the twelve-room villa that Lee Radziwill had rented for her sister, was perched like a swallow's nest on top of a steep, eleven-hundred-foot cliff. The sixteenth-century villa, with its own private beach across the bay, had been inhabited by the last King of Italy, Vittorio Emmanuel III, and his wife, Elena. It was the perfect place for the kind of isolation Jackie seemed to require after the death of Marilyn Monroe. This was actually Jackie's second time in Ravello; she had visited a decade earlier when she was a student in France, but only for a night.

From her room, Lee's view was a spectacular panorama of ice-blue sky and deep aqua water. As she opened her window, a cool sea breeze filled the room. "After breakfast, I'll introduce you to my sister," she promised her friend Nunziata Lisi. "She's so troubled these days. Her husband is making her crazy, you know?"

As they gossiped about Jackie's troubles, the two women stared out the window at the thrilling scenic view. Lowering their gaze, they noticed a lone figure perched on one of the jutting rocks below.

"Why, that can't be her, can it?" Nunziata said.

Nunziata recalls that Lee went to a dresser, opened a drawer, and pulled from it a large pair of binoculars. She then went back to the window and began peering through the glasses at the scene below.

"Oh, my God," she exclaimed. "That *is* her." She handed the binoculars to Nunziata.

"Why, she looks like the loneliest woman in the world, doesn't she?" Nunziata said.

Lee sighed deeply. "That is so like her to be sitting down there by herself," she said sadly. "My poor, poor sister. She has it all, but she has nothing."

"But that's just not safe," Nunziata said, ignoring Lee's comment about Jackie and still looking through the glasses. It had been a long, steep walk for Jackie to get to the coast, three hundred uneven steps ending at a small rocky landing. Alone with her thoughts, Jackie was so still that she seemed at one with the scenery, as if she were a statue. "She shouldn't be sitting down there," Nunziata said, alarmed. "Why, one good wave, and America will have lost its First Lady."

"Oh, let's just leave her," Lee said after a moment's hesitation. "She's thinking. That's why I brought her here, anyway. To think."

"But . . ."

"Don't worry," Lee said. "I guarantee that there's a Secret Service man somewhere."

Lee took the glasses from her friend and scanned the area. "See, right over there, behind that rock, there's one," she said, pointing.

Then, after a beat: "And there! Look—another. And over there—look, still another."

Because of the way Jackie had reacted to Marilyn's death, Lee wanted her sister's vacation to be special. The spot had been recommended to her by millionaire Gianni Agnelli who, with his brother Umberto, manufactured the Italian Fiat automobile. (Gianni had met Jack and Jackie earlier, in 1955, on board Aristotle Onassis's yacht.) Lee had decided that the usual chef employed by the villa was not suitable and instead hired a sophisticated French chef she knew in London. She also organized a ten-car procession with police motorcade to pick up Jackie at the airport.

Mayor Lorenzo Mansi and practically the entire population of Ravello (2,500 people) were on hand to greet Jackie at the bottom of the hill leading to the resort. A troupe of sixteen children, wearing traditional Italian costumes, performed a tarantella dance, much to Jackie's delight. Meanwhile, all of the quaint shops in Ravello had been decorated by the owners in carnival colors to celebrate Jackie's visit.

Paolo Caruso, head of the tourist bureau at that time, recalls, "It was like the arrival of a saint, the way she was treated by the Ravellesi. She looked beautiful in white harem pants and white top, with black belt and matching bag and gloves. She had on a white scarf, tied around her neck, which she took off after a while. She smiled, waved, and was very gracious."

"Privately, I found her to be a very quiet, very sad person when I finally got to meet her," Nunziata Lisi said. "She, the Prince, Lee, I, and a bunch of others went on Gianni's [Agnelli] yacht, *The Agnelli*, on her first evening at the resort. We sailed under the stars to Capri, which was about twenty miles. We ate spaghetti and piccata and drank the local wine. It was an evening of almost intolerable sweetness and melancholy.

"Irene Galitizine-Medici, who was one of the country's top designers, was also aboard with her husband. I remember that Jackie didn't like her at all. At one point, Irene said to her, 'My dear, I would love to design some little frock for you to wear to one of those fabulous White House balls.' Jackie stared at her rather coolly and said, 'Dear, I don't wear little frocks, and I already have a designer, thank you.'

"She was in a bad mood the entire trip, very preoccupied," recalls Nunziata Lisi. "As if things couldn't get worse, she had just gotten a wire from her secretary that her cat (Tom Kitten) had died. The poor dear was upset about that as well. So we were on the yacht, drifting on the Mediterranean, and some person said, 'Have you heard this awful news about Marilyn Monroe?' and I noticed Jackie immediately become very rigid. Lee interrupted quickly and said, 'Oh, please. Nothing unpleasant while on the way to Capri.'

" 'But the poor dear committed suicide, haven't you heard?' the person said, continuing on about Marilyn. 'They found her dead, lying nude in her bed.' At that, Jackie suddenly turned and snapped, 'Isn't it tragic enough without all of us sitting here under a full moon and gossiping about it?' When she said that, everyone stopped and stared at her, stunned."

Jackie got up from her chair and walked to the other side of the yacht. There, with a faint smile, she watched as a couple of mandolin players and an Italian singer performed "O Sole Mio."

The next day, the same party and some other friends of Lee's and Jackie's went to a nightclub in Ravello called Number Two. Wearing green Capri pants and a matching blouse, Jackie had to be coaxed by Lee to dance the cha-cha with Count Silvio Medici del Vascello. "She did not want to dance," said one reporter who sneaked into the nightclub. "She was in a dour mood. Something was bothering her. Lee Radziwill was going around to everyone and apologizing for her sister, saying she was under the weather."

The next morning, Sunday, Jackie attended Mass at the local Catholic church. When she got there, she discovered that the pastor, Father Francesco Camera, expected her to sit on an ornate, sixteenth-century *prie-dieu* with red velvet pillows. Because this seat was usually reserved for the visiting Bishop of Amalfi, Jackie felt uncomfortable about using it and instead sat in one of the wooden pews, next to Mayor Mansi. Later, the Mayor would recall overhearing Jackie say to Caroline in Italian, which she spoke well, "*Caroline, preghiamo per papa.*" ("Caroline, let us pray for father.")

PART FOUR

The Kennedy Women Do Men's Work

In the Kennedy world, politics was a man's game—or at least that's what the men liked to think. It did not appear that they had much tolerance for their wives' opinions. "[Jack] Kennedy could not be swayed by any woman," said Myer Feldman, who was Deputy Special Counsel to JFK. "He might be called a chauvinist today. He did not think most women were his equal."

In fact, though, the wives were not just silent partners. They did have opinions, and they did make them known—whether their husbands were interested or not. Going all the way back to Rose and her relationship with Joe in the 1930s and '40s, Kennedy wives often influenced the course of events.

Rose, who had a fine ear for politics and a keen sense of the right thing to do, was in her glory when Joe was Franklin Delano Roosevelt's Ambassador to the Court of St. James. His position was a huge honor, especially for an Irish Catholic, and the Kennedys were generally approved of in England. They were a breath of fresh air, and the children—especially the older girls, who were popular with London society—made a favorable impression.

Sometimes Joe's democratic ways of doing things were well received, but just as often they were not. Joe had become known for his unusual habits, acting in a less than distinguished—and less than British—manner by greeting people with his feet on his desk, chewing gum, swearing and losing his temper. While Rose was charmingly behaved, Joseph was often crass and undignified. He believed that the British were weak and could not be depended upon in a military conflict, and he made many enemies as a result of his outspokenness.

Even worse was Joe's growing isolationism on the eve of World War II. Rose tried to get him to tone it down because FDR was about to be reelected and he needed the country behind him if he was going to send help to Great Britain. However, Joe was loud in his opposition to the

President he supposedly served. When he went to Washington, he chewed out Roosevelt as though the President were an underling. Furious with him for his insolence, and confused by Joseph's seeming support of some of Hitler's actions ("I can't for the life of me understand why anyone would want to go to war to save the Czechs," he said when Hitler threatened to invade Czechoslovakia), Roosevelt saw to it that Kennedy resigned and he made sure his political career was at an end.

Rose was extremely upset. Yet if she had tried to talk to Joseph about any of it, he wouldn't have listened. He and his sons had always been a stubborn bunch and, like a lot of men of their time, they had to be pushed into thinking of women as more than just the mothers of their children. It was especially ironic, then, that private poll soundings by the Kennedys always indicated that more women than men favored the family and its politics.

In 1946, when Jack ran for the House of Representatives in his first campaign, Rose and Eunice hosted a successful reception for 1,500—mostly women—at the Hotel Commander in Cambridge. It had been anticipated that Kennedy's primary opponent, Mike Neville, would take Cambridge by a landslide, but in the end he barely won. Neville would later cite the Kennedy women's luncheon as "the clincher" that made it such a close race. In the end, Jack would defeat a field of ten in the primaries and go on to an overwhelming victory in November over his Republican opponent, Lester Brown.

Five years later, in 1951, one of the factors that contributed to John Kennedy's surviving the Republican landslide that swept Dwight D. Eisenhower into the Presidency was Rose's involvement in the campaign. The family patriarch was completely perplexed when political strategists suggested that the Kennedy women—Rose in particular—be recruited to campaign. When John Powers, leader of Boston's Democratic drive, wanted Rose to speak at a series of rallies for her son, Joseph roared, "But why? She's a grandmother, for heaven's sake."

"She's also a Gold Star mother," John Powers said, "the mother of a congressman and a war hero, the beautiful wife of Joseph P. Kennedy and the daughter of John F. Fitzgerald—which means she's hot stuff in Boston. I need her and I've got to have her."

Rose loved campaigning and, as the daughter of a legendary mayor of Boston, knew exactly what she was doing when she was on the trail. She became a valuable asset to Jack's senatorial campaign of '51. On a typically busy day, she would change her clothes in the back seat of a car—wearing a glamorous gown and expensive jewels to give one speech to a formal gathering, then a simple skirt and blouse at another function at a union hall. Dave Powers recalls, "She wowed them everywhere."

Rose, Eunice, Jean, Pat, and Ethel—who was the only Kennedy wife at the time—appeared all over the state during the senatorial campaign, at women's clubs, street-corner rallies, and on front door steps after ringing doorbells. It was once calculated that more than 75,000 women attended coffee and tea parties hosted by the Kennedy women during that campaign. In the end, Kennedy ended up beating his opponent, the incumbent Senator Henry Cabot Lodge, Jr., by 70,737 votes.

Jackie's participation in the family's politics can be traced back to the Democratic Convention of 1956, in Chicago. As expected, most of the Kennedy women found a way to participate, except for Pat, who was eight months pregnant, and Rose, who was on vacation with Joseph in France. Jackie, expecting her own child in about a month, probably shouldn't have gone either, since she'd already suffered one miscarriage. However, as the dutiful wife, she didn't want to miss so important a moment in Jack's life. Besides, Ethel was nearly eight months along herself, and she wasn't letting that stop her from participating.

So, even though her doctors strongly suggested that she stay behind lest she jeopardize her health or the baby's, Jackie was adamant that she be in Chicago to campaign with her husband. Adlai Stevenson was the likely Democratic candidate for president but the vice presidential spot was an open field, and the notion of a Stevenson-Kennedy ticket seemed a distinct possibility.

For his part, Jack also wanted his wife in Chicago, but not because he needed her emotional support so much as because he needed her for purposes of public relations. The divorced Stevenson would need a married running mate, and Jackie was the perfect, poster-board wife—not only married, but pregnant. She was also attractive, and since the convention was to be televised, Jack figured that once America got an eyeful of Jackie, he'd have a strong asset in her.

In the end, though Jack Kennedy came close, he fell just sixty-eight votes short of victory, losing to Tennessee Senator Estes Kefauver. Jackie, feeling overwrought and emotional from the entire week, was unable to hold back her tears. "So close," she said, absentmindedly fingering her pearl necklace, "so, so close."

Though he appeared gracious and humble publicly, Jack was bitterly disappointed by his loss and would express a strong private dislike for Stevenson the rest of his life. The problem was that, instead of just selecting his own running mate as had been expected, Stevenson had left the nomination to the floor in a mad race among the leading candidates: Kennedy, Estes Kefauver, Hubert Humphrey, and Albert Gore, Jr.

Jackie stood at her husband's side as he confidently addressed the surging crowd. Even in defeat, he looked like a winner, so handsome, charismatic, and powerful.

Unfortunately, the baby girl Jackie was carrying would be stillborn shortly after the convention. Doctors told her that the stress of the political function may have affected the pregnancy.

Jackie Kennedy wasn't a political person by nature; prior to meeting Jack she had never even voted. But once she became Jack's wife, she wanted to know more and to become more involved. She loved to travel and she took many trips abroad while in the White House, as both sightseer and presidential emissary: five weeks in India and Pakistan, a month in Italy, time in Greece and Paris. Everywhere she went, she was greeted with great enthusiasm.

"I wasn't very interested in politics before I married Jack," she once noted, "but I'm learning by osmosis. People say I don't know anything about politics, but you learn an enormous amount just being around politicians."

"She was intensely interested in all of the political successes of her husband's career," recalls Letitia Baldrige. And here lies the great failure in projecting her real image to the American public, which thought of her as a wonderful wife and mother, which she was, and a beautiful, poised woman of artistic talent, which she also was. But people also saw her as someone who hated politics and hated politicians. In actual fact, although she didn't like events like political conventions and meetings, she was a bright, intelligent person and was interested in the issues.

"All of the Kennedy wives were, in fact. They very definitely shared their opinions with their husbands and interrogated them as to what was going on. They were abreast and helpful," adds Baldrige.

While what Letitia says is no doubt true, it wasn't always obvious.

One of Jack's speechwriters, Ted Sorenson, says, "Offhand, I don't recall hearing about her being his political sounding board. In a meeting, or even to me in private, he never said, 'I was discussing this with Jackie and it occurred to her that we should do this,' or, 'in her opinion, so and so is unreliable.' However, their personal relationship was totally private and kept very private. She could have played such a role without anyone knowing about it."

"Jackie was intensely interested in foreign affairs in particular, and would often write letters to heads of states, friendly, social, chatty letters when she felt she needed to," Baldrige continues. "Of course, we didn't have carbon copies of what she had written and didn't know what she was saying to these people. She would write for pages and pages to General de Gaulle and Prime Minister Nehru. She could have been setting policy for all we knew!

"This was all the result of her working with Jack upstairs [in their private quarters] and seeing how she could help, in her way, to further America's political gains and foreign policies. I am sure no other First Lady has ever done that, and no other President has dared let his wife have so much latitude. I hope that history will one day unearth those letters. She was intensely interested in foreign affairs."

Also, said Baldrige, "Jackie had a fantastic desire for historical knowledge, and she was a sponge once she learned it. She caught every nuance. And she wanted to know American history not just for herself, but for her husband. They were almost competitive in the knowledge they consumed, very much like Henry and Clare Luce in trying to one-up the other on historical facts and so forth, and I think on many points—well, he almost acquiesced that she knew more about history than he did."

According to Kennedy intimate Chuck Spalding, Ethel was also "terribly interested in history and politics, really passionately interested in it. With politics, she had an advantage right from the start over Jackie, because she didn't value her privacy as much as Jackie. Jackie was bigger on writing letters, traveling, and doing her work that way, she wasn't that interested in dignitaries coming to the White House. Ethel had a tremendous enthusiasm for governmental people and for everything they were doing, but above all for everything that her husband was doing and how it related to him. That was a tremendous asset to Bobby.

"You never felt, from the minute you opened that front door at

Hickory Hill, that you were impinging on their time, unless you were dull. Ethel hated dull people. I think it was possibly the most interesting house I have ever been in, and run in a funny kind of opulent simplicity. It was so cluttered. It was done only as Bobby and Ethel could do it, with dogs all over the place, children about, and dignitaries everywhere, all in the same proportion. Ethel was also a good speaker, when that was necessary. She was articulate."

Joan, on the other hand, didn't appear to have the self-confidence necessary to be as successful in politics. She lacked conviction, both in her own views and in being able to express the views of her husband. Like Jackie, she wasn't innately political, either. "Politics never entered her mind, or the thoughts of either of her parents," said Eilenne Harper, who knew the Bennetts in Bronxville.

"Her family was like many in the fifties in that, other than reading the newspaper to stay current on events, there was no interest in anything political until it was time to vote. They were Republican, as I recall. Joan once asked me, 'Public affairs? I couldn't care less about that kind of thing. Why would a girl care about any of that?' It must be remembered that this was back when politics was not a dirty word, just a dull one. Few of the kids of that day were involved in what was going on in government, if only for the fact that little was going on that was of interest to most of them." Joan's lowest grades in college were always in political courses.

It was difficult for Joan to muster the kind of spirit Ethel was known for when it came to politics and quasi-political events, and she definitely did not have the same stamina. Once Joan was asked to christen a ship in Massachusetts, but she had to cancel at the last minute, explaining that she was six months pregnant. Ethel, eight months pregnant herself, stepped in for her sister-in-law and made her apologies. As she stood in front of the local officials and audience, her stomach extended so far in front of her she could barely reach the microphone stand, she quipped, "My sister-in-law Joan couldn't make it today. She's pregnant."

Things would change for Joan, though, by the summer of 1962, for that was when she found herself stumping for her husband in his senatorial campaign. It was Ted's campaign strategists' idea to put Joan's contagious personality and beauty to good use by having her do some politicking for him. Though she was nervous about the prospect, she seemed anxious to take her place among the ranks of Kennedy women who had participated in such campaigns. Perhaps to her it was almost a rite of passage.

Joan had had a certain amount of preparation for such a role, the result of a brief career as a model and actress—something she never liked to discuss much. Because of her success on the beauty pageant circuit, she had considered modeling in her early twenties and had discussed the possibility with her family. Everyone seemed supportive of the idea. By the end of 1957, Joan had blossomed into a beauty. At five feet seven and a half inches, she weighed 132 pounds, with a 36-inch bust, 25-inch waist, and 37-inch hips.

As fate would have it, Joan's father, Harry, and a friend and former model, Candy Jones, were working together on an advertising campaign for a soap product. Jones's husband, Harry Conover, happened to be director of a training school for models and a beauty consultant for Colgate, one of Harry Bennett's biggest accounts. Candy Jones mentioned to Bennett that she and her husband were looking for a model. "Have I got a girl for you," he said. "My daughter Joan." Candy agreed to meet Joan.

Of that meeting, she once recalled, "Joan was one of those rare beauties we got infrequently. I found myself comparing her to an Ingrid Bergman when she was Joan's age."

Soon Joan was posing for photographers in different outfits—everything from casual wear to evening gowns—for consideration by advertising agencies. Within a couple of months, she had her first modeling assignment: sixty seconds on the air in a national commercial for Maxwell House coffee, for which she was paid $2,500.

After that, Joan worked steadily, modeling for beauty products and foods as well as making other television commercials. She became "The Revlon Girl" on The $64,000 Question and sang in commercials during The Perry Como Show (though she lost one Como commercial for Chesterfield cigarettes because she wasn't convincing enough to the advertisers as a smoker). She joined the ensemble on Coke Time with Eddie Fisher and was scheduled to drink a Coca-Cola next to the show's star during a live commercial; she was axed from the bit when Fisher realized she was obviously taller than he was.

When Joan signed with the Harry Conover agency for representation, her career's momentum picked up even more. However, it was a career that would last only about a year and a half. While she enjoyed what she was doing, Joan was really an old-fashioned girl, her values a product of her time and place. She wanted to get married to what she called "my dream husband," have children, and live in a nice home.

Now, with her life's picture so completely different, Joan would use the poise and skill she had developed as a model to stump for her husband on the campaign trail. "Funny how life works, isn't it?" she would observe to family friend Joan Braden.

Ted's campaign manager, the attorney Gerard Doherty, had become a close friend of the couple and was concerned that Joan might not be able to take the emotional rigors of a campaign because he knew her personality. After all, the candidate wasn't exactly a shoo-in: At just thirty, he was at the minimum age required for the position he hoped to win and had little governmental experience. To some he appeared to be just the spoiled kid brother of the President, playing off the family name.

Ted's senatorial platform was a cautious approach to such liberal issues as draft reform and assistance for war refugees, as well as foolproof subjects such as the betterment of education. In time, Kennedy would become a strong politician and a respected Cold War liberal, especially after the death of Bobby. As the years passed, he would be highly regarded for important social legislation concerning the old, the poor, the unemployed and otherwise disenfranchised, as well as race relations. He has always seemed genuinely concerned about the challenges facing what Joan would call "everyday Americans." But at the beginning, he had a long way to go to prove himself, as did Joan.

"The other Kennedy women took to politics like ducks to water," Doherty recalled, "and little wonder, considering their natures and heritage. But we had to remember that Joan was a duck who had never been in water like this, and here she was being dropped into a very full lake. She had to prove to everybody that Teddy wasn't just a smart-ass kid."

Off Joan went in campaign worker Don Dowd's blue Impala—followed by aides in a backup car in case of automotive trouble—all over Massachusetts, visiting hospitals to have her picture taken at the bedsides of sick children and then stopping by housing projects to be photographed with senior citizens. She would visit retired nuns in convents no one knew even existed in Massachusetts, and then attend a backyard afternoon party hosted in her honor by a complete stranger (usually a housewife contacted by campaign headquarters), during which Joan would shake hands and be photographed with about a hundred women.

Most important to the campaign were "coffee hours," where a campaign worker would work with an interested housewife to sponsor a one-hour get-together for about fifty women from the neighborhood. Over delicate little cakes, the women would have the opportunity to meet Joan while drinking hot coffee from paper cups emblazoned with the slogan: "Coffee with Ted." They would ask her questions about family and community services and, if polite, could even expect Joan to answer a few nonintrusive questions about Ted and the other Kennedys.

"Is Jackie really as nice as she seems?" was a popular query.

Also on the list: "Is President Kennedy as good-looking in person as he is on TV?"

"We knew these would pull in votes," recalled Dowd, who was one of the chief coordinators of Ted's senatorial campaign. "They were incredibly successful."

One of the lessons Joan quickly learned was not to ask questions of anyone in the seemingly endless receiving lines that always formed during any guest appearance. Because she was so friendly, and even nervous, Joan sometimes became overly endearing as she would inquire into the lives of the women meeting her. This kind of probing from Joan only encouraged questions to her in return, leaving less time for her to meet the others.

After years of practice, both Jackie and Ethel had "receiving-line etiquette" down to a fine art, realizing that the line would move only as fast as they moved it. "Thank you! How lovely of you to come. So happy to see you," they would say to any well-wisher. "'Bye now." Then they would turn and look to the next person with a warm, engaging smile, thereby signaling to the last visitor that their time was up. If a person stayed in Jackie's vision too long, she would fix him with her perfectly glazed smile and say nothing, creating a moment so awkward it would force the slowpoke on his or her way.

One popular Kennedy family anecdote has it that Ethel became so annoyed at one lingering woman in a long receiving line, she finally snapped at her, "Ma'am, if you don't move along right now, I'll have to sic the police on you. And we wouldn't want that to happen, now would we?"

"Every vote is important," Joan was told over and over. "Make it snappy." (It only added to Joan's dismay, however, when she would hear angry housewives whisper among themselves, "She didn't even ask about me! Those Kennedys, they are so self-involved, aren't they?")

By August, Ted had been nominated by the Democratic Party over the opposition of the older and much more experienced Edward Mc-Cormack, nephew of House Speaker John W. McCormack, who had served as the state's Attorney General. Ted would end up challenging the Republican candidate, George Lodge, son of Henry Cabot Lodge Jr., whom JFK had defeated for the same seat ten years earlier.

It was a bitter battle, and Joan would be an ancillary weapon. Like all of the Kennedy women, she would do anything required of her when it came to her husband's campaigning, even the most absurd tasks. For instance, during one tour of Dalton, a small community in western Massachusetts, Ted gifted one blind boy with a puppy. A few weeks later, the puppy became ill with a hernia and had to be taken to an animal hospital in nearby Pittsfield. When it was learned that Joan would be swinging through Pittsfield on her tour, campaign workers felt it would make for good press if she went to the hospital to visit the sick animal. So Joan's tight schedule was rearranged and, with a motorcade leading the way and news cameras documenting the trip, she went to call on the dog.

Visits to hospitals—for humans and for animals—residences, and churches were not difficult for Joan, though she was unnerved by the way women inevitably gawked at her. More difficult was the seemingly endless schedule of newspaper, television, and radio interviews. "I never know what to say," she complained, "and I'm always so sure I'll say the wrong thing. I'm afraid that I'll be tricked."

Worse for Joan than any other activity, though, was when she had to give a speech. Her first as a Kennedy wife took place on the night of August 18 at the American Legion post auditorium in Springfield, after a fifteen-hour day. Because the Legion post was in an Irish community and had been dedicated by Jack in the 1950s when he was a Massachusetts senator, it was thought that Joan would be among friends. When she walked into the auditorium, she gasped. The place was filled with over a thousand women.

After being introduced, to thunderous applause, Joan walked onto the stage and up to the podium. She took her place as the band played "A Pretty Girl Is Like a Melody," the theme song always used whenever Joan made an appearance, and one about which she had ambivalent feelings because it seemed somehow demeaning. Wearing a powder-blue dress and matching shoes, she began slowly, rustling papers and cue cards on her rostrum, nervously trying to remember how to begin her speech. Then she put the paperwork aside.

"This is not what I'm good at," she told the women, many of whom smiled up at her approvingly. Twisting her wedding band nervously, she continued, "I'm a wife and mother. I just happened to marry into the Kennedy family, and to one of the best-looking of the bunch." The audience laughed at her little joke. "I don't do this kind of thing because I enjoy it," she said. "And I don't do it for myself. I do it for Ted. And why? Because he's the right man for the job, that's why."

Joan then spoke about her husband, his ideas about government ("a better, more enriched life for the elderly of Springfield"), and, at the end of her talk, why she believed Ted would be a good senator. "It's because he really cares," she said, "about all people. He may be young and he may be inexperienced, but he wants to do a good job. I so hope you'll vote for my husband, Ted Kennedy."

The place erupted into applause as Joan stood in the spotlight, beaming.

Of course, while Joan was doing her part, Ted was on a similar campaign trail, giving well-thought-out speeches, using his great charm and charisma as compensation for his lack of experience. He seemed sincere; voters liked him. In fact, the final tally on voting day would be 1,162,611 votes for Ted Kennedy and 877,669 for his opponent, Lodge. Just shy of thirty-one, Edward Moore Kennedy would become the youngest senator in Washington and the only brother of a sitting president to serve in the Upper House.

Jackie's Wicked Scheme

While Joan Kennedy campaigned for her husband, her sister-in-law Jackie was still away on her European vacation, of which Ravello had been a highlight. It was as if she couldn't spend enough time away from the White House. In mid-September, she joined Jack for th

America's Cup races. Then she was off to New York for the opening of Philharmonic Hall, accompanied by John Rockefeller III. She finally returned to Washington on October 10, 1962, now more relaxed and with the Marilyn Monroe tragedy in some perspective.

"Lee told me that Jackie had finally had it out with her husband about Marilyn after they both attended the America's Cup races," recalls Nunziata Lisi. "He apparently told her that he had stopped seeing Marilyn before her death, and that he shouldn't be held accountable for it. He said that she was actually in big trouble long before he started dating her. In the end, from what I understood, Jackie decided there was really no point in blaming him for what happened."

Lee told Nunziata that, in speaking of Marilyn's death, she and Jackie had agreed that "we're all responsible for our own lives and for the choices we make." However, Jackie made the observation that "it doesn't help if one is a weak woman with a powerful man in her life influencing her to make all of the wrong choices."

Lee said that she had to agree with that observation.

When she was in Ravello, Jackie befriended an Italian designer whose name she didn't even remember by the time she got back to Washington. Having had a little too much to drink, she invited him to stay at the White House if he was ever in Washington. As soon as she returned, there was a message from the Italian Embassy: The designer was in town and wanted to take Jackie up on her offer.

"Oh, no!" she cried. "Why did I ever invite him? He was so dreary, I can't bear to be in his presence again."

"She came up with a wicked scheme," recalls Jim Ketchum, "and got all of us who were working on the White House restoration to help. The Queen's Room and the Lincoln Room were the principal guest rooms on the family floor. There was also a floor above with guest rooms, which she said we'd have to ignore for our present purposes. We were her partners in crime, she said. At her direction, we got tarps, paint buckets, ladders, even ashtrays with cigarette butts in them, and redecorated the rooms to make them look a complete mess, as if they were in the middle of construction.

"Then Jackie invited the designer to the White House for a visit and took him on a little tour."

"As you can see, this is the Lincoln Room, one of the guest rooms," Jackie told her guest. "Now, Mrs. [Rose] Kennedy sometimes naps here when she visits, even though it's really for a gentleman. But heavens, look at it," she added, feigning extreme disappointment. "Completely unavailable! What a shame. And look at all of those cigarette butts! I really must talk to the wallpaper hangers about that."

Then she took her guest to the Queen's Room. "And this is where you would have stayed, had it all worked out," Jackie said, showing the man a room covered with dropcloths with all of the pictures off the wall and the paint buckets everywhere. "Oh, well," she said cheerily. "Perhaps next time!"

The scheme worked, and the disappointed man went back to Italy without having stayed at the White House. But as Ketchum and his crew were preparing to straighten out the rooms and return them to their former majestic grandeur, Jackie realized she couldn't resist one more hoax. "I want to play a trick on Jack," she said.

She found the President, escorted him to the Lincoln Room, and said, "I just wanted you to see what we're doing here, Jack."

"Jackie, no!" a bewildered JFK exclaimed. "Not again. You already did the Lincoln Room. When is this going to end?"

Jackie broke into a grin, then into convulsive laughter.

"The two of them laughed themselves silly," recalls Jim Ketchum.

The Cuban Missile Crisis

On the unseasonably warm Tuesday morning of October 16, 1962, John Kennedy received alarming news that the Russians had broken a diplomatic promise and begun setting up bases in Cuba for nuclear-armed, long-range missiles that would be able to penetrate deep into America. This crisis actually had its origins at the Bay of Pigs, eighteen months earlier, when Cuban leader Fidel Castro decimated a U.S.-sponsored invasion in what was one of the worst fiascos in America's political history and an early blight on the JFK Presidency. Now, with the Russians' latest action, there were two options: an immediate air strike and invasion of Cuba, or a naval blockade of the island to prevent Russian ships delivering more missiles. Kennedy opted for the blockade. His decision was taken as preliminary to a declaration of war. For the next several days, citizens of the United States could do nothing but worry, pray, and wait.

With Washington, D.C., in direct range of the Cuban missiles, if they were to be launched, there would be little time to escape—it would be only a matter of a few minutes to oblivion. Perhaps Jackie and Ethel would have time enough to be rushed with their families to the special air-raid shelter that existed outside the District of Columbia. Since Ted was not a member of Jack's cabinet, it's difficult to say whether he and Joan would have had immediate care taken for their safety. While Jackie and Ethel met for lunch at the White House that day, top-level advisers whipped in and out of side entrances to avoid being questioned by reporters as to the unfolding of the dramatic events.

The days of the crisis were tense; at night, a greatly concerned Jackie discussed the matter with her husband. "JFK turned to his wife whenever a crisis arose," said one of Jack's military aides, Major-General Chester Clifton. "The Berlin Wall, the Cuban missiles, the Bay of Pigs—he would talk with her about it. She wouldn't advise his staff, she would advise him at night."

"She made a point of not calling me up or anybody else on the substantive side to say, why don't you do this or make sure you don't do that," adds Ted Sorenson. "I don't think she saw herself as somebody who was involved substantively on policy questions beyond the specific areas of the arts or preservation. She was not involved except for dinner table conversation or pillow talk that might involve her. And that, we'll never know."

Recalled Chuck Spalding, "I remember there was a little squib in the *New York Times*. It said that 'at four o'clock in the afternoon, the President had called up Mrs. Kennedy and they went and walked out in the Rose Garden.' He was sharing with her the possible horror of what might happen."

Letitia Baldrige adds, "Jackie would leave cartoons and limericks for Jack in unexpected places to cheer him up [during the crisis]. She would arrange for a special treat—like Joe's Stone Crabs from Miami; old friends would pay morale-boosting calls at her prompting. Her most effective weapon was a surprise visit to his office with the children. Many days she would be waiting by the elevator to help him when he emerged from it, dragging himself on crutches [because of his bad back]."

By day, as their husbands and their aides and advisers huddled over documents and aerial photographs, Jackie and Ethel busied themselves in the White House school with Jackie's two children and three of Ethel's. Ethel Kennedy would remember these times as "the most troubling I can ever remember" as her husband and Jackie's, the Attorney General and the President, strategized to avoid the kind of holocaust most Americans couldn't even begin to fathom. Dorothy Tubridy, a friend of the Kennedy family from Ireland, happened to be visiting the White House at this difficult time. "Obviously, everyone was tremendously upset and worried about the whole thing," she said in an oral history she gave in August 1966. "Naturally, we girls, all of us, didn't say much about anything to anyone. We stayed to ourselves and let the men handle it. I do regret now that I didn't ask more questions. But you felt you were bothering . . . you know, a little person like me."

As Jackie played with Caroline in the kindergarten, Ethel walked over to Maud Shaw and, according to what Shaw once recalled, told her she was afraid that the Kennedy children would never know adulthood.

"Well then, maybe we should all go to Middleburg or Hyannis Port," Maud Shaw suggested.

"As if we're going to be safer *there?*" Ethel snapped at her. She added that if the missiles were launched, "no one on this side of the country will be safe anywhere" and concluded that "seventy-five million people will be annihilated. We must be prepared for the worst."

Poor Maud Shaw looked as if she'd been stricken. Ethel suggested that if Jackie was seen leaving the White House at such a crucial time, "people will be evacuating their homes all over this side of the country! Here," Ethel said, "you'd better read this if you're supposed to be taking care of Jackie's children."

She reached into her purse and pulled out a pamphlet from the Child Study Association of America: "Children and the Threat of Nuclear War."

Maud Shaw began reading aloud: "American children four years old and up are aware of a danger to life and they connect this danger with the language of nuclear war, fallout, Russia, radiation, and H-bombs. Children are likely to ask questions like: Is a bomb going to hi our house? Where will Daddy go if we're bombed? Will he get to us in time? Will I die?"

Shaw stopped reading. "Oh, dear me," she said, flustered. "Dear, dear me."

" 'Oh, dear me' is *right*," Ethel concurred as she walked away, leaving the frightened nanny with her thoughts of doom.

A few moments later, Jackie walked over to Maud Shaw and asked her what she was reading. When Shaw showed Jackie the pamphlet and told her where she got it from, Jackie snapped it from her hands.

"Just what we need around here," Jackie said, narrowing her eyes at Shaw. "Don't you know that panic is catching? And that children are susceptible?"

That night, after Jack's address to the nation, only a few were asked to remain for a private meal: Ethel and Bobby, the Radziwills, Oleg Cassini, Dorothy Tubridy, artist and Kennedy family friend Bill Walton, and Mary Meyer.*

At 6:50 P.M. the Kennedy guests sat in the eighteenth-century, Louis XVI–styled Oval Room on the second floor, decorated by Jackie in the shades of yellow favored by Dolley Madison. As they sipped a 1959 *pouilly-fumé* (it was nearly the end of the world, and the best they could do was a three-year-old wine?), the President prepared to go on national television to address the nation from his study. Wearing a dark-blue suit, blue tie, and crisp white shirt, Kennedy looked tired but determined. The gray at his temples seemed more pronounced than usual, the lines in his face deeper. As he gave his speech, his words sent chills down the spines of millions of Americans: "Each of these missiles in short is capable of striking Washington, D.C., the Panama Canal, Cape Canaveral, Mexico City, or any other city in the southeastern part of the United States, in Cental America, or the Caribbean area."

Calmly, the President added, "Any nuclear missile launched from Cuba against any nation in the Western Hemisphere" would be re-

---

*Raised on the Pennsylvania estate of Grey Towers, Mary Meyer, like Jackie, was a Vassar graduate and New York debutante. Jack had known Mary—whose father was one of the founders of the American Civil Liberties Union—since 1935; they met at a dance when Jack was a senior at Choate. They became reacquainted when Jack was a senator, and she soon became one of his lovers. An attractive, shapely blonde with short, windswept hair, she was a frequent guest at the White House.

garded as an attack from the Soviet Union "requiring a full retaliatory response." He concluded, "The cost of freedom is always high, but Americans have always paid it."

After his fifteen-minute speech, Jack joined his guests for a dinner of sole Hortensia, *canard à l'orange*, wild rice, and *épinards aux croutons*. Typically, Jack was able to compartmentalize his world and enjoy a nice meal, wild rice and all, even though Armageddon seemed a distinct possibility. Oleg Cassini recalls, "The President seemed unshaken. Jackie, in colorful Pucci pants, was, as always, the perfect hostess. She tried to be cheerful and upbeat, but you could see the tension on her face. It was a difficult, difficult evening."

At one point during the meal, McGeorge Bundy, the former Harvard dean turned adviser to the President for National Security Affairs, told Jack that he had heard the Russians might back down. Jack took a puff from his cigar, turned to Oleg Cassini, and said "Well, we still have twenty chances out of a hundred to be at war with them."

"One wonders how Eleanor Roosevelt would handle this situation," Jackie mused. The former First Lady, who was lying deathly ill in a New York hospital, had been on Jackie's mind all day. Jackie couldn't help but admire her, even though she still felt slighted over Eleanor Roosevelt's initial refusal to support Jack's presidential campaign. ("Well, you know, you liked Mrs. Roosevelt better than we did," she once told Bill Walton.)

"How she got through World War II, well, I'll never know," Jackie said, shaking her head incredulously. "She must be such a brave lady. I pray to God to give me the strength to be half as much help to Jack as she had been to her husband." (Eleanor Roosevelt would die on November 7, 1963; Jackie, Lady Bird Johnson, and Bess Truman would attend her funeral.)

Upon hearing Jackie's words, Jack looked up from his meal and gazed lovingly across the table at his wife.

"If this is the end of the world, it's God's will," Ethel said, ignoring Jackie's sentiment. "There's nothing we can do about it. We're in God's hands now."

"Well then," Jackie said, raising a glass of inexpensive Piper Heidsieck (vintage 1955!) in a toast, "God bless us all, everybody."

"Yes, God bless us," Mary Meyer repeated.

Everyone clinked glasses around the table, except for Ethel, who happened to be seated next to Mary, the interloper. As far as Ethel Kennedy was concerned, this woman was probably as much an adversary as Khrushchev.

The Cuban Missile Crisis was over in a matter of days—days during which America's streets and stores were practically deserted, the air thick with apprehension and dread. In the end, it was said by Jack and his advisers that he was able to face down Khrushchev, thereby forcing the removal of the missiles. Other factors were at work as well. Robert McNamara, Kennedy's Secretary of Defense, explains, "Khrushchev had sent us two conflicting cables, and we came up with the brilliant idea of sending a cable as though we'd never received the second one. Khrushchev's second cable contained a proposal we couldn't accept, with the implied threat at the end of the cable, 'Give me an answer or it's war.' It was Bobby who came up with the idea of sending a cable back as if we hadn't gotten the second one. Kennedy's cable put forth our proposal and closed, 'Let us know within twenty-four hours.' That gave Khrushchev an out with his people." Also a deal was made, of which the public was unaware, whereby the United States traded its armed missiles positioned in Turkey for Russia's missiles headed for Cuba. This agreement was struck with an understanding between the United States and Russia that they would not make it public.*

By the end of the week, as the ordeal drew to a close, Jackie decided to spend the weekend at Glen Ora. She played with the children, rode, and hunted, happy and secure in the knowledge that Jack and Bobby had made the right moves and decisions and that Jack had also probably gained the respect and support of even his most vocal dissenters. On the Sunday after the crisis passed, Jack attended morning Mass at St. Stephens Catholic Church in Washington before joining Jackie in Virginia. Ethel and Bobby went back to their chaotic life at Hickory Hill.

Jackie considered the Nuclear Test Ban Treaty to be Jack's greatest achievement. "There was nothing that caused greater concern in 1961 and 1962 than that there was no control over nuclear weapons," she said. "So many countries would have atomic weapons and be testing

---

*Many years later, in an interview with Jack's adult niece Maria Shriver, Fidel Castro said, "With the information I have now—the experience of the Soviets' hesitation—no, I would not have accepted the missiles. I think that according to the steps taken by each side, we were quite close, quite near to nuclear war."

them, and the world would be that much closer to total destruction. The Test Ban Treaty was finally signed. It was more a sense of enormous relief, and our future generations, and our children and theirs, would be safe."

"She was immensely interested in the limited Test Ban Treaty and thought it an immense achievement," recalled Robert McNamara. "I had been very involved in pushing for it, so [the President] gave me one of the pens he used to sign it. Subsequently, because she spoke of it with such pride, I gave her the pen."

After the Cuban Missile Crisis passed, life went on for the Kennedys as it did for the rest of the country. "But there would always be that nagging in the back of our minds that such a thing could happen again, though we didn't know how or when. It was just a sense of unpredictability about life in general," said Joan, who waited out the ordeal at her and Ted's home with their children. "I don't think we ever forgot it, or took life for granted again, it was that close." (True to their distinct personalities, Jackie took a more optimistic view about the future than Joan. In a letter to a friend, she wrote: "Perhaps saving old buildings and having new ones be right isn't the most important thing in the world—if you are waiting for the bomb. But I think we are always going to be waiting for the bomb. And it won't ever come.")

At this time, Jackie's concerns ranged from the nationally urgent, such as nuclear war; to the personally relevant, such as Jack's ongoing affairs; to the ridiculous—such as what to do with a herd of cows.

At the end of the year, the Kennedys' lease at Glen Ora was to expire. Because the owner was unhappy about the way Jackie had modified the home to suit herself—she had even made structural changes!—the lease would not be renewed. So Jackie was faced with the dilemma of what to do with a gift Lyndon Johnson had given her for the children: two cows that, over a period of two years, had become legion in number.

Jackie wrote to the vice president in October 1962, saying that she didn't know what she would now do for a retreat, but "I can see myself plodding down a dusty lane, beating the rumps of a lowing herd in front of me, which is what your cows have now grown into." (Actually, the Kennedys decided to build their own retreat elsewhere in Virginia.) Jackie wrote that she felt bad that she and Jack could no longer

care for the cows, but because there were so many due to the "great fertility of LBJ cattle," they would have to either give them to the Johnsons or sell them. She suggested that with the profit she would
purchase a present in the Johnsons' name for the White House. Jackie
noted that the "sad thing about having cows is the little calves you
love the most always end up at the butcher! One thing I won't do is
eat any of them!" She closed by joking, "Now I know how Nehru feels
about population control!" (Johnson decided to buy back the cows
himself, and he gave the money back to Jackie so that she could purchase a gift in his name. Problem solved. Jackie wrote back that the
gesture "almost made me weep.")

Joan—The Senator's Wife

In January 1963, twenty-seven-year-old Joan Kennedy would start a
new life as the youngest wife of the youngest senator ever elected in
the United States. After Ted won the election and Joan realized that
a move from Boston was imminent, she recruited help from Jackie and
Ethel in finding a place to live. Both women had gone through the
same process when they had to move to Washington with their husbands, so they were eager to help Joan. Jackie was busy with her duties
as First Lady, however, leaving Ethel to do most of the searching.

Ethel jumped at the opportunity to assist Joan, combing newspapers
for rentals, speaking to real estate agents, and contacting friends to ask
for referrals. By the time Joan got to Washington in December to take
a look at potential residences, Ethel had forty places for her consideration. The two sisters-in-law looked at about fifteen of them before
Joan made a decision: a four-bedroom, redbrick home at 31st Street in
Georgetown. Ethel was at first adamant that Joan should see the rest
of the homes. "But this is your house, and you have to live in it," she
said finally, yielding to Joan's wishes. "I just think you won't be here
long. It's too small."

When Joan finally was moved in, though, Ethel loved the modest surroundings. "Pretty good choice, this place," she told her sister-in-law at one luncheon there. Joan beamed.

Joan's days became filled with the activities of a senator's wife, doing such things as shuttling electorates down from Boston on sight-seeing trips to Capitol Hill, attending fund-raisers and luncheons with the other—mostly older—wives, and greeting large tours at the White House, one of the responsibilities of the Kennedy wives. She was also chairman of the Hope Ball and worked for the Joseph P. Kennedy Jr. Foundation.

Joan's had become an exciting, unpredictable life. For instance, shortly after moving to Washington, she vacationed at the Kennedy compound in Palm Beach for a few days. Jack was also there and offered to take Joan—whom he referred to as "The Dish"—back to Washington aboard Air Force One. So off went Joan and the President in the private presidential plane, opulently decorated by Jackie. ("You asked for barbecue steak on that plane, and you were served barbecue steak," said Secret Service agent Marty Venker. "It was barbecued before your eyes—three inches thick.") After landing at Andrews Air Force Base, sister- and brother-in-law hopped into a helicopter, took off, and landed a few minutes later on the well-manicured lawn of the White House. Jack went straight to the Oval Office, already late for a meeting, while Joan decided to do a little snooping on the second floor in areas of Jackie's private living quarters where no one ever dared venture.

Of course, Joan had often been a guest for dinner at the White House and had attended innumerable parties in the entertaining rooms. Jackie often urged Joan to play piano for the entertainment of the other guests. Joan always complied. After a few songs, Ted would jump up and sing "Heart of My Heart" to everyone's delight. Joan's playing was always in tune, while Ted's baritone was always off-pitch.

On this day, Joan was alone in Jackie's bedroom, and while she surely would never have dreamt of looking in the First Lady's dresser drawers or medicine cabinet, she did sneak a look at her enormous clothes closet. "There was no one home," Joan once explained of her private moment in the White House, "so one of the maids asked me in and showed me around. And there I was, like any tourist, rubbernecking in my very own sister-in-law's house."

Joan quickly became a popular fixture in Washington, so much so that when columnist Art Buchwald compiled his Top Ten list of the city's most beautiful women for *The Washingtonian* magazine, Joan was right on top. She wasn't particularly happy about Buchwald's compliment, however. "I'd like to be noted for something a little more substantial," she said.

There were days Ted would spend in Boston, where he would be invited to a political function. Joan would have to drop whatever she was doing, leave instructions for the help, catch a cab to the airport, race for a plane, and be at his side, looking like a fashion plate, in just a matter of hours. Then she would be off to Japan with Ted as guests of the Japanese Council for International Understanding. Standing next to Cary Grant in the receiving line, Joan wold marvel at the fascinating turn her life had taken. Then back to Washington.

Those nights alone in Washington were problematic. It had been Ted's decision that they attend few social gatherings on Capitol Hill because he was hoping to change his image. Ted knew that he was in office largely because of his name, and he was determined to prove himself a capable legislator. He didn't want to be perceived as a young, frivolous person, and he felt that the less of a presence he and Joan had on the party circuit, the better. He said he didn't want the Washington gossips to have "anything to chew on." So Ted spent his nights working in the Senate office building next to the Capitol, while Joan stayed at home, bored and alone.

While Ted did work hard, his effort to refashion his image into that of a serious politician seemed disingenuous to some observers. Their skepticism might have stemmed from the fact that once he became a senator, his philandering became almost as high-profile as any legislation he hoped to pass.

Most memorable to all concerned was Ted's prostitute in Belgium. When he first became a senator, Ted took a trip to Europe, leaving Joan at home. While in Antwerp, Belgium, he was invited by the American ambassador to a dinner party hosted by a wealthy couple in honor of the King and Queen. Ted showed up at the couple's grand eighteenth-century home obviously inebriated and with a hooker on his arm. Hoping to keep Ted's guest away from the view of royalty, the hostess hurried Ted and his date into a large, opulently appointed sitting room. Unfortunately, the hooker was so drunk that, while sitting on the antique couch and making out with Ted, she accidentally relieved herself, thereby ruining the priceless fabric. Details of this distasteful incident did make their way back to Joan, who was so humiliated by her husband's actions that she even sent the Belgian couple a note of apology.

Despite their problems, Joan and Ted always had a passionate life of their own together. He had been her first lover. "Our good times together were so good," Joan said many years later. "People look at a relationship from the outside and feel they can then be judgmental about it." She pointed out that "the little moments, the times that are shared with each other," were the times that kept the two of them together. "That's why it makes me so mad when people say, 'Oh, how could you stay with him?' " she observed. "What do they know? How dare they?"

It's obvious that Ted and Joan shared a history of not only personal disappointments but also marital highlights, such as the births of their children. She felt that he was one of the few people who knew and understood her. "To think it would be easy for her to end that marriage would be to minimize her feelings for him," said her friend Joan Braden. "No one can understand another woman's marriage, not really. The history of their relationship was so important to Joan. It gave her an anchor. She loved Ted, faults and all, whether it made sense to do so or not. I'm sure a lot of people can relate to having had such blind adoration at one point or another in their lives."

Of course, the fact that Ted was so important to her was the very reason it hurt so much when he wasn't with her, and when she suspected he was with another woman.

"Before I confronted my alcoholism as a disease, I had withdrawn into myself," Joan would say many years later. "Because I looked pretty, people kept telling me I had everything: a fantastic husband, terrific kids, talent at the piano, brains. They didn't see how much I was hurting inside. Being a senator's wife and a Kennedy didn't help me. Many of my women friends later told me they didn't call because I seemed unapproachable. So being painted as perfect and pretending everything was terrific was a terrible burden.

"I'm fine when I'm busy," Joan added, perhaps alluding to Jackie's advice to focus on things other than Ted and her marriage to him. "But when I'm alone . . . well, then it's often not so good. The darkness sets in."

PART FIVE

Delighted to Be Pregnant

"Sacred Heart alumnae, a thousand strong, are taking over the White House for a morning tour. And Mrs. Kennedy is out of town. We need someone to greet them. I promised them a Kennedy wife."

It was May 1963 and White House Social Secretary Letitia Baldrige was on the telephone with the President, explaining a situation she had termed "a terrible, terrible dilemma." Jackie, now pregnant again and due in September, was out of town, and there was no one to greet the Sacred Heart visitors.

"Well, call Ethel," said the President. "She's a Kennedy wife, isn't she?"

"Impossible," said Letitia. "She's eight months pregnant and feeling big as a house. She says she won't leave Hickory Hill."

"Then call Joan," suggested the President. "What about her?"

"She has morning sickness, too. She can't even get out of bed, the poor dear is so weak."

"Joan's pregnant, too?" he asked, his tone incredulous.

"Yes," exclaimed Letitia. "Two months. You knew that, Mr. President. We just made the announcement."

"Well, I'd like to keep track," he said with a chuckle, "but I have a country to run."

All three Kennedy wives were pregnant at the same time: Ethel with her eighth child due in June; Joan with her third due in August; and Jackie also with her third due in September. "We're all delighted to be pregnant again," Ethel had told the press when Jackie finally announced her pregnancy, five months into it. (She had decided to wait until she felt certain all would go well. Nature did its part in helping Jackie conceal her pregnancy—even in her fifth month she did not look as if she were expecting.)

"Well, what'll we do?" Letitia asked the President.

"I'll be right down."

When the President walked into the White House lobby, he was greeted by a thousand former students of Sacred Heart schools all across the country.

"I know you wanted to meet one of the Kennedy wives," he told them, "but they're all expecting babies, as you may know, and unavailable at this time. My sisters may all be expecting as well," he joked. "I don't know. Don't quote me on that."

Everyone laughed.

Letitia Baldrige recalled, "He gave them five minutes of his time, mentioned every cousin, aunt, or niece who had ever attended Sacred Heart, and he said, 'You ladies are the best-looking group of women in the world. It has been my honor and privilege to come and speak to you. I'll tell Jackie, Joan, and Ethel what they missed.'"

The Deaths of Infants Arabella and Patrick

Jackie Kennedy already had two children—Caroline, born on November 29, 1957, and John Fitzgerald Jr., on November 25, 1960—but John's was a particularly difficult birth and it was thought that the baby wouldn't survive because of respiratory difficulties. "Anyone who knew Jackie knew that she loved being a mother," recalls Jim Ketchum, White House Curator during the Kennedy administration. "I saw a mother who spent a great deal of time with her children and who made it very clear that they were a priority, from the way they were watched over by the Secret Service—she always had problems with that—to the way they were taken care of on a daily basis by Maud Shaw when Jackie was busy. More often than not, though, it would be Mrs. Kennedy pushing the carriage on the South Lawn, Mrs. Kennedy taking them on pony rides, Mrs. Kennedy tending to them day and night. Before anything else, she was a mother, and whatever else happened afterward had to take second place with her time and energy. She got everything done, though. Youth had a lot to do with it, I suppose."

Jackie had also been dealt the blow of a miscarriage early in her marriage, as well as a tragic stillborn baby. For the perfectionist that she was, the failure to carry any of her pregnancies successfully to term was devastating. Throughout her life, she had been able to work hard, give her all, and ultimately triumph—she had done everything that was expected and had always managed to exceed expectations. But having a baby was something completely out of her control. It wasn't like mastering a foreign language, or winning a horse-riding competition, or finding the perfect husband.

The stillbirth was the most difficult for Jackie to accept. It happened in 1956, just after the Democratic Convention. Jackie's misfortune at that time was compounded by the fact that Jack had chosen to be on a Mediterranean cruise around Capri and Elba during the final months of her pregnancy. Meanwhile, she had gone to Newport to be with her mother at Hammersmith Farm and wait for the baby there.

On August 23, 1956, a hemorrhaging Jackie was rushed to Newport Hospital. An emergency cesarean was performed and the baby was stillborn. When she awoke, Jackie found Bobby sitting in a chair, staring at her with tears in his eyes.

It had actually been Ethel's idea that Bobby go to Jackie. Though Ethel was in the final stages of another pregnancy herself, her concern was with her sister-in-law. "She's not as strong as she likes us to believe," Ethel observed of Jackie. "I know the *real* Jackie, and she'll be devastated."

The first thing Jackie wanted to know from Bobby was whether the child she had given birth to was a boy or a girl. She still didn't know that the baby was stillborn. Bobby had to break the news to her: The baby was a girl, and she was dead. In fact, he had already arranged for the infant's burial. Through a flood of tears, Jackie managed to say that she had chosen a name for a girl: Arabella.

When Jackie asked if Jack knew what had happened to his daughter, it fell on Bobby to deliver more bad news: Jack could not be reached at sea, "but Eunice is trying her best to locate him." After a couple of days, when Jack was finally located at the port of Genoa, he claimed to be upset about the news but decided not to return immediately. There wasn't much he could do about it, he said, ignoring the obvious fact that his wife would need his emotional support during this terrible ordeal, and causing some observers to wonder just what kind of man he really was.

Some had already been critical of Jack for not being at his wife's side in the last days of her pregnancy. The fact that he didn't return at once when his child was born dead was inexplicable, even to his closest friends.

Two days after Jackie's tragedy, her sister-in-law Pat Lawford gave birth to a daughter, Sydney. Then, two weeks later, Ethel would give birth to her fifth child, Mary Courtney. At just twenty-eight, Ethel would now be the mother of three boys and two girls, the oldest about to turn six years old.

It was difficult enough for Jackie to endure the death of her baby, but to be confronted by happy Kennedy pregnancies and successful births all around her made her feel even more inadequate. Making matters worse, doctors speculated that the rigors of the recent convention—which she had insisted on attending because she wanted to support her husband—had probably been "too much" for her. She actually may have lost the baby *because* of the convention, which made her feel all the more sad about her husband's abandonment and which also forced her to question her own responsibility in the child's death. It was a terrible, dark time filled with deep sadness, self-doubt, and recrimination, and she was alone.

In the end, Jack would be forced to return to the States when the press learned of the stillbirth. George Smathers and Joseph Kennedy convinced him that if he ever wanted to run for President, he had better first run to Jackie, lest he lose the potential vote of every woman in the country.

Seven years later, in 1963, Jackie was pregnant again, as were her sisters-in-law. However, in May 1963, Joan suffered a miscarriage of a child that was due in August, a month before Jackie's. (Joan would have another miscarriage in June 1964, and yet another in August of 1969.) Joan had had some difficulty becoming pregnant, and her miscarriages would affect her deeply, especially since Ted had announced early in their marriage that he wanted at least ten children—and he wasn't joking!

"It was discouraging and depressing for Joan not to see her way through her pregnancies as Ethel had," the Kennedy's family nurse, Luella Hennessey, once said. Hennessey had tended to the births of twenty-six children, including all of Ethel's. She added that Joan's self-confidence and self-esteem were further whittled because "she felt she wasn't as healthy as the others because she had trouble carrying to full term, even though Jackie also had trouble. The problem [with Joan] was in a hormonal deficiency."

Two months later, in July 1963, Ethel Kennedy gave birth to her eighth child, another boy, Christopher George—the second son to be delivered on the Fourth of July. Although he was born a week early, the latest addition to the ever-expanding Kennedy brood was healthy in every way. Ethel, on the other hand, was wiped out from this latest pregnancy, and took months to recover fully.

Although Ethel's first pregnancy had resulted in deep depression and difficult delivery, her next five had been relatively easy. Being pregnant had never stopped her from going on with her life as usual, including the heated, competitive tennis matches with Bobby (which she usually won). She also continued to participate in the wild games of touch football that took place on weekends at Hickory Hill. With her first six pregnancies, Ethel continued to be extremely active right up to the time of delivery.

But during the birth of Kerry, her seventh child, there had been some complications during delivery and Ethel had been forced to undergo her first cesarean section. When it became clear that her eighth pregnancy, in 1963, would be troubled as well, Ethel was so determined to see it through that, uncharacteristically for her, she gave up all heavy physical exertion. She also became less social, spending most of her time at home. On weekends, when the Kennedy clan gathered for their usual touch football game, Ethel refrained from joining in and instead stayed indoors, resting. On the day of Bobby Jr.'s ninth birthday, she appeared only long enough to see him blow out the candles before scurrying back upstairs to bed. She seemed nervous, even upset, during the entire time she was "expecting," and was extremely relieved when the baby was born safely.

As for Jackie, because of her history of troubled pregnancies, doctors were being particularly cautious this time, sharply curtailing her schedule by having her spend as much time as possible at Glen Ora or Squaw Island. But then, on a gray morning on August 7, after returning from the children's horseback riding lessons on Squaw Island (she and Jack were no longer staying at Morton Downey's at this time, but at another estate, called Brambletyde), Jackie went walking along the beach. Suddenly, she stumbled and fell. Normally, she would have gotten up, brushed off the sand, and continued walking. But she couldn't get up this time—there was something wrong, she knew. She was experiencing pains. She dug her nails into the sand and screamed for help. Within seconds, she was surrounded by Secret Service agents, who helped her back to her home, and into bed.

When the pains did not subside, Jackie called her physician, who, fortunately, was vacationing nearby. Dr. John Walsh, professor of obstetrics and gynecology at the Georgetown University Medical School, arrived immediately. With the tragedy of her earlier unsuccessful pregnancies weighing heavily on her mind, Jackie was nearly hysterical with fear and dread. A helicopter was summoned, and she was taken to the military hospital at Otis Air Force Base, where she would give birth by cesarean—which had been anticipated all along, as all of her deliveries had been made in this fashion—to a four-pound ten-ounce baby boy. The child was so frail, however, it was decided that he be immediately baptized. He was given the name Patrick Bouvier Kennedy in honor of Jack's grandfather and Jackie's dad, Black Jack Bouvier. By the time Jack arrived, Patrick had been placed in an incubator. This time no one had to tell him that he should be by her side; their relationship had deepened at least that much in the years since Arabella's death.

Sadly, Patrick Bouvier Kennedy died on August 9 from hyaline membrane disease, a lung ailment common to premature babies. The President was hit hard by his son's death; many—including Jackie—said they had never before seen him cry. "That was the one time I saw him where he was genuinely cut to the bone," recalls Secret Service agent Larry Newman. "When that boy died, it almost killed him, too."

The First Lady was so overcome with grief that she sealed herself off in her makeshift suite at the military hospital while the press swarmed outside her window. Of course, Jackie received many letters of condolence, but probably none more perplexing—and filled with double meaning—than the one from Jack's mistress, Mary Meyer. According to Secret Service visitation logs, Jack had been with Mary Meyer at the White House just two evenings before Patrick was born.

"Dear Jackie," Mary wrote. "Anything I write seems too little—but nothing that I feel seems too much. I am so, so, so very sorry."*

Baby Patrick was the first Kennedy to be buried in the large family plot at Holyhood Cemetery, in Brookline, recently purchased by Joseph Kennedy. As the little white casket was being lowered into the ground, Jack, overwhelmed with grief, put his hand on the coffin as if in a final farewell.

After Patrick's funeral, it was Joan who provided the most comfort to Jack during the time he secluded himself at home.

"She was a rock through this for him," said Joan Braden. "It was surprising to some. Joan was usually the one you needed to rally around in times of crisis. But for this one, she was there for Jack. I think she wanted to do it for Jackie, too. She felt terrible for what the two of them were going through. In so many ways, Joan was—is—probably the most sensitive person in the family. It's easy to say someone would do anything for another person, but with Joan Kennedy, it was always the truth."

Former Kennedy aide Dave Powers who stayed with Jack at Squaw Island recalled, "The first night [after the funeral], she just sat with him for a long, long time and just talked. There was none of the orthodoxy you might expect from Ethel. No talk about how Patrick was in heaven and happy, but rather just warm, human, simple talk."

Jack and Jackie's Squaw Island home was sparsely and simply furnished with comfortable, upholstered chairs and thick, woven rugs. It was large and airy, and spotlessly clean. On the walls were watercolored seascapes that had been painted by Jackie. As Joan and Jack stood before one of the paintings, Powers heard Joan say, "There's no explaining what happened. I'm not like Ethel. I don't know that all things happen for a reason. I just know that things happen."

"That they do," Jack said, his blue eyes tearing up.

"And when they happen," Joan continued, "we just have to go on, somehow, and know that we have the strength to carry on. It's in every one of us, Jack. That strength. It's our birthright."

*Mary Meyer would meet an unfortunate demise on October 12, 1964, when she was murdered while walking along the Chesapeake and Ohio Canal towpath in Georgetown. A twenty-three-year-old laborer was arrested, tried, and acquitted. The case has never been solved.

"Do you have that strength, Joansie?" Jack asked, using Ted's nickname for her. "Can you get through this life God has given us?"

Rather than answer the question, Joan embraced the President.

"I know one thing, Jack. *You* do," she said as she held him. "Of all people, you do."

"The President listened and was deeply moved," said Dave Powers. "She left at eleven that night and the President walked with her out to the driveway. 'You know,' he told me when he returned to the house, 'she's a great girl.' She was there the next night and the next, and the President was grateful. She did a great deal for him."

It would seem, based on the remembrances of others close to the President, that Jack developed a new respect for his sister-in-law and for her unique brand of simple, common, and good sense. She wasn't afraid to address difficult subjects, which was unusual in the emotionally closed-off Kennedy family and was behavior worthy of admiration, and she was even insightful in her clear-eyed assessment of emotional occurrences.

Thirty-four-year-old Jackie Kennedy's mourning after the death of her infant was a private misery, and one the rest of the Kennedys were ill-equipped to handle. It's never easy for a family to address the tragic death of any newborn. For the Kennedys, who rarely communicated their true feelings to one another, it was nearly impossible to come to terms openly with Patrick's death. Jackie's seeming emotional detachment—"I don't really want to discuss it, thank you"—made some feel that she was "doing just fine under the circumstances." She wasn't. This was a darker time for her than most people knew.

For his part, Jack thought he was helping his wife by sparing her the specific details of Patrick's illness prior to the baby's death. "He did so much to protect Mrs. Kennedy at that time," recalls Pam Turnure, Jackie's secretary. "I didn't realize until after Mrs. Kennedy had come home that she hadn't understood how serious the boy was until he died. But he really protected her from all of this. He had a double concern—for her and for the child."

During the grieving process, Jack, at a loss, did the best he could. When Jackie mentioned that she hadn't heard from Adlai Stevenson, of whom she was very fond, Jack called Arthur Schlesinger to ask him to call Stevenson and have him drop her a note of condolence, "because I think it'll make her feel a little better."

Of course, Jack also had his insensitive moments. "Jackie," he told her on one blue day, according to what Janet Auchincloss, Jackie's mother, once said, "we must not create an atmosphere of sadness in the White House because this would not be good for anyone—not for the country, and not for the work we have to do." One might imagine that those words did little to lift Jackie's spirits, though she would never say one way or the other. Jackie's well-meaning mother was also at a loss as to how to deal with the matter. "It'll get better as time goes on," was all that she could offer her daughter.

While pregnant, Jackie had decorated a nursery in the White House for Patrick with a white crib, rug, and curtains. The walls were done in blue, as if she had been expecting a boy. Now she was back at the White House, but without a baby. As days turned into weeks, Jackie fell into a disturbing melancholy, staring off into space, crying unexpectedly, and losing her appetite. No one knew what to say to her to console her, nor did they know how to handle her sudden crying jags and her many questions about her own responsibility in Patrick's death. Perhaps if she hadn't traveled so much in the early months of her pregnancy, if she had taken better care of herself, the baby would have lived. Hospital psychologists who had been recommended by Jackie's doctor were not able to convince her to discuss her loss openly with them, nor could the priest that the family had asked to visit her on a regular basis. Feeling that it was the proper course of action to take, everyone in the family avoided the topic of Patrick's death altogether and tried to act as if it hadn't occurred.

It would be Joan, who had suffered her own miscarriage a month earlier, who would prove to be the most sensible when it came to understanding Jackie's torment about Patrick.

"I think it hurts her so much more when we're silent about it, acting as if it hadn't happened," Joan said of her sister-in-law at a luncheon with Pat, Eunice, and Ethel. According to what Ethel later explained to her friend Joan Braden, the women were sitting in Ethel's kitchen in Hickory Hill eating clam chowder, which she always served from a large tureen her mother had given her, a family heirloom of sorts. Ethel had never had a miscarriage or stillbirth, but her last pregnancy had been troubled.

Ethel looked at Joan with a bewildered expression. "I just can't believe that's true," she said, "that it hurts her for us to be quiet." She added that if she had suffered such a tragedy, she would want to forget it had ever occurred and certainly wouldn't want anyone reminding her of it. "I say we should just ask her how she's doing, but never bring up what happened," Ethel suggested. "Besides," she concluded, "Jackie doesn't *want* to talk about it."

"Then we should force her to," insisted Joan. "It's for her own good. A grieving mother needs to know that she's not the only one missing her child."

"I don't know," Ethel relented. "Maybe you're right. Maybe Jack should talk to her. But every time he starts, he gets nervous and goes and changes his shirt." (Kennedy, always conscious of perspiration, would sometimes change his shirt four times a day.)

Eunice and Pat disagreed. The topic of Patrick's death should definitely be *verboten*, they insisted, regardless of Joan's opinion and Ethel's wavering on it.

"Nobody wanted to bring it up, ever," said Rose Kennedy's secretary, Barbara Gibson. "Back in those days, you really didn't know how to handle such a thing."

Because of her own concerns about motherhood, Joan was the most sensitive to Jackie's emotional distress after the loss of Patrick. "A child is the most precious thing there is," she had said. However, because her sisters-in-law so adamantly opposed speaking with Jackie about her sadness, Joan unfortunately lost confidence in her instincts. In the end, faced with so much opposition, she decided not to talk to Jackie about her great loss.

Lee Radziwill Invites Jackie-in-Mourning

Lee Radziwill, Jackie's sister, was also unsure about how to deal with Jackie during this difficult period. Though the two often confided in one another, Jackie was not forthcoming about her sadness over Patrick's death. Besides her emotional torment, Jackie was also in great physical pain at this time. It had been her fourth cesarean, and she was not recovering as quickly as her physician, Dr. John Walsh, had hoped. She was told to curtail all of her social activities for four months. This left Jackie, who was ordinarily a busy woman, completely frustrated. With little to do since Jack's sister, Eunice, had stepped in and taken over many of her engagements, at the end of two months Jackie was ready to scream.

"When all else fails," Lee had said, "try getting away from it all." Just as she had when Jackie was upset about "The Monroe Matter," Lee decided that the best remedy for Jackie's distress would be a vacation. In the fall of 1963, Lee suggested that Jackie take a cruise with her aboard the yacht of wealthy industrialist Aristotle Onassis.

Jackie first met Onassis at a dinner party in Georgetown in the 1950s, when Jack was a senator. Soon after, during a visit to Rose and Joe's vacation spot in the south of France, Jack and Jackie had visited Onassis on his yacht, the *Christina*, docked at Monte Carlo. While Jack was with Winston Churchill, Onassis took Jackie on a tour of his ostentatious cruise liner, a converted 2,200-ton Canadian frigate that cost him a million dollars a year to operate. After that, whenever Aristotle Onassis and his wife, Tina, sailed to the States, they had always made it a point to dine with the young Kennedys.

Jack and Jackie thought Onassis one of the greatest storytellers they'd ever known. He loved telling Greek myths, fables, and other wild stories—he said that he believed in mermaids, for instance, and swore that a "stuffed mermaid" could be found in a secret location on the Suez Canal. He had held them both captive with tales about his rags-to-riches life, how he had amassed his fortune, and how he loved to spend it. (Much of it was fiction, as Jackie would later learn, but Onassis's appeal was in his ability as a storyteller, not in his accuracy for detail.) His personal attorney of twenty years, Stelio Popademitrio, recalls of his client Onassis, "He was a bit larger—no, actually *substantially* larger—than life, and he knew it. Though you could say he was rather ugly, the moment he opened his mouth to speak, he could seduce anyone."

When Lee told Ari, as he was known, that Jackie had accepted his invitation to cruise, Ari glowed at the prospect of entertaining the

First Lady. (The news, however, did not sit well with the woman with whom he was having a romance, opera star Maria Callas.)

During Jackie's recuperation, there had been growing concern about her sister Lee's budding relationship with Ari, an assignation that would only serve to complicate matters for Jackie. (For the previous four years, Lee had been married to her second husband, the exiled Prince Stanislaw Albert Radziwill, known as "Stas," pronounced "Stash," a Polish nobleman who had made his fortune in British real estate.)

David Metcalfe, an insurance company executive in London, and a friend of Lee's, told her biographer, Diana DuBois, of Lee's affair with Onassis: "It was all supposed to be very discreet, but Ari was out in the open because he reveled in publicity. One couldn't be discreet with Onassis."

When the affair was brought to the President's attention, partly because of a gossip item in the *Washington Post,* and then confirmed by his aides, he was uneasy about his sister-in-law's new romance. While he liked Onassis personally, he was not eager to welcome him into the family. Over the years, the Greek millionaire had earned a personal and professional reputation that was shadowy. He had been embroiled in serious legal disputes with the United States government after being indicted for fraud during the Eisenhower years for not paying taxes on surplus American ships. Jack also had a loyalty to Lee's husband, Stas, who had worked hard on behalf of the Kennedy-Johnson ticket in 1960 and had been very effective for him in Polish communities in the Midwest.

Jackie agreed that the romance was a problem and, unless Lee was serious about Onassis, not worth the political risks to Jack. In her weakened and exhausted condition, however, she didn't have much more to say about it.

Of course, as was wont to happen in the Kennedy clan, other family members had plenty to say about the affair. Ethel, with her eye always on the bigger political picture, had heard about Lee's involvement with Onassis and felt that the "situation," as she called it, was a problem in the making.

"Talk to your brother about it," she told Bobby, trying her best to adhere to protocol. "It's a political liability. If it were personal, I'd speak to Jackie. But since it's political, you should talk to Jack."

Bobby agreed with his wife, and mentioned the matter to Jack, who, in turn, told him to bring it up with Jackie. "She'll know what to do," Jack said.

So, during a private White House luncheon, Bobby pulled Jackie aside and said, "Listen, this business with Lee and Onassis, just tell her to cool it, will you?" Wearily, Jackie said she would "try to look into it" once she was aboard the *Christina*.

"Not Ethel's Best Moment"

History has always painted a picture of Jackie Kennedy eagerly joining her sister on Aristotle Onassis's cruise, anxious for a vacation after the tragedy of her baby's death. Nothing could be further from the truth. Based on the best evidence we now have, Jackie didn't even want to go.

Says Lee Radziwill's Swiss friend, Mari Kumlin, "Lee told me that Jackie was adamant that she wanted to stay with her children. She wasn't happy, which was precisely the point of the trip."

Jackie probably decided to take the trip, however, because it was easier than arguing with Lee about it. It was a pattern in her life, anyway, to get away when she needed time alone to think—whether it was to Glen Ora, Hyannis Port, or to some far-off country.

In the fall, the White House made it official: The First Lady was going away to rest, recuperate, and recover her peace of mind on a cruise on the Onassis yacht, though it was suggested in the press release that she was a guest of Stanislas Radziwill's and that Onassis's yacht had just been secured for the trip. Nevertheless, the decision was bound to stir up controversy, and it did. There were protests in Congress against allowing the First Lady to accept Onassis's hospitality because of his ruthless reputation. Also, Jack's advisers warned him that with an election campaign coming up in less than a year, voters would likely be offended at Jackie's reappearance in the jet set so soon after the death of her baby. And, anyway, suggested the naysayers, why couldn't Jackie vacation elsewhere?

Closer to the Kennedy home front, there was one woman who was unhappy about Jackie's upcoming vacation with the controversial Onassis and, as usual, she was not afraid to make her views known: Ethel.

Ethel, still recovering from her difficult pregnancy, also had other matters that weighed heavily on her mind. At this time her sister Ann was involved in an extramarital affair with a wealthy, married New York businessman whom she had met at a cocktail party. Eventually Ann would become pregnant, give birth to a girl, and have to confess to her husband that the child was not his. Divorce proceedings followed this revelation. At the same time, Ethel's brother, George, left his spouse and became romantically involved with a Swedish stockbroker. Ethel, with her high moral standards, was deeply troubled by these turns of events. To her mind, divorce was sinful; she would never have considered it, no matter what Bobby might do.

Ethel became preoccupied with Jackie's controversial cruise plans. Her concern was not unreasonable: Bobby might have a chance at the Presidency one day, and any scandal that tarnished Jack would also, by association, affect Bobby. As sorry as she was for the loss of Patrick, Ethel was distressed by Jackie's decision to cruise with Onassis, a man she referred to as "a known criminal if ever there was one."

Usually a much more politically minded woman than Jackie—and an alarmist as well—Ethel had a meeting with Jackie at the White House and warned her sister-in-law that she could be playing into the hands of one of the world's biggest scoundrels.

In a series of telephone conversations between the sisters-in-law that took place over a three-day period, Jackie stood her ground. She was cruising with Onassis, she said, and it would be none of Ethel's business.

"But there are political ramifications to everything you, as First Lady, do," Ethel protested, as if Jackie didn't realize it. Ethel was amazed that Jackie couldn't see the potential public relations problem of such a cruise, and even more astounded that Jack was allowing her to go.

"Well, I think they're both crazy," she told Lem Billings. "Jack is so cavalier about these things, and so is Jackie. This country will not be happy seeing pictures of the First Lady, so soon after Patrick's death, carousing with the likes of Onassis. When Bobby and I are in the

White House," Ethel decided, "not one decision will ever be made that could cause any controversy whatsoever."

Finally, perhaps out of frustration because Ethel would not drop the subject, Jackie was forced to tell her to keep her opinion to herself. Her patience tried, the First Lady then took the matter up with the Attorney General. According to George Smathers, Jackie told Bobby, "I don't mean to be rude, but someone needs to remind your wife of her place. I'm going on this trip, and that's final. I don't do what Ethel wants me to do. She's my friend," Jackie continued, "but this is not her best moment."

Aboard the *Christina*

At the beginning of October 1963, Jackie Kennedy went off to Greece. This would be her second visit, for she had stayed in Greece previously, in June 1961, for nine days, after accompanying Jack on state visits to Paris, Vienna, and London. Even though she was supposed to curtail all engagements, the day she was scheduled to leave she decided to attend the welcoming ceremony for Emperor Haile Selassie of Ethiopia, reportedly because she just couldn't resist meeting him.

After the African leader presented her with some choice leopard skins, she graciously bowed out and headed to the airport. Before she left, a floral arrangement was delivered to the White House for her—lilies from Ethel with a simple, handwritten card: "Have a safe trip to the land of the Hellenes."

On the way to Greece, during the last leg of her flight between Rome and Athens, Jackie suddenly became nauseous and overcome with fatigue. She called for oxygen, and a stewardess quickly brought it to her seat. "Maybe this was a bad idea, after all," she observed, weakly. Although she used only a small amount of oxygen, the concern for her need was great, and the President was immediately contacted about it. "She'll be fine," he said. "She's strong as a racehorse."

By the time she landed in Athens and was greeted by Lee, U.S.

Ambassador Labouisse and other officials, Jackie looked pale but eager to begin her adventure. She and Lee were whisked by automobile to the villa of Greek shipping businessman Markos Nomikos, at Cavouri Bay, a seaside resort fifteen miles southeast of Athens. Here Jackie would spend the next couple of days in semiseclusion with her hosts and other guests, including Stelina Mavros, who worked as special assistant to Nomikos.

Mavros, who worked for the Greek mogul for three years, recalls, "We were all amazed at how weak the First Lady was. She had to be helped from a chair, for instance. Immediately, Lee began to hover over her, doing this and that for her, until Jackie finally said, 'Please, I am not an invalid. Let me be.' She stayed with us for three days until finally, we all boarded Ari's yacht. She seemed unhappy, dreary, but determined to have a good time, anyway."

A lifetime of living in the affluent homes of the Bouviers, the Auchinclosses, and the Kennedys had accustomed Jackie to luxury, yet even she was impressed by the opulence that awaited her on Onassis's magnificent yacht. First of all, the *Christina* itself was staggering— more than a luxury liner, it was a floating paradise resort, complete with a beauty salon, movie theater, doctor's office, forty-two telephones, and a mosaic swimming pool. There were also nine staterooms, each named for a different Greek island.

Among those aboard the cruise were Lee Radziwill and her husband, Stanislaw; dress designer Princess Irene Galitzine and her husband; Mrs. Constantine Garoufalidis; Stelina Mavros; Lee's friend Accardi Gurney; and several others, including Kennedy's Undersecretary of Commerce, Franklin D. Roosevelt, Jr., and his wife, Susan. (Roosevelt was sent to accompany Jackie, as Jack put it, to "add respectability to the whole thing.")

While wandering about, guests would discover the ship to be lavishly, if gaudily decorated. Bar stools upholstered with scrotums of whales, lapis lazuli fireplaces, and gold-plated bathroom fixtures were a few of the yacht's more garish embellishments.

Delighted to be entertaining the First Lady of the United States, Onassis outdid his own legendary extravagance. On their first morning at sea he had the entire ship decorated with hordes of red roses and pink gladioli. For passengers' snacks, he had the ship abundantly stocked with rare delicacies, vintage wines, eight kinds of caviar, and fruits flown in from Paris especially for the occasion.

To further pamper his guests, the eccentric Greek hired a staff of sixty, including two hairdressers (hired just for Jackie), a Swedish masseur, and a full orchestra to entertain during dinner and for after-dinner dancing. Two chefs, one Greek, one French, were on call to prepare the passengers sumptuous feasts, which included caviar-filled eggs *foie gras*, steamed lobsters, and jumbo shrimp.

For a woman like Jackie, who had a remarkably discriminating eye for the finer things in life, the delicious excess of this cruise and the dazzling lifestyle it represented were not to be soon forgotten. Jackie, it was decided, would take the principal stateroom occupied at various times by Greta Garbo, Lady Pamela Churchill, Maria Callas, and Jackie's own sister, Lee.

"Mrs. Kennedy is in charge here," the sixty-three-year-old Aristotle proudly told the press, which had assembled to gawk at her while she boarded. "She's the captain." It was thought that Jackie would put the ship on course to the Aegean Islands, which she had enjoyed so much on her 1961 cruise. Instead, she said she wanted to go to Istanbul, then Lesbos Island, then Crete.

"By the time we got to Crete—which was, I think, the sixth day—Jackie seemed to be getting some of her strength back," recalled Stelina Mavros. "She was very excited about seeing the relics of the Minoans [a 3,500-year-old civilization]. That afternoon, we all got into our bathing suits and went for a swim off the shore. Where we were headed next was the big question. It really was up to Jackie. She had a map, and she knew just where she wanted to go. We were in her hands."

Jackie's next stop was the harbor of Itea on the island of Delphi, then to the island of Levkas, and finally on to Smyrna. When the ship finally reached Smyrna, Jackie and Lee wanted a tour of Ari's hometown. Up until this point, Ari had not emerged from his cabin when the *Christina* docked and everyone disembarked for tours, out of respect for the First Lady's desire for privacy. He knew that if he made an appearance with Jackie, the paparazzi would descend upon them. But apparently Jackie didn't care as much about that as Ari thought she did. She just wanted to see Smyrna, and so he obliged. The two toured Onassis's childhood haunts as he told her more about his life, his loves, and in particular, his romance with Maria Callas. His father, with whom he had an acrimonious relationship, had been a successful tobacco merchant in the Turkish port of Smyrna. His mother died after a kidney operation when Ari was six years old. He was an only child, driven all of his life by his desire to be successful in order to win his father's approval. A dejected-looking Lee trailed behind with some other friends as Ari and Jackie walked, hand in hand.

After Ari told Jackie his story, he asked her for her own. He encouraged her to talk about the one subject around which everyone else in her life tiptoed: Baby Patrick. "He had a son of his own whom he loved dearly," says Stelina Mavros, "and he had great sympathy for what Jackie was going through. 'You should talk about it,' he told her. 'You shouldn't hold it in. It's not good for you.' First slowly, and then eagerly, Jackie opened up to Ari about her pain, her sorrow. He was a good listener, very sensitive, very compassionate, a good friend. Jackie told Lee that she really appreciated Ari's ear. She so craved attention, she so craved understanding, someone in whom she could confide," recalls Mavros. "I remember thinking, 'How is it that the First Lady of the United States could be so desperate for a human touch?' I overheard her say, 'I would have loved that baby. I would have loved him so much.' It made me cry."

No man had given Jackie so much personal time and attention in a long while. Jackie would not forget Onassis's compassion. It was clear that the two had a chemistry; photos taken of the two of them while they toured Ari's homeland show a Jackie who was glowing once again. When those photos appeared in the press, the President was not happy about their publication, especially after Bobby telephoned him and asked, "Now, how does *that* look? Maybe Jackie should have listened to Ethel."

According to Jack's personal secretary of twelve years, Evelyn Lincoln, Ethel also logged a number of telephone calls to make certain that Jack knew that she had "warned Jackie, but would she listen to me? No. Never. She never listens to me, that one."

Jack Summons Jackie—To No Avail

The President missed his wife, and he wanted her to come home. Rita Dallas, Joe's nurse, remembered that Jack was "listless and moody" in Jackie's absence. Using the excuse that the cruise was generating negative publicity, he called Jackie and demanded that she return. She refused. She was enjoying herself, she said, and she found Onassis a gracious host. When Jack protested, Jackie made it clear she would not be back in Washington a day sooner than the previously agreed-upon date of October 17.

Jack would later receive correspondence written by Jackie from the cruise, making it clear that her feelings for him were stronger than ever. "I miss you very much, which is nice," Jackie wrote, "though it is a bit sad. But then I think of how lucky I am to miss you. I realize here [in Greece] so much that I am having something you can never have—the absence of tension. I wish so much I could give you that. But I can't. So I give you every day while I think of you. [It is] the only thing I have to give and I hope it matters to you."

"Jackie intimate with Ari? Rubbish," says Stelina Mavros. "Everyone would have known about it because Ari would not have been so discreet to not let us all know in some way that he had won that prize. He did want her, I know that, because he said so after the cruise. 'One day, she and I will meet again,' he said, 'and this time, nothing will stand in my way.' He was very dramatic, like a fictional character in a play. That's just how he spoke."

Joseph Paolella, one of Jackie's Secret Service agents, says that because the agents all knew what Jack was doing outside his marriage, they sometimes mused among themselves about the possibility of Jackie also being unfaithful.

"We used to ask, you know, 'Does she have any boyfriends?' She must have *something* going on," recalls Paolella. "Or point to one of the guys on her detail and say, 'How 'bout you? Are you the one?' It was a common joke," he says.

"If anything was going on, it most certainly would have been relayed through the agents. There was never a hint of anything like that going on with her. She spent a great deal of time away from Jack during the week at Glen Ora and if she ever wanted to do anything, she had plenty of opportunities. But she was devoted to her children, to her horses, and to living a good, country life."

Jackie's sexual relationship with Jack had been influenced for years by his roving eye, as well as his health problems, and she just had to learn to adjust to his approach to their private time together. Also, Jackie knew that her husband suffered from the chronic venereal disease nongonococcal urethritis, or chlamydia. A nurse who worked for Dr. Janet Travell, Kennedy's physician, says that Jackie was terrified of the disease.

"It was one of her greatest fears, and certainly made her husband less than appealing as a sexual partner, let's face facts," said the nurse. "She told Dr. Travell that she believed Jack's VD had something to do with the death of Patrick, and the other problems she had with pregnancies. Even John had had a tough time, almost died shortly after birth."

In fact, according to the nurse, Dr. Travell confirmed to Jackie that the female partner is always infected after the first time she has intercourse with a man suffering from Jack's condition. Her pregnancies can then be affected by the disease, sometimes resulting in premature births, sometimes in miscarriages, sometimes in stillbirths. That Jackie suffered from severe periods of postpartum depression after her pregnancies can also be explained by her having been infected by Jack's sexually transmitted disease.

"I'm not sure, but I think I want to be thought of as desirable," Jackie once told Ethel in a candid conversation about their husbands early in their marriages. According to what Ethel later recalled to Leah Mason, Jackie giggled nervously when she made the confession; women of her generation rarely spoke of such things.

"Then you shouldn't have gotten married," was Ethel's response. "You don't get fireworks with marriage. You get children."

Ethel may have been like her mother-in-law Rose in the Victorian approach she took to physical intimacy with her husband: intercourse was not to be enjoyed, it was to be endured; it was a woman's duty, and the reason to do it was to have children—not for joy, or passion. When Rose felt she had fulfilled her marital duty and had enough children, nine of them, she cut Joe off. As a devout Catholic, birth control was out of the question for her, and there was no other way she knew of to limit her brood.

Joan had her own emotional issues surrounding her sexuality, most having to do with self-esteem. Was she good enough for Ted? She never really believed so, and said so time after time. Still, in the first ten years of her marriage, Joan's sex life with Ted was active. When they were together, she was making love to her husband.

Jackie was a healthy, vibrant, young and beautiful woman, brimming with self-confidence, always ready to take on the world. She had none of Ethel's perhaps old-fashioned views about sexuality, and none of Joan's self-esteem issues. Unfortunately, what she did have was a philandering husband who suffered from chlamydia.

"Ari Is Not for You"

Jackie's relationship with her sister, Lee, was at this time what it had always been: complex. They loved each other dearly; each was often the other's closest and most valued friend. In many ways, Jackie was Lee's healer, and vice versa. They helped each other recover from life's blows, from dramatic changes and problems, and from bad relationships.

The flip side of their relationship is that Jackie and Lee engaged in a not-always friendly competition for attention for many years, with Jackie usually the victor. When they were younger, Jackie's mother, Janet Auchincloss, once observed, "Jackie always looked marvelously put together, while her sister Lee seemed blown out of a hurricane." Both were stylish, glamorous, and charming but, as First Lady, Jackie was the one the world really cared about, not Lee.

While in Smyrna, Jackie and Lee had a heart-to-heart talk, during which Jackie explained the harm it would do to Jack's political career if Lee continued the affair with Onassis. Also, Jackie said, Ari's romance with Maria Callas and the way he had so heartlessly left his wife, Tina, did not bode well for Lee if she was considering anything of a long-term nature with him. Jackie said she was genuinely concerned about Lee.

"You really need to think about this," she told Lee, according to Stelina Mavros. "Ari is not for you. Trust me."

"I know this because, afterward, Lee told me that she was in turmoil over Jackie's advice," said Mavros. "Did Jackie want him for herself, was she really looking out for Lee's best interest, or was she only concerned about her husband's political career? Lee was never sure and, of course, what happened between Ari and Jackie just five years later only added to Lee's uncertainty about her sister's true motivations. The fact that she was even suspicious of them, though, I guess says a lot about their relationship."

Only Lee would know what she was really thinking, but at the time that Jackie spoke to her about Ari, she wept openly about how she only wanted a man to "love me for myself." Then she appeared to give in when she made the decision that she would not continue to see Onassis. Instead, she would return to her husband, Stas, the Prince.

"I cannot know for sure, but I personally believe that Lee had already decided to end it with Ari, anyway," says Mavros. "I think she felt that it would make her and Jackie feel closer if she acted like she was doing what Jackie suggested. But most people believe that she had already made up her mind about Ari, and she was only 'acting' with Jackie. She had already decided to go back to her husband."

On the last night of the cruise, Aristotle Onassis presented the Bouvier sisters with expensive gifts: three jeweled bracelets for Lee, and an extravagant diamond-and-ruby necklace for the First Lady, worth $50,000 in 1963 dollars.

"Oh, Ari," Jackie exclaimed. "You shouldn't have."

"Yes, Ari," Lee said, as she gazed at her sister's bauble. "You *shouldn't* have."

PART SIX

Jack's Rapprochement with Jackie: "Getting to Know You"

By the fall of 1963, the President and his First Lady had grown closer, and that much was clear to all observers. Several occurrences had transformed Jack, and thus had changed his relationship to Jackie for the better.

The first was, of course, the death of Patrick. Kennedy's Secret Service agent Larry Newman recalls, "After the baby's death, I saw the President and First Lady on their way to becoming friends as well as husband and wife. He would stop at the car and help her out, instead of getting out and walking ahead of her as he was known to do. They would talk more, spend much more time walking together, talking things over, being a real couple. The death of the baby was something they shared and deeply felt. It made them much closer."

It seemed, also, that Jackie's long absence aboard the *Christina* on the seas had spurred Jack on to greater desire for her, because he was more solicitous than ever before. "The last weekend he was ever home [in Hyannis Port]," said Rita Dallas, "he commented that the one bright thing on the horizon was: 'Jackie's coming back.'"

As well as the death of his son, the Cuban Missile Crisis had a great impact on Kennedy. "It was so close," he had said to the British ambassador. "Too, too close."

In fact, during that crisis, the President asked Jackie to cancel some of her outside appointments and stay at the White House, so that he could spend as much time with her and the children as possible.

Dr. Janet Travell recalled a scene just before the crisis. "President Kennedy was leaving on a trip west. At my office window, I watched him walk briskly from the West Wing across the lawn to Chopper Number One. The usual retinue trailed behind him. They bounded into the helicopter and I waited to see the steps drawn up. Instead, the

President unexpectedly reappeared in the doorway and descended the steps alone. How unusual, I thought. Then I saw why. Jackie, her hair wild in the gale of the rotors, was running from the South Portico across the grass. She almost met him at the helicopter steps and she reached up with her arms. They stood motionless in an embrace for many seconds. Perhaps no one else noted that rare demonstration of affection. A few days later in the publicized hours of the Cuban Missile Crisis, I remembered it. I thought of its deep significance—the unbreakable bond of love between them that showed clearest in times of trouble."

Some have reported that by 1963 Jack was completely faithful to Jackie. As George Smathers put it, "By 1963, Jack was about as faithful as he was ever going to be. It was more than Jackie had hoped for, but less than she deserved."

"I once asked him if he'd ever fallen desperately, hopelessly in love," James McGregor Burns, a friend and adviser of Jack's once said. "He just shrugged and said, 'I'm not the heavy lover type.'"

Jackie's efforts in redecorating the White House also had a positive effect on her marriage. More than a public museum, the White House was now a comfortable home where Jack and Jackie could play out what sometimes seemed to be a charmed existence.

Rita Dallas, who would accompany Jack's father, Joseph, there on visits, recalled the almost mythical appearance the First Family created in their renovated living quarters, "Often, late at night, the upstairs light would be turned low. It gave the whole area a solemn tone. At one end of the hall, the presidential living room would be softly and dramatically lighted. There would be muted music mingling with the shadows.

"The First Lady would be sitting on the couch, outlined by a gentle halo of light, and then the President would step from the elevator that opened out to the living room. He would stand still, waiting, while his wife rose from the couch to come to him. He would rest his hand on her cheek and then take her in his arms in a quiet embrace. How often I thought, if the world had ever seen those moments there would be no doubt that Camelot existed," Rita Dallas concluded.

"She forced a separation between his private life and work," recalls Pierre Salinger. "That was the deal. Unlike Johnson, when

Kennedy was finished, once he went back upstairs, he went to his wife and that was the end of it. No staff, no more interruptions every half hour."

The way that Jack doted on Caroline and John Jr. also made Jackie's feelings for her husband that much stronger. "He loved his children, he spent so much time with them," recalled Dave Powers. "Every night, no matter what was going on, he'd say, 'I want them brought over before they go to bed.' He had breakfast with them and lunch with them. When there was something going on, like the Cuban Missile Crisis, he'd go up to look at that boy. One day, the President was with some ambassador, Caroline was on Macaroni [her pony], and he went and yelled, 'Caroline.' She rode the thing right through the Rose Garden, right into the White House office. He didn't care. He loved it."

Five days after Jackie's return to Washington, on October 22, she and Jack dined with White House correspondent Ben Bradlee and his then-wife, Tony.

Jack had just endured a bad day. In shirtsleeves, he complained to Jackie and Tony that everything had gone wrong, beginning with the Birmingham, Alabama, police department's refusal to hire Negro police officers. Also, Bobby Baker, Secretary to the Senate Majority and a protégé of LBJ's, had just been sued for allegedly accepting a bribe involving a vending machine franchise in the plant of a company from which a lot of governmental business was conducted. Jack said he thought of Baker not as a crook, but as a rogue.

As Jack unwound with a stiff scotch, Jackie told Tony Bradlee that she so regretted the negative publicity her cruise with Onassis had caused—especially an article in *Newsweek* about it—but added that she found Onassis to be "an alive and vital person who has come up from nowhere." She told the reporter of Ari's hesitancy to go on the cruise, and of her insistence that he be aboard. She also said that Jack was being "really nice and understanding" about the cruise.

Jackie's opinion of him aside, Jack made it clear to Bradlee that Onassis would not be welcome at the White House until long after the 1964 election. Jack clearly intended to run again and didn't want the controversy that always surrounded Onassis to become an issue.

The topic then turned to 1968, and of whom JFK was thinking in terms of his successor.

"So who do you have in mind?" Jackie asked, as the guests all walked to the screening room to see a movie.

"Well," answered Jack, "I was actually thinking about Franklin [Roosevelt, Jr.] . . . until you and Onassis fixed that."

Jackie didn't say a word.

Jack also said that he believed Jackie felt a bit guilty about her trip—odd, in that she didn't really want to go in the first place. She said nothing, however, to contradict him. He added that "Jackie's guilt feelings" could possibly work to his advantage.

"Maybe now you'll come with us to Texas next month," he said with a grin. The President's handlers had advised him that he needed to shore up his popularity in that state, so a trip was being planned. The first stop would be San Antonio, then Houston, Fort Worth, and finally, Dallas.

"Sure I will," Jackie answered. "I'll campaign with you anywhere you want."

Then, the contingent joined Ethel and Bobby, who were waiting in the theater for the screening of *From Russia with Love,* starring Sean Connery. Jack had a short attention span for movies. He would usually leave the theater after about an hour and go upstairs to read. This time was no exception; he left before the first spectacular gunplay. Everyone else, however, enjoyed every moment of it, except for Jackie. After the film ended, she observed to Ethel, "To be honest, I find such violence to be deplorable. Don't you?"

Tragedy

How is it that a person's entire life can be so completely changed in just a matter of seconds?

It was Friday, November 22, 1963. The motorcade's progress had been slow. Jackie Kennedy sat next to her husband in the backseat of a Lincoln convertible, wearing a light wool strawberry pink Chanel suit with a navy-blue collar and a matching blue blouse. She held a bouquet of red roses in her lap; on her head sat a pink pillbox hat. Texas Governor John B. Connally and his wife, Nellie, sat in front of her as a police motorcycle escort led the way. Behind the Kennedys' Lincoln was a car of Secret Service agents, trailed by another automobile, this one carrying Vice President Lyndon Johnson, his wife Lady Bird, and Texas Senator Ralph Yarborough.

Jackie smiled and waved at the cheering crowds, accustomed to the manic adulation and blurred excitement that resulted whenever she and Jack appeared in public. Both were surprised and delighted to have this kind of reception—the chanting and cheering, the jostling for position, the shaking of placards—in Texas, a state where the President's popularity was in question.

By rote Jackie turned to her left and waved. Then to her right. Then again to her left.

Suddenly, the shots rang out, followed by a gush of blood. Jack was hit. Jackie went from shock to fear as pandemonium broke out. The governor started shouting, something about "they're going to kill us."

Clint Hill, who still cannot give voice to the terrible memory without great difficulty, recalls, "I heard a sound from my right rear. I was on the left hand, front, of the follow-up car [on the running board]. As I began to turn to my right toward that sound, my eyes crossed the back of the presidential car and I saw the President grasp at his throat and lurch a little bit to his left, and I realized that something had happened. I got off the car as quickly as I could and ran to the presidential car. By the time I got there, two more shots had been fired and he had been hit in the head."

"I've got his brains in my hand!" Jackie screamed. "My God, what are they doing? My God, they've killed Jack, they've killed my husband . . . Jack, Jack!"

A piece of Jack's skull had come off—a "perfectly clean piece," as she would later remember—and he slumped into her lap.

Then, in one of those frantic, dizzying moments when every horrible emotion possible clashes together at once—the blinding panic of fear, the horror of mutilation, the shock and despair of unexpected loss, the unbelievable finality of sudden death, the destruction of life as it once was—Jackie scampered out of her seat onto the trunk of the car. She began crawling to the rear of the vehicle, though she would have no recollection of ever having done so. In a moment of blind courage, Clint Hill jumped off his car and began racing toward Jackie, risking his life. He could have easily been hit by any of the motorcycles or even his own car.

"I slipped when I first tried to get up on the presidential car," Clint Hill recalls. "It took me four or five steps to get there, and in that time Mrs. Kennedy was out on top of the trunk attempting to grasp part of the President's head that had been blown off and had fallen into the street. I grasped her and put her back in the backseat and placed my body on top of her and the President."

"Oh Jack, oh, Jack, I love you," Jackie sobbed.

Six minutes later, the car carrying the First Couple would pull up to Parkland Memorial Hospital. Jackie, still in the backseat, would cradle Jack in her arms. "Please, Mrs. Kennedy," she recalled Clint Hill begging, "we must get the President to a doctor."

She would refuse. Terror mixed with grief still had complete possession of her. As her shoulders heaved with wracking sobs, she would cradle Jack's ruined head in her hands and try to hold the top of his head together, even though there was nothing between her hand and his brain. The entire right side of his head was gone, beginning at his hairline and extending all the way behind his right ear. Pieces of skull that hadn't been blown away were hanging by blood-matted hair. Part of his brain, the cerebellum, was dangling from the back of his head by a single strand of tissue. The memory of how she would try to hold the top of her husband's head on would fuel Jackie's nightmares for years to come.

How would she ever be able to forget Jack's face in those final moments? Though his gray suit and shirt were bloodied and the top of his head gone, his face remained unmarked and exquisite. His skin was so bronzed he appeared to be tanned, a physiological phenomenon caused by Addison's disease, from which he had suffered for years. His blue eyes were open and clear but stared blankly ahead.

Clint Hill had somehow understood that she was unable to allow strangers the unspeakable horror of seeing this great man's shattered skull, his brain spilling into her lap. Hill tenderly wrapped his jacket around Kennedy's head so that the terrible wound would not be exposed. It was only then that Jackie would allow the Secret Service men to lift her husband's body onto the gurney to be wheeled into the emergency room.

A blur of doctors and nurses rushed by her into the trauma room, including Dr. Robert McClelland and Dr. Charles Crenshaw. "The look on her face forever marked my memory," Crenshaw would recall years later of Jackie. "Anger, disbelief, despair, and resignation were all present in her expression. In all the sentiments I have seen displayed and heard expressed in my thirty years of practice by people grieving and hurting over trauma victims, I never saw or sensed more intense and genuine love."

Twenty minutes passed.

Jackie was alone, but not really. All around her, doctors and nurses hurried about, shouting to one another in a scene of total and utter chaos and panic. Kenny O'Donnell, one of Jack's closest friends, a man Jackie never thought of as fragile, his emotions always so impenetrable, sat in a corner, sobbing. Nellie Connally, a woman she barely knew, had suddenly become a kindred spirit as she stood at Jackie's side in stunned silence. In another corner stood Lady Bird Johnson, her eyes wide with alarm and concern, reluctant to approach the two women. What could she say to them as they stood vigil to learn if their husbands were dead or alive?

Standing in front of Trauma Room One, Jackie waited for word about Jack's fate. Drying blood and brain matter caked the right side of her dress and her leg. Her once-white gloves were stained almost completely crimson. If she hadn't been standing, some observers might have thought she too had been shot.

She noticed Dave Powers leaning against a wall and walked over to him. "You'd better get a priest," she said. He stared at her as she walked away, back to her own corner.

A few more endless minutes passed. Then Jackie could take it no more. If Jack was dying, her place was at his side.

"I'm going in there," she told a nurse. "And I'm staying."

There was a scuffle between Jackie and the nurse, attracting the attention of Dr. George Burkley. "I want to be in there when he dies," Jackie insisted to him. Reluctantly, the doctor led Jackie into Trauma Room One, repeating to himself, "It's her right. It's her prerogative. It's her right," as if trying to convince himself that it was the correct thing for him to do, even though he realized what she would see in that room would likely haunt her forever.

"The President's Been Shot"

It was an unseasonably warm day at Hickory Hill, and Bobby Kennedy was inspired to invite two of his associates, Robert Morgenthau, the U.S. Attorney in New York, and Silvio Mollo, the chief of the criminal division in the Manhattan office, to his home for a poolside lunch. Because they had been working hard during a two-day intensive seminar regarding the fight against organized crime, Bobby thought that a leisurely meal away from the office would be a nice break for his coworkers.

Ethel, excited to have her husband home midday and anxious to show off the new baby to his colleagues, had ordered the cook to prepare a lunch of chowder and tuna fish sandwiches.

It was just a lazy, ordinary afternoon. The children were at school and the grounds were quiet. Earlier, Ethel had played a quick game of tennis with a girlfriend. When Bobby arrived home for lunch with his guests, he changed into his swimsuit and took a quick swim before the meal was served. As they ate their soup and sandwiches, workmen painted the new wing of the house. It was 1:45 when Bobby glanced at his watch and decided that he and his associates should return to the office. Just as he was getting up to change clothes, the phone rang. Ethel, who was closest, answered it. A strange expression came over her face. "It's J. Edgar Hoover," she said, dread creeping into her voice.

Because there had always been a certain animosity between J. Edgar Hoover and the Kennedys, the FBI Director rarely called Bobby at home. So his sudden call signaled that something important must have happened. Bobby jumped up and snatched the phone from Ethel.

Just then, one of the workmen painting the house began running in the direction of the poolside table where the guests sat. In his hand, the painter held a small portable radio pressed to his ear. He excitedly shouted something, but no one could understand what he was trying to convey. At exactly the same time, Hoover said to Bobby, "I have news for you. The President has been shot."

Bobby blanched. "What? . . . Oh. I . . . Is it serious? . . . I . . ."

"I think it is serious," Hoover responded without emotion. "I'm endeavoring to get details. I'll call you back when I find out more."

At that precise moment the others finally understood what the workman was shouting: "They're saying the President's been shot."

Ethel rushed to Bobby and put her arms around him. Bobby stumbled forward, clasped a hand over his mouth and, echoing the house-painter, screamed out, "Jack's been shot! It may be fatal."

Joan Kennedy sat at her kitchen table in her home on 28th Street in Georgetown, and over a steaming cup of coffee planned her day's activities with her social secretary. A full day awaited.

First, Joan had to take Kara, almost four, and Teddy Jr., two, to the kindergarten Jackie had organized at the White House for her children and for those of any family members, special friends, and government officials who wished to have their youngsters close by. The school was another project Jackie was proud of, and Joan agreed that having all the children learning together was a plus. "I want them to know their cousins," Joan said at the time. "And you know that if Jackie had anything to do with it, the teachers are the best in the world."

After dropping the children off, Joan would take a taxicab to the posh, seven-story Elizabeth Arden salon at 1147 Connecticut Avenue to have her hair styled. A big evening was planned. She would be hosting a fifth anniversary party for herself and Ted. Joan's sister, Candy, and her husband, Robert McMurray, would be flying in for the occasion. The celebration was to be a week early because all the Kennedys would be going to Hyannis Port for the Thanksgiving holidays.

The next morning, Ted, Joan, her sister and brother-in-law, and some other friends planned to attend the Harvard-Yale football game and then remain at the Cape for the weekend.

It was while Joan was having her hair done in a cubicle on the fourth floor that the salon's manager, Barbara Brown, heard the terrible news on the radio: The President had been shot.

Barbara took an elevator to the fourth floor, found Joan's hairstylist, Marguerite Muguet, and pulled her aside while Muguet's assistant extracted curlers from Joan's long blonde hair. The two women wondered how to tell Joan the news—or whether to tell her at all. Joan had recently told them of how distraught Jack had been over the loss of Patrick, and how close the two of them had become while at Squaw Island.

The two women didn't want Joan to hear the tragic news on the radio, but at the same time they didn't feel that it was appropriate for her to hear such important, life-altering information from them. As they tried to determine a course of action, Joan's secretary, who was back at the Georgetown house with a shaken Ted, called to tell them she was sending Ted's aide, Milton Gwirtzman, to pick up Joan and take her home.

Barbara Brown instructed Marguerite Muguet to finish Joan's hair as quickly as possible and get her downstairs quickly to meet Gwirtzman. Once finished with Joan, they quickly escorted her to the elevator, and then took her down to the ground floor without telling her why they were in such a hurry.

"Don't tell Joan a thing," said the manager. "Let's just get her out of here."

Holy Mary, Mother of God

Once inside Trauma Room One, Jackie Kennedy saw her husband lying on the table. She approached him cautiously, perhaps with the realization that this was only the beginning of a hurt that would not lessen but would spread and deepen over time. She watched as they worked on Jack, stuffing a tube into a hole dug into his lower neck. Another tube had been thrust up his nose, others protruded from his chest. Blood seemed to be spurting from everywhere.

A doctor pounded on Jack's chest. Again and again he pounded, as Jackie looked on, helplessly. Whatever the doctor was trying to do wasn't working. Jack's eyes were fixed and staring up at the ceiling. His frozen expression was one of stunned dismay. His mouth was agape.

As everyone in the room watched, breaths held—doctors, nurses,

Jackie—a thin green line moved straight across the screen of a monitor. The room was in dead silence except for the muffled sounds of weeping.

Dr. Crenshaw looked down into a nearby bucket, and lost his composure. There, mingled with the President's brain tissue and his lifeblood, were a few of Jackie's long-stemmed red roses.

A terrible stillness came over Jackie's face. Then, in an instant she was overcome and fell to her knees in despair, paying no attention to the pool of blood into which she sank.

Another doctor turned to Jackie. Brushing the tears from her cheeks, she rose as he approached.

"Mrs. Kennedy, your husband has sustained a fatal wound," he said.

"I know," she whispered, the words barely escaping from her lips. Later she would say her very life ended on that warm day, November 22, 1963, at one o'clock in the afternoon.

Dr. Burkley came over to her, his face inches from hers. "The President is dead," he said, his voice choked with emotion. Jackie looked at him and, noticing his great and obvious despair, touched her cheek to his. The doctor openly wept.

Jackie approached her dead husband and stood by his shoulders. The wound was hidden from her, but Jack's face was visible and still so handsome. She was completely transfixed. How could this man's expression be so peaceful after experiencing such violence? A priest's presence shook her from the spell under which she seemed to have fallen as he murmured his condolences and then began the Last Rites, followed by the Lord's Prayer and then the Hail Mary.

"Holy Mary, Mother of God," Jackie spoke the words. "Pray for us sinners, now and at the hour of our death. Amen."

Another priest had entered the room. He blessed himself and said, "Eternal rest grant unto him, O Lord."

"And let perpetual light shine upon him," Jackie intoned, the words rising from her by rote.

The second priest approached Jackie to quell any fear she may have had about the legitimacy of the Last Rites having been performed on the President so clearly after he was dead. "I am convinced that his soul has not left his body," the priest said, as Jackie nodded. "This is a valid last sacrament."

Jackie seemed faint. She was about to pass out when a nurse approached her with a cold towel. She held it to her forehead while the wave passed over her. Then she left the room.

Emerging from the madness of humanity rushing in and out of Trauma Room One was Jackie's friend Lady Bird Johnson. She had just been informed of Jack's death. "You always think of someone like her as being insulated, protected," Lady Bird recalled of Jackie. "She was quite alone. I don't think I ever saw anyone so much alone in my life."

"Jackie, I wish to God there was something I could do," she said as she embraced her. Jackie stared straight ahead, her face a frozen mask.

Meanwhile, inside the emergency room, nurses washed down Jack's body as janitors mopped up the blood before Jackie was allowed back into the room for a few final moments with Jack. When Jackie reentered, she noticed her husband's white foot sticking out from under the hospital sheet. Shockingly white. She bent down and kissed it.

Then, Jackie slowly pulled away the sheet, revealing his face, his still-perfect face. The staring blue eyes—she kissed his eyebrows. The open mouth—she kissed his mouth.

Several other doctors entered the room. Like most of the times during their life together, this sacred moment would not be a private one. Perhaps last night had been her last truly private time with her husband. After a busy day, she had turned in for the night but couldn't sleep. Later, she would remember, something didn't feel right to her. Something was very wrong, in fact. She needed Jack, she wanted him to hold her in his arms. She didn't feel safe and she didn't know why. So, as she would later remember it, she let herself into her husband's room at about 2 A.M., slipped into his bed, and roused him from a sound sleep. Then, after making love, husband and wife fell asleep in each other's arms.

Now he was dead. In full view of the doctors and nurses, Jackie took her husband's hand and pressed it to her cheek. She kissed his fingers.

Then Jackie took off her blood-soaked gloves and removed her wedding ring, also stained with blood. She was remembering her own father, the first man she had ever seen dead, at his viewing. Black Jack had given her a bracelet when she graduated, a gift she treasured. At his funeral, she took it off and placed it in his hand. Now Jackie wanted to slip her wedding ring on Jack's finger. An orderly managed to get it over Jack's knuckle, using cream.

She stood at his side and gazed down at her husband. He was so handsome.

———————

"The Party's Been Canceled— The President's Dead"

Mother Odeide Mouton of the Stone Ridge County Day School was getting a world scoop. Ethel Kennedy was on the phone with her and she had just told the principal that the President was dead.

"The announcement hasn't been made yet to the country," Ethel informed the nun in a hushed but controlled voice. Then she added, "Please tell Kathleen and Courtney. I'll come to pick them up."

Mother Mouton choked back tears. "But you needn't come," she managed to tell Ethel. "Couldn't I make some arrangement for someone else to take the children home?"

"No," Ethel replied. "It's my day for the car pool." And then, remembering the grieving Eunice, she added, "And will you please tell my niece Maria [Shriver], I'll pick her up too so that her mother won't have to come out." Ethel did not want the children to hear the terrible news from strangers, and began to compose herself as best she could for the task at hand.

The nuns at the school had heard on the radio that the President had been shot during the motorcade and had been rushed to Parkland Memorial, but no one knew how seriously he had been wounded. They had already taken the students to the chapel to pray for his recovery. When Ethel arrived to pick up the children, they were still in the chapel praying. Ethel herself knelt down in the back, deep in prayer. In actuality she was still in a state of near hysteria.

Just a short time earlier, Bobby had been dressing hurriedly for the flight to Dallas when the phone rang and he was given the news. "Oh my God. He's dead," Bobby exclaimed as Ethel burst into tears. "Oh those poor children," she cried, referring to her young niece and nephew.

"My brother had the most wonderful life," Bobby had said.

Now, in the chapel, Ethel prayed for her slain brother-in-law and the premature end to his wonderful, tragic, history-changing life. It didn't seem possible he could be gone. She slowly rose and walked to the front pews where the children were praying. She walked her two daughters out to the car and told them that their uncle had been killed. As she was hugging them, Maria was led to her aunt, and Ethel put her arms around her and told her niece the news as well.

Less than an hour after hearing of her brother-in-law's murder, Ethel had been able to hide her suffering behind a shield of take-charge composure. As she drove away, Mother Mouton, who had been watching the scene, marveled at the strength and self-control of this religious woman in the face of such tragedy.

As Joan Kennedy was rushed to the lobby of the Elizabeth Arden hair salon, Ted Kennedy's aide, Milton Gwirtzman, arrived to take her to her husband. In the car heading back to her home, Joan was told the news that Jack had been shot. By the time Gwirtzman pulled up to her home, Ted was waiting at the front door with tears in his eyes. He had been trying to call the White House, he said, but couldn't get through. The lines were dead. No dial tones, no operators. Nothing. It was as frightening as it was unprecedented, and seemed to have some ominous connection to what had happened to the President.

"What is going on?" Joan said, frightened. "Is there some kind of national reason the lines are down?"

"They're not down," Ted said, reassuring her. "The circuits are busy."

"He's not dead, is he? Please, God . . ." Joan said, crying. "Oh my God! Oh no. Poor Jackie. Not Jack. Not Jack."

"I don't know what's going on," Ted said. It was decided that Milton Gwirtzman would stay with Joan while Ted and another friend of the family's, Claude Hooten, ran around the neighborhood looking for an active phone line. The breakdown of the Chesapeake and Potomac telephone system was not due to any national crisis, but rather just a result of overloaded circuits caused by the unprecedented demands upon them. Finally, going door to door, Ted found someone whose phone, mysteriously enough, did work. He immediately telephoned Bobby at Hickory Hill. "He's dead," Bobby said, succinctly. Bobby was too busy at that moment to provide details. "Better call Mother and our sisters," he said before abruptly hanging up, leaving Ted with a dial tone. Then, mercilessly, the tone was suddenly gone and this phone, too, was dead—before Ted even had a chance to call Rose. Perhaps there was a sense of relief about that, though, for what would he have told Rose? She would have had a thousand questions, and he had no answers.

By the time Ted got back to his and Joan's home, Joan and Milton Gwirtzman had heard the news on television that Jack was dead. As soon as Joan saw Ted, she ran to him sobbing uncontrollably. Chalk white, her eyes wide and blank with shock, she went limp in his arms. Ted caught her just in time. "Oh my God, not Jack," she said. "Poor Jackie. Poor Jackie."

"Not now, Joan," Ted said, seemingly frustrated with what he may have viewed as nothing but histrionics. He guided her back to the couch. Ted, perhaps feeling completely isolated from the tragic events taking place, desperately sought more details of what had happened. Leaving Joan with Claude Hooten, Ted and Milton took off in Milton's Mercedes, again looking for a working telephone, first at Gwirtzman's home and then, unsuccessful there, finally driving to the White House. Once there, he used a private White House line in Dr. Janet Travell's office that went through the Army's Signal Corps rather than the civilian telephone system, to call Rose at Hyannis Port. Rose had already heard the news; with nothing else to do about it, she was going for a walk on the beach to pray for her son. Soon Eunice showed up at the White House and, exasperated with Ted for not forcing more information from Bobby, called Bobby herself. The two then decided that she and Ted should take a private plane to Hyannis Port to be with Rose and the rest of the family. Ted called Joan from the White House to tell her he was headed for Connecticut.

To Joan, this was upsetting news. Of course, she wanted to accompany him. However, he wouldn't hear of it. He apparently didn't want to deal with what he viewed as Joan's overwrought emotionalism at this time. "Let me help," she begged him. "I know there's something I can do." There wasn't, Ted assured her. "You're too weak," he told her. "Just go to bed," he told her. "Take a pill, or something." Cruelly, at least for now, Joan would be completely shut out—from his grief and the family's.

Of course, the other Kennedy women were busy and involved. Ethel, seemingly in complete control, tended to Bobby's needs and

those of her children, and also telephoned different Kennedy aides
and associates around the world, giving them details of the terrible
news and assisting in making arrangements for them to get to Washington. Eunice Shriver had knelt in prayer in her husband's Washington office at Peace Corps headquarters and then gone to the White
House, where she consoled members of Jack's staff before heading to
Hyannis Port with Ted. Pat Lawford, who was in Los Angeles, took
the first flight to Washington, where she would join Jean and the rest
of the family in making the dreaded funeral arrangements. Rose
walked the sands in front of the Hyannis Port compound, determined
not to buckle under the pressure, perhaps more certain than ever that
God's will—as difficult as it was to fathom—would prevail. Jackie, of
course, was doing her best to hold up, though she was clearly traumatized. Joan, left alone, was the only one who took to her bed.

In her solitude, perhaps Joan's mind drifted back to a happier time,
just two years earlier in November 1961, a couple of days after
Thanksgiving when the family had an impromptu gathering at Joe and
Rose's. As well as the senior Kennedys and Jackie and Jack, present
were the Kennedy sisters, Eunice, Pat, and Jean, and their husbands,
Sargent, Peter, and Steve; Ethel and Bobby; Ted and Joan; and Paul
"Red" Fay and his wife, Anita.

"We ended up playing one of those Kennedy living room games,
but did it kind of like a variety show," Joan would recall. "I played
some Chopin. Jackie read a poem, probably Edna St. Vincent Millay."

After Jackie's reading, Jack suggested that Paul Fay sing his campy,
bombastic rendition of "Hooray for Hollywood," always a family favorite. Joan accompanied Fay during his number, which received a
wild ovation, as it always did. Then it was Ted's turn. As Joan played,
he sang his favorite, "Heart of My Heart," just as off-pitch as ever, and
to everyone's delight. After Eunice performed a little number, everyone began insisting that the President offer up a performance. Smiling,
Jack rose and walked over to Joan.

"Joansie, do you know 'September Song'?" he asked her. Of course
she did. She scooted over to allow room for Jack to sit on the bench
next to her. He sat facing the family. Then, as she played, the President of the United States sang his song gently, almost ethereally, its
poignant lyrics about the inevitable passage of time.

"The earlier performances had been greeted with boisterous,

friendly clapping," Red Fay would recall, "but now, we were all silent. Suddenly, I realized as I never had before that these days were rushing past, that we were living in a time that could never be regained."

As Joan continued to play, Jack suddenly stopped singing and, turning serious, began reciting melancholy lyrics having to do with the dwindling down of days, "to a precious few." The Kennedy family was held in rapt attention by Jack's sensitive, heartfelt delivery. When he was done, there was a moment of contemplative silence before everyone broke out into rousing applause. Joan sat at the piano, dabbing her eyes.

It was a wonderful moment, but Jack was obviously a better orator than singer. "I managed to follow his voice," Joan would recall years later with a smile, "but Jackie knew what I was doing. She came over to me afterward and said, 'Joan you are a terrific musician. You even made Jack sound good!'"

No one would have dreamed then that John Kennedy would not reach the September of his years but, rather, would be cut down in the prime of his life. Now, with his sudden death, the memory of that family night in Hyannis Port was just as painful as it was touching.*

At 3:30, Joan's sister Candy telephoned her from the airport. They had just arrived in Washington. Should they stay? Or turn around and go back to Texas?

"Oh, no, you must stay," Joan said, her voice trembling. "There are going to be so many people calling. I'm going to be besieged by reporters. Ted is gone, and I don't know what to do."

An hour later, Joan's sister and husband arrived. Soon after, there was a knock on the door. With Joan in bed resting, Candy answered it.

It was the caterer, along with a truckload of food and supplies for Joan's dinner party.

"The party's been canceled," Candy intoned. "The President is dead."

The next couple of days would be some of the most difficult in Joan Kennedy's life as she stayed behind in Georgetown while all of the

*In a 1970 interview with Sylvia Wright of *Life* magazine, Rose Kennedy said, "Joan used to play the piano while we sang in the evenings in Hyannis Port. Once, after we had lost Jack, we tried to sing some of the songs that he had liked. But one of us got depressed and that was, well . . . we all collapsed. So we closed the piano quickly, and everybody went home. We discontinued our singing after that."

other Kennedys were together at Hyannis Port and then at the White House. For the most part, Joan would be about as connected to these historic events as anyone else in the country—any other anonymous citizen—via televised news reports. She would lie in her bed watching the bulletins and the televised images of Jack's flag-draped coffin in the East Wing of the White House.

Dejected, wondering how everyone else in her family was faring, and perhaps feeling inadequate, the weeping Joan would probably never feel less a part of the Kennedy family than she did the weekend after her friend and brother-in-law Jack's death. As if somehow fulfilling her husband's prophecy, she became weaker until, finally, she had become just what he said she was: helpless. Somehow, she would manage to drag herself to the private mass said by Father Cavanaugh for the family at the White House on Saturday, but by that time she wasn't at all well.

At the service, Joan was too distraught to do anything but stare ahead, as if in a trance, on the verge of collapse. Ted didn't seem to want to have anything to do with her at the White House. To him she was apparently an embarrassment. While Jackie and Ethel, his sisters, and even his mother somehow managed to get through it all, Joan had crumpled. She wouldn't be able to attend any of the White House functions prior to the funeral or even pay tribute to Jack by visiting his coffin as it lay in state, as would everyone else in the family. After the Mass, Candy took Joan back to her Georgetown home as quickly as possible, where she would stay as though in exile, until the funeral on Monday.

In Mourning

As Air Force One carried John F. Kennedy's casket back to Washington from Dallas, his successor, Lyndon Baines Johnson, was sworn in on board as President of the United States. LBJ was under considerable pressure at this time, wondering whether or not an organized plot had been behind the death of the President, or even if such a conspiracy would also be suddenly carried out against the Vice President. Johnson was well aware that the CIA had been involved in plots to kill Castro in Cuba and Diem in Vietnam. Suspecting that Kennedy's death was the result of some form of retaliation, perhaps a Communist force coming against America, he was concerned about the United States appearing weak in the face of such an emergency. The new President was anxious to see the country move forward—or at least appear to do so—in a strong, assured manner, and made swift moves in that regard. For instance, it was Johnson's idea that a picture of him actually taking the oath be distributed to the media so that an anxious and bewildered country would know that the Constitution worked, or, as Jack Valenti, a key member of the Johnson White House staff (and today president of the Motion Picture Association of America), says, ". . . that while the light in the White House may flicker, the light just never goes out."

Though she didn't have to do so, Jackie said she wanted to be at Johnson's side during the swearing-in ceremony. "I owe it to the country," she told Kenny O'Donnell. She stood at LBJ's left, her clothes still stained with the blood of her late husband, while Lady Bird Johnson stood to his right. Twenty-seven people witnessed the swearing-in ceremony officiated by Dallas Federal Judge Sarah Hughes in the private presidential quarters of the jet. Later, Jackie would say she barely remembered any of it. Photographs of the moment show her with a blank, hollow expression.

It could be argued that John Fitzgerald Kennedy was not the best husband to Jackie Kennedy, at least based on his disregard for her feelings about his philandering with Marilyn Monroe, Mary Meyer, and the rest. But, his relationship with his wife aside, Jack is still viewed as one of the most memorable of this country's leaders, and it is not because of any of his domestic programs or foreign policies. It was really the way he ignited the American imagination, like few before him, that made Kennedy so memorable.

No doubt, he would have run again. His popularity was high. Of course, one wonders what secrets might have been revealed about Kennedy's private life during that second campaign. At the time, most Americans had no idea—and probably never would have believed it, anyway—that Kennedy's personal life was in such disarray. What Jackie was going through as a result of her husband's personal choices also remained a closely guarded secret. Now, the challenge ahead for young Jackie Kennedy would be to go on with her life, though to some she seemed beaten before she even began. "I want you to know that I consider that my life is over," she wrote to Ben Bradlee shortly after the assassination. "And I will spend the rest of it waiting for it really to be over."

During the loneliest time of night before the funeral, the hours just before dawn, Jackie thrashed in her bed unable to sleep, in spite of the massive doses of tranquilizers administered by her doctor. Impulsively, she sprung out of bed and fervently wrote on her pale blue stationery an impassioned letter to Jack, probably as a way of releasing the fiery emotions burning inside her. She addressed the letter to "My Darling Jack," and went on to write about the sense of loss that was only just beginning, and about her deep love for him.

Soon she began crying, but she kept on writing, her tears blotting the stationery. In page after page she scrawled about Caroline and John Jr., about Patrick, and about their marriage and what it had meant in her life.

Earlier in the evening she had asked the children to do the same, marching into the playroom and saying, "You must write a letter to Daddy now and tell him how much you love him." In block letters Caroline wrote, "Dear Daddy, We're all going to miss you. Daddy, I love you very much, Caroline." John Jr., not old enough to write, simply scribbled on a piece of paper.

The following morning Jackie slipped the letters, along with a set of cuff links she had given him, into the President's coffin, which was lying in the East Wing. Bobby added a PT-109 tie pin and an engraved set of rosaries to the items Jackie placed in the casket. Jackie continued to stare at her dead husband, stroking her hair. Then a Secret Service man, realizing what Jackie wanted, brought Jackie a pair of scissors and she clipped a lock of hair from her husband's corpse.

On Monday, November 25, 1963, the United States mourned the death of its President, John F. Kennedy. Kennedy's casket was carried on the very same gun wagon caisson that had carried the body of Abraham Lincoln. In fact, when planning it, Jackie had patterned the funeral after Lincoln's. It seemed appropriate. Both Kennedy and Lincoln had captured the imagination of their fellow Americans, firing up the conscience of humanity through words and deeds, meeting the emotional needs of their constituents. Both were struck down while at the height of their persuasive power.

Jackie approached Jack's funeral with the same fierce loyalty and dedication with which she approached all her activities during the Kennedy administration, from the restoration of the White House to the planning of her celebrated wardrobe. A riderless horse with stirrups reversed walked alongside the carriage. Behind it strode the First Lady, a model of self-control and dignity.

Like some beautiful, ancient Greek heroine Jackie would become immortalized in a national tragedy. The meticulous manner by which she planned the funeral created images that were seared into the minds of a generation and of generations to come—the serene and composed widow holding the hands of her small children walking on either side of her; later, Jackie, followed by Bobby and Ted and an array of world leaders, walking erect and poised behind the carriage carrying her husband's coffin, her stoic face covered by a black translucent veil. The nation was pierced by the gesture of the slain President's little son saluting the casket, gently urged on by his young mother. It was an image that would be constantly broadcast thirty-six years later when, tragically, John Kennedy Jr. would follow his father in unexpected, violent death.

It really was her public strength and impeccable dignity that had enabled Jackie Kennedy to help America endure one of the saddest and longest weekends it has ever known. Regal and poised, her resolve held the country together. "During those four endless days," Ted Kennedy would say thirty-one years later at Jackie's own funeral, "she held us together as a family and as a country. In large part because of her, we could grieve and then go on."

Inside, however, Jacqueline Kennedy was shattered. Those close to her often took note of the way the full extent of the horror she had experienced would suddenly overwhelm her. One witness, an assistant to Sargent Shriver, recalled his observation of Jackie at a small Mass for the President's friends, family, and servants preceding the television funeral: "She takes the five steps to the casket and quickly kneels down, almost falling on the edge of the catafalque. Her hands hang loosely at her sides. She lays her forehead against the side of the casket. She picks up the edge of the flag and kisses it. Slowly she starts to rise. Then, without warning, Mrs. Kennedy begins crying. Her slender frame is rocked by sobs, and she slumps back down. Her knees give way. Bobby Kennedy moves up quickly, puts one arm around her waist. He stands there with her a moment and just lets her cry."

Somehow, the night of the funeral, Jackie and other family members managed to celebrate John Jr.'s third birthday. After the party, Jackie and Bobby visited Jack's graveside at Arlington National Cemetery. Followed by Secret Service agents, they approached the burial site slowly, Jackie supported by Bobby, who seemed to hold her up by her elbow. The two knelt by the grave and said a silent prayer. Then they walked away from Jack, though he would never be far from their hearts. A bouquet of lilies of the valley was left at his grave by his wife.

Tea with Lady Bird

The day after the funeral Jackie stayed at the White House, dwelling on all that had occurred and writing emotional, heart-wrenching letters to those whose support meant so much. Also on her calendar was a date for tea at 3 P.M. with Lady Bird Johnson in the private family sitting room on the second floor, called the West Hall.

"Lady Bird had that kind of warm, Southern hospitality and personality that Jackie needed at this time," recalls Secret Service agent Joseph Paolella, who observed the two women from time to time. "She was nurturing during a time when Jackie was in such a state of shock. As a woman, she understood what Jackie was going through. In fact, I used to wonder how a guy like LBJ could get such a sweet wife, because he wasn't a real nice guy."

Liz Carpenter, Lady Bird Johnson's press secretary, recalls, "People were always asking Lady Bird if she and Jackie were good friends. Lady Bird felt awkward about being so presumptuous as to say that they were, so she asked me to talk to Letitia Baldrige about it. 'How should we answer the question?' I asked. 'Why, say yes, of course,' Letitia told me. 'She is a close friend, because Jackie doesn't have many close friends. Definitely say yes.'"

In some ways Lady Bird thought of Jackie as a daughter and was always available to her for emotional support whenever she needed it. She saw a side of Jackie that most people wouldn't have dreamed existed. For instance, it was known by all that the sophisticated and worldly Jackie "simply adored" (as she once put it) expensive jewels, but Lady Bird liked to tell of the adolescent enthusiasm Jackie would display when gifted with new pieces. For Christmas 1961, Lady Bird gave Jackie a black pearl ring. In her promptly written thank-you note on the day after the holiday, Jackie wrote that, in her view, the black pearl "was always the most romantic, exotic piece of jewelry!" Like a schoolgirl she gushed, "I never imagined that I would be fortunate enough to have such a jewel!"

Now, just two years later, such simple frivolity was the farthest thing from their minds. Both women were dressed in simple, black, knee-length dresses, Jackie in matching high heels and Lady Bird in more "sensible" shoes. Jackie wore no jewelry; her face seemed drained of all color. Looking painfully thin, she seemed barely able to walk without leaning against the furniture she would pass.

"You really don't look well, dear," Lady Bird told her.

"I don't feel well, either," Jackie said. "In fact, I never will again, Lady Bird. I'm sure of it."

"Have you eaten?"

"Why should I bother?" Jackie answered. "Who cares what happens to me now?"

The new First Lady didn't know what to say to her predecessor. She herself was suffering from persistent chills and insomnia, all the result of being so affected by JFK's gruesome murder. For Lady Bird, it was as if the tragic images had been indelibly etched into her consciousness. For instance, immediately after the shooting, as she and Lyndon Johnson were being rushed into the hospital, Lady Bird took a quick look over her shoulder to see if she could find Jack. "I saw in the President's car a bundle of pink, just like a drift of blossoms, lying on the backseat," she recalled. "It was Mrs. Kennedy, lying over the President's body."

According to a family member of Lady Bird's (who would speak only under a condition of anonymity as long as the former First Lady is alive), it was during the course of their tea together that afternoon that Jackie and Lady Bird had their first and only discussion about their husbands' philandering, veiled as the topic was during their talk.

Like Jackie, Lady Bird also knew that her husband had mistresses over the years. (The competitive LBJ would become incensed when he would hear about Kennedy's female "conquests." He would bang his fist on the table and say, "Why I had more women by accident than he ever had by design.")

According to what Lady Bird later told her relative, Jackie seemed as if she needed some confirmation that Jack truly loved her. "Know that our husbands have loved us greatly, Jackie, but in their own time and in their own way," the older and more experienced woman told her.

"Why, I wonder, have we put up with so much?" Jackie wanted to know.

Grabbing Jackie by the hand, Lady Bird no doubt looked at her with warm, understanding eyes as she said, "Because we know that thing that only women like us can understand. Great men have great flaws."

Then, while Lyndon met with Alliance for Progress members in the East Wing, Jackie and her successor walked through the White House discussing furniture and staff members. All the while, Jackie passed on helpful tips, patiently explained her work, and reminisced about her days there with Jack. Lady Bird was moved by Jackie's passion for the place, and remembered "an element of steel and stamina somewhere within her to keep her going."

The French chef was excellent, Jackie told Lady Bird, but the food he made was too rich. "Jack never likes those rich foods," she said, reminding Lady Bird of JFK's weak stomach. Lady Bird noticed that Jackie referred to her husband in the present tense.

As they walked into the Yellow Room—Jackie's favorite, where the Cezannes were hanging—Lady Bird noticed a folded flag on the table, from the funeral. It was intended for Joseph Kennedy; Jackie would be bringing it to Jack's father later in the week.

"Leaving here is the hardest thing for me to do," Jackie told her.

"Please stay as long as you like," Lady Bird told her. "We want you here for as long as you want to be here."

Jackie asked Lady Bird if the White House school on the third floor—where Caroline and twenty other youngsters of White House employees attended kindergarten and the first grade—could stay open until the semester's end. She said she didn't want to disrupt Caroline's education. After the semester, the school would be moved to the British Embassy. Lady Bird was happy to oblige.

"Don't be frightened of this house," Jackie told Lady Bird before they parted company. "Some of the happiest years of my marriage were spent here."

After the new First Lady departed, Jackie sat down and wrote a long letter to Lyndon Johnson to thank him for his involvement in Jack's funeral.

Jackie and Bobby had led a march from the White House to St. Matthew's Cathedral, where the funeral service was held. President Johnson overruled the Secret Service's wishes that he not participate in the march saying, "I'd rather give my life than be afraid to give it." He walked behind the casket, and Jackie was moved by the gesture.

"Thank you for walking yesterday, behind Jack," she wrote on blue onionskin paper on her first night in the White House alone, after the funeral. In the letter that, many years later, she agreed to have displayed in the Lyndon Johnson Library, she noted that she realized that Johnson had probably been surrounded by people who were concerned that he should take such a risk, and that she was grateful that he had been unmoved by their wishes.

Previously, on the night of the assassination, Johnson had written letters to John Jr. and Caroline, telling them of Jack's importance to the country, and recognizing their deep, personal loss. In her own note to the new President, Jackie now mentioned how much Caroline and John Jr. "loved" LBJ, and said that she believed his letters to her children would have great sentimental value to them in the future.

"And most of all, Mr. President," she continued, "thank you for the way you have always treated me. The way you and Lady Bird have always been to me before, when Jack was alive, and now, as President."

Jackie then mentioned that she had gleaned from the history that she'd read since first going into the White House that the relationship between the President and vice-presidential families was often a strained one. She was grateful that, in her view, this had never been the case between the Kennedys and the Johnsons. She considered the four of them—herself, Jack, Lyndon, and Lady Bird—to be close friends, she wrote. Before signing off, Jackie Kennedy reiterated her admiration for Lady Bird Johnson, the new First Lady. In her estimation, she wrote, "I always thought . . . that Lady Bird should be First Lady," and then she cited Mrs. Johnson's dependability, loyalty, and eagerness to take on new challenges. "I love her very much," Jackie concluded.

Thanksgiving, 1963

Wednesday, November 27, 1963—it was just three days after the funeral and tomorrow would be Thanksgiving. How could anyone think of being thankful at a time such as this?

"It was as if such a thing was unthinkable," Joan Kennedy would say. "Thankful? For what? Jack was dead. There was nothing to be thankful for, or at least that's how we felt."

Ethel agreed. In an interview, she once remembered, "That was the worst Thanksgiving of all. We had always been a grateful family with so much to be thankful for, but that year it was impossible to find gratitude."

Rose Kennedy had returned to the Hyannis Port compound two days after the funeral to be with Joe. Ted and Joan arrived shortly thereafter. Then Pat, Jean, the then-pregnant Eunice, and their husbands showed up. Somehow, they decided, they would have Thanksgiving dinner together, even though a darkness that was almost palpable seemed to envelope the entire household. It was as if Joseph and Rose's home had been enfolded by a shroud of death.

Where there had once been optimism and hope, now there was hopelessness and despair. This kind of negativity seemed incongruous in the Kennedy home, a place where high spirits and "vig-ah" had always been the dominating forces, but things were different now. Jack was gone. The presidential flag, which was always illuminated by floodlights at night, was flying at half-mast in front of Joseph and Rose's white clapboard home.

Inside, everyone was emotionally exhausted and seemed deflated. Joan remembered, "We wanted to pull it together, somehow. Ted tried to be jovial. People tried to laugh. The Kennedys always tried to rise above the worst of circumstances. I don't know if it was healthy though. In fact, I think maybe it wasn't. I know I had so many feelings bottled up, afraid to let them go, let them out, because I didn't want to be the only blithering idiot in the bunch, you know?"

As the Kennedys tried to talk among themselves, the servants gossiped about the funeral in order to ease the tension. Chauffeur Frank Saunders marveled to Rita Dallas about the fact that Rose had worn the black dress she had been saving for Joseph's funeral. "Not only did she expect him to die," Frank said of Rose, his voice a hushed whisper, "she even bought the dress. How awful that she had to wear it for her son's funeral."

Bobby couldn't manage to make it home for this holiday. He was so distraught that he took his family to Hobe Sound, Florida. Ethel was concerned because he would go for hours without speaking to her; rather, he would stare straight ahead and burst into tears unexpectedly. Ethel and Joan agreed that Bobby and Ted needed to spend more time together after these morbid holidays. "They're all they have left now," Ethel said, ignoring the fact that there were other family members, but perhaps referring to the fact that two Kennedy brothers were now gone, leaving only two more.

No one expected Jackie to be at the compound for this holiday, so when the telephone rang and Rose was told that Jackie had just landed at the airport, she couldn't believe her ears. "Jackie's here!" she exclaimed. "Oh my God! What will we say to her?"

The room became quiet as all the Kennedys silently wondered how they would ever be able to comfort Jackie and how she would react to them. She had been through an ordeal that was more than any of them could imagine, and that she still wanted to be with them for Thanksgiving dinner demonstrated her continued allegiance to the family.

"It's family," Ted reminded everyone. "She is family, still. Thank God she's coming."

Joan agreed. "Yes," she said. "Thank God for that, at least."

Kennedy intimate Chuck Spalding, who went to Harvard with Jack, sank into one of the comfortable stuffed chairs. "Oh, man," he said, sighing. "Jesus Christ almighty."

It was thought that Jackie would probably go straight to her and Jack's home on Squaw Island and not be seen until Thursday, if even then.

But there was a knock on the door at about 8 P.M. Ted answered it. It was Jackie. She looked frail in tight black Capri slacks and a gray pullover sweater. Her hair was combed back behind her ears.

Jackie's dark eyes widened when she saw Ted. "Oh, Teddy," she said, her voice faltering. The two of them pressed each other close. Then Jackie turned and hugged Joan tightly.

"Joan," she began. "I want to tell you everything. I must tell you. . . . It was awful, just awful. . . . We haven't had a chance to talk. . . . In all of this time, we haven't even had a single chance to talk."

"No, you mustn't say a single word about it," Joan said, tears falling from her eyes. "You must try to forget it all now. Come in and sit down, now."

"My heart went out to her, standing there, surrounded by people but still seeming so alone," Joan once recalled. "I wanted to be there for her but I didn't know how. I felt a desperation about it, an inadequacy, I guess. I felt that if the tables had been turned, Jackie would have known just what to do. And I wanted to kick myself because I didn't."

"Where's Grandpa?" Jackie wanted to know. "I have to see him."

Rose entered the room at that point and rushed over to Jackie, hugging her warmly. She suggested that Jackie not see Joe at that moment, perhaps feeling that Joseph was not strong enough to see her—or maybe even suspecting that Jackie would break into pieces at the sight of him. However, Jackie was adamant, so much so that she became upset when Rose, Ted, and Joan began to insist that she not see Joe.

"But I must," she said, displaying a slight show of temper. "I'll rest after I see Grandpa. Now, please!"

Eunice and Jean took Jackie by her arms and tried to guide her into the living room.

"You poor, poor dear, you must rest," Eunice told her.

Jackie broke free, explaining that she had told Maud Shaw to take John Jr. and Caroline to her home specifically so that she could be alone with Joe. "And I'm going upstairs," she said. "Enough of this."

"The scene downstairs got so loud that Mr. Kennedy again motioned for me to find out what was actually happening," said Rita Dallas who was upstairs with Joe during the fracas. "Reluctantly, I went out into the hall and stood there for a moment, trying to decide what I should do. Just then, the First Lady came running up the stairs, alone. I suppose I felt she would carry a horrible and visible mark of her tragedy, but there were no changes in her at first glance."

Jackie ran down the hall toward the nurse, saying that she needed to see Joe. Jackie stood before Rita, holding a furled flag. She hugged the flag and, with tears in her eyes, she gave it to the nurse, telling her that her intention was for Joe to have the flag.

"It was Jack's," she said, explaining that she wanted Rita to give it to Joe after she was gone. "I can't do it," Jackie said. "I just can't."

Jackie and Rita then went into Joe's room, and as Jackie approached Joe's bed, Rita put the flag on the dresser, behind some papers and books. Jackie sat down on a footstool next to Joe, and took his hand.

"Jack is gone," she told the old man, "and things will never be the same, Grandpa. Never."

Caressing his deformed hand, Jackie asked Joe if he wanted to hear what had occurred. He nodded. She then unfolded the entire story, from the time she and Jack arrived in Dallas, through the grisly murder, all the way to the funeral. The telling of this story may have been therapeutic to her; Rita Dallas said that Jackie didn't leave out a single, painful, even gruesome detail.

After she finished, Jackie kissed Joe on the forehead and explained that she was exhausted and needed to rest. Joe stared at the ceiling, tears in his eyes.

"You know how I feel," Jackie said, "and how I'll always feel. Don't you?"

She squeezed his hand, pulled his covers up to his chin, and turned away. Then she left the room and walked down the hallway as Rita Dallas watched, "and I have never seen a woman who looked so alone," said the nurse. (In the middle of the night, Joseph's niece, Ann Gargan, decided to cover the old man with the flag. When he woke up and found that his dead son's honorary flag was draped over him, Joseph screamed out so loudly the family thought he was having a seizure. It took hours to calm him down.)

When she got downstairs, Jackie hugged everyone warmly. As she stood talking to Rose and Joan, she noticed Jack's favorite chair in its usual place in his mom's home, a large bath towel wrapped around its ladder rungs so that they might ease the pain in his back. Jackie went over to the chair and touched it, gently. Then, her eyes brimming with tears, she left as quickly as possible.

Jackie spent the night at her home with her children and their nanny, Maud Shaw. The next day she did not emerge for Thanksgiving dinner. Instead, Maud Shaw arrived at Rose's home with John Jr.

and Caroline in tow, explaining that Jackie would not be coming. "She can't bear it," the nanny explained. "She is just much too distraught. She didn't sleep a wink. Instead, she cried all night."

After dinner, Joan drove to Jackie's Squaw Island house with a plate of turkey, cranberries, stuffing, and sweet potatoes that had been fixed by Rose. A strong, cool wind blew in from Nantucket Sound; a roll of thunder signaled an approaching storm.

Ten Secret Service agents stood guard on Jackie's property—the first time a President's widow was given round-the-clock protection. There was a checkpoint set up at the bottom of the hill that led up to the house, which in itself was not unusual, as well as agents roaming the area. It still wasn't known, after all, if Jack's assassination had been a communist plot, or some other conspiracy, and whether or not the lives of Jackie and her children were in danger. After identifying herself to a guard who shone a blinding flashlight in her face, Joan was let through an opening in a barricade. She proceeded up the driveway, got out of the car, and walked to Jackie's front door. She rang. She knocked. She rang again. But Jackie never answered the door.

Jackie's Camelot

The former First Lady spent Thanksgiving evening alone in a melancholy mood, writing letters and making telephone calls to people she felt particularly close to as a result of the tragedy. The murder of her husband would define a new Jackie in many ways, one of which would be the emergence of her true vulnerability. Prior to the assassination, most people really didn't know what she was thinking. If she had problems—and she obviously did—she handled them in her solitude, in her own very discreet way. She wasn't the type to whine, complain, or cry on the shoulders of friends and relatives during difficult times. But after the shock of Jack's death, it was as if a reservoir holding back Jackie's raw emotions was unleashed. From it came forth hurt, pain, and anguish, as well as feelings of love and appreciation. It was a different Jackie who would allow all of her friends to bear witness to her emotional turmoil.

To Nellie Connally, who was sitting in the front seat of the car that carried John and Jackie on that fateful day, she wrote, "The thing I'm glad about is that on that awful ride to the hospital we were two women who really loved their husbands, those two brave men."

She telephoned the new President Johnson and Lady Bird.

"I'm so sad," she told Lyndon. "But I'm here with all of Jack's things. And it's helping. In an odd way."

LBJ asked if she planned to join the family for dinner.

"It's best for me to be alone now," she said.

The Johnsons were moved to hear from Jackie on this sad Thanksgiving. In a letter he wrote to her [on December 1], which he had delivered by messenger from the White House, LBJ would marvel at her strength.

"How could you possibly find that extra ounce of strength to call us Thanksgiving evening?" he asked her. "You have been magnificent and have won a warm place in the heart of history. I only wish things could be different," he wrote. "That I didn't have to be here. But the almighty has willed differently, and now Lady Bird and I need your help. You have for now and for always our warm, warm love."

Although it seemed that Jack at times had treated Jackie callously during their marriage, it was by marrying this man that many of her dreams and ambitions came true. It was through her marriage to Jack that she became the woman she had always dreamed of being. In fact, it was as if by marrying, these two ambitious people coming together created one whole. With his political savvy and her class, style, and culture, they were the perfect match. Both had created images of themselves that they projected to the world, and those images would have impact on our culture even after both were gone. Without Jack, it was as if Jackie was only half a person, or at least that's how it felt to her once she realized she had to face life alone.

Although in the years following Jack's death, Jackie sometimes may have had a tendency to romanticize their relationship, she was always aware of his infidelities, particularly his affair with Marilyn Monroe. However, she had long before accepted this flaw as part of his character and continued to love him in spite of it. She knew only too well that she too had her flaws, and he had accepted her despite them.

With an eye on Jack's place in history, Jackie granted an interview with writer Theodore White to put her relationship with her husband, and what they had achieved together, in a glowing, warm light. The journalist, who was working on a story about the assassination for *Life* magazine, was driven by limousine from New York to Hyannis Port the day after Thanksgiving. To White, she said she envisioned Jack as a little boy, reading about the Knights of the Round Table, reading Marlborough, molding himself into a great hero to whom, one hoped, other young boys would one day look for inspiration. She told White that she wished to "rescue" Jack's memory from the "bitter people" who would one day write about him. Some skeptics would later feel that what she really wanted was to ensure that the inevitable revelations of Jack's many secrets would seem sacrilegious upon their discovery, and that one way to do that would be to mythologize him. "Jack's life had more to do with myth, magic, legend, saga, and story than with political theory or political science," she added. She also told him that "men are such a combination of good and bad."

Spinning a golden mythology, Jackie carefully laid out her Camelot tale to the rapt writer. To Jackie—as to many people back then and, certainly, to a lot more in years to come when this Camelot analogy took hold—the image of her husband was youth, glamour, vigor, and idealism personified. "I want to say this one thing," she told White. "It's been almost an obsession with me. All I keep thinking about is this line from a musical comedy. At night before we'd go to sleep, Jack liked to play some records. His back hurt, the floor was so cold, so I'd get out of bed at night and play it for him, when it was so cold. And the song he loved most came at the very end of this record, the last scene of *Camelot*. Sad Camelot. 'Don't let it be forgot, that once there was a spot, for one brief shining moment that was known as Camelot.'"

Jack did enjoy the original cast recording of Alan Jay Lerner and Frederick Loewe's show. (Starring Richard Burton as King Arthur and Julie Andrews as Guenevere, the Broadway show *Camelot* opened at the Majestic Theater on December 3, 1960, about a month after Jack was elected. The reviewer for the *Wall Street Journal* said that costar Robert Goulet as Lancelot had a "Kennedy-like mop of hair.") Jack had gone to prep school and college with lyricist Alan Jay Lerner, and Jackie thought it would be interesting if her husband had the opportunity to meet composer Frederick Loewe. So she invited Loewe to the White House for an informal dinner. After the meal, and much to

Jackie's delight, Loewe sat at the piano and played selections from his and Lerner's shows *My Fair Lady*, *Gigi*, *Brigadoon*, *Paint Your Wagon*, and, finally, at Jack's special request, *Camelot*.

"There'll never be another Camelot again," Jackie told White, wistfully. Her choice for an analogy was actually a good one, for the Camelot story is a fable about how idealism and right can endure in spite of human frailty and envy, even after the flawed heroes of the story are destroyed. White didn't mind Jackie's wanting him to incorporate the Camelot analogy in his story, considering what she'd been through. However, during a telephone call White placed to the *Life* magazine editorial offices, the editors balked at what they saw as a trivialization of presidential history. Jackie stood her ground, though, and insisted that the Camelot references remain. "So the epitaph of the Kennedy administration became Camelot," Theodore White would write, "a magic moment in American history when gallant men danced with beautiful women, when great deeds were done, when artists, writers and poets met at the White House, and the barbarians behind the walls were held back."

The Camelot mystique would actually live on long after Jack's death. In fact, the romantic notion of Camelot would go on to encompass the full Kennedy experience in the 1960s, the family's greatest time of power and influence—and high drama—when it seemed that every waking moment of those who were a part of the house of Kennedy was of the most potent interest to the world at large.

"Let It All Out"

In the midst of all the postassassination turmoil in her life, Jackie Kennedy had gone ahead with plans for the birthday parties of her children. Since they were born in the same week three years apart, it was decided that it would be easier to combine their celebrations. John's earlier party (the evening of the funeral) had been marked by so much sadness that Jackie thought it only fair for him to have another with his sister. Concentrating on the planning of such a party would be a much-needed distraction for Jackie, but more important, she wanted the children to be as happy as possible during this dark time. Already the loss of their father had robbed them of so much; both children were emotionally devastated, reacting to the news in their own way.

At the direction of Jackie's mother, Maud Shaw was given the unhappy and difficult task of telling the children that their father had died. It was feared that they would hear the news from elsewhere before Jackie's return from Dallas if Shaw didn't act quickly.

"I can't help crying, Caroline, because I have some very sad news to tell you," the nanny began. "Your father has gone to look after Patrick. Patrick was so lonely in heaven. He didn't know anyone there. Now he has the best friend anyone could have."

On hearing the news, Caroline cried so violently that the nanny feared she might choke. Later when Shaw told John Jr. that his father had gone to heaven, the uncomprehending three-year-old asked, "Did he take his big plane with him?"

Shaw couldn't help smiling. "Yes, John," she replied. "He probably did."

"I wonder when he's coming back," the bewildered child then asked.

The party was held in the kindergarten that Jackie had instituted in the White House solarium for her daughter and her friends. "The first year, it had been a cooperative nursery school with mothers, and Mrs. Kennedy included, taking turns as teacher," recalled Jackie's secretary, Pam Turnure, of Jackie's "schoolhouse." "Their school life would be integrated into what was going on in the White House. If there was going to be a ceremony on the lawn, then part of the day's activities would be to watch from the balcony."

John and Caroline had eight childhood friends each—including a few of their cousins—seated at two tables, with two separate birthday cakes.

Jackie showed up at the noisy little affair dressed simply in a black cocktail dress, without jewelry. She appeared thinner, her shoulders, though, seemed somehow broader.

Maud Shaw remembered: "She still looked pale and drawn, but smiled for the first time since the tragedy hit her. She chuckled aloud when John took a huge breath to blow out his three candles, but the sadness was still heavy in her eyes."

Later, Ethel, just back from her trip with Bobby, stopped by the party to give each child a wrapped gift and to pick up two of her children who were in attendance. In spite of Jackie's smile, Ethel immediately recognized the pain on her face, so clearly visible in the newly etched lines on her forehead. With some trepidation, Ethel approached her.

There had obviously always been a certain uneasiness between the two Kennedy wives. The boisterous, wisecracking Ethel had watched Jackie follow her in marriage into the family, and stood aside as she was eclipsed by the reserved and elegant younger woman. But Ethel saw her now not as a woman to envy but rather as one to pity because of the tragic turn of events in her life. In years gone by, Ethel had been stoic in her reaction to tragedy. Jackie recalled that even when her parents were killed, she seemed unaffected, until Jackie made a point of telling her how sorry she was for her loss. But the enormity of the tragedy that had befallen the Kennedy family was enough to break even the unflappable Ethel.

"Oh, Jackie, I don't know what to say to you," Ethel emotionally told her, in front of Maud Shaw and the others, including the kindergarten teacher, Jacqueline Hirsh. "I just wish I knew what to say, or how to help you. You know that Jack is with God, don't you?"

Ethel realized that Jackie didn't have her faith. Jackie was a Roman Catholic who felt that religion was really at its best with rituals. She had gone to confession after Jack's murder, but didn't know what to confess. All she wanted to know from the priest was why God would have done "something so terrible as to take my husband from me." Perhaps Ethel asked that question because she was at a loss for anything else to say that might bring her grieving sister-in-law some comfort.

"I know," Jackie murmured back. She smiled genuinely at the other Mrs. Kennedy, visibly touched that Ethel would want to pass on to her the one thing that had never failed to help her through her own troubles—her unwavering faith. She told Ethel that they would "always be family," even if they did have their differences.

Upon hearing Jackie's reaffirmation of familial ties, Ethel let loose a torrent of words and tears so uncharacteristic of her it stunned everyone in the room. It was all "too terrible," she cried. She didn't know how she was going to go on with her life, and feared that Bobby couldn't go on, either. "Everything has changed," she said.

Ethel allowed herself to go on for several minutes before taking a deep breath of resolve. "But we just have to be strong, Jackie. We have no choice but to be strong, do we?"

Jackie nodded. "For them," she agreed, motioning toward the table of laughing tots.

The two women embraced, with Ethel burying her head in Jackie's shoulder. Then she fled from the room, so upset that she forgot to take her two children with her.

Jackie, left alone in the corner, began to cry. She looked around for her purse, but before long Maud Shaw approached with a handkerchief. "I was doing fine until Ethel came," Jackie said with an embarrassed smile. "Now look at me. What a sight." Both women began laughing.

After Ethel left, Joan arrived with Eunice and Pat. Eunice and Pat immediately walked over to Jackie, who was still sitting at the table alone, and began talking quietly with her. Joan, however, stood in a corner watching her children Kara, four, and Teddy Jr., two, who were playing with the other children.

When Jackie noticed Joan standing awkwardly alone, she excused herself from Pat and Eunice and went to her. The two embraced and, almost immediately, Joan began to sob. Jackie, who had just been through her own crying jag following Ethel's, appeared strong and tearless.

"It's all right, Joan," Jackie whispered. "Let it all out. Let every bit of it out."

Then, still embracing her sister-in-law, Jackie gently patted Joan on the back as Joan cried softly.

Aftermath

After the funeral for John Fitzgerald Kennedy, while the nation continued to mourn its slain President, the government began to resume its normal operations. It had been the idea of Secretary of State Dean Rusk and Secretary of Defense Robert McNamara to move Johnson into the Oval Office quickly in order to get down to the business of running the country. However, Bobby asked LBJ to stay out of the Oval Office until at least three days after the funeral. "And there was Jack's rocking chair," Ethel later recalled ruefully, "upside down in the hallway, ready to be moved out."

Jackie had no interest in any of the inner-office workings of the Presidency at this time. In the months following the tragedy, her moods swung wildly from anger to hopelessness to resolve and back to anger. Whereas she once chose her words with care, now they tumbled out indiscriminately. "I never had or wanted a life of my own," Jackie said publicly at the time, a statement that really was not true but did demonstrate her level of confusion.

She had grown so accustomed to being First Lady that having to relinquish that life so unexpectedly left Jackie feeling utterly lost and without direction. Always a contemplative person, though, she instinctively knew that she had to get a grip on herself and think about her future, if only for the sake of her children. But in the silence of her heart, she must have also realized that her life as a president's wife had left her unprepared for her desolate existence as his widow and single mother of his children. Also, the tremendous guilt she felt at having lived through the Dallas experience, while her husband died, was almost overwhelming.

"Why, oh why, did I survive?" she asked Kenny O'Donnell. "Why Jack instead of me? Why wasn't I killed?"

As Jackie Kennedy struggled with memories of her husband's brutal murder, she worried she would now be doomed to spend her life in the public eye as a living, perpetual reminder of the nightmare—a tragic symbol of a nation's inconsolable grief. She might have been able to accept that fate, but would her children ever be able to exist with such a shroud of death over their lives? Jackie wanted them to have as normal a life as possible, and she would do what she could to shield them from public scrutiny and curiosity, yet she knew that circumstances would probably make this an impossible task. "Everywhere I go, I am his wife," she said. "With his kids. Seeing us in person somehow brings him back to life for them."

While John was too young to fully comprehend what had happened in Dallas—he just knew that Daddy was "in heaven"—six-year-old Caroline not only understood it fully but was also deeply affected by it.

She would vehemently spit out the word "assassinated" with great, and very adult, anger. Whereas she was once a happy, carefree, and precocious child, Caroline became withdrawn, sullen, and troubled in the weeks after her father's murder. Jackie, horrified to find her daughter walking about with her fists clenched, decided to consult Erik Erikson, a celebrated child psychoanalyst and author of the then-popular book *Childhood and Society*.

After the scholarly, gray-haired Erikson, a Harvard professor, counseled the two children on several occasions, Jackie was happy with their progress. It would take years, though, for Caroline to accept the fact that her father had been senselessly murdered.

So distraught was Jackie at this time that she actually considered giving John Jr. and Caroline to Bobby and Ethel to raise for a short time. What kind of mother could she be, she reasoned, under the circumstances? She couldn't even care for her own emotional needs, she reasoned, how would she care for her children's? She felt inadequate as a parent. The thought that she would probably be alone for many years to come made her feel even more helpless and desperate.

It had actually been specified in Jackie's 1960 will that if anything happened to her and Jack, their children should be raised by Joan and Ted (further testimony of Jackie's strong feelings for Joan because she certainly didn't seem to have much of a rapport with Ted at this time). However, after the President's assassination Jackie perhaps realized that Joan was in no shape to care for Caroline and John Jr., even if just for a short time.

Jackie and Ethel had a number of conversations about the possibility of John Jr. and Caroline moving into Hickory Hill, if only for a year. After that time, if she was able to do so, Jackie would take her children back and they would attempt to start a new life together without Jack. But then Jackie changed her mind.

The reality of the chaos that was Hickory Hill—no order, no discipline, a lot of people coming and going, children screaming and hollering from morning to night—came flooding back to her. She had never felt comfortable with the way Ethel reared her family, a rowdy fend-for-yourself kind of environment. In the end, with Jackie's unyielding sense of propriety, she could not envision her children being raised at Hickory Hill as part of what she viewed as practically a platoon from a guerrilla army.

Besides, she now saw herself as the chief protector of what used to be called "the sanctity of the home." After carefully considering the idea, she realized it was unthinkable to give her children away, even for a year. She loved them too much.

Of course, Jackie Kennedy wasn't the only one torn apart by the President's assassination. Jack had been the center of the family, adored by everyone. His career had been their life's work. Now that he was gone, none of the Kennedys—sisters-in-law Ethel and Joan included—would ever be the same. As well as the overwhelming sense of grief they felt, for they loved Jack dearly, there was also an aching for something they all knew they would miss: the joy of the White House experience in the way Jack and Jackie had created it. They might try to have joy in the future—and they would have plenty of good times elsewhere—but it would never be exactly the same as it was during the Kennedy administration. Jack and Jackie had been at the center of a crazy, golden time for everyone. But it was behind them now. As a result, the family's infrastructure was knocked off-kilter. Joan's and Ethel's husbands, Jack's brothers Ted and Bobby, found themselves trapped in their own private hells because of their older brother's murder, and their wives were powerless to assist them in any way.

Ted's deep sorrow seemed to find its outlet in promiscuity. More than ever, he also found solace in the bottle, drowning his misery in alcohol.

Unfortunately, Joan's grief also plummeted her into a deep, dark depression. She had great affection for Jack and could not comprehend such violence. She was also concerned about Jackie, her niece Caroline, and nephew John Jr. Soon she also found herself relying on alcohol to get through her long days and endless nights. Kennedy intimates were concerned that Joan often seemed to be a bit dazed at social gatherings—even those during the day—and whisperings began to be heard that she was drinking too much. "It was true," said her good friend John Braden. "I do believe that the assassination pushed Joan over the edge in terms of her drinking. That was the turning point. Ted became more difficult, she was wracked with grief and sorrow, and she began to drink."

While there was enough suffering to go around, perhaps nobody felt the agony as deeply as Bobby Kennedy. He feared that one of his campaigns—whether against organized crime, union racketeers, Castro, or other dark forces—had brought about the assassination by retaliation. "I thought they would get one of us," Bobby had said on the afternoon of the assassination. "But I thought it would be me."

Bobby's aide, John Seigenthaler, recalled that his emotional torment was so deep that he took on the look of a man in physical pain, "almost as if he were on the rack or that he had a toothache or that he had a heart attack . . . it was pain and it showed itself as being pain."

"He was virtually nonfunctioning," said Pierre Salinger. "He would walk for hours by himself."

Jackie's cousin, John Davis, concurs. "On the day of the funeral, I had never seen such a destroyed man in my entire life as Bobby Kennedy. He could hardly hold out his hand to shake another."

Ethel didn't know how to deal with Bobby as the silent, brooding, and moody man he had become since Dallas and, as she would always do in times of crisis, she decided to rely on God to get her and her husband through this time. "If he only prayed more," she said of Bobby, "he would find solace in God's healing power."

Ethel did what she could. On a trip to New York, she would take him to see *Hello Dolly!* in hopes of cheering him up. "That did more for Bobby than anything else," she would tell writer Bill Davidson. "As he entered the theater, the sophisticated, blasé New York audience rose to its feet and applauded. The only other time I ever saw an audience do that was when Jack Kennedy went to the theater. I try to expose Bobby to that sort of thing as much as possible, but it doesn't always work."

It's interesting that Ethel would choose to have Bobby bask in public attention as a way to help him get over his grief. When he was with his sister-in-law Jackie, it was a different story. Jackie was more contemplative, shunning the public eye and encouraging Bobby to do the same thing. She and Bobby were in perfect understanding about their mutual torment and how they wanted to deal with it. As a result, the two reached out to each other for comfort and formed a special bond during this dark time. Jackie shared the loss of Jack with his brother, and he with her, in a way that didn't involve Ethel. Bobby would often visit Jackie at her Georgetown home, and the two would sit in front of her drawing room fireplace, reading poetry, sharing tears, and feeling their mutual pain and sense of loneliness. Together they would visit Jack's grave, leave flowers, and weep. He was beginning to fill a role as substitute father for Jackie's children as well.

At Easter that year, Jackie and her children vacationed in Stowe, Vermont, with Bobby.

"It was on that trip, I believe, that Bobby suggested Jackie leave Washington," said Kennedy intimate Chuck Spalding. "He felt that she was unhappy in that Georgetown fishbowl, and that she would be better off in New York. She could get lost in the city, he told her. She would find a measure of privacy there. She took his advice.

"At this time, she was concerned about her financial future. The public assumed she was rich, but she was far from it. Jack had left her about $70,000 in cash, plus all of his personal effects. There was also the interest income from two trusts, which I believe were valued at something like ten million. In all, she would have about $200,000 a year to live on. For Jackie, that wasn't much. Bobby was trying to arrange for her to receive roughly $50,000 a year from the Kennedys, but the whole thing was absurd. Jackie on a budget?"

A few weeks later, while house-hunting in New York, Jackie, Ethel, Bobby, Nancy Tuckerman (Jackie's good friend and secretary), and a large group of friends enjoyed dinner at Le Pavilion, an elegant Manhattan restaurant. The evening began with champagne, served as an aperitif, and with the first course, caviar with dry toast. The main course was *navarin d'agneau* (lamb stew), with which a red wine was served. Dessert was a *chocolat soufflé*, followed by *café filtre*, and then more champagne. The subject of Jackie's future came up.

"Well, I need to do *something*," she reasoned as she held her cup of *café filtre*, her pinkie finger extended delicately. "The Kennedys aren't going to support me forever. I have to face facts. But what can I do? Get a job? Me?"

Everybody laughed, knowing a good joke when they heard one.

PART SEVEN

Moving Out of the White House

As it would happen, it would be for her children that Jackie Kennedy would force herself to go on after Jack. "There's only one thing I can do now," she told Pierre Salinger, "save my children. They've got to grow up without thinking back at their father's murder. They've got to grow up intelligently, attuned to life in a very important way. And that's the way I want to live my life, too."

The first order of business, though, would be for her to move out of the White House, a prospect that was difficult in some respects, easy in others. She had spent so much time and energy redecorating the presidential quarters and had taken such pride in what she'd done that to abandon it now was not an easy thing for Jackie. On the other hand, everywhere she looked she was reminded of her husband. For that reason alone, she couldn't wait to leave.

The Johnsons graciously offered to allow her to stay for as long as she wished. Jackie felt it important to move on with her life quickly, yet it was also true that, as she said, "I really have no place to go." So even after Johnson took possession of the Oval Office, Jackie and the children continued to live in the family quarters. "What? *You're* the President now," the former President Harry Truman told Johnson when he heard that Jackie was still living in the White House. "Clear that bunch out of there and move your people in."

One afternoon, Jackie met with Ethel, Joan, Eunice, Pat, and three other Kennedy intimates for tea at the White House. As they chatted, Ethel offered Hickory Hill as a temporary residence for the former First Lady and her children. Jackie didn't want to offend her sister-in-law, but she had already made the decision that she didn't want her children to be raised there, and she was certain she didn't want to live there herself.

"But why?" Ethel wanted to know. "We have plenty of room."

"With ten children?" Jackie asked, her tone buoyant. Perhaps she hoped to keep the mood light.

"Oh, I'll make you so comfortable," Ethel promised, pushing forward in a determined manner. "And Bobby will love it, just wait and see."

Suddenly, Ethel became excited by the prospect. She began rattling off all the "wonderful things" she and Jackie would do together, "just like sisters." She said that Jackie could stay at Hickory Hill for as long as she wished, and that this would afford the two of them the opportunity to know and understand one another. "It's been a terrible time," Ethel told her. "Let me take care of you. You can sleep all day."

The other ladies present didn't say a word. They all realized from the frozen expression on Jackie's face that she did not want to stay at Hickory Hill. "Well, maybe Jackie would prefer her privacy right now," Joan said carefully, perhaps trying to rescue Jackie.

"Oh, Joan, only you would think a person who'd just been through what Jackie went through would want her solitude," Ethel snapped at her. "That's nuts." Ethel continued, saying that in her view Jackie needed people to surround and comfort her during this difficult time. "Lots and lots of 'em," Ethel said.

Observers say that Joan was quickly defeated. She sank into her chair, a stillness over her face.

"I absolutely do *not*," Jackie said, trying to put a finish to this discussion. "Not ever. No offense, Ethel. But I need my privacy," she explained. She further elaborated that her friends, Mr. and Mrs. Averell Harriman (he had been Jack's patrician Undersecretary of State), had offered Jackie their three-story, eleven-room colonial-style brick home at 3038 N Street in Georgetown until she could find more permanent quarters. Jackie intended to move in by the end of the first week in December, she said, and the Harrimans would move temporarily into the Georgetown Inn.

"You just don't like me very much, do you, Jackie?" Ethel suddenly asked. It was a question that seemed to have come from nowhere.

"Jackie's eyes opened wide," said a Kennedy intimate who was present at the tea. "From the expression on her face, you could see that she was surprised. Ethel truly did want Jackie to stay at Hickory Hill in the hope that it would somehow help her, and she was hurt when Jackie wouldn't even consider her proposal. One could also see that Jackie was getting angry by the way Ethel was pushing."

"Why, Ethel, how can you say that?" Jackie asked, truly concerned.

"Because it's true," Ethel responded, sadly. Looking deeply

wounded, she observed that if the two women hadn't married brothers, they wouldn't be interested in even knowing one another. They would have nothing in common, and probably wouldn't even tolerate one another. "And you know that's true, Jackie," Ethel concluded. She then rose, turned and walked out of the room leaving Jackie, Joan, Eunice, and the others with their mouths agape.

"You know something?" Jackie said, suddenly seething. "I have so much on my mind right now with everything going on. How dare she?"

"Yes," Joan said softly. "How dare she?"

Perhaps Joan was looking for a moment of agreement with Jackie. But Jackie was too angry to make Joan feel a part of things. "Ladies, please excuse me," the former First Lady said as she got up to leave.

It was clear from the outset that the Presidency under Lyndon Johnson and Lady Bird would return American politics to a style to which the country had once been accustomed—sober and staid, without the youth, vigor, and allure of the Kennedys. Even though she knew that the house on Pennsylvania Avenue would now probably take on an air of the "Old Americana" background of its present occupants rather than reflecting her own more cosmopolitan ways, Jackie still hoped that the Johnsons would at least finish the refurbishing work she had started. She was almost done with her "project" at the time of Jack's death, but there were still a few tasks left incomplete. During a lengthy telephone conversation with Lady Bird, Jackie was relieved to find that the new First Lady did want to continue with the restoration. In fact, Mrs. Johnson said she would not only establish a permanent Committee for the Preservation of the White House, of which Jackie would become a member, but would also expand the notion to the beautification of all of Washington as well. Jackie was thrilled. (Lady Bird would also, during her husband's administration, pioneer concern for the environment.)

From her home in Hyannis Port, Jackie wrote Lady Bird an eight-page letter about her hopes for the White House. "Maybe I will be remembered as the person who restored the White House, but you will be remembered as the one who preserved it, and made sure for all time it would be cared for," she wrote. She added that she had often feared that "the next President's wife [would] scrap the whole thing as she was sick to death of hearing about Jacqueline Kennedy."

Jackie further told Lady Bird not to worry about saving the group of donors and advisers known as the Fine Arts Committee, explaining that it was really just a group of her friends and acquaintances that she thought could be persuaded into giving valuable donations to the White House if she organized them into a committee they would find prestigious. She said that they had only had about two meetings anyway and that she had really done "all the work myself," along with whichever member had a special interest in the particular project she was undertaking. "I can't stand ladies' committee meetings," she explained. "They never accomplish anything."

Always one to encourage a sense of appropriateness, Jackie suggested that Lady Bird write a letter to all of the committee members showing her appreciation for their participation up until that point. Also ("MOST IMPORTANT"), she advised her to write to the head of the White House Historical Association and praise the members for their work. She suggested that Lady Bird remind them that a curator (such as Jim Ketchum—upon whom Jackie said Lady Bird could rely completely) should always be in residence in order to know which pictures need repairing, which pieces of furniture have been damaged, "and which ashtray has been stolen by a tourist!"

In her very detailed letter, she then provided a list of the members of the association and their duties. She also reminded Lady Bird that the curator of the White House is hired and paid for by the Smithsonian Institute, which should never change, she suggested, lest some future First Lady appoint as curator her "Aunt Nellie who ran a curio shop," which she feared could be "a disaster."

In closing her letter, Jackie mentioned that she would be leaving the White House for the Harrimans' at lunchtime on Friday, December 6, and she asked Lady Bird not to fear—she would be sure not to move out on Pearl Harbor Day. (Fretting how it would be viewed historically, Lady Bird did not want Jackie moving out of the White House on Pearl Harbor Day.)

"Well," Jackie concluded in a letter that still tugs at the reader's heart strings, "Jack and I did a lot in 2 years, 10 months and 2 days— so I can surely move out for you in 4½ days."

Lyndon Johnson "Using Jackie"

"Hell yeah, me and Miz Kennedy are close friends," Lyndon Johnson said as four female reporters took notes. "She and I have a special relationship. She picks up the phone, calls me up, talks. You know? Poor thing. We're like this," Johnson said, crossing his middle finger over his index finger. He was vibrant and excited, his whole being seemingly charged with adrenaline at the thought of Jackie.

It was the evening of December 23, 1963—a month after the assassination—and the new President had just enjoyed a libation or two at the White House Christmas party. Now he was sitting back in an upholstered chair in the Cabinet Room with four reporters and, at least from all evidence, showing off. He snapped his fingers; an idea had come into his head. "Let me just call Miz Kennedy right now," he offered. After pushing a button to activate the speakerphone on a desk, he dialed Jackie's number. As it rang, he put his index finger to his mouth, warning the women to "hush up." Meanwhile, a dictabelt (an early means of recording telephone conversations) would document the entire conversation.

Unbeknownst to Jackie Kennedy, the day after he took office as President, LBJ had instructed his secretary, Marie Fehmer, to be sure that all his White House phone calls were recorded. Lyndon Johnson would become the only President in history to record his telephone conversations throughout his Presidency—without the permission of anyone on the other end of the line. (Those recordings were then stored after his death in the Johnson archives in his home state of Texas.)

"You're so nice to call me, Mr. President," Jackie said when she picked up. "You must be out of your mind with work piled up."*

"I have a few things to do," he told her, "but not anything that I enjoy more than what I'm doing now." He took a look around at the wide-eyed expressions on the women's faces; no one had heard a word

*After accidentally addressing him as Lyndon on the plane after he was sworn in, Jackie vowed that in the future she would only refer to him as Mr. President, even though he insisted that she do no such thing.

from Jackie—probably the most popular woman in the country—since the funeral. He smiled to himself.

"You're nice," Jackie said.

"I just wish all of you a Merry Christmas, and I wish there was something I could do to make it happier for you."

"You've done everything you could," Jackie said, "and thank you so much."

"Do you know how much we love you?"

"Oh, well," Jackie said, unsure of how to answer him. "You're awfully nice."

"You don't know?" Johnson said, pushing. The reporters took feverish notes.

"No, I don't," Jackie answered, sounding extremely uncomfortable. "Well, yes, I do," she said, changing her mind.

"All hundred and eighty million love you, dear," he said.

"Oh, thanks, Mr. President."

"I'll see you after Christmas, I hope," he continued. "If you ever come back here again and don't come to see me, why there's going to be trouble," he added. "You don't realize I have the FBI at my disposal, do you?"

"I promise. I will," Jackie said, unconvincingly.

"I'm gonna send for you if you don't come by," LBJ told her, "and someday they're [the FBI] gonna create a traffic jam up there in Georgetown. You have a good Christmas, dear."

"Thank you, the same to you," Jackie answered.

"Good night."

"Good night, Mr. . . ." he cut her off before she could finish. Johnson turned to the impressed reporters. "What'd I tell you," he said of the former First Lady. "Like this," he concluded, again crossing his fingers.

While he genuinely seemed to care about the former First Lady, Johnson recognized Jackie's political influence, and her easy, almost homespun, sense of diplomacy. Her poll numbers, he kept reminding everyone, had been higher than her husband's at the time of Jack's death. With Jackie as his chief supporter, he believed that Americans would more readily accept his role of leadership, which had been foisted upon them in the most tragic of circumstances. Also, he needed a friendly conduit to the Kennedy infrastructure, someone he could have in his corner to help sway Bobby.

Still, Johnson resented Bobby, was always convinced that Bobby had attempted to sabotage his nomination for the Vice Presidency in 1960, and felt that the defiant younger Kennedy brother had no respect for his knowledge and experience. For his part, Bobby was revolted by Johnson's personality and style, and his lack of "refinement." He also didn't like LBJ's politics. Somehow, though, they managed a working relationship, but—as historians have demonstrated in books about their tenuous alliance before and after Jack's death—it was not easy.

A bit more than a week after the murder in Dallas, on the afternoon of December 2, 1963, LBJ spoke to Jackie, whom he called "Sweetie," and told her, "You just come over and put your arm around me. That's all you do. And when you haven't got anything else to do, let's take a walk. Let's walk around the backyard, and let me just tell you how much you mean to all of us, and how we can carry on if you give us a little strength."

Jackie liked Johnson personally but had never really gotten over his 1960 primary challenge to Jack. When historian and Kennedy insider Arthur Schlesinger once mentioned to her Johnson's "mild personal thrusts" at Jack, Jackie lashed out at him, "Were they mild? Didn't he say his father had been a Nazi? And having Connally talk about Jack's Addison's disease? They were not mild."

Also, Jackie was always a bit uneasy about Johnson's flirtatious manner toward her. However, because she understood that it was his nature—some have called it a Southern trait—to forge an extremely familiar relationship with the people in his life, she was not offended by it as has been previously reported. "To say 'honey,' or 'sweetie' or 'darling,' well, that was just LBJ's way of expressing himself, of expressing concern," says George Christian, who was press secretary to Johnson from 1966 to 1969. "Of course, he was not flirting. He liked to tease." However, probably because of her own more formal upbringing, Jackie did not know how to respond to LBJ's informal personality and would, at a loss, just dissolve into giggles.

Jackie thanked Johnson for a letter of support he had sent her earlier in the week. "I *know* how rare a letter is in a President's handwriting," she said, her voice cracking as if on the verge of tears. "Do you know that I've got more in your handwriting than I do in Jack's now?"

Johnson reminded her that he was depending on her for emotional support. "You got the President relying on you," he said. "And this is not the first one you had. They're not many women, you know, running around with a good many Presidents. So you got the biggest job of your life."

Jackie had to laugh. "She ran around with two Presidents, that's what they'll say about me," she joked. "Okay. Anytime."

"Good-bye, darling," he said to her. He asked her to "do come by," before signing off. She said she would.

When Jackie finally left the White House permanently on December 6—accompanied not only by Clint Hill and two other Secret Service agents but also, at LBJ's direction, by two Navy stewards—she didn't say good-bye to anyone, explaining later that she "couldn't bear the scene." Rather, she left a simple, handwritten card for Lady Bird in her bedroom that read: "I wish you a happy arrival in your new home, Lady Bird. Remember, you will be happy here." She signed it, "Love, Jackie."

The next day, Jackie and the President spoke about the Johnsons' move into the White House. That evening, December 7, would mark the first that the new President and his wife would spend in their new home. When LBJ admitted that he was "afraid," Jackie noted that "it's worst on your first night . . . the rooms are all so big, you'll get lost."

"Darling, you know what I said to Congress," Johnson told her, chuckling nervously, "I'd give anything in the world if I wasn't here today."

Johnson asked her when she was "going to come back and see me," as he did every time they spoke. "Someday I will," she promised, halfheartedly. But when he pushed her for a specific date, she tried to return to the subject of the Johnsons' first night at the White House. "Anyway," she said, "take a sleeping pill." But, pushing for that photo opportunity with the most famous woman in America, Johnson insisted that he would sleep so much better if she would just promise to visit him. "Please come," he pleaded, "and let me walk down to the seesaw with you, like old times." When Jackie agreed, he seemed almost giddy. "Okay, darling. Give Caroline and John Jr. a hug for me. Tell them I'd like to be their daddy."

Ten days later, on December 17, Jackie would visit the White House for the last time. The occasion was a Christmas play performed by Caroline's class, which would be meeting there until the end of the year. Jackie said that she planned to call on Johnson, but realized from reading the newspaper that day that he was in New York to address the United Nations. In a letter to him, she wrote that she felt "so stupid" to have forgotten and would, instead, see him after the holidays as he had suggested.

Four days before Christmas, on December 21, 1963, LBJ called Jackie again. "I love you," he began. "Aren't you sweet?" she said, her voice sounding demure, but somewhat exhausted. Johnson joked that he was angry with her for leaving "without coming by and hugging me and telling me good-bye," and that he should have her "arrested." Then Jackie and Lady Bird spoke for a few moments before LBJ took the phone and went back to the business of getting Jackie to agree to visit the White House. He told the former First Lady that he would "spank" her if she didn't "come by." Jackie promised that "As soon as you get back [from Texas for the holiday], I'll come and get a vitamin B shot from Dr. [Janet] Travell, and see you."

So by the time LBJ telephoned Jackie two days before Christmas, she knew what he wanted: for her to visit the White House. What she didn't know was that he was trying to prove to four reporters that he and Jackie were "like this."

An hour after LBJ's Christmas call to Jackie, her secretary Nancy Tuckerman received a telephone call from a fact checker at the Associated Press. It seemed that AP reporter Francis Lewin, one of the reporters present in the Cabinet Room during the call, intended to file a story about it. Would Jackie like to comment?

"You must be joking," Jackie exclaimed when Tuckerman told her about the story. "But how did they even know that the President called me?" When she was told that there were reporters listening on the speakerphone during the conversation, she was angry. "I think that's going just a bit far," Jackie told Nancy Tuckerman. "I don't like it at all. I think you should talk to Pierre [Salinger] about this. Tell him I'm very angry."

Before Tuckerman had an opportunity to call Salinger, Bobby had already done so. "Look, he's using Jackie," Bobby said. "Tell him we know it, and we want him to fucking stop it."

Salinger telephoned the President and, during another conversation recorded by Johnson, carefully asked if there had been newspaperwomen present during the time Johnson made his Christmas call to Jackie. Sounding defensive, LBJ confessed that there had been, and added he had cautioned the reporters to report only that he had talked to the former First Lady, and nothing more about their conversation, "because I didn't want a private conversation to be recorded." (Meanwhile, Johnson had not only recorded Jackie, but was also surreptitiously recording his conversation with Salinger.)

"I see nothing wrong with the President calling Miz Kennedy and the children and wishing them a Merry Christmas," Johnson told Salinger, his tone testy. "I want to be as nice and affectionate and considerate and thoughtful of Miz Kennedy as I can during these days. I just think that's good politics."

The Kennedy Camp on LBJ: "A Blight on the New Frontier"

In early January 1964, Ethel Kennedy telephoned Jackie to ask if she would have lunch with her and Bobby at Hickory Hill. She explained that she had something important to discuss with the former First Lady.

With three Secret Service agents in tow (including the trusted Clint Hill) as well as Maud Shaw, John Jr., and Caroline, Jackie arrived at Bobby and Ethel's home just after noon. She wore a simple, black pantsuit, a white blouse, an elegant strand of pearls, and a black scarf tied at the chin. She also wore large sunglasses, foreshadowing the mysterious "Jackie look" of the 1970s.

Ethel, Bobby, and Jackie—still wearing the scarf but having taken off the glasses—sat at the kitchen table. Over a meal of stuffed eggplant, which Jackie didn't touch, Ethel got right to the point. "This thing with Johnson is out of hand," she said. "Do you realize that every time he talks to you, he goes to the press. He's using you, Jackie. You know that, don't you?"

Ethel turned to Bobby for support. He nodded absentmindedly.

"Oh, of course I know that," Jackie said. "I'm not stupid, Ethel." Jackie went on to say that, in her opinion, Johnson was "a sweet man." She felt that what the two had gone through in Dallas had cemented a relationship between them.

Ethel strongly disliked the Johnsons, as did many in the Kennedy circle. She couldn't relate to their folksy ways, thought of them as argumentative, and believed that they looked down upon the Kennedys. She had customarily deleted Lyndon and Lady Bird from the guest lists of her extravagant parties at Hickory Hill under the Kennedy administration, and when she was forced to invite them as a matter of protocol, she usually ignored them once they arrived. "Look at her standing over there glarin' at us like we're dentists," LBJ once said of Ethel at a Hill party he and Lady Bird managed to attend.

Most people in the Kennedy camp felt that LBJ was a blight on the New Frontier. He just didn't fit. Kennedy had offered him the Vice Presidency only to keep him safely tucked away. JFK realized early on that if he won the election, it would probably be by a small margin and, as he put it to Kenny O'Donnell, "I won't be able to live with Lyndon Johnson as the leader of a small Senate majority." So with Lyndon out of the way as Vice President, Kennedy would have Mike Mansfield as the Senate leader, someone upon whom he could depend.

For all intents and purposes, Bobby had taken over the position as Jack's right-hand man, and Johnson was either ignored or placated by most of Kennedy's administration. LBJ had it right when he once said that the Kennedys thought of him as "a good ol' country boy with tobacco juice on my shirt." When friends gave Ethel and Bobby an LBJ voodoo doll a month before the Dallas tragedy, "the merriment was overwhelming," recalls *Time* magazine's Hugh Sidey, a frequent visitor at Hickory Hill. But were it not for LBJ, Kennedy probably would not have won the election. With Johnson on the ticket, Kennedy took not only Texas but also the important Southern states of Alabama, Georgia, Missouri, and South Carolina.

Jackie had always felt a strong empathy for Lyndon Johnson. Jack had been killed in Johnson's beloved Texas, and Lee Harvey Oswald was killed there, as well. "He thinks Americans will never accept him as President," she said, "and if he wants to use me in that regard, well, can you blame him?" Though Jackie realized that Jack didn't have much of a relationship with Lyndon Johnson and, in fact, practically never relied on him for anything, she liked Johnson anyway.*

When Ethel called him "a worthless President," Jackie disagreed, citing his eagerness to see Jack's civil rights programs passed (which were actually LBJ's first civil rights programs as Senate Majority Leader).

Jackie turned to Bobby for rescue, but he just stared straight ahead. He was in a dour mood with a pinched look around his mouth, perhaps still depressed over Jack's death. He probably looked smaller and more frail than Jackie had ever seen him, for this is what others who knew Bobby have said about him after his brother's murder.

"Oh, you would *so* like Lady Bird if only you'd give her a chance," Jackie said—and she was right about that: Lady Bird Johnson was much more Ethel's kind of woman than was Jackie. Whereas Jackie was the epitome of the modern jet-set age, her life brimming with action and excitement, Lady Bird's idea of fun was a trip to wide open spaces where she could don Levi's and tennis shoes and tramp around the countryside to her heart's delight. Just like Ethel. But Ethel wasn't interested in developing a kinship with Lady Bird.

"They really don't like us at all, you know," Ethel said as she continued railing against the Johnsons, even bringing up the old story about the time LBJ took Bobby deer-hunting, hoping to make a fool of him because he realized that Bobby would never be able to handle a rifle. "I think we should be careful about how they exploit us for their own gain."

"Well, I couldn't care less about any of this," Jackie said finally, hoping to end the discussion. After a few moments of silence, Jackie dug into her purse for a cigarette, lit it, and took a deep drag, making its tip turn red. She exhaled with a loud sigh. Then, with a sad smile, she

---

*At this time, in his continuing effort to involve Jackie in his administration, Johnson was considering making Jackie the Ambassador to Mexico. "She doesn't want to do anything, but God almighty, all she would have to do would be to just walk out on her balcony about once a week," he told Pierre Salinger. "I talked to her a while ago and she just *oohed* and *aahed* over the phone," he said of Jackie. "She was just the sweetest thing. She was always nicer to me than anybody in the Kennedy family. She always made me feel like I was a human being. God, it would electrify the Western Hemisphere. It would do more than any Alliance for Progress," Johnson continued, excited by the thought of it. "And she could go and do as she damn pleases. She can just walk out on that balcony and look down at them and they'll just pee all over themselves every day." A skeptical Salinger said he needed time to consider the idea. It is not known if LBJ offered her that post, though Pierre Salinger says he did offer her the position of Ambassador to France, and she turned it down.

shook her head and said, "What an awful world this is, isn't it? An awful, awful world when you can't even accept another person's kindness without endless debate about the motivation behind it. It's all so dreary."

Ethel shrugged her shoulders, as if to say, "So, what else is new?"

Bobby, who detested LBJ and had never tried to hide his feelings in the past, stared straight ahead as if he had not heard a word the two women had said.

Jackie had already set her boundaries with Johnson, anyway. She knew he would be able to use her only so much, because she wouldn't allow him to push it. "I will tell you one thing," she said at the time. "They will never drag me out as a little old widow like they did Mrs. Wilson when President Wilson died. I will never be used that way. I don't want to go out on a Kennedy driveway to a Kennedy airport to visit a Kennedy school. I'm not going around accepting plaques. I don't want medals for Jack."

It would take some time for Johnson to understand that Jackie had set limitations. Two days after her luncheon with Ethel and Bobby, Jackie was at her home in Georgetown, trying to sleep. It was 11:30 P.M. when she was jolted by the sound of the ringing telephone. Again it was the President of the United States, the biggest pest in her life these days, wanting to know when she would come by and visit him. He said he would finally be able to relax and start taking naps during the afternoon "on the day you come down here and see me." To Jackie, his constant pestering had become exhausting.

"Oh, Mr. President," Jackie said, wearily. "I can't come down there. I was going to tell you. I've really gotten hold of myself. You know I'll do anything for you," she said. "I'll talk to you on the phone. I'm just scared I'll start to cry again."

"Oh, you never cried," LBJ said.

He must have quickly realized the callousness of his statement. At the church during the service for Jack, Jackie had cried uncontrollably, and anyone near her—as he was—knew it. Clint Hill handed her a handkerchief and tried to comfort her, but to no avail. The wracking sobs and uncontrollable spasms would not stop. Caroline, at her side, had reached out, grabbed her mother's hand, and held it tightly. Jackie had managed to compose herself before going for Communion, but it had not been easy.

LBJ nervously corrected his statement. "Honey, I never saw anyone as brave as you."

"But, I mean . . ." Jackie seemed at a loss for words. "It's . . . you know . . ."

". . . or as great," LBJ continued.

"I just can't," Jackie insisted.

"You know how great we think you are?" LBJ said, pushing.

"Well, you know," Jackie said, sounding as if she was at the end of her rope. "I'll talk to you. I'll do anything I can for you. But don't make me come down there yet."

"Well, I got to see you before long," Johnson said.

"Anytime you say, Mr. President," Jackie responded, her tone one of resignation, as if she understood that it didn't matter what she said, he wasn't listening.

Then, they signed off. It was the last time LBJ ever asked Jackie to visit the White House.*

Joan's Bottled-Up Anxiety

Ethel Kennedy had predicted that the home originally chosen by Joan when she and her family moved to Washington would prove to be too small. Perhaps she felt vindicated when she learned that after less than a year, in January 1964, Joan and Ted decided they needed more space, and moved into another home in Georgetown. The red-brick, vine-covered home with white-trimmed windows, selected by Joan, was a real find, boasting a large drawing room, library, and dining room. This five-bedroom, five-bathroom home was truly a palace, possibly fit more for a queen than for a senator's wife. The house was such a large, formidable structure that taxicab drivers often mistook it for a hospital. Because it was a completely uncharacteristic environ-

---

*In fact, it would be eight years before Jackie would return to her former home, in 1971 when President Nixon and his wife, Pat, invited her and her children for dinner to view her and Jack's official portraits.

ment for the rather simple tastes of Joan, some in the Kennedys' circle began to wonder about the reasons behind the purchase.

"We knew there was a problem afoot when she moved into that house," said one of Joan's friends, today the wife of a senator but at the time married to a newspaper reporter. "She was overcompensating for something that was missing in her life, or at least that's how most people saw it. We knew that her drinking was getting worse. You couldn't keep that kind of thing a secret in Washington. Whenever Joan would go to lunch and have one too many cocktails, people talked."

Whether or not Joan was "compensating" for some lack in her life, she was now truly living the full Kennedy experience: She had a governess for the children, a cook for the family, and a social secretary (Theresa Dubbs, an attractive blonde who had worked for the Kennedy presidential campaign in 1960) to tend to her own needs. She had money at her disposal and, even though she was usually frugal, she was living a life that was not exactly the norm for most women in America.

Joan's days were increasingly busy with social activities, charity work, and luncheons with the wives of other senators. For instance, Joan and Marvella Bayh, wife of Indiana Senator Birch Bayh, both became members of "the Senate Ladies," an informal organization formed in the early 1900s to aid the Red Cross during the First World War. The Vice President's wife was always the leader of the group, which met on Tuesdays. The women spent hours after lunch sewing and rolling bandages, which were then sent on to Bethesda Naval Hospital.

As long as Joan was consumed with and preoccupied by her duties as a senator's wife, she seemed in good spirits. Many of her days and nights were busy, which was the way she liked it; when alone, however, she would inevitably sink into a dark depression. She loved her two children and enjoyed caring for them, but Ted was seldom around. He was either off to Vietnam, looking into the plight of war refugees, or when in town, at his office until the wee hours of the morning working on duties having to do with the Senate committees (the Labor, Veteran's Affairs, Aging, and Judiciary subcommittees) on which he had been placed. Even when her husband was home, though, Joan knew that she did not have his undivided attention. She could not adjust to having a philandering husband, and it still tormented her that she wasn't "good enough" for Ted.

Making matters worse for Joan, most of the senators' wives, the women with whom Joan would spend the bulk of her days, were from another generation, being as much as thirty years older than her. Rather than think of her as a peer, a "girlfriend," they were maternal toward Joan and treated her like a daughter. They spoke of their grandchildren, while Joan was still raising her children. Because there wasn't much common ground upon which to establish solid friendships with these women, Joan felt alone and isolated. Jackie could not be depended upon at this time; she had her own ordeal. Ethel could never be depended on, and she had never gotten close to her other sisters-in-law on the Kennedy side of the family.

After Teddy Jr. and Kara went off to bed, Joan would find herself alone, night after lonely night, with nothing to do but pace the floors of her large home. When Ted would come home and crawl into bed with her, they still had what she thought was passion in their lovemaking, "which kept her on a hook," said one friend of hers. "I don't know if, for Ted, it was passion or just great sex. But most nights, she was alone."

"I'm going stir-crazy," Joan recalls having complained to Ted. "I can only listen to Bach so many hours." On evenings when she wasn't expected at a political function, she had no one to chat with on the telephone or to visit, and so she drank.

Unfortunately, Joan Kennedy's frustrated nights alone, with only her supply of liquor as her companion, had become a matter of routine. In the process, the youngest senator's wife would follow a genetic leaning and emotional pattern set by her own mother, Ginny, and one that, in time, would nearly destroy her life: alcoholism.

Jackie's Saddest Days

At the same time that Ted and Joan moved into their new rented home, Jackie purchased a fourteen-room, brick town house close to them, at 3017 N Street in Georgetown, just down the street from the temporary home offered her by the Harrimans. Jackie's new three-story, mottled-brick house featured a spacious drawing room with a fireplace and French doors leading out to a flagstone patio. To the right of a center hall was a dining room, and behind it, the kitchen, laundry room, and servants' quarters. A large master bedroom was on the second floor, along with a study, a large dressing room, and a small office. On the third floor were four large bedrooms and a small workroom. All floors were accessible by an elevator at the front of the house.

While Joan never had any company at her home, Jackie had more than she could handle at hers—and not anyone she had invited, either. Unfortunately, her new home had become a tourist mecca. Fans would line the street in front of it, hoping for a glimpse of the former First Lady, and would shout out "Jack-eee, Jack-eee." Some of the braver ones would actually attempt to peer into her windows or knock on her door to ask for an autographed picture before being told to leave by Secret Service agents. "I'm a freak now," Jackie complained to Secretary of Defense Robert McNamara one day when he came calling. "They're like locusts," she said of the fans. "They're everywhere. It's getting worse. Every day, it's getting worse."

Night after lonely night, she would sort through Jack's books, papers, and personal mementos, many of which she planned to send on the road in a traveling exhibit of JFK memorabilia. There was the tiny ancient statue of Herakles and the Skin of a Lion, which Jack had bought for himself while in Rome the June before his death; a book of poetry he had borrowed from Eunice and enjoyed too much to return; a handful of family snapshots that he carried with him everywhere he went—it all now had special and heart-wrenching meaning.

Like Joan, Jackie found solace only by artificial means, by taking sedatives and antidepressants such as Amytal to get through the days and sleeping pills for the nights. She drank heavily, with vodka now her liquor of choice. Later, she would say that she played the events of the assassination over and over in her mind, wondering what she could have done differently, how she could have saved Jack's life. She developed a pattern of awakening in the middle of the night, her body torn by dry sobs and shudders. During the day she would be completely fatigued, an exhausting kind of sadness hanging over her.

One afternoon, according to Jackie's Secret Service agents, Jackie and Joan met in Washington for one of their intimate lunches, which in the past had usually centered on Jackie counseling Joan about Ted's philandering. This time, there was no consolation coming from Jackie. The tables were turned.

"Jackie, you have to pull yourself together," Joan said, concerned by the former First Lady's haggard appearance. Her hair had been combed, but defied order. She wore little makeup. Her clothes weren't "Jackie Kennedy crisp." "We all love you," Joan said. "We're so worried."

Jackie just shook her head, dismally. "I'm fine," she said. "Just fine."

Then, as she picked listlessly at her food, Jackie began once again to tell the story of what happened in Dallas, running a checklist of each awful occurrence. She said that the previous night she had suddenly awakened screaming after a nightmare. "I've heard that gun go off ten thousand times," she said. "I picture my own head splattering. I'd give my own life gladly, if I could just get back Jack." Joan looked horrified.

With nothing further to talk about, an awkwardness that had never been a part of their relationship began to set in. The two women just sat and stared over each other's shoulders, according to the agent. After one more drink, they kissed each other good-bye and parted company.

Recalls the agent, "As she was leaving, I heard Joan call after Jackie, 'Give me a ring, will you?' Jackie didn't respond."

Even when trying to be social, Jackie couldn't help but talk about the grisly murder. "My God, his brains were all over me," Jackie would say, as if she still could not believe the carnage she had witnessed. "All over my dress. Just brains. And blood. So much blood."

Those close to Jackie, such as Ethel, called Jackie's nightmarish tale of the assassination the "story from hell." Whenever Jackie would tell it, Ethel would shake her head vigorously, put her hands to her ears, and run from the room. Ethel, who feared that Jackie was becoming an alcoholic (yet didn't notice that Joan was becoming one), told Joan Braden, "My poor sister-in-law is losing it, I'm afraid. And there's nothing anyone can do. Maybe time will take care of this."

Among the sisters-in-law, Jackie had always been the "strong one," and as much as Ethel had quarreled with her, she still had grudging admiration for her strength and her determination to live her life in a strong, powerful way. "You can count on Jackie," she once said to a re-porter. "She's dependable. You may not know what she's thinking, but she has a certain resolve. She loves being First Lady, that's for sure."

It's true that Jackie's personality—imperious at times, usually fair (though she could be unreasonable if the mood struck her), often a voice of reason among the women in the family—had been a constant in the lives of her family members over the years. To see her in such a weakened state was frightening to all. "We lost Jack," Joan told Ted, according to what he later told friends. "We don't want to lose Jackie, too. What can we do?"

Moreover, because she was one of their own, a Kennedy, her family had great affection for her. Ethel, Joan, and all the Kennedys had known the private Jackie for many years and had watched—with mixed emotions, at least for Ethel—not only her public glory as First Lady but also her moments of great despair, such as the deaths of her babies. All of her experiences, personal and professional—her wedding, the birth of her children, her campaigning for Jack, her White House transformation, her dealing with the Marilyn Monroe drama—had meshed with their own lives' events to compose a family history of memories and emotions that only those in the inner circle could or should fully understand. "I couldn't bear to watch what she was going through because it was *Jackie*," Joan once said of this black period in her sister-in-law's life. "It broke my heart in a million pieces."

Jackie may have wanted to tell her terrible story repeatedly, but she really didn't want others to discuss what had happened or ruminate over the sensational details. One topic of discussion in which Jackie steadfastly refused to engage—and it often came up after she told her "story from hell"—had to do with whom to hold responsible for her husband's murder. Was it a conspiracy? Or had Lee Harvey Oswald acted alone? To this day the question remains a source of fascination. Throughout her life, though, Jackie never wanted any answers. In fact, none of the Kennedys did.

"I think she was afraid of what she would learn, and also what the country would learn, in terms of Jack's personal behavior and the Kennedys' connection to the mob, the CIA . . . all of it," says Jackie's cousin John Davis. "She had enough to deal with. She knew that any further investigation over the years could open up all sorts of possibilities about affairs, both governmental and romantic. She didn't want to know." Doubtless, she didn't want the world to know, either.

Davis says that the only time he ever spoke to his cousin about a further investigation into Jack's murder was more than ten years later, in 1974.

"Do you think more should be known about it?" he asked her.

She looked at him blankly, and then said, "So, what have you been up to, John? Are you well?"

"She completely changed the subject, which is what she would do if you tried to discuss the assassination with her," said John Davis. "I don't know if she got over it . . . I suppose, maybe, she found a way to move on. But she wasn't about to dredge it all up. Finding out the truth meant nothing to her. It wouldn't bring back Jack so, in her mind, what good would it serve?"

Rita Dallas recalled, "I once overheard Jackie tell Rose, 'You know, I don't think that I care how Jack was killed. Does it matter? Will it bring him back?'" Jackie did not give her mother-in-law a chance to answer. "No. No. No!" she exclaimed.

"She couldn't have cared less about the myriad of theories," Ted White, who interviewed Jackie for *Life* magazine after the assassination, once said. "What difference did it make whether he was killed by the CIA, the FBI, or the Mafia, or some half-crazed misanthrope? He was gone, and what counted for her was that his death be placed in some kind of social context."

The only Kennedy who seemed interested in what really may have occurred in Dallas was Ethel, who felt strongly that the family should get to the bottom of what happened to her brother-in-law. "They took him away from us," she told one family member, "and I want to know why. I'm sorry, *but I want to know*." It was interesting that Ethel referred to "they" when speaking of responsibility for her brother-in-law's death.

"She tried to have conversations with Jackie about it," said Lem Billings, "but Jackie wouldn't have it."

One afternoon after the Warren Commission, which investigated the assassination, released its report, which concluded that Oswald acted alone, Ethel and Eunice visited Jackie at her home (she was living in New York by this time). "I think you owe it to the country to lead the way and demand more of an investigation. Do you believe this report?"

Jackie was very clear. "Ethel, I don't want to know," she said, her temper rising. "It won't bring back Jack, will it? I was in that car," she reminded her. "Do you think I'm over it? Do you think I can bear another second of it? Why would you think I would want to open further investigation into it?"

Perhaps Ethel's curiosity about what had really occurred in Dallas had to do with the fact that her husband, Bobby, believed there was more to the story than what was presently known. He told Arthur Schlesinger that while he believed that Oswald was guilty of the crime, there was question in his mind as to whether Oswald acted alone or had been a part of a larger plot organized by either Castro or the mob, or, as he put it, "who knows who." Bobby realized, though, that to probe too deeply in matters having to do with these possibilities would open the Kennedys to heavy scrutiny and, as he might have put it, "who knows what" might have come to light. "Bobby asked some questions and did some follow-up," says George Smathers, "but I think he was unhappy with what he was learning—whatever that was—because he backed off."

"He asked me to stay on top of the investigation, and I did," recalls his press secretary from 1965 to 1968, Frank Mankiewicz. "I would relay information to him from time to time. But, really, it wasn't a primary concern. Jack was gone. No one needed more, I suppose, than that."

"As Attorney General, Bobby had all sorts of information about what had happened that no one else knew," adds John Davis. "But in the end, he agreed with Jackie to just take the simpleminded Warren Commission report at its word: Oswald acted alone. He was just a nut, and that was that. . . ."

For the most part, Bobby eventually put the question of who killed his brother out of his mind. On April 4, 1968, after Martin Luther King was murdered and Bobby spoke to a crowd of a thousand, mostly black, in Indianapolis, he went back to his room, slumped into a chair, and said to his speechwriters Jeff Greenfield and Adam Walinsky, "You know, that fellow Harvey Lee Oswald—or whatever his name was—set something loose in this country."

"That was the only time I ever heard him mention his name," recalls Greenfield. "When the news of John Kennedy's death first came out, the news reports had the name backward and that's the way he always remembered it, because he never took a look at it again."

Jackie and Brando—The Rumors

After her husband's death there were whisperings of an affair between Jackie and the handsome, forty-year-old Academy Award–winning actor Marlon Brando.

It was in January 1964 when Jackie first met Brando over dinner with her sister Lee and Brando's friend George Englund at the Jockey Club in Washington. Brando couldn't have been more charming; he and Jackie seemed to have an instant rapport, as he regaled her with stories about things she usually didn't care about, such as the celebrities with whom he made movies and had friendships. "Tell me about Frank Sinatra," Jackie said, teasingly. "Isn't he just an awful man?" Brando agreed. After making *Guys and Dolls* with Sinatra almost a decade earlier, he believed the singer to be a self-absorbed lout.

As the night wore on, all were having a good time. However, the press had been tipped off, and when reporters showed up at the restaurant, Jackie became completely enraged. "How is it that they always, always, *always* know where I am," she cried. "Let's get the hell out of here. Those goddamn parasites!"

The quartet vanished through a kitchen exit. Once back at Jackie's house, the four of them had more martinis, listened to a Wayne Newton record, and danced—Lee with George, Jackie with Marlon. As he danced with Jackie, according to what he later told a friend, he decided to kiss her. His lips touched hers, and Jackie froze in his arms. The look in her eyes said it all: The dance was over and he should leave.

Embarrassed, Brando said his good-byes and staggered out to a waiting car. As he drove off, Clint Hill noticed Jackie Kennedy standing in the doorway with a sad expression on her face.

"It's too soon," she said later. "Much, much too soon. I doubt I'll ever be ready to be a woman again."

The next day Marlon Brando sent Jackie a dozen yellow roses with an accompanying card. While the specifics of what he had written on the card remain unknown, Jackie was touched. Lee suggested that her sister telephone Marlon to apologize, but she couldn't bring herself to do so. "I just hope he forgets all about it, and all about me, and never, ever says a word to anybody about any of it, ever," a mortified Jackie said. She and Brando never saw one another again—at least not that anyone close to them can remember.

PART EIGHT

Ted's Plane Crash

It was one o'clock in the morning on Saturday, June 20, 1964. Twenty-seven-year-old Joan Kennedy was sound asleep when a persistent knocking on the bedroom door jarred her to consciousness. After the assassination, she rarely slept deeply. So distraught had she been that, just two weeks earlier, she had suffered a miscarriage, her second. She went to the door, wearing only her slip. When she opened it, she found her chauffeur, Jack Crimmins. The concerned look on his face told her that something was very wrong.

"Joan, I don't know how to say this to you," Crimmins remembered telling her. "Maybe you should sit down."

Joan stood, frozen. No, she would not sit down, she said. "Please just tell me. Tell me now."

"There's been an accident."

Joan gasped and leaned against the door frame. "Oh no. Who?"

"Ted."

"Oh, my God," she exclaimed, tears immediately coming to her eyes. "Not Ted, too."

"I'm sorry, Joan," Crimmins apologized. "Ted's plane went down, somewhere near Springfield."

"Not another nightmare," she said. "Please, God."

The scene between Joan and Jack Crimmins was played out at the home of Alan and Ann Biardi, friends of Kennedy campaign worker Don Dowd and his wife, state Committeewoman Phoebe Dowd. Joan had gone to West Springfield to watch Ted accept the nomination at the Massachusetts State Democratic Convention for a second term as senator. It seemed clear that he was headed to victory in that he had done so well filling the two unexpired years of his brother Jack's term. With the usual preconvention festivities—receptions, parties, dinners—it promised to be a good time.

A day earlier, the Senate had voted on the civil rights bill, which was approved by a wide margin. Because JFK had introduced the bill (which Lyndon Johnson then championed), Ted had understandable sentimental attachment to remaining on the Senate floor until its passage. So Joan would go ahead to West Springfield alone, with Ted intending to join her there as soon as the final vote was tallied.

Because the Senate was, as usual, running over schedule, Ted would be late in arriving in Springfield. Before even getting on the plane, he wanted to go to Arlington to visit Jack's grave. Head bowed, he would kneel alone at the eternal flame, spending just a moment with his brother and telling him of the passage of the bill—the final tally was 73 to 27—that had meant so much to him.

In a telephone hookup to the Massachusetts delegates, Ted's voice crackled through the loud speakers at 7:30 P.M., just ten minutes before that final vote. "I want everybody to know that I am a candidate this year," he announced. "We are now fifteen minutes away from the vote for civil rights." At that announcement, a loud cheer erupted from the floor. Ted added that he would join them all as soon as possible. "And I ask you," he concluded, "not to get so impatient that you decide to nominate Joan instead." (This was in reference to the strong reaction Joan received earlier when she gave a brief speech to the delegates.)

Joan wasn't at the hall, however. She was in bed, at least until she was awakened by Jack Crimmins, who had driven Joan from Washington, with the horrifying news that he had heard on the car radio.

The plan was that Ted would land at the Barnes Airport in Westfield and then be whisked to the Coliseum in West Springfield, where Joan would meet him. There he would accept his nomination, and the two would share his victory with the nearly two thousand delegates. She hadn't planned to sleep, just to rest her eyes. Somehow she drifted off.

Flying through a heavy fog and drizzling rain, the twin-engined, six-seat Aero Commander plane carrying Ted and his party crashed into an apple orchard. Ted was taken to Cooley Dickinson Hospital in Northampton. Crimmins had gone to Bradley Field, the commercial airport that served Springfield, to meet Ted's plane, but when he heard the news, he turned around and headed back to the house where Joan was staying. Once he was sure there was no mistake, he knew that he had to tell Ted's wife what had happened.

When an announcement of the accident was made from the platform of the Coliseum in West Springfield, delegates reacted in shock and horror. There were audible gasps and female screams at the mind-numbing news. Surely, it was not possible that God would take another Kennedy brother, and at the young age of thirty-two! The chairman asked for a moment of silent prayers.

Gerry Doherty, Ted's campaign chairman, would later recall that he knew in his heart that Ted was probably dead. "How to tell Joan?" he wondered. He knew he had to get her to the hospital, "but I didn't know what she would find there. My mind raced through all the possibilities, and the most likely was that Ted was dead. After what happened to Jack, we were all pretty fatalistic." Doherty found Phoebe Dowd in the crowd and sent her to pick up Joan and take her to the hospital. Phoebe's husband, Don, followed shortly after in his own car. By the time the Dowds got to Joan, though, she had already been told the news by Jack Crimmins.

Joan dressed quickly. Looking drawn and pale, she quickly walked downstairs, outside and into Don Dowd's car. She saw Phoebe on the way. "Isn't this terrible?" Joan said. Phoebe would recall that her voice was almost inaudible.

It was a foggy, difficult, twenty-six-mile ride to the hospital known as Cooley Dick, a drive during which Don could barely see the road ahead. Joan sat in the front seat with him; Phoebe sat in the back with Jack Crimmins. She remembered that Joan kept chattering to herself. "I hope everyone is okay," she said. "Ted, [Senator] Birch Bayh [who was to deliver the keynote speech], and [his wife] Marvella, and Ed [Moss, Kennedy's administrative aide]. Sometimes they say a plane has crashed, when really it's just landed. Isn't that true?" Joan asked, her eyes hopeful. Phoebe agreed. "Sure, that happens all the time."

Don didn't say a word. Later, he would remember that he truly felt that the worst had occurred, and he didn't want Joan to read his fatalistic attitude into anything he would say.

When Joan and Don finally arrived at the hospital, reporters were already there, waiting. Jack Crimmins was so rattled that when he got out of the car, he slammed the door in Phoebe's face, bruising her badly. "Oh, my God," Joan exclaimed. "What's next?" After tending to Phoebe for a few moments, the four headed to the hospital.

Without showing any emotion whatsoever, and very much like her sister-in-law Jackie in her impassive demeanor during a crisis, Joan hurried past the waiting reporters without looking directly at any of them, only straight ahead. "He's going to be fine," she said to one writer who shouted out a question at her. "He's going to be fine."

Joan was taken directly to the emergency room to see Ted; she was horrified by what she saw before her: her battered husband lying on a bed inside an oxygen tent with tubes sticking out of his nostrils, one coming from his chest, and blood flowing into his body by transfusion. He looked up at her and tried to force a weak smile. Saying her name seemed to sap him of any strength he had left. "I'm okay," he said. "I'll be fine." Then he drifted off.

After the plane hit the ground, its wings sheared off by tree branches, it cartwheeled in a death roll, its roof torn off. At the moment of impact, Ted had been half standing, looking at the control panel and trying, in his panic, to assist the pilot in some way. He was thrown about the cabin like a rubber ball. Birch and Marvella Bayh were miraculously uninjured. The pilot of the plane, forty-eight-year-old Ed Zimny, was killed instantly. (A year and a half earlier, Zimny had flown Jackie's mother, Janet Auchincloss, to Rhode Island to accompany baby Arabella Kennedy's body after it was exhumed to be reburied next to her father, JFK.) Ted's aide, forty-one-year-old Ed Moss, died seven hours later after brain surgery.

Ted was not expected to live through the night. With his back broken in three places, he had no feeling in his legs and was bleeding internally. His left lung had partially collapsed, he had two broken ribs, and his blood pressure reading was erratic and dangerously low. It was feared that if he did survive, he would be a paraplegic. The doctors decided not to tell Joan of the gravity of Ted's condition, however, because they sensed that she would not be able to take the news. In fact, Joan was so shaken that she had to be helped from the room. Hospital officials suggested she get immediate rest.

After Phoebe helped her undress, Joan climbed into the bed in the room that was reserved for Ted should he ever be well enough to leave the emergency ward. Later, the Dowds and some other visitors swarmed around Joan in her hospital bed. The hospital sent in coffee.

"Call Cardinal Cushing," Joan said. "He should know what has happened. He should pray. Tell him I spoke to Ted," she said, weakly. "He looked terrible. Oh, my God. What if he can't walk? He'll be in a wheelchair for the rest of his life. Oh, my God, poor Ted." By the time

Bobby arrived at four in the morning, Joan was asleep. When she awakened at eight, she and Bobby began a vigil at Ted's bedside.

On Saturday afternoon the other Kennedys began arriving, while Bobby held an impromptu press conference. Eunice, Jean, and Pat joined Joan at Ted's bedside. Ethel stayed behind at Hickory Hill with the children. When Jackie arrived later in the day, the scene outside the hospital was one of sheer pandemonium. She looked at the reporters with disdain and hurried into the hospital, muttering under her breath.

"Where's Joan?" she asked as soon as she saw Pat. "I have to see her."

When Jackie found Joan at Ted's bedside, the two women walked into the hallway and embraced tightly.

"Thank God he's alive," Jackie told her as doctors and nurses gawked at her. "We just have to thank God he's alive."

"What would I do if he had died?" Joan asked.

With no answer to that question, Jackie just shook her head.

"It's a curse," Joan said, as members of the medical staff listened in on the conversation. "I know now that it's a curse."

Joan told Jackie she had once heard that a gypsy had put a curse on the entire Kennedy family in the late twenties after having been evicted from a housing project owned by Joseph Kennedy.

"This woman spat in Grandpa's face and gave him the evil eye," Joan told Jackie. "And now we're supposedly all doomed."

"Oh, my God," Jackie exclaimed. "Do you believe that, Joan?"

"What if this is true?" Joan said, anxiously. "I mean, can we just discount it? Look at the things that have happened. Can we chalk it up to coincidence?"

Jackie was speechless. "I . . . I . . ." she began. "I suppose anything is possible." Jackie urged Joan to relax; she was concerned about her sister-in-law because she was well aware of the emotional and physical strain that could result from a miscarriage, and Joan's was so recent.

Meanwhile, Bobby reaffirmed to the reporters who had congregated in a conference room that this latest tragedy would not force the family out of politics—even though, privately, he wasn't so sure about that.

"The Kennedys intend to stay in public life," he said. "Good luck is something you make. Bad luck is something you endure."

Afterward, Bobby pulled columnist Jimmy Breslin aside and said, "I was just thinking—if my mother hadn't had any more children after the first four, she would have nothing now. I guess the only reason we've survived is that there are more of us than there is trouble."

By Saturday evening, Ted's condition began to stabilize and it had become clear that his spinal cord had not been severed. In time he would walk again, but his recovery would be a slow and painful one. Joan was relieved, though still extremely shaken by the deaths of the two men who were also aboard. That night she asked to be shown the hospital's chapel. She went inside and knelt at the altar for ten minutes, perhaps thanking God for sparing her husband, perhaps praying for the immortal souls of the two men who died in the crash. Soon after, Jackie followed her into the chapel and the two women knelt together, not saying a word. How far they had come in such a short time, from the discussion of Jack's victory on a Hyannis Port beach three and a half years earlier to a chapel in a strange hospital, thanking God for not taking Ted the way He had so violently taken his brother. The three Kennedy sisters joined them, and together the five women prayed in silence.

The next morning, Joan had three dozen red roses delivered to the chapel in honor of the deceased. (On Sunday, truckloads of candy and flowers would arrive for Ted, which Joan then graciously sent on to cheer other hospital patients.)

After his press conference, Jackie cornered Bobby in the cafeteria.

"Oh, Bobby, we have such rotten luck, don't we?" she said as soon as she saw him. The two embraced tightly.

"It's going to be okay, Jackie," Bobby said. "Don't worry about Teddy. Nothing can stop him."

"I'm just so . . ." Jackie began.

"Tired?" Bobby said, looking at her with a smile.

"Yes, tired. I wonder how much more are we expected to take."

"Hopefully, not much," he responded. "Hopefully, not much."

At 6:45 P.M., after Jackie and Bobby had enjoyed a light snack together, they were summoned to a telephone. It was President Johnson calling from the Beverly Hilton Hotel in Los Angeles. Johnson had sent four Walter Reed Army Hospital specialists to Cooley Dickinson

Hospital to assist in Ted's treatment, and was calling to express his concern. Of course he was taping the conversation.

"He's got a lot of broken bones and his back is in bad shape, but he's not paralyzed," Bobby told Lyndon. "It's going to take anywhere from six months to a year, but he's going to be fine."

"Looks like you have more than you can bear," LBJ said. "But you're a mighty brave fellow and you have my sympathy and all your family, and any way in the world I can help, I'm just as close as the phone. . . ."

"Jackie just wants to say hello to you, too," Bobby said, handing her the phone. Drained, Jackie leaned up against a wall, the phone in one hand, a cigarette in the other.

"Mr. President?"

"My dear, it looks like you have more than you can bear," LBJ told her.

"Yeah, oh boy . . . for a day," Jackie said. "I just wanted to say, you were so nice to call."

Johnson then told Jackie that he had spoken to Dr. Thomas Corriden, one of Ted's doctors, and that he had assured him that Ted would live. "Yes, everything'll be all right," Jackie agreed.

"Give Joan a hug for me," Lyndon told Jackie.

"I will," she said as she tried to rush off the line.

"Thank you, Jackie."

"Thank you, Mr. President."

Joan Wins the Election for Ted

On the Monday after Ted Kennedy's plane accident, a strategy meeting was scheduled with Ted's political planners, Gerry Doherty and Eddie Boland, and Kennedy's press representative, Ed Martin. Joan also attended. She had been told that Ted would be out of commission for some time—many months, probably. Not only was he physically impaired, but he was emotionally devastated by the crash. Ed Moss had been a close friend, much more than just an administrative aide.

The two had enjoyed a special relationship; Ted could always count on Ed as being one of the few people not so intimidated by the Kennedy mystique that he would not give him an honest appraisal. He would be greatly missed.

What now? Ted would not withdraw from the race; that was for certain. He was practically a shoo-in. The Republican Party had selected Howard Whitmore, Jr., a former Massachusetts state representative, to run against Teddy. Poor Whitmore was, at best, a reluctant candidate. So strong was the sympathy for Ted—and so grateful were many of the polled voters that he, unlike Jack, had been spared—that the odds were in his favor from the beginning. In fact, Whitmore would spend much of his campaign apologizing for his presence in the race and hoping that Ted, the other Kennedys, or the citizens of Massachusetts would not be angry at him for even being in the race. Ted was bound to win, but someone needed to campaign for him, anyway.

Someone in his camp suggested that Joan stump for her husband. Kennedy wives were known to be strongly influential on the campaign trail, and if ever such influence was needed, it was now. Yes, she immediately decided, "Of course I will." Recalls Joe Gargan, "She made up her mind to do all she could to help him to recover physically and to win re-election.

"The first thing that had to be done, though, was to pick a hospital in Boston where Ted could spend the nine long months of required recovery," said Gargan. "Joan and I went together to look at Mass [Massachusetts] General Hospital and also New England Baptist. We finally decided that New England Baptist was the best place for Ted because it had porches off the rooms where he could be pushed out onto to enjoy the fresh air. This was a good decision, because Ted spent as much time out in the sun and fresh air as he could."

While Ted would film a few television commercials from his bed, it would be Joan who would have to do all the real work. She had done it before in the summer of 1962 when she campaigned for Ted, and now, for the next five months of 1964, Joan Kennedy would campaign for her husband again, keeping to a grueling schedule that had been carefully organized by Ted's handlers. "Joan became the candidate herself," Joe Gargan recalls, "and was willing to go to every village and town in Massachusetts to appear for Ted."

President Johnson called Joan on July 3, six days before Ted was transferred to the Lahey Clinic in the New England Baptist Hospital. He had visited Ted earlier in his recuperation, a midnight visit to avoid the media. "Lady Bird and I just wanted to let you know that we're thinking about you kids," he told Joan.

"Oh my, Mr. President," Joan said in a whisper, sounding so much like Jackie. "Thank you for calling, and thank you for the flowers. Ted's fine. He's doing so much better."

"I hear you're goin' out there on the [campaign] trail," LBJ told her. "It's hard work, you know. Sure you can handle it?"

"Oh, I know it is, Mr. President," Joan said. "But I must do it. I know I can. It's my responsibility."

"It is," the President agreed. "So you go on out there and be a good little girl, and do a good job. They need you, gal."

Now here was a strange, ironic turn of events for Joan Kennedy: not only was she needed by her husband, Ted, but she had been encouraged by the President of the United States to "do a good job." She had always felt like the useless Kennedy wife, but it seemed that this was beginning to change. She was probably astonished at the way her life had evolved, and would even ignore LBJ's condescending tone, realizing that it was just who he was. (In a couple of years she would have her appendix removed, and the President would send her a note that said: "You're sure a big girl to be having your appendix out.")

For the next five months, the routine would be the same: Early in the morning, Joan's chauffeur would pick her up from her home on Squaw Island, where she would bid farewell to the children, Edward Jr., three, and Kara Anne, four, and then be driven to Lahey, seventy-five miles away. There, in Ted's fifth-floor suite of the Lahey Pavilion, she would confer with him over the rigorous schedule of appointments she was expected of keep. He was strapped into an orthopedic frame, unable to move, his spine held rigid while it healed. In the morning he would awaken, facedown. He would shave in that position and also eat that way. Between his face and the floor was a fixed tray on which he would place a phone, newspapers, books, writing material, and food. He would be rotated several times daily, "like a human rotisserie," he joked. Still, after his 9 A.M. therapy, he and Joan would somehow review her speeches, discuss the important campaign issues, and deal with whatever other business they needed to handle for that day.

Joan would then leave for a suite across the hall from Ted's that had been set up as a second campaign headquarters, the primary one being Ted's Province Street campaign post. She would carefully review the list of people who wanted to see Ted that day—other politicians, reporters, friends—and decide which should have entrée and which should be turned away. Then she would conduct as much telephone business as possible before having to leave at about noon for her first of sometimes as many as eight stops. In all, in ten weeks—six days a week—she would visit 39 cities and 312 towns. "She went to the Fish Pier in Boston, the factory gates in Lowell, Lawrence, and Fall River," recalls Joe Gargan. "Whether it was a ward party in wards six and seven in South Boston, or a music festival in the hills of the Berkshires, Joan was willing to try. . . ."

Joan was grateful for the support of the media and Ted's constituency; however, she couldn't help but wonder if people she met while campaigning were reacting to her personality or to her beauty. To compensate for her insecurity, and because she wanted to be good as a campaigning wife, she would say or do whatever she had to on the road—and if she had to dance, she would do that, too, as she did when she and State Comptroller Joseph Alecks performed a fast polka at the Pulaski Day banquet in the hall of the Kosciuzko Veterans Association Building.

At the end of the day, if she had energy, she would go back to the hospital and with great exhilaration would fill Ted in on all that had happened. Joe Gargan recalls that "Ted was very pleased with what Joan was doing, and proud because the reports he was getting about her were positive." That may be true; however, Ted didn't act that way when he was around Joan. Though he tried to act grateful, he was distant.

"It was okay at the start," Joan recalled, "but as the months went on, it became too much of a good thing." She said that she didn't like being rushed through crowds by police officers as thousands of hands reached out to her. It felt "so unreal and impersonal," she said. Soon, she began to bend under the pressure of such nerve-wracking work, her stomach constantly in knots. She would carefully rehearse her speeches in the car on the way to each stop, hoping that she would not buckle under the pressure and go blank in front of the crowd. Toward the end of the campaign, she began to seem lost.

Unfortunately, for Joan, more pressure in her life eventually led to one thing: more alcohol. As the tour continued she began to drink, just to deal with the stress. "Her face seemed hard," said one observer who had followed her progress on the tour. "She didn't seem to smile as much as at the start. A couple of times I saw her she looked like she had crawled through a rat hole. The old Joan wasn't like that, never in a million years. The old Joan was so beautifully dressed. Jesus, the old Joan would have charmed a bird out of a tree. But there was something very wrong about her, now."

So much was expected of her—people loved meeting her, being photographed with her, touching her, feeling as if they were getting to know her—that she feared she would never be able to live up to their expectations. Rather than applaud her own successes, she couldn't help but focus on the times she would fumble on the platform, give a wrong answer, or just not be as effective as she had hoped. She would wring her hands with nervousness before each speech, making some of those sitting ringside almost as anxious as she was.

One of Joan's biggest problems while on the campaign trail for Ted was that she felt like a fraud when having to tell reporters that she and Ted were happy in their marriage, that they enjoyed operas together, that Rose had sent them Shakespeare's complete plays on records and that they loved listening to them together—all fiction.

Except on rare occasions, Ted had seemed uninterested in Joan romantically. It was crushing for Joan to realize that when Ted would finally leave his hospital bed, it would be for the bed of one of his many consorts and not Joan's. He was thinking about his political future, about a book of reminiscences about his father he was compiling called *The Fruitful Bough*, but certainly not about Joan.

"You have an opportunity to do something here, Joansie," he told her of the campaign in front of volunteers. "So do it. For yourself."

The problem, of course, was that Joan would rather have been doing it for Ted. Or, as Joe Gargan so aptly and succinctly put it, "I was not surprised at how hard she worked, because Joan loved Ted."

On Election Day, November 3, 1964, Ted would win by the largest majority ever recorded to that time in Massachusetts. He would manage 1,716,908 votes, almost 75 percent of the total, practically obliterating Republican Howard Whitmore.

"Joan won the election for you," Bobby would tell his brother, only half joking.

Jackie sent Joan—not Ted—a note: "Congratulations, and a job well done. How wonderful! I hope this shows you how much you can accomplish. . . . I am so excited for you."

Even Ethel would be impressed, and she was not often impressed by Joan. She telephoned her sister-in-law and told her, "The whole family is proud of you. What a wonderful job you did."

Rose, the "political pro" of the Kennedy women—who had presided at the tea parties that first introduced Jack to the voting public—sent Joan two dozen roses with her congratulations.

Somehow, though, despite all of the kudos, it would be a hollow victory for Joan Kennedy because the approval of the most important person—Ted—was not forthcoming. In fact, he acted strangely aloof, as if he didn't want to give her any credit at all. Demonstrating his lack of graciousness, he would tell one reporter that he would have won the election anyway, that Joan's work was just "icing on a cake that I had baked myself."

Despite the fact that he had cheated death, Ted Kennedy was not a changed man. He was still too self-centered and busy to be grateful for anything his wife ever did for him. In the end, he would treat Joan as if she had done what any Kennedy wife would have done under the circumstances: her duty.

―――――――――

Jackie on the Anniversary of November 22, 1963

The first anniversary of Jack's death hit Jackie hard; all the agonizing memories rushed back and she could barely function during the month of November. She complained to her hairdresser, Rosemary Sorrentino, that she wished the world would celebrate the day of her husband's birth, not his death. "Why commemorate the most awful day in our history?" she asked Sorrentino, who probably didn't have an answer.

"Time goes by too swiftly, my dear Jackie," LBJ wrote to her shortly after the anniversary, "but the day never goes by without some tremor of a memory or some edge of a feeling that reminds me of all that you and I went through together." The note brought tears to Jackie's eyes. Surely she was touched by the President's gentle reminder that, though life had gone on and the business of government had not ceased even for a second, no one who witnessed those dark days in Dallas would ever be quite the same.

By this time—November 1964—Jackie had moved into a fourteen-room apartment at 1040 Fifth Avenue in Manhattan for which she paid $200,000. Jackie and her secretary, Nancy Tuckerman, had found an interesting way of looking at prospective homes before Jackie settled on the Fifth Avenue apartment. Nancy recalls, "You could never be bored when you were with Jackie, because you never knew what to expect from her. She had this love of intrigue that often led to some sort of conspiratorial act. For instance, when she decided to move from Washington to New York and we went apartment-hunting, to avoid publicity she came up with the idea that I would play the part of the prospective buyer while she'd come along disguised as the children's nanny!"

In a sweeping move to rid herself of the past, the thirty-five-year-old former First Lady also sold Wexford, a weekend retreat in Virginia that she and Jack had purchased after their Glen Ora lease had expired. Now she would live at the Carlyle Hotel while her new home was being renovated.

As the day of the anniversary approached, Jackie wrote a letter about her late husband for a tribute issue of *Look* magazine. "I don't think there is any consolation. What was lost cannot be replaced," she wrote. "I should have guessed that it could not last. I should have known that it was asking too much to dream that I might have grown old with him and see our children grow up together. So, now, he is a legend when he would have preferred to be a man."

But Jackie was also a legend when she would have, most of the time at least, preferred to be just a woman. For the rest of her life, she would be the subject of heavy scrutiny in Manhattan and everywhere she went.

After the first anniversary, Jackie decided it was time to force herself to move on with her life. Soon, new clothes in the pale pastels and vibrant rich colors Jackie so loved began to replace the somber blacks and whites of her mourning wardrobe. Having spent enough time in her dreadful limbo of loss and indecision, she now began appearing in public more often, lunching with old friends like historian Arthur Schlesinger and novelist Truman Capote. As she had done with the Warren Report, she would avoid, instead of seek out, all that reminded her of Jack. For instance, she refused to read a volume of poems published after the assassination to honor him. Even her visits to the grave in Arlington, once so poignantly frequent, became fewer. And, more importantly, at her small dinner parties she no longer told her "story from hell," as Ethel called it.

After a year of misery, Jackie Kennedy would begin turning away from the past and look ahead to the future, to the passage of years ahead. As a former First Lady and widow of a national hero, her date book would be filled with fund-raisers in America and abroad and public appearances with other Kennedys for political reasons. Of course, she would never get over her husband's senseless death; rather, she would just learn somehow to live with the reality of it, and live past it as well.

Two days after the anniversary, while with family friend and artist Bill Walton, Jackie was mobbed by a crowd as she attempted to go shopping in Manhattan. After they escaped by taxi, Walton said to Jackie, "That kind of thing must drive you absolutely nutty."

"No, not really," she sighed wearily. "I'm all they have left."

Using Jackie—Yet Again

That summer, Jackie would be with the family in Hyannis Port for the Fourth of July. To First Lady historian Carl Anthony, Joan Kennedy recalled, "We would both go off alone [together] and do what we enjoyed. For me, it was music and reading, for her painting and reading. When she painted, she said she liked to listen to chamber music, not symphonies or concerto music, but chamber music because it was more subdued and allowed her to concentrate intently without distraction. The rest of the Kennedy family were all off doing things together. And with great glee she said to me, 'Joan, they think we're weird! *Weird!* We're the weird ducks!' She said the word *weird* in the funniest way. She just made you laugh.

"She took me waterskiing with her," Joan continued of her favorite sister-in-law. "The Secret Service agent would drive the boat, and I would be the one getting her signals—go faster, go beyond the wake. And she'd stay on those water skis for a good hour, then drop off, and I'd get on while she rested up. After that, she went out again! Then we'd both swim for about a mile from the breakwater back to the shore. She was an incredible swimmer, and in great shape. And she always used flippers when she went swimming because, she said, 'If you wear flippers, it's a great way to trim your thighs.'"

Meanwhile, against this backdrop of summer frivolity, the political rivalry between the Kennedys and the Johnsons continued—with Jackie as bait. Earlier in the year, Ethel had again complained to Jackie that LBJ was using her. Soon after, it seemed that Bobby began exploiting Jackie as well. He had asked Jackie to call upon her "friend" LBJ to have the Space Center at Cape Canaveral renamed Cape Kennedy. Jackie agreed to do so, and LBJ granted her wish (but later Jackie regretted having asked for the favor because she believed Jack wouldn't have thought it appropriate). Afterward Jackie complained to Charles Bartlett that "Bobby keeps making me put on my widow's weeds and go down and ask Lyndon for something."

At 7:30 P.M. on the night of the Fourth, the telephone rang at Bobby and Ethel's. President Lyndon Johnson was calling from the LBJ Ranch in Texas. After a brief discussion about civil rights, Bobby asked Johnson if he wanted to talk to "your girlfriend," at which point he put Jackie on the line.

After exchanging holiday greetings with her, Lyndon complained to Jackie that he was "sunburned" and "blistered" because he had been out on his boat all that day. Jackie giggled. "You'll look *marvelous* with a sunburn," she said. Johnson also mentioned that his daughter Luci had not joined them in Texas, as she was in Washington, "having dates." Again, Jackie laughed coquettishly. "I though it [her absence] was something sinister like that," she said. Johnson then mentioned that, as a birthday gift to Luci on July 2, he granted her one wish: that she be allowed to go an entire day without a Secret Service agent at her side. Jackie, who generally loathed Secret Service protection, exclaimed, "Good work!" When LBJ, his voice carrying a lascivious tone, asked Jackie what she thought might have occurred while Luci was on her unchaperoned dates, Jackie said, "I'd hate to think! And don't you!"

As he always did when signing off with Jackie, LBJ said that he "longed" to see her. And, as she always did, Jackie promised that they would do just that, "soon." Then they hung up.

According to his secretary, Marie Fehmer, Johnson was the one feeling "used" after that telephone call. He believed that the only reason Bobby had put Jackie on the line was so that he [Johnson] would feel somehow indebted to the Kennedys when deciding upon a running mate for his upcoming presidential campaign. Johnson believed that Bobby wanted to be that running mate. Of course, the last thing Bobby wanted to be was Vice President, certain that he would be even more useless as LBJ's Vice President than LBJ was to Jack. Still, Johnson, a master manipulator who felt he knew when the tables were being turned, believed that Kennedy was using Jackie to wrangle such a position.

Says Marie Fehmer, "I remember afterward the look of bemusement on his face. He felt that it took a very ambitious and callous man to use a grieving widow as leverage. I can only say that he thought a lot less of Robert Kennedy after that call than he did before he took it," if such a thing were even possible.

Joan the Emissary

The month of November 1964 would be not only a time of renewal for Jackie Kennedy but also an important month for her sister-in-law, Joan. The John Fitzgerald Kennedy exhibition, which had been successfully touring the country, was now ready to be taken to Europe, and a representative of the Kennedy family would have to accompany the tribute and speak about displayed items. The Presidential Seal, Jack's rocking chair, his golf cart, certain paintings, plaques, letters, and other mementos from trips around the world, and even the coconut shell on which the young lieutenant Jack wrote a message asking for help after his PT-109 boat ran into trouble would all be part of the traveling show. This exhibit, which had opened in May in New York, was the family's way of showing its gratitude for the worldwide outpouring of sympathy following Jack's assassination; it was also organized to raise funds for the Kennedy Library, to be built at Harvard.

When it came time to decide who should go to Europe with the exhibit, it was Jackie's immediate idea to send Joan. She felt strongly that Joan should, once and for all, claim her rightful place in the family by representing the Kennedys in Europe. Jackie had been particularly struck by an odd moment in the White House a year earlier, one that said a great deal about Joan's inability to feel a part of the "dynasty."

Shortly after Jack's funeral, Jackie had asked James W. Fosburgh, a well-known art collector who had assisted her in choosing artwork for the renovation of the White House the year before, to help her and the family choose a painting that would be hung in the White House in Jack's memory. It was customary for departing presidents to add one painting to the permanent collection. Fosburgh went to New York and quickly returned with twenty paintings from art galleries and collectors there. He displayed them all in the family room, in front of Jackie, Eunice, Pat, Ted, and Joan. Together, they had narrowed the selection down to six.

"Okay, now, another vote," Jackie had said.

"Not me," Fosburgh said, bowing out. "You should decide this without me. I'm not a family member, after all."

Jackie had smiled and nodded her head appreciatively.

"Me, too," Joan blurted out. "I'm not a family member, either."

Everyone had turned and looked at her, confused expressions playing on their faces. Joan squirmed. "Well, I mean, I . . . I wasn't *born* into the family, you know?"

"Well, neither was I," Jackie had said. "We're all Kennedys, Joan."

"I'd rather not vote," Joan said, uneasily standing her ground. "It's not my place."

"Oh my God," Pat said, impatiently. "Let's just vote and get it over with."

In the end, the Kennedys settled for a painting of the River Seine in Paris by Claude Monet. It was hung in the Green Room.

Jackie had never forgotten that day in the White House when Joan made it clear that she did not feel a part of the family. "She had decided that she would one day find something for Joan to do that would solidify her position in the family," Lem Billings once said. "She had also been impressed by the way Joan had campaigned for Ted earlier in the year. No other Kennedy wife had done anything like that for her husband and everyone in the family was excited by Joan's accomplishment."

"She's beautiful and articulate," Jackie explained, "and Jack loved her. I want Joan to do it. I believe she'll do a wonderful job."

Eunice, Pat, and Jean, and even Ethel, agreed that Joan had acquitted herself so nicely while stumping for Ted that she could most certainly handle the exhibit. Some thought that Ethel should go, since Bobby was Jack's right-hand man, but she wanted to stay home with her children. "I love her like a sister," Ethel said in a statement, "and I'm proud to see her representing the family in this way."

Of course, Ethel had a funny way of showing that she loved Joan "like a sister," especially since she often seemed to go out of her way to belittle her. Richard Burke, who was a senatorial aide to Ted, recalled that "Ethel had a very condescending attitude toward Joan because Joan was really sick [referring to her drinking]. Ethel didn't deal very well with anybody's illness. It was like Ethel had two personalities. She could show compassion and be very attentive to people who were ill, but if they were people who were close to her, or people she relied on, she took that as a weakness and acted resentful toward them. That's the way she treated Joan—in a condescending manner [as if she were] a little girl."

Alcoholism was a serious problem in the Skakel family. Ethel's grandfather, James Curtis Skakel, was an alcoholic, as were her parents, George and Ann. Ethel's sister, Georgeann, would eventually die of the disease, and her brothers were heavy drinkers as well; George Jr. was a particularly troubling alcoholic whose drinking caused decades of problems for the family and his wife, Pat (also, unfortunately enough, an alcoholic).

Ethel believed that she had been strong enough not to succumb, and in her view anyone who did was weak. "Ethel despised weakness of any kind," George Terrien once explained. "It was just so un-Kennedy in her mind."

Interestingly, Jackie also feared that the disease could be passed down to her. She saw the way alcoholism had ravaged Black Jack, and she was smart enough to know that she was genetically predisposed. Luckily, she somehow managed to get ahold of herself after Jack's death because she seemed headed down the same road as her father.

If Joan somehow symbolized their worst fears, Jackie and Ethel reacted to it in vastly different ways: Jackie by reaching out to Joan and treating her kindly, Ethel by castigating her.

Whatever Jackie could do to see to it that Joan would shine, that's apparently what she wanted to do. So, in the second week of November 1964, Joan Kennedy and her sister, Candy, whom she took for emotional support, departed for Europe. Their first stop was Dublin.

Cead Mile Failte

Back in the summer of 1963, when President Kennedy visited Ireland, he had said that it had been "one of the most moving experiences" of his life. While he walked through the U.S. diplomatic residence, he mentioned that he hoped one day to become the ambassador and live there. He and members of his family, including his sister, Jean Kennedy Smith, traveled from city to city, meeting and speaking to the Irish, who pressed rosary beads into his hand as he greeted them. He was an icon for the Irish (just as 1922 marked Ireland's legal independence from the United Kingdom, U.S. election year 1960 defined its psychological independence from hundreds of years of British domination) and his sister Jean watched, awed by the reception.* Jack also spent time with a third cousin there, Mrs. Mary Kennedy Ryan. Experiencing the warmth and enthusiasm of the Irish was not only a career highlight for Jack but a source of personal satis-

---

*Many years later, Jean Kennedy Smith would be named ambassador to Ireland by President Bill Clinton. She would be instrumental in easing tensions in Northern Ireland, her first two years marking abrupt changes in U.S. foreign policy.

faction as well. (While there, he also addressed a joint session of the Irish Parliament, to resounding success.)

"It wasn't just a sentimental journey," Jackie later explained. (She wasn't with her husband because she was pregnant at the time and couldn't fly.) "Ireland meant much more. He had always been moved by its poetry and literature because it told of the tragedy and the desperate courage that he knew lay just under the surface of Irish life. The people of Ireland had faced famine and disease, and had fought against oppression, died for independence. And all through the tragic story, they dreamed and sang and wrote and thought and were gay in the face of their burdens."

"I'll be back in the springtime," John Kennedy said just before he left Ireland. Sadly, he would never see the spring.

Now a little more than a year had passed. Much had changed. Jack was gone, and Joan Bennett Kennedy was representing him and his family in the country that had shown so much love and respect to the Kennedys. From the start, the response Joan received was enthusiastic and heartening. For instance, 50,000 Dubliners came to see the JFK exhibit at the Municipal Art Gallery in Dublin. More specifically, though, it would seem that they came to see the blond-haired, blue-eyed beauty, Joan.

"Look at this, Joan. Just *look*," Candy exclaimed as thousands of Dubliners stood in a winding line in front of the gallery just to catch a glimpse of Joan. The line of patient people seemed endless as it circled around the block. *"Cead mile failte"* (Gaelic for "a hundred thousand welcomes," the national slogan), they shouted at Joan as she finally got up the courage to walk down the street outside the art gallery, shaking hands and greeting all of those who had come to remember Jack, and to meet her.

Though she had been in the public eye for some time now, this reception was unlike anything Joan Kennedy had ever experienced. Perhaps she thought, "So *this* is what it's like to be Jackie," as she shook the sweaty hands of hundreds of excited fans and was offered so many bouquets of flowers that she was forced to leave them on the ground at her feet. Eventually, she was hip-high in colorful bouquets.

There was such a turnout, in fact, that the exhibit would be forced to stay open long after the scheduled closing hour of 9 P.M. Inside, the crowd turned reverential once the people were in the presence of all that displayed history.

Joan later recalled, "It was almost as if they were in church, the way they were hushed and the way they examined each of the objects."

The next day, Joan and Candy drove south to Dunganstown, where they had the opportunity to meet Mary Kennedy Ryan and other relatives. "She was lovely," one reporter said of Joan. "She and the Kennedy relations sat down, stared at one another for a moment, and then they burst into tears. 'I can't believe he's gone, and I can't believe *I'm* here,' Joan said, weeping. They gave her a wonderful reception, made her feel like a queen. They said, 'Look at how much they love you here,' to which Joan responded, 'It's not me they love. It's Jack.' When she left, everyone was all smiles. People were saying, 'Why don't we see more of Joan Kennedy?'"

The next stop for Joan and the JFK exhibit was London, then Paris, Frankfurt, and finally Berlin, where she would be appearing on November 21 at Congress Hall the night before the first anniversary of Jack's death. That evening, the Berlin hall was packed with devotees all anxious to be in the presence of any Kennedy. Many had actually seen the President in person when, in June of the last year of his life, more than half of West Berlin's population came to hear him speak.

Now, a year and five months later, it was Joan's turn to be the Kennedy of choice. The Berliners would not let her down.

There was such enthusiasm for Joan Kennedy's appearance that overly enthusiastic officials almost caused a riot when they decided to open the doors to everyone—those with tickets as well as those who weren't able to purchase any because they were sold out. Everywhere Joan looked from the platform on which she stood, she saw people were smiling up at her, cheering her, loving her. It was surreal, she would later admit.

Under a bright spotlight, Joan stood in front of a microphone on the platform of Congress Hall before the shadowy silhouettes of thousands of figures. She hesitated a moment as the crowd hushed itself.

In a small, trembling voice that was amplified so loudly she was startled at the sound, Joan thanked the throng for its devotion to Jack. "Your love for him is so clear to me, to all of us," she said. A woman interpreter translated her remarks, and after only a few sentences, Joan had to stop and wait once again for the applause to die down. Her sister, Candy, sitting on the side of the platform, looked at her in amazement.

For a moment, Joan seemed helpless in the face of such overwhelming adulation, but then she must have called upon some hidden resolve because she managed to continue. Suppressing her nervousness, she rose to the occasion.

"I am so proud of John F. Kennedy," she said, her voice echoing louder and stronger, "and all that he stood for, and all that he was to America, and to the world—the great, truly great, man he was."

At the end of her brief speech, Joan Bennett Kennedy spoke the words that had caused such a torrent of emotion when last heard spoken by her brother-in-law, the President: *"Ich bin ein Berliner,"* she declared, her voice clear and authoritative, her arms outstretched to the cheering throng.

The audience rose to its feet in a standing ovation. Flashbulbs popped all about as Joan Kennedy, tears streaming down her face, stood on the stage and let the crowd's adoration wash over her, a tidal wave of love, respect, and admiration.

Joan's Continuing Struggle

The week following Teddy's accident, Bobby appeared on the cover of *Life* magazine and was quoted as saying that Teddy's accident had convinced him not to run for the Senate, that his priority should be his family. In truth, Bobby had already decided he was going to run for the Senate if LBJ did not choose him as a running mate. The *Life* story was actually a calculated attempt to force Johnson's hand.

Bobby didn't hold out much hope for a position on the LBJ ticket, though, and he really didn't want the job, anyway. However, he would waffle on the matter for some time, strategizing what to do if asked, and how to proceed if not asked. For his part, Johnson became so determined to avoid having Bobby on the ticket that he soon announced his intention to bypass all members of his cabinet for the position.

Richard Goodwin, speechwriter for LBJ, told Bobby, "If Johnson had to choose between you and Ho Chi Minh as a running mate, he'd go with Ho Chi Minh."

Two days after Johnson chose Minnesota Senator Hubert Humphrey as a running mate, Bobby announced his Senate candidacy. It was a difficult campaign, however, and Bobby was worn down by comparisons to his late brother. Also, long a Massachusetts resident (although he spent his boyhood in New York), Bobby's decision to take a residence in New York and seek public office there was resented by many who accused him of being a "carpetbagger," insisting that a senator should represent the state where he lived and knew its problems.

He considered leaving the race after just a month, until he received an encouraging letter from Jackie. "It was a most feeling letter, in which she implored him not to give up, not to quit," said Lem Billings. "She told him she needed him and that the children, especially John Jr., needed him as a surrogate father, somebody they could turn to, now that their own father was gone.

"Jackie also wrote that the country needed Bobby, and that the time had come to honor Jack's memory rather than continue to mourn it."

Partly emboldened by Jackie's missive and also by his desire to be of public service and continue Jack's work, Bobby continued in politics by resigning as Attorney General, turning down the Cabinet position offered him by LBJ (which he never really wanted), and running for the Senate, representing New York.

Jackie was enthusiastic about Bobby's decision. She gave interviews about him, appeared at his campaign office, was photographed with him, and made her support of him clear. Her willingness to make public appearances for him was not surprising to those who knew of their relationship. Of him she had said, "Bobby is a man for whom I'd put my hand in a fire."

Jackie met for tea with *New York Post* publisher Dorothy Schiff to promote her brother-in-law's ideals and, she hoped, to win an important endorsement from that publication. "He must win," she told her, "he *will* win. Or maybe it is just because one wants it so much that one thinks that. People say he is ruthless and cold," Jackie observed. "He isn't like the others. I think it was his place in the family, with four girls and being younger than two brothers and so much smaller. He hasn't got the graciousness they had. He is really very shy, but he has the kindest heart in the world." (Bobby did win the *Post's* endorsement, though it's doubtful that it was solely because of Jackie's intervention.)

Bobby's New York campaign against incumbent Republican Kenneth Keating was an uproarious one, with wild crowds everywhere he went in New York just wanting to glimpse him and his wife, Ethel. When he went on to win the election to the Senate, there was no doubt that Jackie's quiet assistance helped him win many votes that would have otherwise gone to his opponent.

On January 4, 1965, Bobby Kennedy took the oath of office alongside Ted. "What's it like to have a wife who is becoming so much a part of history?" a reporter for the *Boston Globe* asked Ted. The writer was obviously referring to Joan's successful campaign on Ted's behalf, and also her triumph in Europe. As Joan smiled broadly by his side, Ted shrugged. "She's a good girl," he said, dismissively. "Don'tcha think?"

With those words, Joan seemed to shrink, the sadness on her face clear to any observer.

By mid-1965, some in the Kennedy camp thought of Joan Kennedy as a diamond in the rough. Though she had always maintained that she didn't want to be a public person, even she—with all her doubts and insecurities—had to admit that much of what she set out to do in front of an audience she seemed to do well, whether it was campaigning for her husband in Massachusetts or talking about her deceased brother-in-law's personal effects in Europe.

Later, in the spring, Joan would have an opportunity to distinguish herself as more than another Kennedy wife when asked to do something she enjoyed that had little to do with politics: narrate *Peter and the Wolf,* by the Russian composer Sergei Prokofiev, for a fund-raiser. With her background in music, perhaps Joan had an advantage over most narrators; her work in this regard was touted by some Washington critics. She would be so successful at this new endeavor—at a lectern at the front of a stage with an eighty-member orchestra playing behind her—that she would be asked to narrate *Peter and the Wolf* several more times over the years.

Still, Joan was conflicted. While she may have appeared to be comfortable with crowds, it was all an act. The truth was that, except in fleeting moments, whenever she put herself in the public forum she was doing something she didn't enjoy.

"You need to bring her out more, like Ethel," Bobby told Ted at a New York charity event in front of a group of Kennedy aides. "She's too shy, too quiet. No one knows what to make of her."

"I'm lucky to get her out of the house," Ted replied.

"But why?" Bobby asked. "She was great when you were flat on your back, she was great in Europe. She needs to continue in that vein, like a Kennedy."

It seemed as if almost everyone around her—Jackie, Ethel, Bobby, Rose, and even the Kennedy sisters, Pat, Jean, and Eunice—saw the great potential in Joan Kennedy to do anything to which she set her mind. However, it seemed that because she could not win her husband's approval, nothing she accomplished meant anything to her. So, rather than be energized by those accomplishments, she appeared exhausted by them, possibly because they did nothing to ingratiate her to Ted. Perhaps she saw each achievement as really just another failure.

During one cocktail meeting with political allies in New York at the 21 Club, Joan and Ethel seemed to be the focus of attention of every person in the club. In typically sixties' outfits, the two sisters-in-law were a sight: Ethel was in a vinyl dress with large black-and-white squares and spaghetti shoulder straps made of rhinestones, and Joan was in a short miniskirt of a silver fabric, with enormous plastic bubble earrings. Recalls Jerry Summers, one of the security guards on duty that night at the club, "Everyone wanted to stare. It was like having major movie stars in the place."

At one point, the two Kennedy wives got up to go to the ladies' room. Suddenly at least thirty women rose to follow them, all headed to the small bathroom. As soon as they saw the stampede, Bobby's security men leapt up to run interference, attempting to pull the fans away from the Kennedy women. Ethel helped by screaming at the women, "Get back right now. Can't a woman even go to the bathroom? What's the matter with you people? My God, you're *animals*."

Joan, who had enjoyed a few drinks, looked terrorized. Her hair was mussed, and mascara tears ran down her face as she spun about in the same spot, being pushed and pulled from all directions. She was a

Raggedy Ann doll in a bad miniskirt. One of the guards grabbed her by the arm and practically dragged her to safety. When she finally got back to her table, she broke down crying. She and Ted left, quickly. Ethel and Bobby stayed behind, however, signing autographs, smiling, and shaking hands.

PART NINE

The Rumor Mill

Was Camelot's Guenevere having an affair with Lancelot now that King Arthur was dead and buried?

As soon as Jackie Kennedy had settled in Manhattan, rumors began anew about the nature of her relationship with her dead husband's brother Bobby, giving the East Coast gossip columnists something new upon which to focus in welcoming Jackie to town. Throughout the years, and in many biographies of the two Kennedys, just such a "romance" has been confirmed by people who claim to have had intimate knowledge of it.

Kenny O'Donnell once told of an instance in the spring of 1965 when Jackie called Bobby in tears. "She was in her apartment with her kids, and the police were scouring the place with the bomb squad," said O'Donnell. "Someone had apparently phoned in a bomb threat. Jackie was frantic, Bobby said, crying on the phone that she was going to be blown to bits with her kids, and asking what she had done to deserve this fate. It was a terrible thing.

"She was a prisoner in that place. They were afraid to get her out of there because the caller said there was a sniper waiting for her to leave the building. She was going to be picked off as soon as she walked out. It was a night of terror; she was trapped like a caged animal. Bobby took the next plane to New York and was there in a few hours. By the time he arrived, though, the scare was over . . . no bomb was found. Jackie was so upset, Bobby spent the night at her place.

"That's where rumors got started," said O'Donnell. "If he had been seen leaving there, then there would have been stories." O'Donnell, who knew both Bobby and Jackie well, doesn't believe the stories. "How could anyone be romantic after a hysterical scene like that one? She needed him, he was there for her. But as a close friend, a protector, which is what she needed, believe me."

The rumor of an affair between Jackie and Bobby has also been fanned by people whose relationship with both parties had been somewhat strained over the years. Gore Vidal wrote derogatorily in his memoirs, *Palimpsest*, that "the one person she [Jackie] ever loved, if indeed she was capable of such an emotion, was Bobby Kennedy." However, Vidal's animus for Bobby was well known.

Another writer of note, Truman Capote, was quoted as having said that he was surprised "that the Jackie-Bobby love affair remained under wraps as long as it did."*

"Such a hurtful rumor," observed Joan Braden, "but so typical of the kinds of stories that floated around about the Kennedy women, started up by people who didn't think of them as real, flesh-and-blood human beings. Besides the obvious fact that Jackie was so devastated and would never be able to have a man in her life at that time, look at how bereaved Bobby was! People can't just push all of that hurt and anger aside and jump into bed together. Maybe on a TV soap opera they can, but not in real life. It was so demeaning a rumor, to everyone concerned."

"Rubbish," concurs Bobby Kennedy's former spokesman, Frank Mankiewicz. "In people's fantasy world of what the Kennedys were like, yes. In the real world, no."

Rose Kennedy's secretary, Barbara Gibson, adds, "It's just absurd and the kind of thing that people whispered about because it was such a juicy bit of speculation. Untrue, I am sure of it."

Also underscoring the rumors over the years has been the slow release of classified Secret Service documents that have indicated that Jackie and Bobby were in each other's constant company throughout the last six months of 1964. "Considering the way J. Edgar Hoover felt about Bobby Kennedy, is it any wonder that he would attempt to turn his relationship with Jackie into something tawdry?" said Frank Mankiewicz.

However, one person who apparently did believe the stories was Ethel. According to George Smathers, "Though there was no affair, I believe Bobby's wife thought there was one."

---

*Jackie and Joan were once discussing Truman Capote when Joan asked, "Is it true, Jackie, that he's queer?" Jackie, who was always amused by Joan's naïveté, acted as if she didn't know what her sister-in-law meant by "queer." Joan persisted, "You know, Jackie, gay. *Gay!*" Jackie had to laugh. "Oh, Joan, you are too much," she said, kidding her. "Gay? He's as gay as *paint*! We'll never be able to corrupt you, will we?"

Ethel seemed to find it difficult to accept that her husband was spending so much time with his attractive sister-in-law. It is interesting to note that in the early fifties, Bobby first fell in love with Ethel's older sister, Pat Skakel. After his first few dates with Ethel, the shy and moody Bobby had slowly drifted to her sister, who better matched his temperament. Soon, Pat and Bobby were seriously involved. "They fell in love and dated for two years," Ethel admitted some two decades later, but added that she didn't like to talk about that "terrible period."

It was Pat whom Bobby first seriously considered marrying. However, Pat wasn't in love with Bobby and, in time, broke it off with him. Bobby, on the rebound, began dating an alluring young actress named Joan Winmill.

But the ambitious Kennedy boys, with their sights set on politics, were brought up to be practical in their decision-making. Every move they made, from the schools they attended, to the wives they chose, was a choice made with a careful eye to the future marks they would leave in the political arena. The women they married would have to be exceptional in many ways and provide more than just temporary infatuation. The athletic, competitive Ethel, with her deeply held Catholic beliefs, fitted in perfectly with the Kennedy clan. Ethel, like Bobby and his mother Rose, attended Mass every day; she was intelligent and loyal, and what she lacked in glamour she made up for in devotion. Her offbeat humor and boisterous behavior also melded in effortlessly with the rowdy Kennedy clan; she made the perfect Kennedy wife.

At the time of her great concern about her Bobby's alleged affair with Jackie, Ethel subscribed to a magazine called *Photoplay*, a movie fan magazine that was a popular monthly at the time. Jackie and Ethel enjoyed reading about themselves in such silly fan magazines, even though much of what they read was completely untrue. Says Leah Mason, who worked at Hickory Hill as an assistant to Ethel, "Ethel always had a huge stack of these magazines, and one of my jobs was to clip out the articles about her and the other Kennedys, and keep them for posterity."

The three Kennedy wives were written about more than any other political wives of the sixties and seventies, sharing covers with Hollywood stars such as Elizabeth Taylor and Frank Sinatra. While reading about themselves in such magazines, the women would privately marvel at how journalists would create pure fiction around innocent photographs. Ethel, however, was prone to believe that the stories about other family members were true.

Said Leah Mason, "Ethel would call up Joan and say, 'Why didn't you tell me you were angry at me?' and Joan would say, 'What in the world are you talking about?' Ethel would reply that she had read about the 'feud' in a movie magazine, and believed it. She just assumed that Joan would speak to a reporter about it before she would speak to her. Then, after hanging up with Joan, she would say to me, 'Cut that article out and file it. I may need it for future reference.' Sometimes she would have me send an offending article to someone, like Andy Williams, and tell me to write in the margin something like, 'We must be more discreet!' Once, Andy called and said, 'What is she *talking* about?'"

Jackie and Ethel—not Joan, who couldn't even bear to read what was being written about her, let alone save the stories—would spend hours writing letters and making telephone calls to friends, pleading with them to completely disregard some untruth that had been printed. One odd letter from Ethel to Andy Williams explained that an article implying a romance between Bobby and Williams's wife, Claudine Longet, was "inaccurate as far as I know." One might assume that famous women, so accustomed to this kind of publicity, good and bad, would not be concerned about what was written in cheap magazines, but that was not the case. It's also interesting to note that they would even have the time to devote to such pursuits.

For her part, Jackie loved to gossip, and always had. However, when the gossip was about her, she didn't much like it. She would read the fan magazines and circle the names of the sources for the articles, and then write them off forever, never speaking to them again. If one of those sources happened to be someone with whom she was friendly, she would clip the article, circle the offending passages, send it to the sinning friend, and then she would never speak to that person again.

She, like her sister-in-law, often feared that others would believe what they read in these publications. For instance, while stories had persisted that Jackie found Lyndon Johnson to be offensive, there is little evidence in their correspondence over the years—more than seventy-five letters in all—that Jackie and LBJ shared anything but a friendly, respectful relationship; he was very solicitous.

Yet, during the holidays of 1966, Jackie was disturbed by the reprinting of an article by William Manchester in a fan magazine called *Modern Screen* with the headline: "Jackie Hates LBJ—She Thinks He's a Dirty Old Man!"*

Jackie feared that once Johnson read this story, whether in this magazine—as if the President actually read *Modern Screen!*—or elsewhere, his feelings about her might change. The fact that she would be worried about such a thing not only demonstrated her concern for the feelings of people she cared about, but perhaps it also spoke volumes about her own insecurity.

To set things straight, she wrote Johnson a letter (addressing the envelope simply to "The President; The White House, Washington, DC") and sent it off on January 6, 1967, from Antigua in the West Indies, where she was vacationing after New Year's.

She started by saying that she feared he would think she was "childish" by sending the letter, and she understood that he had more important matters on his mind other than what she was about to express to him. She then explained that she had been misquoted in the magazine article as having said that she objected to his use of the term "honey" when speaking to her. It may have said something about the state of Jackie's emotions when she then wrote, "The rage I have been trying to suppress and forget down here boiled up again." She conceded that the misquote was probably inconsequential, but was typical of the way Manchester had, in her view, "twisted" whatever she may have told him.

Jackie assured Johnson that any term of endearment he had ever used with her over the years was genuinely received, and she noted that she thought of "honey" as being a term that she appreciated hearing from him. She further wrote that she wished there were more people in her life who would use that term when referring to her and that

*Jackie had filed a highly publicized lawsuit against William Manchester to prevent him from using, in his book *The Death of a President*, highly personal material he had gotten from her in an interview. In the end the material was deleted from his work, but not until it was reprinted in newspapers and magazines everywhere as the result of reports about the lawsuit, all much to Jackie's dismay. "I am so dazed," she wrote during the litigation, "I feel that I will never be able to feel anything again."

she hoped Johnson would continue to use it. She also hoped that he would "not become embittered by all this [the article], and by all life, really."

Jackie apparently had second thoughts about drawing attention to what was probably a trivial matter because, in her letter, she then asked LBJ to forgive her for even having written it, and said that she would probably later regret not having torn it up rather than sending it off to him. However, in what she termed as "some blind way," she said that she just wanted to reaffirm her great affection for him. "No matter what happens, no matter how your feelings might change towards me. Once I decide I care about someone," she concluded, "nothing can ever make me change." (Perhaps Jackie's comment to LBJ about her loyalty to her friends was ironic, considering the way she would ostracize those she felt had talked about her to the press.)

When these same kinds of fan magazines began publishing stories about Bobby and Jackie, Jackie didn't mention anything about them to Ethel, at least not to anyone's recollection. Perhaps she never imagined that Ethel would believe such stories to be true. However, Ethel did seem upset about the rumors. Her secretary arrived for work at Hickory Hill one day to find a stack of fan magazines on her desk, each with a Bobby-Jackie headline. "Just look at those," Ethel said, clearly exasperated by the press coverage. "Look at what they're writing about Bobby and Jackie. Do you think any of it is true?"

The secretary didn't respond.

"This is so unlike Jackie," Ethel continued. "I don't know what to think." She then gathered the magazines and hurled them into the trash can. "Why do I read this garbage, anyway?" she asked, rhetorically.

Joan Braden and a number of other family friends said that Ethel, perhaps in some desperation, asked her brother George to talk to Bobby about the stories, which was odd in that the two men disliked each other. Predictably, George refused to become involved. When Ethel then asked Ted for his opinion of the matter, he told her to "forget about it. It's ridiculous." Finally, Ethel decided to just confront Jackie about the rumors, but both Joan Braden and Lem Billings, in separate conversations with her, managed to persuade her not to do so. Years later, Braden recalled convincing Ethel that Jackie would be hurt by the insinuation, and that the result of such an inquiry would only permanently damage their relationship.

Two weeks later, Ethel saw Jackie at a party. Afterward, she told her friends of "an epiphany" that had occurred at the gathering. Joan Braden recalled, "She told me that she looked Jackie straight in the eye until it suddenly hit her: It couldn't be true. 'It just *couldn't* be,' she said, reaching out for me. We embraced, and she held on as tightly as she could." As she hugged her, Joan sensed that Ethel was sobbing. "It's very stressful, very upsetting for a woman to go through this kind of thing, what with all of the terrible indecision and worry," Braden said. "However, when Ethel pulled away, she turned quickly. She wouldn't let even me see her tears."

RFK for President

By early spring 1968, Bobby Kennedy still had not made up his mind about running for the Presidency. The family was split in its opinions. With the exception of Jackie, the women all seemed to agree that he should run. Ethel wanted nothing more than for him to one day be President. It had been her dream for years.

Rose, along with Eunice, Jean, and Pat, and their husbands, all had that "ol' Kennedy spirit" as well, and felt that Bobby had much to offer the Democratic Party. Ted, however, disagreed, fearing that Bobby's life would be in jeopardy should he ever become President. He now seemed to actually believe in the Kennedy curse Joan had spoken to Jackie about at the hospital after Ted's plane accident. Jackie agreed with Ted, saying that the thought of Bobby as President was chilling to her. She said that she couldn't bear the idea, and when anyone wanted to discuss it with her, she would become grim.

Because the race had already begun (it was too late even to enter most of the primaries), Bobby feared that his late entry might split the party and perhaps even strengthen Republican support. He was also afraid that his running would appear to be a vendetta against Johnson.

LBJ's popularity was all but completely ruined, anyway, by the Vietnam War, as well as the protests and violence across the country.

In the end, it would be Ethel who would convince Bobby to run. "She believed he should do it, and she pushed for it," said Ted Sorenson. "She wanted it for him, and perhaps for herself."

Sorenson, who opposed Bobby's candidacy, recalled one meeting with the family at Hickory Hill in which he voiced his opinion. Ethel railed against him. "But why, Ted?" she demanded to know. "And after all of those high-flown praises you wrote for President Kennedy?" As the meeting went on, Ethel and some of her children disappeared and went to an upstairs bedroom. From a window, they rolled down a banner that read "Kennedy for President." Then, Ethel put "The Impossible Dream" on the record player. It would later become the campaign theme.

"She was a major factor, without question," said Frederick P. Dutton, Bobby's political campaign adviser, of Ethel's influence on Bobby's decision.

"She wanted to be First Lady, that's true," concurred Barbara Gibson. "But she also believed that Bobby had so much to give, that he could make changes, do good things for the country. She was his main cheerleader, most definitely."

Bobby made his announcement on Saturday, March 16, 1968. (At about this same time, Ethel learned she was pregnant with her eleventh child. The pregnancy would be kept a secret for the time being.) The road to the 1968 Democratic nomination had been a long one for this young Kennedy, a man who had undergone authentic interior changes and growth. The once-puny-but-pugnacious member of the tight-knit Kennedy clan was a sibling who now spoke from the same podium where his brother, Jack, had announced his campaign just eight years earlier. If he were to win in November, Bobby would be the youngest man ever elected to that office; 175 days younger than Jack when he was sworn in.

Bobby's historic announcement would once have been greeted with wild enthusiasm by the anti-war movement. But now, to many, his candidacy seemed opportunistic. Some felt he'd had his chance; when his supporters had wanted him to run in 1964, he hadn't. In the end, there would be no time to build the kind of mammoth political machine that had characterized past Kennedy campaigns. Ted Sorenson recalled that allies had to be lined up at a moment's notice without much effort to determine who was best for the job, "who could deliver and who was full of hot air."

Meanwhile, Kennedy took a strong position against Lyndon Johnson and the bombings in Vietnam. "Some of his speeches got very close to demagoguery," recalled Richard Harwood of the *Washington Post*, who traveled with the Kennedy campaign. "And I said so in a couple of pieces in the *Post*. When I went back to the airplane to take off on the next leg of the trip, some young woman tried to stop me from boarding the plane, saying I wasn't welcome there. But I got aboard. And a little while later, Ethel Kennedy came down the aisle, with my story wadded up, and she threw it in my face."

On the evening of March 31, things changed when Johnson finally bowed out of the race. A Gallup poll showing that only 26 percent of those questioned approved of his handling of the war seemed to seal his fate, at least in his own mind. The Democratic race would now be between Kennedy, Eugene McCarthy, and Vice President Hubert Humphrey.

Ethel accompanied Bobby on his campaign tour, leaving her children at Hickory Hill, where they were being cared for by the couple's servants. Two of the oldest were at boarding schools: Kathleen, seventeen, was finishing her final year at Putney School in Vermont, and Joe, now almost sixteen, attended his father's alma mater, Milton Academy. The rest—one-year-old Douglas, three-year-old Matthew Maxwell, five-year-old Chris, eight-year-old Kerry, ten-year-old Michael, twelve-year-old Courtney, thirteen-year-old David, and fourteen-year-old Bobby Jr.—would watch their father on the nightly news and cheer mightily at his image on the screen. The children missed their mother, however, and made life difficult for the servants, acting in an undisciplined manner and, as one who also worked for Jackie from time to time put it, "raising so much hell, we were afraid there'd be nothing left to Hickory Hill by the time Mrs. Kennedy returned."

While on the campaign trail, Ethel would visit hospitals, industrial plants, and children's institutions, make speeches, sign autographs, shake hands, and do whatever necessary to support her husband. She was usually gregarious in front of a crowd, displaying a great sense of humor. "This is my first day speaking," she said at Marion, Ohio, "so I confess I'm a little hesitant. In 1960, Bobby sent me to Kentucky, Utah, California, Oregon, Virginia—and we didn't win one of those states."

She wanted to do her best, but this campaign meant a lot. Nervous, she made some embarrassing gaffes. In Fort Wayne, Indiana, she relied on a taxi driver to give her information that the city was named after "Mad Anthony" Wayne, the American patriot who had fought the British in the War of 1812. Later that day, in giving a speech to students, Ethel mentioned the bit of trivia to them. Later, their teacher informed Mrs. Kennedy that not only was Wayne really a famous Indian fighter, but that by 1812 he had been dead for sixteen years. "Oh no!" Ethel exclaimed. "That cab driver had it all wrong!"

Later, when she landed in Los Angeles, she announced to a crowd how happy she was to be in Anaheim. "For Christ's sake, Ethel," Bobby said, scolding her. "If you're going to get the name of the town wrong, at least say it in a whisper."

While she gave a few on-air television interviews, she appeared wooden and clearly afraid of saying the wrong thing and hurting Bobby's chances. For Ethel, the pressure was on like never before.

The atmosphere of Bobby's campaign was electric. With the fury and hopelessness that set in among the black community following the murder of Martin Luther King, minorities became even more passionately devoted to Bobby. In turn, Bobby was more devoted to civil rights than ever. His energy seemed ceaseless, as if he thrived off the frenzied admiration from the zealous crowds. The country seemed at the dawning of a new era and it was Bobby, the oldest surviving Kennedy brother, who became the personification of the nation's deliverance.

Enter "The Greek"

After her husband passed away, Jackie did not share details with other members of the Kennedy family about the men she saw socially. First of all, she was a discreet woman and thought it inappropriate to give details of her personal life to the family of her deceased husband. She also must have realized that most of the Kennedys would view anyone with whom she chose to share her life as an unworthy replacement for Jack.

But Jackie wasn't sitting at home alone. She had a number of men interested in her at the time, though no one she took seriously as a romantic partner. She was seen with the widowed David Ormsby-Gore, former British Ambassador to the United States, as well as with family friends Roswell Gilpatric, Lord Harlech, Mike Nichols, and Arthur Schlesinger, Jr. She was fascinated by Truman Capote and other gay men who idolized her, recognized her status as an icon, and treated her like a queen. She had also dated John Carl Warnecke—the architect she had hired to design a permanent memorial grave for the President—on and off for the last two years. Friends of Jackie's have differing memories of her relationship with Warnecke. Some insist she truly cared for him, while others say that he was merely a diversion.

As the press vigorously covered Jackie's "romantic" liaisons, she laughed at the way they focused "on the fanciful embellishments" (as she told Rudolf Nureyev over dinner one evening) while leaving "the essence still untouched."

It was Aristotle Onassis who was the essence of Jackie's interest at this time. During her years of mourning, she began keeping company with the wealthy industrialist who had been so kind to her in 1963 when she visited him on his yacht, the *Christina*, after baby Patrick's death. He encouraged her to talk about her loss when no one else wanted her to do so, and she had never forgotten his sensitivity. He was also charming and personable, spoke fluent Spanish, French, and English as well as his native Greek, and enjoyed poetry, music, and quiet times as much as he did wheeling and dealing, negotiating tough deals, and making money. "A strange man in many ways," she had said, "such a rogue, but also so understanding. I was fascinated by him from the beginning."

When Jack died, Onassis had been at the White House to express his sympathies, and was one of the few visitors, outside of family and a few heads of state, whom Jackie allowed upstairs to the private quarters to visit her. He consoled her as she spoke to him of the terrible ordeal she was enduring at that time, and just as he had won her favor after Patrick's death, he impressed her with his understanding and patience after the death of her husband. He understood how difficult it was for Jackie to begin her life again, and he encouraged her to be strong.

"But every day I feel I'm losing a little more of him," she said, crying to Onassis about a year after Jack's death. "As time goes on, he becomes more a part of my past."

"You have done all the mourning that anyone can humanly expect of you," he told her. "The dead are dead. You are living."

The two stayed in communication; Onassis began sending Jackie roses almost daily for nearly a year, and soon they were seeing each other socially, with Jackie traveling back and forth to Greece and Ari commuting to the States. Although Ari was not as handsome as Jack or her father, he had the same dynamic qualities as the two men she had adored. He was attractive to women, and vice versa, an important quality to Jackie. And he was rich and generous, and she did have a need for the money.

The fact that Jackie found Onassis to be charming and sensitive made for a pleasant dating experience, but wouldn't have been reason enough for her to allow him into a position of prominence in her life. After all, she was a woman who had been raised to consider a man's wealth when making a decision about her future with him, and the fact that Onassis was one of the richest men in the world no doubt helped Jackie in making certain choices about him. His money would afford her not only a glamorous lifestyle but also a sense of freedom and protection, important to her and to her children at this time.

Many of the Kennedys closest to her were unaware of how truly frightened Jackie was just to walk out onto the street in public. Crowds terrified her. The constant popping of cameras when she was in public never ceased to jolt her. Was it a bullet? she would wonder. Or just a flashbulb? The memory of watching helplessly as the lifeless body of her husband slumped into her lap had been burned into her consciousness. The nightmares had never ended; no matter how much time passed, she was still traumatized. Much to her dismay, she felt like a victim. If there was one thing Jackie Kennedy never wanted to think of herself as, it was a victim. Ari would be able to protect her and her children at this time when she felt most vulnerable. He could whisk her to far-off lands when she felt most threatened in America by paparazzi, the media, an adoring public, and worse.

Jackie's relationship with Ari was kept from the family in the first few months because both believed that if the Kennedys knew of it, they would stop at nothing to end it. Bobby, who referred to Onassis as "the Greek," felt he was a criminal, and nothing would change his mind about that. Even though Onassis was spending nights at Jackie's Fifth Avenue apartment and she was flying off to Europe to be with him, Bobby and the rest of the Kennedys really did not know that anything serious was developing between them.

Jackie happened to be in Mexico in March 1968 when she learned that Bobby had decided to run for President. For her, this was not good news. She was convinced that it was open season on Kennedys, and that if he were to become President, his fate would be the same as Jack's. He would leave behind ten children whose lives would be ruined, she believed, and a widow who would never be able to pick up the pieces of her shattered dreams. She had told Bobby of her fears but, apparently, he wouldn't listen. So Jackie prepared a statement for the press, indicating that she "will always be with him with all my heart," and began to hope and pray for the best outcome.

In March of 1968, shortly after Bobby announced his candidacy, Aristotle Onassis was interviewed at a cocktail party at the George V Hotel in Paris. In comments that have been published innumerable times over the years, Onassis said that, in his estimation, Jackie was a woman who had, for years, been held up as a model of propriety, constancy, and "so many of those boring American female virtues." He said that she was "now so utterly devoid of mystery" that she needed "a small scandal to bring her alive. A peccadillo, an indiscretion. Something should happen to her to win our fresh compassion. The world loves to pity fallen grandeur." Ari knew his words would have a great impact not only on the media, but also on the Kennedys. "That should set the cat among the pigeons on Hickory Hill," he said, with a snicker, after making the statement. The next morning, newspapers across the country trumpeted his critical assessments of Jackie.

Ethel didn't like it when she picked up the morning paper and read Onassis's summation of her sister-in-law. "How well does he even know Jackie?" she wondered. "Why would he say these things? How dare he?" She convinced Bobby that he should discuss the matter with Jackie. However, Bobby was so angry at the report that he didn't need much coaxing.

When Bobby telephoned Jackie to ask what she felt about Onassis's comments, she confessed that she was actually thinking of marrying him but that no decision had been made. He was upset and said so, telling her that her decision could "cost me five states." He further cast aspersions on the relationship, calling it a "family weakness," alluding to Ari's previous romance with Lee Radziwill. Jackie knew he was hurt, so she refrained from doing what would have come naturally for her at that point—hanging up on him.

Jackie still felt a close relationship to Bobby, and in the past had often tried to abide by his wishes and the wishes of the family. "But it's time for me to live for me," she finally told him. "Not for the Kennedys."

After Bobby seemed to get nowhere with Jackie, it was Ethel's idea to visit Jackie herself and to bring Joan along. Joan, who always cared about Jackie's well-being, was concerned that her sister-in-law was making a terrible mistake and that she would get hurt in the process. She didn't trust Onassis—though she didn't know exactly why, rather it was just a sense that she had—and she felt that, based on what she read, he had underworld connections.

Ethel's uneasiness was more specific. She wanted to know more about Onassis's complex and allegedly illegal business dealings as much as she wanted to know the truth about his well-publicized, volatile relationship with opera singer Maria Callas. She believed that a wedding between her sister-in-law and Onassis should be canceled or at the very least delayed, because it would most certainly jeopardize Bobby's political chances.

The Appeal to Jackie

Ethel and Joan paid their visit to Jackie on a brisk, New York afternoon in early April 1968. As always, Fifth Avenue in Manhattan was alive with bustle and movement: horns braying in congested traffic, taxis screeching to a halt and then starting off again, people colliding with one another as they walked—along with an assistant of Ethel's—

to their destination. On this afternoon a small gathering of people, about fifteen in all, had congregated on the sidewalk at the entrance of Jackie's fashionable pre–World War I apartment building at 1040 Fifth Avenue, hoping for just a glimpse of the former First Lady. Later that day, Jackie and one of the Secret Service agents protecting her at this time would walk out the front door and right into the middle of this mass of humanity. At first the fans, who had been waiting for hours, would be stunned by her sudden appearance, as if they were in the presence of a religious apparition. Then after just a moment (because she wouldn't be with them very long), the air would be filled with applause and shouts of "God bless you" and "We love you." Quickly, Jackie would be ushered into a waiting car and driven away from the worshipping assembly, leaving each of its members feeling a bit faint in her wake.

"Will you just look at these nutcases," Ethel muttered to her assistant as they worked their way through the group, none of whom seemed to recognize either her or Joan. "Who the heck lives here? Elvis?"

Once past the crowd, Ethel, Joan, and the assistant walked through the ornate, black, wrought-iron gate and into a small foyer with French doors, which opened into the large main lobby of 1040. The floors were black-and-white diamond-shaped marble tile. Above them hung a large, expensive-looking, crystal chandelier, beneath which stood an ornate, antique table holding a huge vase of fresh, seasonal flowers. To the left were the elevators, and to the right a fireplace in front of which sat a plush couch with end tables.

"What floor?" Ethel asked as they approached the elevator.

When the three women got out of the elevator, they stepped into a long entrance foyer with gilt-framed mirrors and nineteenth-century French paintings on the walls; Jackie's was the only residence on the floor. Ethel turned to her assistant: "That's it for you, kiddo," she told her. "Time for you to go." The assistant then handed her boss a couple of coffee-table books about French art, which Ethel intended to give to Jackie as gifts and, with a disappointed look on her face, said, "Are you sure, Mrs. Kennedy, that you won't be needing me in there?"

Ethel said no. The downcast assistant turned and walked back into the elevator, just as Ethel rang Jackie's doorbell.

After a butler welcomed the two women into the apartment, Ethel and Joan walked into a parquet-floored foyer that opened into a vast rectangular gallery with fourteen rooms radiating outward from it, including five bedrooms, three servants' rooms, a kitchen, and a butler's pantry. The living room, with its windows facing Central Park and its reservoir, was forty feet long and ran parallel to Fifth Avenue. The furniture, much of which came from the family's quarters at the White House, was an eclectic mix that spoke of Jackie's varied tastes, from dark, heavy, and formal pieces such as her most cherished possession— an ormolu-mounted Empire fall-front desk that once belonged to her father—to light and airy colored sofas and bright floral throw pillows. Striking watercolors by noted painters decorated the walls. In a corner stood a large telescope, which Jackie liked to use to watch people as they enjoyed Central Park. There were no pictures of Jack to be seen; the only photo of JFK in the apartment was a small, silver-framed one on Jackie's bedside table in her bedroom. Outside, on the wraparound fenced terrace were large crab apple trees in wooden boxes painted blue. The whole place cried out for magazine photography.

About a month earlier, Jackie had hired a Greek chef, recommended to her by Aristotle Onassis, who went by the name of "Niko," short for Nicolas (Konaledius). "I worked for her part-time for just six weeks preparing Greek foods for special occasions," he recalls from his home in Greece, the walls of which are covered with photographs of him and Jackie from his brief employ. "I was fired, then returned again six months later for another three weeks. Then I returned to Greece where I worked for friends and relatives of Onassis's."

Niko walked into the living room just in time to hear Joan muse, "Gee, I wonder how many windows face the park."

"Fourteen of twenty-three," came a voice from behind Niko. It was Jackie, entering the room, smiling and looking radiant in beige harem pants and a matching top. Her long feet were bare and her toenails meticulously manicured and painted. The three women embraced and then walked about the apartment admiring Jackie's collection of animal paintings and Indian miniatures on the walls. They then went into the library where they would chat privately for about thirty minutes before gaily going into the dining room for lunch.

All three seemed to be in good cheer as they sat in Jackie's spacious and elegant dining room with its view of the George Washington Bridge. The room boasted of overstuffed couches, a baby grand piano, and a marble fireplace. On one wall was a large map with small pins all over it denoting places President Kennedy had visited, which was used as an educational tool for Jackie's children, Caroline and John Jr.

After they were seated in the warm room, the walls of which were covered in crimson damask wallpaper with matching drapes, Niko served a Greek salad with tomatoes, peeled onions, cucumber, and *bunch roka* (Greek watercress). "I am completely fascinated by Greek culture now," Jackie said as the salad was being served. "I thought it would be fun if I treated you both to some Greek food. Isn't this special?"

Following the salad, Niko displayed a Greek vegetable casserole with eggplant, zucchini, potatoes, and green peppers, which the women seemed to enjoy. For dessert, he offered *kouradiedes* (Greek cookies) and Greek cheesecake with feta, ricotta, and Swiss cheeses.

"Oh my God, this cheesecake is so rich," Ethel complained. "How can anyone eat this stuff?"

"I know," Jackie said with a nod, not realizing that Niko was standing directly behind her. "Isn't it absolutely awful? The ghastly, rich foods those Greeks eat! Niko!" she called out. When the servant showed up instantly over her shoulder, she looked startled for a moment before she sweetly asked, "I wonder, do we have any of those lovely madeleines?" He then ran to fetch the cookies, bringing them to the table a few minutes later.

Finally, over the madeleines and tea, Ethel got to the point. "Please tell me that you're not serious about this Onassis character," she said to Jackie.

"Oh, Telis?" Jackie answered, using her pet name for him, short for Aristotelis (the Greek form of Aristotle). "Why, he's completely charming. Yes, I do like him very much." When Ethel expressed surprise that she already had a nickname for Onassis Jackie smiled coyly.

At this point, Niko left the women to their conversation about Onassis's life, his family, and his wealth. Joan sat silently sipping her tea, not really participating and at one point getting up to admire the baby grand piano in the room. As Ethel and Jackie spoke, the servant overheard bits and pieces of their conversation.

Ethel said, "Please tell me you will not marry him, Jackie. At least not until after the election, and even then . . ."

Because the women noticed Niko, who had entered the room, they stopped talking. He leaned over to pour tea for Joan, then walked to a serving cart a few feet away, but still within earshot of the conversation.

Niko recalls, "Ethel said something about not wanting to court controversy at this time. She also said that she wouldn't allow Jackie to 'ruin this for me,' probably referring either to Bobby's campaign or, perhaps, her chances to get into the White House. I don't know which. I was too nervous to pay attention."

Tense about what he was overhearing, Niko accidentally dropped two pieces of silverwear onto the glass top of the serving cart. Jackie, startled by the racket, turned to face him. "Will you please leave us?" she snapped. "Where in the world did Ari find you, anyway?"

After she scolded him, Niko sequestered himself in the kitchen. Shortly thereafter, he heard Ethel and Joan leave. "From what I could glean, no one was very happy with the way the luncheon went," he recalls. "I actually think Mrs. Kennedy asked them to leave, but I can't be sure since I was hiding in the kitchen.

"As soon as they left, Mrs. Kennedy came bursting into the kitchen, seeming upset, and told me to go clean the table. Then she disappeared into her bedroom and didn't come out again until the next morning. I knocked on her door at about seven P.M. to ask if she wanted something to eat. She opened it, wearing a robe, and with a completely different attitude. She smiled at me, said, 'No, thank you. I can wait for breakfast,' and then closed the door."

Ethel's Thoughtless Remark

In May, around a month after Jackie's luncheon with Ethel and Joan about Aristotle Onassis, Jackie joined him on the *Christina* for a four-day cruise. While sailing under the stars, they discussed marriage. According to what they would later tell friends, Ari promised that should they wed, Jackie would still be a free woman, able to do whatever she pleased and see whomever she liked. As his wife, not only would she be one of the richest women in the world, but she and her children would also be protected by an arsenal of security: an army of seventy-five trained, machine-gun-toting men and their vicious attack dogs. What would Onassis get out of the deal? He would get Jackie, of course, someone to worship, the most famous woman of all, and a prize to any collector of famous women. He would also be able to stake his claim of legitimacy in the business world, for surely she would not be with him if he weren't someone special, a man of integrity.

Did they love each other? "Jackie was never in love with another man after Jack," said her friend Joan Braden. "It wasn't a matter of love with Ari. It was about security, protection . . . and money. Onassis was worth $500 million, right up there with J. Paul Getty and Howard Hughes in terms of wealth. She was not mercenary, but rather a practical woman in the way she handled her marriage to Jack, and in her relationship to Ari. She had children to consider, and a lifestyle in the public eye that she could not escape. She had to make certain decisions with an eye toward what made sense."

Stavlos Pappadia, who at the time was a reporter for the government-controlled Greek newspaper *Acropolis,* and also a friend of Onassis, recalled, "Ari told me that Jackie said she was under pressure from Bobby and her sisters-in-law to delay the marriage. He said he agreed to it because, really, he was in no hurry.

"Ari told me, 'She's a lovely woman, very self-centered, very egotistical, but fascinating in every way.' He spoke of her as if he were a fan, not her future husband. In fact, he collected photographs of her from newspapers and magazines, he told me. He said he had hundreds of them. She was his idol, really."

Even though Jackie had decided to delay a decision regarding a marriage to Onassis, she didn't want Ethel to believe that she had had anything to do with it. "I don't want Ethel to start thinking she can run my life," is how she put it at the time to a friend of hers. When news leaked out to family members that the wedding was being postponed, Ethel was the first on the telephone to Jackie.

"I think you made the right decision," she happily told her, according to Leah Mason.

Jackie hung up on her.

A few weeks later, in the middle of May, Jackie was with the family at the Hyannis Port compound. She flew in from New York because she wanted to see Bobby and congratulate him for his recent successes at the polls. Jackie still felt a sense of union with the Kennedys. As far as she was concerned, the family's successes were hers, as were their failures.

It's true that Jackie had not wanted Bobby to run for the Presidency because she feared for his life. She hadn't changed her mind about that, but since he was pushing forward anyway, she wanted to support his effort, which was the reason she had decided to postpone any decision about marrying Onassis. Jackie was struck by Bobby's courage, awed by his wisdom. He so reminded her of Jack that watching him deliver a speech on television never failed to bring a tear to her eyes. She said that she wished she could attend more of his speeches in person, but feared that her presence might detract attention from him. "I've been shopping for an awful wig that would provide enough concealment to let me watch from the crowd," she joked, "but I look so stunning in all of them, there's no way I wouldn't be recognized!"

Jackie's backing was a double-edged sword for Ethel, however. Even though it was Ethel who shared with Bobby the thousands of small intimacies that actualized not only their marriage but also the true essence of who he was as a man, it still always seemed that she was in Jackie's shadow. Once again, just as after Jack's death, it felt to Ethel as though Bobby's need for Jackie was greater than his need for her.

After Jackie's return from Greece, there was a family gathering at Rose and Joseph's to fete Bobby. It soon grew into a raucous affair with plenty of drinking and friendly (and sometimes not-so-friendly) ribbing, so typical of a Kennedy gathering. Joan, Eunice, Pat, Jean, their husbands . . . the whole gang was present and, for the most part, in good spirits. However, tension between Jackie and Ethel was palpable, and seemed to be growing thicker as the evening wore on.

Bobby began reading the results of recent promising polls. With every "win," the family would raise a cheer and someone would make a toast. "Jacqueline did not applaud politely, as she usually did," recalled nurse Rita Dallas, who was also present. "She led them all."

When Bobby had finished reading the results, he grinned broadly. "Well, looks like we just may make it," he said.

"Three cheers," Rose said. "Hip, hip . . ."

And everyone joined in—"Hooray!"

"Hip, hip . . ." Ted added.

"Hooray!"

"Hip, hip . . ." Eunice shouted.

"Hooray!"

Jackie, caught up in the jovial spirit of the moment, called out, "Won't it be *wonderful* when we get back in the White House?"

"What do you mean, *we?*" answered a female voice from across the room. All eyes turned. It was Ethel.

The room fell silent. Rita Dallas remembered that Jackie "looked as if she'd been struck. She flinched as though a blow had actually stung her cheek."

Ethel's comment seemed to beg an explanation, something along the lines of "Oh, I was just kidding. Let's have another drink." However, Bobby's wife just shrugged her shoulders at the deafening silence her remark had caused, then disappeared into the kitchen.

Jackie looked about the room helplessly, waiting for someone to come to her rescue. But everyone, it seemed, was too stunned. Without saying a word, Jackie stood from her chair, head high, and walked over to Bobby. She kissed him on the cheek. Then she walked out of the front door.

During her years as First Lady, Jackie had enjoyed sharing her glory with all of the Kennedys. Even though Ethel clearly resented the attention Jackie got, Jackie had done what she could to make Ethel feel as if she were a part of Camelot. She had never snubbed her, never intentionally set out to hurt her. It was difficult to reconcile Ethel's callous remark, but its effect on Jackie would force a defining moment in the former First Lady's relationship with the Kennedy family.

The next morning, Jackie arrived early at Rose and Joseph's to visit Joe. "Her hair was tied back with a silk scarf," Rita Dallas recalled. "She looked somber and very tired." Dallas said that Jackie stayed for just a few minutes before telling Joseph that she had some "thinking to do." Before leaving, she stopped to talk to Rita Dallas. Sitting at a chair in front of Rita's desk, she fidgeted with a paper clip and then asked Rita, "You've been a widow for a long time, haven't you?"

"Almost twenty years," Rita said.

"It's hard, isn't it—being alone, I mean."

Rita Dallas recalled telling Jackie that widowhood had been difficult for her. However, she took it upon herself to suggest that Jackie should not make the same mistake that she had made—devoting all her time and energy to the Kennedy family, only to find that her hard work was barely appreciated.

Without wanting to seem presumptuous—but since Jackie had brought up the subject—Rita suggested that Jackie consider moving on, forging a new life for herself, and perhaps breaking some of her close ties to the Kennedys in the process. It would be impossible to end her relationship with the family completely, Rita reasoned, and Jackie shouldn't even attempt to do such a thing. She had her children to think of, after all, and they would always be Kennedys. Moreover, Jackie would always feel a sense of responsibility to keep Jack's memory alive through the Kennedy Library, the many exhibit showings, or in any other way she thought appropriate. No doubt, in keeping Jack alive in the hearts of those who loved him, Jackie felt that a part of herself continued to live on in her so-called "Camelot." She could never give that up completely. But perhaps a little distance would do her some good, Rita advised.

The nurse chose her words carefully, hoping that Jackie would not be offended. She wasn't. Rather, she listened carefully and said she would give thought to all that Rita had said.

Jackie spent the rest of the day walking to all the places in the area that had been special to her and Jack: the patches of beach in front of the compound that they had most enjoyed together, Squaw Island, the horse barns, the private picnic areas. She must have thought about her life at Hyannis Port with her husband and children and wondered how it had all turned out the way it had. "Life is all about change, isn't it?" she had rhetorically asked her friend Joan Braden. "The only constant we can count on, I guess, is that nothing is constant, and you can't depend on anything or anyone, just yourself, which I have learned the hard way."

"I think she was beginning to find an inner strength she didn't even know she had," said Braden. "She wasn't a religious person, not really. Mostly, I think, Catholicism was, for her and most of the Kennedys, a family ritual rather than a true belief system. But in the years after Jack's death, she found strength where she least expected it, within. She told me that she felt that God was most certainly pulling her through the ordeal, 'sometimes kicking and screaming all the way,' she said, laughing."

When Jackie returned to the house, she found that Joseph had been waiting for her, concerned about the hour. She apologized for having worried him and explained that "I've had a lot of thinking to do today, some decisions to make." Joseph raised his eyebrows as if to ask what Jackie had decided. She grabbed his paralyzed hand and put it to her cheek. "Well, you know that no matter what happens, I'll always love you," she said. With those words, she kissed him on the cheek and left quickly. There were tears in her eyes.

For the next few days, no one at the Kennedy compound saw Jackie. Before leaving Hyannis Port, Joan had a brief moment with Ethel in front of some of the other sisters-in-law and a few friends. She could see, as could everyone else, that Ethel was jealous of Jackie, and she decided to address the issue head-on. It must have taken a great deal of courage for Joan to do this, however, since she and Ethel were not known for their heart-to-heart conversations.

"Bobby is very complicated," she told Ethel. "Not just one person can be everything to him. He needs a lot of different people in his life, and Jackie is just one of them. But when it comes down to it, Ethel, *you* are his wife, not Jackie. You're the one who matters most." Ethel stared at Joan, seemingly stunned by her uncharacteristic candor with her. She hugged her sister-in-law warmly and whispered something in her ear which made Joan smile broadly. Then Ted took his wife by the arm and walked out to the car with her.

Later, Ethel decided to go to Jackie's home to speak to her about what had happened the night of the party, but the agent guarding Jackie said she didn't want to talk to anyone. "But I want to apologize to her," Ethel said. "I didn't mean it. I swear. It was just—oh, I don't know why I said it. I would never want to hurt Jackie, not after what she went through. You must believe me."

Clearly distraught, Ethel babbled on. "How could I have been so thoughtless? You know, I was drinking. I mean, we *all* were. We were having a *party*."

When Ethel apparently realized that she was apologizing to a Secret Service agent—opening her heart to someone who was in what she considered a subservient position—she stopped herself short. "What in the world am I doing?" she asked. "Look, just tell Jackie that I must see her. Please. It's urgent."

"Will do, ma'am," the Secret Service agent said to Ethel, as she walked off, shaking her head in distress and muttering to herself.

The next day, Jackie left Hyannis Port for her apartment in New York, without seeing Ethel.

———

Another Tragedy

There was the sound of gunfire, six shots in all, like firecrackers popping, and then, amid the aftermath of chaos and confusion, the life of another Kennedy hung in the balance—Bobby's.

It was Tuesday, June 4, 1968, voting day for the presidential primary in California. Bobby Kennedy had won the Democratic primary in the state of Nebraska, but despite this and other victories, he still trailed Hubert Humphrey two to one in the race for delegates. He had pushed on to Oregon; and after he lost there, he decided that the state "just doesn't have enough poor people, black people, or working people." Everything would now depend on the California primary. Bobby had campaigned throughout the state, drawing huge crowds. But by Election Day it was still too close to call, and much depended on the black and Latino neighborhoods, where the turnout was usually low. With this election, though, the response from those groups was particularly high; Latino voters would go for Kennedy fifteen to one. In the end, Bobby won California with almost 50 percent of the vote.

Bobby walked onto the speaker's platform in the Embassy Room of the Ambassador Hotel in Los Angeles to wild applause from two thousand elated supporters. Ethel was at his side, basking in the moment. For her, it was a feeling of great excitement, happiness, and joy. Ethel looked out at the adoring crowd and waved giddily to familiar faces.

Bobby's victory speech was a short one. "We are a great country, an unselfish country, and a compassionate country," he told the cheering crowd, "and I intend to make that my basis for running. My thanks to all of you, and now it's on to Chicago and let's win there."

There was an effortlessness and grace in the way that Bobby appeared before the throng, which had been missing in recent speeches. He had always had great passion and strong ideas but was often awkward in his presentation. On this evening, though, he seemed more at ease with himself than ever before. He was confident and ready for the future, or as one observer remembered, "I looked at him and I said, 'My God. The guy looks like a President.'"

After giving the victory sign, Bobby jumped from the podium and headed to an impromptu press conference in the nearby Colonial Room of the hotel. Having been told that there was a shortcut to his destination through the kitchen, he decided to take it. Bobby passed through the kitchen area as the employees there, energized with excitement about the presence of the famous Kennedy, reached out to touch him as if he were a deity. Just as the presidential car carried his smiling, waving brother past throngs of admirers in Dallas five years earlier, a jubilant Bobby made his way toward the press room through an adoring crowd, smiling and shaking hands, unaware that an assassin lurked amongst the worshippers.

Bobby relied on his bodyguard Bill Barry, a former FBI agent, for protection. The unarmed Barry was Bobby's only trained security. To assist in crowd control, Kennedy enlisted the help of Rosey Grier, a former Los Angeles Rams lineman, and Rafer Johnson, an Olympic decathlon gold medalist. He didn't want to be surrounded by police, he said, because he felt it created a barrier between himself and his constituency. No one pushed the issue with Bobby. It was as if, with the assassination of John F. Kennedy, everyone but Jackie felt that the worst had occurred, and now they could relax under the umbrella of protection that bad luck could never strike twice in the same family.

He turned to look for Ethel. Rosey Grier brought Ethel down from the podium and was leading her through the door at the back of the stage that led to the pantry. Though she was only about fifteen feet away from Bobby, they were separated by a crush of supporters and hotel staff. About seventy-five people in all had crowded into the small pantry to try to get a glimpse of Bobby, pushing forward to shake his hand, slap him on the back, wish him well.

Then gunshots rang out, followed by pandemonium. In a flash, joy turned to horror. Hysterical screams and shouts filled the air as terrified onlookers reacted in disbelief, causing mass hysteria. The hotel ballroom had quickly become what reporter Roger Mudd later called "something out of Hades." Not sure of what was happening, Rosey Grier threw Ethel to the ground, covering her petite frame with his hulking 285-pound body.

Unnoticed among the zealous admirers had been a dark, slight, twenty-four-year-old Palestinian, Sirhan Bishara Sirhan, carrying a .22 caliber handgun. Sirhan, who had been crouched by the ice machine waiting for Bobby, had approached the senator, pointed a gun at his head, and started firing. Bobby had thrown his hands to his face, stumbled back, and collapsed on the dirty concrete floor. Five others were wounded. Now a crowd of people swarmed around Bobby's crumpled body. Juan Romero, a seventeen-year-old busboy who, just moments before the shooting, had been chatting with Kennedy, now placed his rosary beads in Bobby's hands. The pandemonium continued as a crush of men tried to wrestle Sirhan to the ground. Finally, after a struggle, they managed to get the gun from him.

Roger Mudd helped the trembling Ethel to her feet and tried to shoulder her through the crowd to get to Bobby. "Let Ethel through," he said as he forcefully pushed forward, "let Mrs. Kennedy through." The crowd cleared a narrow path for Ethel and, as they did so, the shifting bodies revealed her worst nightmare. Bobby was hit. He lay on the floor, his eyes staring vacantly, muttering a steady stream of unintelligible babble. His head was oozing a stream of blood. His cheeks were a deathly white. "Oh my God," she gasped, kneeling down in the pool of blood by his head. "Oh my God."

Ethel cradled Bobby's head in her lap. Gently, she unbuttoned his shirt and rubbed his chest, all the while talking tenderly to him. Jean Kennedy, the sister who, years earlier, had introduced Bobby to Ethel, knelt down beside them. Spectators gawked, flashbulbs popped, people screamed. "Get back," Ethel pleaded to the crushing throng. "Give him room to breathe."

"This is history, lady," one cameraman barked back at her. Another television newsman pleaded with his own cameraman to keep rolling as the candidate lay on the floor.

Over the hotel's address system, Ethel's brother-in-law Stephen Smith frantically called for a doctor. Dr. Stanley Abo, a diagnostic radiologist who had been in the ballroom, responded and found his way to Bobby. He saw the senator sprawled on the floor, his legs twisted underneath him, blood rushing from his head and neck.

One of his eyes was now closed, the other open and staring vacantly, but there was still a pulse—slow but strong. At this point Bobby turned to Ethel and, with his one open eye, recognized her.

"Ethel. Ethel . . ." he said weakly. Tears streaming down her face, she leaned very close to his face and whispered, "It's okay, Bobby. It's okay." He lifted his hand and she took it, both of their hands clasping the rosary. Grimacing as the pain increased, Bobby then sighed deeply as his wife tightly held him. He started to say something else, and then went limp in her arms.

Twenty minutes later the police arrived and took Sirhan away. Apparently, the gunman, who had immigrated to the United States from Jerusalem, blamed Kennedy for the problems of his people. "I did it for my country," he shouted. While they were leading him down the stairs, the ambulance arrived for Bobby.

Two ambulance attendants, Max Behrman and Robert Hulsman, fought their way toward Bobby with a rolling stretcher. "Don't lift me," Bobby said weakly, as they wrapped him in a blanket. "Don't lift me." Ethel, hovering over her husband's body, had become what some witnesses described as a lioness protecting her young. "Keep your hands off of him," she screamed, trying to push the attendants away. "I'm Mrs. Kennedy!" she added with authority.

The medics were there to do a job, however, and didn't want anyone, including a Kennedy wife, telling them how to do it. They proceeded to lift Bobby onto the gurney.

"Gently, gently," Ethel called out as they placed him down.

"No, no, no . . . don't," Bobby said. These were the last words Bobby Kennedy ever uttered in public. Then he lost consciousness.

The two ambulance workers were brusque and professional as they quickly rolled Bobby toward the elevator with members of the Kennedy entourage, including Ethel, Jean, and the campaign aides Fred Dutton and Bill Barry running alongside them. Behrman wheeled the stretcher so quickly that, at one point, he almost lost control of it. "Gently, gently," Ethel again called out. Barry became furious at the sight. "That attendant handled the stretcher like a madman," he said later, "bouncing it around, pushing it hard, with a wounded man on it."

By now relations between the Kennedy party and the ambulance attendants were volatile. When they were all in the elevator, Behrman loudly barked out orders. Ethel didn't like his attitude and told him to keep his voice down. Tempers flared, an argument ensued, and one of the women in the Kennedy entourage slapped Behrman. "If you do that again, I'll crush your skull," the enraged medic exclaimed.

When they finally reached the ambulance, Behrman ordered that "Only Mrs. Kennedy is allowed in the ambulance with us." Ethel brushed him aside, however, and allowed Fred Dutton into the car. Bill Barry and Warren Rogers, a correspondent for *Look* magazine, both climbed into the front seat. It was only a two-minute, one-mile drive to the hospital, but during the trip there, tension continued to build in the ambulance. When Behrman attempted to put an oxygen mask over Bobby's face, Ethel screamed at him, refusing to allow the medic to touch her husband.

As the banshee sirens of the ambulance wailed and its red lights flashed, an emotional Ethel, seemingly out of control, continued to rage, at one point becoming so angry at Behrman she threw his log-book out the window. "I tried to check his wounds and she told me to keep my hands off him," Behrman later said. "I tried to put bandages on him and she wouldn't let me." When Bobby's breathing became very heavy, however, Ethel relented and let Behrman put an oxygen mask on Bobby.

Dr. Vasilius Bazilauskas, the emergency doctor on call at Central Receiving Hospital, had been alerted that Bobby Kennedy had been shot and that he might be on his way to that hospital. As Bazilauskas waited on the ramp leading to the emergency room, he could hear the blaring sirens. The ambulance turned a corner, pulled in, and backed up to the platform. "Somebody ripped the back door open, and there was Ethel," recalled Bazilauskas. "She looked frightened, and her eyes were very wide."

Ethel focused on the doctor. "Please help him. Please help him," she moaned. But when hands reached out to pull the stretcher out of the ambulance Ethel, panicked and frightened, began inexplicably slapping at the hands. "Somehow she didn't want hands reaching out to handle him," recalled Dr. Bazilauskas. "Maybe it was because one of those clawing hands that she had seen in the past few months of the campaign had held a gun that shot her husband."

By the time they reached the hospital, Ethel was panic-stricken and acting out of sheer terror. "Please don't hurt him, please don't hurt him," she kept repeating in a frantic litany. When she saw a lone photographer near the emergency entrance, she screamed at him and pushed him with her shoulder, sending him reeling backward.

"When he [Bobby] was on the platform I could see that he was like a blob of Jell-O that you took out of the refrigerator," recalled Bazilauskas. "I immediately realized that he was probably gone, but of course I couldn't be sure of it. There was an oxygen mask on his face, put there in the ambulance. I put my hand underneath his shirt, which had been partially opened, to feel his chest for warmth and it was halfway to the coldness of death."

"The Hand of a Dead Man"

The tiny hospital emergency room was crowded with people. A team of nurses cut off Bobby's clothes while others tried to clear the area, though they weren't having much success. The doctor, not hearing a heartbeat in Bobby, started massaging his chest. When Ethel complained, thinking that he was hurting her husband, the physician patiently explained to her what he was doing. Earlier, when the doctor had repeatedly slapped Bobby's face to see if he reacted to pain stimulus, Ethel had asked him not to be so rough. The doctor ignored her.

When Dr. Bazilauskas injected adrenaline into Bobby's arm muscle, his heart started beating on its own.

"Why did you stop massaging him?" Ethel now wanted to know.

"His heart is going now," the doctor replied, "and we have some hope."

"I don't believe you," Ethel said quietly, drained of emotion. "He's dead. I know he's dead."

Placing the stethoscope's diaphragm over Bobby's heart, the doctor then handed Ethel the ear portion. She leaned forward, listening. "Her face lit up," Bazilauskas later recalled. "She looked like a mother who had just heard the heartbeat of a child she thought was gone."

Ethel's joy was short lived, however. She heard a scuffle outside the emergency room and rushed out to see what was happening. Two policemen were guarding the door, refusing entrance to Father Mundell, a family friend who had been with them at the hotel but who had gotten lost in the crowd. He had finally found his way to the hospital. Ethel rushed out and pushed one of the officers aside. The startled policeman then shoved her back, sending her reeling. When others surrounded the officer and broke up the shoving match, Ethel was able to usher the priest into the room, where he gave Bobby Absolution. Shortly thereafter another priest from a nearby parish, Father Thomas Peacha, was also allowed to enter the room. He had heard of the shooting on his car radio and rushed over to the hospital, where he performed the Last Rites.

The decision was made that Bobby should be transferred to the nearby Good Samaritan Hospital, which was better equipped for delicate brain surgery. Wearing an oxygen mask, and with tubes sticking out of his body, Bobby was transferred to Good Samaritan. Because a crowd of a thousand or more had gathered outside the hospital, they were forced to sneak the stretcher out of a side door.

"Will he live?" Ethel asked the doctor before they took off in the ambulance.

"Right now he's doing all right," Dr. Bazilauskas replied. "Let's hope, let's just hope."

Privately, the doctor knew the worst. "I had seen the senator's legs go into convulsions," he said later, "which meant that the damage to the 'switchboard' [nerve center] was just too much. He could not survive. But of course I didn't want to tell her that, and there was always hope."

Ethel rode with Bobby in the ambulance, and when they arrived at the hospital she was joined by all the members of the Kennedy entourage, including his sisters Pat and Jean, all there to keep vigil.

At 2:45 A.M. a team of surgeons—brain and chest specialists—started a last-ditch effort to save Bobby Kennedy's life. The doctors discovered that one of the bullets had passed through Bobby's brain, but didn't have the firepower to escape. Instead it hit the skull opposite the entry wound, splitting into many particles and ricocheting back, ripping into the brain tissue. The doctors' mission was to clean out as much of the debris from the brain as they could without destroying more tissue, and then repair as much damage as possible. Meanwhile Police Detective Sergeant Dan Stewart was ordered to Good Samaritan to help take charge of security.

Nurses had tried to get Ethel to lie down, but she refused, opting instead to pace the floor and pray in a tiny room near the operating room, where two policemen kept guard. Three hours and forty minutes later, when the double doors swung open, Ethel was still there, waiting. When Bobby was wheeled into the recovery room, Ethel, still in her orange and white minidress, climbed onto the bed and lay next to him.

At 7:20 A.M. Frank Mankiewicz emerged outside, exhausted and grim, to talk to reporters and to tell them that Ted Kennedy had recently arrived. In fact, just hours earlier, Ted had turned on the television in his hotel room in San Francisco to see a surreal scene of people screaming and panicking. Someone had been shot. Ted and his friends had somehow misunderstood what was happening and thought the madness was occurring at a victory rally for Bobby they had just attended in San Francisco. Had the shots been a near miss at Ted? Suddenly, the reality hit him: It was Bobby who had been shot, and the nightmare being broadcast was from Los Angeles. Stunned, Ted took the next plane to the City of Angels.

Mankiewicz admitted that Bobby's condition was "extremely critical" and that "the next twelve to thirty-six hours are crucial. He's living. He's not conscious. He's breathing on his own."

What Mankiewicz did not tell the reporters is that Bobby's situation was hopeless. He was going to die. Shortly after surgery, head surgeon Dr. Henry Cuneo had told Mankiewicz as much, though Mankiewicz says today that that's not what he heard. "What I heard was that Bobby was in critical shape and that there was always a chance he could live," he says. "I don't care what they told me. I only know what I heard. There was a sense among us, somehow, that he would pull through. It was hard to imagine that he couldn't, and harder to imagine that this terrible thing could happen twice in the same family. I don't think we were listening to what we were being told, as much as we were listening to our hearts."

Dr. Cuneo called John Miner, Deputy District Attorney of Los Angeles, to inform him of what was happening. "He's on life support, but he's dead," Dr. Cuneo reported to Miner on the telephone. "Oh, my dear God," Miner said. "His poor wife, all those children. How could this have happened?"

Miner rushed to the hospital. "I went to the room where he was,"

Miner now recalls. "It was very sad. I noticed that the door was ajar and I peeked in. There was Ethel sitting beside his bed, holding his hand. 'It's all right, Bobby,' she was telling him. 'We're going to take you back home where they have the best doctors and you'll be all right. You'll see, you'll be just fine. I promise.'

"She didn't know that she was really holding the hand of a dead man."

"No God of Mine"

"How's Bobby?" Jackie wanted to know as soon as she got off the plane that had taken her from New York to Los Angeles. Large sunglasses covered her reddened, puffy eyes as she looked at Chuck Spalding, who had picked her up at the airport. "I need to know. Please give it to me straight."

"Jackie," said Spalding, "he's dying."

Visibly stunned, Jackie took three steps backward, closed her eyes and dropped her head to her chin as if mortally wounded. "Oh, dear God," she said. "My dear God in heaven above . . . why?"

Earlier that day, at 3:45 A.M. New York time, the ring of her telephone had awakened Jackie. Just hours earlier, she had paid a brief late-night visit to Bobby's campaign headquarters in New York, where the mood was jubilant. "I feel just wonderful. I'm delighted," she exclaimed with a broad smile when asked how she felt about Bobby's success. She was escorted back to her apartment at about midnight; after just a few hours' sleep, Prince Stas Radziwill awakened her, calling from Europe to ask about Bobby's condition. But Jackie didn't even know he'd been shot. In an instant, the shocking news caused her reluctant memory to go reeling back to that November afternoon in Dallas. "Oh, no," she exclaimed. "It can't have happened again."

"I got there at about five in the morning," Roswell Gilpatric recalled. "It was a bad time, she was very, very emotionally distraught, but it was the way Jackie got upset. Very internally. But she thought Bobby might make it, or at least that's what she had been told, by

Teddy I think. She needed a private plane, so I called Tom Watson, head of IBM, a personal friend. I knew he had a number of planes at his disposal."

After meeting Stas Radziwill at Kennedy Airport, Jackie, Roswell Gilpatric, and Tom Watson all left for Los Angeles, where they were met by Chuck Spalding. He describes Jackie as "slowly withering away from the inside. You could just feel it."

Jackie immediately went to the hospital, where she joined Jean, Pat, and Ted in their awful vigil in the Board of Directors' room. Jackie seemed to be sedated, almost in a zombie-like state. She had been fortified by pills from Dr. Max Jacobson, the infamous doctor who had kept her husband drugged through much of his time at the White House and who continued to supply her with "downers" from time to time in moments of great stress. Soon Ethel joined the sad group while finally taking a break from her bedside vigil. Jackie and Ethel hugged, a desperate embrace with no tears, just stunned silence between them.

Everyone milled about, trying to think of what to do, what to say. Jackie walked over to Frank Mankiewicz. "The church is at its best only at the time of death," she said, for no apparent reason. "The rest of the time it's often rather silly little men running around in little suits. We know death. As a matter of fact, if it weren't for the children, we'd welcome it."

Mankiewicz now recalls, "I don't believe that she was speaking of the Kennedy family in particular, which is how it has been reported in the past. She was speaking about she and I when she said 'we.' We were having a private conversation, which some must have overheard, and it's been misconstrued for years. I don't know why. She was in shock. It was an awful night."

Two by two, they visited Bobby, whose head was heavily wrapped in white bandages. George Plimpton, a friend of the Kennedys who had been just a few feet from Bobby when he was shot, has recalled, "It was a horrifying deathwatch, like visiting a tomb at Westminster Abbey."

"It was terrible," recalls Claudine Longet. Just two days earlier, Bobby had joined her husband Andy Williams in an off-key chorus of "Moon River" during a rally at the very same Ambassador Hotel in which he would be slain.

"Bobby loved to sing," said Andy Williams, "and, boy, what a voice!

It was terrible! He always sang loudly and off-key. I used to kid him about it."

Those happy days with Bobby seemed over now as he lay in a coma. "Bobby never recognized us, never saw us," Longet recalls of that night at the hospital. "It was the longest night of my life. We kept thinking he was going to make it, because if anybody could make it, he could. We were just pacing back and forth, drinking coffee, and feeling empty. It was like another world."

However, no one, even Ethel, was more on edge than Jackie. As the evening wore on, it was as though an already-taut wire was being drawn one final notch tighter around Jackie's sanity. Suddenly, it snapped. "Get away from me," she ordered her Secret Service agent. "I don't ever want to see you around me again. I mean it." Before astonished witnesses, she began to cry. "What good are you, anyway?" she asked the agent through her tears.

Frank Mankiewicz recalled, "Jackie had a wild, hunted-animal look in her eyes, and she just wanted to escape, to lash out and reject an intolerable situation."

After turning on her Secret Service agent, Jackie lashed out at Ethel. "How dare God do this to us?" she said, her voice filled with raw emotion. "If there is a God in heaven, Ethel, he is a cruel God," Jackie concluded, her voice seeming slurred, her manner a bit medicated. "He is an unfeeling God, a heartless God, and no God of mine."

Jackie Kennedy then turned and walked toward the hospital room of her dead husband's younger brother for one final visit.

Senator Robert Francis Kennedy Is Dead

At 1:44 A.M., on June 6, 1968, about twenty-five hours after he had been shot, Senator Robert Francis Kennedy died a few minutes after being taken off life support and without ever having regained consciousness. With him at the time of his death were Ethel; his brother, Ted; sisters Jean and Pat; Jean's husband, Stephen; and Jackie. He was just forty-two years old.

"When the President was assassinated, the family became very stoic," remembered Rita Dallas, Joseph Kennedy's nurse. "But when Bobby was shot, the whole house crumbled. Mrs. Kennedy fell apart and she kept saying, 'My son, my son.' Mr. Kennedy cried. I cried. It was too much."

Roger Wilkins, Assistant Attorney General, put it best when he encapsulated the feelings of the family and perhaps of the entire country, exhausted by a decade of turmoil: "It was over. The whole thing was over. The whole period of lift and hope and struggle. It was all over. It was just over."

It would fall upon Ethel's family—including Jackie—and friends, in particular Joan Braden, Sarah Davis, Sue Markham, Kay Evans, and Ann Buchwald, to support Ethel emotionally during this awful time. While Jackie was at Ethel's side, Joan couldn't be because she was in Paris with Eunice. Joan had been visiting the Shrivers in France after opening a Kennedy Memorial Library exhibition in London. (In recent years, Joan had continued touring the world with exhibits of JFK memorabilia, an active and effective Kennedy ambassador.)

One of Ethel's friends remembers having taken three telephone calls from Joan at the hospital, wanting to speak to Ethel. Ethel would not get on the line, but Ted did speak to his wife. Slumping over, he began to sob. "Bobby's gone, Joansie," he said. "He's gone."

Jackie and Ethel sat together on the Air Force One flight that the Kennedys and their friends and coworkers—including Rafer Johnson, Rosey Grier, Frank Mankiewicz, Pierre Salinger, Jesse Unruh, and others—took from Los Angeles to LaGuardia, which had been sent by Lyndon Johnson to carry Bobby's body home. Three of Ethel's children, Bobby Jr., Joe, and Kathleen, were also aboard. Accompanied by Lem Billings and a Secret Service agent, they had flown to be with their mother in Los Angeles after the shooting. Of course, a deeply upset Ted was aboard, along with his sisters Jean and Pat, Jean's husband, Steve Smith, and Lee Radziwill and her husband, Stas.

Jackie and Ethel both cried on the flight, though the tears flowed more easily for Jackie. She was still raw with grief over Jack, even after five years. She had even hesitated to get aboard the plane because she thought it was the same one that had carried Jack from Dallas back to Washington, "and I could never get on that plane again, ever. Is it the same one?" she demanded to know. "Because if so, I must know."

Crewmen assured Jackie that, while both planes were blue and silvery-white, this 707 was not the same aircraft.

Ethel tried to maintain her composure throughout the flight, sometimes falling into a fitful sleep lying next to Bobby's coffin. At other times, she would bound up the aisle telling everyone to "cheer up."

Sander Vanocur, one of the few reporters on the flight, recalls, "Ethel tried to cheer up everyone. She tried to lift everyone's spirits in that moment of great sadness and grief for herself. People would come up to her and offer their condolences and she'd say, 'But are *you* all right?'"

"There was a doctor on that flight [Dr. Blake Watson, Ethel's obstetrician, present because Ethel was pregnant with Rory, her and Bobby's eleventh child] who tried to give Ethel sedatives," Lem Billings once remembered. "Jackie took all the pills from him, except for one, which she gave to Ethel. 'I think you should feel as much of the pain and misery now as you can stand,' Jackie told Ethel. 'Better now than later, believe me.'"

Also on that flight was Coretta Scott King, widow of the slain Martin Luther King, Jr., who had flown to Los Angeles to be at the hospital with Ethel. Ethel and Jackie, along with Bobby and Ted (but not Joan), had attended Martin Luther King's funeral, and Bobby had arranged for the plane that would take King's body back to Atlanta from Memphis, where he was killed.

"On the flight, I looked up at one point," Lem Billings recalled, "and there they were, three of the bravest women in the country, Jackie, Ethel, and Coretta, speaking to one another about their mutual despair. It was very touching. Very touching."

"I witnessed a lot of love between Jackie Kennedy and Ethel Kennedy," recalled Coretta Scott King. "I felt that I was in the midst of true family. Jackie cared for Ethel, tried to be there for her. There were a lot of special, memorable moments on that flight, which I would never discuss publicly for fear of invading the privacy of these great women.

"Ethel Kennedy was so brave, such a truly heroic person," Mrs. King continued. "Having already gone through what she and Jackie went through, one would think I could relate entirely to their experiences. But the truth is that every woman's relationship with her husband is special and unique. No outsider can completely understand the intense loss suffered by a wife when her husband is taken from her . . . it's just that personal to their relationship."

"What can I do for you, Ethel?" Jackie wanted to know about an hour into the flight. "Please, tell me how I can help you."

Ethel looked at her sister-in-law with sad, lost eyes. "Help me with the funeral," she said, finally. "The way you did Jack's, it was so perfect. It's what Bobby should have. It's what Bobby would want."

"Well, I arranged Jack's funeral the way *I* wanted it done," Jackie said. "They're for us, really, these terrible ceremonies. They're for the living, for the heartbroken who've been left behind. So you tell me what you want, Ethel, and I'll take care of it."

Ethel said that she wanted the service to take place at St. Patrick's Cathedral, and that she wanted Leonard Bernstein, a friend of the family's since Jack's presidential campaign, to help select the music. She wanted the nuns who had taught her at Manhattanville to sing during the mass. She also wanted Andy Williams to sing "Ave Maria." (Williams and his French wife, Claudine Longet, were also aboard the plane.) Bobby should be buried next to his brother, Ethel concluded, at Arlington National Cemetery.

Jackie raised her eyebrows. Leonard Bernstein? The nuns from Manhattanville? Andy Williams singing "Ave Maria"? To Jackie, it sounded like a network television special. But these were Ethel's wishes just the same, so Jackie would see to it that they be honored.

"Immediately, she began making telephone calls," Lem Billings remembers. "As I recall it, Bernstein told Jackie that women were not allowed to sing in the cathedral. 'So what?' was Jackie's response. 'This is special. This is Bobby. They will make an exception.' She was determined to see to it that Ethel get everything she wanted."

Jackie asked Bernstein to make the necessary arrangements and keep her apprised of his progress. After the plane landed at LaGuardia, where a thousand Kennedy friends, celebrities, politicians, and other supporters waited, a motorized lift slowly lowered Bobby's coffin to the ground. Noticing that Ethel suddenly seemed ready to faint, Jackie rushed to her side and put her arm around Ethel's shoulder. As the coffin was lifted into the waiting hearse, Jackie whispered words of comfort in her ear. Ethel stood limply at Jackie's side, seemingly dazed, as the two women stared at the completely unfathomable sight of Bobby Kennedy's maroon-draped, African mahogany casket being sprinkled with holy water by Terence J. Cooke, Archbishop of New York. The family and friends would take the body to St. Patrick's at Fifth Avenue and East Fifty-First Street, and then go to Bobby and Ethel's three-bedroom apartment at 860 United Nations Plaza. Rose Kennedy, dressed in black, was already at St. Patrick's when everyone arrived.

"Oh Grandma," Jackie said when she saw her. "I'm so sorry." Jackie collapsed in tears as the stoic old woman held her firmly, her eyes lifted to the heavens in a blank stare. "If I ever feel sorry for myself, which is the most fatal thing, I think of Rose," Jackie would say later. "I've seen her cry just twice. Once, her voice began to sort of break up and she had to stop talking. Then she took my hand and squeezed it and said, 'Nobody's ever to feel sorry for me.'" (Rose's personal secretary, Barbara Gibson, recalls the day that the priest who gave JFK his Last Rites passed away. Barbara was reluctant to show the obituary to Rose for fear that it would upset her. It did. Rose began to sob in a display that was completely uncharacteristic of her. Barbara was so moved, she too began to cry. Suddenly, Rose stiffened. "You must be tired, or coming down with something, to break down like that," she said firmly as she quickly dabbed at her eyes.)

Jackie didn't have Rose's or Ethel's faith, but even if she had, some felt it wouldn't have eradicated the great despair she felt over Bobby's death. Not concerned with what people thought of her, Jackie knelt in front of his coffin and broke down in deep, wracking sobs. Clearly, this repeating nightmare was more than she could bear.

When Rose found Ethel, the Kennedy matriarch walked over to her and hugged her, warmly. The two women shared a moment of silence, but no tears.

John Glenn, the astronaut and a close friend of the family's, had arranged for all of Bobby's clothing to be taken to another apartment in the building, owned by Truman Capote. But another friend of the family convinced him that Ethel would be distraught to find Bobby's possessions already gone, so they were put back into place before Ethel arrived.

Later, Jackie and Ethel stood together in front of one of the floor-to-ceiling windows and gazed out at the twinkling lights of Manhattan—a thousand-mile stare out to nowhere—lost in their thoughts, saying not a word to one another, the twin tragedies of Texas and California merging into one: Ethel in Los Angeles, pushing away the pressing crowd while trying to give Bobby room to breathe; Jackie in Dallas, jumping onto the trunk of a car hoping somehow to retrieve fragments of Jack's skull; Ethel kneeling over Bobby's bullet-riddled body, cradling his head in her lap; Jackie in Dallas, holding Jack's ruined head to her bosom. Each had known so much anguish and loss, and there were no words to express any of it.

Bobby's Funeral

"The flight to New York, six hours to think, that was the worst thing," said Joan Kennedy, describing her return from Paris to attend Bobby's funeral. Some family members had felt that it was probably best that Joan had been in Paris when she heard the news about Bobby. The separation from Ted gave her the chance to bring under tight control her own grief for Bobby and her concern for Ted. "I thought of Ted more than anyone else, and his family burdens," Joan remembers. "None of us cried," she said of herself and the Shrivers upon hearing of Bobby's death. "We were just so numb."

The delivery of a eulogy for his brother would be Ted's first public act as the effective head of the family. Ted's former law school roommate, Senator John Tunney, remembered Ted and Joan huddling over the eulogy, discussing it in great detail, "trying to help Ted get it right. He had gone fifty hours without sleep and then was only getting two hours a night. He was in terrible pain because his back injury from the plane crash still made it impossible for him to be on his feet for long periods of time. Joan was there if he needed her, but she never flitted around the way some women would, saying 'Please get some rest.' She knows what motivates him, how he expects her to behave: no tears, never any tears . . . I've never known him to cry. Joan had to bottle it all up, just as she always did when she was around him."

On June 8, the morning of the funeral, more than a hundred television cameras invaded St. Patrick's Cathedral, capturing for generations to come the agonies of the bereaved and pregnant widow and her ten fatherless children. Wires and lights were strewn about the floor.

Reporters and photographers huddled among those seated in the pews. The solemnity of the funeral service was punctured again and again by the popping of flashbulbs and the momentary electric brilliance of dozens of lights.

Lyndon and Lady Bird Johnson led the two thousand invited mourners as a hundred million people in the United States alone watched transfixed. Tears were shed, prayers were offered. The sentiment was just as it had been for Jackie. Perhaps the only differences were the month and the year. In November, the air was chilled and a cool breeze blew. In June, humidity hung heavy, forming a visible blanket of mist. Otherwise, the coverage and the circumstances were practically identical as the cameras zoomed in to catch Ethel's tears, just as they did for Jackie's five years earlier. Jackie was in a daze through much of the service for Jack's brother, so much so that when her good friend Lady Bird Johnson approached to offer her condolences, Jackie barely seemed to recognize her.

Rather than "Ave Maria," as Ethel had originally requested, Andy Williams sang "The Battle Hymn of the Republic," the marching song of the Union forces during the Civil War. The number was listed in the program as "Glory, Glory, Hallelujah," because Ethel refused to have the word "Battle" associated with Bobby on the day of his funeral. Williams sang the song *a cappella,* and using cue cards. "All the while, I was wondering what I would do in that big cathedral if I tried to sing and no sound came out," he recalls. "Here, I drew strength from Ethel Kennedy, a truly magnificent person."

Soft but clear, Andy Williams's voice surrounded the mourners as they filed out of St. Patrick's Cathedral. He sang the song not in triumph, but tenderly, as if it were a mother's prayer, and he touched the emotions of thousands present, many of whom now began to sob after having remained reverentially stoic throughout most of the service. Gaunt, drawn, purposely without expression, and completely oblivious to the television cameras, this was an Andy Williams completely different from the cheerful one Americans had, for years, welcomed into their homes on various television programs. Ethel had certainly been right in her selection of Andy, who had also escorted her to and from St. Patrick's on this sad day. He barely recalls the entire week, saying he was "in a fog the whole time. They needed a tie for Bobby," he remembers. "I got a tie from my closet, and, to my knowledge, that is the tie they put on his body for the flight back to New York. I think it was in my tie that he was buried."

For Ted, the eulogy for his brother Bobby would be one of his finest moments. "We loved him as a brother, as a father, and as a son," Ted said, his voice cracking with emotion as he spoke just a few feet from his brother's flag-draped coffin. "He gave us strength in time of trouble, wisdom in time of uncertainty, and sharing in time of happiness. He will always be by our side."

Ted, who had held up admirably through the service, finally broke down on the funeral train that carried Bobby's body from New York to Washington for burial at Arlington National Cemetery. Two million people solemnly lined the 226-mile route, waiting for the train to pass. Overcome by grief, Ted sobbed through much of the trip, barely able to stumble through the railway car. At one point, he tried to lock himself in a private compartment to use as a hiding place where he could get away from the sight of the mourners at the side of the tracks along the train route. Rose said later that she could "see it coming over him" even before Ted cracked. As she explained later, "I watched his face drop and I could see him slipping. There wasn't anybody on that train that I was worried about—except Teddy."

Rose insisted that Teddy pull himself together, get back to his window seat and conduct himself "the way Bobby would have" if it had been Ted's last journey. Ted straightened up immediately, as if hypnotized by his mother's edict. Observing her instructions, he returned to his seat at the window, although he never once lifted his head to even look up at anyone, much less glance out. He sat motionless until the train came to its last stop. Joan was powerless to help him. Distraught, she sat alone and quietly stared out the window.

Thirty years later, Jack Newfield, Bobby's biographer who had been in Los Angeles with him the night he was shot, and who was on the train after the funeral afternoon, recalled in the *New York Post*, "It was heartbreaking. There were eight hundred people on the twenty-one-car train: his closest friends and supporters, family, all the people who'd been in his brother's Cabinet, who worked in his campaign, a lot of celebrities—Shirley MacLaine, Harry Belafonte, Warren Beatty. It was like a rolling Irish wake. But what was most amazing was to see the numbers of African-Americans along the poor side of the railroad

tracks through New Jersey into Baltimore and Washington, D.C. That
was just one of the most depressing, heartbreaking scenes."

Jackie wandered about, speaking to relatives, friends, and campaign
workers, while Ethel, who appeared cheery, consoled others. Recalls
Claudine Longet, "Andy and I were so sick on that train, inconsolable, really. Me, I died a little when Bobby died, knowing that life
would never be the same. She [Ethel] came and comforted us. She
gave us strength and asked if we were all right, instead of us doing it to
her. Her courage was unbelievable. She was like Jackie Kennedy that
way—the same qualities."

But this afternoon, Jackie was not the same strong, stoic woman she
had been at her own husband's funeral. Today, she was coming apart.
When finally she sat down in her Pullman car about thirty minutes
into the trip, she seemed dazed and disoriented. One high-ranking
Cabinet member under JFK who paid Jackie a visit reported that she
said, "The first thing I intend to do when this goddamn thing is over
is get me and my kids the hell out of this country. If anyone expects to
see me this time next year, they'd better forget it, because I won't be
found."

By the time the funeral train arrived in Washington, night had
fallen. The mourners, carrying thin, lit candles, followed the coffin
into Arlington National Cemetery. In this wavering, trembling light,
the assembled priests spoke their last solemn words, and Bobby was
laid to rest. Joan, too distraught to handle any more emotion, would
not be at Ted's side for this ceremony.

The American flag was lifted from the coffin and folded, just as the
flag on Jack's coffin had been folded, and passed from brother, to son,
to widow. Ethel, tears streaming down her face, took it. Holding it
tightly to her breast, she walked the few steps to Bobby's coffin and
knelt beside it. She pressed her lips to the wood in one last kiss, one
final farewell to her husband of eighteen years. Then, alone, she
turned and walked away toward the waiting limousine. Behind her,
Jackie knelt at the coffin, bowed her head, and said a silent prayer. She
rose and, bending over, picked up a delicate spray of daisies at the foot
of the casket. With her children, Caroline and John Jr., at her side,
Jackie walked slowly to the quiet place nearby where, beneath stone
and eternal light, her own husband lay at rest. There, as Ethel

watched, Jackie placed the flowers, Bobby's flowers, tenderly on his brother's grave.

"We Shall Carry on with Courage"

One week after Bobby's funeral, Ted Kennedy appeared on national television with his father and mother, his eyes dark-rimmed from sleepless nights. His voice occasionally threatened to break, as it had in St. Patrick's Cathedral. It was Rose who appeared strong and Kennedy-like. "We cannot always understand the way of Almighty God, the crises which He sends us, the sacrifices which He demands of us, but we know His great goodness and His love," said Rose, her demeanor composed, her voice almost robotic. "And we go on our way with no regrets of the past, not looking backwards to the past, but we shall carry on with courage."

"This was like a gruesome nightmare replayed, and there was only darkness and terrible feelings of emotional anxiety and depression," said Ted's friend John Tunney. "I remember walking with Teddy after Bobby died and saying to him, 'You know, you have got to get away. You must not allow yourself ever to think about you being next in line for this terrible treatment.'"

At this time Jackie became concerned that Joan would be obsessed with her husband's safety because of what had happened to his brothers, "and that's no way to live," she said. When she called Joan to ask how she was, Joan said she was worried that the Secret Service protection that had been afforded Ted after Bobby's assassination would end before any danger was over. "We're getting threats," Joan said, "and I'm scared to death. Who lives like this?"

"Sadly, we do," answered Jackie, according to what Joan later told Joan Braden.

Jackie immediately telephoned Secret Service official Joe Barr to request that the protection be in place for as long as possible. (Ethel was under temporary Secret Service protection as well.) When Barr telephoned Ted to ask if he wanted the protection to continue, he said that it wasn't necessary. The agents' presence only served to remind Ted of the tragedy that had befallen his family, he said. Declining protection so soon after Bobby's murder seemed foolhardy to most observers, and when Joan found out about it, she became angry. Oddly, though, she didn't discuss the matter with Ted. Instead, she told Jackie about Ted's decision, who then telephoned Ted and spoke to him of Joan's fears. She encouraged him to continue with Secret Service protection. "You must do it for all of us," Jackie said. "My God. We don't want to lose you, too. Think of the children, mine, Ethel's, and your own." So Ted agreed to Secret Service protection for another few months, after which the FBI would be called in should a problem arise.

Two weeks later, Joan was musing to a friend about the Kennedy dynasty, about all that had happened in recent years and what it all meant to the family and to the nation. It was difficult not to be bitter. So many had invested so much, and for what? "What is that 'monolith' of Kennedy power now?" Joan asked, disgusted. "Just Teddy and me," she answered. "All of the others are either dead . . . or old." Or too young to answer the call.

After Bobby's death, a friend of Joan's noted, "She seemed to be a shell of herself. She acted oddly, so much so that even Ethel—who had her own grief to deal with—said that she thought Joan was on the verge of a breakdown."

Her assistant, Marcia Chellis, recalls that Joan "just disappeared" rather than attend Bobby's burial. Joan later told friends that she watched news reports on the television, never feeling more removed and isolated, and all by her own doing.

Despite the fact that Ted received hundreds of letters saying he should retire for the sake of his own safety, he decided that he must continue in politics. All of his life he had been a cheerful, open, and optimistic person, but suddenly, with the deaths of his brothers, he had to become the holder of the dreams, frustrations, and hopes of millions of Americans who had supported the Kennedys. Could Ted go on and be the happy-go-lucky guy he had always been, or would he now have to become something different, someone more serious—a real politician? "If it were up to me, he'd get out now while he still can," Joan told a reporter. "But," she added sadly, "it's not up to me, now is it?"

When one reporter wondered if perhaps Joan was exaggerating the danger of being a Kennedy in politics, she blew up. Very uncharacteristically for her, she ripped into the journalist, saying, "Exaggerate? *Exaggerate?* How can you say that? Let's get in my car and I'll drive you down the road just a mile to Hickory Hill where Ethel lives. Let's go there and you can look at a house filled with children without a father, and then tell me if I exaggerate the dangers of being a Senator Kennedy."

For the next two months Ted would remain out of the public eye, mostly in the home he shared with Joan and the children in McLean, Virginia. It was easy to isolate himself within these glamorous trappings—tennis court, football field, swimming pool, servants' quarters, and a French chef who cooked for the Duke of Windsor. If it were up to Joan, he would never leave.

Much thought was given to the children at this time—eight-year-old Kara, six-year-old Ted Jr., and year-old Patrick, all of whom came down with chicken pox right after the funeral—in terms of how to protect them from jumping to the conclusion that since both of their beloved uncles had been murdered, their father might be next. Joan refashioned some of Kara's fairy tales, for instance, so that they would be completely happy and nonviolent. "Have you ever noticed how awful fairy tales are?" she said after Bobby's death, "what with poisoned apples and mean stepmothers. There's enough pain in the world without exposing my children to that."

True to Kennedy form, though, Ted kept his emotions inside and asked the same of Joan so that even employees were unaware of the turmoil they felt in their lives. Frank Corsini, who along with his twin brother, Jerry, worked part-time for the Kennedys, saw them two weeks after the assassination to see if they needed help. "Joan was in the pool when I drove up," Frank says. "To look at her and talk to her, you would have thought the only worry she had in the world was arranging for a caretaker to keep the pool and tennis courts."

At just thirty-six, Ted had become the effective head of an extended family, responsible in part for the welfare of fifteen children—Jack and Jackie's two, Bobby and Ethel's ten, and his and Joan's three. Along with that personal responsibility, he carried the political burden foisted upon him by being next in line, whether he liked it or not. One person who most definitely did not like the notion of her husband as savior was Joan.

"Why must it be *my* husband?" she asked writer Barbara Kevles.

"Why must he be the one to carry these terrible problems of the world on his shoulders?"

"It had been a difficult summer," Joan remembered. She was the one to tell the children about what had happened to their Uncle Bobby. "Ted couldn't do it," she remembered. "It was too painful for him. I often wondered how he managed to stay sane."

Joan's sanity never seemed to be anyone's concern, though it should have been. No one—especially Ted—saw her cry after Bobby died. Determined to provide a cheerful atmosphere for her family, she always kept their home gay and bright. Eager to support Ted in his hour of need, Joan would stay up long nights with him, trying unsuccessfully to encourage him to open up to her, share his emotions, his misery. On the many nights when he couldn't sleep, she would stay awake, too, out of sympathy and a sense of duty. The next morning it was her responsibility, she believed, to look refreshed for the sake of the children, while Ted slept into the late afternoon hours.

One day, when Ted suggested they charter a yacht and cruise Cape Cod, to "get away from it all," Joan dutifully packed hampers of food, rounded up a dozen Kennedy children (her own, some of Bobby's, and John Jr.), and sailed off with him as if it were just any pleasure excursion, casually undertaken. On that trip, she and Ted never once talked about the tragedy or about anything that was bothering anyone. In ignoring their dilemma, there was not much else to discuss. So they were distant toward one another, focusing on the children at play.

"I began to drink alcoholically," Joan recalls. "But at the time, I didn't know it. No one really ever does know. I mean, sure, once in a while you have too much to drink and you wake up the next morning and you have a hangover and you think, 'Oh, I'm not going to do that again.' A week or two goes by . . . and then you go and drink too much again. It becomes a pattern that starts to creep up on you."

Dazed and dizzy, there were nights when Joan Kennedy would fall asleep sitting at the kitchen table, her head on the table. Ted would be infuriated when he'd find her there, passed out.

"You think this helps me?" he would bellow at her. "Seeing my wife out cold? How does that help me, Joan? How does that help?"

Out of a deep sense of shame, Joan Kennedy would then retire to a guest room and do the only thing she could do to make the world go away—she would drink. Ted's ongoing grief became Joan's personal failure. If only she were smarter, if only she understood what to do, if only she could be there for him.

Ethel—Just a Shell

After Bobby's assassination, Ethel Kennedy retreated to her home, Hickory Hill, in McLean, Virginia, where she would continue to raise her soon-to-be eleven children with the help of two horses, three ponies, one donkey, four dogs, one kitten, ten ducks, five chickens, two roosters, one goose, five rabbits, four pigeons, several sparrows, a parakeet, a cockatoo, three secretaries, two cooks, and a governess. (A sea lion named Sandy, which was kept in the swimming pool, had recently escaped when he learned how to climb out of the pool. Soon, he was flipping down the road on his way to downtown McLean. He was later given to the Washington Zoo.)

For the first couple of days it was difficult for anyone who visited to notice much of a change in her. She seemed to be her old self as she read and responded to the condolence letters she received, and had even mellowed somewhat—especially in her opinion of the Johnsons. In a letter to LBJ, which Ethel had hand-delivered to the White House on June 19, she wrote that she was especially grateful to him for the manner in which he had made Air Force One available to transport Bobby's body back to New York from Los Angeles. She also thanked the President for meeting Bobby's funeral train in Washington and escorting the family to Arlington. "Your kindnesses, both known and unknown, were many but they were all surpassed by the feeling of personal human sympathy which you and Mrs. Johnson gave to my children and me and the entire Kennedy family. We shall always be grateful to you, Mr. President." She signed the letter, "Love, Ethel."

(On the day he received the letter, LBJ sent a quick response back to Ethel: "Practical assistance of the kind I could give is necessary, but it is never enough to assuage the loss. Only time and faith can do that, and the support of people who love you.")

Ethel also made plans to take Bobby's place on the planning board that had been attempting to find solutions to poverty in the Bedford-Stuyvesant slum in New York—as well as tending to the many responsibilities of her household. Pregnant with her eleventh child, she seemed eager for the birth. She enjoyed being a mother, and patiently consoled and comforted her children if any of them were having a particularly difficult day dealing with their father's death. In fact, she would be so exhausted by the end of her busy day that she would sleep straight through the night.

"For Ethel, the sun rose and set on Bobby," said his aide Frank Mankiewicz. "Without him in her life, we all wondered what would be left." It's true that Bobby, his goals and his political ambitions, had been the focal point of Ethel's life for years. They shut out the world. To forget others' needs, to finally give way to personal sorrow, was what people expected of Ethel at this time. At first Ethel refused to give in to those understandable reactions. She said she was a Kennedy, not only in marriage but also in spirit. She insisted that she would not give up on life. Her religion gave her a sense of peace, she said, and she was determined to rebuild her life upon faith.

Joan was amazed. "How does she do it?" she asked.

Jackie was not convinced. The former First Lady knew the emotional devastation she had endured when the President was murdered—she was still carrying the heavy weight of grief, and she also knew Ethel's temperament and personality. "She's the type who doesn't deal with human conditions," Jackie so accurately observed in a conversation with Roswell Gilpatric. "She never was. She wouldn't even be around Joe when he had his stroke. When Patrick died, I didn't hear a word from her. If she doesn't crack now, I'm going to be afraid for her," Jackie added. "It's not normal. Believe me, Ross," she said, "I still am not over Jack. How can she be okay? *How can she be?*"

To most of the Kennedys, Bobby's widow seemed to be the same "Ethie" as always. However, because these were people who were accustomed to stifling their feelings, they couldn't recognize when someone else was doing the same thing. Only Jackie, who went through the gamut of emotions when her husband was murdered, could see that what Ethel was portraying as her true self was not organic—it was fake. She was doing an imitation of Ethel Kennedy—the Ethel people expected to find when they visited Hickory Hill, and not the one left in the wake of her husband's assassination—and

Jackie saw through it. "I'm telling you here and now, she's in trouble," Jackie told Jean Kennedy Smith after visiting Ethel one day and eating soft-shell crabs with her for lunch. Jean blithely responded by saying, "Well, I don't know, I think she's doing remarkably well."

In the mornings, Ethel would awaken early and play tennis with fierce conviction until completely exhausted, as if exorcising demons of grief, even though she was pregnant. "I refuse to let this get to me," she said of Bobby's death. "I know that God has a plan. I just don't know what it is."

"She wouldn't allow herself to feel the grief that would have been understandable," said Lem Billings, "which is so typically a Kennedy trait."

"It was disturbing," concurred Rita Dallas. "At least, to me, as a nurse, it was. The rest of them [the family] didn't seem to recognize it."

Ethel bottled up her emotions—her fear, her anger, her pain—just as she had done all of her life during times of great tragedy, such as when her parents were killed in the plane crash. In fact, the only memory anyone had of her breaking down in public was when Jack died and a weeping Ethel had to be consoled by Jackie at the small birthday party Jackie had hosted for her children at the White House. No doubt Ethel had her moments of wrenching emotion in private, but those were times she did not share with anyone. However, it would seem that the stress of putting on a happy face for friends and family was having an effect on her, or as Barbara Gibson put it, "She was never a great actress."

"She would snap at her children, smack them, and be very impatient," said Leah Mason. "In the months, and even years, after Bobby's death, it got so that it was actually hard for Ethel to put her arms around her children and kiss them. She would hate herself for it. 'How can I be like this?' she would ask. 'What kind of terrible mother am I? It's not their fault Bobby died.' Then she would push herself even harder to be a good mother to them, and in doing so seemed to resent them even more. She was a single mother with all of these kids. It was so unfair. She was never the same. She lost her spirit, her fire, that spark that was always Ethel's that you either loved or hated was gone, never to return.

"She wanted nothing to do with Jackie and Joan, Eunice, Pat, or Jean. She had her circle of friends, but these were people in whom she did not have to confide, people who didn't expect her to reveal herself. She knew that if she had lunch with Jackie, it would be all about, 'How do you *really* feel?' And she didn't want to discuss how she really felt about anything and, really, she never discussed anything, ever, with anyone that I ever heard about."

Barbara Gibson adds, "It was as if she had just internalized it all, the hurt, the pain, the loss . . . and then, it no longer existed. To me, it was like she had hollowed out all of her insides and now she was just a shell."

One Secret Service agent recalls the weekend in the fall of 1968 when Ethel telephoned Ted to tell him that she believed she had nothing left to live for and that she was considering suicide. She had been drinking heavily. Even though everyone who knew her thought it inconceivable that Ethel would do such a thing, Ted was alarmed enough that he and Jackie and two Secret Service agents decided to go to Hickory Hill for the weekend, ostensibly to watch over her. However, Ethel refused to come out of her bedroom, locking herself in and not emerging the entire weekend. Instead, she slipped a handwritten note under the door that said she was humiliated by her threat, would never actually go through with it, and apologized to both Ted and Jackie "for being so ridiculous." Though she pleaded with them to leave from the other side of her bedroom door, they decided it was best if they stayed.

"So Ted and Jackie and the two of us ended up spending the weekend taking care of all those kids, and supervising all of those servants," said the agent.

In the months after Bobby's death, the Kennedys' New York office (run by Stephen Smith, where most of the family's business was conducted) forced Ethel to sell off art, horses, and other assets, and insisted that she dramatically reduce her staff, explaining that her expenses at Hickory Hill were so high that she would have to learn to economize. Just as it was with Jackie, Ethel wasn't left with the millions the public assumed she would have after Bobby was buried. In fact, she was advised by one callous family member to marry a wealthy man, "and as soon as possible." When there was a delay in the Kennedy office in setting up an account from which Ethel would now draw for expenses, three months went by without any money for Ethel from the Kennedys. Jackie was appalled at the way Ethel was being treated. "With all of those children?" she said. "This should never happen."

Jackie knew what Ethel was up against; the Kennedys had put her on a strict budget as well after Jack died. It was an ongoing annoyance in her life that the Kennedys' New York office constantly questioned her expenses, and it was especially embarrassing when Rose involved "the help." Rose's chauffeur, Frank Saunders, recalled that just a year earlier (in 1967), Rose had a discussion with him about Jackie's expenses.

"Are you doing food shopping for Jacqueline?" she wanted to know. Her tone was one of great suspicion. She had heard a rumor that her chauffeur was shopping for Jackie and charging the Kennedys' account for the former First Lady's groceries. Frank explained that he wasn't actually doing any major shopping for Jackie but that when her maid needed "a few things" he would go to the store and fetch them. Perhaps, all told, it added up to about fifty dollars a week.

"And you're then charging that to the Kennedys' account?" Rose asked, her temper rising.

"Yes, ma'am."

"Well, I want a stop put to that immediately," Rose said with controlled rage. "I don't want Jacqueline putting her food on our bill."

Frank said he would do as he was told. "We must keep these things separate," Rose reminded him.

Now Rose—who routinely ran around the Hyannis Port home shouting at the servants, "Lights out! Lights out!" in an effort to save on the electric bill—was on a roll about her former daughter-in-law's spending ways. "And Jacqueline is going to have to cut back on her personal staff, too. This cannot continue. She's just going to have to learn to manage within a budget. Mr. Kennedy's [Joe's] office cannot pay for every whim of Jacqueline's, you know. And, by the way, those people are always wanting raises," Rose continued, speaking of Jackie's staff. "And they always want overtime. The maid and her secretary. Overtime! Can you imagine?"

It's always been reported that Jackie spent the Kennedys' money freely and without regard after Jack's death, but it would seem that she only did what she felt she must to live the lifestyle to which she had become accustomed, without gouging the family—and the country—for every cent she could get. For instance, on January 12, 1967, Jackie wrote a letter to the President about the financing of her office space in New York. She had it delivered to LBJ from Ted's office, by messenger.

In her letter, Jackie noted that for the previous three years, "Congress has been most understanding and generous in granting me the funds to maintain an office for my official business." She explained that this office had made it possible for her to handle the volume of mail that she received after Jack's death. "As you know, in the fall of 1965, I felt that the volume of business and mail was such that my staff and expenses could be cut back," she wrote, "and I asked that the appropriation be reduced accordingly. Now, the work at my office, although still considerable, has diminished enough so that I can personally assume the burden of my own official business. Therefore, I no longer wish a government appropriation for this purpose."

"She basically only wanted what she felt she needed when it came to financing," said George Smathers. "No more. No less. She spent a lot, don't get me wrong, a whole hell of a lot—which was always a problem for JFK who thought she was out of control. But after his death, she wasn't inconsiderate about it, as has been painted in the past. The Kennedys were pretty cheap."

In order to assist Ethel during this troubling time, Jackie lent her $50,000. Though she signed a promissory note, Ethel never paid back the loan. Many years later, in 1974, Jackie's attorneys demanded payment in a strongly worded letter to Ethel, to which they attached a copy of the promissory note. Ethel refused to remit, however, saying that she did not have the funds. When Jackie learned that her lawyers had confronted Ethel without her authorization she was extremely angry with them.

"It's completely uncalled for," she wrote to one of them. "Please do not allow this matter to become an issue between me and Mrs. Kennedy. It is now my direction to you to write her back immediately and tell her that the loan I gave her in 1968 is now a gift. Also, please send me a copy of the correspondence to Mrs. Kennedy, so that I may be sure that it is properly worded."

PART TEN

Ted Negotiates Jackie's Nuptials

"You know, Mrs. Kennedy is not just an ordinary woman," Ted Kennedy said, thoughtfully. "In fact, you might say she's a saint."

Aristotle Onassis looked at Ted from the other side of an imposing mahogany desk. "A saint?" he repeated, bemused. "Like the Blessed Mother."

"The Blessed Mother is not a saint," Ted said, correcting him. "She is the Blessed Mother."

"That she is," Onassis said, chuckling.

It was August 1968, and the men were in Onassis's office on Skorpios negotiating the terms of Jackie's impending marriage to the Greek businessman. Jackie had asked Ted to go with her to Skorpios to negotiate the possible union. Though he did not approve of the marriage, Ted decided that he should be the one to make the deal. So, at Jackie's insistence, they told the other Kennedys what they would also tell the press: that Onassis had extended the invitation as a gesture to take the two away from the strain that followed Bobby's assassination.

While on this trip, Jackie hoped to acquaint herself with Ari's children, eighteen-year-old Christina (whom Jackie had previously met) and twenty-year-old Alexander. At first, Ari insisted that they call her "Mrs. Kennedy," but Jackie insisted that they call her by her first name. Over the years, as it would happen, they would both call her many names, but seldom "Jackie."

"They resented her from the start," says Onassis's personal assistant, Kiki Feroudi Moutsatsos, "because they were always thinking one day that their mother and father would be together."

Despite the fact that Jackie had indicated she wanted to be involved in the negotiations, she decided to go on a two-day shopping trip to Athens and let Ted handle the business at hand. Because Ari thought of Ted as nothing more than a pretender to the throne in the wake of his brothers' deaths, and because Ted was oblivious to those feelings, the ensuing negotiations bordered on the ludicrous, according to what Ted and Ari both later told friends and associates, which corroborates what has previously been reported about the meeting.

"Look what she went through in Dallas," Ted continued. "You must understand that because of that alone she is one of the most revered people in our country. And for Americans to accept her being married to you would take a leap of faith. Her image could be forever tar-nished. That has to be worth *something*."

"Of course," Onassis said, with a patient smile. "Such a thing surely must have value."

Ted went on to point out the obvious: that if the marriage occurred, Onassis would be stepfather to Caroline and John Jr. Without wanting to be offensive, he observed that Americans who still felt great affection for Jack Kennedy would be unhappy by the paternal replacement in his children's lives. "And that, too, has to be worth *something*," Ted said.

Not the least bit offended, Ari smiled. "One would imagine . . ."

"And what about security?" Ted pushed on, adding that if Jackie married Onassis she would lose her Secret Service protection.

Ironically, Jackie so loathed the Secret Service protection that by 1968 she would desperately try to get it reduced from what she felt was a completely unreasonable number of eight agents on duty protecting her and her children, to just three (and, when in Greece, only one, agent John Walsh). In a lengthy letter to Secret Service Director James J. Rowley, she complained, "The children are growing up. They must see new things and travel as their father would have wished them to do. They must be as free as possible, not encumbered by a group of men who will be lost in foreign countries, so that one ends up protecting them rather than vice versa." She further wrote that while in New Jer-sey, the agents lost track of the children for two hours because they had followed the wrong car out of the driveway, "and the mother of nine had to leave her children just to bring mine home!" She also com-plained that an agent had "forcibly dragged" her children home for sup-per even though she had given them permission to dine at a friend's. Rowley responded by saying that the FBI was still receiving letters from mentally ill people threatening Caroline and John, and that there was the "ever-present threat of a kidnapper." Because Jackie persisted, a compromise was eventually reached in security measures reducing the number of agents, at least while in Greece. So she would not have been at all pleased to hear Aristotle Onassis tell Ted Kennedy, "Why, my army of security will dwarf in size whoever is presently guarding Mrs. Kennedy." Onassis further explained that Jackie would have around-the-clock security by what he viewed as the best trained agents in the world for her, her children, her maids, her butlers, and anyone else she cared about. Not only that, Onassis continued, but Jackie would also have German shepherd police dogs at her disposal.

"I might also note that if Jackie marries you, she will lose her income of $175,000 from the Kennedy trust," Ted cautioned, seriously.

Finally, as Ari would remember it, he had to reveal his true feelings in a laugh so loud and hard he almost lost his breath.

"You mean to tell me that you are giving this saint, as you call her, only $175,000 a year?" Onassis asked. "Why, I could give her more money than she could ever dream of." He said that he would give her what he felt was her true value, "and it would be much more than $175,000 a year."

"Well, don't forget that she's going to lose her $10,000 annual widow's pension plan," Ted added, perhaps not understanding the weakness of his position.

Onassis laughed again. He spent that much a week on shoes, he said.

The negotiation went on like this for an hour, until a rough deal was finally struck for Jackie as if she were an expensive racehorse.

"One-point-five, that's a fair price," Ari said. "And we can work out the other details later. But if she marries me, Mrs. Kennedy will get one-point-five million."

"I believe that's a fair deal," Ted said as he rose to shake the Greek businessman's hand.

"I agree," Ari said.

Later that day Onassis said he felt strongly that the nuptials should occur in America. He obviously wanted the publicity and credibility that such a service in that country would bring to him. But Ted was against the idea. "That would mean that mother, Joan, Ethel, and all of us would have to attend," he said, "because if we didn't, how would that look? And we can't. It would be completely inappropriate. It would be a nightmare. I won't be moved on this point."

"Then, fine," Onassis said. "We'll leave it as it is. One-point-five."

"One-point-five," Ted agreed.

By the time Jackie returned to Skorpios with a dozen pairs of shoes and matching handbags, the deal—such as it was—seemed to be in order. Everyone was satisfied. One-point-five it would be.

Or would it?

A few weeks later, Aristotle Onassis sent the proposed agreement to Ted for signature, who then forwarded it to André Meyer, Jackie's financial adviser. In the deal draft, Jackie was described only as "the person-in-question." Because Meyer had "some problems" with it, Onassis ended up having a contentious meeting with him about the "acquisition" on September 25, 1968, at Meyer's apartment at the Carlyle.

Meyer felt that Onassis should pay at least $20 million to marry Jackie. Onassis thought that was a preposterous amount of money for a former First Lady, saint or no saint. In fact, the price was so high that it had the potential to hurt the feelings of all concerned, he said, "and might easily lead to the thought of an acquisition instead of a marriage."

In the end, after much haggling, Onassis agreed to pay three million dollars for the privilege of marrying the former First Lady, which was twice the amount for which Ted had almost sold her. Jackie could take the three million dollars outright, or the money could be used to buy nontaxable bonds. Also, each of her children would receive a million dollars, and the annual interest on that money would go to Jackie. In the event of Onassis's death, Jackie would receive $200,000 a year for life.

While Jackie was satisfied, it was said that Onassis was struck by buyer's remorse and had agonized over the matter for some time, wondering if he had paid too much for Jackie Kennedy. One day, as the story goes—and it was probably concocted by Onassis—it came to him that he could actually buy a supertanker for that amount. However, he then realized that, considering the cost of such a supertanker's fuel, maintenance, insurance, and other extras, he probably made a good deal in buying Jackie instead.

Lynn Alpha Smith, who was the executive secretary to Constantine (Costas) Gratsos (director of Ari's New York operations), remembered, "We used to call Jackie 'supertanker' around the office. Onassis didn't mind. It made him laugh. 'It's supertanker on the line,' I'd announce whenever she called. In my eyes, and in the eyes of many people, Jackie was an acquisition, nothing more or less. The dowry system was acceptable in Greece, only in this case it was Onassis who had to pay the dowry."

But Ari had the last laugh.

Under the laws of Greece, Jackie would have been entitled to at least 1.5 percent of Onassis's $500-million estate in the event of his death: roughly $62.5 million. It's difficult to imagine, yet astonishingly true just the same, that with all of their combined business acumen, Ted and the other attorneys who worked out this "deal" somehow neglected to realize that Jackie didn't need a prenuptial agreement and, moreover, that the existence of one all but guaranteed her less money than she would otherwise receive at Onassis's death. Moreover, the payment Jackie would receive at the time of her marriage meant that she had legally renounced her right to any future money, other than what was stipulated in the agreement.

It wouldn't be until after Ari's death that Ted and Jackie's other attorneys would scramble to try to figure out a way to pull the submerged supertanker from the drink.

Jackie Kennedy married Aristotle Onassis on October 20, 1968, in a Greek Orthodox ceremony, witnessed by several other members of the groom's family, as well as Jackie's own mother and stepfather, Mr. and Mrs. Hugh Auchincloss, her sister, Lee Radziwill, and her late husband's two sisters, Pat Lawford and Jean Smith, who were there representing the Kennedy family. Probably the most significant two witnesses, however, were Caroline and John Jr., who carried lighted candles as they stood behind their mother.

Andy Williams

Ethel Kennedy was not only a Kennedy widow, but also a relatively attractive woman whose wide-set bright blue eyes and broad, winning smile were her greatest attributes. Ethel was a perfect size eight at the time of Bobby's death, and her consistent waistline—even after all those pregnancies—had always been the envy of Jackie. Whereas Jackie had to diet constantly, Ethel never bothered. Skating, skiing, swimming, sailing, shooting the rapids, and running after eleven children was all she needed. Whereas Jackie and Joan both spent hours on their hair, constantly experimenting with new styles (especially Joan), Ethel kept her light-brown hair in a short, casual style, the better to brush it back into shape after falling off a raft into the river. To the public, she was a woman of inexhaustible energy and ample charm, fascinating in every way. No one outside of her private circle knew of the brooding, and often contentious Ethel, the private Ethel.

Being young, being a widow, and being a Kennedy made Ethel, in the years after Bobby's death, prime fodder for tabloid speculation about her private life. Her biggest "romance," resulting in widespread publicity, seems to have been with popular singer Andy Williams.

Ethel and Bobby had known Andy and his then-wife Claudine Longet since the mid-sixties. Recalls Andy Williams, "The first time I ever really talked with Bobby Kennedy was in 1964 at a birthday party [Universal Studios president] Lew Wasserman gave for his wife, Edie, at the studio. I had done a TV show earlier that night and came over to sing 'Happy Birthday' to Edie. Bobby and Ethel came over to our table afterward, and my first impression—Claudine's, too—was how young he looked. And how he looked and talked directly to you. I danced with Ethel, and Claudine danced with Bobby. The next day, I was playing golf when Claudine called and said the senator had invited us to visit with them in Palm Springs. He hadn't had a vacation in a while."

Upon the return of Andy and his wife from their vacation, it was clear that they had fallen under the spell of Camelot. "We stayed up all night, talking and singing. That's where our friendship really started," recalled Williams. "It was a gradual thing, and there is no point where I can say that's where I knew he would be one of the closest friends I'd ever have."

Before long the couples were constantly traveling and socializing as a foursome. When Bobby and Ethel entertained at Hickory Hill, Andy and Claudine were always at the top of the guest list. The Williamses spent many hours with the Kennedys, skiing in Sun Valley, rafting on western rivers, playing touch football at the Kennedy compound at Hyannis Port. As proof of their special friendship, photos of the Kennedys and the Williamses together were positioned all over their households.

On June 6, 1970—the two-year anniversary of Bobby's death—Ethel (kneeling), Joan, and Ted visit his grave. (GLOBE PHOTOS)

Despite the fact that his presidential aspirations would be forever ruined by Chappaquiddick, Ted was re-elected to the Senate in November 1970. Here he thanks his campaign workers, flanked by Ethel, on the left, and Joan. Behind him is another reminder to the skeptical press of his "ideal" family life—even though the relationship he shared with Joan at this time was anything but. (UPI/CORBIS-BETTMANN)

Joan did have her own fashion taste, controversial though it sometimes was. Here she is seen in London's Heathrow Airport in 1971, looking smart in leather. (POPPERFOTO/ARCHIVE PHOTOS)

Though no one could ever replace Bobby in Ethel's life, she and Andy Williams did date. Ethel loved reading stories in the press of their budding romance, which was actually short-lived. When Jackie, feeling that Andy was perfect for Ethel, tried to move the relationship forward, Ethel resisted. (GLOBE PHOTOS)

Ethel convinced Andy Williams to allow Joan to demonstrate her piano-playing skills on his TV show in March 1971. Joan performed a solo, then accompanied Williams as he sang. (PHOTOFEST)

It was sometimes difficult for Ethel to feel compassion for Joan's alcoholism, because she believed it to be a weakness, not an addiction. Unlike Jackie, Ethel also believed that Joan should be more tolerant of Ted's unfaithfulness because, as Ethel once put it, "at least Joan has a husband." (PHOTOFEST)

Jackie joined Joan and Ted on a ski trip to Idaho during the Christmas holidays in 1975. Joan and Ted's son Patrick is in the foreground. (PHOTOFEST)

Always behind her man? Maybe not. By 1976, when this photo was taken (on the day Ted won re-election to the Senate for his third full term), Joan had other things on her mind. She had been in and out of rehab centers and was at a low ebb in her life. (PHOTOFEST)

In December 1979, Joan held a press conference at her Boston apartment to demonstrate that she was sober and ready to compaign for her husband in his bid for the presidency, even though they were separated. Photos of her family were placed on the piano in hopes of convincing the media that the separation was temporary, and that Joan would be a proud First Lady should Ted get elected. (UPI/CORBIS-BETTMANN)

Despite her drinking problems and troubled marriage, Joan was still able to hold it together and look stunning in her stylish maxi coat as she, Ted, and children Ted Jr. and Kara took a stroll in Boston, followed by the ever-present paparazzi. (PHOTOFEST)

Even though Jackie had ambivalent feelings about Ted, she and Joan remained close. It was Jackie in whom Joan confided about her alcoholism, and about her desire to finally put an end to her marriage. Jackie blamed herself for not suggesting that Joan end the marriage many years earlier and was concerned that she was somehow at least partly responsible for Joan's alcoholism. (UPI/CORBIS-BETTMANN)

In May 1981 Joan received her master's degree in education from Lesley College. By this time she had taken control of her life and had filed for divorce from Ted, using Jackie's attorney. Joan and Ted pose with their children (l–r): Patrick, Kara, and Edward Jr. (UPI/Corbis-Bettmann)

"There are certain people you love despite everything else, just because you know they're being so completely true to who they really are," Jackie Kennedy Onassis once said. "In my life, Ethel Kennedy is one of those people." Here Jackie and Ethel share a light moment during a Robert F. Kennedy Pro-Celebrity Tennis Tournament at Forest Hills Stadium in New York. (AP/Wide World Photos)

A distraught Ethel Kennedy kneels at the coffin of Jackie Kennedy Onassis during funeral services for the former First Lady on May 23, 1994, at Arlington National Cemetery in Arlington, Virginia. Despite their often contentious relationship, Ethel had great admiration and love for her former sister-in-law, whom she visited the day she died. Behind Ethel is her son Joseph, his wife, Beth, and his sister Kathleen Kennedy Townsend. (AP Photo/Greg Gibson)

At the time they met the Kennedys, Andy and Claudine's marriage seemed headed for certain trouble because of his hectic touring and television schedule. She was lonely, she complained, and longed for more attention from him. Then they met the Kennedys and, she now recalls, "Just being around that family changed our whole lives. Andy watched Bobby with their kids and saw how they all got involved in activities together. He got an entirely new viewpoint of what a family is supposed to be like. Bobby got him involved in doing things he would have never tried otherwise—skiing, tennis. We'd go camping and sit around the campfire and Ethel would ask Andy to start a song, and we'd all join in and sing, even Bobby, who had the worst voice in the world and, of course, sang the loudest. We'd break up laughing until our stomachs hurt. It brought Andy and me together again—at least for a time—I have no doubt about it."

When Claudine became pregnant, Ethel sent her a box of maternity clothes that she had worn during some of her own pregnancies. While Bobby was alive, Ethel had gotten into the habit of buying maternity clothes even when she wasn't expecting, knowing that sooner or later she'd be needing them. After his death, she decided that she'd never have that need again. Claudine said later that she sobbed as she thought of what it must have meant to Ethel to pack all of those dresses for the last time and send them off to a pregnant friend. To one especially pretty cocktail dress, she had pinned a note: "This was Bobby's favorite. Wear it in good health!"

But it was Bobby and Claudine who seemed to have made the most intense bond. Years after Bobby's death, Claudine hinted that her relationship with him had developed into something deeper than the friendship the two couples shared. "We could talk in the way a girl and a man could talk," she said, "the way women are almost never able to talk, the way I was never able to talk with Ethel . . . not chitchat. When Bobby died, I lost interest in the Kennedys. There was no one for me to talk to. I drifted away."

Because she was a Kennedy widow, the press was naturally interested in Ethel's private life, always linking her with everyone from New York Governor Hugh Carey to Cary Grant. Andy Williams's marriage to Claudine Longet began to sour shortly after Bobby died, so Ethel began recruiting the entertainer to be her escort. Of course, this innocent coupling started a flood of rumors and speculation about an impending marriage, a story that would continue to be a headline-grabber in fan magazines all the way into the late seventies.

For Ethel the flurry of headlines her "affair" with Andy (whom she had nicknamed "Andy Baby") generated was just another madcap adventure which she took in stride. "She thought it was all a riot," George Terrien once said. "She loved the attention she was getting; she loved the fact that she was suddenly considered a *femme fatale*."

"Every week she had me cutting articles out of *Photoplay, Modern Screen, Movieland,* and all of the rest of the silly fan magazines she used to read religiously," said Leah Mason. "Once they started writing about her and Andy, well, she loved that more than anything. 'We'd make a good couple, don't you think?' she'd ask me. She would stare at the pictures longingly, as if she wished that they actually meant something romantic was going on in her life. I sensed she needed someone, some human contact. They went to a lot of concerts together, spent time in Hyannis Port, played sports. Andy was a lot like Bobby, small and wiry, a great smile. He was a gentler man, though, than Bobby. Not as argumentative. A softy, maybe too soft for Ethel, who was used to fireworks."

It would seem that it was actually Jackie who tried to foster a more serious relationship between Andy Williams and Ethel Kennedy. "Jackie liked Andy very much," said Joan Braden. "She wanted to see Ethel move forward with her life, not only because she, from her own experience, realized that this was best, but also because she knew that this was what Bob would have wanted. And Bob liked Andy so much. But Ethel was not the same kind of woman as Jackie. Ethel was satisfied to stay home, to live an almost cloistered life. Jackie would never have been able to deal with that. They were very different women."

"Jackie thought Andy was perfect for Ethel," said Leah Mason, who stopped working for Ethel in 1968 but resumed on a temporary basis in the seventies, "and she worked behind the scenes to orchestrate something romantic between them."

Trying to play matchmaker, Jackie telephoned Andy to tell him that Ethel was romantically interested in him, without having obtained her permission to do so. Then, as if she were a tenth-grader, the forty-three-year-old former First Lady called Ethel and told her that Andy wanted to move the relationship forward. "It was so juvenile of her, I was completely amazed that she would be involved in such nonsense, but I know she was," says an associate of Ethel's, "because she later admitted it. It showed a side of her that people might not expect to find, one that certainly surprised me because I thought she was too self-involved to have ever done such a thing. I think it worked, too . . . for a while."

According to people close to Ethel Kennedy, Ethel and Andy stepped up their relationship in 1972 into a romantic realm. Leah Mason diplomatically concedes that there was a period of time that year when Ethel and Andy were sleeping in the same room, in the same bed. However, she adds that "it's entirely possible that they were platonic, even in the same bed."

These sleeping arrangements lasted for the entire year, whenever Andy would visit Hickory Hill. However, it would seem that Ethel wasn't comfortable with even the illusion of closeness to Andy Williams, that she felt that she was somehow betraying Bobby's memory by moving ahead with her life. Friends remember seeing Ethel and Andy together on the patio, holding hands and kissing, but they hasten to add that it did not seem like a happy, lighthearted experience for Ethel to be close to another man while still wearing her wedding ring—which she refused to take off—at Hickory Hill, in front of Bobby's children. Ethel, with one foot firmly planted in the past and the other tentatively feeling for the future, could never commit herself to Andy Williams under the circumstances.

"Andy Williams cared deeply for Ethel," Lem Billings once told a journalist. "Maybe enough to know that she was not ready for romance in her life—and maybe never would be ready. Her devotion to Bobby wouldn't allow it. No matter how hard he tried, and I saw him try on several occasions, he couldn't break through. Since he couldn't wear Ethel down, I think he began to feel he wasn't man enough to fill Bobby's shoes, that he was inadequate."

Bobby Kennedy was still the center of Ethel's world; no one—not Andy Williams or anyone else—was ever going to replace him. One associate of Ethel's remembers overhearing a telephone conversation between Ethel and Jackie, during which Ethel said, "Listen, Jackie, just forget it. Andy and I tried it, and it just didn't work. Nobody can replace Bobby. You should know that by now." To that associate's knowledge, Jackie then abandoned her matchmaking efforts.

"I thought it was sweet that she [Jackie] cared," says Leah Mason. "But Ethel didn't. She said to me, 'How dare she try to match me up with Andy Williams! It could never work.' Then she shook her head sadly and said, 'He deserves better, anyway.' She seemed so very alone as she walked out of the room. I thought to myself, 'Such a sad woman, with no one in her life.' I wondered how this had happened to such a lively, effervescent person. It seemed unfair."

(In the end, sixteen years after his divorce from Claudine Longet, Andy Williams married a hostess who was some twenty-five years his junior. Through the years it seems that Andy and Ethel remained what they always were: good friends.)

Like Andy Williams, the gentlemen Ethel would see socially after Bobby's death were all men left over from her friendships with Bobby who happened to be widowers or who were going through marriage difficulties and divorces. Ethel often needed an escort to social events, and the men with whom she felt most comfortable were naturally her choices. Such was the case with Frank Gifford, who had been a friend of Ethel and Bobby's dating back to the days when RFK was Attorney General. During the mid- and late seventies, while he was going through a divorce with his then-wife Maxine, Gifford became a frequent escort of Ethel's. The relationship, from all appearances, looked serious enough for Maxine to cut off Ethel, a woman she once considered a friend.

But, as with Ethel's other relationships, nothing seriously romantic developed between Ethel and Frank. (Gifford eventually married TV personality Kathie Lee Gifford. Then, in 1981, Gifford's daughter Victoria married Ethel's son Michael—they would later divorce—bonding Ethel and Frank together as in-laws.)

The fact is that Ethel enjoyed men simply for the sake of their company. Always the jock, she preferred playing doubles with her male friends and rarely hit the courts anymore with other women. "Women's tennis bores the tears out of me," she declared. (In the mid-seventies, though, she would become an ardent fan of female tennis pro Martina Navratilova, dubbing her "magnificent.") She also said that she would never become involved with anyone who was not Catholic or who was divorced, though everyone who knew her well felt that this was just an excuse.

Recalls Frank Mankiewicz, "She would often joke with me and say,

'What am I going to do if the Pope one day says that it's okay for a Catholic to marry a non-Catholic? Or it's okay for a Catholic to marry someone who's been divorced? With my luck,' she would add, 'the Pope would say, "And guess what, everyone? It was okay all along!"' Seriously, though, I never felt that Ethel was interested in anyone; not that I would ever presume to know what she was thinking when it came to her personal life."

Ethel Pushes Jackie Too Far

After Bobby's death, thirty-eight-year-old Ethel Kennedy's main interest seemed to lie in keeping Bobby's memory alive. She put most of her energy into the RFK Foundation, and would continue to talk to Bobby and about him to friends, as if he were still alive. This is precisely how she felt Jackie should live her life, after Jack. In her view, Jackie should devote the rest of her life to Jack's memory out of a sense of duty and obligation. She was adamant about it: Once married to a Kennedy, always married to a Kennedy, whether he was dead or alive.

Also, she resented Aristotle Onassis—just on principle. Ethel, as a Kennedy widow, was completely devoted to the Kennedy legacy now and thought Onassis was a crook who would somehow taint the family's image. She couldn't imagine why Jackie wanted to be involved with him in any way.

One afternoon in September 1968, Jackie, a Secret Service man, a nanny named Susannah Walker (who was temporarily replacing the vacationing Marta Sgubin), and Jackie's children went to Ethel's Hickory Hill estate for a visit—rare in 1968, because the two women were angry with each other about Onassis's intentions. However, Jackie had a gift for Ethel's soon-to-be-born baby and wanted to give it to her personally.

"Where are all the kids?" Jackie asked when she arrived. Usually, as soon as she walked through the front door at Hickory Hill, she was besieged by excited children lunging at her and screaming, "Aunt Jackie! Aunt Jackie!"

"What kids?" Ethel answered, joking. "Oh, *those* kids. Bobby and I just had those to get into the papers. I farm them out now." The two women laughed and greeted one another with a hug.

After settling in, Jackie went with Ethel out onto the well-manicured, flower-bedecked grounds to talk. As they walked along, exchanging polite generalities, a great black Newfoundland dog leapt into the air between them. Ethel kept repeating "Down, Brumus! Down, Brumus!" while Jackie pretended the animal did not exist. Soft music played in the background, seemingly from nowhere (actually there were camouflaged speakers placed all along the pathway).

During the course of their discussion, the two women apparently became embroiled in a heated argument. As Jackie stormed into the house to retrieve her children, she said to Ethel, "You cannot tell me how to live my life. I deserve to be happy. If you choose not to be, that's your choice."

"Just the same old selfish Jackie Kennedy," Ethel observed bitterly as the Secret Service agent and nanny looked on, no doubt with discomfort. "Poor Jack. He's probably spinning in his grave right about now."

According to the agent, at the mention of her late husband, Jackie stopped struggling to get John into his coat. Her control slipped another notch. Standing to face Ethel, she raised her hand as if she were about to strike her. Perhaps thinking better of it in front of the children, Jackie instead ran her fingers nervously through her shoulder-length hair. Behind her on the wall was a framed letter from President Franklin D. Roosevelt to young Robert Kennedy, giving advice about Bobby's stamp collection.

"After all these years, and all we have been through," she said, spitting out the words in a harsh, guttural whisper so as not to frighten John as she finished putting his coat on him, "how dare you say that to me?" She further stated that she would never speak to Ethel again, that Ethel was "no longer a part of" her life.

Ethel's eyes opened wide. She had gone too far and, judging from her expression, she knew it. "But . . ." she began.

However, before Ethel had a chance to collect her thoughts, Jackie hurried her entourage from the house. They were followed out of the vestibule and down the flagstone path by a contrite Ethel who, by now, was apologizing in every possible way. "I'm so sorry, Jackie," she said, stammering. "I didn't mean it. Come back. Let's talk. Please."

The thought that Jackie would never again speak to her was, it seemed clear, more than Ethel could bear. After all, for the past fifteen years, she could always count on Jackie. No matter how unkind Ethel had been to her, Jackie was always there for her. However, it now seemed that their relationship was going to change forever as a result of Ethel's temper, and she couldn't allow it to happen. She wanted to take it all back, start over again, act as if the last five minutes had never occurred.

"Jackie, you know me. You know how I get," she said, according to what the agent would later recall. "Forget what I said. Thank you for the gift, Jackie. The baby will love it. I'll open it later, Jackie. I'll love it, too."

Now, she was speaking almost incoherently through her tears. "I love you, Jackie. Bobby loved you, too. Please . . ."

But Jackie was too angry to stop and console Ethel, be there for her, take care of her. In fact, it seemed as if she wasn't hearing a word of Ethel's apologies. "You just leave me alone," she hollered back at her.

Once outside, Jackie got into the passenger seat of her automobile as the Secret Service man and the nanny positioned the children in the back. The nanny sat next to Caroline and John Jr., the agent got into the driver's side, started the ignition, and began to drive off. As they drove away, they could see a pregnant Ethel Kennedy with tears streaming down her face, standing in the driveway, mouthing the words: "I'm sorry."

"Bobby's Little Miracle"

As her due date crept up on her, Ethel Kennedy began to become more anxious about the notion of giving birth. The child she was carrying was all that remained of her husband, kept safe inside of her. Its safe journey into the world was her priority. Since her last baby,

Douglas, had been born premature, Ethel feared that the stress of the last few months would cause this new child to be born prematurely as well. In fact, on October 12, two months before the baby was due, she awoke with a start, feeling that she was possibly having contractions.

By noon, she was certain she was going into labor. Panicked, she immediately telephoned Joan to tell her what was occurring. Joan put Ted on the extension, and it was decided that Ethel should telephone her doctor, John Walsh. By six that evening, Ethel was in the labor room at Georgetown Medical Center. Ted arranged for the Kennedy family nurse, Luella Hennessey, to be at Ethel's side. "The whole family was afraid she'd go into premature labor," Luella Hennessey remembered. "Senator Kennedy said to me, 'I don't know what will happen to Ethel if anything happens to this baby.'"

By the time Hennessey got to the hospital, though, the crisis was over. It had been a false alarm. Still, to be safe, Walsh suggested that Ethel spend the rest of her pregnancy on bed rest. Hennessey, who stayed with Ethel during this time, told Laurence Leamer, author of *The Kennedy Women,* "She had very strong faith and believed that if this is what the Lord had planned for her, he would also provide for her. She was truly an optimist. Ethel talked as if Bobby was away. She never said, 'Oh, he's never going to come back, isn't it awful?'"

On December 11, 1968, Ethel checked back into the hospital for a planned cesarean. She hoped her arrival would go unnoticed, but of course it did not. Reporters waited for her at the entrance to the hospital. She ignored them as she and her coterie, including Luella Hennessey and Ted Kennedy, rushed into the lobby and were taken to a private room in the maternity ward, which had just been painted pink for her arrival. Hennessey was given a private room across the hall. In Ethel's room was a bouquet of pink and blue flowers waiting for her on the bed stand. They were from Jackie and the card read: "Boy or Girl? It matters not. How wonderful for you! Love, Jackie."

The next morning, with Ted and Luella at her side, Ethel was wheeled into the delivery room. Ted seemed in almost as much distress as Ethel. He began to tremble so ferociously that Ethel instinctively grasped his hand and squeezed it reassuringly. He turned pale, gagged, and wavered on his feet as though he was about to faint, as Ethel was finally wheeled into the delivery room.

Within the hour, Ethel gave birth to an eight-pound four-ounce daughter, her fourth. Afterward, Ted, still shaking, had to be helped on his wobbly feet from the room by two very concerned nurses.

Ted and Joan, along with some of the Kennedy children, waited in Hennessey's room for the news. When Hennessey burst in and made the announcement, they let out a unified scream of excitement. The baby was named Rory Elizabeth Katherine; Joan called her "Bobby's little miracle."

"Bob would have loved to see his baby girl, but we can't talk about things that never can be," Ethel Kennedy would later say at a press conference where photos of mother and child were snapped for the international media. "So I will take her home to Hickory Hill in Virginia and let her grow up among her brothers and sisters and let her learn from them what her father was and how lucky she is to be a member of this family . . . the older ones take care of the smaller ones, and the smaller ones take care of the very little ones . . . and they all take care of me.

"Teddy and Joan have been just wonderful to us," she continued. "With an aunt and uncle like those two, this new Kennedy can't miss."

Three days after Ethel gave birth, she found Jackie at her bedside. She was probably not surprised. Despite their differences about Onassis—and the recent, terrible outburst at Hickory Hill—theirs was a bond of tragedy shared by no one else in the family. Both women's husbands had been shot down with a bullet into the brain during a moment of triumph. Both had felt their husband's lifeblood running through their fingers. Both had seen them die. They had borne so much of the same kind of sorrow that they would always be spiritual sisters in some way. Of course Jackie would be at the hospital when Ethel gave birth to Bobby's child, this baby who would never know the warm, secure touch of her father's hand.

Jackie seemed happy and in good spirits when she showed up at Georgetown Hospital. She had on no makeup and her hairdo was not the usual fresh-combed style she always wore when there was a chance her picture might be taken. She was wearing the same navy blue dress and matching jacket in which she'd traveled back and forth for her wedding in Greece, the dress she'd been wearing so often that a reporter from *Women's Wear Daily* tartly suggested it was time she gave it to charity.

A week after the birth of her daughter, Ethel and the infant went home, driven by Ted. On the way, Ethel asked that they stop at Arlington National Cemetery. Carrying the baby, Ethel walked to Bobby's resting place and stood at the foot of the grave. While Ted waited in the car, tears streaming down his face, Ethel introduced Bobby to his new daughter.

PART ELEVEN

Chappaquiddick

It was early Saturday morning, July 19, 1969, when the phone rang in Joan Kennedy's bedroom in Boston. It was Ted.

"There's been an accident," he told her. His voice sounded weak and strained, as if he had been crying. "A terrible, terrible accident."

As the breath whooshed out of her, a chill ran down Joan's spine. "Oh, no, Ted. What now?"

It was then that Joan heard the words that would forever change her life: "A girl drowned, Joansie. And there was nothing I could do. I swear it."

By the end of the sixties the smoke was just settling over cities that had been burned during the civil rights unrest. The country still had not recovered from the deaths of Bobby Kennedy and Martin Luther King, Jr., and a lingering sense of hopelessness stemming from Jack's assassination five years earlier was still felt by many. With the war in Vietnam continuing as an explosive, divisive factor, it could be said that Americans had not had a chance to catch their breaths in a decade that had been chaotic, emotional, and troubling.

On Friday, July 18, 1969, as the Apollo 11 crew approached the moon in fulfillment of a goal set by Jack in 1960, Ted was en route to Boston to attend a weekend party with some male friends and six single young women who were fondly referred to by friends and family as "The Boiler Room Girls" (an appellation given them because of the countless hours they had put in for Bobby's 1968 presidential campaign.) This party—attended by five men, all married—was held in a cottage that had been rented by Kennedy cousin Joe Gargan on Chappaquiddick Island, just off Martha's Vineyard.

A bit after eleven o'clock, as the festivities wound down, Ted emerged from the seaside cottage with blonde, blue-eyed Mary Jo Kopechne. At twenty-eight, Mary Jo had earned herself a degree in business and a treasured job on Robert Kennedy's presidential campaign. Ted then asked his chauffeur, John "Jack" Crimmins, for the keys to his black 1967 Oldsmobile, and the two motored off into the night.

Ted would later explain that he was giving Mary Jo a ride to the ferry, which would be headed back to Edgartown, where Mary Jo was staying. Tragedy occurred, though, when, according to his own account, he took a wrong turn onto a dirt road that led to an unlit, narrow wooden bridge. His car plunged off the bridge, landing upside down in the cold, dirty water. While Kennedy managed somehow to escape, Mary Jo did not. Later Ted would claim that he had alerted Joe Gargan and friend Paul Markham to the accident, and the two dove repeatedly into the water in an effort to save Mary Jo.

After two teenage boys discovered the car on an early-morning fishing trip, police were summoned, and the young woman's body—her identity a mystery—was eventually pulled from the murky water. It would be ten hours before Ted would contact the police and explain that the body was Mary Jo's. No matter how one looked at it, everything about Mary Jo Kopechne's death seemed to point to Ted's lack of integrity and responsibility, or maybe worse.

Saturday, July 19, 1969, was three days before Rose Kennedy's seventy-ninth birthday. Still healthy and active, that morning she planned to attend a charity bazaar at her church, St. Francis Xavier, and was dressing to leave when Ted called to tell her that something tragic had occurred. He warned her not to go to the bazaar for fear she would be confronted by the press, and told her he was on his way to the compound.

When Ted finally arrived in Hyannis Port, he went to Joseph's room to tell him that an accident had resulted in a woman's death, even though he had tried to save her. Joseph couldn't do much but squeeze his distraught son's hand. Then Ted patiently explained the situation to Rose. As usual, she was composed.

Rose knew of Mary Jo, even admired her, and was deeply troubled and saddened by her death. However, looking at a bigger, practical picture, she could predict serious trouble in the offing, and summoned her family to the compound to deal with it. Pat flew in from California, and Jean and Eunice both arrived from Europe, all three with their husbands. Jean's husband, Steve Smith—who had taken over much of the Kennedy business in the wake of Joseph's stroke—began to make logical decisions about strategy.

Once he got to his home on Squaw Island, some might be surprised to know, Ted's first call was to Greece in search of Jackie Kennedy Onassis. In fact, Ted had demonstrated a great degree of caring and generosity not only to Jackie and her two children but also to Ethel and her eleven in the wake of the family's twin tragedies. "No one outside the family can ever know how much his efforts have meant to the shaping of their [Jack's and Bobby's children's] lives," Rose wrote in her memoirs. Jackie was so impressed with his sense of responsibility that she had even suggested he become Caroline's godfather by proxy.

Upon hearing from Ted, Jackie said that she would join the family in Hyannis Port as soon as possible.

Ted's next call was to a woman he had dated sporadically over the years and was involved with at this time, the Austrian-born, blonde Helga Wagner. Alarmed by Ted's predicament, Helga asked if she should come to Hyannis Port to be with him. Since her presence would only cause more turmoil, he wisely advised her to keep her distance.

After he called Jackie and Helga, Ted called Joan.

"Don't worry. I believe you when you say it was an accident," Joan promised her husband, according to what she later recalled.

"I knew you would," he said, relieved. "I could always count on you."

After they hung up, Joan Kennedy sat on her bed, stunned by the news and overwhelmed by a deepening sense of dread. Just six weeks pregnant, Joan realized that she shouldn't take on any stress, but that would now be impossible. She packed a small bag and left for Hyannis Port to be with the rest of the family.

Two hours after Joan's arrival at the compound, Ethel arrived directly from Storrs where she had made an appearance at the opening of the first Connecticut Special Olympics at the University of Connecticut. She was upset, angry, and confused, as were most of the family members.

When Ethel saw Joan, she must have immediately noticed that the young Kennedy wife seemed to be in a trance, as if on heavy medication, walking about aimlessly, biting her lip, and wringing her hands.

Ethel took Joan into her arms, and the two embraced warmly. "We've had our problems in the past, but now is the time to pull together," Ethel told Joan.

"Tell me what really happened," Ethel said to Joan as they walked arm in arm into Rose's living room.

"I don't have the vaguest idea," Joan answered, and she wasn't lying. "Do you know if Jackie is coming, or not? I heard that she was."

"I don't have the vaguest idea," Ethel answered, echoing Joan's response.

Jackie Tells Ari:
"I Have to Be There"

By 1969, Jackie Kennedy Onassis was living a life far removed from the concerns of the Kennedys. She sometimes seemed determined to reinvent herself as a woman who had never been Queen of Camelot. During a vacation to Italy's Isle of Capri in the Gulf of Naples, she ignored any autograph-seekers who referred to her as "Mrs. Kennedy," and would indulge only those who referred to her as "Mrs. Onassis." She also had her checks changed to read "Jacqueline Bouvier Onassis," eliminating "Kennedy." However, Jackie and Ari actually led separate lives from the start of their union. He told his biographer, Will Frischauer, "I was with Jacqueline for only thirty days during the first ninety days of our marriage."

As soon as he married Jackie, Ari reignited his obsessive affair with Maria Callas. He went to be with Callas as soon as he returned to Paris, right after his honeymoon with Jackie. Jackie didn't seem to mind.

"In his own way, Onassis was good to her," observes Jackie's cousin John Davis. "Who can say what kind of marriage that was? His two children, Christina and Alexander, hated her. But she seemed unaffected by their bitterness. Of course, it never much mattered to Jackie whether you liked her or not. Onassis got her away from the Kennedy tragedies, the publicity, the hellishness . . . and the next time I saw her after she married him, she seemed a completely new woman. Just lighter, better. . . . She had gotten on with things."

Despite her new life, Jackie's sisterly bond with Joan and, to a lesser extent, Ethel, still existed. Jackie had also stayed in touch with Rose, and had even arranged for the Kennedy matriarch to join her, Aristotle, and the children for a two-week cruise in the Caribbean in March of 1969 for the Easter holiday.

Rose couldn't help but marvel at the jet-set lifestyle Jackie now enjoyed. The Onassises maintained fully staffed homes in Monte Carlo; Glyfada, Greece; two in New York; London; Skorpios; Montevideo in Uruguay; Paris; and aboard the *Christina*. Each residence was kept in complete readiness should the wealthy couple decide on a moment's notice to hop off to South America and their Montevideo hacienda, or fly to Paris for an art exhibit or to take a peek at "the collections," where the latest fashions were shown.

Rose once described the opulence she found on the *Christina* as "overwhelming." While some of the interior of the luxury craft, such as the bar, represented masculine tastes, the nine staterooms were now decorated in pink satins and silks, refurbished to represent Jackie's style (even though Ari would have preferred her not to redecorate). A rare, jade Buddha sat on display in the main salon. Expensive oriental vases were securely strapped to the walls in case of turbulent high seas. El Greco, Pissarro, and Gauguin paintings decorated the passageways. At night, the base of the Olympic-size, mosaic-tiled swimming pool was hydraulically lifted level with the deck, forming a dance floor under multicolored lights.

The Onassis's French household staff—accustomed to serving such personalities as Winston Churchill, Greta Garbo, and Cary Grant—served breakfast on trays in the staterooms on the lowest of the three decks used as living quarters by the family. At lunchtime, John and Caroline would eat with their mother on the shaded top deck while the ship was anchored, or by the saltwater pool near the game room when at sea. Onassis continued to make the final decision as to what food would be served in the oval dining room for dinner, selecting one main course from the three suggested by the French chef. Jackie ordered only for the children, usually beef and poultry dishes, which they would eat not in the main dining room but rather in the "officers' mess"—a warm, intimate, wood-paneled breakfast room—with their nurse.

Ellen Deiner, who worked as a publicist for the Greek National Theater, was aboard the *Christina* as a guest of Aristotle Onassis on that particular cruise with Rose and Jackie. She recalled, "Rose reminded me of a typical tourist, with the big floppy hats and sunglasses, and cheap, cheap, *cheap* clothing. She and Jackie got along well, but they did have an ongoing discussion having to do with the children's schooling."

As the only offspring of her son, John Fitzgerald, Caroline and John Jr. were dear to Rose Kennedy. It was her wish that they be brought up to understand Kennedy values, a sense of family being chief among them. Rose feared that as they went through their impressionable adolescent years with Onassis as their stepfather, the children would grow away from the Kennedy tradition of serving country and family. Because she also wanted them to be available for frequent family visits to Hyannis Port and Palm Beach, she was upset when Ted told her Jackie was thinking of sending the children to Le Rosey, a Swiss boarding school attended by the children of the wealthiest of European society.

Recalled Ellen Deiner, "While the two were sunning, Rose and Jackie talked about the fact that if the children went to the Swiss school, they would be away from their mother for long stretches of time. She said that Joan and Ethel were so adamant about being with their children that they were known to fly back from political rallies just to make breakfast for them. I was sitting two chairs over, but could clearly hear Jackie protesting, 'Well, I am not Ethel, and I am not Joan. I'll raise my children my way.' I had the feeling that the two bickered like any mother-in-law and daughter-in-law, but that at the core of it was a deep, abiding love and respect for one another."

Rose seemed to crave information about her former daughter-in-law. To her, Jackie was almost a stranger these days, living a life of privilege away from Hyannis Port and away from her watchful eye. In an attempt to learn about Jackie's life, she tried to ferret out some tidbits from Ellen Deiner, who, she knew, was close to Onassis. "Rose asked me if it was true that Ari wanted to change the children's names to Onassis by adoption," recalls Deiner. "There had been news reports to that effect. In fact, I did once overhear Ari complain about seeing references to 'John Kennedy, Jr.' and 'Caroline Kennedy' in the papers. He wanted the children to have his name, since they were now his responsibility. But Mrs. Onassis said, 'They are not your responsibility, they are *my* responsibility.'"

"An adoption will never occur," Rose told Ellen Deiner as she rubbed suntan lotion on her pale but still remarkably taut thighs. "Never! Once a Kennedy, always a Kennedy." She put on her sunglasses and turned to Deiner. "The blood of the Kennedys runs through those children's veins," she insisted. "They are Americans, not Greeks. We will fight an adoption in court, believe me. They will be Kennedys, those children, and they will live in America. Even in death, my son has a right to expect *his* son to carry on his name."

"But I don't know how you will be able to stop an adoption," Ellen Deiner said, hesitatingly.

"We'll just see about that, now won't we?" Rose said confidently. "I am certain we could at the very least get a decision that the adoption and name change would not be recognized in America."

Deiner was surprised by Rose's observation. It sounded as if she had already begun to look into the legalities of the matter.

"This kind of discussion went on and on throughout the two-week cruise," said Deiner. "As we went to Nassau, then the Virgin Islands, the children were the subject of ongoing discussions between Rose and I [sic]. I am sure that she brought up all of these points to Jackie as well, which is what I suggested she do."

On the last day of the cruise, Rose told Ellen Deiner that, as a result of her discussions with her former daughter-in-law, Jackie not only had agreed to let the children continue their educations in New York, she also would not allow Onassis to adopt the Kennedy children. She would not remove the children from either their national or family heritage.

"My daughter-in-law is not a foolish woman. I can't imagine why you ever thought she would have allowed an adoption," Rose said, pointing an accusatory finger at Ellen Deiner.

"But I *never* said that," Deiner countered in her defense, her face by now reddened. "You asked me if . . ."

Rose placed her finger on her lips for silence, cutting off the mortified Deiner. "Well, I believe you did say just that, and I have told Jacqueline as much," Rose countered. Then, before taking her leave, she concluded, "Jacqueline told me to tell you that *some* people should learn to mind their own business."

At the time when Jackie got the telephone call from Ted about the Chappaquiddick tragedy, she was on the Isle of Scorpios with her husband, her children, their cousin Victoria Lawford, and a playmate of John's, Eric von Huguley. She immediately decided that she wanted to be in Hyannis Port to support the family, but she didn't want the media to know of her presence there.

"But why must you go?" Aristotle asked. "That is their problem, not ours."

"You're right. It's not our problem," Jackie agreed, "it's *my* problem," she added, underscoring the separate nature of their lives. "I have to be there. I have to know what is going on."

Nicholas Stamosis, who worked in the travel department of Olympic Airways, which was owned by Ari, also knew Jackie well. He recalls, "Ted's call came at a convenient time because Mrs. Onassis already had business in New York—meetings to arrange for the children's schooling. So she was planning to go to America anyway. We just scheduled her trip a week early when she got the call."

"I don't want anyone to even know I'm in Hyannis Port," Jackie told Stamosis. "This trip has to be done very carefully. No photographers. Is that understood?" Presumably, Jackie didn't want it to appear that Ted was using her and the memory of her husband in a bid for sympathy.

"I can guarantee you that I will at least try, Mrs. Onassis," Stamosis said.

"Well, you will have to do better than that," Jackie snapped. *"Just do it."*

"I will, Mrs. Onassis," he said, finally.

"We got her out of Greece and into Hyannis, and nobody was the wiser," recalls Stamosis, "at least as far as I know."

A couple of days later Nicholas Stamosis ran into Jackie's disgruntled husband in Athens at the Architectoniki Bar. "He was drunk and talking about how angry he was that Jackie went to be with the Kennedys," he recalls of Onassis.

"Those damn Kennedys, they have some kind of dirty hold on her," Onassis said, exasperated. "Just look at what has happened. Ted

Kennedy drives a girl off a bridge, she drowns, then my wife flies around the world just to pat him on the back and tell him it's all right."

"Well, she is a very caring woman," said Stamosis in Jackie's defense.

Onassis slammed his fist down on the bar, his mouth turned down at the corners. "She just wants to make sure the Kennedy kingdom doesn't come tumbling down, for if it does, what will that do to her children's inheritances and trust funds?" As he tossed back another vodka and soda, Onassis concluded, "*That's* what she cares about."

Joan Accuses:
"All You Care about Is How It *Looks*?"

In the days after the death of Mary Jo Kopechne, the Kennedy family closed ranks as it always had in times of trouble. Maria Shriver, Eunice's daughter and Ted's niece, speaks of the Kennedy credo that was at work at that time and which, she says, still exists today. "My grandparents [Rose and Joseph] emphasized family loyalty, which my parents then emphasized in turn," she explains. "'This is your family and you stand by it no matter what,' they told their children, and their children then instilled it in us, and I have handed it down to mine. 'If you have something negative to say, you say it in the house. You don't say it out there. These people are family. You may not like them sometimes, but they are the most important people in your life, and don't you forget it.'"

Soon the Hyannis Port home was filled with concerned Kennedys, many of whom, perhaps, didn't have particularly fond feelings for Ted at this time but who would stand by him just the same. "There was rage, horror, and anger," recalled Joseph's nurse, Rita Dallas, "a lot of anger. Not at any particular person, not at Teddy, but I really think at fate."

When Jackie Onassis arrived, she greeted all of the family members, and then quickly departed for her own home next door to Joseph and

Rose's. Something had changed, and it was painfully clear to everyone. "She didn't really belong there," said John Davis. "Things were different now. She wasn't really a Kennedy anymore, and they knew it, and they treated her like it."

The last time Jackie was at Rose and Joseph's was during Bobby's campaign. She had run off in tears after Ethel reminded her that "we" would never again be in the White House. Since that time, Bobby had been killed and she had married Onassis, much to Ethel's dismay and, it would seem, many other people's as well.

"The sisters—Jean, Eunice, and Pat—never treated Jackie the same after she married Onassis," said another relative of Jackie's. "No one really knew how to deal with her. There were those who felt she was so far above them, they couldn't relate. And there were those who felt she was just an outsider now. She could feel it in the air, and didn't want to be around it. Even Joan seemed as though she couldn't relate to Jackie anymore. So Jackie retreated to her own home and stayed there, almost in a 'wait and see' position."

Ted's explanation of what had occurred on the tiny island was relayed to Jackie by others. In fact, she and Ted had no discussion about the events in question, or about anything at all, at least not in anyone's memory.

"Her emotions were mixed, I believe," said the late author Leo Damore, who wrote a book about the Chappaquiddick tragedy titled *Senatorial Privilege: The Chappaquiddick Cover-Up*. "She was there because she had a stake in what happened to the family, because of her children. My research indicated that she was reluctant even to be there, that she wanted her presence to be a secret, and didn't want a public show of support. I believe she felt that Ted was guilty of something, even if she didn't know what it was."

Her friend Roswell Gilpatric once said that he believed that Jackie was "probably very angry at Ted, and perhaps even feeling guilty because of her very human reaction to his obvious lack of judgment. I'm sure she was confused, trying to sort it all out. One thing she did say sticks out in my mind as being amazingly perceptive. 'I believe Ted has an unconscious drive to self-destruct,' she told me. 'I think it comes from the fact that he knows he'll never live up to what people expect of him. He's not Jack. He's not Bobby. And he believes that what he is, is just not enough.'"

Jackie knew that with the Chappaquiddick tragedy, the Kennedys' chances of ever getting into the White House again were killed along with Mary Jo Kopechne. "Never will he be President now. *Never*," Jackie told Roswell Gilpatric. "He would never allow it for himself, anyway. And now, with this tragedy, it's over. We should just face it."

After meeting with Ted and with Kennedy adviser Burke Marshall, Ethel would volunteer to call upon some influential people in Washington, the first being former Secretary of Defense Robert McNamara, to help with strategy. At Ethel's urging, McNamara arrived quickly.

More "troops" were summoned from far and wide. Soon, an army of Jack's loyalists (a court that was, at least to some extent, in exile and still dreaming of Washington) had descended upon Cape Cod. There were fifteen in all staying at Ted and Joan's ten-room home on Squaw Island, and at Ethel's, Jackie's, and Rose's homes in the compound as well.

"Mrs. Onassis was asked if they could use her home—the President's home—as a headquarters, and she agreed," recalls Rita Dallas. "She then became deeply involved in seeing to it that the meetings went smoothly. These men were all dear friends of hers, so she was a big part of what being decided. However, she spent her time with them, not with the family. There were a lot of questions to be addressed."

Most troubling was the fact that Kennedy had failed to report the accident for almost ten hours, choosing instead to return to the hotel in which he was staying in Edgartown and spend the night there before returning to Chappaquiddick and then going to the Edgartown police. Why had he waited so long? Of course, there was also speculation about Ted's relationship with Mary Jo Kopechne. Had they been lovers?

These meetings were not about what had occurred as much as they were about what to *do* about it.

The first order of business was to have Joan Kennedy place what some aides referred to as "the call." Prior to this time, Joan had been secreted away in a bedroom, concerned about her husband and anxious about whatever was being plotted downstairs. While Ethel and Jackie had been the involved, "important" Kennedy wives, busy discussing strategy with aides, Joan was thought of as the weak, fragile wife locked away upstairs. Now, though, she had a role to fill.

Joan was asked to telephone the Kopechnes to extend the Kennedy family's condolences. Strategically it was decided that the way the Kopechnes felt about the Kennedys could make a huge difference in what they would seek from Ted. The Kopechnes had to be persuaded that the Kennedys were also grieving the loss of young Mary Jo, that they were a caring, sensitive family. In fact, Ted had already telephoned Mary Jo's parents, Joseph and Gwen Kopechne, in Berkeley Heights, New Jersey, to tell them personally the awful news about their daughter. However, Ted's call did little to ingratiate him to the Kopechnes because he failed to mention that he had been driving the car or that he had even been in it.

"We must align ourselves with the Kopechnes," Joan was told by one senior adviser. "And it starts with you, Mrs. Kennedy."

The senior adviser, who would only speak off the record, remembered that Joan became incensed, lashing out at him in a manner uncharacteristic of her. "There's a dead girl, and all you care about is how it *looks?*" she said to him, angrily.

Joan sat motionless in front of the rotary telephone. A slip of paper with the Kopechnes' number on it was slid across the table toward her. By now, Ted was standing at his wife's side. "But what if they ask me questions?" Joan asked her husband. "What if they want details?"

"Well, you don't *have* any details," Ted said, speaking softly to placate her. "That's not what this call is about, Joansie. Just be nice, be sympathetic . . . and get the hell off the line. Do you understand?"

As Ted dialed the phone, Joan seemed to choke the receiver in silent protest.

"Now just make the call, and maybe later I'll take you to Mildred's," he told her, referring to a nearby restaurant, Mildred's House of Chowder.

"Hello, Mrs. Kopechne?" Joan began when the connection was made. "Yes. Why, this is Joan Kennedy, Ted's wife."

As Ted listened to every word she said, Joan told the dead girl's mother how terribly sorry she and "the whole Kennedy family" were about what had happened. "We have had tragedy in our own family, as you know," Joan said, her voice small and miserable, "and so we empathize with you, and I am . . . I mean, we, are so, so sorry."*

Ted patted her on the arm and walked away while his wife com-

*In an interview years later, Gwendolyn Kopechne would say that, while Joan Kennedy was pleasant enough and seemed genuinely saddened, the call was a disappointment to her. "It was a sympathy call," she said. "Nothing was explained."

pleted the brief call. As twilight deepened into darkness, a cool wind blew in from Nantucket Sound through an open window in the living room. Shivering, a pregnant Joan Kennedy hugged herself.

Ethel to the Rescue

Thirty-nine-year-old Ethel Kennedy had always been politically savvy, ambitious, and determined. Throughout the years, she would do anything it would take to help the Kennedy family—her family—achieve whatever it had set its collective mind to in terms of public service and power. However, like Jackie, she was not a naïve woman. Mary Jo Kopechne's death was a crushing blow to Ethel's morale in that she—like just about everyone else—immediately seemed to recognize that it would mark the end of an era for the Kennedys. Or, as she put it during one family meeting with top advisers, "There's no way out of this. This is it. Jack and Bobby are rolling over in their graves."

However, her dismay aside, Ethel had always proved herself to be capable in times of crisis, and during this one she would do her best to keep the Kennedy machinery in proper tune. In fact, she had the entire weekend organized like a two-ring circus.

On the one hand, Ethel was summoning Democratic party spin doctors to chisel out the "family's position" on the tragedy. On the other, she was organizing a series of casual sporting events at the compound, ostensibly to keep everyone's mind off the tragedy that had befallen them. One moment drafting a statement for the press, the next hunting down a badminton birdie, even a minor medical emergency didn't slow her down. Her fourteen-year-old son David broke an arm while playing football, and it was Ethel who examined it, then dispatched a few family members to the hospital with him.

While her actions were seen by many as further evidence of Ethel's strong will and commitment, others viewed them more skeptically. Her ability to compartmentalize her efforts on that weekend seemed more than just deft managerial talent, but a total disregard for any true emotional attachment to the events that had brought about the situation.

After Joan's phone call, and because it was known that the grieving Kopechnes were devoutly Catholic, it was decided that Ethel should telephone them to talk about their shared religious convictions. This, even more than the call from Joan, seemed a blatant manipulation. Ethel was the "religious one," it was reasoned, and the public knew as much from press interviews with her in the past. The memory of her televised grief during Bobby's funeral was still fresh in the minds of most Americans and, it was hoped, in the minds of the Kopechnes. It was thought that Ethel would be able to appeal to the Kopechnes on a deep, very personal level. So while Joan may have been the family's reluctant personal emissary, Ethel would be the Kennedys' loyal spiritual ambassador.

"God has a plan for all of us," Ethel told Gwen Kopechne during her telephone conversation with her. "And I just wanted to let you know that Mary Jo is in her rightful place in heaven."

Before Ethel knew what was happening, Mrs. Kopechne was consoling her over Bobby's death. However, Ethel didn't want to be swayed from her purpose. She went back to the subject at hand: Mary Jo's passing. "Please, let us pay for the funeral," Ethel offered. "The Kennedy family would like to do that, if you'll let us."

The offer was politely rejected. When Ethel was told that the funeral would take place in Plymouth, a coal-mining town in northern Pennsylvania, she said, "Ted, Joan, and other members of the family, of course, will be there." It hadn't been an easy call for Ethel, even though she made it seem as if it had been. As soon as she hung up, a tiredness seemed to come over her like a high wave from the crashing Sound. "I have to go lay down," she told Robert McNamara, wearily. "This is too much for me."

Later that evening, after resting, Ethel wrote a tribute to Mary Jo that would be released to the press. "Mary Jo was a sweet, wonderful girl," she said in the forty-word release. "She worked for Bobby for four years and was in the boiler room [the phone room used for delegate counts]. She often came out to the house, and she was the one who stayed up all night typing Bobby's speech on Vietnam. She was a wonderful person." Ethel's comments served only to anger some members of the media, however, because they didn't mention the fact that an accident had occurred or that Ted had been involved. "It wasn't supposed to be a press release," Ethel said in its defense. "They were just my little thoughts."

Then, in what seemed like another strategic public relations move, Wendell Pigman, a former employer of Mary Jo's, issued a statement that compared Ethel and Mary Jo favorably, saying that Mary Jo "was like Ethel in that she would grimace if anyone said anything dirty or tasteless. You can spot people who are swingers and she [Mary Jo] was not one of them." It was as if Mary Jo's reputation as having been puritanical was now being exploited in order to help clean up the mess at hand.

Mary Jo's Funeral

Monday morning dawned bleak and humid. "Joan doesn't want to attend the funeral?" Rose asked Ted over breakfast. "Why, she must. She has no choice. She's the wife!"

It's not known how much Rose knew about Joan's emotional distress at this time, or whether or not she was aware of Joan's drinking. Previously, she would not accept that her daughter-in-law had a problem. But in a few years it would be so clear even Rose wouldn't be able to ignore it. She would handle Joan's alcoholism by trying to keep Joan so busy during visits to Hyannis Port that she wouldn't have time to drink. Once, according to Barbara Gibson, she put Joan to work sorting through hundreds of old books looking for valuable signed editions. Another time, she had her inspecting all the lampshades in the house. "It was as if she figured Joan wouldn't drink if she had something else to do," says Gibson.

In fact, Rose Kennedy was usually kind to Joan, though it was apparently difficult for her to empathize with or even understand her daughter-in-law's problems. "She certainly knew that Joan was in a bad marriage and it bothered her," says Barbara Gibson. "She was unhappy about the fact that Joan and Ted had separate bedrooms, for instance. When she stayed with them, she realized that Joan would sleep late just so that she wouldn't have to have anything to do with Ted. But she, too, had a bad marriage, and she suffered through it as best she could. To Rose's thinking, a woman simply put up with marital problems, which she didn't really think of as problems, anyway, if the trade-off was worth it. The money, the power, the glamour, the status of being a Kennedy should have been worth it to Joan to just accept the drawbacks, as far as Rose was concerned. Rose used to say, 'She has it all. She's beautiful, has a handsome husband, wonderful children, a wonderful home . . . why is she always so sad? I simply do not understand it. Please, someone, explain it to me.'"

Throughout the ordeal of Chappaquiddick, Joan made herself available to her husband for support and encouragement—or at least as much as he would allow her to do so. On some days the two would spend hours walking on the beach arm in arm, not saying much. Then when he would suddenly turn on her or lash out at her, she would once again feel the great divide between them.

As much as she may have wanted to be supportive of Ted during what promised to be an emotionally difficult day, Joan Kennedy was concerned that she would not be able to maintain her composure at Mary Jo Kopechne's funeral in Pennsylvania. She was also concerned about the effect of such stress on her pregnancy. After suffering two previous miscarriages, she worried about the child she was now carrying.

"She knew she had difficulty holding a baby in early pregnancy," explained her nurse, Luella Hennessey. "And so, this time, she was being very, very careful. She rested a lot each day, stayed close to the house, gave up tennis and swimming and other sports that required exercise, exercised only by walking. She wanted this baby very much."

When Joan attempted to discuss her anxiety about attending the funeral with Ted, he was completely unresponsive. When prodded for a reaction, he would walk out onto the deserted beach that stretched in front of the house. He would be gone for hours, leaving Joan to agonize over whether or not he had drowned himself, only adding to her stress. If Joan did not want to attend the funeral, that seemed to be fine with Ted. He was in his own world of misery, and he probably would not miss her in the least, she may have thought.

Rose and Ethel felt strongly, however, that it was Joan's familial responsibility, and her political one as well, to be at her husband's side at such an important, public event. Both women tried to reason with

Joan and convince her to go, but were not successful. In the end, Rose felt that Jackie would be able to make the difference, and so she asked her to speak to Joan. Observers recall Rose's hands shaking badly as she reached for a glass of orange juice and said, "If Jackie can't convince her to go, no one can."

In a scene reminiscent of their heart-to-heart walk along the beach of Hyannis Port on the day of Jack's election, Jackie and Joan took a stroll on the sand of Nantucket Sound—this time, not followed by Secret Service agents. There, Jackie and Joan had what is believed to be their only private conversation about Ted and Mary Jo Kopechne. What they said remains unknown; one witness recalls seeing, from afar, Jackie tenderly touch Joan's cheek. However, by the time they returned, Joan had decided to attend the funeral.

"Whereas Rose might have expected Jackie to convince Joan to go to the funeral, that's not what happened," said a friend of Joan's at the time from Boston. "Jackie felt that if Joan didn't want to go, she shouldn't go. They discussed it calmly, and Jackie said she wasn't sure Joan owed it to Ted to go. However, she did feel that, if only for the sake of public relations, Joan might want to consider it. 'I've never been one to care how things look,' she told her, fibbing, 'but it will really look bad if you're not there.' Later, according to what Joan once told me, Jackie added, 'In the end, they've always been bastards, haven't they, these Kennedy men? Nothing has changed, I suppose.'"

According to Joan Braden, Jackie also suggested that Joan consider psychiatric help. "It wasn't as if Joan hadn't already thought of it," said Braden. "But Jackie was the first to mention it to her, and tell her that there was no stigma attached to it. Joan said she would consider it."

So Joan would accompany her husband to Plymouth. Ethel, too, would go to the funeral as the widow of Bobby, Mary Jo's former employer. Jackie, however, would stay behind in Hyannis Port. Wisely, she realized that her presence at the Kopechne memorial would cause sheer chaos and turn it into a bigger media event than what was already promised by its circumstances. No doubt, she also did not wish to be so closely associated with the ensuing scandal. The other Kennedy women, and their husbands, would also not attend the funeral.

On the humid Tuesday after the drowning, Ted, Joan, Ethel, a phalanx of aides and friends, as well as cousin Joe Gargan, headed to

Pennsylvania for Mary Jo Kopechne's funeral. Joan seemed to be in a trance, never looking anywhere but straight ahead. Ted seemed dazed while Ethel, true to her nature, seemed almost cheery.

The funeral Mass took place at St. Vincent's church in Plymouth. It was a mad scene, with Kennedy fans and supporters, along with reporters and photographers, all converging upon the church. Outside, a woman stood in the crowd of onlookers holding up a sign that said "Kennedy for President, 1972." Of course, the eyes of most of the seven hundred mourners were on the Kennedys.

After the service, Joan and Ethel flanked Ted as the three walked down the aisle and exited the church. Outside, the Kennedys were greeted by a throng of photographers; flashbulbs went off and reporters began shouting questions.

At the graveside, the Kennedys and Kopechnes took their places on folding chairs around the open grave. At one point, Joan reached for her husband's hand and squeezed it.

Of Joan, Bernie Flynn, a detective lieutenant who worked on the Chappaquiddick case, recalled, "To me she was just this shadow of a woman who showed up when her husband did, always following behind him, just sort of there, but not really there. I never saw her talk to anyone. I never saw her smile. I never saw her cry. I don't know what kind of relationship she had with Ted Kennedy, but I can tell you that it looked to me like she hated his guts. I remember once he was answering some questions from me, and she said something like, 'Ted, don't forget to tell him,' and the guy gave her a look like he was about to smack her. She drew back as if she truly feared him. It was a tense moment. At the funeral, she was almost as dead as Mary Jo, I thought."

Ted Asks for Forgiveness

After Mary Jo Kopechne's funeral, there was a lack of information coming out of the Hyannis Port Compound. Upon landing at the Hyannis airport, Kennedy was confronted by NBC newswoman Liz

Trotter who repeatedly asked when he would be releasing a statement. Kennedy refused to answer. Instead, he hurried into a white car and, with Joan at the wheel, sped off, leaving shouting reporters and desperate photographers in their wake. The next day, a Kennedy aide made a threatening telephone call to NBC, demanding that Trotter be removed from the story. "It was raw power reaching out," Trotter remembered, years later. "I thought, 'Gee, there's not even a velvet glove on this. It was just naked. Lay off. Take a fall. Throw the fight.'"

Eventually, Ted Kennedy's legal team offered a deal, and the authorities accepted it. Three days after the funeral, on Friday morning, July 25, Ted appeared at the courthouse in Edgartown and, with Joan at his side, pleaded guilty to the relatively minor charge of leaving the scene of an accident. Kennedy was sentenced by Judge James Boyle to two months at the House of Corrections at Barnstable and a year's probation. The sentence was suspended, as was his driver's license, for a year.

That evening Ted appeared on all three television networks to plead his case not only to his constituents in Massachusetts, but also to all of America, to try to explain what had happened, to appear contrite, to ask for forgiveness.

However, anyone expecting certain questions to be answered during Ted's speech had to have been sorely disappointed. In the speech, written by Ted Sorenson, the lack of specificity only served to underscore the growing public suspicion that a massive cover-up was taking place.

The reaction to Ted's speech was sharply divided. Many Americans found his explanation inadequate, his speech mawkish. Even some Kennedy loyalists had to admit that, as he gave the speech, Kennedy looked and sounded guilty.

While the nation's opinion of Ted was divided, Massachusetts still seemed to want him. In the end, Massachusetts would rally to the last of the Kennedy brothers and Ted would be re-elected—with Ethel's help and unequivocal support—to another Senate term in November 1970.

The Chappaquiddick matter would not end with Ted's explanation of it, however. District Attorney Edmund Dinis soon reopened an investigation into the circumstances of Mary Jo Kopechne's death. At a hearing that took place in January 1970, Ted gave evidence, as did the five "Boiler Room Girls" and other witnesses, but Judge James Boyle was not convinced of the veracity of Ted's story. In his inquest report, Judge Boyle concluded that Ted Kennedy was probably guilty of operating his automobile in a negligent manner and that, if so, his recklessness had contributed to the death of Mary Jo Kopechne. Despite this outcome, the Kopechnes chose not to file a civil suit against Ted saying, as Joseph Kopechne later explained, "We figured people would think we were looking for blood money." Instead, they received a settlement of $140,904—$90,904 from Kennedy and $50,000 from his insurance company.

With Ted's probable guilt now recognized by the courts, Joan began looking at her husband in a different light. First of all, he never apologized to her for any of what had occurred. Investor Bill Masterson, a friend of Ted's from Boston, said, "Ted—all of the Kennedy men for that matter—were not the kind of men who apologized for anything. As far as he was concerned, it was over, and Joan just had to get past it. He didn't ask for her forgiveness, as he had his constituency."

After Joan had ample time to get over the shock of what had occurred—that Ted had almost died in the accident—she began to feel a deep sense of betrayal. Those closest to her say that she was now more certain than ever that Ted had planned a romantic liaison with Mary Jo. "It was terrible," Joan recalls of the months following the accident, "one of the worst times of my life. And it was the beginning of the end for Ted and me."

The reality of Ted's extramarital affairs had been difficult to take in the past, but the situation with Mary Jo Kopechne felt vastly different to Joan Kennedy. From all Joan could gather, Mary Jo was not like the others. She was the star daughter of Catholic parents, a respectable member of society.

Not surprisingly, Joan began to see Mary Jo as a victim—and not just a victim of a horrifying accident, but still yet another victim of the Kennedy men. In that regard, Joan would identify with Mary Jo, feeling that she and the deceased were kindred spirits. Joan even felt compelled to reach out to the Kopechnes after the judge's final word on the case had been delivered. "She phoned us on several occasions asking us for forgiveness for what had happened," said Mary Jo's mother, Gwen. "What could we say to her? Not much. She was in pain, but so were we."

The few close friends Joan Kennedy had in her life all echoed the same refrain: "Divorce Ted, now!" However, as Joan told Joan Braden, she believed she could never do it: "My whole life is tied up with this person [Ted]. Why would people think it's so easy to end it with him? To think of my children as being upset and distraught because of our mistake. I couldn't do it."

Moreover, even after Chappaquiddick, Joan believed that she was more to blame than Ted for their unhappy marriage. While she was just married to an irresponsible philanderer who may have contributed to someone's death, Ted was married to an even sorrier sight: a drunk. At night, she would lie alone in her room and ponder her situation while waiting for Ted to come home from wherever he had been. When he finally got home, she would listen in the dark as he stumbled into the kitchen. His routine there was always the same. She wouldn't hear the refrigerator open, but she would hear it slam closed. Then, silence as Ted ate leftovers. He always got hungry after having sex.

"It wasn't my personality to make a lot of noise," Joan would later explain. "Or to yell, or scream, or do anything. My personality was more shy and retiring. And so rather than get mad, or ask questions concerning the rumors about Ted and his girlfriends, or really stand up for myself at all, it was easier for me to just go and have a few drinks and calm myself down as if I weren't hurt or angry. I didn't know how else to deal with it. And, unfortunately, I found out that alcohol could sedate me. So I didn't care as much. And things didn't hurt as much."

After Jackie returned to Greece, she tried to stay apprised of Ted's situation. One woman who worked in the office of Ted's press secretary, Richard Drayne, recalls, "The day after the speech, we got a call from Mrs. Onassis. . . . Jackie asked, 'So, how did the speech go?' Before I had a chance to answer, she quickly asked, 'And how's Mrs. Kennedy?'"

The woman reported that Jackie went on to say, "You know what Mrs. Kennedy needs. She needs a good temper tantrum. She should wave her arms, stamp her feet, kick, scream, gnash her teeth, and get furious at Ted. She would get it out of her system, feel so much better and then start working on herself," she concluded. "She should cause a scene, make a spectacle of herself."

In the weeks after Ted's speech, a public outcry rose against the way

matters were handled at Chappaquiddick. The controversy monopo-
lized the news to such a degree that Joan didn't even want to turn on
the television. She was ill-equipped to deal with the campaign of
whispers and innuendo that had mounted against her husband and her
marriage. "You just have to ride with it," Luella Hennessey suggested
to Joan. "We won't bother listening to the news. You can't do anything to stop it, so we'll talk about something else."

Joan recalled, "It seemed to drag on and on. It went on for months."

"The stress was overwhelming," recalled Luella Hennessey. "Under
ordinary circumstances, this would have been a difficult pregnancy for
Joan. But with all that was going on, and the sleepless nights and anxiety . . . it was difficult."

No doubt making matters worse for Joan were the death threats
constantly being made against Ted. One, received at his office, was
made on a day that Ted was set to go to the Justice Department to attend a ceremony honoring his slain brother, Bobby. Because the FBI
viewed the threat as "serious," the police were directed to maintain
surveillance on Ted and Joan's home. Their presence outside her windows did not calm Joan but, rather, served only to make her more anxious and afraid.

"Can it get any worse?" Luella Hennessey asked one night before
she and Joan retired for the evening. (Hennessey would often stay
with whichever Kennedy family needed her assistance.)

"Sure it can," Joan told her. "You betcha it can. Just wait and see."

The two women laughed, as Luella recalled it, and couldn't stop
giggling for ten minutes. "Be sure your hair's dry before you go to bed,"
the nurse finally said as she hugged Joan good night.

Joan's joking answer to Luella's "can it get any worse?" turned out
to be prophetic: It got worse. Much worse.

Joan Loses the Baby

On the evening of Thursday, August 28, 1969, Joan Kennedy—who would turn thirty-three in a week—found herself alone at home. Ted had two of their children, Kara and Teddy, on a camping trip to Nantucket with Jackie's son, John Jr.

Shortly after nightfall, Joan felt a sharp abdominal pain, the kind all pregnant women fear. Joan stumbled to a phone and called Ethel, who rushed to Joan's side with the Kennedy family nurse, Luella Hennessey. Both women knew the seriousness of Joan's condition and quickly prepared her for the drive to Cape Cod Hospital in Hyannis. After spending agonizing hours in admissions there, Joan came to terms with the fact that she had lost her baby.

She was completely shattered and, as she would later say, now believed that Chappaquiddick not only robbed her of her self-esteem and perhaps her marriage, but her baby as well. Ted arrived the day after the miscarriage, but Joan didn't want him with her. "I just wanted to be alone," she recalled, years later.

Almost as unbearable as the miscarriage was the fact that all of this personal drama in her life had been played out in the public's view. Joan loathed being perceived by outsiders as weak, as a victim, even if that was truly how she often felt.

"I'd get mad at people for making little comments like, 'Oh, poor Joan,' or 'You poor thing.' You know how people love to think that you love sympathy: [mimicking] 'Oh, you poor thing, you must have gone through *hell*.' And I'd say to them, 'You know, I don't need, I don't *want*, your sympathy. Don't feel sorry for me. Don't feel sorry for us.'"

As Joan made plans to leave the hospital two days later, it was Ethel who insisted that she stay with her family at Hickory Hill. Ethel and Joan had grown closer in recent months, and their new relationship was one that surprised some members of the family. "It was as if they had found something in each other that served to make them truly sisters," Lem Billings once recalled. "They were older. Things changed. Ethel was the one Joan called when she thought she was going to have a miscarriage. And Ethel was the one she began to depend on. Ethel liked being depended on, as everyone knew. She was sorry that Jackie was out of her life, I think. She filled the void—if there was a void—with Joan."

Joan had plans of her own, however. She wanted to visit her mother, Ginny, who had just been released from a sanitarium a week earlier, where she had been battling her own alcoholism. Ethel objected strongly, arguing that Ginny was going through a difficult time herself, and that Joan needed to concentrate on her own health. Yet all the objections were halted by a simple statement from Joan: "I want to be with my mother." Ethel surrendered.

In her mother's convalescence Joan had found a safe harbor. Only a short explanation about Ginny's own fragile health was enough to keep well-meaning visitors away. Most of her mother's day was spent in her room under a shawl, quietly dozing away the hours, which left Joan plenty of solitude. Unfortunately, it may have been that same solitude which laid the groundwork for the deep depression to which Joan was headed.

While alone, Joan probably couldn't help but study the events of the previous few months: Ted's affair with Helga, the mystery of his relationship with Mary Jo, the truth of Chappaquiddick. She would later admit that she began once again mulling over the genetic predisposition that may have contributed to her own alcoholism, and reaffirmed that there was no way out, no matter what she did. After a few days of this kind of torturous self-examination and self-delusion, Joan sent for Ethel.

During her visit with Joan, Ethel suggested to Joan that she continue her recuperation at Hickory Hill. "It's time for you to start living your life again," Ethel told her and, because she was persistent, Joan agreed. She also arranged for Teddy, Kara, and Patrick to be there, which seemed to lift Joan's spirits. She had missed her children, who were not with her while she was at her mother's.

At Hickory Hill, dynamic Ethel would be in absolute charge, and for the first time in weeks, Joan would feel the beginnings of some sense of security, the smallest stirrings of contentment. Two good months followed, filled with the sounds of playing children, the smells of savory and nourishing food, the brightness of country sunlight. But, from time to time, a shadow would fall over Joan's happiness—in the form of her husband, Ted.

Ted was a frequent visitor at Hickory Hill, and his somber face after a day of meetings with his aides reminded Joan of how serious the Chappaquiddick situation still was for him, and for her as well.

―――――――――――――

A Final Gathering for Joseph

In the weeks after Ted Kennedy's *mea culpa* speech, his father, Joseph, fell into a deep depression. After he lost his appetite, it was clear to his family that he was giving up on his life, such as it had been for the last eight long, difficult years.

One evening, Joe suffered a cardiac arrest at the Hyannis Port home while he was getting ready for bed. Hearing a ruckus, Jackie, Joan, Ted, Ethel, Rose, Eunice, Pat, and some other family members rushed to Joe's room to find Rita Dallas pounding frantically on the old man's chest, trying to bring him back to life. Ted, in particular, was horrified by the sight; Joan held on to him, tightly. Ethel stood transfixed, while Jackie kept repeating, "He'll be fine, he'll be fine, he'll be fine" in a hypnotic litany.

Finally, Joe began breathing. Though he pulled through, the family was reminded of the sad fact that this was a very sick man. Next time, Rita warned them, he might not be as lucky.

After the incident, Joan found Rita Dallas in the kitchen, having a cup of coffee with the Norwegian cook, Matilda.

"I'm glad I found you," Joan said. "The senator has been wanting to speak to you, but he's still with his father. He wants to tell you how glad he is that you saved his dad's life tonight." (Just as Ted always referred to his brother as "the President," Joan referred to her husband as "the senator.")

As Rita Dallas said that no thanks were necessary, Joan crumpled into a chair. "How much more of *that* can any of us take?" Joan wondered wearily, her hands shaking. "No wonder Kennedys don't cry. They're always too traumatized."

During recent times, Joseph Kennedy had spent most of his days in bed watching television, his eyes fixed on the daily news broadcasts.

However, that small luxury was taken from him when he began going blind. Shortly after losing his sight, his vocal chords began to atrophy. Joseph hadn't actually spoken in years, but now he could no longer make the guttural sounds he had used for years to communicate with others. When he could no longer swallow, doctors realized that it was just a matter of time before he would die. Rose Kennedy, emotionally drained by having to witness the daily deterioration of a husband who was once so strong and vital, sat in a chair next to his bed and wept quietly for hours before deciding that the time had come to summon the family.

On November 15, the first to arrive was Jackie from Greece. She and Joseph had always been close, and when she came from his room after visiting him, her face was drawn and her eyes red-rimmed. "It's really time for him to go now," she told Rose, who sadly agreed. "This isn't the way he would want it. He's ready. Why must life be so hard?" Jackie wondered. "The slow decay of body, mind, and spirit—all the money we have, and we can do nothing."

Joseph's daughters arrived the next day. Eunice was first, with her husband Sargent Shriver, from Paris. Then came Pat and Jean.

Soon after his sisters, Ted arrived with Joan. Then Ethel. She had the flu and, after a short visit with Joseph, was forced to go to her own bed next door. "In some ways, I think she's been sick ever since Bobby died," Rose remarked.

The ongoing death vigil became unbearable for all the Kennedys, especially by November 17, when Joseph fell into a deep coma. That night Jackie stayed with him, sleeping in a straight-backed chair in his room. Early in the morning, she went downstairs and found Ted sitting by a weak fire. He, too, had been up all night, while a distraught and exhausted Joan had gone to their home on Squaw Island for some rest. Jackie and Ted spent the next few hours together sitting in front of the hearth, engaged in a calm, private conversation, the details of which are unknown.

The next morning, Luella Hennessey telephoned Rita Dallas to tell her that the end was near. By the time Dallas got to the house from where she lived nearby, Joseph's pulse was so weak she was afraid he would expire without having any of his family members around him, as all had retired to their own homes to shower and prepare for the day. So Dallas sounded an alarm in Joseph's room, the awful clanging noise of which alerted everyone in the compound that the time had come.

Jackie came running out of her home next door in her bare feet, wearing just a pair of blue slacks and a short-sleeved white blouse, never considering the frigid temperature. Ethel, still very ill, met her in the backyard, and the two women raced upstairs, Ethel first. Joan and Ted arrived moments later, as did the Kennedy sisters, their husbands, and Joseph's niece, Ann Gargan, who had cared for him for years. Soon, Joseph's room was filled with his immediate family.

Almost as a matter of protocol, his children encircled his bed, while the wives (Jackie, Ethel, and Joan) and the husbands (Steve Smith and Sargent Shriver) took a few steps back. It was decided not to allow Rose into the room until the last possible moment, just in case Joseph should begin to convulse in his final moments. Finally, when Rita Dallas and Luella Hennessey decided it was safe to do so, Ted left the room and returned in a couple of minutes with his elderly mother, stooped and sobbing.

At the first sight of her barely breathing husband, Rose fell to her knees at the side of his bed and put her head down upon his deformed hand. She stayed in that position for about ten minutes, crying all the while, as the others looked on, each lost in his or her own moment of grief.

Rita Dallas thought it might be best if Rose, always a woman of great faith, had her rosary with her at this time, and so she asked that someone fetch it. Jackie, who had noticed the beads on a dresser in the room, brought them to Rose. Rose then put them gently to her husband's lips and into his open hand, which she closed around them. Tears washed down Jackie's face, but not Ethel's; she remained stoic. Joan, standing next to them, was unable to speak.

After a few moments of heavy silence, Eunice began to say the Our Father, aloud, with Ted, Jean, and Pat each taking a line.

"Forgive us our trespasses," Ethel said when, after a pause, it seemed as if it should be her turn.

"As we forgive those who trespass against us," Jackie added, reaching over and taking Ethel's hand in her own.

"And lead us not into temptation, but deliver us from evil," Rose intoned, finally, her head hanging low.

Then, from behind, in a small, barely audible voice, someone said, "Amen." It was Joan.

In agreement, everyone else echoed Joan Kennedy's final word, as Joseph Patrick Kennedy passed into history.

The End of Camelot

Rose Kennedy would live another twenty-five years after her husband, Joseph's, death, finally dying at the age of 104 in January 1995. In her later days, Rose was paralyzed on her left side, unable to walk or speak, partially blind, and had to be fed through a tube. It would be Ted's agonizing decision to have his mother removed from life-support systems; she had been confined to her rose-colored bedroom for years. Rose had thirty grandchildren and forty-one great-grandchildren. She would be buried next to her husband in suburban Brookline. Ethel, who, along with Rose's children, had been at Rose's bedside when she died, would read passages from the Bible during the funeral for her mother-in-law.

However, long before the Kennedy family's matriarch would pass away from complications of pneumonia, a confluence of events in the family's history would cause the Kennedy generation of the fifties and sixties, which had so fascinated the world, denizens of Camelot, so to speak, to begin a slow and final decline. With Joseph Kennedy buried, this generation of Kennedys began focusing on their own lives, careers, marriages, and children, to make way for the next generation, which would one day include more than a few of its own politicians. Like the other family members who began to consider their lives separately and apart from the Kennedy infrastructure, Jackie, Ethel, and Joan also began looking to the future—a future after Camelot.

While Jackie Kennedy's life changed when she married Aristotle Onassis, one thing that remained was the public's intense interest in her. During her marriage to Onassis—and beyond—tons of newsprint would be devoted to her and eagerly devoured by a world famished for the beauty and elegance she continued to represent. She would continue to be deified and, despite the disappointment the public had expressed about her marriage, she would remain for many an object of great adoration, obsessive interest, and intense scrutiny. To the millions who would continue to read about her every move and scrutinize her every action, she would transcend human confines and become something called "Jackie O," an appellation that she would deplore.

While some who knew them insisted that they loved one another, others say that Jackie and Ari wanted little to do with one another. Ellen Deiner, publicist for the Greek National Theater and a friend of Onassis, recalls a remarkable incident that said much about Onassis's feelings about his wife. Apparently, Onassis had been collecting pictures of Jackie for years and by 1969 had, without exaggeration, probably over a thousand photos in his possession. In fact, according to Deiner, he had a secret room at his Paris penthouse that was, for lack of a better word, a "shrine" to Jackie.

Onassis himself seemed to have realized that this was a somewhat unusual tribute to his wife, because he took measures to make sure his wife didn't find out about it. Though Jackie often asked what was in the room, she was never told. One day, while at the Paris apartment working on a project involving the theater and Onassis, Deiner heard a loud woman's voice saying, *"What in the world is this?"* She went rushing upstairs and down the hallway, and there was Jackie standing in the doorway of the "closet," staring at the huge, black-and-white and color framed posters of herself on the walls, and smaller photos of herself all about.

"What is all of this?" the shaken Jackie demanded. Somehow, she had found a key to the room; she was holding it in her hand.

Ellen Deiner, in a moment of panic, could do little more than shake her head helplessly. She had never seen the inside of the room, either.

The two women stepped into the secret room and slowly took in the surroundings, moving from photo to photo, each one a documentation of Jackie's ever-changing image through the years. It was a veritable museum of Jackie Kennedy memorabilia. (Ironically, the home of Jackie's father, Black Jack, had also been something of a shrine, filled with pictures of his daughter Jackie.)

Jackie paused at a small silver-framed photo on an end table, picked it up and stared at it for a moment, then put it back down. It was a picture of her wedding day to Jack. On the wall was a large framed photograph of her on that horrible day in 1963 when she stood next to Lyndon Johnson as he took the oath of office. However Jackie interpreted all of this, she was visibly shaken, especially after looking at the photo of Johnson's swearing-in. She turned and walked from the room, shaking her head in dismay.

The next day, at her direction, the room was completely cleared of all photos of Jackie Kennedy Onassis. Ari's reaction to that remains unknown.

Aristotle Onassis would die on March 14, 1974, after catching pneumonia during recovery from an operation for gallstones. He had never recovered from the emotional devastation of his son Alexander's death in a plane crash a few years earlier. Alexander's death had changed him; he became embittered and filled with hopelessness. He treated Jackie poorly, according to those who knew the couple best. Jackie was not at his side when he died in Greece; she was in New York.

Neither Joan nor Ethel would attend his funeral. ("Maybe I can get out of it if I call Ted and see if he'll represent the Kennedys," Ethel told her assistant Noelle Fell.)

Three days after his death, Jackie's good friend Lady Bird Johnson wrote her a lovely letter saying that Onassis's death "sent my heart winging your way. The shadow of grief, which has pulled at your family life, seems an unendurable one," she wrote. "I know your strength and composure has been put to the severest tests, always in the public's watchful eye. I dearly hope the years ahead bring the balm of happier days for you and the children."

Jackie would contest her ill-conceived marital contract and, after much legal wrangling, ended up with $26 million. She would then go on to become an editor in the publishing world, first at Viking (which she left after Viking published a fiction book that supposed a death threat against Ted Kennedy), and then Doubleday. Her two children, John and Caroline, would become living testaments to the common sense and wisdom she, as a mother, had always demonstrated. (Jackie's own mother, Janet, would die in July 1989 at the age of eighty-one, six years after having been diagnosed with Alzheimer's, a disease Jackie had always feared would be passed down to her, at least according to her stepbrother Yusha Auchincloss.)

At the end of the sixties and into the seventies, Ethel Kennedy retreated to her home at Hickory Hill in McLean, Virginia. In staying close to home, hearth, and family, she hoped to raise her eleven children—with the help of an army of nannies, nursemaids, cooks, and social secretaries—by drawing comfort from the familiar and embracing the past rather than running from it.

In years to come, Ethel would change little in the house; pictures of Bobby would remain where they'd always been—throughout the home, on walls, on top of the television sets, the piano, and everywhere else. In some ways, it was as if he would live on almost as large as life at Hickory Hill, his memory counseling and guiding his wife and children. Or, as Ethel put it, "Bobby is here, in every smile, in every joke . . . in every tear."

One moment that says a lot about Ethel is remembered by Ray Springfield, a young landscaper employed by Alex Johnson (who worked for Rose Kennedy every year planting flowers on the grounds of the Hyannis Port home). It was the spring of 1974 as Johnson walked about with Rose, who was dictating the kinds of flowers she wanted planted and where. As they walked up the steps of Rose's back porch, they noticed Joan and Ethel sitting side by side on large wooden chairs. "As I walked by them, I heard a brief snippet of a conversation, Joan saying to Ethel, 'Maybe you shouldn't spend so much time living in the past. It can't be good for you.' And Ethel snapping at her, 'Well, what choice do I have? You tell me.' That's all I heard, as Mrs. [Rose] Kennedy and I rushed by."

An hour later, Johnson and Rose Kennedy walked by the same spot. The Kennedy sisters-in-law had left. Rose motioned to a thick book on the porch floor between the two chairs upon which they had been sitting.

"Would you bend down and pick that up for me?" she asked the landscaper. When he did so, she looked at it for a moment, then held it to her breast as they walked back into the house. It was Bobby and Ethel's wedding album.

* * *

Joan Kennedy's personal life had been challenging ever since the day she married into the family. Unfortunately, it would not get better for her in the seventies, and in many ways the death of Joseph P. Kennedy would mark the beginning of a ten-year stretch of even tougher times. As a result of a series of difficult events in her life— Ted's ongoing philandering, her mother's death from alcoholism, and her own vast insecurities and emotional problems—Joan's alcoholism would spin out of control for the next ten years. Though she would take Jackie's advice and begin seeing a psychiatrist in 1971, it would be years before she would reconcile her emotional problems. "It's sad to say," she recalls, "but I think I had to suffer an awful lot and cause my family and friends a lot of trouble in coming to terms with myself."

Joan was becoming a lonely, desperate woman. The one thing she and Ted had always enjoyed together was a satisfying sex life. However, that was long gone, according to those in whom Joan had confided. The more Ted drank, the less he was able to function. "Joan once told me she missed more than just physical passion," said a friend of hers from Boston who is still close to her today. "She longed for simple physical intimacy. She so wanted a man to be close to, to hold, to make her feel that she wasn't alone."

Then, there would be Ted's affair in the spring of 1972 with Amanda Burden, the daughter of William S. Paley, chairman of the board of CBS. It would get to the point where Joan would be afraid to pick up the newspaper for fear of reading about this particularly well-publicized relationship.

In the fall of 1973, her twelve-year-old son Teddy would be diagnosed with cancer. His leg would have to be amputated, and the tragedy would drive Joan deeper into self-destructive behavior with alcohol.

"I remember the time that Ted had a dinner party while Joan was knocked out in the bedroom," recalled Barbara Gibson. "Ted dressed the children's nanny in Joan's chic clothing and had her act as hostess. The implication was obvious, especially given Ted's reputation. Ethel was outraged when she showed up, demanding to know, 'What the heck is that woman doing in Joan's clothes?' She wanted to see Joan, but it was impossible that evening."

"What happens to the human spirit is like what happens to a high cliff when the waves are too strong and too high and too constant," noted Joan's good friend Muffy Brandon. "The cliff erodes and the underpinnings get shaky. That's what happened to Joan. When you have two brothers-in-law assassinated, when your son has cancer, when your husband almost died in an airplane crash, when you've had several miscarriages—how much can the human spirit endure?"

Joan had a three-week stay at Silver Hill Foundation, a small private hospital in Connecticut, in June of 1974. Two weeks after her release, she was back for a longer stay. In October of that same year, she pleaded guilty to drunk driving after slamming her Pontiac GTO convertible into another automobile in McLean. She was fined and lost her license.

Ted and his aide, Richard Burke, would rifle through Joan's bedroom in search of stashed-away liquor bottles, or "contraband," as Burke called them. After so many years of drinking, though, Joan would be able to find relief in many ways: she would use a mouthwash, for instance, with a high alcohol content.

Meanwhile, as Joan continued giving interviews to the press about her drinking, insisting to one reporter that hers was "a recovery in progress," the public would remain unaware of the fact that the interviews were Ted's idea, not Joan's. "The senator urged her to acknowledge openly her chronic difficulties in order to stave off further innuendo," recalled Richard Burke, "[all the while] we were spiriting more bottles out of her bedroom."

After finally separating from Ted in 1977 thanks to thrice-weekly psychiatric sessions, Joan would move into a seven-room condominium on Beacon Street in Boston and begin doing interviews about her alcoholism and how she was working to overcome it, as well as about her terrible marriage. A year later, she would be back at McLean Hospital, drying out once again. Meanwhile, at that same time, her mother would die of alcoholism-related disease.

The years after Camelot would be difficult ones for Joan Bennett Kennedy. She would leave her children—Kara, seventeen, Teddy, sixteen, and Patrick, ten—with Ted, when she moved to Boston. She realized that she couldn't take care of herself, so how was she able to care for her children? This is what it would come to for Joan and her children—weekend visits.

PART TWELVE

Ted Hurts Joan Again

It wasn't until the 1970s and the beginning of the women's movement that things began to change for many females in this country, including two of the Kennedy wives—Jackie and Joan. Both women's experiences, as they would unfold throughout the next decade, would prove to be emblematic of their time.

Interestingly, Ethel would choose to stay out of touch with the women's movement. She never really understood the notion of uplifting the feminine consciousness, and believed that a woman's place was in the home, subservient to her husband—if she were still lucky enough to have one. So, while Jackie and Joan would each go on to expand their horizons, Ethel would stay home at Hickory Hill, surrounded by her children, mourning her late husband, and often lamenting what might have been.

By the end of 1971, Joan had taken Jackie's advice and had begun therapy with a Washington psychiatrist. At this time, many people still believed that only those with the most severe emotional problems consulted psychiatrists. At the urging of Jackie and other friends, Joan was able to get past that kind of archaic thinking in an effort to help herself with her "issues."

Some of her choices—particularly her fashion choices—were often still the subject of controversy.

For instance, earlier she had worn a shimmering minidress, cut low at the neck, to a formal reception hosted by President and Mrs. Nixon at the White House to honor the country's senators and their wives. The invitation had specified formal dress, suggesting floor-length skirts for the ladies. The next day practically every newspaper in the country ran photos of the formally attired First Lady, in a gown with white gloves to her elbows, sneaking an astonished look at Joan's long legs while being greeted by her in the receiving line. Fashion reporters across the country noted that "Jacqueline would never have dressed that way."

Helen N. Smith, Pat Nixon's press aide, later said that the First Lady was more "concerned about Joan" than she was angry because "it did seem a bit odd." However, though Joan's wardrobe was often eccentric—ranging from funky miniskirts to typically sixties bell-bottoms and garish flower-printed gowns—it was probably no more bizarre than Ethel's plastic minis with their asymmetrical designs. Joan just got more attention for her clothing, probably because she was known to have troubles ("poor Joan") and the public and press were watching her for clues to her state of mind.

Joan had wanted to speak to a mental health professional for some time, but Ted had always objected to the notion. First of all, like Ethel and many other members of his family, he mistrusted psychotherapy. Also, he may have feared that certain family skeletons would come to the surface during the course of Joan's sessions. He actually asked Joan, "How do we know whoever you see isn't going to go running to one of those fan magazines with everything you've told him?"

However, for the first time Joan didn't care what Ted thought. She went into therapy and would become only the second family member to voluntarily do so (Bobby being the first, after Jack's death, but for only a couple of visits before Ethel convinced him to stop). "This was the first step in a long, long process," said Luella Hennessey. "But it was a beginning."

Finally, Joan was looking for ways to empower herself. She was now thinking about what might be best for her and how she might want to consider living her life from this time onward. As Hennessey indicated, it would be a long and sometimes torturous process, for it would be years before Joan would accept that she was an alcoholic. As Joan herself would later note, "I found that small steps add up to big strides . . . for me, though, it wasn't one day at a time, it was more like one moment at a time."

As it sometimes happens, Joan's life changed in small but significant ways as soon as, during therapy, she started to review, recognize, and at least try to understand the reasons behind not only her perceived weaknesses but also her inarguable strengths. "It just started rolling, like a snowball down a hill—good things," Joan said, "all as soon as I started looking within, as soon as I started trying to figure me out."

For instance, in late summer of 1970, thirty-four-year-old Joan received an invitation to appear as a piano soloist at an October fundraiser for Governor Milton Shapp of Pennsylvania at the Academy of Music in Philadelphia. During her performance, she would be accompanied by musicians from the esteemed, sixty-strong Philadelphia Orchestra. The great Metropolitan tenor Jan Peerce would sing. The event would mark her concert debut, and before an audience of almost three thousand people. While she had narrated *Peter and the Wolf*, first in 1965 and every year since, this was a completely different experience for Joan in that she would be performing as a pianist for the first time in front of such a large audience. After giving it some thought, Joan eagerly accepted the invitation, viewing it as an opportunity to challenge her potential and, she hoped, grow as a woman.

It was not surprising that Ted, who would be up for reelection in November, was not happy about Joan's decision to accept the invitation. "I'm going to need you out there stumping for me, Joansie," he told her. "The timing for this thing, it's not good."

When Joan somehow assured her husband that she would be able to rehearse for her engagement and still find the time to do her part as a Kennedy wife on the campaign trail, he relented. By the fall she was on the road, wearing an "I'm for Ted" button, and hitting briefly on subjects that were unique for Joan. "Women should stick up for their rights," she told one packed house, "but never, never become so aggressive that they lose their femininity." While she was clearly sitting on the fence between a fifties' conservatism and a seventies' feminism, the changes in Joan Kennedy seemed profound to some observers just the same. "She's stronger, more focused, more in charge," wrote a political analysist for the *Boston Globe*. "She does Ted proud, even after the Chappaquiddick debacle."

A week before her performance, William Smith, assistant conductor of the Philadelphia Orchestra, joined Joan at her sixteen-room home overlooking the Potomac River in McLean to help her rehearse her material. "She struck me as a very unconfident young lady who had to do this to prove she could do something on her own," recalled William Smith, who said that Joan seemed a little out of place among the McLean trappings of tennis court, playing field, swimming pool, and servants' quarters. "She didn't seem as confident as I imagined a Kennedy woman would be. It clearly showed in her demeanor, in the way she had of wringing her hands. She had the feeling of filling very large shoes in that royal family atmosphere, where she had to prove herself or be submerged. But it was her grit that impressed me."

After two more days of campaigning for Ted, Joan was on her way to Philadelphia, accompanied by just one family friend who would double as her publicist, Pat Newcomb (who, eight years earlier, had represented Marilyn Monroe in the same capacity).

The next evening, Joan walked onto the stage in an elegant, black lace Valentino gown with sloping neckline and long sleeves. As the applause rang out, she walked confidently to the black Steinway piano, followed by conductor William Smith. For her performance, Joan had selected the second movement of Mozart's Piano Concerto No. 21 in C major, which was more popularly known at the time as the theme to the motion picture *Elvira Madigan*. She would follow that selection with Debussy's Arabesque No. 1.

As the lush strings came up behind her, Joan played beautifully, her hands moving adroitly over the keys, her head tilted back, her eyes sometimes closed as if in a meditation. As she played she would weave back and forth, seemingly in a musical trance, surrendering herself to her music.

A private woman who had, for the last twelve years, lived her life in crowds, Joan Bennett Kennedy had always seemed alone in a serene world of her own choosing whenever she played piano. Now, on this stage, as she would later recall, the music carried her away to private places in her soul, "places only I could know or understand." At the end of her first number, the applause rang out loud and strong. Bolstered by the enthusiastic reaction, she began the next song. After it was over, she stood and took her bows to a rousing standing ovation.

Of course, the theater that evening was filled with friendly Democrats, but it didn't matter to Joan. Even though the marquee outside the theater read "Mrs. Edward (Joan) Kennedy—World Piano Debut," the audience appreciated her not because she was Ted's wife but because she had proven herself as a musician and, as a performer with limited experience on the stage of such a prestigious venue, a courageous woman as well. Overwhelmed by the moment, Joan walked off into the wings in tears, only to be brought back on for three curtain calls. During the last, she was presented with a large bouquet of red roses. A smile spread across her face as she cradled the flowers with her right arm and dabbed at her eyes with her left hand.

While cheers continued to ring out, a beaming Ted made his way down to the backstage area to greet his wife. Joan's eyes immediately zeroed in on his ruggedly handsome face when she finally walked off-stage. She ran over to him, giddy as a schoolgirl, and reached out to her husband. Flashbulbs popped all around her.

Rather than lovingly embrace his wife and congratulate her for her stellar achievement, Ted put his arm around her shoulder as if she were a pal and not a lover. "Well done, Mommy," he said. "Well done." Joan glanced downward, the color rising in her face. Suddenly she looked gloomy.

It was a humiliating moment, and not only for Joan but for Ted as well. He had made his dismissive appraisal of her accomplishment in front of a reporter, who then passed it on to the public the next morning in the *Philadelphia Daily News*. "'Well done, Mommy'? For God's sake!" wrote Tom Fox. "This is the way the Irish talk when they have made it to the drawing room. He should be ashamed of himself."

In his defense, Ted Kennedy—like his brothers Jack and Bobby— had always been incapable of expressing unabashed affection for anyone in public, even for his wife. Still, for the sake of the newspeople and cameras he might have at least tried. Ordinarily his actions would have been crushing to Joan, but not this evening. She recovered quickly. Judging from the smile on her face as she greeted well-wishers, even Ted could not dampen Joan Kennedy's sense of achievement on that victorious October evening in 1970.

Ethel's Troubled Brood

While Joan Kennedy battled alcoholism and fretted about her marriage, Ethel Kennedy had her own personal problems, many of which must have seemed overwhelming at times.

By the early seventies, Ethel's sons Joe and Bobby along with some of their brothers and cousins had begun using drugs and rabble-rousing about the Cape Cod area—shooting BB guns, racing cars, and mugging other youngsters—to the point where the Kennedys' neighbors had actually begun to fear for their safety. Once, three of her children tied the family cook to a tree and threatened to set her on fire. "Look, I'm just a single mother trying to raise all of these kids," Ethel explained to her by way of an apology. "I'm sorry for your trouble, but I can only do what I can do."

When the cook threatened to press charges, Ethel said she would welcome the police intervention, saying, "Maybe *they* can do something about these boys, because I can't."

At one point, when Ethel needed a new governess, she called Ted's assistant Richard Burke to ask him to find one for her. He suggested hiring a woman who had worked as a nurse at Georgetown University. Ethel agreed. A month later, the governess telephoned Burke, crying. "She was hysterical because the kids had planted a big snake in her bed," said Burke. "I drove to Hickory Hill and spirited her away from the madness. Ethel wasn't really concerned, would never discipline the kids over something like that. Bigger things, yes. I think she had to pick and choose her battles, but to say she was an effective parent would be, I think, a mischaracterization."

It's true that with all of her suppressed anger and heartbreak over her beloved Bobby's murder, Ethel wasn't as available to her children as she may have wanted to be. For instance, when her sixteen-year-old Bobby and Eunice's sixteen-year-old son, also named Bobby, were arrested for possession of marijuana, Eunice and her husband, Sarge, sat down with their boy and tried to reason with him. They finally convinced him to curtail his friendship with his cousin.

Meanwhile, Ethel chased her Bobby around the yard with a broom stick, yelling, "I'll beat the daylights out of you if I ever get my hands on you!" The youngster ran to Jackie's home, rushed in and began pleading to her for protection. "Look, Jackie, you can keep him," Ethel told her sister-in-law when Jackie tried to talk to her about Bobby. "I don't want him. Maybe you'll have better luck with him."

The teenager stayed with his Aunt Jackie for a few hours before Ethel finally retrieved him.

"Please promise me you won't kill him," Jackie told her, perhaps only half-jokingly.

"I can't promise you that," Ethel answered.

"Well, I guess I can't blame you," Jackie said, trying to keep the mood light for fear of further antagonizing her sister-in-law. "If John ever smoked marijuana, *I'd* be the mother chasing her boy around the yard." (Little did Jackie know that John often smoked pot . . . and that he got it from Bobby!)

"One summer, we started realizing that we were missing a lot of food from our basement where we stored canned goods and other non-perishables," recalls Kennedy neighbor Sancy Newman. "When we looked into it, we found that our children were harboring a bunch of Ethel's kids whom she had kicked out of the house. They were living in our basement! When they were found out, the boys refused to go back home to their mother. Instead, they dug a hole in the woods, covered it up, and began living there."

In 1972, a real tragedy occurred when Joe, his brother David, and David's girlfriend, Pam Kelley, went on a joyride in a jeep on Nantucket that resulted in an accident leaving Pam paralyzed from the neck down. The Kennedys would take care of Pam's medical costs, and provide for her as well, for the rest of her life.

"Ethel broke down when she heard about that accident," says Leah Mason. "She was inconsolable. 'My own boys are responsible for this,' she said, 'which makes *me* responsible. If Bobby was still here, none of this would be happening. Why did God do this to us? I tried to live a good life,' she said, crying. 'Why punish me further?'"

Mason says that Ethel often tried to reason with her rebellious children, "but there were simply too many of them, and they all had their own agendas as to how to get into serious trouble. They looked at her as the enemy. It was her against them. 'I'm outnumbered,' she used to say, 'and it's hopeless.' The boys, especially, were as angry on the inside as their mother was about what had happened to their father, and so they acted out terribly."

Sometimes, the monkeyshines pulled by the boys were humorous. For instance, teenage sons Joe, Bobby, and David spent one summer selling what they called "Kennedy Sand" for a dollar a bag to fascinated tourists parked outside the gates of Hickory Hill. For an extra quarter, they would even answer "Kennedy Questions." One day, when someone asked the name of Jackie's favorite designer, Bobby ran into the house and called his cousin Caroline for the answer. Caroline said she would ask her mother the question for him. When Jackie later telephoned Ethel to ask why Bobby needed the information, Ethel laughed and said, "Oh, I guess he's trying to make an extra buck out at the front gate again."

At other times, the pranks got out of hand. Once, one of Ethel's teenage sons pulled a knife on Leah Mason and demanded money. When she handed over her purse, he laughed, threw it back at her and said, 'I don't need your money, bitch. I'm a Kennedy. You're a *secretary*!' Then he ran off. To him, it had all been a joke. However, Mason was "frightened half to death," she recalls. "When I told Ethel about it, she looked at me squarely and said, 'Don't tell me. Tell a cop. Here's the phone.' And she handed me the telephone! I shook my head and thought to myself, 'Oh my God.'"

Mason adds, "There was a time when Rose asked Jackie to talk to Ethel about the children. Apparently, the boys had shot holes into all of the windows at the Catholic church that Rose regularly attended. She was mortified, and had gotten nowhere with Ethel when she brought it up to her. I was standing in the room with Jackie and Rose and heard Jackie say, 'Grandma, why would you think, after all these years, that Ethel would ever listen to a word I have to say about anything?' Rose looked at her with an astonished expression. 'Why, Jackie, she has always respected you more than anyone else in the family. Don't you know that?' Jackie seemed stunned by that observation. 'Still in all,' she said, 'I think it would be assumptive for me to tell another woman how to raise her children.'"

With Ethel's hidden rage and great remorse over the way her life had turned out, to have so many misbehaving children under one roof was more than she could handle. She would often be seen on the rocker on her porch at the Hyannis Port home, rocking back and forth for hours while staring out at the panoramic ocean view. "She would have such a look of sadness on her face that any person would have felt compelled to hug her," Barbara Gibson said. "But she didn't want to be hugged. She didn't want anyone to feel sorry for her. 'I can handle it,' she would say." Or, as Ethel also often said, "God is my partner in this ordeal."

Will Ted Run? The Joan Factor

It was spring 1979. After nine difficult years, during which she had battled her alcoholism in the glare of a very public spotlight, forty-three-year-old Joan Kennedy found herself sitting on a couch in a hotel suite being scrutinized and judged by an assembly of family members and doctors.

"Well, I think Joan's done pretty well with things," a smiling Ethel said, as she walked over and grabbed her sister-in-law's hand. "I mean, just look at her, Teddy. Look at how *wonderful* she looks."

"She does look wonderful," Ted agreed.

"Doesn't she, though?" Ethel asked. "And what's that scent? My God, she smells so good . . ."

"It's Opium," Joan answered, studying Ethel.

"Well, I just *love* it," Ethel offered, a bit too enthusiastically.

"Thank you," Joan said, with a thin smile.

Though Joan and Ethel had never fulfilled the promise of a loving, sisterly relationship that seemed to be in the offing after the Chappaquiddick incident, they had remained close over the last ten years. Though she often seemed exhausted by so many troubles with her children, by the end of the decade, Ethel seemed newly energized by the prospect of Bobby's brother Ted running for President.

In the decade after Chappaquiddick, Ted Kennedy had served as one of the leading liberal spokesmen in the Senate, building a legislative record unmatched by either of his brothers. In fact, as his aide Richard Burke put it, Ted was considered by many as "the torchbearer of liberalism" in America, though there were some liberal issues he still found thorny, such as gay rights. As time went on, though, many people in Ted's circle began to believe that, since it rarely came up in the press anymore, the public had forgotten about Mary Jo Kopechne's death. Perhaps, it was being whispered, Ted would have a chance at the Presidency. He would wait through 1972 and then 1976, when another Democrat, Jimmy Carter, won the White House. But by 1979, with the Chappaquiddick issue ten years old, Ted thought he had a chance and decided to take on the unpopular Jimmy Carter in the Democratic primaries. Successfully challenging an incumbent President of his own party would be difficult, Ted knew, but he and his handlers believed it to be possible.

A meeting in the spring was called to discuss the "Joan Problem," and the likely pitfalls during the campaign of a presidential candidate whose wife was a well-publicized alcoholic. In fact, by 1979, Joan knew that her alcoholism was still not completely under control, though she hadn't had a drink in about four months. Working with her therapist, Dr. Hawthorne, from Boston as well as a number of recovery programs, Joan seemed on her way to sobriety. But she knew it would not be an easy road ahead. She was now a forty-three-year-old woman and, tough as it may be for her to do so, she realized that she was ultimately the only one with the power to turn her life around.

When the couple unofficially separated in 1977 (with Joan moving to Boston and Ted and the children staying at the McLean home), Ted, oblivious to how it would affect his wife, took that opportunity to begin a heated affair with a woman he had met in Palm Beach. It was not a secret; Ted's friends and business associates knew about her, as did Joan and their children. Even Ted's eighty-seven-year-old mother, Rose, knew.

After Joan moved to Boston, Kennedy historian Lester David had a conversation with Rose Kennedy—who was in her late eighties—during which he asked her if Ted's marriage was ending. When Rose said she didn't know, David asked why Joan was now living in Boston while Ted had stayed behind in Virginia. "Virginia!" exclaimed the hearing-impaired Rose. "Who's she? I've never even heard of *that* one."

Ted had asked his aide Richard Burke to call together some of the most renowned psychiatrists in the nation, all specialists in the treatment of substance-abuse problems, along with members of his family, so that they could deal with the "Joan Problem." Because Joan's psychiatrist, Dr. Hawthorne, warned Burke that such a meeting should occur only on "neutral territory" and not at Hyannis Port or any home deemed Kennedy territory, Burke booked a number of suites in a moderately priced hotel in Crystal City, Virginia, for the doctors. The family meeting would be held in one of the doctors' suites.

"I organized all of it in a secretive fashion, without Joan's prior knowledge," confessed Richard Burke. "The thought was that if she was aware of the meeting in advance, she might panic and not go along with it. At the last possible moment, when all of the players were in place, Marcia Chellis, I believe, told Joan about what was going on, and then had her show up for it at the appointed time. However, if I'm not mistaken, I don't think Joan was told until the second before she and her kids walked into the room, after having flown in from Boston, the extent of what was going to occur—that Ethel, Eunice, and Jean would be there, as well as all of the doctors and Ted's aides. Any person would have been unnerved by such a confrontation, most certainly."

Prior to the meeting, Dr. Hawthorne and three other specialists from Yale, the Mayo Clinic, and UCLA reviewed hundreds of documents pertaining to Joan's case in order to determine how to proceed. By the time Joan and her children got to the hotel, the doctors had already had a private conference with Ted, Ethel, Ted's aide Richard Burke, and Ted's sisters.

When Joan showed up at the appointed hour, it was with her children at her side—nineteen-year-old Kara, who had grown to be a beautiful woman with long brown hair and was now a student at Trinity College; eighteen-year-old Ted Jr., blond and solidly built like his dad and a student at Wesley; and twelve-year-old, brown-eyed Patrick, who attended school in Washington. To her left was Ethel, and Ted's sisters Eunice and Jean were to her right. (Jackie, who was living in New York City, was not summoned. While she was still involved in many of the personal aspects of the Kennedy family, Jackie had so distanced herself from its political concerns by 1979 that she would never have been invited to a strategy meeting, nor would she ever have attended.)

Richard Burke, who was present, recalls that the meeting began with one of the doctors stressing that Joan would "only get better when she wants to get better. But she's got to do it herself."

"Well, personally, I think she's licked it," Ethel said of Joan, looking over at her warmly. Disregarding the earlier warning of one of the doctors that "there is no cure for alcoholism," Ethel pushed on, "Isn't that right? Haven't you licked it, Joan?" Like many people, Ethel thought of a serious drinking problem as a sign of weakness or lack of will power, not a disease. So to Ethel, it was something that could just be "licked."

Joan didn't say anything. Everyone else exchanged uneasy smiles.

"Didn't you hear what the doctor said? He said that you don't cure this kind of thing, Ethel," Eunice, who was always very concerned about Joan's well-being, said impatiently. It was as if everybody in the room except Joan was hearing about alcoholism for the first time. "So, no, she is not cured," Eunice observed. "And I don't think she can take a campaign right now. I really don't."

Joan opened her mouth to protest, then closed it again.

"Oh, sure she can," Ethel argued. "Can'tcha handle it, Joan? C'mon, now."

"Look, may I have your attention," Dr. Hawthorne interrupted. "What we need is for each person to have a say." Richard Burke recalls Joan raising her eyes to the ceiling in dismay.

The psychiatrist then moderated a discussion as each person in the room gave his or her opinion on how Joan would fare in a presidential campaign. Eunice said that she was worried that Joan would not be able to handle the stress, that it would drive her back to the bottle and maybe even cause a rift with her children. Jean was silent, as she often was in situations such as this one. (Usually, when she had concerns about family matters, she would take them up with her husband, Steve, and he would then bring them to the attention of whoever was involved.) For her part, Ethel felt that Joan could deal with the pressure of a campaign, and she took it a step further to say that she would do anything in her power to help Joan, even though some observers found her reasoning to be a bit curious.

"Oh, I so want Ted to be President," Ethel said, dreamily. "My God, wouldn't it be great to be back in the White House? It's what we've always wanted, after all. And now it can happen. Whatever I can do to help Joan through this, that's what I'm going to do. She should come and stay with me at Hickory Hill," Ethel suggested. "I would keep an eye on her."

Suddenly, Joan spoke up. "Look, I'm not a child, Ethel. I don't need to be looked after."

"Oh, I know that, dear," Ethel said, her tone just a bit condescending. "You're not a child. Of course not."

Joan looked at Ethel menacingly.

"Okay!" Ethel said, holding up her hands defensively. "I just agreed with you."

There was silence in the room.

Kara, sitting at her mother's side, finally offered, "I'll only go along with Dad running for President if Mom's okay with it," she said, squeezing her mother's hand. Her brothers agreed wholeheartedly. It speaks well of Joan that her children were so supportive of her. Though she had moved away from home, they visited her on weekends. It hadn't been easy for them to see Mommy move out, but they seemed to understand that Joan was taking care of herself.

Finally, it was Ted's turn to speak. "I want nothing more than to be President," he said, catching Ethel's wide grin. "The timing is right. I can do this. I believe I can win. People are sick of Carter. The energy crisis, the economy . . . people need a change, and that's me." He walked over to Joan, stood behind her, and put his hands on her shoulders. "If it will hurt Joan, though, forget it. I won't do it. I will only proceed if I have the full support of everyone in this room, including my wife."

Ted's magnanimous speech aside, the fact was that he could not mount a successful campaign without his wife's cooperation. But what responsibility did she have as a political wife when she and her husband had been estranged for three years, and how could she resolve the conflict between that duty and the one to herself?

Joan was no longer eager to camouflage her feelings and put on a happy face for the media as she had done for so many years as a Kennedy wife. She had made that much clear about a year earlier, when a *Good Housekeeping* reporter visited her at her Boston apartment and asked if she thought Ted still loved her. She answered, "I don't know. I really don't know." Then, when questioned about her feelings for him, she remained silent. Asked if the marriage was going to end, she explained that her focus was on her recovery, not on her relationship. "I'm working on myself," she said, "then maybe I can make up my mind from a position of strength." This was a "new" Joan Kennedy, one who had no pictures of any of her family—or any other

Kennedys—anywhere in her apartment, the only reminder of her past being a framed letter to her from President John Kennedy.

Now the "new" Joan was being called to act like the "old" one and sublimate her own feelings for the greater good: the Kennedy good. However, Joan felt that there was more at stake than just the personal and political image of the family. This time she believed she could extend her motivation so that there would be some benefit to her, as well as to the family. Ted's and the family's presidential aspirations could provide her with the motivation she needed to continue her recovery, or so she thought. She believed—as she would later explain—that the discipline required to remain sober during a difficult campaign would keep her that way. If she were to start drinking again during such a high-profile time, it would prove to be humiliating not only for herself, but also for Ted and everyone in their family. She would never do that to them—at least not intentionally—and so, for the next year, she would feel that she had a strong impetus to continue her recovery. Yes, she would stop drinking for the campaign. But was this a good enough reason? She never thought of what would happen after the campaign was over.

Finally, after each person had made his or her opinion known, it was Joan's turn to speak. All eyes were on her as she stood up. "I want Ted Kennedy to be President, too," she said, avoiding eye contact with her estranged husband, a man she now almost always referred to as "Ted Kennedy." She continued, and not too convincingly, "I think he'd make a great President." Then, looking around at all of the smiling, relieved faces, she hastened to add, "I need more time, though. I really do. I have a lot of work to do on myself. . . . But I'll do it. Yes. I can do it," she concluded firmly, "and I will do it."

"Then that takes care of that," Ted said happily as he jumped to his feet. He walked over to Joan and reached out to her. She ignored him. Ted took a few awkward steps backward.

"Well, this is just the beginning of a process," cautioned Dr. Hawthorne. "We don't need to make any final decisions right here, Joan."

"We're on our way, though," Ted said.

"Oh boy! We sure are," Ethel agreed enthusiastically. It was as if the old Ethel Kennedy had suddenly emerged, the one filled with joy at the thought of herself and Bobby in the White House, the one whose zest for life seemed to have died along with her husband.

Joan and Ted:
Creating the Illusion of a Marriage

After the meeting of Kennedy family members and doctors in Virginia, quickly laid plans went into action to—as Richard Burke would remember it—"create the illusion of a marriage" between Ted and Joan Kennedy, all for the sake of public relations and good politics. Joan would spend more time in McLean (with the liquor cabinet always locked in her presence), Ted would spend less time with his Palm Beach mistress (though he would not give her up), and the two would attend the children's school functions together and make other personal appearances that would generate the news that they were working on their marriage.

"I think she was searching for her own identity," observes Richard Burke of Joan at this time, "and appeared to want to hold on to the concept of defining herself as Mrs. Kennedy. I believe she was terrified of losing that label."

In the intervening months, Ted's brother-in-law Steve Smith agreed to act as his campaign manager (a post he had held during Bobby's ill-fated campaign). Others came along to fill other positions, including Ted's former press representative Dick Drayne, who signed on to do battle with the media for the Kennedys.

By August 1979, the decade-anniversary of Chappaquiddick, the Kennedy handlers had put together briefing papers for Ted relating to his Chappaquiddick fiasco: There was nothing new to say, he accepted full responsibility, and all questions have been answered. Ted even called the Kopechnes at their ranch home in Pennsylvania, "to see where they stood, whether or not they were going to say anything damaging," recalled Mary Ann Kopan, Mary Jo Kopechne's aunt.

It might have been understandable that Ted didn't know where the Kopechnes stood because, years earlier, Mary Jo's family sent Joan and Ted a card when twelve-year-old Ted Jr. had his leg amputated because of cancer. It seemed odd under the circumstances. Joan responded with a nice note of her own to the Kopechnes.

In fact, the Kopechnes had strong feelings against the Kennedys, and yet they said nothing to Ted that would indicate that they would be the slightest political liability. Ted's call remained completely innocuous.

"Thank God that's over with," Ted reportedly said when he hung up.

On September 6, the Kennedy office leaked a new story to the media indicating that neither Rose nor Joan would oppose a possible candidacy by Ted. (Carter ridiculed the announcement, saying, "I asked my mama, and she said it was okay [for Carter to run for reelection]. And my wife, Rosalynn, said she'd be willing to live in the White House for four more years.") The next day a CBS-TV poll showed that Ted had a 53–16 lead over Carter and that he could probably have the Democratic nomination if it was what he wanted.

In a couple of months, Ted would be on the cover of *Time* magazine with the bold headline: "The Kennedy Challenge" and an accompanying story about Joan called "the Vulnerable Soul of Joansie" that did nothing to enhance her image: "Public life has not been kind to Joan Kennedy. Its wounds can be seen in the puffy eyes, the exaggerated makeup, the tales of alcoholism. Today, she is a sadly vulnerable soul and an unknown factor in her husband's electoral equation." In speaking of her marriage, she was quoted as saying, "Subconsciously, I'd like to have been like Ethel and had one baby after another." The distressing article implied that Joan wasn't even good at being an alcoholic: "She passes out after only three drinks." The feature also reported that Joan was at her Boston home a few months earlier when Ted's car pulled up. "Oh Christ," she reportedly said. "Here he comes. I'm getting out of here." Then, she strode away rapidly. Though Ted was angry at Joan when the story was published, she stood up to him well.

The article listed as Ted's "dalliances" alleged girlfriends Amanda Burden, Paige Lee Hufty, skier Susie Chaffee, and Margaret Trudeau, "among others." Joan closed the magazine after reading the feature and walked away muttering, "Nice list . . ."

October 20 marked the dedication in the Boston suburb of Waltham, Massachusetts, of the John F. Kennedy Presidential Library, giving Ted an opportunity to make remarks, along with President Carter, who was also a scheduled speaker. Jackie flew in from New

York for the ceremony. (When President Carter kissed Jackie on the cheek as he moved through the crowd on his way to the podium, Richard Burke recalls, "She recoiled as if bitten by a snake.") While there, Jackie enjoyed a warm reunion with Joan. Though the two women rarely saw each other because their lives had taken them in completely different directions, when they did have the occasional reunion, affection was deeply felt between them.

"Oh my God, Joan! Just look at you," Jackie exclaimed. "I've never seen you look so . . . so . . . together."

As Joan smiled, she reached out and embraced her sister-in-law.

It was true; Joan had never looked better. She had lost the bloated look that had diminished her attractiveness in recent years. Her blonde hair was cut in a stylish pageboy, she had shed some weight, and hadn't had a drink in almost six months. Jackie must have taken a certain amount of pride in Joan's recovery, because, just a few years earlier, Joan showed up unannounced at her apartment on Fifth Avenue, needing to talk. She was torn, she said. Should she move out on her own to Boston, or stay with Ted and the children in McLean? Would she be abandoning her children? Would they hate her?

"When I realized my drinking was becoming a real problem, I went to see Jackie," Joan later recalled. "I'd been told that an alcoholic by nature starts to blame everything and everybody except himself. And that's when I knew that I had to get away and have some time for myself. So Jackie and I talked about all that. I felt close to Jackie because both of us needed space to be alone.

"I was always a person who could be alone and like it. Jackie and I were the Kennedy wives who were different that way. We treasured our privacy and, for instance, enjoyed slipping away and reading a book on the beach. I believe that private time is growth time. Although I don't talk about this much to the children, I think I've provided an example that having a camaraderie and private time is equivalent to having a full life."

Jackie had been a bit ambivalent about the notion of Joan leaving her children. However, she also must have related to Joan's desperation. A little more than fifteen years earlier, she had considered leaving Caroline and John with Ethel and Bobby, so distraught was she after Jack's death. Ultimately she had decided against it. However, her situation was different from Joan's. In time, Jackie would be able to pull herself together, whereas Joan's alcoholism had made it impossible for her to be a good and dependable mother. Her sobriety had to come first now—which is what she had been told at Alcoholic's Anonymous—above everything else, even her children. Because Jackie had alcoholism in her own family and had often fretted that she, too, could fall prey to it, she understood Joan's misery.

"Listen, you do what you have to do, *for Joan*," Jackie told her favorite sister-in-law, according to what Joan later recalled to Joan Braden. "If you take care of Joan, the rest will fall into place. How many years have I been telling you that?"

"Too many years," Joan said, with a laugh.

Now, just a short time later, Joan seemed like a new woman, in control and ready to face the future. "Is it true?" Jackie wanted to know. "Is Ted going to run?"

Joan confirmed the information, saying, "We're going to give it our best shot, anyway."

"Well, if Ted runs," Jackie warned her, "you'll have to be twice as strong as I was when Jack and I were in the White House, Joan. It's much worse now than it was for us then," she said, probably referring to the post-Chappaquiddick Kennedys' world and the media's ever-growing interest in the private lives of politicians. "It feels to me like everyone is watching," she said. Joan had to agree.

Jackie and Ethel were pleasant to one another at the library's dedication, but it was clear to all observers that, even after all these years, they had never resolved the differences between them brought about by Jackie's marriage to Aristotle Onassis. Sometimes they were thrown together, though, in situations involving their children, and for those times they were cooperative with one another, such as when Jackie's son John ran away from home when he was about eleven—to Hickory Hill.

When young John had informed his mother that he was leaving, she not only told him to go but also packed a suitcase for him. As it would happen, John Jr. would be one of those rare children who would run away from home with his own Secret Service agent, John Walsh, in tow. Defiantly the youngster, suitcase in hand, walked down Fifth Avenue to the corner of 83rd Street, where he and Walsh hailed a cab. The two were driven across the Triborough Bridge to LaGuardia, where John and the agent caught a plane to Virginia. Once there, Jackie arranged for them to be picked up and taken to Hickory Hill.

(After dropping John off, Walsh turned around and went back to Manhattan.) Before the boy's arrival, Jackie had already spoken to Ethel and explained that he was having trouble in school, refused to apply himself, and said he would rather live with his cousins than hear his mother nagging him about his studies. Ethel agreed to make it as tough as possible for John at Hickory Hill.

In just a few days John found that visiting Hickory Hill and living there were two very different things. After Bobby's death, Ethel ran Hickory Hill like a boot camp, never letting up on her children when it came to chores—painting the house, doing the gardening, picking up after the assortment of animals. And there were always the competitive sports that John was never good at as a youngster. Baseball, football, tree-climbing—it was all more than the young prince could take. On the plus side, he could eat anything he wanted to. Ethel's cook was instructed to prepare for the children anything they demanded, whenever they demanded it. John was used to a prearranged menu; he would ordinarily eat whatever was placed before him, or he wouldn't eat at all. However, after four days of his favorite peanut butter and jelly sandwiches, he was on the phone begging his mother to rescue him from his banishment. He promised to study, and with the threat of all those Hickory Hill chores hanging over his head, he did his best in the future to apply himself to his schooling. "And if you don't," Jackie would tell him, "I'm sending you back to Aunt Ethel's."*

Shortly after the *Time* magazine feature, CBS aired an hour-long special, "CBS Reports: Teddy," which would turn out poorly and would bode ill for Ted's campaign and his hopes of ever being elected President. No matter how much preparation, no matter how much strategizing, no matter how much everyone in the Kennedy camp hoped to fool everyone else, the simple fact that Ted was not being honest—about his life, perhaps, Chappaquiddick, and most certainly his marriage—would be his ruination. The interview, taped earlier at his home in Squaw Island, was conducted by Roger Mudd, who wasted little time before asking Ted about "the present state" of his marriage.

---

*During this period, a bully was taunting John daily in the third grade, saying "John-John wears shorts." One day John drove his fist into the child's nose, almost knocking him out, much to Jackie's dismay. Alarmed, she asked her son where he learned to hit like that. He replied, "The Secret Service, Mom!"

Ted, never a spontaneous speaker, seemed caught off guard, though the question was inevitable. "Well, I think it's a—we've had some difficult times, but I think we'll have . . ." he began, stumbling. "We've, I think, been able to make some very good progress and it's—I would say it's—it's—it's—I'm delighted that we're able to share the time and relationship that we—that we do share."

"Are you separated or are you just, what?" Mudd asked, pressing.

"Well, I don't know whether there's a single word that should—have a description for it," Ted said, sputtering along as if about to run out of gas. The expression on his face indicated that he knew he was in trouble.

After a commercial, the report reexamined the Chappaquiddick tragedy—one decade and two months later—bringing back into focus that there were more than a few unanswered questions regarding the matter. Then, as if to drive any remaining nails into his own coffin, Ted botched the answer to the most important question of the evening, why he wanted to be President. It seemed as though he was unable to articulate his goals; he mumbled something about it being "imperative for this country to either move forward, that it can't stand still, otherwise it moves back."

The broadcast was devastating; no one in the family was pleased about it, least of all Ted, who felt that he had been sandbagged by Roger Mudd. If anything, it set the tenor for the way the media would handle Ted for the rest of his campaign: suspiciously. While Jackie's reaction to the interview was unknown (though she probably wasn't surprised by the way Ted had seemingly sabotaged his own campaign, since she had always believed that he would never allow himself to be President), when Ethel saw it on television, she ran to her bedroom, slammed the door, and did not emerge for three hours. Joan watched with Marcia Chellis. Afterward, the two women sat in utter astonishment, before Joan finally got up and turned off the television.

Joan in Control of Joan

A week before Ted's official announcement, a meeting was held at Joan's Boston apartment with Milton Gwirtzman and Ed Martin, both of whom had worked for Ted in previous campaigns. Gwirtzman—an excellent speechwriter as well as media strategist—had been one of JFK's aides, and was sent to Ted's office during Jack's administration to watch over him and make certain that the junior senator didn't say anything to the media that would conflict with Jack's or Bobby's points of view. It had been Gwirtzman who picked up Joan at the beauty parlor the day Jack was shot, and stayed with Joan while Ted tried to find a telephone with a working line so that he could figure out what had happened to his brother in Dallas.

The two men from Ted's office had been sent to divine how Joan hoped to handle tough questions about her alcoholism and her marriage and, it was hoped, convince her not to say too much about anything. During Ted's 1976 senatorial campaign, a drinking Joan—who looked puffy and much older than she would just three years later—was led around like a dog on a leash, and it was hoped that, this time, she would be just as compliant. However, Joan was a different woman now. She had strong feelings and wanted them known.

Also present when the advisers met with Joan were Sarah Milam and Sally Fitzgerald, both friends of Ted's and Joan's who would assist with campaign decisions, and Marcia Chellis, Joan's assistant. Gwirtzman and Martin were both opposed to Joan's making a statement at the time of Ted's announcement.

"Here's what I think," Joan said, after everyone had their say. "We need to deal with these issues head on. It's the thing that's going to cause us the most problems early on, the so-called 'Joan Factor,'" she said, with a smile. "They think I'm in trouble, a sorry sight. But I'm not, and we need to prove it. Ted can't talk about this," she continued, "only I can. I should make a strong statement of support at the press conference, and then deal with the other questions later in other forums. And during the course of this campaign, I should answer every question about my alcoholism and life with Ted. If I rehearse and know what I'm doing, I can pull it off."

Everyone in the room looked at her with amazement.

"Well, I disagree," Ed said. "I say she should just sit up there with the family. Ted makes his announcement. She looks at him with adoration. She leaves with him. Everyone smiles, and that's it. No problems."

Joan became clearly annoyed that she was being talked about as if she were not present. She rose and walked over to Martin. "I'm here, Ed. See me? I'm right here," she said as she waved her hand in front of him. "And I am not just going to sit up there and look like an idiot," she declared. "Everyone knows that Ted and I are having problems, and everyone knows that I'm an alcoholic. I need to say *something*."

Milton Gwirtzman's mouth opened and stayed that way as Joan walked past him and sat back down.

"The problem, Joan, is that people don't care about your marriage as much as you think they do," Ed said, directly. "They want Ted to come out strongly and powerfully and confidently because deep down they're afraid that . . ." he paused, perhaps for dramatic effect, ". . . they're afraid that he'll be *assassinated* like Jack and Bobby. And they want to see that he's not afraid of it too."

For a moment, Joan looked as if she'd been punched in the stomach. She could not meet Martin's gaze. "She was obviously fearful for Ted's life," said Joe Gargan of Joan, now voicing her then-secret apprehension, "because of what had happened to Jack and Bobby."

"Look, if anyone asks questions of a personal nature, well, Ted can handle it," Ed continued, his tone more conciliatory now that he thought he had Joan back in control. "For instance, if they ask about your alcoholism or your marriage, Ted can deal with it."

"Oh, yeah?" Joan said, her anger suddenly rising. "How? That's what I'd like to know. Ted doesn't know what he's talking about half the time when it comes to me, my problems, and my marriage. The political issues? Yes, he obviously can handle those. But when it comes to me, forget it, Ed. He doesn't know what the hell he's talking about."

It was difficult to argue with her when she was so determined and confident. "I know what I want," she told the group, "and I think, I really do, that we should do it my way."

Finally, it was decided that a person who would be situated in the assembly of reporters in advance would ask a question—the third one of the conference—about whether or not Joan was supportive of Ted's efforts. Then Joan would come forward and answer quickly and briefly. She would look happy and in control, "like I really feel," she offered.

"And what are you going to do if some idiot asks about Chappaquiddick, Joan?" Ed said. "Or the other women in Ted's life. What are you going to do then? Have you thought about that?"

Joan seemed annoyed, but she must have known that the questions could come up. She admitted that "those are some tough areas for me," adding that "if you think about it, they have nothing to do with me. Those are Ted's screwups, not mine." She said that she felt comfortable speaking about her mistakes, but not Ted's. "I can speak about my own, but when it comes to his, well, I don't know if I want to . . ." She hesitated for a moment. "The best I can offer, I guess, is that, yes, he has his problems, I have mine, and we're both working on our problems," Joan concluded. "That's the truth. That's what I'll say."

The Announcement: EMK for President

Throughout the month of October, Ethel Kennedy had attempted to make contact with Joan. She had said that she wanted to help her sister-in-law in any way she could, and so she hoped to share with her some advice on how to campaign as a potential First Lady. After all, she campaigned with Bobby. Besides that obvious fact, though, she did care about Joan, understood (or thought she did, anyway) her frailties, and wanted to make good on her promise at the hotel meeting a few months earlier to do what she could to be of assistance.

Margaret (Meg) Leaming was a friend of Ethel's at this time. The two had met in Aspen during one of the Kennedys' skiing trips there. In two years, she would be ousted from the Kennedy circle for giving an interview to a biographer of Ethel Kennedy, for a book that would go unpublished. She now recalls, "Ethel wrote Joan a letter asking for a luncheon, but Joan didn't respond. From my understanding, Ethel then telephoned her a few times. Joan ducked her calls, but finally did have to speak to her. She told her that she appreciated her offer, but she had

a full staff of people at her disposal advising her on the very topics that
Ethel wanted to discuss with her—people like Marcia Chellis. Ethel
was very hurt. 'I've been there for her in the past,' she told me, 'and I
don't know why she's cutting me out now. I have so much to offer. I've
done this. I know what I'm doing. I want to do my part.'

"I don't think Joan realized that Ethel was a very different person by
1979," continues Leaming. "Ethel was much more withdrawn. She
had become a hermit, really, only going out for charity causes and special Kennedy functions. True, she was still unkind to her servants—
wouldn't think twice about slapping them if they talked back—but
that was just Ethel. She had only a few friends. She trusted no one, really. She wanted to be a part of Ted's campaign, she so wanted to do
something. When Ted called to ask her to do some commercials for
him, she jumped at the chance."

In fact, Joan still thought of Ethel as the critical, difficult woman
she had been during the Camelot years, and she didn't want Ethel
around lest she would undermine her hard-earned self-confidence.
After years of successfully doing so, Ethel knew how to push those
"buttons" in Joan that would set her into a tailspin; and so, perhaps
wisely, Joan avoided her as much as possible. Unfortunately, Jackie
avoided Ethel as well. In the end, it seemed, Ethel had fixed it so that
both of her sisters-in-law, and many others, didn't want much to do
with her by the end of the seventies. Ethel had her children, though.
And her memories.

On November 7, 1979, Ted Kennedy was scheduled to make his
big announcement at Faneuil Hall in Boston, in front of an assembly
of reporters, other politicians, and campaign staff members. Present
and seated in one heavily guarded section were members of the
Kennedy family, including Ted's sisters Eunice and Jean (with their
husbands Sargent Shriver and Steve Smith) and Pat Kennedy Lawford, as well as the eighty-nine-year-old Kennedy matriarch, Rose.
Also there was Ethel, looking a bit vacant-eyed and lost. The big surprise of the day, though, was the appearance of a radiant Jackie
Kennedy Onassis.

Ted had called Jackie personally to ask her to be present, and she
had agreed. However, with the exception of a quick hello and a hug,
Jackie, who had seen Joan two weeks earlier at the dedication of the

JFK Library, would have no contact with Joan on this day, and neither would Ethel, for that matter. The event would be so hectic, and there were so many security guards and Secret Service agents around Ted and Joan, that it would be impossible for anyone to have a real conversation with them. As she walked onto the stage, Joan spotted Jackie in the audience. She smiled broadly as Jackie raised a thumbs-up sign. With Ted at a podium and Joan and their children behind him, Ted made his announcement.

"It just seemed as you watched him that the weight of his brothers' legacy was on his shoulders and that he was only a human being, but that they were expecting him to be Jack and Bobby all together," recalled one observer. "And I think he knew that very day that there was no way he could be that. No one could."

After formally announcing his candidacy, Ted took questions from the media.

"Senator, is Joan in favor of your running for President?" the "plant" asked.

Ted paused for a moment then, acting as if the question was impromptu, he turned to Joan and offered to let her address it. Joan, wearing a short lavender dress with a pleated skirt and matching jacket, glanced at Ted and smiled broadly at the assembly. Shedding the pitiable image of the wronged wife, Joan seemed refreshed and positive.

"I look forward to campaigning for him," she said in a small sound so reminiscent of Jackie's on-camera voice. "And not only that, I look forward very, very enthusiastically to my husband's being a candidate and then as being the next President of the United States." Suddenly, her voice lifted and strengthened. "I will be talking with members of the press and at that time I hope to answer all of your questions that you might have on your minds today." The crowd applauded as Joan bowed out and took her seat, indicating that this was really Ted's big moment, not hers. Still, she had made her point, not only with her brief words but with her presence. She looked completely at ease, totally in control, and ready for whatever lay ahead. In the audience, Jackie seemed delighted as she clapped her hands, her eyes aglow at Joan's triumph.

A couple of months later, Joan had the promised press conference at her home in Boston, a group of reporters pummeling her with a barrage of personal questions about Chappaquiddick, her marriage, and alcoholism. A well-meaning but, perhaps, somewhat naïve Eunice had told Joan to avoid all questions about the death of Mary Jo Kopechne, refuse to discuss her drinking problem, and refer to her marriage as a stable, good one.

"Eunice was usually the one Kennedy less concerned about the politician and more concerned about the person," observed Richard Burke. "She was always interested about the human aspect of any decision, what would be the easiest for the person involved. Once, I was in the car with Eunice and Ted and we were discussing the fact that Ted was going to be forced to divulge all of his financial information during the campaign. Eunice said, 'Absolutely not. That's personal.' It was a normal person's reaction rather than a politician's. That's how she thought."

Joan had also telephoned Jackie in New York for moral support. When she asked Jackie what she thought of Eunice's opinion, the former First Lady had to laugh. She said that Eunice was "still stuck in the sixties," and that "someone needs to tell her that Camelot is over."

Jackie maintained that the media would no longer buy a perfect picture of a perfect marriage, the way it had with her and Jack's, if it wasn't absolutely true. Jackie told Joan to be as forthcoming as possible, "without losing a shred of dignity."

After Joan followed Jackie's advice, the press conference was a success, though it did have its tough moments, such as when one reporter observed that Ted's "number one love is politics" and asked her how it felt "to be second." Joan's hands seemed to tremble as she responded, "I am not second. Just ask Ted Kennedy."

Joan's White House Fantasies

At first, Joan Kennedy decided to go along with Ted's presidential campaign—and with the charade that the two of them had a sturdy, albeit troubled union—as incentive for her to stop drinking. However, after Ted made his official announcement, it would seem that the confidence Joan felt at having pulled herself together so well up until this point gave her reason to believe that she could fulfill even greater aspirations. Her self-esteem had been raised to the point where the idea of being First Lady had actually become appealing to her. Not only was she in the process of learning how to handle life's pressures without the need to fortify herself with liquor, she also had years of experience as a political wife. She believed that she had much to offer. She may have reasoned, "Why not?"

Said Richard Burke, "Being First Lady began to take hold for her as a personal dream. She used to talk about it quite often. I remember being in her apartment many times as she was getting ready for interviews, and we would converse about what life would be like for her in the White House, some of the things she wanted to do, the plans she hoped to implement. 'I really do want this,' she told me. 'I think I could contribute a lot, like Jackie did.' I think she almost felt a sense of destiny at work that Ted be in the White House, and she there at his side. The effort she was putting forth became not only about Ted's future, but also about her own."

Of course, the happily married couple Ted and Joan had been portraying for the media was a complete charade; they had been separated for years. How, should Ted actually be elected into office, did they intend to perpetuate this farce in the White House?

The senator told Richard Burke and others on his staff that, if elected, he had reason to believe he would be able to continue with the "Big Lie" (as he called it) just based on the fact that, in his view, he and Joan had been successful with it up until this point in the campaign. He would have his girlfriends, and his wife, and somehow he would do it all as President. (It's been done before, and has certainly been done since.)

For her part, Joan was now operating under the notion that, as unhappy as she was in her marriage, she was willing to put up with it if it meant she would be in the White House. Apparently, whether she realized it or not, she had been sucked into the unrealistic whirlwind of Ted's campaign, just like everyone around her.

"I also believe that, deep in her heart, she hoped that she and Ted would reconcile once they were in the White House," observed Marcia Chellis, "that he would so appreciate all she had done for him during the campaign and be so happy with her at his side that he would want to do anything to reunite the family. As angry as she was at him, I always believed that if he had at least tried, Joan would have still wanted to save the marriage and transform it into the happy union they were trying so hard to convince the press existed between them."

Adds Richard Burke, "But most of the press didn't buy the happy marriage bit, anyway. With the heavy scrutiny they would have gotten as First Couple, this huge deception was bound to be revealed. Looking back, there was a certain amount of total unreality within the bubble in which we were running the campaign."

"[Joan's doctor] Hawthorne didn't think any of this was at all good for Joan," continues Burke. "In time, as he more fully understood what was going on and what Joan was setting herself up for, he became very unsupportive of Ted's campaign, of Joan's White House fantasies, the whole bit. But no one—least of all Ted and Joan—was willing to listen to him. We all had our eyes set on the White House, no matter what."

EMK's Candidacy: Not Meant to Be

Throughout the campaign, Ted Kennedy seemed troubled, distracted, and ill at ease. He was never able to pull himself together, which was clear from the erratic nature of his speeches and television appearances. Try as he might, he also couldn't avoid sweets and liquor, and continued to pack on the pounds. He always seemed out of breath and appeared to be unhealthy and unhappy.

At the time that the senator announced his intention, he was leading two-to-one in the polls. But during the months to come, Ted would fall behind President Carter and never regain the lead. Not only had Chappaquiddick not been forgotten, but times had changed. The country was moving away from the Kennedys' brand of liberalism. Also, Ted never seemed to be either prepared or in control, and the resulting gaffes eroded his image. "We should expedite the synfuels program through the process of expediting," he said in one speech. "We must face the problems we are facing as we have always faced the problems we have faced," he said in another, as his speechwriters looked at one another with stricken expressions.

Also, to his detriment, the "Joan Problem" was never really solved.

Whenever reporters looked at his wife standing at his side beaming, they couldn't help but think of Ted's questionable character—a line of thinking that inevitably pointed them right back to Chappaquiddick.

Perhaps to his credit, it was difficult for Ted to completely lie about the state of his marriage, though he tried.

"We have had our problems, and we're working them out," Ted said, not too convincingly. For the most part, Ted barely looked at Joan when they were in public together, often embarrassing her by walking away while the cameras were rolling, or when she was in the middle of a sentence. He displayed no warmth toward her whatsoever. Joan, ironically, was better able to act the part of a happy wife if called upon to do so. However, the "act" bothered her. In truth, according to those who know her best, Joan couldn't stand to be in the same room with this man who had betrayed her so many times.

One close friend tells this story: "Joan and Ted were doing a photo session for a newspaper, and the photographer was saying things like, 'Look at her with love, Ted. Now, hold her hand. Now, Joan, hug Ted.' He was trying to get that great shot. Joan was fine with all of it, but Ted was less eager, acting wooden and distant the whole time. Joan apologized for Ted, saying, 'Oh, he has such a headache, what with this schedule.' But afterward, when the photographer left, Joan lit into Ted. Raw emotion erupted from her. She called him a bastard and said, 'I'm trying. The least you can do is the same. Do you think it helps my sobriety to lie like this? I'm supposed to be honest about every aspect of my life, and so this is real hard for me, Ted.' She was very angry, and just went on and on. Before she stormed out, she said, 'If we make it into the White House, all I can say is, God help us both. Some President and First Lady we're going to make . . . we can't even hold hands. . . . What a farce.'"

By the end of the summer of 1980, Ted was lagging badly in all the polls; a *New York Times*/CBS poll showed that 24 percent of the Democrats polled would not vote for him under any circumstances because of "the character issue." The Kennedy camp tried everything, even trotting Jackie out for a fund-raiser at Regis College in Westin, Massachusetts, and having Ethel star in a campaign commercial during which she sang Ted's praises as a surrogate father to her children. It didn't matter. While Ted seemed to fail at his venture, Joan was a smashing success at hers.

At every stop along the way, Joan could feel the difference in the way people looked at her. By attending regular meetings of Alcoholics Anonymous, Women for Sobriety, and other support groups, she had managed to remain sober throughout the entire campaign. It wasn't easy. "I don't know how many times she told me she needed a drink," said one friend of hers. "Sometimes, she would shake. It was a physical addiction as well as an emotional one. But she did it, by God. She sure did stay sober."

Now Joan Kennedy radiated nothing but good health; her attitude was enthusiastic and positive. The courage and strength she exhibited, and the fact that she seemed to be conquering her demons, all worked to redesign Joan's image. Marcia Chellis remembered: "[Joan's] successful struggle to overcome alcoholism and her decision to live her life for herself had made a difference in the lives of others. One evening in Helena, Montana, when she walked up the long center aisle of the Shrine Temple to meet Vice President Mondale, the entire audience rose to its feet in applause and cheers."

Joan was greeted with great enthusiasm everywhere she went. When she gave a speech about the Equal Rights Amendment at the Parker House, the response was overwhelmingly positive.

After all she had been through to forge her own identity within the Kennedy family (or as Jackie told her long ago, "Build a life for yourself within this Kennedy world"), Joan told her audience that she now understood and related to the women's movement. She once thought of it as for "other women," she said, "but no more." During her speech, Joan discussed some of the issues facing working mothers, and called for an end to economic and social injustices facing women. She ended her speech by saying in a strong, authoritative voice, "I know that one of my husband's top priorities is to see that the Equal Rights Amendment becomes at last the twenty-seventh amendment to the Constitution. And I know that if Ted is elected President, I will commit myself to the ongoing struggle for women's equality with everything I have and everything I am."

Afterward, Joan shook hands with members of the audience— mostly young and very appreciative, mostly female but some male— for an hour or so. For years, she had craved affection and intimacy—just the touch of another person other than her children so that she could perhaps feel cherished and safe—and so the acceptance shown by these kinds of crowds on the campaign circuit was fulfilling in many ways. Joan found a great comfort in their acceptance of her, in the way they held on for a second longer than appropriate when shaking her hand, in the way they enveloped her with their arms in an embrace of approval. It all meant more to Joan Kennedy than her fans would probably ever know.

By August, Joan was tired of running in and out of limousines and being shouted at by anxious Secret Service men to "step on it," yet she rarely complained. She felt strong and in control, though she knew Ted's campaign was in deep trouble, especially when, during a trip to Alabama, she saw someone holding a placard saying "How Can You Rescue the Country When You Couldn't Even Rescue Mary Jo." After Ted gave a speech at Columbia University, he and his contingent drove down 114th Street—Fraternity Row—and blaring from one of the windows as if to greet the motorcade were the strains of Simon and Garfunkel's "Bridge Over Troubled Waters," as an intentional and un-kind ode to Chappaquiddick.

"There was no fighting it," observed Frank Mankiewicz, Bobby's former press representative who also advised Ted from time to time during the campaign. "The sentiment against him was too strong. We all knew it. We knew it going in, but we just hoped that maybe . . . maybe . . . But it wasn't meant to be."

The decision was made by Ted to bow out of the race. He didn't re-ally have much choice; his candidacy was roundly rejected by the del-egates. Joan was never consulted, even though so many of her hopes and dreams for the future would be dashed by Ted's choice.

In fact, by the time Ted finally withdrew his candidacy in August at the Democratic Convention at Madison Square Garden—on the same stage where Marilyn Monroe had sung "Happy Birthday" to his brother eighteen years earlier—he had left behind a Democratic polit-ical landscape of scorched earth that had created great divisiveness within his own party, and which some say aided in Ronald Reagan's election. But in his hour of defeat, he spoke with an eloquence that banished for a moment all the shadows on the Kennedy legend. It would be the speech of a lifetime for Ted Kennedy, evoking what his brothers had come to mean for many Americans of their generation.

"May it be said of our party in 1980 that we found our faith again," he intoned, a look of total defiance and determination on his face.

"And may it be said of us both in dark passages and bright days, in the words of Tennyson that my brothers quoted and loved, and that have special meaning for me now: 'I am a part of all that I have met, too much is taken, much abides, that which we are, we are. One equal temper of heroic hearts, strong in will, to strive, to seek, to find, and not to yield.'"

A teary-eyed Joan came forward on cue and stood at Ted's side, as did their three children, Kara, Ted Jr., and Patrick. "For me, a few hours ago, this campaign came to an end," concluded Ted, the last Kennedy of his generation. "For all those whose cares have been our concern, the work goes on, the cause endures, the hope still lives, and the dream shall never die."

As the family was enveloped by applause, Joan put her arm around Ted's neck. Their heads close together, they faced the assembly smiling, Ted with his arm around her waist. "It was the closest I had ever seen them," recalled Marcia Chellis, who watched with great emotion from a far-away balcony. As everyone clapped and stomped their approval, Ted embraced his wife warmly. She melted into his arms. The family smiled and waved at their supporters and detractors, all of whom were by now standing and cheering—thousands of people in blue-and-white hats waving hundreds of blue-and-white Kennedy placards as similarly colored balloons floated in the air—for one final farewell, a send-off to Ted Kennedy, a twenty-three-minute standing ovation. "For an instant," recalled Richard Burke, "Camelot was revisited."

While Ted's and Joan's appearance at the 1980 convention was one of its greatest moments, the most memorable and significant occurrence to many was the petty and divisive behavior Ted displayed on the podium when he absolutely refused to join hands with Jimmy Carter before the assembly.

In years to come, other Kennedys would share the dream and take their chances in public life. But on that evening in Madison Square Garden, the quest for the Presidency had finally come to an end for the sons of Joseph P. Kennedy.

Afterward, there was a party at the Waldorf-Astoria, where the family was staying. Joan seemed happy and relieved. As she spoke to supporters, Ted sidled over to her and invited her to lunch the next day. He wanted to thank her for all she had done, and maybe talk about their future. Joan looked at him suspiciously for a moment, but since she was in the company of others she smiled, reached for his hand, and said, "I would love to have lunch with you tomorrow, of course!" After a few hours, the gathering broke up and Joan retired, alone, to her suite in the hotel.

The Last Straw for Joan

The morning after Ted Kennedy dropped out of the race, Joan awakened to find her picture on the front page of the *New York Times*, kissing her estranged husband as they left the podium during the convention. Ethel telephoned Joan in New York that morning, as did Eunice, Pat, Jean, and a few other friends and relatives. Everyone who called complimented Joan on her perseverance during the campaign, even Ethel, who told her, "Kiddo, I feel so bad. But there's always 1984!"

From Jackie, Joan also received a telegram with a decidedly positive—and maybe even prophetic—message: "All's well that ends well."

"After it was over, I think Joan felt what we all felt," said Richard Burke, "which was 'What the hell was I thinking? What the hell did I just do?' It had all been so unrealistic. It was like waking up from a bad dream with a hangover."

The only one who had not said a word of thanks or encouragement had been the one whose opinion had always mattered, and maddeningly so, Ted.

Joan seemed lost in thought when Marcia Chellis arrived to help her dress for her lunch date with Ted. All else had failed, she realized, but perhaps she could still salvage her marriage. "She held out hope that maybe this lunch with him might be the beginning of a new relationship with her husband," said Chellis. "I think that, in all of the hysteria, she had even started to believe the illusion set by the campaign that he actually cared about her. She left for lunch with Ted with a great sense of expectation."

Accompanied by Secret Service agents, Ted and Joan lunched at The Box restaurant. One of the agents recalls, "It was a madhouse.

There were reporters everywhere. Ted didn't say two words to Joan. He barely looked at her. She sat there, picked at her salad, and tried to smile as photographers shot pictures. Afterward, as I helped push her through the crowd, she was furious. 'That bastard,' she said, looking at Ted. 'He set this thing up as a photo opportunity, didn't he?' She looked at me as if I had an answer. I didn't. But it sure looked like she was right. He just wanted the little wife by his side for the press."

The next evening, Joan and Ted hosted a party at their home in McLean, and then they were to fly to Hyannis Port. "Ted and I should have a chance to talk things over on Squaw Island," Joan told Marcia Chellis, hopefully.

The party in McLean was a success. While Joan was dancing with a Secret Service agent, Ted tapped her on the shoulder to tell her that it was time to go to the airport and catch a plane to Hyannis Port. They rushed to the airport, and while on the plane, Ted seemed relaxed and happy to be with his wife, though he never mentioned her work on his campaign. Suddenly they were landing, much too soon and not in Massachusetts. Much to Joan's surprise, the aircraft touched down on Montauk Point in Long Island.

"Okay, Joan, see ya later," Ted said, kissing her on the forehead. "And, oh yeah. Thanks a lot," he added as he got up and walked away. Joan bore the cruelty of it all without a word or sound of protest, just a look of dismay. Through the small, circular window she watched her husband disembark from the aircraft and gather his luggage. Her stunned gaze followed him as he walked to a waiting car and got in. He was driven off into the night.

Joan was flown onward to Hyannis Port, alone. Later she would learn that Ted had ordered that his yacht, the *Curraugh*, be sailed in from the Cape and be waiting for him in the harbor. From there, accompanied by a female guest, Ted went sailing in the Caribbean to unwind from his grueling campaign experience.

While on her flight from Long Island to Hyannis Port, as Joan would later tell it, something inside of her was "adjusted." As she gazed out at the vastness dotted with heavenly stars, the possibility of her life suddenly seemed as wide open as the soft, engulfing darkness. Another world awaited her. It was not the manic, almost unnatural one inhabited by the Kennedys, but one that perhaps made more sense, populated by reasonable-thinking, "normal" people. Maybe it was for this world that she had been destined before becoming derailed so many years ago, on that day when Ted came to speak at Manhattanville College. Perhaps she would be the only one of the sisters-in-law to escape by her own volition; Jackie and Ethel certainly had no choice after the deaths of their husbands, though she often wondered whether they would ever have ended their marriages had those tragedies not occurred. Joan did have a choice—it could be argued that she had it all along, though she didn't seem to know it—and now she seemed ready to make a decision.

Joan would remember years later that as she assessed her past and wondered about the future, a sense of tranquillity washed over her. Ted's abandonment that evening in Long Island was truly a defining moment. With astonishing clarity she could now see the man she had known for the last twenty years for who he really was, not what she wanted him to be or hoped he would one day become. Clearly, the senator would never change. As a politician he had always been without peer—at least in her view. As a suitor he had been irresistible. As a lover, generous and caring. But as a husband, he'd been intolerable. It no longer mattered to Joan. There was no anger, resentment, or judgment, as she would tell it, just a certain sadness about all of the wasted years, "and a sense of relief, like exhaling," she recalled, "because, finally, I got it. *I got it.*"

Once she landed in Hyannis Port, Joan Kennedy knew what she had to do.

Postscript:
Jackie, Ethel, and Joan after Camelot

The official announcement was made on January 21, 1981: Ted and Joan Kennedy were divorcing. Barbara Gibson was in the servants' dining room of the Palm Beach estate with Rose when Ted called his mother to tell her the news before it hit the press. "Oh, really?" Gibson heard Rose ask her son, with great interest. "Well, is there someone else?"

Before making her decision, Joan discussed her intention with Jackie Kennedy Onassis, which was appropriate considering that she had depended on Jackie's counsel about Ted's unfaithfulness for more than twenty years. The two women spent four hours discussing the state of Joan's marriage and her future.

"I'm so sorry," Jackie told Joan, according to what she would later recall, "because now I feel that I should have told you to do this fifteen years ago. I just didn't know back then what we know today." Jackie said she felt "terrible" about the way Joan's marriage had turned out.

Joan acknowledged that Jackie had always been one of the few people she could depend upon when she needed help. But Jackie said that she now wished she had advised Joan to divorce Ted years earlier instead of telling her to learn to live with his unfaithfulness, "then maybe you wouldn't have gotten so sick." She was apparently referring to Joan's alcoholism.

"I couldn't have done it, anyway," Joan observed. "Times were so different. We did the best we could back then, though, didn't we?"

"We sure did," Jackie agreed. "With what we had to work with, anyway."

The two former sisters-in-law shared a laugh. Then the ever-practical Jackie recommended that Joan be represented by her New York attorney, Alexander Forger. Joan took her up on the offer.

Before she hung up, Jackie said, "My wish for you, Joan, is that you are always surrounded by people who love you, no matter what—without hesitation or condition." Jackie's words so touched her sister-in-law that Joan cried upon hanging up the phone.

Later Joan would recall, "Back then, I probably couldn't have taken Jackie's advice if she had suggested divorce, which she never would have done. There was so much to consider. The times were different, I was Catholic, we had children, not to mention Ted's career. Nowadays, women have choices. Back then, we had few."

Longing to expand her horizons, Joan continued her education and later, in 1981, received a Master's in Education from Lesley College. "I didn't know after all that drinking if I had any brain cells left," she joked to one writer. Her estranged husband was present for the ceremony, as were her three devoted children, and, much to the amazement of many observers, he seemed proud of her. "I want the personal credibility that little piece of paper gives me," Joan said at the time. "Now that I have that, I'm no longer just Joan *Kennedy*."

For Joan, as for many alcoholics, her sobriety would not be easy to maintain. Joan would have several relapses in the years after the 1980 campaign, including a particularly embarrassing setback in the summer of 1988 when, while vacationing in Hyannis Port, she crashed her Buick Regal into a chain-link fence, narrowly missing a woman crossing the road. Russell Goering, who was vacationing at a rented house, witnessed the accident: "When I approached the car, she was slumped down against the door on the driver's side. She was very thin and looked sick. Her face was deathly white and her pupils were really dilated. She looked like a whipped dog, with no spirit at all." After seeing what occurred, five local youngsters came to Joan's aid. One of them locked her keys in the car's trunk so that she wouldn't be able to do any further driving. Joan, whose license was suspended following a similar offense in 1974, was arrested for drunk driving.

All throughout the 1980s Joan would find herself in a series of drug and alcohol abuse centers as she waged her battle against alcoholism, with the media as her watchdog, nipping at her heels every uncertain step along the way.

Joan's last relapse was in 1992. With floundering times then behind her, she began building block by block a sturdy foundation for her future, as she once explained. Some of the blocks were marked "I'll never drink again," others, "I'll live a good and fulfilling life." They interlocked; they were interdependent. Never again, she believed, would one stand without the other. Never again would she waste another moment under the influence of anything other than the exhilaration she felt at finally overcoming her illness. "I couldn't believe how hard it was to stop," says Joan, who has not had a drink in eight years. "Alcoholism is a baffler. God knows, toward the end of my drinking, talk about being enslaved."

Today, sixty-two-year-old Joan Kennedy writes in a letter dated November 8, 1998, of the joy she experiences daily, "spending a lot of my time with my four grandchildren and enjoying my part-time job as chairperson of Boston's Cultural Council and serving on the board of directors of four great Boston institutions. I am blessed with many dear friends whom I have known since my college days, and I still play the piano or narrate with orchestras for a favorite charity," she concludes. "Fortunately, I am well and happy in this present stage of my life."

Joan remains close to her three children, Kara, now thirty-nine, Ted Jr., thirty-seven, and Patrick, thirty-two. Patrick went on to follow his father's example in becoming a politician, as a congressional representative from Rhode Island. With a note of facetiousness, Joan says she will write her memoirs when "I'm about ninety years old, because only then will I feel safe about writing everything truthfully. I don't want to speak about a lot of what took place. I have to think about my children."

Ted Kennedy is, as of this writing, in his sixth full term as a Democratic senator from Massachusetts. A passionate advocate of liberal causes such as universal health care and gun control, Ted has, over the years, earned great admiration as a leader in the United States Senate. He is credited with raising the minimum wage and reforming campaign finance laws. "He's one of the most effective senators of this century," observes Senate Minority Leader Tom Daschle.

In July 1992, Ted married the former Victoria Reggie, a Washington, D.C., lawyer eighteen years Joan's junior. In what some observers felt was a cruel twist of fate, considering all that Joan Kennedy had endured as a Kennedy wife, Ted had their twenty-three-year marriage annulled so that he could marry Reggie in the Catholic Church. In effect, he invalidated his very union to Joan Kennedy in the eyes of the Church, so that he could move forward with his life.

According to one priest in the Boston diocese, Ted's annulment was granted for "lack of due discretion," a term which covers cases in which a person had wed in the Catholic Church but did not fully understand the nature and responsibilities of the sacred commitment. The standard is also used for purposes of annulment when one of the spouses was addicted to drugs or alcohol and could not live up to the requirements of the union. After the annulment, Ted took Communion at his mother's Funeral Mass in 1995.

Joan's feelings about the annulment of her marriage are unknown; she simply refuses to discuss it. As a result of years of therapy, reflection, and self-examination, she says that she has managed to move from her old self through a new self, to, finally, her true self—a woman who fully embraces who she is and the life she has lived, both the good and the bad. She has no need to explain any of it to anyone; there will be no further *People* magazine cover stories touting her liberation from alcoholism and a bad marriage. Indeed, with no more false smiles needed for the purpose of Kennedy family public relations, Joan is now free to simply not say anything at all, if that is her choice.

Joan Bennett Kennedy sees her former husband, Ted Kennedy, from time to time and reunites with him every Thanksgiving and Christmas for the sake of her children and grandchildren.

The years after Ted Kennedy's unsuccessful bid for the Presidency in 1980 were not easy ones for Ethel Kennedy. In 1983, her son Bobby was arrested and pleaded guilty to possession of heroin. He was sentenced to two years' probation. Then a tragedy occurred in 1984 when another son, twenty-eight-year-old David, was found dead in a Palm Beach hotel from a heroin overdose. At the age of twelve, David had watched his own father's assassination on television and, as has been repeatedly reported, never really recovered. "Nobody ever talked to me about my father's death," he told Peter Collier and David Horowitz, authors of the book *The Kennedys: An American Drama*, a year before his death. "To this day in fact, my mother has never talked to me about it."

In January 1998, Ethel Kennedy endured still another tragedy when her thirty-nine-year-old son Michael was killed in a skiing accident. Michael, married to Frank Gifford's daughter Vicki, had been accused of improper relations with his children's teenage baby-sitter. Just as the uproar was fading, his life was suddenly taken on the wintry slopes in a perilous—and typically Kennedyesque—game of touch football on skis. Shortly after David's death, Ethel's brother, Jim Skakel, died from a painful kidney disease. Later that year, she was faced with the thirtieth anniversary of Bobby's assassination. Somehow, though, her deep religious convictions have continued to sustain Ethel Kennedy, which seems the greatest miracle of all.

While Jackie was supportive of Joan's divorce, Ethel was not. No matter the circumstances, she did not understand why Joan would not want to remain a Kennedy. Ethel talked about the divorce on the telephone to friends and relatives, saying that her sister-in-law should have just been grateful to still have a Kennedy husband in her life, despite the problems he presented. "I don't have one anymore, and neither does Jackie," she told one confidante. Ethel claimed to not understand what it was that Ted had done to Joan that she should "treat him so spitefully." She felt that Bobby's brother had served Joan as well as any Kennedy husband had ever served his wife, which certainly wasn't saying much (though no one would dare tell Ethel so). It had been enough for her. It had been enough for Jackie. Why not Joan?

Today, Ethel's surviving children, all of whom had troubled childhoods, are an impressive brood who have gone on to fulfilling and respectable adult lives, some in public service: Kathleen, forty-eight, is Lieutenant-Governor of Maryland; Joe, forty-seven, after a congressional career, is now the head of Citizen's Energy, a nonprofit organization that provides home heating oil to low-income families in Massachusetts; Bobby, forty-six, is founder of New York's Pace University environmental law program; Mary Courtney, forty-three, is a homemaker with her husband, Paul Hill, the Irish independence activist; Mary Kerry, forty, is presently writing a book and is the wife of HUD Secretary Andrew Cuomo; Christopher, thirty-six, is vice president of the Kennedy family's Chicago Merchandise Mart; Matthew Maxwell, thirty-five, now a teacher at Boston College, is the former District Attorney in the Juvenile Crime Unit of the Philadelphia prosecutor's office and also the editor of *Make Gentle the Life of This World*, a book of poems loved by his father, as well as other written tributes to the late Bobby; Douglas, thirty-two, is a cable television news reporter; and Rory, thirty-one, is a documentary filmmaker.

In 1999, seventy-one-year-old Ethel Kennedy was asked, at a ceremony marking the eightieth birthday of John Fitzgerald Kennedy, about her ambitions at this time in her life. "A long life, to watch my children grow," she quickly answered, with a warm smile. "I have the most precious gift of all . . . my family."

Jacqueline Bouvier, Ethel Skakel, and Joan Bennett probably would not have known each other except that they had happened to marry sons of Joseph P. and Rose Kennedy. Though their relationships with each other encompassed a wide range of human emotions over the years—from jealousy, compassion, indifference, and anger to joy and triumph—they shared a unique history, forever joined in that sliver of time and place historians would call Camelot, forever joined as sisters-in-law, and as Kennedys. Though they lived a privileged existence, one that many on the outside viewed as a surreal fantasy, the irony is that they were really just everyday women—sisters, wives, and mothers—who often found themselves desperately attempting to make some sense of troubled, turbulent lives.

Jackie, who always somehow expressed the appropriate sentiment, once made an observation about her life that seems fitting in describing not only her personal experiences but also those of her sisters-in-law Ethel and Joan. "I have been through a lot and have suffered a great deal," she said, her words evoking painful memories and quick flashes of the past. "But I have had lots of happy moments, as well. Every moment one lives is different from the other. The good, the bad, hardship, the joy, the tragedy, love and happiness are all interwoven into one single, indescribable whole that is called *life*. You cannot separate the good and the bad," concluded this woman of Camelot, who certainly had encountered her share of both. "And perhaps there is no need to do so, either."

Sadly, Jacqueline Bouvier Kennedy Onassis passed away on Thursday, May 19, 1994, after a brief but painful battle with the swiftly moving cancer non-Hodgkin's lymphoma. Because she had always taken such exceptional care of herself—dieting, swimming, jogging, riding her horses—and had enjoyed good health nearly all her life, her illness seemed incomprehensible. (The worst ailment she had previously faced was a persistent sinus inflammation in the winter of 1962.) She described her feelings of pride at the way she had taken care of herself as "a kind of hubris," when she spoke to Arthur Schlesinger about her surprising sickness. She was determined to beat the cancer, however, as she wrote to friends.

The last of more than forty years of correspondence to Lady Bird Johnson is not dated, but it seems to have been written in February 1994, just after the terrible news of Jackie's illness was confirmed to a shocked public by Jackie's longtime spokeswoman, Nancy Tuckerman, in the *New York Times*. The years had never diminished the deep fondness Jackie and Lady Bird felt for one another, and Jackie still considered her successor in the White House a close friend; she had hosted Lady Bird at her Martha's Vineyard home just six months earlier. Whereas Jackie's handwriting was ordinarily a perfect backhand, the penmanship in her last letter to Lady Bird seemed unsteady, perhaps a result of the many anticancer drugs she was taking, which were almost as debilitating as the illness itself.

The always optimistic Jackie wrote to her elderly friend that everything in her life was going well, and that she looked forward to seeing her "in the Vineyard again next summer." She signed the note, "Much love, Jackie." (Apparently, Jackie passed to her married daughter [to Edwin Schlossberg], Caroline, her penchant for letter-writing. She would write personal notes to all of those friends of her mother who attended the funeral, including Lady Bird, whom she thanked for "coming to New York to wish my mother farewell.")

Though the weather was gloomy and drizzling the evening Jackie died, it was a glorious, spring morning—warm and sunny—on the day of Jackie's funeral. Seven hundred attendees began arriving at 8:30 A.M. to go through a series of security checks before they could enter St. Ignatius Loyola Roman Catholic Church at the corner of Park Avenue and 84th Street in New York. The mourners had been called by phone or had received hand-delivered notices.

John F. Kennedy, Jr., said the family wanted the funeral to reflect his mother's essence, "her love of words, the bonds of home and family, and her spirit of adventure."

(Perhaps the only blessing of Jackie's death was that she would not have to experience the terrible grief she no doubt would have suffered when John was killed after the private plane he was piloting plummeted into the Atlantic Ocean. John and his wife of nearly five years, Caroline Bessette [whom Jackie had never met], and her sister Lauren, were on their way to Ethel Kennedy's home on the Cape to attend the wedding ceremony of her daughter Rory—the child with whom Ethel was pregnant when Bobby was assassinated. John, Caroline, and Lauren were all buried at sea on July 22, 1999, which was, coincidentally, the anniversary of Rose Kennedy's birthday.)

In accordance with Jackie's wishes for privacy, no television cameras were allowed in the church, though an audio feed was transmitted by speakers to the 4,000 people who waited outside behind police barriers, and to the media. The service began promptly at 10:00 A.M., with John Jr. reading Chapter 25 from the Book of Isaiah. Ted gave the eulogy. Caroline read the poem "Cape Cod," by Edna St. Vincent Millay, an evocative reminder of the place that was so identified with the Kennedy family. Perhaps the most moving was New York diamond merchant Maurice Tempelsman's reading of "Ithaka," a celebration of Odysseus' voyage by the Greek poet Constantine Peter Cavafy. At the end of the poem, Tempelsman added his own personal and emotional sentiments about Jackie.

A portly, balding diamond merchant, Tempelsman had always seemed an unlikely companion for a woman who had so epitomized style and grace, yet he had been her friend and lover for more than ten years. He had lived with Jackie since the early eighties, and he and his wife of thirty years, Lily, never legally divorced, though his wife did grant him an Orthodox Jewish divorce. They had three children.

Sixty-four-year-old Tempelsman's friendship with Jackie began after Aristotle Onassis's death, when Jackie turned to him for investment advice. His astute handling of her affairs would quadruple her worth after 1975, eventually leaving her with a fortune estimated at $200 million at her death, the bulk of which would go to John and Caroline. (Interestingly, Jackie made no provision for her sister Lee in her will, "because I have already done so during my lifetime.") Jackie and Maurice began dating in 1981. "Jack was a politician, and he was busy. Need I say more?" said Paris attorney Samuel Pisar, a family friend. "With Onassis, she was a trophy. Tempelsman didn't look on her as a trophy."

"M.T.," as Maurice was called by Jackie's family, spoke fluent French and was also a collector of African art. He did not place any demands on Jackie, and she reciprocated. Throughout the years, Jackie's consort treated her with respect and dignity. He was with her in her living room to lend emotional support when she broke the devastating news of her cancer to John Jr. and Caroline. Tempelsman was the kind of man she deserved to have in her life after so much disappointment in relationships and so much personal growth.

When asked by David Wise, author and White House correspondent during the Kennedy administration, if she might one day write her memoirs, Jackie said that it would probably never happen. For her, a book editor at Doubleday in the last years of her life, it was a matter of perspective and objectivity. People change, she noted, and the person she might have written about thirty years earlier "is not the same person today. The imagination takes over. When Isak Dinesen wrote *Out of Africa*, she left out how badly her husband had treated her," Jackie observed. "She created a new past, in effect."

Now Camelot was just a distant dream, its Queen being laid to rest, her life's history as a woman and national treasure left to biographers and historians to analyze and explain. Ironically, if it had been left up to Jackie, she too might well have "created a new past," much as she did when Jack was murdered. Image and fantasy had always played major roles in the house of Kennedy, and never was that more true than in the way Jackie wished her relationship to Jack be remembered.

The people who were invited to say good-bye at St. Ignatius Loyola were a varied crowd. As well as friends not in the public eye, there were also those present who were famous enough to be instantly recognized—such as a feeble Lady Bird Johnson, using a cane and barely seeming able to walk with the help of an assistant, and the present First Lady, Hillary Rodham Clinton—as well as close family, such as her sister Lee Radziwill (married to stage and screen director Herbert Ross since 1988). Except for the Kennedy matriarch, Rose, who was almost 104 years old and in failing health (and was never even told of Jackie's death), the Kennedy family was all there—those who were born Kennedys and those, like Joan and Ethel, who became Kennedys by the sacrament of marriage. Even though Jackie had remarried, she was still considered a Kennedy, evidenced by the fact that she would be laid to rest next to Jack in the immaculately tended velvet lawns of Arlington National Cemetery. The name of the late Aristotle Onassis was never mentioned by any speaker during the service. Though Ethel was a widow and Joan divorced, as far as the public was concerned they were indelibly and permanently part of the Kennedy family as well.

Jackie and Joan had drifted apart after Joan's divorce simply because their experiences had taken different paths, a natural order of events in the lives of busy women whose own children have children upon whom they begin to focus. In the last couple of years, though, Jackie and Joan became close once again.

In 1992, Joan parlayed her talent and interest in classical music into a book, *The Joy of Classical Music: A Guide for You and Your Family*, which was published by Doubleday and edited by Jackie. Joan frequently found herself in New York for meetings with her editor about the work, and over a two-year period Joan had many visits with Jackie in her New York office and over lunch. "We talked not only about the book, but about everything," Joan would later recall to First Lady historian Carl Sferrazza Anthony. "We congratulated ourselves on how well our children turned out—and said we hoped we had something to do with it. Here we were, things were so different, but through all the changes, we were still sisters-in-law."

"May you always have your beautiful family around you," Jackie had told Joan one day before they parted company. "That's everything, you know."

Outside the church, after the Mass, Joan walked over to Ethel, who was speaking to someone else. As soon as Ethel saw her, she reached out and took both of her sister-in-law's hands into her own. The two spoke privately for a few moments before finally embracing. "Now, you be sure to call me," Ethel was heard to say as Joan walked away. "Oh, I will," Joan said, with a weak smile. "And we'll have lunch." Ethel smiled, seeming eager to see Joan once again, soon.

As a result of Jackie's death, Ethel probably couldn't help but reminisce about the good times as well as the bad that she and her sisters-in-law had shared over a nearly forty-year-long relationship. Friends and relatives say that she was truly distraught by what had happened to Jackie. Just five weeks earlier, Jackie had called Ethel to acknowledge her sixty-sixth birthday. According to what Ethel later recalled, the two shared a laugh when Ethel complained, "I feel more like *ninety*-six." Jackie responded by saying, "Well, if you ask me, you don't look a day over fifty-six."

"If Ethel had only been able to discuss it with her, she would have been surprised to know that Jackie had actually loved her all of those years without reservation," said Joan Braden, who had been a close friend of both women since the early sixties. "Jackie once told me, 'There are certain people you love despite everything else, just because you know they're being so completely true to who they really are. In my life, Ethel Kennedy is one of those people.' The tragedy is that, like most of us, I think Jackie and Ethel always thought they had more time to reach an understanding. But, as it always does, time just slipped away."

One of Ethel's sons, who asked not to be identified, says that his mother took solace in the fact that she had attempted to set matters straight with Jackie. "When she visited Aunt Jackie the day she died, she told her how much she loved her," he says, "and how much she had always meant to her, no matter their differences. However, she said that she wasn't sure that Aunt Jackie understood what she was saying, or if she was even awake. My mother was devastated when she died. I don't think she ever thought it possible that Aunt Jackie would not be here."

"Oh, I'm sure that Ethel was bereft," says Barbara Gibson. "As contentious as their relationship was from time to time, I still think Jackie meant a lot to her and for many reasons, not the least of which is that Jackie was one of the last links to mythical Camelot. They also both experienced the nightmare of witnessing their husbands—brothers— murdered in very much the same truly horrible way. That's a bond they would share, no matter what happened between them."

Leah Mason says that she heard through her connections to the Kennedy family that Ethel was on the verge of collapsing after hearing of Jackie's death. While she wasn't present to witness Ethel's grief, she says, "One of Ethel's friends called me to ask if I still had contact with Ethel. I don't. I haven't seen her in many years. They wanted to know if I was close enough to the Kennedys to go to the reception at Hickory Hill for Jackie, and said that Ethel was much too distraught that day to extend invitations. As she gets older, these Kennedy tragedies are harder for her to take. I didn't feel it appropriate for me to attend any gathering since it had ended so badly between Ethel and me. But I wasn't surprised that she was grieving so terribly. I always felt that losing Jackie would be extremely difficult for Ethel."

At the reception hosted by the family at Hickory Hill after Jackie's burial, Ethel began to cry when speaking of Jackie to Ted in front of a few startled friends. Some observers were surprised at Ethel's emotional display because, as it has been said by those presumptuous enough to think they would know such things, Ethel Kennedy ordinarily never cried. Or, as her husband, Bobby, once decreed, "Kennedys don't cry." It's true that, more often than not, Ethel's eyes showed only the merest flicker of emotion in times of extreme sadness. However, on that afternoon, tears came to Ethel's eyes, perhaps for all that had existed between her and her sister-in-law Jackie.

"I wonder if she knew how much I . . ." Ethel began. She left her sentence hanging. When Ted embraced his deceased brother's wife, she buried her face in his shoulder. After a few moments she forced a smile and, dabbing tears from her eyes, she quipped, "Oh, my! How Jackie would love *this!*"

Acknowledgments and Source Notes

My mother, Rose Marie Magistro Taraborrelli, passed away in August 1996, so she is not here to see the realization of this idea, which she and I had spent so much time discussing over the years. On some level, I know that she is vitally aware of this book, happy about its completion, and pleased with the way Jackie, Ethel, and Joan come to life on these pages. So, as I do with all of my work, I dedicate this book to my mom.

Of course, *Jackie, Ethel, Joan: Women of Camelot* would not have been possible without the assistance of many people and institutions. As mentioned earlier, Maureen Mahon Egen, president of Warner Books, was also my editor on this project. Working with Maureen has been an honor and a pleasure; she set the tone for this work, and she shared my determination that the women be presented in a way that was fair and honest. I so appreciate her encouragement and her thoughtful, insightful viewpoints.

After so many years of developing this project, I was grateful to finally find the right agent to represent it, Mitch Douglas at International Creative Management (ICM). Mitch has taught me much in a short time. He is a true gentleman, and he has remained one in a business that, sadly, sometimes seems short on manners.

Paula Agronick Reuben has been an important ally of mine for so many years now, I am beginning to lose count. However, I do know that this is our fourth book together, and I would like to pay homage to her sense of professionalism and keen editorial eye. Paula also spent untold hours of library time researching the early lives and background history of the Kennedy family, saving me valuable time to concentrate on my immediate subject matter.

A new addition to my team is Charles Casillo, a fine journalist in his own right, who spent seemingly countless hours working with me on this manuscript, fine-tuning the ideas behind it, thinking about the women involved and how to present them fairly and objectively, and adding so very much to this work. I am so indebted to Charles for his time and his great attention to detail. I thank him for not only his professionalism but also his friendship.

John Drayman worked with me as an editor and fact-checker on my previous book, *Sinatra: A Complete Life,* and now again on *Jackie, Ethel, Joan.* Without John, this would be a very different work. I thank him for setting me straight on so many points along the way. He's a fine editor—who came up with the subtitle of this book—but, more important, a good and trusted friend. Great job, Johnny!

This is my fourth book with Cathy Griffin, who is, in my opinion, the best investigative journalist in the business and also an author in her own right. Cathy conducted scores of interviews for this work, locating sources who had lost contact with those in the Kennedy circle. Because there have been so many Kennedy-related books, it would have been easy for her to focus on those who have told their stories many times over. However, it was Cathy's task to find the sources who had not recited their memories so often that they'd become routine. With this work, I believe she has done just that, and I thank her for her perseverance, tenacity, and uncanny ability to not accept no for an answer. Ms. Griffin also provided hundreds of pages of interview transcripts culled from many hours of interviews spent with Sydney Guillaroff regarding Marilyn Monroe's relationships with Jack and Bobby Kennedy.

I must acknowledge Dorie Simmonds for all of her wonderful work for me abroad. She's a delight, always one to keep her head when everyone else's is long gone. We've had many victories along the way.

I can also always count on my extremely capable fact checker and personal copy editor, James Pinkston, to swoop in at the last minute and find that one small yet important error that had somehow managed to evade everyone else's attention. Jim's knowledge of the political landscape of the sixties was invaluable to me during the many editing phases of this book, and I am so fortunate to have him in my corner. He's one of a kind, and most appreciated.

I am so proud to have this book published by Warner Books, and I owe a debt of gratitude to a number of individuals who have contributed to this work. Editorially, I am grateful to Bob Castillo, Gill Kent, Torrey Oberfest, and Frances Jalet-Miller, all of whom did such a wonderful and conscientious job. The wonderful production of this book was the brainchild of Jackie Merri Meyer, Ana Crespo, and Thomas Whatley. My thanks to Emi Battaglia, Jimmy Franco, and Jonathan Hahn for their work in publicity. And I am indebted to Erika Johnsen, Rebecca Oliver, and Nancy Wiese in the Rights department. Also, I was happy to once again work with deputy general counsel Heather Kilpatrick, who always does such a wonderful and thorough job. Finally, I am so appreciative to the two women who assisted me in many different and important ways, Jackie Joiner and Doris Bonair: None of this would have worked without their facilitation of so many of the annoying details. Thank you, ladies.

Thanks also to Iake Eissinmann for his excellent photography.

I owe a debt of gratitude to Wayne Brasler of the University of Chicago, who read this book in early manuscript form, in order to correct any inaccuracies. In fact, Mr. Brasler has read all eight of my books in advance in order to render a much-valued opinion, and I have appreciated his assistance over the years.

Without a loyal team of representatives, an author usually finds himself sitting at home writing books no one ever reads. I thank mine: James Jiminez, Esq., of Gilchrist & Rutter; Ken Deakins, Rae Goldreich, and Terina Hanuscin of Duitch, Franklin and Company. Also, Bart Andrews was a trusted adviser.

Thanks to John Carlino for so many hours of dedication to this project. It would seem that he now understands the Kennedys and Johnsons about as well as anyone I've ever known. Good work, John!

My thanks to James Spada, author of *Peter Lawford: The Man Who Kept the Secrets*, for sharing contacts, telephone numbers, and ideas with me. Thanks also to James Haspiel for tips and advice. Haspiel, once a teenage fan of Marilyn Monroe, is today the foremost authority on her life and career.

For years, Kennedy historian Lester David and I were with the same publisher, Carol Publishing. I had the opportunity to meet with him on several occasions; he provided a wealth of information, and I am indebted to him. I thank the late Mr. David for transcripts of his interviews with the late Kirk LeMoyne Billings and Stephen Smith.

I must thank Barbara Gibson, Rose Kennedy's former secretary, for her cooperation. Ms. Gibson gave much of her time and shared many memories of Jackie, Ethel, Joan, and the other Kennedys. I so appreciate the many interviews.

Jackie Kennedy Onassis's first cousin, John Davis, is the consummate Kennedy scholar, whose books have provided a wealth of information to historians and biographers along the way. I am so grateful to him for his assistance.

Thanks also to Ethel Kennedy's former assistant Leah Mason, who—reluctantly at first out of loyalty to Mrs. Kennedy—gave of her time. Ms. Mason eventually granted me a dozen interviews from Europe, where she now makes her home, and I do appreciate her time.

Thanks to Dale Manesis for all of his help with Kennedy memorabilia that I would never have had access to otherwise; to Linda Robb for support and insight; to Dum Gifford for his advice and encouragement; to Lucianne Goldberg for certain telephone numbers and other assistance; to Jacques Lowe for his encouragement and for the use of his wonderful pictures of the Kennedy family through the years, particularly that used on the jacket of this book.

Thanks to Camille Sartiano-Glowitz for all of the travel accommodations. You've been so helpful, and are appreciated.

My appreciation, as always, to Stephen Gregory, who encouraged me in this project in its early days with Warner. He is, and will always be, a dearly valued friend on whose care and judgment I can truly depend.

And thanks also to all of those who assisted me in a number of tangible and intangible ways, including Richard Tyler Jordan, Dan Sterchele, Ray Trim, Jeff Hare, Al Kramer, RuPaul, David Bruner, George Solomon, Tony O'Dell, Sven Paardekooper, Billy Barnes, Hillel Black, Tony and Marilyn Caruselle, Roby Gayle, Kathryn Christy, Louise Schillaci, Barbara Cowan, Sonja Kravchuk, David Spiro, Barbara Ormsby, Rick Starr, Geordie MacMinn, John Passantino, Linda DeStefano, Ken Bostic, Mr. and Mrs. Joseph Tumolo, Daniel Tumolo, Reed Sparling, Mr. and Mrs. Adolph Steinlen, David and Frances Snyder, Abby and Maddy Snyder, Maribeth and Don Rothell, Mary Alvarez, Mark Bringelson, Hope Levy, Tom Lavagnino, Iake and Alex Eissinmann, Michael Bonnabel, and Anne McVey.

All of my thanks and gratitude is also extended to Andy Steinlen. He is an important person not only in my life, but also in the lives of so many others he has touched, inspired, motivated, and—sometimes even more important—made laugh. He gives of himself so unselfishly, and always with love.

Thanks to my wonderfully supportive family, Roz and Bill Barnett, Zachary and Jessica Barnett, Rock and Rosemarie Taraborrelli, Rocky and Vincent Taraborrelli, Arnold Taraborrelli, and of course, Rydell and Dylan. Special thanks to my father, Rocco, who has always been my inspiration. He has taught me more than he knows just by shining example.

And to those readers of my work who have followed my career over the years, who have sent me so many letters of support and encouragement (and who have also doled out harsh criticism when necessary), I thank you for taking my books to bed with you. If reading this one keeps you up for just a fraction of the number of nights it kept me awake while writing it, then I've done my job.

A note about the Secret Service agents interviewed for this work: Cathy Griffin and I interviewed a number of Secret Service agents while doing research for this book. They provided great insight into the private lives of the Kennedy wives and how the women dealt with their husbands.

On October 10, 1998, in Louisville, Kentucky, the Association of Former Agents of the U.S. Secret Service Inc. chastised several colleagues at its annual meeting for speaking to reporters such as myself about their work during the Kennedy administration. The group passed a resolution expressing disapproval of the agents' actions, and—according to George Lardner, Jr., of the *Washington Post*—P. Hamilton Brown, the association's secretary and one of the leading advocates of the resolution, went so far as to say in a speech that it would have been better if a contract had been put out on the agents who spoke to Seymour Hersh for his 1997 book, *The Dark Side of Camelot.* James E. LeGette, the president of the association, declined to discuss the resolution, saying, "It was a private business meeting, a private affair. I wouldn't say we censured anyone. There's no physical action or anything coming out of this." Brown, who also worked on the Kennedy detail, added, "We got a lot of heat from our members. A lot of people thought they [the agents] were talking out of school."

A copy of the resolution was sent to Secret Service Director Lew Merletti who, in turn, sent a memo to agents that sternly cautioned

them to never disclose any aspect of the personal lives of their pro-
tectees.

Afterward, several of the agents who had been interviewed for the
first time about Jacqueline Kennedy, specifically regarding her feelings
about her husband's relationship with Marilyn Monroe, asked that
their names not be used in this work. Also, though the participation of
certain other agents may be clear in the text, they asked to not be formally acknowledged in the source notes. Others asked for quote approval, meaning that they wanted to review in advance quotes of
theirs that would appear in this book. In all fairness to these brave
men who took such pride in their work for the Kennedy administration, the author honored each of their wishes. I so appreciate their
input and cooperation.

Finally, my appreciation goes out to the following agents who spoke
openly and freely and did not ask for anonymity: Larry Newman,
Joseph Paolella, and Anthony Sherman.

A note about documents from the Federal Bureau of Investigation: First
of all, my thanks to Michael J. Ravnitzky for his assistance in helping
me obtain FBI files and for his understanding of the complicated procedures involved.

Over the years, many authors have attempted to utilize FBI documents to research books involving the Kennedys. However, those who
have been successful have done so without ever explaining exactly
which of the thousands of documents compiled by that organization
over the years are of any value. Many are filled with rumor and innuendo and, as such, are worthless. Others actually have real value as
source material.

As a researcher and author, I have always wished that other writers
who had covered this particular territory would have provided the FBI
file numbers for the more reliable documents used as source material.
It's never happened, to my knowledge, making it necessary for every
writer along the way to start from the beginning in tracking down per-
tinent FBI files, reviewing thousands of documents in search of those
few that are worthwhile. One of the most time-consuming aspects of
the FOIA process—the search through an agency's holdings for requested information—can be eliminated if one is able to provide the
FBI's own file number. I am herein providing those numbers for future

researchers, historians, and authors. These numbers will mean nothing to the general reader but hopefully will save other writers months of research time and expense.

These are the documents that were utilized for this book:

For Marilyn Monroe: HQ-1050040018; LA-1630001398; LA-1000022505.

For John Fitzgerald Kennedy: HQ-0090037991; HQ-0090037800; HQ-0940037374; HQ-0090039836; HQ-0560002534; HQ-1570000929; HQ-0620109060; HQ-0870138553; HQ-0620107481; HQ-0620107506; HQ-0620108641; HQ-1050111811; HQ-0940037374; (Assassination) HQ-0620109060.

For Joseph P. Kennedy: P.HQ-0940037808.

For Robert F. Kennedy: HQ-0440024721; HQ-0620076943; HQ-1180005869; HQ-1200009166; HQ-0770051387; HFO-0770037011; HQ-0440089006; HQ-1570000768; HQ-0890003213; HQ-0620107624; HQ-0620000587; F. HQ-0620109131.

To obtain any file, write to: FBI Freedom of Information Act Unit, Office of Public and Congressional Affairs, Federal Bureau of Investigation, 935 Pennsylvania Avenue N.W., Washington, DC, 20535-0000, and request, by name and file number, the files of interest under the provisions of the Freedom of Information Act (5 USC 552). List which files are needed, and also agree to pay reasonable fees up to twenty dollars without additional permission, so that the FBI can quickly process the request. (Files are just a dime a page, with the first hundred pages free.)

As well as documents about the Kennedys from the Federal Bureau of Investigation, I reviewed J. Edgar Hoover's Official and Confidential Files. A word to the wise about Hoover's papers: Most are filled with rumor, innuendo, and stories that cannot be substantiated. It was my decision not to use any of J. Edgar Hoover's files as source material for this book.

I also reviewed papers from the National Archives II in College Park, Maryland, released under the Assassination Records Review Board.

A note about correspondence and telephone conversations between the Kennedys and the Johnsons: I am so greatly indebted to the staff of the Lyndon Baines Johnson Library for their help in compiling documents from the decades of correspondence between Jackie Kennedy Onassis and President Lyndon Johnson and his wife, Lady Bird Johnson, used as research material in this work. In particular, the letters exchanged between Jackie and Lady Bird over more than a forty-year period speak to a strong friendship. Mrs. Johnson, a wise woman who has always understood the importance of historical documentation, also made available certain letters that are not available for general usage in the library. I have such admiration for her and thank her so much for her generosity and understanding.

I would also like to acknowledge Linda M. Seelke, the library's archivist, for her dedication to her work and for her assistance to me and my researchers. As well as Ms. Seelke, I would like to thank Harry J. Middleton, director of the library, for his help in many ways, and also for the personal interview he granted to Cathy Griffin on September 28, 1998. My thanks also go to Tina Houston, the supervisory archivist. Also a special thanks to Matthew Hanson, Deirdre Doughty, Mollie McDonnold, and Kate Bronstad.

I urge any researcher working on a book involving President Lyndon Johnson even tangentially to contact the Lyndon Baines Johnson Library in Austin, Texas, for they will make your work much easier.

Thanks also to Lady Bird Johnson's assistant, Shirley James.

Oral Histories

I could not have written *Jackie, Ethel, Joan* without using as source material the many Oral Histories provided by the John F. Kennedy Library.

Begun in 1964 with a grant from the Carnegie Corporation, the Oral History program is one of the oldest continuing activities of the Kennedy Library. Modeled on the Columbia University oral history program, its goal is to collect, preserve, and make available interviews conducted with individuals who have recollections of events and people associated with the Kennedy family.

Many of these interview subjects have given not just one but numerous Oral Histories, some as many as five conducted over a span of years.

In the past, these Oral Histories have been criticized by some

Kennedy historians as not containing anything of a revelatory nature. My researchers and I did not find that to be true. Of course, the usefulness of these interviews to a biographer—and the informative nature of the stories found in these histories—depends on what the writer is searching for exactly, and whether or not his particular subject matter has been written about in the past. For instance, if one were writing a so-called exposé on Jackie Kennedy, this material would not prove to be beneficial. (However, the Jacqueline Kennedy Onassis Newsclipping Files at the John F. Kennedy Library do contain hundreds of printed articles and full-length stories that I found to be useful in my work.) Also, a great deal of material has been archived—hundreds of thousands of pages, in fact—and one has to go through all of it to find the fascinating nuggets. Because my subject matter, the relationship between the three Kennedy sisters-in-law, has never before been examined (and because my researchers and I have been diligent over the years in reading these many transcripts), we found a wealth of stories, remembrances, and other fascinating details.

My thanks to the following staff members of the John F. Kennedy Presidential Library who assisted me and my researchers: William Johnson, Ron Whealon, June Payne, Maura Porter, Susan D'Entrement, Kyoko Yamamoto, Allen Goodrich, and James Hill.

Also, I would like to mention that David Powers, former special assistant to President John Kennedy, was the first curator of the late leader's library. Mr. Powers was an unemployed veteran living with his widowed sister and her ten children when he first met JFK after the Second World War. The man who would become president was looking for help in running his first political campaign for the House of Representatives. After Mr. Powers signed on, a friendship was formed that lasted until JFK's assassination in November 1963. David Powers, always the Kennedy loyalist, was extremely reluctant to speak to me for this book. However, he did fill out two lengthy questionnaires and then, finally, submitted to a followup telephone interview. No mention of the Kennedy Library is complete without a nod to Mr. Powers, who died in April 1998, at the age of eighty-five.

The John Fitzgerald Kennedy Library collection of Oral Histories totals more than 1,800 interviews. I stand in particular debt to the Oral History interviewers, the volunteers who conducted interviews with JFK's and RFK's family, friends, and associates, most notably L.J.

Hackman and Roberta Greene. I utilized the following interviews throughout *Jackie, Ethel, Joan* for a more complete understanding of the Kennedys, as well as background about the major events and personalities of their times. (Except where noted, all of the Histories can be found in the John Fitzgerald Kennedy Library archives.) I am also grateful to Marianne Masterson, Leanne Johnson, and Doug Anderson for assisting me in the reading and analyzing of all of these transcripts.

It would be impossible—and impractical, given space limitations—to cite paragraph by paragraph how these Oral Histories were used; they were that important in the general shaping of this work. However, anyone interested in reading the Oral Histories should avail himself of that opportunity by contacting the John Fitzgerald Kennedy Library in Boston.

The following Oral Histories were utilized in this work:

Joseph Alsop, journalist, author, Kennedy friend and associate; Lawrence Arata, White House upholsterer; Janet Lee Auchincloss, Jackie's mother; Isaac Avery, White House carpenter; Letitia Baldrige, White House social secretary; Joanne Barboza, waitress at Kennedy home, Hyannisport.

Albert Wesley "Wes" Barthelmes, press secretary to Robert F. Kennedy; Charles Bartlett, journalist, friend of President Kennedy; Jack L. Bell, journalist, Associated Press; Leonard Bernstein, composer, conductor, New York Philharmonic Orchestra; Kirk LeMoyne "Lem" Billings, Kennedy family friend and associate; Dinah Bridge, Kennedy friend and associate, Great Britain; Edmund Pat Brown, governor of California (interview conducted by the Lyndon Baines Johnson Library); Preston Bruce, White House doorman; Traphes L. Bryant, White House electrician; McGeorge Bundy, special assistant to the President for National Security Affairs; Carter Burden, New York society and political figure, worker in Robert F. Kennedy's New York Senate office (interviewed for RFK Oral History Project); Kenneth Burke, White House policeman; George Burkley, physician to the President; Elaine Burnham, office worker, John F. Kennedy's presidential campaign, Oregon.

Rev. John Cavanaugh, Kennedy family friend, associate, Roman Catholic priest, University of Notre Dame; Barbara J. Coleman, journalist, White House press aide, member of Robert Kennedy's Senate staff, and presidential campaign aide; Peter Cronin, reporter, United Press International; (Cardinal) Richard Cushing, Roman Catholic Archbishop of Boston.

Andrew Dazzi, journalist, *Boston Globe*; Margaret Dixon, journalist, managing editor, *Baton Rouge Morning Advocate*; Angier Biddle Duke, chief of protocol, White House and State Department; Frederick Dutton, special assistant to President Kennedy.

John English, New York political figure, political aide to Robert F. Kennedy (interview conducted for the RFK Oral History Project); Rowland Evans, journalist, *New York Herald Tribune*, syndicated columnist.

Paul B. Fay, Jr., friend of President Kennedy and undersecretary of the Navy; Richard Flood, friend and classmate of Joseph P. Kennedy, Jr., at Harvard and worker for John F. Kennedy's congressional and Senate campaigns; Edward Folliard, journalist, *Washington Post*; Hugh Fraser, Kennedy family friend and associate.

Edward Gallagher, Kennedy family friend; Elizabeth Gatov (interview conducted by the Women in Politics Oral History Project, University of California, Berkeley); Dun Gifford, legislative assistant to Senator Edward M. Kennedy, national presidential campaign assistant to Robert F. Kennedy, staff member, secretary's office, Department of Housing and Urban Development (interview conducted for the RFK Oral History Project); Roswell Gilpatrick, deputy secretary of Defense; John Glenn, Project Mercury astronaut; Grace DeMonaco, Princess of Monaco; Katherine Graham, publisher, *Washington Post* (interview conducted by the Lyndon Baines Johnson Library); Edith Green (interview conducted for the RFK Oral History Project); Jeff Greenfield, legislative assistant to Robert F. Kennedy, member of Robert F. Kennedy's presidential campaign staff (interview conducted for the RFK Oral History Project); Josephine Grennan, Irish cousin of John F. Kennedy; Michael Gretchen, West Virginia labor leader; Charles E. Guggenheim, film producer, political media consultant for Robert Kennedy's Senate campaign and presidential campaign, producer of *RFK Remembered* (1968) (interview conducted for the RFK Oral History Project); Edwin O. Guthman, editor, *Seattle Times*, director of public information, Department of Justice, press assistant to Robert F. Kennedy; Milton Gwirtzman, presidential adviser, speechwriter, Robert Kennedy's senate campaign, director of public affairs, Robert

Kennedy's presidential campaign, co-author (with William vanden Heuvel) of *On His Own: RFK, 1964–1968* (interview conducted for the RFK Oral History Project).

David Hackett, friend of Robert F. Kennedy, executive director, President's Committee on Juvenile Delinquency and Youth Crime, member, John F. Kennedy's and Robert F. Kennedy's presidential campaign staffs (interview conducted for the RFK Oral History Project); Kay Halle (Katherine Murphy), author and Kennedy family friend; John Harlle, Kennedy associate, chairman, Federal Maritime Commission; Averell (William) Harriman (interview conducted for the RFK Oral History Project); Harrison Gilbert, editor, publisher, *New Republic*; Andrew J. Hatcher, assistant press secretary to John F. Kennedy; Anne Hearst, West Virginia political figure; William Randolph Hearst, owner, editor, Hearst Newspapers; Mary (Welsh) Hemingway, wife of Ernest Hemingway; Louella Hennessey, Kennedy family nurse; David P. Highley, John F. Kennedy's Washington barber (written statement); Jacqueline (Provost) Hirsh, French language instructor to President Kennedy's children (1966); Harry G. Hoffman, journalist, editor, *Charleston Gazette*; John Jay Hooker, member, John F. Kennedy's presidential campaign staff; Claude E. Hooten, member, John F. Kennedy's presidential campaign staff; Ralph Hooten, classmate of John F. Kennedy at Choate Academy and Princeton University, member, John F. Kennedy's presidential campaign staff, special assistant, Equal Opportunity Program, Department of the Army; Oscar L. Huber, Roman Catholic priest who administered Last Rites to President Kennedy in Dallas; Hubert H. Humphrey, Vice President of the United States, presidential candidate (interview conducted for the RFK Oral History Project and also by the Lyndon Baines Johnson Library); Francis T. Hurley, Roman Catholic monsignor, assistant secretary, National Catholic Welfare Conference.

Benjamin Jacobson, Kennedy associate, Boston; Jacob Javitz, Senator from New York (interview conducted for the RFK Oral History Project.); Rafer Johnson, friend and aide to Robert F. Kennedy (interview conducted for the RFK Oral History Project.)

Joseph J. Karitas, White House painter; Nicholas Katsenbach (interview conducted for the RFK Oral History Project.); Mary Kelly, Oregon political figure; John H. Kelso, journalist, *Boston Post*; Robert Francis Kennedy, brother of President Kennedy, Attorney General of the United States, Senator from New York; Rose Fitzgerald Kennedy, wife of Joseph P. Kennedy, mother of President Kennedy (interview conducted by the Herbert Hoover Library Foundation.); Fletcher Knebel, journalist, Cowles Publications, *Look*; Laura Bergquist Knebel, journalist, *Look* (interview conducted for the RFK Oral History Project); John H. Knowles, classmate of Robert F. Kennedy, Harvard College, general director, Massachusetts General Hospital (1962–72) (interview conducted for the RFK Oral History Project); Joseph Kraft, journalist, syndicated columnist (interview conducted for the RFK Oral History Project); Jerome Kretchmer, member, New York State Assembly from Manhattan, campaign worker, Robert Kennedy's Senate and presidential campaigns (interview conducted for the RFK Oral History Project); Arthur Krock, journalist, *New York Times*, Kennedy family associate.

Donald Larrabee, journalist, Griffin-Larrabee News Bureau; Fridda Laski, wife of Harold Laski of the London School of Economics; Peter Lawford, actor, brother-in-law of President Kennedy (edited draft transcript); William Lawrence, journalist, *New York Times*, news commentator, American Broadcasting Company; Helen Lempart, secretary, Senator John F. Kennedy's Washington office and White House; Anthony Lewis, journalist, *New York Times*, Washington bureau, London bureau (interview conducted for the RFK Oral History Project, portions closed); Samuel B. Lewis, vice president, general manager, Carlyle Hotel, New York; Evelyn Lincoln, John F. Kennedy's personal secretary (interview conducted by Barry Goldman for *Manuscripts* magazine in 1990); Gould Lincoln, journalist, editor, *Washington Star*; Walter Lippmann, journalist, *New York Herald Tribune*, *Newsweek*; Kathleen Louchhmeim (Katie Scofield), director, women's activities, Democratic National Committee, deputy assistant secretary of state for Public Affairs.

Torbert MacDonald (Hart), roommate of John F. Kennedy at Harvard, Representative from Massachusetts; Ralph McGill (Emerson), publisher, *Atlanta Constitution*; Mary McGrory, features writer, *Washington Evening Star*; Mary McNeely, Massachusetts political figure; Frank Mankiewicz, press secretary to Robert F. Kennedy (interview conducted for the RFK Oral History Project) (unedited transcript); Andrew Minihan, Irish cousin of John F. Kennedy, mayor, New Ross;

Patrick J. Patsy Mulkern, Kennedy friend and political associate, Massachusetts political figure.

Esther Newberg, staff assistant to Robert F. Kennedy (interview conducted for the RFK Oral History Project).

Kenneth O'Donnell, special assistant to the President (interview conducted by the Lyndon Baines Johnson Library); Andrew Oehmann, executive assistant to the Attorney General (interview conducted for the RFK Oral History Project); Frank O'Ferrall, Kennedy family friend, London; Jacqueline Kennedy Onassis (interview conducted by the Lyndon Baines Johnson Library, 1974).

Nelson Pierce, White House usher; Charles Roberts, contributing editor, *Newsweek*.

Pierre Salinger, press secretary to John F. Kennedy (interview conducted for the RFK Oral History Project); Dore Schary, playwright, motion picture producer; Arthur Schlesinger, special assistant to the President; John L. Seigenthaler, reporter, editor, the *Tennessean*, Nashville, aide to Robert F. Kennedy; Maud Shaw, Kennedy family governess; Sargent R. Shriver, director, Businessmen for Kennedy, director, Civil Rights Division, Democratic National Committee, director, Farmers for Kennedy; Carroll Kilpatrick, journalist, *Washington Post*; Eunice Kennedy Shriver, sister of President Kennedy, executive vice president, Joseph P. Kennedy, Jr. Foundation; Hugh Sidey, journalist, *Time*, *Life*; George Smathers, Senator from Florida (interview conducted by the U.S. Senate Historical Office); Theodore C. Sorenson, staff assistant, speechwriter to Senator John F. Kennedy, special counsel to the President; Charles Spalding, Kennedy friend and campaign aide.

George Taylor, John F. Kennedy's valet and chauffeur, Boston; Cordenia Thaxton, White House maid; Janet G. Travell, physician to President Kennedy; Stanley Tretick, photographer, United Press International, *Look*; Dorothy Tubridy, Irish friend of the Kennedy family.

Jack Valenti, special assistant to Lyndon Baines Johnson; Sandy Vanocur, journalist, NBC News (interview conducted for the RFK Oral History Project); Sue Mortenson Vogelsinger, secretary to John F. Kennedy; William Walton, artist, friend of Robert Kennedy, coordinator of Robert Kennedy's 1968 presidential campaign in New York (interview conducted for the RFK Oral History Project).

Ernest Warren, reporter, Associated Press; Bernard West, chief usher, White House; Irwin M. Williams, White House gardener.

Personal Papers, Archives, and Manuscripts

As important as the Oral Histories were to this book, the personal papers, archives, and manuscripts housed at the Kennedy Library were just as vital. I must thank the many authors, historians, and researchers in the Boston and Washington area—too many to note here, but all have received personal letters of gratitude from me—who spent, literally, years going through all of the hundreds of archives and manuscripts, narrowing them down to what follows, and then making them available to me for *Jackie, Ethel, Joan.*

Archival materials and manuscripts relating to the following individuals were used as source material for this book:

Kirk LeMoyne (Lem) Billings (includes letters from JFK); McGeorge Bundy (includes fascinating and useful transcriptions of presidential recordings on the Cuban Missile Crisis); Clark Clifford (Kennedy family attorney, 1957–61; includes insightful memos); Barbara J. Coleman (journalist and White House press aide and aide in Robert Kennedy's presidential campaign; papers include miscellaneous correspondence between Jackie and Ethel); Dorothy H. Davies (staff assistant to JFK; includes correspondence and memorandums).

Katherine Evans (including condolence letters and correspondence to Mrs. Robert F. Kennedy, drafts and copies of acknowledgments); James J. Fahey (author; includes originals and copies of newspaper articles about the Kennedys); Paul Fay (personal friend of JFK's and Under Secretary of the Navy; includes personal correspondence between Fay and JFK, as well as original manuscript and notes relating to his book, *The Pleasure of His Company*); Dun Gifford (including correspondence and campaign materials having to do with Joan Kennedy's involvement in Ted Kennedy's senatorial campaigns); Roswell Gilpatrick (deputy Secretary of Defense, friend of Jackie Kennedy's; contains copious correspondence, memorandums, appointment files, and daily diaries, with correspondence to and from Jackie Kennedy Onassis); Doris Goodwin Kearns (historian and author; contains copious and fascinating notes, drafts, interview transcripts, edited and unedited material from her book *The Kennedys and The Fitzgeralds*).

Dave Hackett; Chester (Chet) Huntley (broadcast journalist; contains correspondence and notes relating to his coverage of the assassination and funeral of JFK); Edward (Ted) Moore Kennedy (Senate files); John Fitzgerald Kennedy Personal Papers; John Fitzgerald Kennedy President's Office Files (the working files of JFK as maintained by his secretary, Evelyn Lincoln; includes correspondence, secretary's files and special events files through the years of the administration); John Fitzgerald Kennedy White House Social Files (includes papers and records of Jackie Kennedy's and the White House Social Office under the direction of Letitia Baldrige and Pamela Turnure); Robert Francis Kennedy (the author's researcher utilized only the Attorney General Papers 1961–1964); Rose Fitzgerald Kennedy (correspondence, family papers, research, background materials and drafts of her memoirs, *Times to Remember*).

Evelyn Lincoln (personal secretary to JFK; includes research materials, notes, and other papers pertaining to her book, *My Twelve Years with John F. Kennedy*); Frank Mankiewicz; Jacqueline Kennedy Onassis (includes condolence letters, tribute, Mass cards relating to JFK's death; not particularly enlightening); Kenneth O'Donnell (special assistant to JFK; includes correspondence, audiotapes, news clippings, pamphlets, and memorabilia, as well as notes and drafts of *Johnny, We Hardly Knew Ye*, written with Joe McCarthy); David Powers (includes copious correspondence, audiotapes, news clippings, and memorabilia).

Pierre Salinger (press secretary to JFK; includes correspondence, press briefings, and, most important to my research, press releases and telephone memoranda); Arthur Schlesinger (special assistant to the President; includes correspondence, drafts, and copious research materials, book drafts, and manuscripts for his wonderful books *A Thousand Days* and *Robert Kennedy and His Times*; a treasure trove for any Kennedy historian); Theodore Sorenson (special counsel to the President; includes manuscripts and personal papers, as well as magazine and newspaper articles); Jean Stein (author of *American Journey: The Times of Robert Kennedy*; another treasure trove that includes tapes and transcripts or Oral History interviews, unedited drafts of her excellent book, as well as notes and other background material).

Janet Travell (physician to JFK; includes correspondence relating to his health); William Walton (journalist, painter, and Kennedy family friend; includes copious correspondence); Theodore White (journalist and author of *The Making of the President* and other works; the mother lode for any Kennedy biographer, including all of White's outlines, notes, drafts, proofs with annotations, correspondence, notes and transcripts from his interview with Jacqueline Kennedy after JFK's assassination); United States Secret Service Papers and Files (includes all records of JFK's and Jackie's activities from 1960 to 1963; also lists visitors to the White House).

Also utilized:

Clay Blair Jr. Papers (American Heritage Center at the University of Wyoming); Charles Higham Collection of Papers (Occidental College, Eagle Rock, California); Joseph Kennedy Correspondence (House of Lords Library, London); Peter Lawford Files (Special Collection Division, Hayden Library, Arizona State University, Tempe); Jacqueline Onassis Oral Histories (Lyndon B. Johnson Library); Secret Service Gate Logs (JFK Library, visits filed chronologically); Sidney Skolsky Papers (Academy of Motion Pictures Arts and Sciences); Special Collections of the Mugar Memorial Library (Boston University, including the papers of Laura Bergquist, Fletcher Knebel, and David Halberstam); Donald Spoto Papers (Academy of Motion Pictures Arts and Sciences); Gloria Swanson Papers (Hoblitzelle Theatre Arts Library, University of Texas, Austin); Harold Tinker Papers (Brown University); White House Central Subject Files (JFK Library); White House Files of Chester Clifton, Jr. (JFK Library); White House Press Releases (JFK Library); White House Telephone Logs (JFK Library, calls filed chronologically); Zolotow Collection (Humanities Research Center, University of Texas).

In January 1999, the Secret Service released Jacqueline Kennedy Onassis File 1968: Protection of President Kennedy's Children. Material from this voluminous file was utilized throughout this book.

Arts & Entertainment

The Arts & Entertainment Network *Biography* series was invaluable to my research. My thanks to the staff of A&E who assisted me in my research, providing me with tapes, transcripts, and other materials. The following documentaries were reviewed as part of my research, and can all be obtained at biography.com, or by calling 1-800-344-6336: "Assassination and Aftermath: The Death of JFK and the Warren Report"; "Bay of Pigs/Cuban Missile Crisis"; "Chappaquiddick"; "Conspiracies"; "Kennedy and Nixon"; "Joseph Kennedy, Sr.: Father of an American Dynasty"; "John F. Kennedy: A Personal Story"; "Ted Kennedy: Tragedy, Scandal and Redemption"; "Magic Moments, Tragic Times: Camelot and Chappaquiddick"; "The Men Who Killed Kennedy"; "Jackie O: In a Class of Her Own" (from which some quotes by John Davis, Letitia Baldrige, and Pierre Salinger were culled); "Christina Onassis"; "Jacqueline Kennedy Onassis"; "RFK Assassination/'68 Democratic Convention"; "Helen Thomas: The First Lady of the Press"; "Lady Bird Johnson: The Texas Wildflower"; "Lyndon Johnson: Triumph and Tragedy"; "Presidents in Crisis: Johnson Quits and Nixon Resigns"; "Secret Service."

Institutions and Organizations

Numerous organizations and institutions provided me with articles, documents, audio interviews, video interviews, transcripts, and other material that was either utilized directly in *Jackie, Ethel, Joan* or for purposes of background. Unfortunately, it is not possible to thank all of the individuals associated with each organization who were so helpful and gave of their time; however, I would at least like to express my gratitude to the following institutions:

American Film Institute Library; Amherst College Library; the Archdiocese of Boston; Assassinations Archives and Research Center (Washington, D.C.); Associated Press Office (Athens, Greece); the Bancroft Library (University of California, Berkeley); Baylor University Institute for Oral History; *Boston Herald* Archives; the Beverly Hills Library; Boston Public Library; British Broadcasting Corporation; Brooklyn College Library; University of California, Los Angeles (Department of Special Collections); California State Archives (Sacramento); Columbia University Rare Book and Manuscript Collection; Cornell University Libraries; Duke University Library; Federal Bureau of Investigation; Gerald R. Ford Library; the Glendale

Library; Hayden Library; Arizona State University; the Hollywood Library; the Houghton Library (Harvard University); Lyndon Baines Johnson Library; John Fitzgerald Kennedy Library; the Margaret Herrick Library (Academy of Motion Pictures Arts and Sciences); Manhattanville College Library; the Andrew Mellon Library (Choate Rosemary Hall); National Archives; National Security Agency (Central Security Service); New York City Municipal Archives; New York Public Library; New York University Library; Occidental College (Eagle Rock, California); Palm Beach Historical Society; Princeton University Library; Franklin D. Roosevelt Library; the Stanford University Libraries; Department of the Treasury; United States Secret Service; Westport Public Library; Harry S Truman Library; Yale University Library.

Sources

It is impossible to write accurately about anyone's life without many reliable witnesses to provide a range of different viewpoints. A biography of this kind stands or falls on the cooperation and frankness of those involved in the story. Not surprisingly, Jackie Bouvier Kennedy (via her spokeswoman, Nancy Tuckerman), Ethel Skakel Kennedy (via a sharply worded letter from a Kennedy family attorney), and Joan Bennett Kennedy (via a friendly and forthcoming letter about her present life that—so typical of Joan—was one of the nicest declines I've ever received) all chose to not be formally interviewed for this work. However, a great number of other people went out of their way to assist me over the years. More than three hundred friends, relatives, politicians, journalists, socialites, lawyers, celebrities, Kennedy business executives and former executives, Kennedy family political associates, as well as foes, classmates, teachers, neighbors, friends, newspeople, and archivists were contacted in preparation for this book.

The Kennedys (just by virtue of their annoyance at the heavy scrutiny they have been under for years) have always been an extremely private and sometimes suspicious family, who have been known to oust those from their circle who speak of them to the press. As recently as July 1999, certain longtime friends of the family were ostracized and not invited to John Kennedy Jr.'s funeral simply because they had spoken kindly of John on television programs paying tribute to him. For what they view as good reason, many of my sources asked for anonymity. Some of these sources are not only close friends of the Kennedys but also family members anxious to set the record straight on certain issues but not eager to see their names in print. As I always do, I am respecting all requests for anonymity. I sincerely thank those sources for their assistance, and for putting their relationship with the Kennedy family on the line for the sake of this book's accuracy.

Of course, those many people who spoke to me and my researchers on the record, allowing their names to be used, are truly courageous, for they are willing to risk their relationships with the family for truth's sake. It's never easy for a source close to the subject of an unauthorized biography to give his or her permission to be identified in the text of such a book. Who knows what the ramifications will be when the work is published? I am so grateful to all of the people named below who gave of their time and energy, and allowed the revelation of their identities.

Whenever practical, I have provided sources within the body of the text. The following notes indicate just some of the sources used for each part of this book, and the names of some of those who were interviewed from the beginning of official research for this book to the end, January 1990 through January 1999. These notes are by no means comprehensive—for instance, they do not repeat the earlier-cited names whose important Oral Histories, papers, and manuscripts I utilized—but are intended to give the reader a general overview of my research. Also included here are occasional comments of an extraneous but, hopefully, informative nature.

Since chapter notes are usually not of interest to the general reader, I have chosen a more general—and practical, for space limitations—mode of source identification, as opposed to specific page or line notations.

Also, because of their voluminous nature, I have made the choice of not including complete listings of the scores of magazines and newspaper articles that were referenced. It would simply be impractical to do so, considering space limitations. The few mentioned within these pages are included because I felt they were important to recognize.

As a note to the researcher: It is no longer necessary for scholars, historians, and other interested readers to know the date of publication and name of the company that published any particular book in order to obtain it. Virtually all of the volumes I utilized for this work can be obtained on the Internet by simply referring to the title of the book and/or the author. The author recommends amazon.com or barnesandnoble.com.

Also, I would like to especially cite the work of biographers C. David Heymann (*A Woman Named Jackie* and *RFK*), Jerry Oppenheimer (*The Other Mrs. Kennedy*), Laurence Leamer (*The Kennedy Women*), Peter Collier and David Horowitz (*The Kennedys: An American Drama*), John Davis (*The Bouviers*), Carl Sferazza Anthony (*First Ladies* [volumes 1 and 2] and *Jackie Kennedy Onassis: As We Remember Her*), and Doris Kearns Goodwin (*The Fitzgeralds and The Kennedys: An American Saga*), for their published words provided great insight and illumination.

Joan . . . ; Jackie . . . ; Ethel . . . ; and the Secret Service; Jack Defeats Nixon; The Pre-Inaugural Gala; Jack; The Five Inaugural Balls; Bobby

As well as having utilized the previously cited Oral Histories, personal interviews were conducted with Secret Service agents Larry Newman, Joseph Paolella, and others requesting anonymity who assisted in reconstructing certain conversations; Jacques Lowe, Leo Damore, Liz Carpenter, Sancy Newman, Oleg Cassini, Helen Thomas and John Davis (both present at the inauguration), Hugh Sidey, Jim Whiting, Lem Billings, James Bacon, Nancy Bacon, Marvin Richardson, Morton Downey, Jr., Barbara Gibson, David Powers (questionnaire), George Smathers, Letitia Baldrige, Raymond Strait, Jack Valenti, Walter Cronkite, and Stanley Tretick.

Volumes consulted: *John F. Kennedy, President*, by Hugh Sidey; *A Very Personal Presidency*, by Hugh Sidey; *With Kennedy*, by Pierre Salinger; *The Coming of the New Deal*, by Arthur M. Schlesinger; *A Tribute to Jacqueline Kennedy Onassis* (privately printed, by Doubleday, 1995); *In My Own Fashion*, by Oleg Cassini; *A Thousand Days of Magic*, by Oleg Cassini; *Kennedy and the Press*, by Allen H. Lerman and Harold W. Chase; *Counsel to the President*, by Clifford Clark; *A Hero for Our Times*, by Kenneth O'Donnell and David Powers, with

Joe McCarthy; *Of Diamonds and Diplomats*, by Letitia Baldrige; *The Making of the President 1960*, by Theodore White; *Sargent Shriver: A Candid Portrait*, by Robert A. Leston; *Kennedy Justice*, by Victor Navasky; *Those Fabulous Kennedy Women*, by H. A. William Carr; *The Kennedy Family*, by Joseph Dinneen; *The Cape Cod Years of John Fitzgerald Kennedy*, by Leo Damore; *JFK: Reckless Youth*, by Nigel Hamilton; *The Founding Father*, by Richard J. Whalen; *The Power Lovers*, by Myra MacPherson; *A Hero for Our Time*, by Ralph G. Martin; *Kennedy*, by Jacques Lowe; *Ethel*, by Lester David; *Bobby*, by Lester David; *The Consent of the Governed*, by Arthur Krock; *Six Presidents, Too Many Wars*, by Bill Lawrence; *Atget's Gardens*, by William Howard Adams; *Life with Rose Kennedy*, by Barbara Gibson and Caroline Latham; *Rose*, by Gail Cameron; *My Twelve Years with John F. Kennedy*, by Evelyn Lincoln; *The Dark Side of Camelot*, by Seymour Hersh; *Jacqueline Kennedy: First Lady*, by Jacques Lowe; *An Honorable Profession*, edited by Pierre Salinger, Frank Mankiewicz, Edwin Guthman, and John Seigenthaler; *Seeds of Destruction*, by Ralph G. Martin; *Johnny, We Hardly Knew Ye*, by Kenny P. O'Donnell and David F. Powers; *One Special Summer*, by Lee Bouvier Radziwill and Jacqueline Bouvier Onassis; *I Was Jacqueline Kennedy's Dressmaker*, by Mini Rhea.

Videos, articles, and other material reviewed and consulted: various news accounts about and photographs of the Kennedys on inaugural day; Secret Service files from the John Fitzgerald Kennedy Library; Secret Service documentary, PBS (air: June 1999); biographical information on Jackie, Ethel, and Joan from published accounts; "What You Don't Know about Jackie Kennedy," by Laura Bergquist, *Look*, July 4, 1961; correspondence from Lady Bird Johnson to Ethel Kennedy, courtesy of Lyndon Baines Johnson Library; "Jackie: An Exclusive First Look at Her Private Letters," by Oleg Cassini, *In Style*, October 1995; *The New Jackie* (entire magazine devoted to Jackie), Summer 1970; *Jackie: A Photo Biography*, by Beverly Maurice, August 1971; interview with Jackie Kennedy by Charles Collingwood (video): *The Secret Lives of Jackie Onassis* (BBC documentary, includes interviews with Evelyn Lincoln and Priscilla McMillan); "The Clint Who Really Could Have Saved JFK's Life," by Sharon Churcher, *Mail on Sunday*, September 26, 1993.

Anyone seriously interested in the personal life of John F. Kennedy before he knew Jackie should consult the JFK personal papers and correspondence, 1933–1950, Box 4A in the JFK Library.

The Skakels; Not One to Feel Sorry for Herself; White House Infidelities; The Bouviers

As well as having utilized the previously cited Oral Histories, personal interviews were conducted with Joan Braden, Sancy Newman, Luella Hennessey, Leah Mason, Gore Vidal, Anthony Sherman, George Smathers, Betty Beale, Lem Billings, Bess Abel, James Bacon, Letitia Baldrige, Ben Bradlee, George Christian, Leo Damore, John Davis, Joseph Gargan (questionnaire), Jeanne Martin, Joseph Paolella, Pierre Salinger, and George Smathers.

Volumes consulted: *To Jack with Love*; *Black Jack Bouvier: A Remembrance*, by Kathleen Bouvier; *The Bouviers*, by John Davis; *The Auchincloss Family*, by Joanna Russell Auchincloss and Caroline Auchincloss; *Our Forebears*, by John Vernou Bouvier, Jr. (privately printed); *The Kennedy Legacy*, by Theodore Sorenson; *With Kennedy*, by Pierre Salinger; *Upstairs at the White House*, by J. B. West; *Diamonds and Diplomats*, by Letitia Baldrige; *Power at Play*, by Betty Beale; *Ethel Kennedy and Life at Hickory Hill*, by Leah Mason (unpublished manuscript); *The Other Mrs. Kennedy*, by Jess Oppenheimer; *Ethel*, by David Lester; *The Kennedy Women*, by Laurence Leamer; *Jack and Jackie*, by Christopher Andersen; *All Too Human*, by Edward Klein; *The Sins of the Father*, by Ronald Kessler; *Seeds of Destruction*, by Ralph C. Martin; *First Ladies*, by Carl Sferrazza Anthony; *Jacqueline Kennedy*, by Gordon Langley Hall; *The Kennedy White House Parties*, by Ann H. Lincoln; *Jacqueline Kennedy: La Premiere Dame des Etats-Unis*, by Peter Peterson; *Jackie: The Exploitation of a First Lady*, by Irving Shulman; *Jackie, Oh!*, by Kitty Kelley; *The Pleasure of His Company*, by Paul B. Fay, Jr.; *The Bouviers*, by John Davis; *Kim Novak: Reluctant Goddess*, by Peter Harry Brown; *Jacqueline Kennedy: Beauty in the White House*, by William Carrl; *Jackie: The Price of the Pedestal*, by Lee Guthrie; *The President's Partner*, by Myra Gutin; *The Kennedy Promise*, by Henry Fairlie.

Videos, articles, and other material reviewed and consulted: news and other published accounts of Skakel and Bouvier family history; questionnaire answered by John Davis; transcript of Stephen Smith interview by Lester David; Ted Sorenson interview on *Today Show*, 1998; Rose Kennedy obituary, January 23, 1995, by John J. Goldman, *Los Angeles Times*; "A Left Coast Kennedy: Max Kennedy," by Susan Salter Reynolds, *Los Angeles Times Magazine*, March 14, 1999; *The Kennedys* (APB Video); *Jackie O.* (APB video).

Jackie's First Meeting with Ethel; Jack Proposes Marriage; All of This, and More; Joseph and Jackie's Deal; Sisterly Advice; The Bennetts

As well as having utilized the previously cited Oral Histories, personal interviews were conducted with Joan Braden, George Smathers, Mary Fonteyn, Paul B. Fay, Jr., Sancy Newman, Chuck Spalding, Lawrence Alexander, Larry Newman, Joseph Paolella, Joseph Livingston, Ted Livingston, Joe Gargan, Mary Lou McCarthy, Bess Abel, Betty Beale, Oleg Cassini, Paul Fay, David Lester, Lem Billings, Morton Downey, Jr., Geraldo Rivera, Luella Hennessey, Frank Mankiewicz, and Jeanne Martin.

Volumes consulted: *Changing Habits: A Memoir of the Society of the Sacred Heart*, by V. V. Harrison; *The Society of the Sacred Heart in North America*, by Louise Callan; *Ethel*, by David Lester; *A Woman Named Jackie*, by C. David Heymann; *All Too Human*, by Edward Klein; *Living with the Kennedys*, by Marcia Chellis; *Kennedy Wives, Kennedy Women*, by Nancy Gager; *The Kennedys: An American Drama*, by Peter Collier and David Horowitz; *America's First Ladies*, by Christine Sandler; *Jackie*, by Hedda Lyons Watney; *Torn Lace Curtain*, by Frank Saunders; *JFK: The Man and the Myth*, by Victor Lasky; *My Story*, by Judith Exner, as told to Ovid Demaris; *Bitch*, by Buddy Galon; *The Censorship Papers*, by Gerald Gardner; *The Whole Truth and Nothing But*, by Hedda Hopper and James Brough; *Uncommon Grace*, by J.C. Suares and J. Spencer Beck; *Remembering Jackie*, by *Life* editors; *The Woman in the White House*, by Winzola McLendon; *Ethel Kennedy and Life at Hickory Hill*, by Leah Mason (unpublished manuscript); *Presidential Wives*, by Paul F. Baker.

Videos, articles, and other material reviewed and consulted: "Kennedys in Hollywood" (E-Channel broadcast); news accounts of the deaths of George and Ann Skakel; Secret Service record at John Fitzgerald Kennedy Library; various news accounts of Bennett family history; John Davis questionnaire; "With Kennedy," by Pierre Salinger, *Good Housekeeping*, August 1966.

A Legacy of Infidelity; Jack's Affair with Marilyn

As well as having utilized the previously cited Oral Histories, personal interviews were conducted with Peter Summers, Leo Damore, George Smathers, Helen Thomas, Michael Selsman, Barbara Gibson, David Powers (questionnaire), Joe Gargan (questionnaire), Jimmy Haspiel, Micky Song, Cindy Adams, Liz Carpenter, Hildi Greenson, Jim Ketchum, Joseph Paolella, Larry Newman, and Pierre Salinger.

Volumes consulted: *Gloria and Joe: The Star-Crossed Love Affair of Gloria Swanson and Joe Kennedy*, by Axel Madsen; *Swanson on Swanson*, by Gloria Swanson; *JFK: The Presidency of John F. Kennedy*, by Herbert Parmetl; *John Kennedy: A Political Profile*, by James MacGregor; *Honey Fitz*, by John Henry Cutler; *John F. Kennedy and American Catholicism*, by Lawrence H. Fuchs; *JFK: Reckless Youth*, by Nigel Hamilton; *Rose Kennedy: A Life of Faith, Family and Tragedy*, by Barbara Gibson and Ted Schwartz; *The Fitzgeralds and the Kennedys: An American Saga*, by Doris Kearns Goodwin; *The Kennedy Women*, by Laurence Leamer; *Times to Remember*, by Rose Fitzgerald Kennedy; *Marilyn: The Last Take*, by Peter Harry Brown and Patte B. Barham; *The Decline and Fall of the Love Goddess*, by Patrick Agan; *The Masters Way to Beauty*, by George Masters; *Marilyn Monroe: An Uncensored Biography*, by Maurice Zolotow; *Marilyn Monroe: Confidential*, by Lena Pepitone; *Robert Kennedy and His Times*, by Arthur M. Schlesinger, Jr.; *Jacqueline Kennedy Onassis*, by Lester David.

Videos, articles, and other material reviewed and consulted: questionnaire answered by Joe Gargan; *Marilyn: The Last Word* (documentary); "Jacqueline Kennedy," by Mary Van Rensselaer, *Ladies Home Journal*, April 1961; "Of Man, Myth and Might-Have-Beens," by Bob Adams, *St. Louis Dispatch*, November 22, 1988.

Jackie's Expensive Diversion; Madcap Ethel during the Kennedy Presidency; Joan's Social Impasse; Trying to Understand Each Other; Jackie's Documentary: A Tour of the White House; The Voice; "Secrets Always Come Out"

Interviews with Jim Ketchum, Larry Newman, Pierre Salinger, Hugh Sidey, Mickey Song, Joan Braden, Helen Thomas, Paul Fay, Betty Beale, C. Wyatt Dickerson, Letitia Baldrige, Barbara Gibson, Rita Dallas, Luella Hennessey, Ben Bradlee, Mari Kumlin, and David Powers (questionnaire).

Volumes consulted: *In the Kennedy Style*, by Letitia Baldrige; *Designing Camelot: The Kennedy White House Restoration*, by James A. Abbott and Elaine M. Rice; *The Kennedy White House Parties*, by Anne H. Lincoln; *Uncommon Grace*, by J.C. Suarez and J. Spencer Back; *A Woman Named Jackie*, by C. David Heymann; *My Life with Jacqueline Kennedy*, by Mary Barelli Gallagher; *The Other Mrs. Kennedy*, by Jess Oppenheimer; *The Last of the Giants*, by Cyrus Leo Sulzberger; *Joan: The Reluctant Kennedy*, by Lester David; *A Tour of the White House with Mrs. John F. Kennedy*, by Perry Wolf; *JFK: The Memories*, by Hugh Sidey, Chester Clifton, and Cecil Stoughton; *John F. Kennedy, President*, by Hugh Sidey; *Office Hours: Day and Night*, by Janet Travell; *Upstairs at the White House*, by J.B. West; *The White House Chef Cookbook*, by Rene Verdon.

Videos, articles, and other material reviewed and consulted: news accounts of Joan's fifteenth anniversary party for Ethel and Bobby; "Jackie Kennedy: A Tour of the White House" (broadcast); "At Home with the Kennedys" (broadcast); transcript of David Lester's interview with Lem Billings; "A Visit to Camelot," by Diana Trilling, *The New Yorker*, June 2, 1997; "Havanas in Camelot," by William Styron, *Vanity Fair*, July 1996; "Say Good-bye to the President," 1985 BBC documentary; "In Step with Ethel Kennedy," by James Brady, *Parade*, April 3, 1988; "A Last, Loving Remembrance of JFK," by Jim Bishop, *Good Housekeeping*, March 1964; "Jacqueline Kennedy: The Future of a Noble Lady," by William V. Shannon, *Good Housekeeping*, April 1964; "Smashing Camelot," by Richard Lacayo, *Time*, November 17, 1997; "The Dark Side of Camelot (Judith Exner)," by Kitty Kelley, *People*, February 29, 1988; "The Exner Files," by Liz Smith, *Vanity Fair*, January 1997.

A note regarding President Kennedy's indiscretions: The Secret Service kept handwritten logs in which were recorded the names of all visitors entering the White House and the person they intended to visit. When a visitor was going to see the President, the gate logs would indicate it by noting a visit to "Evelyn Lincoln," "Residence," "President," or "Mansion." When the visitor was a woman being smuggled in for JFK, the gate log would read "David Powers Plus One" or "Kenny O'Donnell Plus One." These logs, organized chronologically by month and year, were used as research for this book and made available to the author by the John F. Kennedy Library in Boston.

A note regarding the oft-reported press conference to be held by Marilyn Monroe in 1962, during which she planned to reveal government secrets: In 1985, when Ethel Kennedy was told about the supposed press conference by an associate at ABC News during a meeting with her at Hickory Hill, she said, "Oh my God! Bobby didn't discuss those things with me unless I pushed and pushed for information—and I almost never did unless it involved the safety of the family. He would never have discussed anything like that with Marilyn Monroe. Please, let's be sensible. It's ridiculous." (Ethel made these comments in a meeting at Hickory Hill with high-level executives at ABC-TV to voice her extreme unhappiness about a planned twenty-six-minute segment of the show *20/20* detailing the intimate relationship between the Kennedys and Marilyn Monroe. The program was ultimately canceled, some have alleged, because Ethel used as leverage her close relationship with ABC president of News and Sports, Roone Arledge. Also, David Burke, a vice president of ABC News, was a top aide to Ted Kennedy; and Jeff Ruhe, an assistant to Arledge, was married to Bobby's and Ethel's fifth child, Courtney Kennedy, twenty-nine at the time.)

Also regarding that episode of *20/20*, Geraldo Rivera, who worked for the program at the time, told me during one appearance of many I made on his show: "I alleged at the time and have said repeatedly that, in my opinion, the story was killed not because it lacked journalistic merit—because I think the story was absolutely solid journalistically—but rather because of the relationship between certain members of ABC News management and the Kennedy family. I said at the time that it smacked of cronyism. I will say it until the day I die."

Hugh Downs has a two-word explanation as to why the show didn't air: "Cold feet."

Bobby Meets Marilyn; "Life's Too Short to Worry about Marilyn Monroe"; Jackie's Ultimatum to Jack; Bobby's Rumored Affair with Marilyn

Personal interviews with Peter Dye, Max Block, Nunziata Lisi, Jeanne Martin, Patricia Brennan, Joan Braden, James Bacon, Clint Hill, Gore Vidal, George Masters, George Smathers, Chuck Spalding, Leah Mason, Jim Whiting, Micky Song, James Haspeil, Ben Bradlee, Morton Downey, Jr., Jim Ketchum, Sancy Newman, Anthony Sherman, Geraldo Rivera, Bernard Flynn, and Paul Fay.

Volumes consulted: *Marilyn: The Last Take*, by Peter Harry Brown and Patte B. Barham; *Marilyn Monroe: The Biography*, by Donald Spoto; *Marilyn Monroe: An Uncensored Biography*, by Maurice Zolotow; *The Curious Death of Marilyn Monroe*, by Robert Slatzer; *Marilyn Monroe in Her Own Words*, by Robert Taylor; *Robert Kennedy at 40*, by Nick Thimmesch; *Marilyn Monroe: A Complete View*, by Edward Wagenknecht; *The Fitzgeralds and The Kennedys: An American Saga*, by Doris Kearns Goodwin; *The Kennedy Men*, by Nellie Bly; *The Marilyn Conspiracy*, by Milo Speriglio; *Marilyn: The Last Months*, by Eunice Murray with Rose Shade; *The Ultimate Marilyn*, by Ernest W. Cunningham; *The Last Days of Marilyn Monroe*, by Donald H. Wolf; *Chief: My Life in the LAPD*, by Darryl Gates; *The Intimate Sex Lives of Famous People*, by Irving Wallace, et al.; *RFK*, by C. David Heymann; *Marilyn and Me*, by Susan Strasberg; *The Kennedys in Hollywood*, by Laurence Quirk; *Peter Lawford: The Man Who Kept the Secrets*, by James Spada; *The Unabridged Marilyn*, by Randall Riese and Christopher Hitchens; *Crowning Glory*, by Sydney Guilaroff as told to Cathy Griffin; *Hollywood Is a Four Letter Word*, by James Bacon; *Show Business Laid Bare*, by Earl Wilson; *Sinatra: A Complete Life*, by J. Randy Taraborrelli; *Sinatra: The Man and the Myth*, by Bill Adler, *Where Have You Gone Joe DiMaggio?*, by Maury Allen.

Videos, articles, and other material reviewed and consulted: transcripts of interviews with Milt Ebbins (August 6, 1992), Pat Newcomb (August 3, 1994), Joseph Naar (December 18, 1994), Rupert Allan (March 13, 1995), and Ralph Roberts (March 2, 1992), by Donald

Spoto, all from the Academy of Motion Pictures Arts & Sciences Library; "The Legend of Marilyn Monroe," ABC- TV, 1967; *Monroe's Last Picture Show*, by Walter Bernstein; "Marilyn Monroe: A Serious Blonde Who Can Act," *Look*, October 23, 1951; "Nine Kennedys and How They Grew," by Jerome Beatty, *Readers Digest*, April 1939; "Kennedys in Hollywood" (E-Channel), includes interviews with Barbara Gibson, Paul Fay, Oleg Cassini, John Davis, and Lynn Franklin; *Joan Rivers Show*, 1992, special on the Kennedy women, with John Davis, Cindy Adams, Barbara Gibson; James Bacon (column), *Beverly Hills 213*, August 26, 1998.

Joseph's Stroke; At Horizon House; The Walking Cane; Life at the Hyannis Port Compound; The Fourth of July in Hyannis Port, 1962

As well as having utilized the previously cited Oral Histories, personal interviews were conducted with Barbara Gibson, Elliot Newman, Steven Silas, Betty LeRoy Thomson, Peter Dilliard, Frank Mankiewicz, Stephen Webb, Inez Foxworthy, Sheridan Bonswell, Patricia Moran, David Powers (questionnaire), Joe Gargan (questionnaire), and George Smathers.

Volumes consulted: *The Kennedy Case*, by Rita Dallas and Jeanira Ratcliffe; *Living with the Kennedys*, by Marcia Chellis; *Kennedy*, by Jacques Lowe; *Torn Lace Curtain*, by Frank Saunders; *Peter Lawford: The Man Who Kept the Secrets*, by James Spada; *The Peter Lawford Story*, by Pat Seaton Lawford; *The Kennedy Women*, by Laurence Leamer; *Times to Remember*, by Rose Fitzgerald Kennedy; *The Sins of the Father*, by Ronald Kessler; *Seeds of Destruction*, by Ralph G. Martin; *Rose*, by Gail Cameron; *Life with Rose Kennedy*, by Barbara Gibson and Caroline Latham; *Jackie after Jack*, by Christopher Andersen; *Among Those Present*, by Nancy Dickerson; *My Twelve Years with John F. Kennedy*, by Evelyn Lincoln.

Videos, articles, and other material reviewed and consulted: transcript of Frank Saunders interview by Jeffrey Stephenson (from the Academy of Motion Pictures Arts and Sciences), "Joseph Kennedy: A Life" (MGM video); "Jackie Onassis" (APB Video).

Joan's Many Faux Pas; *Pat Finds Jackie "So Insecure"; Marilyn Monroe's Death; Jackie Goes Away to Think*

As well as having utilized the previously cited Oral Histories, personal interviews were conducted with Helen Thomas, James Bacon, Nunziata Lisi, Patricia Brennan, John Bates, Leah Mason, George Smathers, Pierre Salinger, and Gore Vidal.

Volumes consulted: *Joan: The Reluctant Kennedy*, by David Lester; *My Life with Jacqueline Kennedy*, by Mary Barelli Gallagher; *Marilyn: The Last Six Months*, by Eunice Murray with Rose Shade; *The Kennedys in Hollywood*, by Lawrence Quirk; *The Curious Death of Marilyn Monroe*, by Robert F. Slatzer; *Marilyn: The Last Take*, by Peter Harry Brown and Patte B. Barham; *The Fifty Year Decline and Fall of Hollywood*, by Ezra Goodman; *Who Killed Marilyn Monroe?*, by Charles Hamblett; *From under My Hat*, by Hedda Hopper; *Hollywood's Unsolved Mysteries*, by John Austin; *The Strange Death of Marilyn Monroe*, by Frank A. Capell; *Marilyn Monroe*, by George Carpozi; *RFK: The Man Who Would Be President*, by Ralph De Toledano; *Marilyn Monroe Story*, by Joe Franklin and Laurie Palmer; *Confessions of a Hollywood Columnist*, by Sheila Graham; *Don't Get Me Wrong, I Love Hollywood*, by Sidney Skolsky.

Videos, articles, and other material reviewed and consulted: James Brady in *Parade* magazine, January 1999; notes, transcripts, and correspondence between Bobby and Ted Kennedy and original manuscript of *What Makes Teddy Run*, by William Peters, in *Redbook*, obtained from the Kennedy Library, by James Spada; the Hedda Hopper Collection (of published and unpublished columns with notes) housed in the Margaret Herrick Library at the Academy of Motion Pictures Arts and Sciences; "JFK's Women," *Time*, December 22, 1975; "The Kennedys in California," *Los Angeles Times*, March 23–28, 1962; the 1982 report of the Los Angeles district attorney on the reinvestigation of Marilyn Monroe's death; "The Bobby Kennedy Connection," *New York Post*, 1986; Justice Department memorandum of August 20, 1962, quoting Robert Kennedy on his relationship with Marilyn Monroe (he denied it was anything more than passing); "The Bobby–Marilyn Affair," *National Review*, August 1988; "Camelot after Dark," by Paul Chin, Joe Treen, and Karen S. Schneider, *People*, May 27, 1991.

A note regarding the *Redbook* story: Bobby found a myriad of problems—at least a dozen—with the feature that Ted hadn't noted, none of which had anything to do with Joan. For instance, a college roommate of Ted's, Ted Carey, recalled at the time that he (Carey) wasn't doing well in school and mentioned to Kennedy that he'd give anything to chuck it all and take off for Africa. Ted encouraged his friend's whim and, daring him, offered to buy both of them a one-way first-class ticket to Cairo for a trip that would commence immediately after Carey's final exam. They made the bet, but Ted never thought Carey would follow up on it. However, Carey called Ted's bluff and, after the final exam, sent word to Ted that he was on his way to Boston's Logan Airport. Much to Ted's surprise, Carey got on a plane headed to New York, en route to Cairo. Ted got cold feet and had Carey paged at the New York airport and told him that he had stopped payment on the check for the tickets because he'd changed his mind. Instead, he paid for Carey to spend a weekend in New York, as a consolation prize. The writer observed, "I think the main reason Teddy backed down was if Carey didn't get back in time to register for the new term, the story might get in the newspapers. His father has always had almost an obsession about keeping the family name out of the papers in affairs like this, and Teddy knew it." Of that and other stories from Carey, Bobby wrote: "I would also tell him [author] that you are not enthusiastic about the stories from Ted Carey. Tell him the story about the canceled check is not accurate. Perhaps with a smile, you can get him to eliminate the whole thing."

A note regarding Frank Sinatra's investigation into Marilyn Monroe's death: Says Thomas DiBella, a former underworld figure on the East Coast and once a close friend of Chicago mob leader Sam Giancana's, "Sinatra tried to call JFK about Marilyn's death, but the President would not take his calls, which only made Frank angrier. Then in November [1963], Jack was assassinated. Frank was very distraught about that. By this time, he was really on an emotional merry-go-round. In December his son, Frank Junior, was kidnapped. Bobby [Kennedy] used his influence with the FBI to help him get the kid back. So, out of gratitude, and also respect for the Kennedy family, Frank decided to drop the whole thing about Marilyn."

"What was he going to do with the information, anyway?" added

Dominic Santori, also once a friend of Sinatra's. "Have a press conference and spill the beans? Frank Sinatra? Not likely. But I know he always had a great distaste for the way the Kennedys treated Marilyn
Monroe." Santori concluded, "Decades later, all these books came out
about Marilyn, Jack, and Bobby, but Frank Sinatra had all this information in his hands over thirty years ago. But like the gentleman he
was, he never said a word. And, in the end, he took all the anger and
resentment he had about it to the grave with him."

The Kennedy Women Do Men's Work

As well as having utilized the previously cited Oral Histories, personal interviews were conducted with Eileen Harper, George Smathers, David Lester, Lem Billings, Rita Dallas, Stanley Tretick, David
Powers (questionnaire and followup interview), John Davis (questionnaire), Helen Thomas, Walter Cronkite, Oleg Cassini, Pierre Salinger,
Lisa Conners, Thomas Stanwick, Liz Carpenter, Nancy Bacon, Larry
Newman, Bess Abel, Jim Ketchum, and Andrew Martinelli.

Volumes consulted: *Dark Side of Camelot*, by Seymour Hersh; *A
Very Private Woman*, by Nina Burleigh; *Conversations with Kennedy*, by
Ben Bradlee; *A Good Life*, by Ben Bradlee; *All Too Human*, by Edward
Klein; *The Kennedy Women*, by Laurence Leamer; *Times to Remember*,
by Rose Fitzgerald Kennedy; *Life with Rose Kennedy*, by Barbara Gib-
son and Caroline Latham; *Rose*, by Gail Cameron; *Iron Rose*, by Cindy
Adams and Susan Crimp; *Rose*, by Charles Higham; *Rose Kennedy and
Her Family*, by Barbara Gibson and Ted Schwartz; *Joan: The Reluctant
Kennedy*, by Lester David; *The Dark Side of Camelot*, by Nelson
Thompson; *The Joy of Classical Music*, by Joan Kennedy; *The Kennedy
Imprisonment*, by Gary Wills; *Tell It to Louella*, by Louella Parsons; *One
Brief Shining Moment: Remembering Kennedy*, by William Manchester;
Portrait of a President: John F. Kennedy in Profile, by William Manches-
ter; *The Kennedy Library*, by William Davis and Christina Tree.

Videos, articles, and other material reviewed and consulted: Secret
Service logs from White House and John Kennedy Library; comments
by Candy Jones, Gerald Doherty, Donald Dowd, and Phoebe Dowd
are from interview transcripts conducted by David Lester; "Dangerous
Minds" (an ABC-TV special based on Seymour Hersh's book *The
Dark Side of Camelot*, which includes interviews with Larry Newman,

Julia Reed, G. Robert Blakely, Ben Bradlee, Hugh Sidey, Anthony Sherman, Joseph Paolella, George Smathers); CNN *Talk Back Live*, interview with Seymour Hersh, December 26, 1997; "JFK: The Truth as I See It," by Arthur Schlesinger, Jr., *Cigar Aficionado*, December 1998.

Jackie's Wicked Scheme; The Cuban Missile Crisis; Joan—The Senator's Wife

As well as having utilized the previously cited Oral Histories, personal interviews were conducted with Jim Ketchum, Nunziata Lisi, Oleg Cassini, Robert McNamara, George Smathers, Liz Carpenter, Pierre Salinger, Letitia Baldrige, Jim Whiting, Stanley Tretick, and Helen Thomas.

Volumes consulted: *Marvella: A Personal Journey*, by Marvella Bayh; *Presidential Anecdotes*, by Paul F. Boller; *Dog Days at the White House: The Outrageous Memoirs of the Presidential Kennel Keeper*, by Traphes Bryant and Frances Spatz Leighton; *Edward Kennedy and the Camelot Legacy*, by James MacGregor Burns; *The Hidden Side of Jacqueline Kennedy*, by George Carpozi; *Jacqueline Kennedy: A Portrait of Courage*, by Hal Dareff; *Remember the Ladies: Women of America*, by Linda Grant De Pauw; *A Thousand Days*, by Arthur Schlesinger, Jr.; *Kennedy and His Women*, by Tony Sciacca; *John F. Kennedy's 13 Great Mistakes in the White House*, by Malcolm E. Smith; *The Severed Soul*, by Dr. Herbert Strean and Lucy Freedman; *Sex and Politicians: Affairs of State*, by Kerry Segreve; *Jackie: A Truly Intimate Biography*, by Frieda Kramer; *Hidden Hollywood*, by Richard Lamparski; *Kennedy: A Time Remembered*, by Jacques Lowe; *Controversy and Other Essays in Journalism*, by William Manchester; *The Kennedy Case*, by Rita Dallas and Jeanira Ratcliffe; *Bobby Kennedy: The Making of a Folk Hero*, by David Lester; *RFK: The Man Who Would Be President*, by Ralph De Toledano; *Those Wild, Wild Kennedy Boys*, by Stephen Dunleavy; *In His Own Words: The Unpublished Recollections of the Kennedy Years*, by Robert F. Kennedy; *Joan: The Reluctant Kennedy*, by David Lester; *The Pleasure of His Company*, by Paul "Red" Fay.

Videos, articles, and other material reviewed and consulted: Maria Shriver interview with Fidal Castro, *Oprah Winfrey Show*, April 1999;

correspondence between Jackie Kennedy and Lyndon Johnson courtesy of the LBJ Library.

Delighted to Be Pregnant; The Deaths of Infants Arabella and Patrick; Lee Radziwill Invites Jackie-in-Mourning; "Not Ethel's Best Moment"; Aboard the Christina; Jack Summons Jackie—To No Avail; "Ari Is Not for You"

As well as having utilized the previously cited Oral Histories, per-
sonal interviews were conducted with Jim Ketchum, Pierre Salinger,
George Smathers, Chuck Spalding, Mari Kumlin, Dora Kumlin,
Bessie Jaynes, Stelina Mavros, and Joseph Paolella.

Volumes consulted: *A Very Private Woman*, by Nina Burleigh; *The Search for JFK*, by Clay Blair, Jr., and Joan Blair; *The Remarkable Kennedys*, by Joseph McCarthy; *Jack and Jackie*, by Christopher An-
dersen; *All Too Human*, by Ed Klein; *White House Nannie*, by Maud
Shaw; *The Radziwills: The Social History of a Great European Family*, by
Tadeusz Nowakowski; *The Kennedy Case*, by Rita Dallas and Jeanira
Ratcliffe; *In Her Sister's Shadow*, by Diana DuBois; *The Other Mrs.
Kennedy*, by Jerry Oppenheimer; *Onassis*, by Willi Frischauer; *The
Fabulous Onassis*, by Christian Cafarakis; *Jackie, Bobby and Manches-
ter*, by Arnold Bennett; *Jackie Oh!*, by Kitty Kelley; *Ari: The Life and
Times of Aristotle Onassis*, by Peter Evans; *Onassis*, by Frank Brady;
Ari, by Peter Evans; *Those Fabulous Greeks*, by Doris Lilly; *Oh No,
Jackie O*, by January Jones; *Aristotle Onassis*, by Nicholas Frasier,
Philip Jacobson, Mark Ottaway, and Lewis Chester; *Palimpsest*, by
Gore Vidal; *The Onassis Women*, by Kiki Feroudi Moutsatsos; *Onassis:
An Extravagant Life*, by Frank Brady; *First Lady*, by Charlotte Curtis;
The Joy of Classical Music, by Joan Kennedy; *Maria: Callas Remem-
bered*, by Nadia Stancioff; *Maria Callas: The Woman Behind the Legend*,
by Arianna Stassinopoulous; *Aristotle and Christina*, by L.J. Davis; *The
Kennedy Promise*, by Henry Fairlie; *Endless Enemies*, by Jonathan
Kwitny; *JFK*, by David Lester and Irene David.

Videos, articles, and other material reviewed and consulted: Stelio
Popademitrio quotes from ABC-TV; "Hospital Vigil over Kennedy
Baby," *Life*, August 16, 1963; correspondence from Jackie to Jack from
Jackie Kennedy auction; "Callas in Love," by Stelio Galatopoulos,

Vanity Fair, March 1999; "Maria Was a Weapon," by Arianna Stassinopoulos, *People*, March 23, 1981.

Jack's Rapprochement with Jackie: "Getting to Know You"; Tragedy; "The President's Been Shot"; Holy Mary, Mother of God; "The Party's Been Canceled—The President's Dead"; In Mourning

As well as having utilized the previously cited Oral Histories, personal interviews were conducted with Larry Newman, George Smathers, Pierre Salinger, Ben Bradlee, Nellie Connally, Robert McNamara, Diana Dubois, Walter Cronkite, Frank Mankiewicz, Sancy Newman, Beatrice Lowell, Roz Clark, Johnny Grant, Morton Downey, Jr., Stuart Greene, and Betty Beale.

Volumes consulted: *The Day Kennedy Was Shot*, by Jim Bishop; *The Kennedy Case*, by Rita Dallas and Jeanira Ratcliffe; *The Pleasure of His Company*, by Ben Bradlee; *Conversations with Kennedy*, by Ben Bradlee; *The Death of a President*, by William Manchester; *They've Killed the President*, by Robert Samanson; *My Twelve Years with John F. Kennedy*, by Evelyn Lincoln; *Not in Your Lifetime*, by Anthony Summers; *The Kennedys*, by Peter Collier and David Horowitz; *Times to Remember*, by Rose Fitzgerald Kennedy; *Power at Play*, by Betty Beale; *President Kennedy*, by Richard Reeves; *Ethel*, by David Lester; *The Other Mrs. Kennedy*, by Jerry Oppenheimer; *Joan: The Reluctant Kennedy*, by David Lester; *A White House Diary*, by Lady Bird Johnson; *The Kennedy Women*, by Laurence Leamer; *RFK*, by C. David Heymann; *The Pleasure of His Company*, by Paul Fay; *The Dark Side of Camelot*, by Seymour Hersh; *The Assassination Tapes*, by George O'Toole; *Rush to Judgment*, by Mark Lane; *Counterplot*, by Edward Jay Epstein; *The Imperial Presidency*, by Arthur Schlesinger.

Videos, articles, and other material reviewed and consulted: Clint Hill's comments from Secret Service documentary, PBS, June 1999; *Life* interview with Rose Kennedy by Sylvia Wright (1970); Maria Shriver's comments from *Oprah*, January 1999; Ted Kennedy's eulogy at Jacqueline Kennedy's funeral; "A Matter of Reasonable Doubt," *Life*, November 25, 1966; "Report to the President by the Commission on CIA Activities within the United States," June 1975 (also known as the CIA Commission Report); Jackie's testimony from volume five of "The President's Commission on the Assassination of President John Fitzgerald Kennedy"; "John F. Kennedy Memorial Edition," *Life*, November 1963; "These Are Things I Hope Will Show How He Really Was," by Jacqueline Kennedy, *Life*, May 29, 1964; "Valiant Is the World for Jacqueline," by Laura Bergquist, *Look*, January 28, 1964.

Tea with Lady Bird, Thanksgiving, 1963; Jackie's Camelot; "Let It All Out"; Aftermath

As well as having utilized the previously cited Oral Histories, personal interviews were conducted with Joan Braden, Michael Oliver, Beatrice Moore, Liz Carpenter, Joseph Paolella, Jack Valenti, Susan Neuberger Wilson, Ed Newman, and Pierre Salinger.

Volumes consulted: *In Search of History*, by Theodore White; *On His Own: RFK*, by William Vanden Huevel and Milton Gwirtzman; *Presidential Passions*, by Michael John Sullivan; *A White House Diary*, by Lady Bird Johnson; *The Vantage Point*, by Lyndon Baines Johnson; *JFK and LBJ: The Influence of Personality on Politics*, by Tom Wicker; *To Move a Nation*, by Roger Hilsman; *Containing Central Intelligence*, by Harry Rowe Ransom; *Joan: The Reluctant Kennedy*, by David Lester; *Joan Kennedy: Life with the Kennedys*, by Marcia Chellis; *A Private View*, by Irene Mayer Selnick; *Sinatra and His Rat Pack*, by Richard Gehman; *Mislaid in Hollywood*, by Joe Hyams; *The Thin Veil*, by Frank Saunders; *The Kennedy Case*, by Rita Dallas and Jeanira Ratcliffe; *White House Nannie*, by Maud Shaw; *The Kennedy Men*, by Nellie Bly; *Confessions of an Ex–Fan Magazine Writer*, by Jane Wilkie; *The President's Mistress*, by Irma Hunt; *The Women around RFK*, by Susan Marvin; *The Best of Friends*, by David Michaelis; *Robert F. Kennedy: A Memoir*, by Jack Newfield; *Backstairs at the White House*, by Lillian Rogers Parks with Frances Spatz Leighton; *The Struggles of John F. Kennedy*, by Herbert S. Parmet; *Tell It to Louella*, by Louella Parsons.

Videos, articles, and other material reviewed and consulted: letters from Jackie Kennedy to Lyndon Johnson and from LBJ to Jackie, and transcripts of telephone calls courtesy of LBJ Library; Frank Saunders interview transcript by David Lester; "Lady Bird Johnson Writes about Her Private World," *Life*, August 13, 1965; "What Has Tragedy Meant to Bobby Kennedy," by Bill Davidson, *Good Housekeeping*, July 1964;

"What Kind of Woman Is Our New First Lady," by Ruth Montgomery, *Good Housekeeping*, March 1964.

Moving Out of the White House; Lyndon Johnson "Using Jackie"; The Kennedy Camp on LBJ: "A Blight on the New Frontier"; Joan's Bottled-Up Anxiety; Jackie's Saddest Days; Jackie and Brando—The Rumors

As well as having utilized the previously cited Oral Histories, personal interviews were conducted with Pierre Salinger, Frank Mankiewicz, George Christian, Peter Brent, Joseph Karats, and John Davis.

Volumes consulted: *Taking Charge*, by Michael Meschloss; *A White House Diary*, by Lady Bird Johnson; *The Vantage Point*, by Lyndon Baines Johnson; *Joan: The Reluctant Kennedy*, by David Lester; *Just Jackie*, by Ed Klein; *No Final Victories*, by Lawrence F. O'Brien; *The Kennedy Case*, by Rita Dallas and Jeanira Ratcliffe; *The Kennedy Women*, by Pearl S. Buck; *Jacqueline Kennedy Onassis*, by David Lester; *Ethel*, by David Lester; *Robert Kennedy and His Times*, by Arthur Schlesinger, Jr.; *Bobby Kennedy*, by David Lester with Irene David; *The Kennedy Courage*, by Edward Hymoff and Phil Hirsch; *Palm Beach Babylon*, by Murray Weiss and Bill Hofmman; *There Really Was a Hollywood*, by Janet Leigh; *John Fitzgerald Kennedy: As We Remember Him*, edited by Goddard Lieberson; *Behind Every Successful President*, by Alice Anderson; *Presidential Wives: An Anecdotal History*, by Paul Boller, Jr.; *Dog Days at the White House*, by Traphes Bryant with Frances Spatz Leighton; *As We Remember Joe*, by John F. Kennedy; *Tell It to the King*, by Larry King; *When I Think of Bobby*, by Warren Rogers; *The Struggles of John F. Kennedy*, by Herbert S. Parmet; *Kennedy and Johnson*, by Evelyn Lincoln; *Lyndon Johnson and the American Dream*, by Doris Kearns; *The Tragedy of Lyndon Johnson*, by Eric F. Goldman; *The Kennedy Promise*, by Henry Fairlie; *Recollections of the Kennedy Years*, by Edwin Guthman.

Videos, articles, and other material reviewed and consulted: transcripts of telephone conversations between LBJ and Jackie (and Pierre Salinger and LBJ) courtesy of LBJ Library; "LBJ and the Kennedys," by Kenneth O'Donnell, *Life*, August 7, 1970; "John Fitzgerald Kennedy, 1917–1963," by Laura Bergquist, *Look*, November 17, 1964; "The Unknown JFK," by Fletcher Knebel, *Look*, November 17, 1964; "Eight Views of JFK," by T. George Harris, *Look*, November 17, 1964; "Teddy Kennedy: Is He Running for President?," by Edward R.F. Sheehan, *Saturday Evening Post*, June 5, 1965; "Ted Kennedy On His Own," by Joseph Roddy, *Look*, July 13, 1965; "The Bright Light of His Days," by Jacqueline Kennedy Onassis, *McCalls*, November 1973.

Ted's Plane Crash; Joan Wins the Election for Ted; Jackie on the Anniversary of November 22, 1963; Using Jackie—Yet Again; Joan the Emissary; Cead Mile Failte; Joan's Continuing Struggle

As well as having utilized the previously cited Oral Histories, personal interviews were conducted with Joe Gargan, Joan Braden, Benjamin Strait, Marie Fehmer, James W. Fosburgh, and Jerry Summers.

Volumes consulted: *Ted Kennedy: Triumphs and Tragedies*, by Lester David; *The Kennedys in Hollywood*, by Lawrence Quirk; *Seeds of Destruction*, by Ralph G. Martin; *Good Ted, Bad Ted*, by Lester David; *The Last Brother*, by Joe McGinniss; *The Shadow President*, by Burton Hersh; *Living with the Kennedys*, by Marcia Chellis; *As We Remember Her*, by Carl Sferrazza Anthony; *The Senator: My Ten Years with Ted Kennedy*, by Richard E. Burke; *The Education of Edward Kennedy: A Family Biography*, by Burton Hersh; *The Other Mrs. Kennedy*, by Jerry Oppenheimer; *The Joy of Classical Music*, by Joan Kennedy; *We Band of Brothers: A Memoir of Robert F. Kennedy*, by Edwin Guthman; *Breaking Cover*, by Bill Gulley and Mary Ellen Reese.

Videos, articles, and other material reviewed and consulted: questionnaire filled out by Joe Gargan; news clips about the accident; transcript of conversations between Joan and LBJ and Jackie and LBJ, courtesy of the Lyndon Baines Johnson Library; LBJ correspondence to Jackie also courtesy of the Johnson Library; the transcript of Arthur Egan interview by David Lester; "Celebration of One Year Anniversary of JFK's Death," *Look* magazine; various published articles about the Kennedy Exhibition; *Dateline* report, "Just Jackie," by Ed Klein, 1999, including interview with John Carl Warneckie, Stelio Papadimitriou, and Niki Goulandris; "Ideal Plane, Expert Pilot . . . Why Flying So Low?," by Anne Wyman, *Boston Globe*, June 23, 1964; "Ted Kennedy Escapes Death" (Associated Press), *Daily News*, June 20, 1964; "Kennedy Family Stands Vigil," by Anthony Matejczyk, *Boston*

Globe, June 21, 1964; "Ted Kennedy's Recovery," *Life*, January 15, 1965.

The Rumor Mill; RFK for President; Enter "The Greek"; The Appeal to Jackie; Ethel's Thoughtless Remark; Another Tragedy; "The Hand of a Dead Man"; "No God of Mine"

As well as having utilized the previously cited Oral Histories, personal interviews were conducted with Gore Vidal, Barbara Gibson, Liz Carpenter, John Lewis, Frank Mankiewicz, Jeanne Martin, Leah Mason, Charles Bartlett, Roswell Gilpatrick, Chuck Spalding, Nicolas "Niko" Konaledius, Stavlos Pappadia, John Miner, and Rafer Johnson.

Volumes consulted: *Palimpsest*, by Gore Vidal; *RFK*, by C. David Heymann; *The Kennedy Case*, by Rita Dallas and Jeanira Ratcliffe; *Robert Kennedy and His Times*, by Arthur Schlesinger; *Onassis*, by Willi Frischauer; *The Enemy Within*, by Robert F. Kennedy; *Robert Kennedy at 40*, by Nick Thimmesch and William Johnson; *Robert Kennedy: The Brother Within*, by Robert E. Thompson and Hortense Myers; *The Unfinished Odyssey of Robert Kennedy*, by David Halberstam; *Robert Kennedy: A Memoir*, by Jack Newfield; *85 Days: The Last Campaign of Robert F. Kennedy*, by Jules Witcover; *A Thousand Days*, by Arthur Schlesinger; *Plot of Politics*, by Rosemary James and Jack Wardlaw; *The Kennedy Conspiracy*, by Paris Flammonde; *Cardinal Cushing*, by John Henry Cultler; *Witness to Power*, by Marquis Childs; *The Hidden Side of Jacqueline Kennedy*, by George Carpozi; *Dog Days at the White House*, by Traphes Bryant and Frances Spatz Leighton; *The Woman in the White House*, by Marianne Means; *The Radziwills*, by Tadeusz Nowakowski; *Men, Money and Magic*, by Jeffry Potter; *Jacqueline Kennedy: The White House Years*, by Mary Van Rensselaer Thayer; *Dateline: White House*, by Helen Thomas; *Ambassador's Journal*, by John Kenneth Galbraith; *The Man to See*, by Evan Thomas; *Official and Confidential: The Secret Life of J. Edgar Hoover*, by Anthony Summers.

Videos, articles, and other material reviewed and consulted: Andy Williams interview by Carol Welles for *Photoplay*, October 1971; Andy Williams interview transcript by Byron McCall for *Motion Picture*, April 1970; Claudine Longet interview by Carol Welles for *Photoplay*, October 1971; "AP Reporter Recalls Tragic Scene," by Bob

Thomas, Associated Press wire, June 6, 1998; "Breaking His Silence,"
by Paul Ciotti, *Los Angeles Times*, June 6, 1988; "How L.A. Cops
Botched the Bobby Kennedy Murder Inquiry," by George Carpozi,
Star, May 10, 1988; "The Murder of Robert Kennedy," by Allard K.
Lowenstein, *Saturday Review*, February 19, 1977; "Caroline Kennedy:
A Little Girl in New Turmoil," by Lester David, *Good Housekeeping*,
January 1969; "Son Ted Phones Sad News to Parents," by Alan H.
Sheehan, *Boston Globe*, June 5, 1968; "The Coming of Age of Joan
Kennedy," by Christine Sadler, *McCalls*, February 1965.

Senator Robert Francis Kennedy Is Dead; Bobby's Funeral; "We Shall Carry on with Courage"; Ethel—Just a Shell

As well as having utilized the previously cited Oral Histories, personal interviews were conducted with Coretta Scott-King, Charles
Spalding, Roswell Gilpatrick, Roger Wilkins, Rosey Grier, Rafer Johnson, Frank Mankiewicz, Marva Whitford, Stewart Bodell, Samantha
Wright, John Tunney, Leah Mason, George Smathers, Barbara Gibson, Lem Billings, George Smathers, and Eudora Davis.

Volumes consulted: *My Life with Martin Luther King*, by Coretta
Scott-King; *First Ladies*, by Margaret Brown Klapthor; *Times to Remember*, by Rose Fitzgerald Kennedy; *Torn Lace Curtain*, by Frank
Saunders; *The Joy of Classical Music*, by Joan Kennedy; *A White House
Diary*, by Lady Bird Johnson; *Life with the Kennedys*, by Marcia Chellis;
The Kennedy Case, by Rita Dallas and Jeanira Ratcliffe; *The Diffusion
of Power*, by W.W. Rostow; *Letitia Baldrige's Complete Guide to Execu-
tive Manners*, by Letitia Baldrige; *Front Runner*, by Ralph G. Martin
and Ed Plaut; *No Final Victories*, by Lawrence F. O'Brien; *Deadline: A
Memoir*, by James Reston; *Heroes of My Time*, by Harrison Salisbury;
Mob Lawyer, by Frank Ragano and Selwyn Raab; *Man of the House*, by
Thomas O'Neill; *A Very Special President*, by Laura Bergquist and
Stanley Tretick; *The Kennedys: Dynasty and Disaster*, by John Davis.

Videos, articles, and other material reviewed and consulted: tele-
vised news accounts of Robert Kennedy's funeral; Jack Newfield's
comments to *New York Post*; Claudine Longet interview by Elaine
Harper, *Photoplay*, September 1968; Ethel Kennedy's and Jackie
Kennedy's letters to LBJ courtesy of LBJ Library; "The Ted Kennedys
Conquer Fear," by Maxine Cheshire, *Ladies Home Journal*, September

1968; "The Young Kennedys," by Julia Lawlor, *USA Weekend*, November 4, 1968.

A note regarding Jackie's spending habits: Contrary to her public image, Jackie wasn't always a spendthrift. The popular columnist Cindy Adams, who was a neighbor of Jackie's in New York, recalls this humorous story: "She was chintzy, that's for sure. She would expect huge discounts on clothing, saying, 'Everyone will see me wearing this, and it will do you a world of good as a designer.' At one point, she was having some carpentry work done by a carpenter we both used, and when his work was done, Jackie approached him with a check in one hand and a photograph in the other. 'Now, would you like me to pay you,' she asked, 'or would you prefer this lovely autographed photo of me, suitable for framing?' He chose the check." (Jackie may have gotten the idea from Rose, who, according to Barbara Gibson, would carry cards with Jack's picture on one side and a passage from his inaugural address along with a scripture on the other. After signing them, she would hand them out as tips to cab drivers and bell men, saying, "Keep this. It will be worth a lot of money.")

Ted Negotiates Jackie's Nuptials; Andy Williams; Ethel Pushes Jackie Too Far; "Bobby's Little Miracle"

As well as having utilized the previously cited Oral Histories, personal interviews were conducted with Barbara Gibson, Leah Mason, Frank Mankiewicz, Susannah Walker, Lem Billings, Carmen Bucarelli, Sierra Montez, Chuck Spalding, Stavlos Pappadia, Steven Webber, and an attorney for Ted Kennedy who asked for anonymity regarding Ted's negotiation with Onassis for Jackie's hand, which corresponds with the account by Willi Frischauer in his book *Onassis*.

Volumes consulted: *The Onassis Women*, by Kiki Feroudi Moutsatsos; *The Kennedy Neurosis*, by Nancy Gager Clinch; *The $20,000,000 Honeymoon*, by Fred Sparks; *Aristotle Onassis*, by Nicholas Fraser; *Jackie and Ari*, by Lester David and Jhan Robbins; *Heiress: The Story of Christina Onassis*, by Nigel Dempster; *Ted and the Kennedy Legend*, by Plimpton Stein.

Videos, articles, and other material reviewed and consulted: Kiki Feroudi Moutsatsos interview with *Dateline*, ABC-TV; "The Woman behind Bobby Kennedy," by Pete Hamill, *Good Housekeeping*, 1968; "Battle for the Onassis Millions," by Kim Hubbard, *People*, June 29, 1988.

Chappaquiddick; Jackie Tells Ari: "I Have to Be There"; Joan Accuses: "All You Care about Is How It Looks?"; Ethel to the Rescue; Mary Jo's Funeral; Ted Asks for Forgiveness; Joan Loses the Baby; A Final Gathering for Joseph; The End of Camelot

As well as having utilized the previously cited Oral Histories, personal interviews were conducted with John Davis (questionnaire), Dum Gifford, Joe Gargan, Bernie Flynn, Leo Damore, Mary Ann Kopan, Joseph Kopechne, Gwen Kopechne, Walter Cronkite, Bill Bradlee, Roswell Gilpatrick, Ellen Deiner, Nicholas Stamosis, Barbara Gibson, Frank Manciewcz, Bill Masterson, Betty Newman, and Ray Springfield.

Volumes consulted: *Senatorial Privilege: The Chappaquiddick Coverup*, by Leo Damore; *Days of Wine, Women and Wrong*, by David Barron; *Ted Kennedy: Triumphs and Tragedies*, by Lester David; *Rose*, by Gail Cameron; *Joan: The Reluctant Kennedy*, by David Lester; *The Kennedy Women*, by Laurence Leamer; *Living with the Kennedys*, by Marcia Chellis; *Rose*, by Charles Higham; *Iron Rose*, by Cindy Adams and Susan Crim; *Rose Kennedy*, by Barbara Gibson and Ted Schwartz; *The Kennedy Neurosis*, by Nancy Gager Clinch; *An American Melodrama*, by Godfrey Hodgson and Bruce Page; *Ted and the Kennedy Legend*, by Max Lerner.

Videos, articles, and other material reviewed and consulted: Maria Shriver's comments are from her appearance on *Oprah*, November 1999; Gwen Kopechne's comments from interview with Jane Adams for "Kopechnes Reveal Truth about Mary Jo," *TV Star Parade*, January 1971; "Intimate Portrait of Joan Kennedy," by Barbara Kevles, *Good Housekeeping*, September 1969; Rita Dallas comments from A&E's biography of Ted Kennedy; *Teddy: Keeper of the Kennedy Flame* (entire magazine devoted to EMK), 1968; "Chappaquiddick: What Really Happened?" with guests Leo Damore and Leslie Leyland, *Geraldo* (television program); "Ted Kennedy Talks about the Past and His Future," *Look*, March 4, 1969; "The Kennedys in China," by Joan Kennedy, January 1977; "Teddy Kennedy: Will He?," by Robert Healy, *Los Angeles*

Herald Examiner, June 11, 1979; "Kennedy Women Say OK," Associated Press, *Los Angeles Times*, September 7, 1979; "The Kennedy Challenge," *Time*, November 5, 1979; "Memories of Mary Jo: Interview with Joseph and Gwen Kopechne," by Jane Farrell, *Ladies Home Journal*, July 1989; "Jackie Onassis: Her Life with an Ailing Ari," by Liz Smith, *People*, October 14, 1974; "Jackie's World," *People*, April 18, 1977; "Jackie Twice Widowed," by Liz Smith, *People*, March 31, 1975.

Ted Hurts Joan Again; Ethel's Troubled Brood; Will Teddy Run? The Joan Factor; Joan and Ted: Creating the Illusion of a Marriage; Joan in Control of Joan; The Announcement: EMK for President; Joan's White House Fantasies; EMK's Candidacy: Not Meant to Be; The Last Straw for Joan

As well as having utilized the previously cited Oral Histories, personal interviews were conducted with Helen N. Smith, Richard Burke, Leo Damore, Walter Cronkite, Bill Bradlee, Roswell Gilpatrick, Betty Newman, Ellen Deiner, Nicholas Stamosis, Margaret Leaming, Barbara Gibson, Frank Manciewcz, Bill Masterson, Ed Gwirtzman, Helen Thomas, and John Davis.

Volumes consulted: *The Joy of Classical Music*, by Joan Kennedy; *The Last Brother*, by Joe McGinniss; *The Senator: My Ten Years with Ted Kennedy*, by Richard E. Burke; *Good Ted, Bad Ted*, by Lester David; *The Sins of the Father*, by Ronald Kessler; *The Kennedy Children*, by Bill Adler; *Washington Exposé*, by Jack Anderson; *As We Remember Her*, by Carl Sferrazza Anthony; *The Kennedy Women*, by Pearl S. Buck; *The Onassis Women*, by Kiki Feroudi Moutsatsos; *Cooking for Madam*, by Marta Sgubin; *Jackie O*, by Hedda Lyons Warney; *Joan: The Reluctant Kennedy*, by David Lester; *The Shadow President*, by Burton Hersh; *Kennedy Wives, Kennedy Women*, by Nancy Gager; *The Kennedy Courage*, by Edward Hymoff and Phil Hirsch; *The Kennedy Family*, by Joseph Dineen; *The Kennedy Years*, edited by Harold Faber; *The Education of Edward Kennedy: A Family Biography*, by Burton Hersh; *The Next Kennedy*, by Margaret Laing; *Ted Kennedy: Profile of a Survivor*, by William H. Honan.

Videos, articles, and other material reviewed and consulted: William Smith transcript by David Lester; "Rose Kennedy: She Wanted to Inspire Us, and She Did," by Dotson Rader, *Parade*, July 22, 1990; "A Glittering Array of Kennedy Ladies Center Stage," *Life*, June

11, 1971; "Ethel K. Gives Trashman a Trashing," by Gayle Fee and Laura Raposa, *Boston Herald*, July 17, 1997; "Bobby's Kids," by Michael Shnayerson, *Vanity Fair*, August 1997; "A Life of Challenge," by Maxwell Taylor Kennedy, *Inside Borders*, June 1998; "We Happy Few," by Joseph P. Kennedy II, *Esquire*, June 1998; "After 24 Years, Joan Kennedy Ends Marriage," by Gail Jennes and Gioia Diliberto, *People*, December 20, 1982; "Joan Kennedy Surveys Her Sober Life," by Gail Jennes, *People*, April 7, 1978; "Chappaquiddick Questions Remain," UPI, July 18, 1994; "The Joan Kennedy Book and Ethics," by Eunice Kennedy Shriver, *New York Daily News*, November 4, 1985; "Joan Kennedy: Book Contains Inaccuracies," Associated Press wire, October 18, 1985; "Kennedy Linen Hung on the Line," by Paul Taylor, *Washington Post*, September 29, 1985; "Marcia Chellis," by Cheryl Lavin, *Chicago Tribune*, June 1, 1986; "Joan Kennedy: The Life That Put Her into Silver Hill," by Liz Smith, *People*, June 24, 1971; "Richard Burke: My Ten Year Binge with Teddy," by Frank DiGiacomo and Joanna Molloy, *New York Post*, July 27, 1992; "The Secrets of Joan Kennedy," *People*, September 23, 1985; *The Ted Kennedy Story* (special tribute magazine), 1970; "Rose Kennedy at 85," *People*, September 22, 1975; "The Lucky Life of Sargent Shriver," *Chicago Tribune*, July 30, 1987; "An Intimate Visit: Rose Kennedy at 80," by Sylvia Wright, *Life*, July 17, 1970; "La Vie en Rose," by Carl Sferrazza Anthony, *Fame*, August 1990; "Farewell Rose," by Bob Speyer and Corky Siemaszko, *Daily News*, January 23, 1995; "Rose Kennedy Dies at 104," by Bryna Taubman, *New York Post*, January 23, 1995; "Death of a Matriarch," by Elizabeth Gleick, *Time*, February 6, 1995; "How I Got Over: Interview with Joan Kennedy," by John Stratford, *Star*, August 1, 1989; "Closing Scenes from a Kennedy Marriage," by Myra MacPherson, *Washington Post*, January 22, 1981; "Ted and Joan: Why This Marriage Couldn't Be Saved," *Ladies Home Journal*, March 1983; "Women Stand Up for Joan Kennedy," by Maxine Cheshire, *Washington Post*, October 22, 1980; "Joan Kennedy Silences Reporters," by T.R. Reid, *Washington Post*, January 19, 1980; "The Other Jackie O.," Edward Klein, *Vanity Fair*, August 1989; "Joan's Journey," by Myra MacPherson, *Washington Post*, December 14, 1979; "Watch Them Run: Teddy and the Kennedys," by Dick Schaap, *Look*, March 5, 1979; "Is Teddy Ready?," by Clare Crawford-Mason, *People*, July 2, 1979; "Into the Fray: Joan Kennedy Campaigns Down on the Farm," by

Myra MacPherson, *Washington Post*, December 12, 1979; "Joan Kennedy: Win or Lose, I Win," by Myra MacPherson, *McCalls*, June 1980; "The Tragedy of Bobby Kennedy, Jr.," by Susan Deutsch, *People*, October 3, 1983; "Ethel & David: Troubled Mother, Tormented Son," by William Pulmmer, *People*, May 14, 1984; "A Working Woman," by Gioia Diliberto, *People*, June 18, 1984; "The Quiet Life of Jackie O.," by Lester David, *Los Angeles Herald Examiner*, October 22, 1988; "Kennedy Ladies Take to Gentleman," by Cindy Adams, *New York Post*, August 8, 1994; "What Price Camelot?," by Paul Gray, *Time*, May 6, 1996; "O Jackie, How Tacky," by Jerry Adler, *Newsweek*, May 6, 1996; "How Much Is That Jackie in the Window?," by Barbara Lippert, *New York*, April 29, 1996.

A note regarding concerns about the Kopechnes during Ted's 1980 campaign: When Ted telephoned the Kopechnes in 1979 prior to the announcement that he would be a candidate, Gwen Kopechne was shocked to hear the voice of the man she and her husband, Joseph, derisively referred to only as "The Senator." She once recalled, "He just wanted to say he was running for the presidential nomination. 'I'm calling to see how you are, and I'll be in the area,' he said, pleasantly. He also said Joan would be with him, and I said, 'Well isn't that nice?' It was so transparent, really. If I hadn't been in such shock getting that call, I would have said to him, 'The next time you're in the area be sure to visit my daughter's grave.' He just wanted to make sure we were on his side, as if we could ever be on his side.

"I don't believe anything I've heard so far. I want him to tell me what happened. I don't ever remember him even saying he was sorry. I think there was a big cover-up and that everybody was paid off. The hearing, the inquest, it was all a farce. The Kennedys had the upper hand and it's been that way ever since."

The mystery of what happened at Chappaquiddick, and the names associated to it, will always remain a part of our popular culture, though inaccurate perceptions remain attached to it. For instance, Monica Lewinsky's mother, Marcia Lewis, made reference to the drowning in talking with her daughter about the potential liability should she tell the truth about her sexual relationship with President Bill Clinton (during a sworn deposition in the lawsuit filed against him by Paula Jones). In a tape-recorded conversation, Lewinsky told Linda Tripp that her mother had safety concerns: "She keeps saying Mary Jo Chappaquid-dick, or whatever the fuck her name was." Also, a recent biography of Bobby Kennedy reported that Mary Jo engaged in an affair with Bobby. "Oh, for God's sake," said an exasperated Frank Mankiewicz when asked about the report. "Mary Jo and Bobby? Jesus! Who's peddling *that*?"

On February 15, 1980, Joan was asked to address the Ted Kennedy for President Women's Advisory Committee. She wrote the speech herself. In part, she said:

"My own life experiences in the last few years have brought me to an increased awareness of the central importance of the women's movement. Two years ago, I returned to college, and when I receive my graduate degree, I will be a professional in my chosen field. . . . Yet the reality is that most women who might wish to return to school are unable to afford it and that few of them have the proper counseling to direct them back into the stream of education and work.

"In speaking of my *choice* to work, I fully recognize that the major-ity of women today are working out of necessity, not choice. . . . So great are the economic pressures today that six out of every ten women with children at home are working, and these mothers are contribut-ing twenty-five to forty percent of their family's incomes. This means that millions of women are struggling frantically each day, rising early enough to get their children ready for school, then driving off to a full day's work, then afterward rushing out to do the shopping, to pick up their kids, to make the family meal. . . .

"The ERA is more than a symbol. It can become the mandate for the federal government and for every state to ensure equality in both the law and the life of the land."

Joan called for more child-care facilities, experimentation with dif-ferent forms of neighborhood centers, more flexible work schedules, job sharing, equal pay for equal work, and the best possible health care for children.

Postscript: Jackie, Ethel, and Joan after Camelot

As well as having utilized the previously cited Oral Histories, per-sonal interviews were conducted with Leo Damore, Barbara Gibson, Walter Cronkite, Bill Bradlee, Roswell Gilpatric, Ellen Deiner, Kitty

Carlyle-Hart, Steven Styles, Jim Whiting, Nicholas Stamosis, Barbara Gibson, Frank Mankiewicz, Jeanne Martin, Bill Masterson, and Betty Newman.

Volumes consulted: *A People of Compassion: The Concerns of Edward Kennedy*, by Thomas P. Collins; *Our Day and Generation: The Words of Edward Kennedy*, edited by Henry Steele Commager; *The Kennedys: The Third Generation*, by Barbara Gibson; *Bobby Kennedy: Off Guard*, edited by Sue G. Hall; *The Kennedy Encyclopedia*, by Caroline Latham and Jeannie Sakol; *The Estate of Jacqueline Kennedy Onassis* (Sotheby's catalog); *The Best of Modern Screen*, by Mark Bego; *The Kennedy Women*, by Pearl S. Buck; *Living with the Kennedys*, by Marcia Chellis, *Kennedy Wives, Kennedy Women*, by Nancy Gager; *Jack and Jackie*, by Christopher Andersen; *Just Jackie*, by Edward Klein; *A Woman Named Jackie*, by C. David Heymann; *Ghost of a Chance*, by Peter Duchin; *Good Ted, Bad Ted*, by David Lester; *The Shadow President*, by Burton Hersh; *Jackie under My Skin*, by Wayne Koestenbaum; *As We Remember Her*, by Carl Sferrazza Anthony; *Cooking for Madam*, by Marta Sgubin; *The Uncommon Wisdom of Jacqueline Kennedy Onassis*, edited by Bill Adler; *The Joy of Classical Music*, by Joan Kennedy; *Kennedys: The Next Generation*, by Jonathan Slevin and Maureen Spagnolo.

Videos, articles, and other material reviewed and consulted: numerous press accounts of Jacqueline Kennedy Onassis's death and funeral, including those in the *New York Times*, May 20, 1994 through May 24, 1994; "Jackie, 1929–1994," *Newsweek*, May 30, 1994; *Star* special memorial issue; "Jackie, 1994"; *People* commemorative issue, Jacqueline Kennedy Onassis tribute, Summer 1994; "A Quiet Life with M.T." (Maurice Tempelsman), *Newsweek*, June 6, 1994; interview with Jacqueline Onassis in *Publisher's Weekly*, April 10, 1993, by John F. Baker; "Strange Twilight of Ethel Kennedy," *Star*, April 14, 1987; "A Day of Farewell to a First Lady," by Marylou Tousignant and Malcolm Gladwell, *Washington Post*, May 24, 1994; "America's First Lady," by Peggy Noonan, *Time*, May 30, 1994; "Joan Kennedy: Music Is for Life," by Mary Campbell, *St. Petersburg Times*, January 1, 1993; "Death of a First Lady," by R.W. Apple, *New York Times*, May 24, 1994; "Remembering Jackie," *People*, June 6, 1994; "Jackie Remembered," *USA Today*, May 20, 1994; "The Jackie Mystique," by Anemona Harocollis, May 22, 1994; "The Way She Was," *Life*, August 1999; "Stirring Up Memories of Joan K.," by Gayle Fee, *Boston Herald*, January 23, 1996; "New Divorce Settlement for Joan Kennedy," by Gayle Fee and Laura Raposa, *Boston Herald*, June 26, 1996; "Joan Kennedy Turns a Glittering 60," by Julie Hatfield, *Boston Globe*, October 28, 1996; "Joan Kennedy: Born Again, Beautiful," *Star*, November 17, 1992; "Portrait of a Lady," by Elizabeth Gleick, *People*, February 28, 1994; "Joan Kennedy: On a Campaign Trail for the Classics," by Roberta W. Coffey, *Los Angeles Times*, November 26, 1992; *Larry King Live*, "Remembrances of Jacqueline Kennedy Onassis," with guests Oleg Cassini, Letitia Baldrige, Pierre Salinger, John Davis, and Hugh Sidey, May 19, 1999; "Ari's Fate," (interview with Kiki Feroudi Moutsatsos), by Peter Ames Carlin and Toula Viahou, *People*, November 9, 1998.

A note regarding Joan's divorce: Anticlimactically, especially considering the melodrama of their marriage, the end of Ted and Joan's union would occur in a dull, plodding kind of way. The divorce would not be final until the couple underwent two years of legal wrangling. It was reported that, as her settlement, Joan received the Squaw Island home, the Boston condominium, alimony, and between four and five million dollars in cash. However, in 1994, when Ted was in the middle of a bruising reelection battle with Mitt Romney, Joan demanded more money. "The reports of my previous arrangement were grossly exaggerated," she claimed. "I only received about one-fifth of what was reported." Her new Boston attorney, Monroe Inker, called Joan a long-suffering wife who stood by her husband during the most difficult times and said she was outraged that she had been taken in by her former husband in their previous settlement, implying that Ted had concealed certain details of his finances. The new divorce deal, struck in 1996, did not allow for Joan to receive any additional money, but it did include her in Ted's will, so that she would be protected in the event of his death, explained her attorney.

When Ted and Joan made their divorce announcement, Joan's father, Harry, took the news badly. "I was hoping they would resolve their differences," he told Kennedy historian David Lester. "The whole thing was just plain wrong. It's just over. She'll be happier not being married to him," Bennett concluded of his daughter. "It [the marriage] never should have happened."

A few months later, in August 1981, Harry Bennett suffered a heart attack in Metairie and was flown to a Boston hospital, where he died.

In 1984, Joan received an honorary degree of Doctor of Humane Letters from her alma mater, Manhattanville College. The citation accompanying the award reads: "Today we recognize the quiet courage of one who confronted serious illness and personal tragedy, of one who has prevailed against circumstances to emerge victor rather than victim."

*   *   *

Finally, in conclusion, just a little advice from the very wise Lady Bird Johnson to Jackie Kennedy in one of her many letters to Jackie during their forty-some years of correspondence. "Put your faith in love," Lady Bird offered. "And it will carry you through life . . . no matter what happens and no matter when."

Index

the human**mind**

and how to make the most of it

ROBERT WINSTON

BANTAM PRESS

LONDON • NEW YORK • TORONTO • SYDNEY • AUCKLAND

TRANSWORLD PUBLISHERS
61–63 Uxbridge Road, London W5 5SA
a division of The Random House Group Ltd

RANDOM HOUSE AUSTRALIA (PTY) LTD
20 Alfred Street, Milsons Point, Sydney,
New South Wales 2061, Australia

RANDOM HOUSE NEW ZEALAND LTD
18 Poland Road, Glenfield, Auckland 10, New Zealand

RANDOM HOUSE SOUTH AFRICA (PTY) LTD
Endulini, 5a Jubilee Road, Parktown 2193, South Africa

Published 2003 by Bantam Press
a division of Transworld Publishers

Typeset in 11½/13½pt Bembo by
Falcon Oast Graphic Art Ltd.

Printed in Great Britain by
Clays Ltd, Bungay, Suffolk

1 3 5 7 9 10 8 6 4 2

Papers used by Transworld Publishers are natural, recyclable products made from wood grown in sustainable
forests. The manufacturing processes conform to the environmental regulations of the country of origin.

To
Professor Colin Blakemore
and
Professor Richard Dawkins

This book is dedicated with respect and admiration to two
distinguished scientists who have done such outstanding
work in promoting science in society. They have led where
others of us hope to follow.

Contents

Acknowledgements

This book has many imperfections of which I am only too aware. If there are errors, let me clearly state – and this is not an excuse – I am the only person to be blamed. None of the kind, gifted and intelligent people who examined bits of the manuscript have seen the whole book in its entirety – there simply was not time.

I owe a huge debt to a number of people. Particular thanks go to John Lynch, Head of Science at the BBC. He has been very kind and supportive throughout and I owe the opportunity to work on this project to him. He had sufficient faith to encourage me to present material related to cognitive neuroscience on mainstream BBC television and his enthusiasm was essential to start this project and, indeed, to write this somewhat personal account of the mind.

The book could not have been completed in the time available to me without the solid work, dedication and advice of Matt Baylis. We first met nearly nine years ago when he helped me with the book *Making Babies* and with background to various articles I was writing at the time. His towering intelligence and ability to research, ferret out, and sift information was vital for this book and his constant advice on structure and history has been critical. He has always been available when I was in a panic; it has been a pleasure to work with him.

Secondly, thanks go to Joel Winston, who read most of the manuscript, made numerous corrections and amendments, and prevented me from falling flat on my face at several stages during the writing. I fear though at times he has not been as critical as he should for fear of embarrassing his father. My thanks also go to Sarah-Jayne Blakemore, who has an extraordinarily incisive, analytical brain. Her lucid criticism, kindness and advice have been enormously helpful. Any neuroscience errors in this book remain only because they are in a section I never discussed with her. As an advisor on the television series, too, the quality of her guidance and research has been pivotal in making the programmes. My old friend Alison Dillon and I have worked together previously, and her help with editing part of the manuscript is appreciated.

Mark Hedgecoe was series producer for *The Human Mind*. His acumen, considerate advice, military planning and, especially, his friendship are so appreciated. Many times during the preparation of the manuscript his enthusiastic response to my imperfect writing was a key reason for continuing with this project. I am also grateful to Jessica Cecil, the magnificent executive producer, whose warm support and careful discernment has meant much.

Three people, above all, stand out in the ways ideas have been expressed in both the programmes and this book. The BBC has always ensured that I have been extraordinarily fortunate in working with genuinely gifted producers, whose mixture of scientific sense, calm appraisal, artistic skill and film-making ability has been wonderfully stimulating. The producers on this series, Johanna Gibbon, Diana Hill and Nick Murphy, have all been exceptional (even by the standards of the BBC) and it has been a great privilege, a pleasure and fun to work with each of them. I am also grateful to the powerhouse of assistant producers and researchers who were so diligent in digging out and collating background research – they are Miranda Eadie, James Marshall, Nicola Cook, Stian Reimers and, of course, Sarah Blakemore.

The actual process of filming has been important in writing this book – it gave pause for thought, a change of environment, and the stimulus of working with a crew. It is invidious to pick out individual members of a film crew, but it would be remiss not to mention three extraordinarily talented cameramen who did the bulk of the filming, and with their artistry and commitment to the project set the tone for the whole endeavour. They are Chris Hartley, Rob Goldie and Paul Jenkins.

Acknowledgements

Maggie Pearlstine, my remarkable agent, and Jamie Crawford, her brilliant assistant, have been the usual tower of strength. Their regular comments on the manuscript and enthusiasm for its content have spurred me throughout. I am so grateful for their confidence in me as I am for that shown by my publishers, in particular the keen interest of Sally Gaminara and her outstanding team at Transworld, and the concentrated work of the copy editor, Mari Roberts, and the Managing Editor at Bantam Press, Katrina Whone.

One huge advantage I have is in belonging to a great university, Imperial College. It has a wealth of expertise, excellent libraries, and strong backing for the communication of the ideas behind science to a wider audience. I am grateful for the support of my senior colleagues there, the Rector, and the Principal of Medicine, and my Divisional Chairman, David Edwards, and for the facilities of the university. Also, so many students from the university – the physicists, the drama club, the orchestra and the rowing club, amongst many others – put up with the imposition of a film crew with patience and good humour. It was a real pleasure to meet and work with them.

Finally, as any writer will probably admit, the act of setting down a manuscript is usually miserable for much of the time. My family, as always, have suffered (mostly stoically) and the love and support of my wife, Lira, and her very many helpful suggestions about the text, are deeply appreciated.

Foreword

The first few chapters in this book attempt to describe the basic functioning of the brain and how scientists have used various tools to measure this. Such an introduction is inevitably somewhat technical, but it is important to have a loose idea of the complexity of the anatomical regions of the brain and how it functions. Without this we cannot begin to understand how the mind works. I hope the reader will accept the necessity of this and be encouraged to persevere with the book by my use of anecdote and personal experience. In later chapters there is much more discussion of some of the current problems in our exploration of the science of the mind. One thing I hope will be obvious: there is a considerable amount that is controversial and a great deal that we do not know. Science is about uncertainty, and the topics of the human mind and human consciousness are some of the greatest unsolved scientific issues. Perhaps because, paradoxically, we are using an imperfect tool – the human mind itself – to understand the mind, there will always be unresolved questions. Finally, in the last part of this book I deal with issues like personality and intelligence; and I hope it will become obvious that a determinist view of the mind is not, in my view, at all adequate to explain what makes each of us who we are. We are, of course, invested with genes that direct many broad aspects of character and ability, but the environment in which we are placed can have the most profound influence. I hope, therefore, that it will become clear to those who persist beyond the first two or three chapters that there are indeed numerous ways in which we can improve our minds.

It is highly presumptuous for me, a mere reproductive biologist, to have attempted to write any book of this sort. Cognitive neuroscience is not my field of biology, and it is one of the most complex, rapidly changing and contentious areas of modern science. Moreover, a huge number of people, many of them outstanding scientists and a great number excellent writers, have written very good books on this subject. So I have little excuse. But over recent years I have become so interested in this field that if I had my time again as a medical scientist I think this is the area that would now hold the greatest attractions.

In many ways for me this subject is a natural progression from my general scientific and broadcasting interests. These have increasingly touched on various aspects of brain function. Nearly all the TV series and programmes with which I have been involved recently, from *The Human Body*, *Superhuman* and *Instincts* to *Threads of Life*, *Walking with Cavemen* and *Child of Our Time*, have had the brain – with its development, adaptations and workings – as their unifying interest. Though I genuinely never intended to write such a book, I found myself increasingly persuaded that it might be worth doing so during the filming of my latest BBC project. This book was largely stimulated by my presenting *The Human Mind* series and simple intellectual curiosity. When I was encouraged by numerous colleagues at the BBC to write a book around that subject, I took up the challenge with diffidence but growing enthusiasm. I hope its readers will find my particular approach fresh and interesting.

This is not simply the book of the BBC television series. Of course, it refers to it in many places, but it uses only a limited amount of the material seen on the screen. The book is intended to go further and to act as an independent companion, one that will stand alone. It tries to give the background – scientific, historical, social and philosophical – to what we in the production team found interesting or extraordinary about many aspects of human consciousness. So it is focused on the things that I find interesting and is not intended to be a comprehensive account. Nevertheless, I hope that its readers will enjoy reading this attempt to explain some aspects of what is most topical, controversial and intriguing in this extraordinary field.

chapter**one**
Body, brain and mind

If I were to die later today before finishing this chapter and my brain was removed from my skull, it would weigh about 1,400 grams – roughly the same as a bag and a half of granulated sugar. Before being preserved for posterity by being marinated in a jar of formalin (better still, perhaps, strong alcohol with some flavouring), about 75 to 80 per cent of my brain would be made up of water, with just over 10 per cent fat and about 8 per cent protein. If, once it was fixed, people came to examine it and poke it about a bit, it would appear rather crinkled and whitish, and have the slightly rubbery consistency of a large mushroom. And what is more, if you, dear reader, were to die at the same time and have your brain treated in the same peremptory fashion, it would be so similar to mine that any difference would almost certainly be undetectable.

The chances are that no matter how closely our respective brains were viewed, there would be hardly anything obvious to show that what amused passers-by were gazing at were two totally different specimens of the most complicated structure on this planet. There would be nothing to reveal that these two rubbery objects, which to some bystanders would seem faintly disgusting, respectively comprised the sum total of our very being and personality. Nothing to show that at some time we had both loved in different ways, had known different pains, ambitions and disappointments, and had been angry and taken pleasure at different things. Nor that we had learnt different physical and intellectual skills, had mind-bending experiences in different parts of the world, had totally different memories, liked different food or music, and that each of us had quite different human strengths and failings.

Perhaps it is not so surprising then that it has taken humans such a long time to understand the complex nature of the brain, and that it is the very centre of what makes us who we are. Although surgical drilling of holes in the skull (for whatever now mysterious purpose) goes back to Cro-Magnon man some 40,000 years ago, and knowledge of the mind-altering nature of alcohol and the sap from the poppy plant is longstanding, most old civilizations regarded the heart, not the brain, as the centre of the soul. Ancient Egyptians, when embalming human bodies, religiously preserved the heart but destroyed the brain – because otherwise it would rot – by scraping it out of a hole they drilled in the bones at the back of the nose and palate. But it was an Egyptian surgeon who left the first written descriptions that give evidence of some basic insight into neuroscience.

The Edwin Smith Papyrus is one of the oldest known written documents. It is around 3,700 years old and is a surgical treatise describing injuries, mostly to the head, in forty-eight different patients. The Egyptologist, Edwin Smith, who first handled this extraordinary manuscript brought it back from Luxor in 1862, but he did not understand the remarkable nature of the text. Its real signifi-cance was recognized by James Breasted, director of the Chicago Oriental Institute, in 1930, who realized it was a scribe's copy of a treatise from an even earlier time – possibly some 5,000 years ago. The horrifying injuries of Case Number Six give a description of the pulsating brain under the surgeon's hands:

> If thou examinest a man having a gaping wound in his head, penetrating to the bone and smashing his skull, and rending open the brain, thou shouldst palpate the wound. Shouldst thou find that smash which is in his skull those corrugations* which form in molten copper, and something therein throbbing and fluttering under thy fingers – like the weak place in an infant's fontanelle before it becomes whole . . . then if he suffers blood from both his nostrils and stiffness in his neck . . . thou shouldst say concerning him 'An ailment not to be treated'. Thou shouldst anoint that wound with grease

*The 'corrugations' almost certainly refers to the convolutions seen in the cerebral cortex.

2

but not bind it; thou shalt not apply two strips upon it until thou knowest
he has reached a decisive point.

So even Egyptian physicians knew when it might be more prudent
not to treat a patient actively. These hieroglyphics go on to describe
the delicate membranes lining the injured brain, the meninges,
and the discharge of cerebrospinal fluid from inside the head.
Elsewhere the papyrus records the symptoms of a patient unable to
move one limb after severe head injuries on one side, and loss of
speech resulting from injuries to the temple – presumably damage to
the frontal lobe and Broca's area – several thousand years before Dr
Paul Pierre Broca described the speech centre in the 1860s.

The mind/body debate

Thousands of years elapsed before the brain, rather than the heart, was
universally recognized as the most important organ in the body.
Alcmaeon, who around 500BC was one of the earliest to see the
brain's importance, regarded it as the centre of sensation – he
removed an animal's eye and noted the tracts leading to the brain,
recording that 'all senses are connected to the brain'. Plato believed in
the soul – the essence of ourselves, and what we might in modern
times call the 'mind' – and he thought that it had a separate existence
from the body, to the extent that it could survive after the body had
expired. He believed that the centre of the intellect was in the head.

But Aristotle, who lived from 384 to 322BC, appears to have disagreed with his teacher, Plato. He seems to have regarded the heart as
more important. All the lower animals he examined – worms, insects
and shellfish – had a pulsating organ resembling a heart but they did
not have an obvious brain. All blood vessels led towards the heart, and
he describes how the heart twitched when touched while the brain of
higher animals remained inert. The fact that a chicken ran about after
its head was cut off helped Aristotle to the view that 'the seat of the
soul and the control of voluntary movement – in fact of nervous
functions in general – are to be sought in the heart. The brain is an
organ of minor importance, perhaps necessary to cool the blood.'
Aristotle hugely influenced the medieval scholars who came later;
after all, his view of the importance of the heart fitted with biblical

accounts. The notion of the heart as the centre of human behaviour survived until the sixteenth century. 'Faith sits under the left nipple,' said Martin Luther.

A little earlier than Aristotle, though, the philosopher Democritus argued against the heart being the centre of human functions. He writes: 'The brain watches over the upper limbs like a guard, as citadel of the body, consecrated to its protection,' and adds that 'the brain, guardian of thoughts or intelligence', contains the principal 'bonds of the soul'.

Hippocrates, the father of medical practice, recognized the unique nature of the brain: 'Men ought to know that from the human brain and from the brain only arise our pleasures, joys, laughter, and jests as well as our sorrows, pains, grief and tears . . . It is the same thing which makes us mad or delirious, inspires us with dread and fear, whether by night or by day, brings us sleeplessness, inopportune mistakes, aimless anxieties, absent-mindedness and acts that are contrary to habit . . .'

In the third century BC, Herophilus and Erasistratus, both human anatomists, dissected thousands of bodies and demonstrated that nerves were different from blood vessels and that they originated not in the heart, as Aristotle thought, but in the brain or the spinal cord. Then, almost five hundred years after Herophilus' day, the Greek physician Galen (AD130–200) dissected pigs, cattle and monkeys and wrote meticulous accounts of what he had seen. By cutting various nerves, such as those coming from the spinal cord, he established the lack of function caused by their damage. He also demonstrated that severing the laryngeal nerve resulted in the loss of the ability to make noise. During his career he was a physician to gladiators in Rome. Seeing many head injuries presumably gave him an insight into the working of the nervous system and the understanding that the brain played a central role in controlling bodily and mental activity.

When I was a medical student, one of the organs I found most mysterious in the brain was the pineal gland. It is a tiny rounded protuberance, pretty much deep in the middle of the brain, and is unique because, being in the centre, it is the only structure in the brain that is not paired. It has always been associated with mystery – the ancient Hindu mystics thought of it as the seat of the human soul. In the early seventeenth century, the French philosopher René Descartes took the debate further. He concluded that the pineal gland was vital because it functioned by connecting our physical being with our spiritual side. He decided that these two separate and apparently contradictory attributes – the corporeal body and the entirely non-physical mind – could communicate and act as one using the pineal as a conduit. This idea of a conduit seems odd and I am unsure how Descartes came to believe it. To me, the pineal gland seems rather puzzling, if not totally useless. I know that it is supposed to respond to the light of day and the dark of night via the optic nerves and thus regulate the body clock. Everybody repeatedly tells me how it does this by producing the hormone melatonin. Nowadays, travellers can buy melatonin in airports to combat jet lag. But numerous transatlantic flights to the second laboratory in which I work, in California, have never been made even slightly easier by my taking melatonin. I still wake up in Los Angeles feeling like death at three in the morning.

Though he never sat for ten hours in an aircraft, Descartes felt that the pineal was highly significant. So-called Cartesian dualism, the idea of a physical body and abstract mind (communicating via the pineal), endured for a long time because it helped Science and Faith to co-exist. But historical events lent strength to an opposite point of view. The French Revolution, with the infamous apparatus 'popularized' by Dr Joseph Ignace Guillotin, provided the curious with an ample supply (it is calculated at about 40,000) of freshly decapitated heads – and hence brains – to view. And just over a century later, the horrors of the first world war provided doctors and scientists with a steady stream of conscious but brain-damaged young men to observe. Between these two great historical events, advances in physics and better methods of measurement gave scientists the means to observe fluctuations in electricity and pressure. Thanks to these developments, the early neurologists were able to begin to amass a body of evidence to challenge the Cartesian point of view. Rather than the mind and its faculties floating formlessly in the ether and communicating with the brain and body through the pineal gland, it began to seem that the mind was a product of the brain. Moreover, it became increasingly clear that different and distinct regions of the brain were responsible for different aspects of 'mind'.

One lump or two?

In medieval times, various attributes of the self were thought to reside in different bodily fluids. It was generally believed that the cerebro-spinal fluid, the watery fluid in which the brain and spinal cord are bathed, provided the faculty of thought. Then in the early nineteenth century, before science could really prove its claims, phrenology became popular. It was argued by its many adherents that differences in brain architecture – and hence in the character of individuals – could be felt and seen as differences in the shape of the skull.

Dr Franz Joseph Gall, a Viennese doctor, seems to have been the father of phrenology in the late 1790s. Gall, together with his pupil Johann Spurzheim, established many of the basic notions behind this 'science'. Gall recognized that the brain was where the mind was situated. The essential features of his thinking were that the mind is made up of distinct faculties and attributes. He postulated that because these faculties were distinct, they each should occupy a different location within the brain. The bigger the brain, the bigger a person's mental capacity. It therefore followed, in his thinking, that those parts of the brain that were identifiably larger were larger because the attribute associated with them was particularly well-developed. But the key to the science of phrenology was that the skull takes its shape from the brain – so the surface of the skull, and its lumps and pro-tuberances, gave a clue as to what lay underneath. Although this is ridiculed now, these ideas are not so silly. For example, we now know that people with trained memory, such as London cab drivers, some-times have an area – the posterior hippocampus, a structure deep inside the brain associated with memory – which is larger than average. Another example is that of the estimations made by palaeo-anthropologists – they frequently use skull shape to deduce information about the characteristics of our early, ape-like, hominid ancestors.

By the end of the Napoleonic Wars, phrenology was getting estab-lished as a way of telling a person's character and personality. Phrenologists palpated the head and even made complicated measure-ments with specially designed calipers to find out whether someone was likely to be conscientious or a convict. Soon, phrenology was out of the medical and scientific journals and discussed in the serious literary papers; not all comment was glowing. In June 1815, *The Edinburgh Review*, the serious journal of its day, reported:

The writings of Drs. Gall and Spurzheim have not added one fact to the stock of our knowledge respecting either the structure or the functions of man; but consist of such a mixture of gross errors, extravagant absurdities, downright mis-statements, and unmeaning quotations from Scripture as can leave no doubt, we apprehend, in the minds of honest and intelligent men as to the real ignorance, the real hypocrisy, and the real empiricism of the authors . . .

Such is the trash, the despicable trumpery, which two men, calling themselves scientific inquirers, have the impudence gravely to present to the physiologists of the nineteenth century, as specimens of reasoning and induction.

In spite of this sometimes hostile press, phrenology became increasingly popular, particularly in Europe, Britain and then in the United States. Cesare Lombroso, the Italian physician and criminologist, gained widespread attention when he published his book *L'uomo delinquente* (The Criminal Man) in 1876. His view of criminal attributes was partly stimulated by Darwinian ideas and the notion that primitive man was descended from apes. He believed that measuring the heads of people gave a clue about their criminal tendencies. He based his observations on measurements of both living and executed criminals. He compared these with the skulls of non-human primates and came to the view that criminals were 'throwbacks' – the consequence of atavism.

In Britain, phrenology was used to reinforce conventional arguments and prejudices about class, race and criminality. Soon employers were seeking information from their local phrenologist about the predilections of candidates for a post they might be offering. For some gullible members of the public, a visit to a phrenologist was rather similar to a modern-day visit to a clairvoyant or astrologer. And in addition to the thirty-five areas of the head responsible for such attributes as Fidelity, Musical Talent, and Verbal Memory, several devout Christian theologians saw cranial organs for Veneration and Wonder – clear evidence of divine design.

Phrenology was responsible for even more thoroughly laughable claims, such as the idea that Eastern peoples were less warlike because they had smaller heads. And though phrenology has been long discredited, it still had some uncomfortable echoes in the twentieth century. There seems to be a strong element of this stereotypic thinking

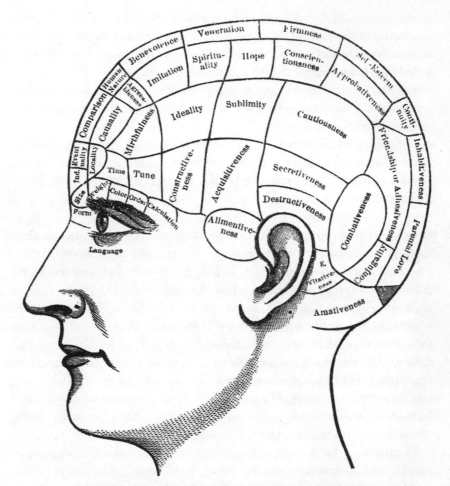

NUMBERING AND DEFINITION OF THE ORGANS.

1. AMATIVENESS, Love between the sexes.
A. CONJUGALITY, Matrimony—love of one. [etc.
2. PARENTAL LOVE, Regard for offspring, pets,
3. FRIENDSHIP, Adhesiveness—sociability.
4. INHABITIVENESS, Love of home
5. CONTINUITY, One thing at a time.
E. VITATIVENESS, Love of life.
6. COMBATIVENESS, Resistance—defense.
7. DESTRUCTIVENESS, Executiveness -force.
8. ALIMENTIVENESS, Appetite—hunger.
9. ACQUISITIVENESS, Accumulation.
10. SECRETIVENESS, Policy—management.
11. CAUTIOUSNESS, Prudence—provision.
12. APPROBATIVENESS, Ambition—display.
13. SELF-ESTEEM, Self-respect - dignity.
14. FIRMNESS, Decision—perseverance.
15. CONSCIENTIOUSNESS, Justice equity.
16. HOPE, Expectation - enterprise.
17. SPIRITUALITY, Intuition—faith—credulity.
18. VENERATION, Devotion—respect.
19. BENEVOLENCE, Kindness—goodness.

20. CONSTRUCTIVENESS, Mechanical ingenuity
21. IDEALITY, Refinement—taste—purity.
B. SUBLIMITY, Love of grandeur—infinitude.
22. IMITATION, Copying—patterning.
23. MIRTHFULNESS, Jocoseness—wit—fun.
24. INDIVIDUALITY, Observation.
25. FORM, Recollection of shape.
26. SIZE, Measuring by the eye.
27. WEIGHT, Balancing—climbing.
28. COLOR, Judgment of colors.
29. ORDER, Method - system – arrangement
30. CALCULATION, Mental arithmetic.
31. LOCALITY, Recollection of places.
32. EVENTUALITY, Memory of facts.
33. TIME, Cognizance of duration.
34. TUNE, Sense of harmony and melody.
35. LANGUAGE, Expression of ideas.
36. CAUSALITY, Applying causes to effect. [tion
37. COMPARISON, Inductive reasoning—illustra
C. HUMAN NATURE, Perception of motives.
D. AGREEABLENESS, Pleasantness- suavity.

Phrenological map (Wellcome Library, London)

8

behind the detailed skull measurements used for some of the Nazi pronouncements on race. In Hitler's Germany, the shape of the skull was frequently evaluated to help determine true Aryan origins, or to detect underlying Jewish racial degeneracy.

In spite of all this, phrenology was vaguely groping in the right direction in a few instances. The so-called 'Organ of Mirthfulness' is a region slightly north-west of the crown of the head. A University of California Medical School surgeon recently applied an electrical current to this region of a patient's brain as part of a procedure to reduce epilepsy, and she burst out laughing.[1] The Organ of Mirthfulness was a happy accident for phrenology, and it shows that there is an extent to which the brain is a box of separate functions. However, these distinct brain regions do not cause protuberances in the skull.

So Gall was not entirely on the wrong track after all. Sadly for him, he lived well before any of the modern-day methods of proving brain function existed. There are many ironies in the history of neurology. In 1828, Gall suffered a fatal stroke and his own head ended up as the last, rather morbid addition to his personal skull collection.

Nowadays, we have clearly arrived at a point where we understand something vital about humankind: that the brain is the key organ responsible for who we are – that the 'mind' is created by the brain. But, as we have seen, this was by no means something we had always understood, or a view that was universally held. In reaching this understanding, the key process, which developed with improved scientific measurement from the middle of the nineteenth century onwards, was brain mapping.

The process of mapping has provided medical science with some of its most crucial information. Thanks to pioneers in this field, we now know that there are regions of the brain that are responsible, at least in part, for movement, sensation and vision, and others even for such things as some religious experiences, and speech. We know that there are sites which store our vocabulary for topics as specific as the naming of vegetables and gemstones. And still others which, when damaged, cause responsible people to become rash, impulsive, promiscuous risk-takers.

The neuron – the basic unit in the brain

A key development was an understanding of the intricate internal anatomy of the brain. Among the first anatomists to look at the brain through a microscope was the Czech professor Johannes Purkinje (1787–1869) who, among other achievements, first classified human fingerprints. Purkinje is credited with describing the first cell identified in the central nervous system in the cerebellum. The cerebellum is the folded structure at the back of the brain that deals largely with balance and coordinated movements. The nerve cell or neuron named after him, the Purkinje cell, is gigantic and it has a most complex web of delicate fronds at its end which connect with other nerve cells. It is almost as thick as a human hair (very large indeed for a single cell) and about ten times bigger than most other cells in the cerebellum, the part of the brain where it mostly resides. It may be of interest to know that somebody calculated that there are around 26 million of these cells in the brain.

Presumably the very size of these large neurons enabled Purkinje to identify them under the microscope and to make drawings. Remarkably, one Purkinje cell with its huge network has been

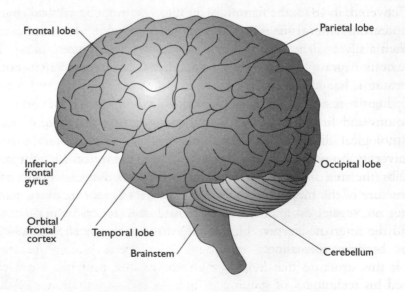

The brain seen from the left side

calculated to receive inputs from up to 200,000 other cells. Jim Bower, a neuroscientist from California Institute of Technology, waxes lyrical about the Purkinje cell: 'They are continuously active at night . . . awake, asleep, or anesthetized,' he writes. 'They are physically stunning, absolutely beautiful. And the ones in your brain are the same shape as the ones in the brain of a fish, bird, reptile, or earliest vertebrate.'

Towards the end of the nineteenth century, the use of tissue stains made it increasingly clear that some cell types were more prevalent in one region of the brain and other types in another. Many great anatomists, among them Nobel Prize winners such as Santiago Cajal from Spain and Camillo Golgi from Italy, were responsible for this key progress, and the basic cell unit in the brain, the neuron, was described in increasing detail.

The respective stories of Golgi and Cajal are interesting and poignant, and eventually clash with a bitter scientific rivalry – not unlike, sadly, scientific jealousies of today. Human nature does not change. Golgi came from Milan, studied medicine at the University of Pavia, but, because he was financially desperate, left academic work to earn a meagre living in the small town of Abbiategrasso as the medical resident in the Home for Incurables. Working by candlelight in his kitchen, which he modified as a crude laboratory, he eventually discovered, in 1873, the famous silver stain that is specifically taken up by neurons. After tissue is hardened in potassium bichromate solution, when a silver salt is applied, nerve cells immediately turn black – 'la reazione negra'. This black reaction is, to this day, rather mysterious because it happens in only a limited number of neurons, and those apparently at random. The Golgi stain, as it is still called, became famous and helped lead Golgi to making a number of important pathological discoveries, mostly after he was able to return to a university hospital. These include the fine anatomy of the olfactory bulbs (the area of the brain largely responsible for taste and smell), the structure of the hippocampus (the area responsible for memory) and, later on, studies on brain tumours, the sensory apparatus in tendons and the internal structure in cells called the Golgi apparatus, which has become increasingly important in modern biology because it is this structure that helps the cell to process proteins. He even used his techniques of staining to help in the understanding of the parasite Plasmodium – the organism responsible for malaria. This last achievement alone is of signal importance and it is not surprising that a kind of shrine devoted to his memory was established at the University of Pavia.

Santiago Ramón y Cajal was born in a small village in northern Spain and studied medicine in the University of Saragossa. He had an ambition to become a painter, but his father was determined that his son should be a doctor. As it happened, his artistic skill was to be of huge benefit. He eventually became Professor of Anatomy in Valencia. Soon after Golgi published his silver stain method, Cajal started to make detailed, quite beautiful drawings of different parts of the brain, viewed down a microscope. In those days, photography down a microscope was of course virtually impossible, so accurate drawing was crucial. His meticulous drawings are still a source of wonderment. He eventually built up a complete picture of the whole of the brain, area by area. As his work developed, Cajal became increasingly convinced that the neuron, the single nerve cell with its minute, fine and delicate processes connecting with other nerve cells, was the key unit in the brain. This is where he had a fundamental disagreement with Golgi. Golgi and his followers were convinced that the brain's tissue was a diffuse net of nerves that were interconnected – a kind of miniature mesh. Of course, the lack of photography meant that the evidence Cajal could produce, a mere drawing, was open to scepticism and ridicule. Many scientists, including Golgi, regarded Cajal's drawings as mere artistic interpretations.

It turns out that Cajal was right, and Golgi wrong. Cajal's genius lies partly in the fact that even though he was using the same kind of microscope and similar staining methods, he was rigorous in drawing what he could see and did not overinterpret what he could not see. But, in 1906, they were jointly awarded the Nobel Prize for their contribution to neuroanatomy, a matter that caused fury and bitterness for Golgi, who was a supreme egotist. To be fair, presumably the appalling way he behaved to Cajal was at least in part because of the difficulties he had repeatedly experienced in getting his earlier methods accepted. It seems they met only once – at the Nobel Prize ceremony in Stockholm. Golgi gave his Nobel lecture first, in which he re-emphasized his belief in a neural mesh – a theory that was then completely contradicted by Cajal's lecture only minutes later. It is interesting to me that, in spite of their rivalry, Santiago Cajal must have been a generous man. Even though his own work had been

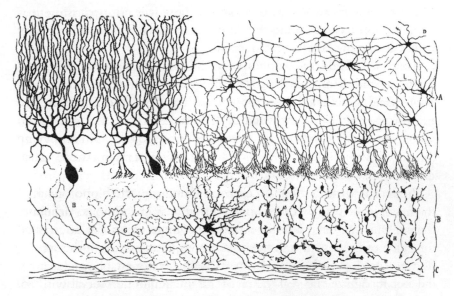

Drawing of neurons by Santiago Ramón y Cajal (Wellcome Library, London)

criticized and ridiculed by some of his opponents, he felt able to write of Golgi's method in 1917:

> I expressed in former paragraphs the surprise and wonder which I experienced upon seeing with my own eyes the wonderful revelatory powers of the chrome-silver reaction and the absence of any excitement in the scientific world by its discovery. How can one explain such strange indifference? Today, when I am better acquainted with the psychology of scientific men, I find it very natural ... Out of respect for the master, no pupil is wont to use methods of investigation which he has not learnt from him.

Korbinian Brodmann was a contemporary of these two famous neuroanatomists. In one way, he is a bit of an unsung hero. His book published in 1909 is regarded as a classic work, but few people have ever actually read it. Nonetheless, the brain maps he published in it, which show the principal areas of cortical function, are extremely well known. He identified around fifty-two separate regions of the cortex, classifying them largely according to the cell types seen in the different areas. Each of the areas was numbered by him, and some of these numbers are still in use today – however, as modern neuro-scientists are starting to understand more about brain function, many of Brodmann's areas are controversial.

Korbinian Brodmann was born on 17 November 1868, and studied medicine in Munich, Würzburg and Berlin. He worked in Switzerland and then Berlin for a while, and he became interested in neurology after he contracted diphtheria. His boss, Oscar Vogt, to whom he owed much of his later career, described him as having 'broad scientific interests, a good gift of observation and great diligence in widening his knowledge'.

Brodmann wrote a thesis on chronic changes in the blood vessels of the brain, in Leipzig in 1898. His meeting with the famous Alzheimer there inspired an interest in the anatomy of brain tissue that he pursued for much of the rest of his scientific career. Even with Vogt's support, he was passed over for promotion in Berlin – the establishment there did not recognize the real value of his meticulous observations. So, again in a relatively short career, he moved institutions. After working in Tübingen, in 1916 Brodmann took over as Director of the Nietleben Mental Asylum in Halle. He left getting married – to Margarete Francke – until the age of forty-eight and by then he was financially secure for the first time in his life, happy and settled.

On 17 August 1918, shortly after the birth of his daughter, he had flu, and septicaemia followed. Brodmann was generally very fit, and was quite pleased to be ill because it gave him a chance to catch up with paperwork. He did not understand how ill he was becoming. One day, his wife saw him making writing motions on his bed with his finger. He then sat back in the bed and died, at the age of forty-nine. Part of the reason I find his death so poignant is the memory of the death of my father, who contracted influenza, did not take it seriously, was quite happy to catch up with work and died of septi-caemia – which led of all things to an abscess on the brain – at the age of just forty-two. I was nine when he died, so, unlike Brodmann's baby, at least I was a child who knew something of his father's attributes – but it was a death that now, with better antibiotic treat-ment, would certainly not have happened.

Brodmann's work is fundamental because it not only involved human brain mapping, it involved work comparing these maps with those in rodents and primates. It led to a much better understanding of how different areas in the cortex might work. Of course, it is only with the development of techniques such as MRI, PET scanning and identification of chemicals in different regions of the brain – mostly eighty or more years after his death – that the principles behind Brodmann's ideas, which were not always appreciated at the time, have been vindicated. But new maps are being produced now that are much closer to how we believe the brain works.

Localizing the workings of the brain

Just before scientists like Brodmann were mapping the detailed microscopic structure of brain tissue, others had started to look at the brain in a more general way. Paul Pierre Broca was one of the most brilliant young men at his medical school in Paris, graduating at the age of twenty. He also held a degree in mathematics, and others in physics and French literature. He was soon appointed Professor of Pathology in Paris at the Hôtel Dieu and Bicêtre hospital. His career was extremely distinguished; he described the spread of cancers through the veins of the body, the effect of dietary deficiency in causing rickets and congenital muscle wasting caused by muscular dystrophy. He also used volunteer medical students to test the temperature of the scalp during various mental activities. Being something of a polymath, he became fascinated by anthropology and this interest landed him in considerable trouble. He was on record in the police files as a 'suspicious person'; the Parisian authorities, particularly the Prefect of Police and the Catholic Church, had him followed and all his movements monitored. At this time discussion of knowledge about human beings was considered to be against the public interest and hence against the interest of the state. His attempts to popularize this science led him to be dogged constantly by plainclothes police and denounced as a subversive, and the public anthropological meetings he organized were infiltrated by agents and informers.

On 4 April 1861, Broca attended a lecture by Ernest Aubertin at the Anthropology Society that was to change his life. Aubertin was a pupil of the phrenologist Gall, and was convinced that the power of speech was localized in the front part of the brain. Paul Broca determined to find a suitable brain on which to work and looked for a patient who had a severe speech disorder. A week later, Monsieur

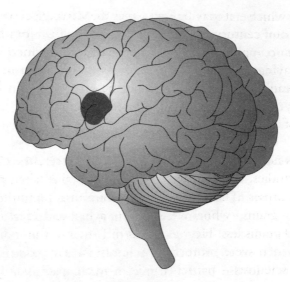

The left hemisphere of the brain, showing Broca's area

Leborgne, a patient who had been incapacitated in Broca's hospital ward for many years, died of septicaemia and gangrene of the right leg and buttock. Leborgne had been paralysed down his right side for some thirty years and was only able to say the words 'tan – tan' in response to any question. His plight was so well known to those who nursed him that they called him 'Tan'. At a post-mortem, Broca found a lesion on the surface of the left side of the frontal lobe of his brain.* Leborgne's pickled brain can now be viewed in Paris at the Dupuytren Museum, a short distance from Odéon Métro station, at no. 15, rue de l'Ecole de Médecine. By 1863, Broca had managed to identify similar lesions in the same part of the brain in no fewer than twenty-five patients who had lost their powers of speech. This area of the brain, the left inferior frontal gyrus, became known as Broca's area, and his reputation was made. The recognition that specific areas of the brain were important for particular functions was an important advance in the history of neurology.

Broca generously paid homage to the maligned phrenologist Franz Gall – at least in general terms. In 1861 he wrote, 'Gall . . . had the undisputable merit of proclaiming the great principle of cerebral

---

*Recent scans of this brain, which is preserved in a glass jar, show that the area of damage in Leborgne's brain was actually considerably bigger than that described by Broca.

localization, which – it may be said – was the starting point of the discoveries of our century concerning the physiology [of the brain].'
Despite this compliment, Broca seemed less inclined to credit
Gall with having identified virtually the same location in the brain
some fifty years earlier, which Gall had called 'Organ 14', the centre
of 'memory for words'; its connected region was known by
the father of phrenology as 'Organ 15' – 'the sense of language, of
speech'.

Broca was not always quite so blessed in his researches. Later in his
anatomical studies, he compared the sizes of brains taken from male
and female corpses. The average weight of a man's brain turned out
to be 1,325 grams, while women, on average, had a brain that
weighed 180 grams less. He was led to the obvious (but wrong) conclusion that men were more clever than women, a view shared by
many other scientists – particularly Darwinians – of his time. Once
the political climate in France changed, Broca ended his career in
1880 as an elected member of the upper chamber of the French
parliament, a senator. He was widely regarded as a fine speaker and
raconteur, and a generous, compassionate Christian. By some cruel
irony, he died shortly after his elevation, following a ruptured
aneurysm in the brain – bleeding from the brain vessels being something he had most carefully documented in his nine-hundred-page
monograph on the subject some twenty years earlier.

Measuring brain function

One of my finest moments was when I acquired my first stethoscope.
Go to any teaching hospital and you can still spot the proud beginners
and the newer students because they will be displaying a form of
designer wear – prominently wearing their stethoscope around the
neck or more casually thrown over the shoulder. As students, our
chiefs were always calling on us to listen to remote, faint and
totally obscure sounds down the tubing, and the usual temptation
was to pretend to hear a noise when you almost invariably couldn't.
As we progressed in my teaching hospital, we weren't required
merely to listen to the sounds of breathing or the heart. Advanced
students even listened to the neck, and I remember on one
occasion mystifying both my elderly patient and myself by listening

to his knee. I couldn't hear a thing but it impressed my class greatly.

In 1928, John Fulton broke new ground when he listened to the back of a man's head. While a doctor in training in Boston, a mere resident at Peter Bent Brigham Hospital, he heard of a patient with gradually decreasing vision on whom surgery to remove a collection of abnormal vessels at the back of the brain had failed. The surgery had left the patient with a gap in his skull where bone had been removed. The man complained that whenever he opened his eyes, he heard a roaring sound. The noise became a bit more intense, the patient said, whenever he was doing something difficult. Fulton wasn't interested in trying to impress his colleagues but he picked up his stethoscope and identified what clinicians technically refer to as a faint 'bruit' or a 'murmur' – a rushing, pulsating sound caused by turbulent blood flow. Fulton decided that the tangle of blood vessels in the visual area of his brain was the cause, and that the roaring noise they could both hear was the noise of chaotic blood flow as it rushed to the area of the brain doing the work when he opened his eyelids and used his remaining vision. The noise was particularly intense when he attempted to read. So the more intense the mental activity, the more the blood flow, because the brain was using more oxygen to complete its task. The remarkably resourceful Fulton even developed a very primitive 'imaging' machine. He rigged up a stethoscope so that the amplified sound vibrations could record changes in the sound of blood flow by dragging a needle across a smoked drum. Thus equipped, he would appear to have provided the first ever 'picture' of brain activity.

But although in recent years measurements of blood flow in the brain have become important in monitoring its activity, it was a long time before suitable instruments for measurement were available. Around the 1880s there was a growing realization that the brain might be producing electrical activity, and the most promising experiments of the time were to try to capture these faint signals. In Liverpool, a physician at the medical school, Richard Caton, was examining what happened to the brains of monkeys and rabbits when he shone lights into their eyes. Electric light wasn't yet available, so a naked flame sufficed, and he needed to take off the top of their skulls in order to apply his crude probes to the surface of the brain. He recorded electrical impulses by means of a mirror attached to a fine coil of wire – the so-called mirror galvanometer invented by the physicist Lord Kelvin. Removing the cranium was hardly a procedure, in those days of relatively crude anaesthetics, that could be applied to humans. It wasn't until the 1930s that we developed electrodes sensitive enough to routinely register changes in charge through the bone and the scalp.

The first person to record electrical activity in the brain of human subjects was probably the Austrian Dr Hans Berger. He started animal experiments before the first world war, but these were mostly inconclusive and unhelpful. However, as early as 1902 he had found a number of human subjects who had defects in the skull bones, and he used primitive electrodes and galvanometers to see whether he could detect faint electrical activity. After his return from the war, he set about using the rather more sophisticated equipment that had become available. Once again, he found a few people with defects in the skull – presumably not so difficult in Germany after the ravages of battle. He tried various approaches to measuring activity in these people, one of which involved stimulating one side of the brain with an electrode and seeing if there were any demonstrable pulses coming through on the opposite side. But he soon realized that it was possible to measure the slight fluctuations in electrical signals that were occurring spontaneously when no artificial stimulus was being given. He first published this work, coining the word 'electroencephalogram', in 1929. This is still regarded as an important milestone in the history of neuroscience because what Berger described were the first rhythms in human brain physiology, the alpha waves, which change in pattern and frequency during activity.

Berger was an odd man. He was demanding and reserved. His experiments were conducted in the strictest secrecy. He refused access to his laboratory and never mentioned to any colleagues what he was researching. He was obsessed with the idea that others might take credit for his work, and was haunted by the many false turns he had made in the thirty years of interest he had had in this work. In 1937, when international recognition was finally accorded to him at the Parisian Psychology Congress, he cried when he said, 'But in Germany I am not so famous.' He was an opponent of the Nazi regime, and watched the rise of Hitler with growing despair and depression, being forced to retire from the University of Jena in 1938. In 1941, he took his own life by hanging himself in the hospital where he had worked.

Electroencephalography – EEG – has limitations when trying to evaluate the function of the mind. It is a rather unselective form of monitoring the brain's electrical signals – like a TV that manages to receive all channels at once. Until relatively recently it has been thought nearly useless for researchers trying to isolate the brain activity associated with a particular thought or feeling or action. However, in the last twenty-five years electroencephalography has become more refined and has been used extensively in neuro-psychology. It is undergoing something of a renaissance for this kind of investigation.

The use of radioisotopes

In the 1970s, a team of Danish and Swedish researchers hit upon a new technique. Using Geiger counters to measure radiation, they injected a tiny amount of a radioactive gas into the bloodstream of the subject: the more blood flow, the more radiation capable of detection. The gas they used was xenon, which is completely inert and harmless, but several of its isotopes are radioactive. Radioactive isotopes decay over time, eventually becoming devoid of radio-activity. The radioactivity of a substance is normally measured by its half-life, which is the time it takes for half the radioactive atoms to decay. Compounds with a short half-life are valuable for medical measurement because the patient receives a rapidly diminishing amount of radiation, and the dose of radiation is greatly limited. Where the radioactive isotopes of xenon that were once used produced radiation that lasted for a few hours or several days, nowadays only isotopes with a very short half-life are used – a few minutes at most.

Once the xenon had been injected by the Scandinavian scientists, its progress could be measured by the Geiger counters close to the scalp as it travelled in the bloodstream of the brain. The injection was not exactly pleasant – to get enough into the head entailed direct injection into the carotid artery in the neck using a hand-held syringe, and the only subjects hardy enough to withstand it were, rather sur-prisingly, big, beefy men drawn from the local fire station in Lund. (In my experience big beefy males would most probably be the worst candidates for this kind of procedure, likely to faint at the mere sight of the needle.) Crude though this procedure might have been, the

20

researchers were able to produce pictures of the blood flow inside the brain as the subjects performed tasks such as listening to speech, tapping fingers, even imagining making sudden movements. From these early eye-watering experiments, the technique of Positron Emission Tomography, or PET scanning, was born.

In PET, a fast-decaying radioactive tracer is injected into the blood, and the resultant gamma rays are read while the subject undertakes the activity being studied – counting to ten, for instance, or thinking happy thoughts. By analysing a few million of these readings at a time using sophisticated computing, it is possible to build a three-dimensional image of the brain as it goes to work. While PET was a step forward, it was undoubtedly a large-scale procedure. The machines were huge and costly – the PET unit at the Hammersmith Hospital in London, for instance, required an army of physicists, engineers, chemists and computer operators. It also required a small nuclear reactor, a cyclotron, to generate the rapidly decaying isotopes with a short half-life that would not give too much radiation to the subject. The Hammersmith cyclotron, which largely started as a possible way to give deep X-ray therapy to cancer patients, was also used to develop radioactive nucleotides for injection into patients having scans other than those done by PET.

When I first arrived at the Hammersmith in 1969, as a very junior physician and research worker, it seemed not so much a proper hospital as a collection of disparate buildings that did not match each other, dotted around in an almost random fashion next to Wormwood Scrubs prison. From time to time the more adventurous among those held as involuntary guests of the Crown would slip over the wall next to the high-security wing and into the grounds of the hospital. One such prisoner was George Blake, the atom spy. The collection of brick, concrete and wooden buildings, old workhouse premises, isolated out-patient facilities, Nissen huts and Portakabins (or whatever was the equivalent in those days) that made up the hospital was ideal territory for a hunted man looking for temporary cover, but not so good for someone trying to get from place to place in a hurry. It was especially difficult when attempting to use short-half-life isotopes for injection into patients who were not in the PET scanner, which was carefully sited in the cyclotron building. One of my colleagues, a junior house physician, was instructed to scan the neck of a patient on the second floor of the main hospital to identify how her parathyroid glands were working. The isotope that would be taken up in this gland and was therefore deemed suitable had a half-life of seven minutes. Several practice runs were made by the overworked houseman so that this highly valuable isotope, freshly made up and incorporated into the carrier compound, could be taken safely from the cyclotron unit, about a quarter of a mile distant. Two aluminium ladders, a huge keep net, a bicycle and a fishing rod with a large reel were prepared. The practice runs went without difficulty and it was found that an ampoule, resembling in size and shape the real container of the isotope, could be delivered from the cyclotron in four and a half minutes.

On the morning of the intended injection, the Geiger counters and the patient were prepared. Her bed was placed close to a window on the second floor. The fishing rod, complete with reel, was placed next to the window. Once the isotope had been delivered from the machine, prepared for injection and placed in a suitable vial and then into a canvas bag, the nearest window, on an upper floor of the cyclotron building, was opened and the vial was dropped vertically into the large-aperture keep net held by the waiting houseman in the car park. He mounted his bicycle, pedalled furiously to the first perimeter wall, shinned up the aluminium ladder, mounted the wall and gingerly felt his way over to the other ladder held firm by a waiting assistant, then sprinted 200 yards to the back of the ground floor of the hospital, two floors below the Endocrine Unit. Right on time, the line from the fishing rod was unreeled, the houseman gave the signal after tying on the bag containing the vial, and the isotope inside it was wound in to the window above, in the ward sister's office. But the patient had felt a call of nature and had locked herself into the lavatory. After various negotiations through the solid wooden door, the patient emerged and a sweating member of the medical team injected the isotope into the patient with just over two minutes to spare – still a new Hammersmith record. I have no idea whether the patient's parathyroid gland showed positive on the Geiger counter.

Picture the brain at work

The presence of the cyclotron at the Hammersmith was extremely important in establishing one of the first PET scanning units in

Europe looking at the brain. The use of compounds such as those containing radioactive oxygen or radioactive glucose meant that both blood flow and brain metabolism could be measured. One powerful technique introduced fairly soon was substraction scanning. The brain might be scanned while the volunteer in the scanner is gazing at a blank screen, and then scanned again, for example when the screen contains a word. Thus physiologists and psychologists could learn what part of the brain is actively associated with reading. But one problem was that all the attention given to generating isotopes and working out the physics of the scanning process meant that the people best able to operate the machines were not the same individuals conducting research into the function of the brain. At that time, psychology was somewhat in thrall to the newly emergent discipline of computer science. The accepted view was that the human brain was no more than a very complex logic machine, one that could be replicated as our skills in programming grew sharper. PET was never going to be the technology that knocked this view from its throne, partly because it was so expensive. But what is more important is that any process that involves injecting radioactive substances into a person is likely to be limited – particularly if its purpose is research, rather than cure.

The resolution in PET scanning is limited, so structures in the brain do not show up very sharply. PET also has the severe disadvantage that volunteers cannot be repeatedly scanned. Repeated exposure to radiation would be harmful, and this is a major limitation, particularly as so much neurological investigation requires repeated evaluation in the same subject under differing conditions. And it is especially unwise to use women and children for this kind of research – women because they might be pregnant, and children because their threshold of what is acceptable and safe is much reduced. Ethics committees are properly cautious about giving approval to techniques involving PET that might expose the subject to any extra radiation risk. So while PET provided some very exciting three-dimensional images of the brain at work, it was never likely to enable us to build a detailed map of consciousness. Consequently, PET scanning is now largely used for specific indications where actual measure of brain blood flow is required, for looking for tumours (which tend to have a high metabolic activity), and in scanning people who might have pieces of metal in their skull when magnetic resonance imaging (MRI) cannot be used. PET is also used extensively for research into drugs that may be active in the brain. PET can evaluate very specific markers for brain activity – not, for example, just blood flow. So, if a researcher is interested in, say, dopamine function, PET can be of considerable value. PET is useful, too, for psychological evaluation of auditory function. This is because the PET machine is very quiet, unlike the MRI machine that has tended to supersede it.

Magnetic resonance imaging has proved to be a hugely important tool for brain and cognitive research. In another book, *Human Instinct*, I have explained in detail how MRI images are obtained. Essentially, if a person is placed in an intense magnetic field, the molecules in the body line up like minute compass needles. Thereafter, the molecules can be knocked off their axis by exposing them to a pulse of radiowaves. The molecules in different tissues spin at slightly different rates, emitting a signal that is detectable by arrays of sensors connected to a computer. Remarkable three-dimensional images can be generated and, as far as we know, without risk. It seems that repeated exposure to even very powerful magnetic fields is harmless and this has led to MRI being used widely to investigate the brains of willing subjects repeatedly. More recently, fMRI, or functional magnetic resonance imaging scanning, has been an important step forward. This utilizes a property of haemoglobin, the oxygen-carrying pigment in red blood cells. The amount of oxygen carried by haemoglobin changes the degree to which the haemoglobin, flowing through the brain, disturbs a magnetic field. By taking many readings from slightly different angles and building up a computed picture, it is possible to construct a three-dimensional image of great clarity.

While writing this book, I had the privilege of meeting Professor Richard Ernst from Switzerland, who won the Nobel Prize in 1991 for his remarkable work on improvements in magnetic resonance technology. This great scientist rather wistfully told the story of how he had recently sat in an MRI scanner to have his own brain imaged. With all the photographs taken, the technician came up to him and said, 'Professor, your brain is completely normal.' Had a technician said this to me I would have been reassured. But then I haven't won a Nobel Prize; it does rather illustrate that a brain that produces great intellectual achievement does not generally stand out from the run of the mill.

MRI not only delivers an image of great clarity in a short period of time, it is cheaper than PET technology. Nearly every major hospital now has an MRI scanner, and in recent years MRI has become increasingly used to replace other kinds of imaging, such as conventional X-rays. Moreover it does not require a large cohort of staff to operate it. As the *New Scientist* writer and author of *Going Inside*, John McCrone, describes it, MRI is 'brain scanning for the masses' – a reasonably accessible technology that nearly any scientist can use to test his or her thesis.

MRI is not the last word in brain mapping technology. In recent years, the technique of magnetoencephalography (MEG) has offered a few further refinements. MEG is a sensitive technology, able to read the minute traces of magnetic activity given off; however, the spacial resolution is limited and not substantially different from EEG. Because the signals are so small and detection of them difficult, it can only be used in specially constructed shielded rooms, and even then experiments can be hampered by the faintest movement. But one of MEG's great advantages is its speed. PET scanners could measure what happened in the brain over a period of minutes, fMRI over a few seconds. But MEG can deal in thousandths of a second. Given that our thoughts take fractions of a second to appear and disappear, any technology that can keep up with them is likely to be a useful tool. Another significant advantage over EEG (when background electrical activity can confuse the picture) is that the scalp and skull bones do not interfere with the underlying changes in the magnetic field occurring in the brain.

Watching single neurons at work

One of the most important advances in brain science has been the development of the ability to assess what an individual neuron is doing at a particular moment. Most of this work has been done in laboratory animals. Studying single cells by assessing their electrical activity is an important alternative to looking at regional activity in the brain, and makes it possible to look at what individual elements are doing within a region of interest.

Interest in single neuron measurement originates from the 1940s and a wonderfully productive partnership by two remarkable scientists. Andrew Huxley and Alan Hodgkin won the Nobel Prize for their work in 1963. Hodgkin is regarded as one of the great physiologists of the last century. Together with Huxley, he illustrated how nerves work electrically and how they 'fire' impulses. Hodgkin and Huxley did something revolutionary by inserting a tiny electrode directly into a nerve cell. Part of their genius was to use an animal with unusually large nerve cells – the squid – which they caught offshore in Plymouth. When I say these nerve cells are big, I am still referring to a cell around the thickness of a human hair – about 0.5mm across. They made a surprising discovery. Far from what was expected, they found that the resting potential inside the cell was −60 millivolts, and during a nerve impulse this changed to reach a peak of around +40 millivolts. They were unlucky in one sense – the discovery was made in July 1939 and a month later Britain was at war with Germany.

Alan Hodgkin was brilliant (and also something of an amateur mathematician), and the War Office commissioned him to work with radar. He was highly instrumental in developing radar in fighter planes so that they might detect Luftwaffe bombers. He worked on the spot and flew many hours strapped into the tiny space in the tail of fighter planes. His experiences must have been hair-raising – literally – because his equipment needed 15,000 volts and in the rare atmosphere 10,000 to 16,000 feet above sea level was prone to spark massively without warning. From time to time he found himself strapped right next to an electrical fire in the equipment surrounding him.

Andrew Huxley, who comes from an extraordinarily gifted scientific family, was an equally talented Cambridge undergraduate. But like many good scientists he kept a sense of proportion about his achievements. When speaking in Stockholm at the time of his being the joint recipient of the Nobel Prize, he modestly paid tribute to Hodgkin as his teacher. His war was also spent involved in radar, but more in the development of radar for gunnery and for use in naval ships. Like Hodgkin, his wartime work must have saved countless lives and was one of the most important defensive advances in recent military history. Also like Hodgkin, he eventually became President of the Royal Society, the most influential position in British science. In recent years his work at University College, London, concentrated more on the action of muscles than nerves.

The award of the Nobel Prize to these two great men somewhat overshadows important earlier work on microelectrodes. Ida Hyde in 1902 at Harvard constructed tiny glass tubes of about three microns' diameter that were filled with salt water and therefore good electrical conductors. She was interested in cells that contracted, like muscle cells. More relevant to neuroscience was the pioneering work of Angelique Arvanitaki, who dissected giant cells from molluscs, initially the sea hare and the land snail. She showed, a little earlier than Huxley and Hodgkin, that nerve cells rhythmically produced electrical impulses and that one nerve cell in close proximity to another could influence the way it discharged.

There have been many refinements in electrodes, making the study of smaller neurons possible. Glass has a valuable property – fine glass tubing can be drawn easily into very thin tubes after being briefly heated, under tension, in a laser beam – a technique I use in my own work studying eggs and embryos. But modern single-cell research does not necessarily require the glass electrode to be inserted into the neuron itself. The electrode can be inserted painlessly into the brain of an animal, and, providing the tip of a very fine glass electrode is in close proximity to a neuron, its activity can be accurately measured. Important observations can be made by watching the change in electrical potential of single cells in this way, for example when an animal moves a particular limb, sees something or performs a given task – or possibly when it learns something new. This approach has been expanded in an exciting way recently. A number of physiologists have made simultaneous recordings from more than one single cell in animals. It is reported that one recent study of the hippocampus involved recordings from no fewer than 150 cells, taken simultaneously. Single-cell science, though, by no means solves all the puzzles of brain function. Studying very many neurons working together in harmony must hold many of the answers to understanding the nature of the human mind.

Animal research

No potted history of neuroscience is possible without a discussion on the use of experimental animals. As we shall see again and again throughout this book, animal experimentation has been central to the understanding of brain function ever since Galen in the second century. A surprising amount of brain research, valuable in understanding human nervous function, can be done in relatively 'primitive' creatures, such as fruit flies and, as we've seen, molluscs. But the mammalian brain has a unique cortex and much of the exploration of mind – cognitive neuroscience – requires work in mammals. Make no mistake about it. The study of a whole range of serious or fatal human diseases, for example cranial tumours, brain damage in babies, depression, schizophrenia and CJD, has required work with mammals, and this work has to continue, in my opinion, if human lives are to be saved. There is a strong moral imperative here. The central tenet of human ethics is the notion of the sanctity of life – human life above all. But we have important moral obligations to the lives and welfare of animals, too. These responsibilities must be taken with absolute seriousness. Not to do so would be to brutalize our society. So the codes of conduct in the human treatment of animals – which are now more rigorously enforced than ever before – must be taken seriously. We have no right to make animals suffer more than is absolutely necessary; they must be treated with humanity and respect at all times.

There are certain basic principles that experimenters must take into account. First, on conducting any research with animals there must be recognition that the studies are worthwhile and likely to lead to measures that have a reasonable chance of benefiting health. In this respect, repeating experiments that have already been done by others purely for the sake of minor advantage is not ethical. Secondly, all experiments must be conducted throughout with the minimum of pain or distress, with anaesthesia or analgesics used if there is any pain, and animals kept clean, comfortable, well housed and respected. Very few experiments cause any pain. Where this does happen – such as when finding out how to avoid or minimize human pain, or how to improve anaesthesia – it is kept to a minimum and pain relief is given. If there is evidence of prolonged suffering, there is a need to destroy the animal humanely and swiftly. Thirdly, the number of experiments must be kept to a minimum and alternatives that might be valuable should always be preferred even if they are more expensive or difficult. Cell culture techniques, human tissue experiments, studies on simple single-celled or invertebrate species are to be preferred if they are a realistic alternative.

Animal research has been attacked with massive hostility in recent years. Most scientists find this puzzling when the majority of the population eat meat and wear leather shoes and belts or carry leather handbags. Animal farming is far less rigorously regulated than laboratory animal usage. Leaving aside the question of food – and an animal diet is certainly not essential for human health – there are the issues raised by therapeutic drugs. All of us in modern society take drugs, use vaccines and employ pharmaceuticals that protect and maintain health. These must be tested for safety on animals, and usually more than one species will be required – sometimes in large numbers. Any alternative, with the attendant risks to human life, would be unthinkable to all but a tiny group of people. It is no accident that a recent House of Lords Select Committee, a body known for its independence of mind, reported of drug testing that it is '. . . essential for medical practice and the protection of consumers and the environment, as it provides information that is not currently available from any other source'. Perhaps, before the animal protesters persuade people that animal research is wrong, every drug bottle and preparation in this and other European countries should be clearly stamped: 'This preparation has been produced, and your safety improved, by the use of animal testing.'

What should be deeply worrying to people living in a democracy is the lengths to which some animal rights groups and protesters will go in their attempts to ban animal research. Their attacks on scientists and on scientific institutions risk human life and have barbaric consequences. Much of their propaganda, put out on the internet for example, is misleading and inflammatory. Their exhortations to criminal behaviour are clearly illegal and often violent. Their boycott of, or attacks on, companies that support animal work, however loosely – such as banks, insurance companies and pharmaceutical companies – are wicked because they frighten and intimidate. It should be a source of deep concern to every democrat in a modern society that governments do not do far more to protect individuals and institutions who are targeted by these protest groups, and by the violent action they frequently use. Until proper and effective measures are taken about criminal action and criminal threats, neuroscience and the health of people who suffer from brain diseases, such as stroke and Alzheimer's, will continue to be in serious jeopardy.

Let me conclude here with a rather surprising statistic. If you can bear it, visit some of the more virulent websites that contain material which violently condemns animal research and those who undertake it. Many canards are repeated: that animal research is done to promote the careers of scientists, that there are strong commercial motives behind it, that research has seldom achieved any scientific knowledge which could not have been achieved by other means. Throughout this book there are references to great scientists who have made significant contributions to our understanding of the brain. The highest accolade of all is reserved generally for the Nobel Prize winners – these are men and women whose science is considered of the highest importance. When a Nobel Prize is awarded for medicine or physiology, it is because the contribution is regarded as of extreme importance for health. Since 1901, no fewer than 132 individuals have won Nobel Prizes whose work would not have been possible had all research on animals been banned. Seven of the last ten Nobel prizewinners have relied at least partly on animal work. Of these 132 Nobel laureates, at least thirty-two individuals have made a direct contribution to neuroscience – indeed, many of them are mentioned in this book. These people did not use animals to further their career. They did so because they believed, and have demonstrated, that their work was important in the battle to save lives and to promote health.

chapter two

How does your brain work?

It is remarkable how controversial the study of the brains of dead people has become in Britain. Since the recent publication of the Isaacs Report by the government, there has been an extraordinary outcry. This is because pathologists have taken it upon themselves to store brains after post-mortem examinations to further knowledge of their possible abnormalities. The British press have made claims that such brains 'were illegally taken' or even that they were 'stolen'. These statements, designed to shock, have not been denied by the NHS, Department of Health officials or ministers of government. This irresponsible failure on the part of officials who should know better is having a devastating effect on brain research in Britain. It is widely agreed among neurologists that detailed study of brain tissue after death is of major medical importance. However, very soon after life ceases, the brain decomposes so fast that its structure can no longer be usefully studied unless it is first rapidly preserved by fixation in formalin. Inevitably, detailed study at the time of a post-mortem is simply impossible, so pathologists – completely responsibly in my opinion – have fixed brains to store them for later assessment when there is time to do detailed analysis. Because government officials have been so unsupportive of brain researchers undertaking this kind of study, there is a serious restriction on our knowledge of one of the most important and expensive issues facing the NHS and our society – namely, mental ill-health.

I hold strong religious views and certainly most religious people rightly desire that respect should be accorded to dead bodies. These religious views are essentially based on a conviction of the sacredness of life. But to preserve life, it is sometimes necessary to study death. Of course, I hold that the religious views of others should be respected deeply. But I do not consider that retarding the progress of society at large by overreacting to the religious sensitivities of a small number of people is acceptable. Of course, the relatives of somebody who may have had misgivings about a post-mortem have a right to refuse that examination and for the body to be buried intact. That is perfectly reasonable. But if relatives give permission for a post-mortem, then it should be understood that certain tissues may be required to be stored for future study – as part of the original post-mortem.

Neural networks

What is it we can see when we look at a brain after its preservation in formalin? Externally, not much. That unprepossessing object weighing roughly three pounds (or 1,400 grams) looks mostly like a gigantic, convoluted fungus. But under the microscope we can see it contains an extraordinary number of cells. Some are neurons, the cells that do the work of thinking: roughly 100 billion of them. Only a small proportion of the brain cells – probably around 10 per cent – are neurons, however. They need a supporting structure of other cells, and these are called the glia. The early anatomists thought of the glia as a 'glue', hence the name.

Glial cells are of various types. Some perform the function of protecting the neurons from undesirable chemical compounds, such as many drugs. Other cells in the glia are used in the healing process – if neurons die, these cells invade the damaged areas and eat up the dead neuronal tissue by engulfing it. Lastly, other cells of the glia form the substance myelin, a fatty sheath wrapped around the neurons that acts as a kind of electrical insulator.

If we zoom in with higher magnification, we will see that each of these neurons is connected to up to 10,000 other neurons by frond-like tendrils. These tendrils that project from the neuron resemble fine branches on a tree, or complex rootlets. They are known as dendrites and axons. Dendrites receive incoming information, and axons

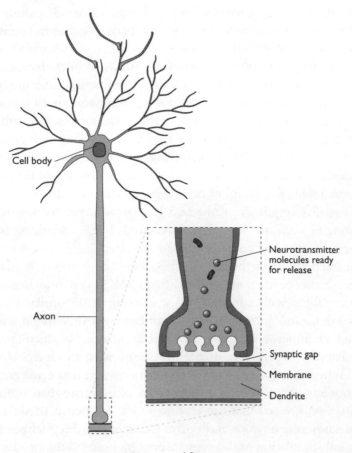

Cell body

Neurotransmitter molecules ready for release

Axon

Synaptic gap

Membrane

Dendrite

A Neuron and Synapse

transmit it. You will already know that the neurons of the brain communicate via electricity that they themselves can generate – but that doesn't mean there are sparks flying inside our skulls. The communication is mostly by the release of chemicals from a neuron. This results in a change in the minute electrical charge of those neurons with which it connects.

The neurotransmitters

If we zoom in even closer, we will see that the neurons of the brain are not joined to each other. Understanding how our neurons communicate using chemical messages was a giant leap forward for neurology. As is sometimes the case, the precise moment of discovery occurred in a rather unlikely fashion. In 1921, the Austrian scientist Otto Loewi (1873–1961) awoke in the dead of night having had an inspirational dream. He scrawled it down on a piece of paper next to his bed and promptly went back to sleep. He woke with a start at six o'clock in the morning, realizing that he had dreamed of something most important, but turning to his notebook he was completely unable to decipher his dead-of-night scrawl. He described the following day as 'the most desperate day of my scientific life'. But the next night, the dream came to him again and, taking no chances, he immediately got up, rushed to his lab at three in the morning, purportedly still in his nightshirt, and began working on the experiment that had come to him in his sleep.

He used two frog hearts which both had their vagus nerve still attached; the hearts were still beating. He placed one heart into a chamber filled with salt water (at a concentration similar to normal body fluid), and connected this chamber by a fluid-filled tube to a second chamber containing the other heart. He then began to stimulate the vagus nerve of the first heart with an electrical current that immediately caused its beat to slow down. Then came the amazing moment of truth. After a short delay of no more than a minute or two, Loewi noticed that the second heart also began to slow down. Loewi drew the obvious and correct conclusion. He realized that his electrical stimulation of the vagus nerve had caused the production of a chemical message. The chemical had passed from the first chamber into the second chamber in the saline, so causing the second heart to slow down without being directly electrically stimulated. By five o'clock that very morning, just two hours after his dream, Loewi had the first proof that nerve impulses were carried by chemical messengers – later known as neurotransmitters – around the brain and body. For this work, Loewi was awarded the Nobel Prize in 1936. But just two years later, being a Jew, he was arrested by storm-troopers. In order to escape their clutches, he had to instruct his bank to transfer all his Nobel Prize money to a Nazi account; and, as a refugee, all his other possessions were subsequently confiscated. He was lucky to arrive in England, penniless.

While Loewi's work showed the chemical message passed between a nerve cell and a muscle cell, what he had observed was precisely the same mechanism by which chemical messages are passed between the neurons in the brain. Neurons aren't joined to each other, so how do they communicate? There is a tiny gap between each axon transmitter site and the dendrite receiver sites of its neighbours. This gap is called the synapse. When communication between neurons occurs, this gap is filled up with the chemicals called neurotransmitters – these carry the electrochemical 'message'. These messages travel at a variety of speeds – between 2 and 20 miles an hour – depending on the size of the axon and the density of that fatty myelin sheath enveloping the neurons. But the human brain, as I say, is the most complicated object in the known universe. There are estimated to be an amazing 1,000 million synapses in a piece of your brain the size of a single grain of sand.

To date, around fifty different neurotransmitters have been identified – though we shall mainly be concerned here with only a few of them, mostly active particularly in the cortex. Most neurons are capable of producing more than one neurotransmitter, depending on the degree of stimulation they receive.

Glutamate is one of the most important and widespread 'general-purpose' neurotransmitters found everywhere in the brain. It is a chemical closely related to monosodium glutamate (MSG), widely used in cooking – particularly in Chinese restaurants. Because monosodium glutamate is so closely related to this ubiquitous neurotransmitter there has been some concern in the past that too much of it added to food might affect the way the nervous system functions. But the latest studies in America tend to confirm that MSG is harmless.

Gamma aminobutyric acid or GABA is the most important inhibitory neurotransmitter in the brain. To prevent the brain being overloaded by too many neurons and all their synapses firing at once, the neuronal circuits have to 'decide' which messages to pass on. GABA is the neurotransmitter that most frequently acts as a controller. If, for some reason, there is insufficient GABA, the system reacts chaotically, and many thousands of neurons send messages simultaneously, which can result in a fit. I have heard neuroscientists describe an epileptic seizure as losing the battle between stimulation by glutamate and inhibition by GABA. GABA helps neurons discriminate about which signals they respond to. Evidence from Rhesus monkeys suggests there may be inadequate GABA in old age. This could be one of the reasons why there is mental deterioration as we get older, and the findings imply that treatment with this compound or others that increase its action may improve well-being in old people.

Dopamine is associated particularly with voluntary movements – and people with low concentrations of it, such as sufferers from Parkinson's disease, generally have problems with initiating action. Low dopamine levels are also found in people with Attention Deficit Hyperactive Disorder, and in depression. Schizophrenia is associated with high dopamine levels. The dopamine pathways of the brain are well defined, and we can see how variations of dopamine secretion are responsible for certain disorders and traits. For instance, one key dopamine pathway travels from an area of the brainstem called the substantia nigra pars compacta up to the basal ganglia, enabling smooth performance of automatic movements – for instance, walking.

Among other things, as we shall see, dopamine is also linked to certain behaviour – such as alcoholism, criminality, thrill-seeking and drug taking. This is not surprising, given that dopamine is particularly important in the pleasure centres of the brain. The American geneticists David Blum and Kenneth Comings believe they have identified a specific change in one gene that is found in 50–80 per cent of alcoholics, drug addicts, compulsive eaters and compulsive gamblers. This gene prevents dopamine from binding to neurons in the 'reward-motivation' pathways of the brain. As a result, people with this gene do not feel sufficiently satisfied when they have engaged in behaviour calculated to give them a sense of reward. So they do it again and again.

Serotonin, among other functions, plays a role in appetite regulation – people with high levels of serotonin may, for example, have a poor appetite. It is also important in the regulation of mood. The anti-depressant Prozac is one of a class of drugs called Specific Serotonin Re-uptake Inhibitors. These work by preventing the action whereby the neuron reabsorbs serotonin after it has done its 'message-relay' job. The result is high levels of serotonin sloshing around the brain – which results in improved alertness and mood.

Adrenaline (or *epinephrine*, its alternative name) is chiefly found elsewhere in the body, though small amounts also act within the brain. Not surprisingly, it is associated with high levels of alertness and excitement. *Noradrenaline* (or *norepinephrine*) is more concentrated within the brain, and its levels increase dramatically once we wake up. This is primarily a vigilance neurotransmitter – not only does it help us focus attention, it also performs the same function at the molecular level within the brain – ensuring that weak neural connections wither away while strong ones are nourished.

We will come across several other neurotransmitters along our journey – among them the *endorphins*, which control pain and stimulate reward centres within the brain, and *adrenocorticotrophin*, which appears to inhibit the analytical left brain and enable creative thought processes.

The regions of the brain

If we now step back once more and look at the brain with the naked eye, we see that this remarkable object is not just composed of two halves; each half is split into four further components (see pages 10 and 38). Right at the back is the occipital lobe, largely responsible for visual processing. Further forward, just around the left and right ears, are the temporal lobes, which deal with, among many other things, language and sound processing. At the top of the brain are the parietal lobes responsible for perception of space and where you are in it, and partially at least for movement and touch. Right at the front are the frontal lobes – responsible for what we call the 'higher functions' of mankind, such as thought and planning. There is also another 'lobe' or region, the insula, deep between the temporal and parietal areas, which is important in processing visceral sensation – for example taste, and temperature.

The frontal lobes play a key role in regulating our behaviour. We shall explore the development of the human brain from conception to old age in a later chapter, but it is worth noting here that the frontal lobes take the longest to mature, in some cases not completing their growth until a person is in their mid-twenties. It is clear that children's capacity for learning to control themselves is something that can only improve with time – a ray of hope for exasperated parents and teachers!

Going in underneath the surface of the brain – that characteristic formation of convoluted ridges (known as gyri) and grooves (known as sulci) – we see a further set of structures, each with a twin in the

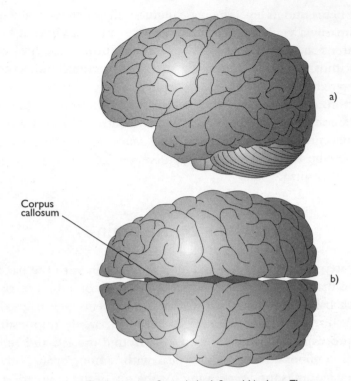

Corpus
callosum

The brain seen from a) the left and b) above. The two
hemispheres of the brain are joined by the corpus callosum

opposite hemisphere. (The only item not replicated in both hemi-spheres, as we saw, is the pineal gland.) Four of these units – the *amygdala, hypothalamus, thalamus* and *hippocampus* – are connected to form what is sometimes called the *limbic system*. The limbic system is thought of as the seat of our emotions, along with many of the instincts, appetites and drives that help us to survive. The amygdala, a tiny, almond-shaped structure, is the area active when we feel emotions. If your amygdala was damaged or absent, you would be likely to lack the capacity to feel fear.

The hypothalamus acts as a processing centre for many of the other regions of the brain and the body, receiving information and sending out appropriate responses. It's the hypothalamus, and in turn its mastery of the pituitary gland, that causes our hearts to race and our blood pressure to rise when we are afraid, for example. People with impaired hypothalamic function may have a tendency towards anorexia or overeating, as if they are unable to communicate with their own appetites. They may also be infertile because if the wrong signals are sent by the hypothalamus to the pituitary gland, the hormonal instructions to produce eggs or sperm may be inadequate. The thalamus, meanwhile, acts as the connection site between the sensory components and the higher functions of the brain. All incoming sensory information – with the exception of smell, the most primitive sense – passes through the thalamus before being sent upstairs to the cortex. The hippocampus is responsible for the storage and retrieval of long-term memory. People with hippocampal damage experience severe memory problems, and it has been shown that people who have been through serious trauma, and subsequently have only fragmentary recall, may have reduced hippocampal tissue.

Above and slightly encircling the amygdala and hippocampus are the basal ganglia. These act as an interface between the rest of the brain and the motor centres of the brainstem below them. Hence they have a distinct role in the planning and production of movements. But, as with many regions of the brain, their function cannot be so neatly labelled. People with damage to the basal ganglia can also have difficulties in understanding the non-verbal communications of other people. The same is true of the structure that sits at the very back of the brain, just above the stem. This area, the cerebellum (which means 'little brain' in Latin), has long been seen as a purely primitive motor, movement and balance centre. But recent research has demonstrated the cerebellum's role in the planning and timing of action, judging the shape of objects and creating properly pro-portioned drawings. And there is increasing evidence of its involvement in language and reading and many other aspects of cognition.

Together with the cerebellum, the bottom-most region, the brain-stem, forms the oldest section of the human brain – the part we have in common with our reptilian ancestors. The brainstem is the site of the most basic survival programmes – those that control eating, sleep-ing, defecation, orgasm and breathing. It does enough to keep an organism alive in the absence of any other functions. Cats whose brainstem has been detached from the rest of their brains can still move around, pounce if they hear a noise and eat food if it is placed in front of them.

These various modules of the brain are connected to one another

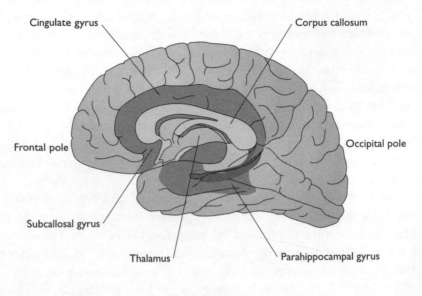

Cingulate gyrus

Corpus callosum

Frontal pole

Occipital pole

Subcallosal gyrus

Thalamus

Parahippocampal gyrus

The limbic system

by densely packed, criss-crossing ropes of axons. There is also a thick band of connecting material that joins the left and right hemispheres of the brain – known as the *corpus callosum*. As its position would suggest, the corpus callosum allows the two halves of the brain to communicate with one another. As we shall see, the left and right hemispheres, and their interaction, play a vital role in the creation of who we are.

A brain of two halves

While the left and right hemispheres of our brain each have identical structures and in normal circumstances are in constant communication with one another, each half also houses somewhat different functions. Having said that, the two sides of the brain do not work in isolation from each other. In most people, the left side tends to do more analytical processing. As well as being the site of language faculties in most people, it is also often responsible for aspects of

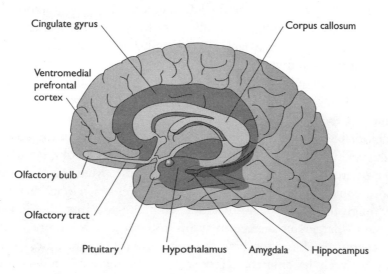

Cingulate gyrus

Corpus callosum

Ventromedial
prefrontal
cortex

Olfactory bulb

Olfactory tract

Pituitary   Hypothalamus   Amygdala   Hippocampus

Right hemisphere seen after bisection of brain (inner surface)

reason and deduction. The right side, in contrast, tends to be a much more holistic machine.

Much has been written, often without good evidence, about the difference between the function of the right side of the brain and the left side. Certainly, under a microscope, a difference between the left and right brain can be seen. Our right hemisphere is made up of more white matter than grey matter. The grey matter is essentially where the processing gets done; the white matter provides the channel of communications. The right hemisphere with its greater amount of white matter is sometimes stated to have more density of connections between the neurons. The connecting axons in the right brain are longer than those in the left brain and they can connect with neurons that are further away. Some writers have claimed, without very good evidence, that the left brain is better at associating logic, ideas and concepts and that the right brain is the seat of creative and intuitive thought. It is claimed that somebody with a dominant left brain (or damage to their right hemisphere) might be better at methodical, analytical work – like accountancy. Meanwhile someone with a dominant right brain might be more skilful at linking seemingly disparate ideas and feelings – skills useful in art, music and literature. In general, right-handed people tend to have a dominant left hemisphere, and the reverse is true for left-handers. But this shouldn't be taken as a universal truth. If this rule was always consistent there'd be no left-handed mathematicians and no right-handed poets!

Recent research investigating the differences in behaviour between men and women has revealed a fascinating fact about the corpus callosum. Generally speaking, it tends to be proportionately larger in women. Ruben and Raquel Gur at the Pennsylvania Medical Center in Philadelphia have confirmed that women tend to be more able to 'multi-task'.[2] Women regularly carry out a number of tasks, say in the office or around the home, all at the same time. Men, on the other hand, are more inclined to focus on and complete each individual task they're given. Ruben and Raquel Gur suggest that the corpus callosum is larger on average in women because it has more neural connections, enabling the brain to communicate more quickly and easily between its different regions. In men, there are fewer connections across the two hemispheres, so neuronal communication is somewhat slower and therefore more effective when a function is taking place in one particular brain region rather than across the two halves. They suggest that this difference in the corpus callosum might even explain some well-known emotional differences between men and women. There is much speculation about this, and some sources claim emotional processing is largely located in the right hemisphere, and that the power to express our feelings through language lives in the left. Could it be that for men, with fewer connections between the two halves, it is harder to talk about emotions? For women, on the other hand, with all those extra fibres in the corpus callosum, expressing emotions is second nature. So, at least, we men perhaps have some sort of excuse for our behaviour.

A splitting headache

In the 1960s, surgeons tried a last-ditch treatment for severe epilepsy. They set about severing the corpus callosum. Often the reason for a major fit with loss of consciousness (and the risk of death) is that the electrical discharges from the damaged area of the brain spread through the cortex, involving both sides. Cutting the connections between the two halves is intended to stop the seizures from spreading to involve the whole brain. More often than not it helped dramatically. However, it wasn't long before the patients began demonstrating some rather odd side effects.

The neurobiologist Roger Sperry, who won the Nobel Prize in 1981, was one of many illustrious scientists to spend part of his career at the California Institute of Technology. He was something of a polymath – one of his colleagues there, for example, records what a fine sculptor he was. But in the annals of neuroscience, he is perhaps best known for his work on these split-brain patients. He once famously declared, 'What it comes down to is that modern society discriminates against the right hemisphere.' In a noted case, he asked a woman to fix her eyes on a screen that had a small dot in the centre. There is a crossover between the eyes and the parts of the visual cortex that receive the information – so that under normal circumstances, information from the right side of the visual fields goes to the left side of the brain, and vice versa. The same is true of hands – the left hand is wired directly to the right brain, and vice versa. But clearly in the split-brain patients, most of the crossovers have been severed. Sperry tested the effects of this by flashing up an image of a cup for one twentieth of a second, just to the right of the dot. This is the amount of time it takes for the eye to register an object but not to focus on it and thereby send information across the two hemi- spheres. So in this woman's case, thanks to her severed corpus callosum, the image went only to the left side of the brain. Because that is also the language region of the brain, she could identify and speak the name of what she had just seen. A cup.

But then an image of a spoon was flashed up to the left of the dot, so that it would enter her right hemisphere. Asked to report what she had seen, she answered 'nothing'. Sperry then asked her to reach underneath the table without looking and select, with her left hand using touch alone, from a number of objects, the one that she had just seen. She immediately picked the spoon. But when asked to identify the object in her hand, she defined it as 'a pencil'.

In this experiment, we can see a clear example of the left and right hemispheres at work. When the cup image was on the right, her left brain could not only identify it, but also allow her to say what it had seen. But when the spoon image was on the left, and went to her right brain, she couldn't tell Sperry about it – because the left brain controls language, and the left brain had not seen it. The only thing her left brain could say was 'I see nothing.' But the image of the spoon was absorbed by her right brain – so it could use the left hand, without language, to select the correct object, even though it couldn't name it properly.

Not everyone has his or her language faculty situated solely in the left brain. A very few rare split-brain patients have been able to communicate from their right hemisphere – giving rise to some eerie results. Michael Gazzaniga, whose fine books on neuroscience I strongly recommend, worked at the University of California and now works in Dartmouth, New Hampshire. He came across a student, a patient whose right hemisphere had the ability to communicate in short phrases. It wasn't an easy task, because spoken questions – unlike images – can't be sent to one hemisphere in isolation. When the left brain hears language, it takes over. So Dr Gazzaniga and his co-researcher Robert LeDoux devised a new method: they would speak the bulk of the question, but flash the keyword up on a screen to be read, thereby letting the right brain absorb what the left brain could not. For instance, they might ask – 'Tell us what are your . . .' and then flash the word 'hobbies' on the screen. The patient would then answer questions directed to his right hemisphere by arranging Scrabble letters.

The patient's right brain began to emerge as a distinct personality with its own likes and dislikes. When asked to rate a long string of items such as foods, colours and names, the right hemisphere consistently judged them to be worse than the left. Even more bizarrely, when asked what he wanted to do after graduation, the left brain vocally answered 'draughtsman' while the right brain spelt out the words 'automobile racer'. So are we all walking around with two separate personalities inside our heads, one of them rendered mute by its lack of language? That would certainly be the most extreme (and somewhat worrying) conclusion to draw here. It might just be the case that your consciousness moves continually from one hemisphere to the other, unless interrupted. Or that there are many different 'versions' of yourself inside your brain, usually integrated and harmonious thanks to your very own corpus callosum.

Professor Gazzaniga also writes of an intriguing episode in which a short piece of distressing film was shown to the right hemisphere of a split-brain patient (in other words, through her left visual field – the left side of both eyes). Having no language capacity in her right hemisphere, she couldn't report what she'd seen – and in fact said that she'd seen nothing at all. But nevertheless she did mention that she felt scared and anxious. Later on, she let slip to another member of the research team, 'I know I like Dr Gazzaniga, but right now, I'm scared of him for some reason.' It seemed that the emotional content of what she'd seen had been picked up, so she had tried to find some explanation for the feeling. The same kind of phenomenon can be seen when more neutral images are shown to split-brain patients – such as ocean scenes and waterfalls. The patients report feelings of tranquillity; they remain unaware that those feelings have been caused by the footage they've been shown.

How do split-brain patients go about living a normal everyday life? Some of them report being unable to perform even the simplest tasks because, while one hand acts according to their will, the other hand carries out all manner of Faustian mischief. Alan J. Parkin, Professor of Experimental Psychology at the University of East Sussex, has reported on patients with so-called 'Alien Hand Syndrome' (AHS), whose one hand takes off their clothes as fast as the other hand can dress them.

Alien Hand is the stuff of nightmares and horror movies. About two years ago, Dr Feinberg, from the Albert Einstein Medical College, on the television Learning Channel described a woman who, awakening from a troubled sleep, found in the pitch black of her bedroom a hand tightening around her neck, vicious and implacable. Using all the strength in her right hand, she tried desperately to pull it off. Then, struggling, she realized that the hidden assailant was her own left hand. So it is hardly surprising that, for the rest of that night, and most nights to follow, she was too scared to fall asleep unless totally exhausted.

While many people with AHS have had radical brain surgery to treat severe epilepsy, Feinberg says it can happen to anyone who has had brain damage. The case of the woman whose hand attempted to strangle her goes back to the earliest study of the disorder, written in Germany in 1908; but in matter-of-fact fashion, Larry, one of the patients on the show, also reported waking up one night to find his left hand around his neck. Sometimes when he is trying to eat, recalled Larry, his left hand will grab his right hand, 'and just won't let me get a fork – or spoonful – of food.'

I quite like this story, which I found on a motorbikers' website:

> I met this Japanese rider yesterday. Nice guy, maybe in his mid-40s. Well, he tells us that he's not working right now. Says he had a medical condition: 'Baka Te'. I'm totally confused. That means crazy hand. What in the world is crazy hand? So he goes on to tell us that at times he loses control of his right hand. It just does what it wants. One night he was coming down the Daishein Keihin something. All of a sudden his right hand locks up on the throttle. Scary, 'cause this guy rides a 1300 Suzuki Hayabusa. This guy accelerated out of control. He told us that he was doing somewhere around 270kph, struggling and beating his right hand the whole way. Eventually, he was caught by the police running over 250kph with his mad hand. He was taken to the police station but later all charges were dropped against him because of his medical condition – Alien Hand Syndrome. He's STILL riding. Can you imagine that?

Clowns to the left of me, mopers to the right

We all differ to some extent in the degree of dominance of one hemisphere over the other – though, as we shall see later on, there need be nothing permanent about this arrangement. But differences across this axis can be responsible for key facets of our temperaments. A 1994 study by Richard Davidson at the University of Wisconsin involved showing film clips to various subjects, and then evaluating the blood flow to their left and right hemispheres.[3] The film clips were of two types – positive, happiness-inducing, and negative, sadness-inducing. Davidson noted that people with more left-side activity seemingly responded more positively to the positive film clips. And those with more right-brain activity responded more negatively to the negative film clips. It seems that, in short, people with more active left brains set up a loop of feedback between themselves and positive stimuli in the world around them, ensuring a more constant positive mood. And people with more right-brain activity do exactly the opposite – as if they have a tendency to be more moved by the sad things they see. This is certainly interesting. People with depression often say that they 'see the world in a different way' to everybody else. Perhaps there is a lot to be said for not always grasping the big picture.

We can see this difference if we look at people who have suffered a stroke that has effectively 'knocked out' one or the other hemisphere. People with damaged left brains are more prone to depression; they tend to treat their problem as a major disaster. In contrast, people with damaged right brains sometimes even fail to recognize that they have a problem.

The left/right split is seen in our reactions to art – quite often we say that we like paintings but cannot explain why. Indeed, art teachers encourage students raised in an academic environment where thoughts are rationalized to leave their preconceptions behind at the door. They ask them to start connecting with the feelings that art produces. This may seem a throwback to 'method acting' and other movements in the arts in the Sixties, but our left brain is where we use language to define and pin things down, and our right brain is where creativity is most at work. That is why advertising makes so much more use of imagery and music than it does of words. If our left brain got in the way and started analysing whether we really needed this revolutionary new nasal hair trimmer, we might not buy it . . .

A similar process can be seen if a written command is quickly sent to the right hemisphere of split-brain patients. In one case, after the command 'laugh' was flashed up, a patient promptly fell about chuckling. When asked why, she responded that the researchers were making her laugh with their absurd experiments. The left brain was seeking to make sense of actions produced by the disconnected right brain.

The Alien Hand Syndrome described earlier does not result solely from damage to the corpus callosum. An area at the top of the brain called the SMA (supplementary motor area) is also implicated. This area springs into action whenever we want to undertake some action of our own free will. It does not initiate the action so much as send signals to parts of the surrounding motor cortex. As we have seen with many functions of the brain, there is cross-wiring, so that the right part of the SMA controls the left side of the body and vice versa. But notably, whichever side of the body is used in the action, areas on both sides of the SMA are active. The action on the right side of the SMA for a right-handed action is fairly weak, but, Professor Alan Parkin believes, enough to initiate some action if not inhibited.

Normally this inhibition comes directly from the side of the SMA opposite the side of the body being moved. It's as if a message is sent saying, 'Do not move – leave this to me.' To get from one side of the SMA to the other, an intact corpus callosum is needed. Hence, in some split-brain patients, there is a tendency for left and right hands to do contradictory tasks. Both sides of the SMA are sending 'Do it' messages to the motor areas and thence on to the limbs themselves.

In Parkin's view, there is nothing mischievous about the work of Alien Hands, nor anything to suggest that we are all inhabited by impish, playful alternative personalities. In his view, Alien Hands are most often to be observed undoing the work that the other hand has done, because that's the only job that seems to need doing. For instance, say, in a case of split brain, the left hand opens the door. The right hand arrives on the scene and sees an open door, but carrying the crucial message 'Door – Handle – Do'. Not being able to communicate with the right brain and thus know that the relevant job has been done, the left brain assumes that the task is to shut the door and duly does so. Frustrating if you are in a hurry.

Whether or not we are seduced by the appeal of plural personalities residing in our right and left brain, it is becoming clear that the view of the brain as a series of separate modules is an oversimplification, for in the execution of the simplest tasks, we call upon a whole array of faculties. Imagine buying a pie in a baker's shop, for instance. We use our motor functions to walk in and not bang into the counter. We use our visual systems to see a pie and our memory to line up former pies with the pies we see in front of us. We call our language and social behaviour faculties into action in order to behave appropriately in our interactions with the counter assistant, and our reasoning capacities to work out how much money we need to hand over. In so much of our daily lives, our ancestors are working for us – the 'reptilian' and 'early mammalian' brain as much as the higher cortex. It might be more appropriate to think of the brain as operating like a large city, where the pie manufacturer needs his neighbours at the paper mill to provide the packaging and the oil refinery to provide petrol for transport. And as we shall see shortly, the brain is not a closed system. Like a city, in which businesses and public institutions and family homes grow and move in and out of different premises, the brain is undergoing constant change. In many cases, a faculty impaired is not a faculty lost for all time, but one that may be taken over elsewhere. But before we can explore this concept, we need to understand in a little greater depth precisely how the different units of the brain communicate with one another.

You might have noticed something unusual about one of the above statements. If not, read the information about noradrenaline again. A key aspect – indeed asset – of the human mind is contained within that paragraph. Namely that the brain which creates it, or at least many areas in it, is subject to a state of constant change. Synaptic connections between neurons grow and become more established. Connections that are seldom used grow weak and eventually wither away, the neurons responsible for them taking on new routes and new tasks. In short, the brain is not something formed during the first twenty years of our lives and in a state of decay ever after. It is a moving, changing, fluid organ that interacts with its environment.

The plastic brain

Do you remember being told that you were born with a finite number of brain cells and that, from the moment you were born, these were dying away, never to be replaced? It's a common misconception. The brain is not only the most complex organ in the body, it is also arguably one with great capacity to reinvent itself. That's why the mind can be the product of a flesh-and-blood organ, and yet be subject to change over time – why we can learn new skills, why we forget others we once knew well, why stroke victims can recover lost faculties with patient practice, even why teenage communists can become high Tories in their thirties. The discovery that this is the case has had far-reaching consequences for medicine and for the whole 'nature versus nurture' debate.

The tale of the plastic brain began in the 1940s with a Canadian psychologist called Donald O. Hebb. At that stage, brain researchers had already begun to discover that communication between neurons was no one-way street. On the contrary, it seemed that whenever a neuron was receiving input from another, it would not only pass its message on to other neurons, but send feedback to the neuron from which it had received the original message. This created a loop, which in turn could amplify the signalling of the original cell, or alternatively dampen it down.

Further to this, Hebb discovered that cells involved in a pattern of communication were changed by it. After the initial process of electrical firing had died down, a secondary activity took place, during which neurons strengthened their connections with one another, growing new axons and increasing their supplies of neurotransmitters, so that it became easier for them to fire again in the same pattern in the future. In other words, the network of neurons in the brain regrouped itself according to what information came in, and it remained primed to regroup if that information should come in again.

This feedback and learning mechanism within the brain means that each synaptic connection is 'told' whether it has contributed to the final outcome of the communication. If it has, it is encouraged to react a little more strongly next time, by growing new connection sites and by sending more neurotransmitters across the synaptic cleft. If it hasn't, it will inhibit its actions.

We will deal in greater depth with the brain chemistry of learning and memory at a later date, but for now, let us use an example from daily life. Imagine, for instance, I start working in a bar. Let's also imagine, for the sake of illustration, that it is an old-fashioned bar without a fancy modern electronic till. And that my mental arithmetic is a little rusty. The first time I am called upon to add up the cost of three pints and then deduct this from a twenty-pound note, the calculation may take up some considerable length of time. Inside the deductive regions of my brain, neurons are firing together, per-haps for the first time in years. But as they fire together, a pattern is established – in the same way as generations of footsteps will beat a path through thick undergrowth, making it smoother and clearer with each journey. When I serve the next customer, and the next, the pathway is that little bit more pronounced as the neurons involved become more tightly enmeshed, and the increasing quantities of neurotransmitter promote ever more vigorous firing. Over time, I become proficient at addition and subtraction – faster, more accurate and more confident. I am Barman of the Year. To some, I may seem to be overstating the obvious maxim that practice makes perfect. But what is significant about it is that this process is built into the chemistry of the human brain. As we learn, the circuitry of our brain learns, too.

The best neuron for the job

Our emergent understanding of this process gave birth to a theory known as Neural Darwinism – coined by Gerald Edelman, an American who won the Nobel Prize for his work on how antibodies protect us against infection. Later in his career, while working at the Rockefeller Institute, he turned his attention to brain development. Edelman's idea was essentially that the architecture of the brain was created in the same way as living beings competed for survival. As animals compete for food and space and mating rights in their bid to survive, so do the synapses within our brain have to compete with one another.

In the womb, at the dawn of life, the foetal brain produces new neurons at a staggering rate of 250,000 a minute. These neurons attach to their neighbours in a frenzy of seemingly random wiring – though, as we shall see later, genetic and environmental factors also play a role at this stage. But in the first year of life, there is a process called apoptosis, a programmed mass suicide of brain cells. Neurons are, in effect, forced to compete for their survival, to show that they are part of a useful circuit in order to maintain their connections with other neurons and their supply of neurotransmitters.

For Edelman, the whole evolution of the human brain can be seen as a tale of ever more efficient competition. The simplest creatures, like worms and jellyfish, he suggests only adapt over many generations. Slightly cleverer creatures, like snails, develop a sort of reflex memory over a lifetime. In humans, this process reaches its apogee, such that we are able to make continuous adjustments to our brain in response to the demands of the environment.

It's that final phrase that stands out as the most important for me. For through an understanding of Neural Darwinism in the human brain, we arrive at a clearer indication of the relationship between nature and nurture. If we say a person is 'nervous', or 'aggressive' or 'a great talker', we do not then have to fall into one of two camps and say that this attribute is *only* something they could have inherited, or conversely *only* something that happened to them because of experiences in early life. It is both. Attributes of mind – traits of personality, habits and skills – emerge as result of the interplay between the brain and the environment.

A classic example is shown in an experiment performed by Michael

Merzenich, a pioneer of the 'plastic brain' theory. Merzenich carefully measured the cortical areas associated with one digit of a monkey's hand. He then amputated the finger and watched what happened to the brain. He discovered that the related area shrank in size, while the areas associated with the other fingers grew. In further experiments, he trained monkeys to use their middle fingers in a certain task – and noted that the related brain area grew in size, as if the increased demand resulted in a need for greater cortical space.

We do not need to look at monkeys to see this process at work. Research has shown that musicians have 25 per cent more of their auditory cortex given over to the processing of music than non-musicians. The greatest amount of extra music area is found in those musicians who started to play an instrument earliest. Similarly, non-musicians given the task of performing a simple finger exercise over a number of days have been found to grow extra connections in the relevant area of their brain.

This is the basis of Cognitive Behavioural Therapy – a process that seeks to correct behaviour detrimental to self or others by replacing 'negative' thought patterns with 'positive' ones. Jeffrey Schwartz at the University of California, Los Angeles School of Medicine performed brain scans on patients undergoing CBT and noted a decrease in the neuronal activity associated with the original, negative impulse.

We might also look at the thoroughly invigorating example of the nuns of Mankato, a religious order based at a remote nunnery in Minnesota. The nuns have been the object of study for David Snowdon, a University of Kentucky professor, due to their remark-able longevity – many of them living for over 100 years. They are not just long-living, but they have a lower rate of Alzheimer's disease and other impairment of their ability to think than is found in the general population. Now, of course, nuns may not be an ideal population to study – there are certain aspects of their lifestyle that exclude activi-ties given to other women. But their secret, Dr Snowdon is convinced, lies in their ceaseless activity. For the nuns, idleness is a sin and so even the oldest of the sisters keep their brain occupied with quizzes, puzzles and political debates. Snowdon has examined a hun-dred brains donated by deceased members of the order and concludes that their intellectual activity stimulates the growth and connection of neurons. Significantly, the nuns who were engaged in intellectual pursuits resisted the debilitating effects of ageing far better than those nuns who were kept occupied with menial work.

The brain deprived

Of course, it therefore follows that brains deprived of stimuli produce corresponding deficiencies in their owners. Only by regular usage does a neuronal pathway remain strong and healthy. If neurons are not being used in a certain pattern – for instance, the patterns associated with doing bar-room maths – they will quickly be co-opted into new groupings for new tasks.

Hence, for example, the sad plight of the Romanian orphans discovered in the late 1980s, practically abandoned by the state in vast, bleak orphanages, devoid of any emotional contact or environmental stimuli. The Harvard Medical School researcher Mary Carlson studied babies abandoned at one such orphanage and found that, in addition to being mentally and physically retarded, they also had abnormally high levels of the stress hormone, cortisol.

A University of Washington study undertaken by Geraldine Dawson found some physical abnormalities in the brains of babies raised by clinically depressed mothers. These babies who were less exposed to smiles or other lively shows of excitement by their ill mothers showed reduced activity in the left frontal region of the brain. At three and a half years of age, these babies were significantly more likely to exhibit behavioural problems. However, thanks to the plasticity of the brain – and the especially plastic infant brain – it is nearly always possible to reverse the negative effects of environment with timely intervention. The brain is remarkably resilient. For those readers following another BBC television series in which I've been involved, *Child of Our Time*, this reversal, and the extent to which it is possible, is poignantly shown by some of the children we have filmed.

The brain can even recover from physical damage. Young children who have had an entire brain hemisphere removed due to severe epilepsy manage to compensate for this loss, often with only minor mental or physical impairment. And stroke victims who lose the capacity of speech may regain it, in a reduced capacity, by using neighbouring areas of their brain circuitry. In general, however, we have to be aware that there are limits to the brain's plasticity. Young children recover from brain injuries significantly faster than teenagers, for example.

A good example of the limits to the brain's plasticity is in language acquisition. As we now know, babies' brains are hard-wired to learn language. Research has shown that newborn babies can recognize and develop a preference for their mother's language by the time they are four days old. Russian babies will suck harder, for instance, when they hear Russian spoken, than when they hear Portuguese. By less than a year old, a baby can only recognize as language the set of sounds particular to its mother tongue. Anything else is rejected as non-meaningful in the language sense. When babies babble at this age, they do it using the set of sounds, or phonemes, particular to their native tongue. The same process occurs in children born with cataracts – if these are not removed before they are six months old, the child will never see. The neural circuits vital to the process will swiftly take on other functions if they are not used.

We can see this most vividly demonstrated in the examples provided by the plight of Genie and Isabelle – children who spent a key period of their developmental years deprived of human contact. Until the age of thirteen, Genie was locked in a Los Angeles attic and beaten if she made a noise. She grew up without human interaction and the language areas of her brain were severely distorted. When she eventually did learn to speak, scientists discovered that she was using the auditory regions of her language faculties – which presumably had been kept working because of background noise, such as birdsong and traffic. With only this narrow facility at her disposal, Genie was able to master basic vocabulary, but never grammar.

In contrast, Isabelle was released from her silent imprisonment at the age of six. Within a year and a half, she had acquired a vocabulary of 1,500 words and could use quite complex grammar. It seems likely therefore that the brain has a window of opportunity when an understanding of grammar can be most easily gained, which becomes more difficult somewhere between the ages of six and thirteen.

In short, what happens to us has a direct and observable effect on the shape of our brain, and this, in turn, informs who we are. But thanks to the brain's plasticity, much can be changed throughout our lives. To deepen our understanding of how we become who we are, we need to know not just that the brain changes in relation to the information it receives, but also how it receives and processes that information. If this feedback relationship between brain and environment makes us who we are, then it follows that differences in the way we perceive the world equate to differences in personality and character.

John Ratey, author of *A User's Guide to the Brain*, and associate Professor of Clinical Psychiatry at Harvard Medical School, suggests psychiatrists stop asking their patients how they feel, but instead ask how they perceive the world, in order to understand the origins of their disorder. In the next chapter, we shall be applying this principle to the broad spectrum of human experience. What goes on inside the brain as we see, feel, hear, touch, run from danger, kick a ball or complete a crossword? And could it be that differences in the way our brains handle these tasks lie at the root of differences in our personalities?

chapter**three**

Coming to your senses

In the twentieth century, there was something of a revolution in opera. An increasing number of composers were aware of new scientific discoveries, public interest in psychology was mounting and the understanding of human consciousness was growing. So composers wrote operatic works focusing strongly on the workings of the mind. Leoš Janáček's opera *Jenufa* (1903), Richard Strauss's *Salome* (1905) and *Elektra* (1909), Alban Berg's *Wozzeck* (1925) and Benjamin Britten's *Peter Grimes* (1945) are all psychodramas that examine the mental state of the main protagonists, whether sane or frankly pathological. Another of these great works is Sergei Prokofiev's *The Fiery Angel*. There can be few more gripping, yet terrifying, operas; it always sends shivers down my spine. In it, the central character, Renata, is possessed of an evil spirit, the Fiery Angel, which haunts and obsesses her to the exclusion of all normal love. Eventually, to escape her spirit she enters a nunnery. In an attempt to exorcise her religious delusions, the Grand Inquisitor visits her, but the Fiery Angel's control over her mind is so powerful that, in an extraordinary hysterical scene at the end, the Abbess and all the nuns become equally possessed, strip naked and have what must be the only full-scale orgy ever put on an operatic stage. I strongly recommend going to see this opera.

Prokofiev's remarkable music, with its vivid orchestration, conjures up a striking and horrifying resemblance to some forms of epileptic attack – initially a sense of foreboding and disaster, altered sensory

56

perception of sounds or smells, a religious illusion that seems totally real to Renata, the rapid repeating phrases in the music reaching a climax, a kind of fit, and then, unconsciousness.

Few disorders have caused more superstition, fear and terror than epilepsy. Its fits, convulsions and loss of consciousness stem from flurries of sudden overactivity within areas of the brain – rather like localized electrical storms. These seizures, sometimes regarded as the work of the devil or the work of God, were recognized since earliest times. Epilepsy is mentioned in the Ayurvedic literature and in ancient Egyptian tablets. One of the most ancient accounts comes from Babylonian times; the tablets (all forty of them) are preserved in the British Museum in London. Each type of seizure these tablets describe was associated with a different god or, more usually, an evil spirit. Many famous individuals suffered from epilepsy, including Julius Caesar, Peter the Great of Russia, Fyodor Dostoevsky and, probably, Lord Byron. Some of the ancients, and medieval scholars such as Maimonides, the great Jewish philosopher and doctor writing in the twelfth century, attached stigma to the disease and wrongly regarded it as mostly inherited. Basic understanding of the mechanism behind epilepsy did not really occur until the nineteenth century, when the neurologist John Hughlings Jackson suggested that the sudden fits were caused by electrical discharges from specific areas of the brain. Jackson, who has been called the father of English neurology, gave his name to the fits – Jacksonian seizure. As we see throughout this book, the study of epilepsy and focal stimulation of the brain has had a huge influence on our understanding of how the brain, and therefore the mind, works.

Penfield pioneering brain mapping

One of my great heroes – ever since I first heard of his work when I was a medical student studying brain anatomy forty years ago – is Wilder Penfield. He pioneered brain surgery for epilepsy in the 1930s. Originally from the USA, he went to Oxford to study medicine. On his return to the USA in 1921 he is reported as saying, 'Brain surgery is a terrible profession. If I did not feel it will become different in my lifetime, I should hate it.' He had what could be a unique experience and one that most surgeons would dread.

When he was in his thirties, and brain surgery was in its infancy, his own sister, Ruth, was diagnosed as having a brain tumour. Once it had been discovered that the tumour was extensive and undoubtedly cancerous, he operated on her himself and removed more brain tissue than most neurosurgeons would have considered remotely safe. This must have been an incredibly difficult decision, but it gave Ruth another three good years before the tumour eventually returned.

Ruth's difficulties motivated him to establish the famous Montreal Institute of Neurology, which he went on to direct. The understanding of epilepsy at the time was primitive and, although it was very common, the treatment was frequently ineffective. The main drugs, barbiturates, with their depressant side effects, frequently did not prevent fits recurring. It is not surprising therefore that, as a neurologist, he decided to specialize in, among other nervous diseases, epilepsy. Sometimes the electrical storms paving the way for a fit emanate from scarred areas in the brain, produced as a result of old injury. They tend, in some patients, to be preceded by warnings – referred to as auras – such as a sensation of tingling, or of a strange or unpleasant odour. It was Penfield's theory that if he could get into the brain and stimulate different areas electrically while the patient was conscious, this might provoke the onset of an aura. He would then identify where the faulty brain tissue was and cut it away.

You possibly cannot help a tiny shudder at these last words – the idea of cutting into the brain seems crude. It feels wrong because it is difficult to believe that it is possible to treat this seat of our being as if it was an ordinary organ. Surely it must be more – something that transcends physics and biology and exists beyond time and space? This is the organ of consciousness, of original thought and inspiration, the means by which we feel soaring joy, burning rage and perceive the glory of God. Could it be improved by simply cutting bits away with a knife?

Even though well over sixty years of serious scientific activity have left us in little doubt that the brain is responsible for each and every attribute of the mind, these personal feelings demonstrate that brain research is emotive. It turned out to be just as emotive for Wilder Penfield. He noted that, when certain parts of the surface of the brain were electrically stimulated, his patients – who were lying awake on the operating table with the top of their skulls sawn off like a boiled egg – reported a range of sensations. It may seem odd but the brain has no pain fibres so it is insensitive to touch or injury. Most pain experienced in the head is perceived through other tissues, such as blood vessels. Penfield's stimuli produced no pain at all but the body underwent a series of involuntary tics and muscle spasms, and some patients experienced sensations of light, heat or cold. Others reported very subtle mental states – such as foreboding, and déjà vu. And some even experienced quite detailed hallucinations – including in one case a man who heard the strains of Beethoven so clearly that he seriously thought Penfield must have had a radio concealed within the operating theatre.

Penfield's findings shocked even himself – to the extent that, towards the end of his life, he backtracked somewhat. Although his research provided a very solid foundation for the view that consciousness itself resides in the electrochemical processes of the brain, he argued that it could never account for the sum total of experience. Attributes like free will, Penfield argued, could never be pinpointed within the structures of the brain. But a good deal of the evidence now points to the contrary. And to an extent, some of the most magical aspects of human consciousness have been de-mystified and almost 'normalized'. This is certainly one of the by-products of some more recent findings in Switzerland.

A more detailed atlas

A Swiss neurologist called Professor Olaf Blanke made an interesting discovery when performing a latter-day version of Penfield's pro-cedure on a woman who suffered severe epilepsy. The surgeon builds his specialized map by opening up the scalp and the skull after it has been treated with local anaesthetic while its owner – the patient – is fully conscious but sedated. Various areas can be stimulated with an electrode, just like Penfield used. The surgeon can ask his patient to perform simple tasks, like counting or reciting a nursery rhyme, or simply to report the sensations he or she undergoes as an area is stimulated. By first painstakingly mapping out areas in this way, any surgery to remove pieces of brain or tumours can be done with minimal risk of damage to other, vital brain faculties that have been clearly identified, such as language or motor function.

Increasingly nowadays, before any surgeon starts cutting into this most precious human organ with his scalpel, he is able to build up a detailed map of his patient's brain, often using methods we have already discussed, like MRI. And fMRI, an increasingly sophisticated technique, has even made it possible for surgeons to watch the brain as it undergoes the 'storms' associated with a seizure and to identify the areas where the activity is most concentrated. But some readers might be surprised to learn that there is no reference book a surgeon can consult at this point, because the geography of each human brain is different. Some might, at this juncture, be hurriedly flipping back to my opening chapter, in which I categorically stated that my brain, your brain, every human brain there ever has been or will be is structurally the same. On the surface, every brain looks more or less the same, even though there are variations in some of the minor contours and divisions. But beneath, at the level of individual neurons and glial cells, there is a vast number of variations.

We can talk about certain brain areas with confidence, because we know they perform the same function for everyone, and when they are damaged, they produce the same symptoms in everyone. For example, if I had a stroke – essentially a disruption to the blood flow – in the left side of my brain, I might well lose the ability to speak. And so would you. If there was a lack of activity in three areas of either your brain or mine – the dorsolateral prefrontal cortex, left basal ganglia and anterior cingulate – then we would display many or all of the symptoms associated with Tourette's syndrome: tics, twitches, a compulsion to utter inappropriate words or make strange sounds.* This, roughly speaking, would be because the dorsolateral prefrontal cortex, among other things, is concerned in all brains with inhibiting inappropriate actions. The basal ganglia are concerned with movement. And the anterior cingulate is associated with control and focused attention.

But, as we shall see on the course of this journey, there are almost as many points of individual difference as there are similarities. We could make an analogy here between a road map and the knowledge that a resident has of his own street. The current state of scientific knowledge about the brain enables us to know the location and purpose of many sectors of the brain – in the same way as a road map can tell us how to get from Leicester to a remote village in the

*Some people who have listened to my lectures might argue that these three areas of my brain are indeed likely to show abnormal activity.

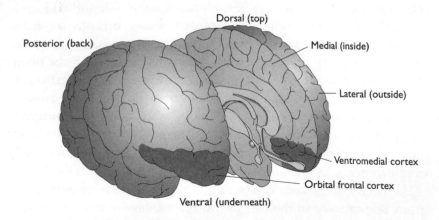

The two hemispheres separated, seen from the right side

Hebrides. We know, for instance, where the long-term memory is situated, or which parts of the brain become active when we listen to music, recognize a friend, solve a crossword, see something dangerous, become angry or sad or fall in love. But to be more specific, to see precisely where discrete functions of those larger categories are situated, it's necessary to talk to the residents.

Awareness: seeing or feeling

Olaf Blanke and his team noticed that whenever they stimulated a certain region of their epileptic patient's brain – the angular gyrus of the right cortex, in this case – she reported an out-of-body experience. 'I see myself lying in bed, from above,' she told them. When she was asked to lift her arm up and look at it, she believed it was trying to punch her. Rather than having tapped into the 'seat of the soul', Olaf Blanke reported in *Nature* that he had simply identified a region of the brain where two functions overlap. The visual system – which we use to see our own bodies as well as the rest of the world – and the system which uses touch and balance to create our physical sense of self-awareness.[4]

Much as Blanke's findings are interesting – and potentially depressing for people who believe that out-of-body experiences are sterling evidence of an afterlife, or of some 'soul' that exists outside the physical body – they are not new to the scientific world. There are numerous, well-documented accounts of people who have experienced the doppelgänger effect, otherwise known as an autoscopic delusion, in which they are confronted by an exact replica of themselves. And they don't need to be lying on a surgeon's table for it to happen, nor overcome by a spiritual revelation. In one case, published by the psychiatrists Louis R. Franzini and John Grossberg, an engineer dogged by his doppelgänger spent large chunks of his day making faces and aiming punches at it – even though he knew quite well that it was his own image.[5]

As Blanke suggested, it is thought that these phenomena result from a disturbance to the part of the brain where visual information intersects with information about the body. As I write this, I am aware of myself as being seated at a desk in a rather noisy lounge at Frankfurt airport, with one foot resting on the other, and my hands over my laptop computer keyboard. I don't need to see a picture of myself in order to know this. I know it from memory, but also from touch and balance, from areas situated at the top-back of my brain known as the parietal cortex, which tell me where my body is in space and what it is doing. On the other hand, I know that in front of me lies a computer screen and an expanse of desk. For that knowledge I rely on my visual faculties, which sit in an area right at the back of my brain, the occipital cortex.

But if, instead of hearing the call for my next flight to St Petersburg, I was to undergo an autoscopic delusion at this moment, it would be as if the current information in my 'touch and balance' files was mistakenly transferred into my 'what's in front of me' files. For a period of time, then, I would end up 'seeing' a version of the information I should normally be 'feeling'. I might then be confronted by an image of myself, seated and typing. Truly terrifying, if I didn't know something about the workings of the brain – and, come to think of it, even if I do. Unsurprisingly, people over the centuries have seen doppelgängers as the harbingers of imminent tragedy.

Dr Blanke's story is more than an intriguing anecdote, for it expresses an important point about something we take all too often for granted. The way we respond to the world, the way we *are* in the world, and the way the world *is* to us, are constructed by this rubbery organ inside our skulls. If, for whatever reasons – genes, the chemical and hormonal environment inside our mother's wombs, childhood experiences, illness or surgical intervention – some tiny modification results in the inner structure of my brain being different to yours, then I will see a different world to the one you see and, what's more, I will be a different person. Two brains may look identical on the surface, but no two minds can ever be alike.

Think about the ways in which we use the word 'mind' in English. For instance – we use it to imply attention and perception, as in the phrase 'Mind out!'. We use it to imply preference for things and, by association, emotion, as in 'I don't mind what music you put on'. We use it to imply memory, as in 'It slipped my mind' or 'Mind my words'. We use it to signify our conscious, calculating selves, in that someone who is 'out of their mind' or who has 'lost their mind' is taken to have lost all ability to behave in a rational way.

Taken together, these four idiomatic expressions provide a neat summary of the chief services that our brains perform for us. Without attention and perception skills, we can't 'mind out' and would hence be in great danger. Without emotion, we would be unable to signal our intentions to other people, or understand theirs. Consequently we would not be able to express whether we 'minded' something, or know whether someone else did. Without memory, we would be in a state of permanent confusion – never knowing where we were, or what we were doing. If our higher cortex could not override our emotions and impulses, we would be uncontrolled, unable to formulate plans and carry them through. So it's clear that the mind, at least in the way we speak of it in a day-to-day sense, is not a single entity so much as a set of skills. It is a toolbox that enables us to function. But to take that analogy further, a hammer might be used by both a carpenter and a sculptor, or to perform a bodged bit of DIY. An artist uses a scalpel and so does a surgeon. The way we use those tools – the way we individually make use of faculties like perception, attention and emotion – informs our individual identities. So let's begin by looking at how we perceive the world.

The senses

Once during a hot summer I was driving over an Alpine pass. At the very bottom of the pass I noticed a simple advertisement on a bend.

It was one word, advertising a local brand of mineral water. I looked away and concentrated on the tricky business of negotiating the pass, with its many bends and twists. The process was rendered less enjoyable than I had hoped, in part because of the relentlessly beating sun, and also because I had landed up behind a very slow farm vehicle which, in addition to belching out thick, black fumes, also happened to be carrying a load of gently baking pig's manure. I was hardly enjoying myself. Then, about halfway up the mountain pass, I saw another sign. This time, the name of the brand of mineral water was repeated – alongside a very simple picture of a bottle of the product. From that point onwards, I became aware of a powerful thirst. I grew utterly unconcerned about the tractor in front of me, the pounding sun or the time my journey was taking. The thirst had taken over – and the only thing that concerned me was finding some means to quench it, as soon as possible.

At the top of the pass, there was a small car park set up so that people could enjoy the view. There was also a small café and – like someone staggering in from the desert – I made a beeline for it. The waiter asked me what I'd like. I immediately mentioned the mineral water whose advertisement I'd seen. As he went away, he laughed. And then, as I settled into my seat, I realized why. Everyone else in the café was drinking the same brand of mineral water. When it came, it was expensive. It tasted like any other mineral water, too. But it didn't matter. Two strategically placed little signs had convinced me, and a whole café full of other motorists, that what I most wanted was a glass of fizzy mineral water.

This experience, which is hardly unique or particularly transcendental, may partly be due to a subliminal message, which we shall encounter later. But haven't you ever looked at a painting of a sunset and thought that it made you feel 'warm'? Seen one of those cleverly manipulative gin and tonic adverts on a hot day and felt unaccountably thirsty? Heard a piece of music and felt sad or at peace? I should hope so, because if not you would be living a considerably compromised sensory existence. In all of us, there is a crossover between the information that comes in through our eyes, ears, noses, mouths and skin, and faculties further down the line, such as emotion and hunger and memory. We see, hear, smell one thing, and we feel, taste and remember another. It all happens so automatically, without us consciously making it happen, that you may not have considered it much before. So what is happening inside your head?

Why not try this? Professor Vilayanur Ramachandran from San Diego, California, in his recent opening 2003 Reith Lecture on BBC Radio 4, asked his audience at the Royal Institution to picture two objects. One he described as a shattered piece of glass with jagged edges, the other an object resembling an amoeba with undulating curvy edges. One he called a 'bouba', and the other a 'kiki'. He then asked his audience which was which. Ramachandran pointed out the amazing thing that 98 per cent of people automatically and spontaneously associated the word 'kiki' with the jagged piece of glass. Try it yourself with the photograph in the plate section. To be fair, this may not be quite as impressive as it first seems. There may be a number of explanations for this association, not least that the 'k' and 'i' of 'kiki' look jagged and the letters of 'bouba' are rather round.

Synaesthesia – blending the senses

Some individuals have a condition known as synaesthesia: they experience an odd blending of their sensory perceptions. They can taste sounds, for example, and feel words. It's a faculty that, as I stated above, exists to a degree in all of us – otherwise we'd be dead to the charms of art or music. But in synaesthetes, the confused perceptions are particularly intense. Vladimir Nabokov, the author of *Lolita*, describes his own synaesthesia as 'coloured hearing'. In his autobiography, *Speak, Memory*, he reveals its peculiarity, and also indicates something of the richness this disorder lends to his experiential life. '. . . I see [the letter] *q* as browner than *k*, while *s* is not the light blue of *c*, but a curious mixture of azure and mother-of-pearl . . .' Arguably, if it weren't for synaesthesia lending such a vivid range of colours to the way Nabokov heard language, he might not have become a celebrated novelist. In his, as in so many cases, we can see that the specific and unique way our brains are wired makes each of us who we are, for better and for worse.

This disorder, if I may call it that, is surprisingly common – it has been suggested that as many as 10 per cent of the population experience some kind of synaesthesia. It tells us something interesting about the way we take in sensory information and what we do to it. If someone feels they can taste the colour green, for example, then it implies that perhaps there is no real, objective, 'out-there' colour green, merely some raw data which goes in through the eyes to be assigned a meaning within the brain. In a non-synaesthetic person, the electrical pulses stimulated when we see a green wall would go directly to the visual cortex of the brain. But in a synaesthete, they might be travelling to the taste centre as well. So there is no real colour green – merely a route of information-processing that is similar within most, but not all, people's brains.

Ramachandran points out that synaesthesia was described by Francis Galton, the distinguished geneticist, in the nineteenth century. Some people who are otherwise completely normal get their senses mixed. Every time they hear a particular tone they see a particular colour. So, for example, when they hear C sharp, the colour red is evoked, while F sharp is blue. One of my friends at university, who was a particularly good pianist, had a strong sensation of a blue colour when listening to music in A minor; when the music modulated to a different key, the perception of this colour faded. What is of considerable interest is that this trait may be genetically determined, says Ramachandran, and indeed Galton pointed out that it runs in families. Work by Simon Baron-Cohen in Cambridge confirms this.

Another aspect of synaesthesia is that some people when shown numerals printed in black and white experience a particular colour. So, for instance, '5' is always seen as red and '6' is always tinged green. '7' may always be indigo and '8' always yellow.

Ramachandran asks why this mixing of signals occurs. Together with one of his students, Ed Hubbard, he studied brain atlases and they were impressed by the fact that the fusiform gyrus is where the colour information seems to be analysed. And the number area of the brain, which represents visual symbols of numbers, is next to it, almost touching it, in the same region. Ramachandran suggests that in some people there is some accidental cross-wiring. In his Reith lecture, he argued that in some people this may be caused by a gene or a set of genes that causes abnormal connections between adjacent brain regions. In this instance, the connections are between the areas perceiving numbers and colours.

Ramachandran devised a test for discovering synaesthetes of this type. Using a simple display on the computer screen, he had a number of blue 5s scattered on a white screen. Embedded among those were a number of 3s. The figure 3s were placed to form a shape like

a triangle, hidden among the other figures. Normal individuals looking at this pattern see a mass of 5s. But a synaesthete who sees
numbers in colour immediately sees the 5s as blue and the 3s as red
and identifies the fact that they are forming a red triangle on a white
background (see the photograph in the plate section).

MRI imaging makes it more possible for us to at least partially
understand what is happening. When subjects are asked to look at a
colour, or to smell an odour (or even to imagine it – though this is a
matter for later discussion), rapid firing of neurons down a well-
travelled sensory path occurs, leading from the organ in question to
various destinations in the brain. As the information travels through
the brain, it is split into streams, which then go to various separate and
distinct 'centres' to be processed. For instance, some information will
go to the visual cortex. Other parcels of information will travel into
the limbic system, to be tagged by the emotion and memory centres.
In this way, we may not just think 'green' when we see green, but
might also be reminded of the institutional corridors at our first
school, for instance, and how fearful they made us feel.

The region in the cortex for each sense is split into further smaller
zones, which deal with more specific properties. So for instance, in
the visual cortex, there are separate regions that interpret shape, size,
depth, colour and movement. Once these areas have done their job,
then the information is sent onwards into larger cortical regions
known as association areas. Here, the sensory information is married
to corresponding cognitive associations – for instance, the sight of a
hammer may be paired up with associations like 'heavy', 'cold' and
'banging', i.e. its function.

Research has shown that kittens, if deprived at an early age of
certain features in their visual environment – such as horizontal lines
or right-angles – are unable to recognize them when they grow to
adulthood. This may seem like a strange phenomenon. If their eyes
are working properly how can they be blind to what is right in
front of them? But because the visual cortex of the brain has been
deprived of a certain kind of input, the cats never developed the
apparatus to perceive it. In my childhood, one of the common threats
made to 'lazy' children was that if they didn't get up and do whatever
was expected of them at that moment, they might lose the use of their
legs. And to some extent, this threat is not far short of the mark.
Hostages kept for months, even years, in conditions of enforced

solitude have great difficulty using their voices once freed. The associated areas of their brains, no longer used for the purpose for which they were originally designated, may take on new functions. As we have already seen, the plastic brain neural connections that are not used die away, and with their death, even vital sensory functions like seeing and hearing can be lost. The reverse is also true – the more use a brain region receives, to some extent the bigger it may become. So it follows that, to an extent, our brains will differ purely because we are each exposed to subtly different environments.

Sensory overload

There is a Zen Buddhist tale of a frog who lived in a well and dreamed of escaping to the river. But when its wish was granted and it saw the river for the first time, the frog fell down dead on the spot. The implication was that, in its narrow little world, the hapless frog had been unable to imagine a thing so vast as a river, and its brain and body experienced a sensory overload. A similar, almost certainly apocryphal story, is reported of Captain Cook's voyages in the South Seas – he claims that the inhabitants of one particular island were unable to see his huge galleon anchored a few yards off the shore. Their brains did not have the sensory capacity to encompass an object so huge. Whether this tale is true or not, consider the fact that some societies only count up to ten. Anything beyond that is simply 'many'. Living in small human groups, with small numbers of possessions and accompanying animals, they do not have any need for larger numbers. This expresses the point that brains develop only the faculties they need. The proportional layout is much the same in everyone, but excessive use or disuse results in individual differences.

I was reminded of this frog recently as I was experiencing another kind of sensory overload. Not so long ago, I visited the Jewish Museum in Berlin designed by the remarkable architect Daniel Libeskind. Part of the museum is a memory of the Holocaust. There I spent a short time in the 'Garten des Exils' (Garden of the Exiles). You can only spend a short time there because the sensory overload becomes unpleasant. Here, in a high-walled space, over which you can just perceive the tops of other buildings, are forty-nine square pillars made of smooth concrete, seven metres tall (each placed a metre from each other made out in rows of seven, so they form a square seven by seven). The planting is on the top of the pillars, so the garden is high above and completely out of reach. The pillars, though regularly placed and parallel, are themselves planted in sloping ground, and this sloping ground is uneven and cobbled. So, within the walled space, vision is giving one sense of horizon, balance on the sloping ground another, and (because of the cobbles) proprioception – the feeling of where one's limbs are in space – another neural message. With the senses so completely confused, the effect is extraordinary and extremely disorientating – indeed, after about five minutes I had an overpowering need to leave because I was feeling dizzy and sick.

Sight

Information derived from our sight has a long way to travel from its initial entry point at the lens of the eye. Firstly it goes to the retina, at the back of the eye, where it is converted into electrical impulses. These travel along the optic nerve and half of them cross over (left visual field information to the right brain, and vice versa). The majority of the fibres connect with an area of the thalamus called the lateral geniculate body and a few with the pulvinar nucleus. As we saw, the thalamus acts as the connection site between the sensory components and the higher functions of the brain. Visual information then proceeds to the visual cortex, situated at the back of the brain, above the cerebellum.

Like all other areas of the brain, the visual cortex needs regular use to grow and remain healthy. A particularly sad example of this is found in the children who received the first lens transplant operations. Born blind, and typically having remained so for ten or more years, the children and their families welcomed this new surgical innovation with great enthusiasm. But after the operations were completed, it became obvious that none of the recipients was able to see without significant problems. They experienced visual stimuli as glaringly bright and painful. They were unable to use visual information to orientate themselves in space. They were, in short, unable to learn to see, because their brain had passed the point of plasticity for that skill – the years of disuse had robbed their brain of the potential. Following the surgery, these children (who had had such high hopes) felt severe depression, and some even committed suicide.

But the future may not be so gloomy. Eventually, it may become possible to train the brain to form a 'new' visual cortex. Dr Susan Blackmore[6] of the University of the West of England, Bristol, points to a preliminary report from Dr Paul Bach-y-Rita of Strasbourg.[7] One of the patients he describes is a woman who was congenitally blind. He showed that, using specially devised electrodes on her tongue, she could learn to see and manipulate objects within a few hours of training. And Dr Blackmore also comments on Dr Mriganka Sur's experiments at MIT, Boston,[8] involving rewiring the cortex of newborn ferrets. They have suggested that there is nothing intrinsically 'visual' about the visual cortex. Visual input was rerouted by these researchers to what should have developed as the part of the cortex that is involved in hearing. But later examination showed that it had, with time, become organized into maps and columns in a very similar pattern to that normally found in the visual cortex. In other words, the characteristic organization of different parts of the brain's cortical areas might be driven by the input rather than being purely pre-wired and therefore determined by genes.

Smell

Smell is detected high up in the nose by two small patches containing around six million or so cells. While our sense of smell is not as acute as it is in most animals, normal humans can detect some chemicals even when they are diluted to one part in several billion of air. Our sense of smell is most acute when we are children and drops off as we age. There is some evidence that premature ageing – such as Alzheimer's disease – results in a more rapid decline in our ability to smell. It is also true that a number of conditions such as schizophrenia, depression and anorexia are associated with decreased ability to smell and at least one study suggests that migraine sufferers may also have a lowered sensitivity to some smells, at any rate during if not before an attack. What is not clear is whether this lowered sensitivity is caused by the migraine.

Smell is perhaps the oldest sense available to us, a remnant of our reptilian past. Whereas all other sensory information takes a lengthy route through the thalamus, into the cortex and thence onwards to the limbic system to be tagged with emotions and memories, the smell route goes directly to the limbic system and then up to the cortex. This might explain why we find smells so instantly evocative of moods and memories. In one study, students learnt new words while sniffing an unusual smell and then sniffed it again when trying to recall the words. They showed a 20 per cent boost in their memory recall.

It is easy to see that, in our evolutionary past, having a quick response to smell information could be vital to our survival. That's why there is so swift a route from nose to limbic centre. It seems that smell was a major factor in the development of our brains, as the original, reptilian brain consisted of little more than some olfactory tissue sitting on top of a nerve cord. The entire limbic system is thought to have evolved from this point – originally interpreting odours and sending out corresponding chemical messages. The olfactory cortex is no smaller in modern humans than in our ancestors, though arguably modern life – with its sensory onslaught of exhaust fumes, perfumes, deodorants and the like – does not help our smell system to guide us as it once did.

Nevertheless, there is evidence that we still unconsciously respond to smells, and sometimes to things that we cannot even smell but perceive through our nostrils. Women may have a sense of smell up to 1,000 times more sensitive than men's, and various studies have shown these powers to be eerily sharp. A study by researchers at the Institute of Anthropology in the Ludwig-Boltzmann Institute at the University of Vienna involved showing a number of female subjects a frightening film while having them wear underarm pads to collect their perspiration. For those of you that are interested, the film was *Candyman* – said in its blurb to be 'the most frightening film since *Silence of the Lambs*'. A further group watched a neutral film while undergoing the same process. And a third group of women were able to distinguish by smell alone those pads that were carrying the 'scent of fear'.

Many animals produce pheromones and there is good evidence for their role in communicating alarm and fear. Fish, insects (such as bees), and some worms even, communicate alarm, which encourages members of the same species to avoid a threat coming from a particular region where the alarm was triggered. Mammals certainly communicate by smell, and it is known that cats can seek out stressed mice by the scent caused by their stress. Until recently, the evidence for the existence of human pheromones has been more controversial.

Pheromones are very volatile substances that affect either the behaviour or the hormones (or both) of an individual who perceives them. There are two different types. 'Signalling' pheromones result in a direct and observable change of behaviour. 'Primer pheromones' have a long-term effect on the receiver, presumably by changing his or her hormonal state. Pheromones act directly on the brain and are generally not recognized consciously by their recipient. They are frequently present in sweat, and in recent years research has shown that they may often play an important part in human sexual behaviour. Norma McCoy and Lisa Pitino, from San Francisco State University, recruited volunteer female undergraduates by asking whether they might like to participate in testing whether a synthesized female hormone, when added to their regular perfume, could 'increase the romance in their lives'.[9] To qualify for inclusion in the study, these young women had to be menstruating regularly, heterosexual, not using oral contraceptives and not cohabiting with a regular partner. During the experiment, some of the volunteers used their regular perfume which had been spiked with a totally odourless pheromone. Others, selected at random, had their perfume spiked with a neutral substance. None of the volunteers was told whether they were using a pheromone or not, and the control group was only recruited with the promise of a free vial of the real stuff for everyone at the end of the experiment.

Each volunteer was asked to use their perfume in a standard fashion and at set times. The women using pheromone-spiked perfume turned out to be three times more likely to have sex, or just share their bed with a male friend, than those in the control group. The researchers demonstrated that, rather than make the women more responsive to sexual advances, this particular pheromone made the women more attractive to men. So men, too, may have a keen sense of 'smell' even when a substance seems odourless. I regret that I am unable to divulge the name of the pheromone – the researchers report that Athena, the American company marketing this product, are in the process of patent application – but no doubt you could try buying it on the internet for a price.

Women are undoubtedly more sensitive to smell at certain times during their menstrual cycle. Their olfactory powers are usually at their sharpest when they are most ready to conceive, at the time of ovulation. Women produce pheromones that not only influence men, but also other females, particularly as regards their menstrual cycles. Thus in a relatively closed environment it is not at all unusual for women, after being together for several months, to have their periods at the same time. One of my senior colleagues at work tells me that in our laboratory, in which 85 per cent of the staff are female, after several months of working together the women tend to have synchronized menstrual cycles.

Dr Laurence Katz and his team at Duke University have discovered that animals have a pheromone-processing machinery in the brain which seems to produce a specific 'pheromonal image' of another animal.[10] Such an 'image' of the other animal's identity, sex and reproductive status governs a range of mating, fighting, maternal–infant bonding and other behaviour. The neurons that process pheromonal signals are similar in many respects to the 'face neurons' in the part of the visual cortex of the primate brain that are specifically triggered by facial features of other animals. A wide range of mammals, from mice to elephants, possess such a 'sixth sense' for detecting pheromones. These animals have a specialized sense organ, the vomeronasal organ, in the nose cavity. This organ pumps samples of pheromones into a sensory cavity, where they are detected by chemical receptors similar to those used in taste and smell – even though they cannot be detected by either smell or taste. These sensory neurons send connections to a structure called the accessory olfactory bulb, where Katz's team made electrical recordings of individual cells. To measure the signals, Dr Katz used a method first developed to measure the activity of neurons in the brains of birds as they sing. Three tiny micromotors attached to hair-thin electrodes are insinuated into the pheromone-processing region of the animal's brain. These electrodes can be retracted or extended by remote control by minute amounts, seeking out individual neurons to record their activity during different behaviour. The electrodes are so tiny that the animal can move freely, interacting with other animals, while their brain is sending signals over a fine wire to a recorder.

But animals like mice live largely in the dark, and generally have rather poor vision. So, as Dr Katz points out, communicating by pheromones would be critical to their survival. Whether a structure like the vomeronasal organ persists in humans remains controversial but it must be likely.

When smell information goes into the limbic system, it passes to both the amygdala and the hypothalamus. Some epileptics report a sensation of unusual smells just prior to having a fit, and brain imaging shows that in these individuals, the electrical activity is concentrated in the limbic area. The amygdala, as we shall see later on, is vital for the expression and interpretation of emotions. The hypothalamus, meanwhile, is the brain's hormonal centre – among other things responsible for the 'fight-or-flight response' when we are startled. That is why certain odours have the power to increase heart rate and blood pressure, and others to induce calm. Aromatherapy is not simply a New Age fad; it may really play a therapeutic role by relieving tension.

Taste

Taste and smell are probably the most linked sensory faculties. Most taste is actually smell – we can discriminate only five tastes with our tongue. These are salt, sweet, bitter, sour and umami. Umami is a kind of savoury taste given by foods that are rich in amino acids – glutamates. This is why monosodium glutamate is such an effective taste enhancer. But a mere whiff of roast chicken or banana and we can imagine the taste so vividly it might as well be on our tongue. Unsurprisingly then, the taste area of the cortex is situated right above the olfactory area in the right hemisphere. Damage to this area can result in some surprising phenomena – a Swiss study identified thirty-four brain-injured patients who had suddenly developed an obsession with food. In all these cases of 'gourmandism', lesions were found in the right frontal lobes. Interestingly enough, though these people developed an obsession with food, buying it, cooking it and eating it, none of them became overweight. Having tasted the dairy-heavy delights of Swiss cuisine on many a ski trip, I find this hard to explain.

It is easy to see how our taste faculties would have been vital to us in our ancestral past. Something that tastes 'bad' to us might well be a source of poison. We are, incidentally, thousands of times more sensitive to bitter tastes than to salt, sweet or sour ones. 'Bitter' is likely to be more dangerous. For that reason, survival manuals advise anyone trying to forage for food in the wild to be guided by their senses – as a rule of thumb, avoid anything that tastes or smells bitter, rancid or otherwise disgusting. The area of our brain that becomes active when we taste something we don't like – the anterior insula – has been reported to light up in the scanner when we see someone else registering disgust. From an evolutionary perspective this could be very useful – if another of our species tries to eat something and registers disgust, we don't need to waste time trying to eat it ourselves. We can concentrate on chasing after that tasty antelope instead.

Hearing

The last sense lost when slipping into unconsciousness, and the first to return on waking, seems to be hearing. For this reason it is important to be cautious when speaking in front of a very ill, apparently unconscious person, or in the presence of a dying relative. Many years ago when I was rather more callow, I was doing a simple Caesarean section operation for Julie, who had already had two previous deliveries by Caesarean section. Consequently, a third delivery by this route was inevitable. In such circumstances, once the baby is delivered safely, the rest of the operation procedures – removing the placenta, stopping the bleeding, repairing the uterus, cleaning out the abdomen and closing the wound – are pretty humdrum. Twenty years ago it was quite normal to give a fairly light general anaesthetic for this kind of surgery, the reason being that the baby would be born fitter and more ready to breathe. My anaesthetist, well known in the hospital to be urbane and totally unflappable, was congratulating himself on the excellent condition of the baby boy as I delivered him – moving all four limbs vigorously and crying with gusto. Some devil got into me and made me want to prick his complacency. 'It's all right for you,' I declared, 'your anaesthetic may be good for the baby but it's resulted in a lot of dilated vessels – we've a brisk haemorrhage here.' Moments later, I complained about spurting from the inferior branch of the left uterine artery, and shortly afterwards asked my assistant who, I regret to say, had just as inappropriate a sense of humour, how many pints of blood had been cross-matched before the operation. On hearing his false-apologetic answer, 'Only two, I'm afraid,' I said with as much alarm in my voice as I could muster that we might need another five. It soon became clear to my anaesthetist we were just trying to shake him and the operation finished without hitch.

Next morning I went to see Julie with her little boy. Both were fine. Then she turned to me and apologized for giving me so much trouble. Uncomprehending, I said that the operation had been easy and routine. 'But what about the haemorrhage?' she asked. 'And the trouble with, what did you call it, the left inferior branch of the uterine artery – and the five pints of blood you needed to order?' She then told me that she had heard – and could recall – everything that had been said up to the time when we started to close her abdomen. She felt no pain, and just at times the remotest sense of touch. After an initial anxiety, Julie said she felt no fear – 'Everything seemed to be under control and there was nothing I could do, anyway.' But we learnt at least one important lesson from Julie's case. We were very lucky that we hadn't frightened her, but this taught us to ensure that sufficiently deep anaesthesia is always maintained.

As in all other faculties except smell, information crosses over from one side to the other: information presented to the left ear travels to the right side of the brain to be processed. Both left and right hemispheres play a distinct role in sound processing, so a person with hearing problems in one ear may perceive auditory information very differently from someone with perfect hearing. For example, the left side of the brain seems to deal mainly with the identification and naming of sounds, rather than their quality. So somebody who can only hear in their right ear may have a blunted perception of aspects of music like rhythm and melody.

It is worth noting that although there is a direct link between the auditory cortex and the language region of the left hemisphere, you do not need to hear to develop language. MRI studies of deaf children born to deaf parents who grew up using sign language reveal a language region just as developed as that of hearing children. Moreover, non-deaf children born to deaf parents never attain the same degree of fluency in sign language as their deaf counterparts – they use a 'broken' version of the language, similar to a foreigner's attempts to master English. Other senses are somewhat similar. Blind people who learn to read using Braille show activity in the visual and language areas of the brain, as well as in the sites responsible for receiving touch sensation through the fingers.

Touch

A sense that develops early is touch – and it is more acute in newborn babies than sight or hearing. The 'rooting reflex' can be seen from day one, when the baby turns its head towards anything that touches its face, the reflex that helps it to find the nipple.

Touch is vital to a baby's development. It seems curious that the practice of giving newborns to their mothers seconds after birth is a development only of the last twenty years or so. Previously, they were often whisked away to be washed and weighed by the nursing staff – hospital etiquette that seems to fly in the face of human need. But, arguably, while this practice might have been injurious to the mother–child relationship, it did not necessarily do any harm to the baby. All the while it was with the nurses, receiving the touch of human hands. But in some countries, of course, babies are routinely wrapped tightly in swaddling and restricted in movement – whether this is harmful is an interesting question. Brain scans of infants deprived of touch show that vital areas of their brains are underactive – like the Romanian orphans I described earlier. Dr Tiffany Field from the University of Miami has reported that premature babies massaged three times a day for ten days gained nearly 50 per cent more weight than premature babies who didn't receive this extra bit of simple tender loving care.[11] Moreover, they were able to leave the hospital an average of six days earlier. She claims that massage stimulates the production of human growth hormone, and hormones such as insulin that aid growth. Although I have not seen hard evidence of this, she maintains massage increases levels of the neuro-transmitter serotonin, an action not dissimilar to that of some anti-depression drugs.

Touch and movement information are processed at the top of the brain. Pain, as distinct from ordinary touch, is received at the site of its production by units called nociceptors. These send signals to the spinal cord, which then pass up through the brainstem to the thalamus. From there, the information travels into the cortex to our sensation regions, telling us what type of pain is being experienced and where it is located. A region in the frontal lobes called the anterior cingulate cortex – one particularly associated, as we shall see, with attention, monitoring and concentration – plays a particular role in pain perception. Many painkillers – particularly the ones that have a similar structure to opium: for example, codeine, found in many cough medicines – act by blocking the receptor sites in the brain's neurons that would normally be filled by the brain's own painkilling chemicals, encephalins. Opioids also decrease activity in the anterior cingulate cortex – and, accordingly, people find that they are paying less attention to their pain. When I was a medical student, after repairing a thick waterproof anorak while lying on my bed, I dropped the massive bodkin I had been using onto the floor. Some minutes later, foolishly forgetting what I had done, I jumped off the bed and rammed the thick iron darning needle into the sole of my foot, the needle breaking into two pieces deep in the muscles of my foot. It could only be extracted after a substantial incision under general anaesthetic. The pain after the surgery was intense, but an injection of pethidine – an opiate-like drug – relieved the unpleasant aspects of the pain completely. I could still perceive a throbbing feeling in my foot but it wasn't unpleasant and it didn't feel as if the rest of me was there at all. I think I can understand why some people become addicted to such drugs.

Have you noticed that if you rub the site of a pain – provided it is not severe – it begins to feel better? Mothers will instinctively rub or kiss the limb of a child who has hurt itself. This is not superstition – it works, because of a process called competitive inhibition. By rubbing the site of the pain we are sending a second set of signals to the brain in addition to the pain signals. The brain now pays attention to two streams of signalling at once, with the result that there is a reduction in the perceived severity of the first, 'pain-type' signal.

This raises some interesting questions. If pain and touch are things perceived inside the brain, do we need a body to feel? The obvious answer would be yes, of course we do. But there are a number of people who have had whole limbs amputated but who feel a ghostly sensation of the limb still being there as part of them, to the extent that they can even feel pain. The Phantom Limb Syndrome is still not fully explained, but neuroscientists know that the areas in the brain that are involved are the thalamus and the touch areas of the cortex. Vilayanur Ramachandran, who has done much research in this area, noted that when pressure was applied to other, intact parts of the body, his phantom-limb patients, missing, say, their left leg, would often say they felt touch in specific, and consistent, regions of the non-existent leg. Ramachandran suggests that, when an area of the brain is not in use, it becomes coopted by neighbouring neurons for new purposes. So the area of neurons once responsible for an arm, now amputated, might be taken over by the face area of the brain. These coopted pathways still carry traces of their original function – and hence the feeling of pain in a leg or arm that no longer exists. There may be other reasons for phantom-limb pain, too. If there has been intense pain immediately before amputation in the limb to be removed, this pain can persist afterwards.

There is a curious, opposite phenomenon, known as apotemnophilia, which might possibly be related to 'phantom limb'. A few people report feeling that normal limbs which are very much a working part of their bodies should not be so. They may go to a doctor asking for amputation of the offending limb. They frequently find it very difficult to explain how they feel except that, for some inexpressible reason, they feel their leg or arm is 'not theirs'. Rather understandably, medical professionals have been apt to treat apotemnophilia as a form of hysteria, a psychotic state such as schizophrenia or associated with severe depression, or sometimes a sexual fixation with limblessness. Some apotemnophiliacs have succeeded in persuading surgeons to perform amputations on them in order to alleviate their mental suffering. The most famous recent cases in the UK resulted in questions being asked in the House of Commons by Mr Dennis Canavan, MP, in February 2000. Mr Robert Smith, a surgeon operating privately at Falkirk and District Royal Infirmary, had cut off the lower legs of two patients who were requesting amputations. One of these patients was British, the other German. The men had previously been turned away by other surgeons from different hospitals in Europe before Mr Smith agreed to operate. Mr Smith said that he saw nothing wrong with his actions but that he did 'not want to specialize in the procedure'. 'The last thing I want to be is a world centre for cutting off arms and legs,' he said. The Health Minister at the time told Mr Canavan that the government did not think a public inquiry was necessary.

Our advancing understanding of brain science may make it possible to alleviate this bizarre syndrome without recourse to bone-saw and ligature, by treating the related area of the cortex. The desperate measures taken by some people with rare disorders of the awareness of their own body are a reminder that it can be hard to communicate your perception of yourself, and the world around you, to anyone else. It's a problem that stems, once again, from that hoary old chestnut of philosophy and language. The only device we have for interpreting and communicating about our brain is the brain itself. Indeed, while microscopy, electroencephalography, MRI and PET scans and X-rays are essential tools in understanding how the brain works, the investigator's own brain – with all its flaws and subjectivity – will always remain the best tool of all. As each person's brain is different, I cannot possibly know what it feels like to be in possession of a working limb and yet want it amputated. If you say you see the colour green, I can only think of my brain's version of green, not your green. When talking about your brain and my brain, we have to accept a certain, necessary amount of indistinctness.

The thingummy-whatsit-doo-dah

Our senses are not really separate and discrete skills, because we tend to use them in combination with one another. Certain linguistic visual cues – the things we see, such as the shape of someone's lips – activate the hearing areas of the brain, while non-linguistic movements of the mouth do not. It's as if our brains are primed for the task of communicating with others. A study at Brandeis University in the United States also found that we sometimes 'see' with our hearing. Volunteers shown an image of two blocks moving towards one another on a screen reported that they had seen the two blocks collide when in fact all that had happened was that they had heard a sharp click. Similarly, subjects playing ping-pong with their ears muffled perform less well than those who can use their hearing, as well as their sight, to judge the trajectory of the incoming ball. Have you noticed, for example, that when you are trying to park your car in a tricky space, it helps to turn down the music on the car radio? This might be purely because you need to concentrate. But equally, although you are not immediately conscious of it, you are relying on hearing, as much as visual and motor skills, to get your car safely into that tight spot.

One of the chief areas in which all our sensory faculties work together is in recognition. Recognition is one of the mind's most vital skills – we call upon it daily in the most simple and complex of tasks. When I go into my laboratory office in the morning there is a tiny, unconscious 'Aha!' inside my brain as I pick out the familiar surroundings from the other laboratory offices immediately next door. The familiar smell of old coffee and the odour of damp paper underneath the leak from the top window, the unique view of the high-security wing of Wormwood Scrubs prison just over the hospital wall, and the depressing sight of mounds of correspondence which my secretary has thoughtfully left on my untidy desk (still with a soggy packet of biscuits) all inform me that this is indeed my office. As I look downwards, I can pick out from the huge mound of post the really important letters in the pile. All this happens so swiftly that my conscious brain barely registers the process at all. Indeed, I am already thinking about a whole host of other things.

In the BBC TV series of *The Human Mind*, I wear a 'magic hairnet', a series of hundreds of electrodes covering the whole of my scalp, while watching a TV screen on which there is an optical illusion. At first difficult to identify, there is a still photograph of a Dalmatian dog hidden against a background of a wider pattern of large and small blots of black. Only when the dog starts to move do I recognize the image. When I recognize it, Gaynor Evans, a doctoral student of the University of Warwick, is on hand with an EEG machine to measure the electrical activity inside my brain as the 'aha' moment dawns.

In order to get clear results, it is necessary to perform the test many times. Each time I was asked to recognize the dog, there were two significant bursts of gamma waves. The first occurred as my brain registered that I had seen 'something'. The second, very shortly afterwards, occurred at exactly the point where I experienced a little internal 'aha' – I had 'got' the trick. This gap between the two bursts of activity is likely to be the time it takes for the brain to match what it sees with a meaning. In other words, the gap is where my brain matched up the 'something' with my own internal images of dogs.

Our faculty for recognition does sometimes break down. This American patient described a very familiar object in the following way: 'I can see a lot of lines. Now I see some stars. When I see things like this, I see a lot of parts . . .' The man was suffering from a brain disorder known as agnosia and was attempting to identify the

American flag. His speech demonstrates that his problem was not merely that he didn't know the correct word. He quite genuinely had no idea what the item in front of him was. He was having difficulty because agnosia is, in essence, an inability to recognize objects. The disorder tends to be very specific – for instance, sufferers may be unable to recognize faces, or other body parts, or items of food, or man-made objects. The discovery that such disorders can result from a single bit of damage to a specific area in the brain suggests that there are compartmentalized sections of our memory in which we store items of particular kinds. Biological objects are generally stored by how they look in parts of the brain that do perceptual analysis – while inanimate objects are commonly represented in the brain by their function, so they are stored in regions associated with actions that might use those objects.

One of the problems for me in writing about the working of the brain is that it is easy to descend into a description of what may be seen as a 'freak show'. But the truth is that in research into the way the brain functions it is so often the study of the disordered state that enables us to understand what's happening in a normally functioning brain. Studies into agnosia have found that the brain seems to make a strong distinction between living and non-living objects. Rather more bizarrely, people who are unable to recognize living things are also often unable to recognize food and musical instruments. Yet these same people have no problem identifying other man-made objects or human body parts.

These pairings may seem weird but they led scientists to conclude that the recognition faculties of the brain are both rigorous and at the same time quite generalized. From the examples above, for instance, we can say that the brain seems to put food, animals and musical instruments in one compartment, and man-made objects and body parts into another. A study at the University of Iowa, led by husband-and-wife team Antonio and Hannah Damasio, tried to pinpoint the exact location of the brain's various recognition categories. They found a whole range of possible 'storage sites'. For instance, lesions in the right temporal lobe seem to be related to difficulties in facial recognition. An inability to recognize tools and instruments was associated with lesions in an area of the left hemisphere where the temporal and parietal lobes join together.

Recognition units

One explanation for this is that the brain stores and categorizes things, not according to how they look or what they do, but according to our individual relationship with them. Take a hammer: it could be used for work or it could be an instrument of violence. A musical instrument could be seen, felt, played or heard. It seems that each quality of an item is stored in a separate region of the brain – in her book *Mapping the Mind*, the medical writer Rita Carter terms these 'recognition units' or RUs. So a musical instrument like a trombone would have not one 'unit', but several: a shape recognition unit in our visual areas, a word RU in our vocabulary area, a touch RU in the touch area, a sound RU in our hearing area. Each region of the brain may be stacked up with the recognition units of objects that might, on the face of it, not seem to have anything in common. They are together because they share the particular quality that concerns that region of the brain. So our trombone might sit in the same little corner of the brain's library as a cigarette or a straw – because all are non-food items that we put in our mouths. When we think of a trombone, all of our separate trombone RUs are drawn together from their separate storage regions and united to give us what we recognize as a long, sliding brass instrument that makes wonderful sounds in Tchaikovsky's Fourth Symphony.

So once again we see that our own particular experiences of the world create the geography of our brains, and these in turn inform our behaviour. A life-long vegetarian, for example, would not have a taste recognition unit for a chicken or a cow. A musician would have different RUs for a trombone than a casual jazz listener. I have it on good authority that a colleague's mother is unable to bear the taste of bananas because, as a child during the second world war, she was given mashed turnip doused with vanilla essence and told that this was the rationed fruit. Now, when she eats a genuine banana, she still tastes its distinctly unappealing substitute. Clearly some trick of the recognition facilities is at work here – for her, the word RU for 'banana' still has a connection to the original turnip-and-vanilla-taste RU, a connection so strong – and probably reinforced by the emotional memories associated with her disgust – that more recently formed RUs, such as what a real banana looks and feels and tastes like, cannot break it. Seemingly some qualities of both are filed next to each other in her brain's recognition site.

Nearly all of us are familiar with the dreadful experience of arriving at a party and being greeted by someone who seems to know us intimately, but whom we cannot remember. Some people suffer permanently from this, in a condition known as prosopagnosia, and cannot recognize people they have known all their lives and see every day. Still others suffer from its equally alarming opposite, known as Fregoli's Delusion (or Syndrome), in which they believe total strangers to be completely familiar. Leopoldo Fregoli was a famous actor from Rome, who died in 1936. The syndrome is named after him because of his mastery of disguise. It is said that, in one performance, he played no fewer than sixty different characters – a sort of forerunner to that great comic satirist Rory Bremner. Sufferers from Fregoli's Syndrome, on encountering people they have never previously met, may come up with very convoluted reasons to justify their belief that this really is an old friend. They may argue, for example, that this friend or relative has adopted a clever disguise.

But we cannot blame our lapses on another person's delusion. At the cocktail party, it is not that the other person is suffering from Fregoli's Syndrome, but much more likely that we have forgotten their face. Why does this happen? Why do we forget one face and yet remember another – even though both might be similarly unstriking faces?

Partially the answer boils down to the 'use it or lose it' maxim. Humans are social animals. We live as we have always lived, in groups, and we depend upon the ability to communicate with others of our species for our survival. For that reason, we have evolved with special brain wiring for face recognition – such that even a newborn child will orientate itself towards objects that resemble faces, like a balloon with eyes, nose and mouth drawn on it, and also show a preference for symmetrical faces over non-symmetrical ones. Faces occupy a special category of our recognition faculties – and brain scans show heightened activity in these areas not only when we see faces, but even when we imagine seeing them. If a face is seen or imagined frequently, its RU stays active, the neural connections remain strong. If on the other hand we do not see or think about a person for a long time, the facial RU for that person falls into disuse. Try remembering someone you have not seen for a very long time – the likelihood is that you can remember many of their attributes, but not accurately recall their face.

Of course, some other faces from long ago remain very vivid – and we will be examining the relationship between intense experiences and memory at a later point. For now it is enough to say that facial RUs do not necessarily need a strong stimulus to become activated, or to remain active. Imagine that the car-park attendant near your office has a strong resemblance to a cousin who emigrated to Australia. In seeing the car-park attendant five mornings and evenings a week, you are also keeping the facial RU for your Antipodean cousin stimulated. We can also see this at work in the grief process: someone in mourning is imagining the lost person more or less constantly, and the process is keeping that person's facial RU permanently switched on. Hence it is not uncommon for bereaved people, or people who have recently separated from a lover, to keep thinking they have seen their deceased or lost loved ones in the street. In reality, the 'heated' state of the facial recognition unit merely predisposes it to be triggered by the weakest of stimuli – so the sight of a face only vaguely similar to the face of our loved one, or the object of our grief, is enough to convince us, momentarily at least, that we have really seen them.

Facial recognition of all kinds involves a strong emotional content. This is why we are never entirely neutral in our dealings with other humans – however much we would like to be. Some people 'look' trustworthy or kind to us. (In fact, research has shown that men with softer, more feminine features are more likely to be found 'not guilty' in court.) Other people may seem sad, or threatening – without us being able to find any solid evidence for our verdict. This is because facial recognition takes place along two pathways within the brain – one conscious, and involving the higher cortex, and one unconscious, taking place within deeper structures of the brain. The unconscious pathway runs through the limbic system – and includes the amygdala – which you will by now recognize as one of the centres for our emotions.

The conscious pathway works at a slower speed – it is here that we work out, for instance, whose face we are looking at, and how we should behave towards them. This is why we often have an almost instantaneous 'first impression' of a person, which is chiefly an emotional feeling – of unease, for example, or affection – which we might find hard to put into words, and which might, upon further inspection, turn out to be quite wrong. As we shall see time and again throughout this book, the amygdala does not merely generate emotions, but seems to encode very basic emotional memories. So meeting someone whose face has vague similarities to the feared and hated maths teacher at school, for example, triggers a swift, brief and shadowy reliving of our feelings towards the original figure.

And now we can go some way towards accounting for the bizarre recognition disorders I mentioned earlier on. Prosopagnosia – a generalized failure to recognize faces – results from damage to the higher cortex – in particular the temporal and occipital lobes. In other words, it affects the higher, conscious recognition pathway. Patients with this problem, when shown photographs which include familiar faces, will typically say they recognize no one. But brain scans show that there is activation in their lower, sub-cortical pathway. Electrical changes in their skin also suggest that their brain is registering more than they are capable of saying. It remains, in effect, possible for them to recognize someone without being conscious that they are doing so.

This also helps to explain why people suffering from Fregoli's Delusion – in which they believe strangers to be familiar – feel the need to come up with complex and creative justifications for their beliefs. The same is true for people with the opposite disorder: Capgras Delusion – in which familiar faces are perceived to be those of strangers. People with Capgras suggest, for instance, that their friends or loved ones have been replaced by aliens or androids. They no longer have any emotional attribution to familiar faces. In both cases, their explanations are a noble attempt by the conscious brain to make sense of information coming up from the unconscious.

Walk a mile in my moccasins

So differences in the way our brains receive and assess incoming sense information create differences in the way we each see the world. In fact, it might be more accurate to speak of individual sense-worlds rather than some objective World. A Native American Indian proverb states that in order truly to understand a man, one must walk a mile in his moccasins. And we can see how this wisdom applies to our enquiry into the mind. The way we see, hear, touch, taste, in all respects sense the environment we're in, makes us who we are. It is possible to gain insight into someone else's character, if not our own, by understanding how they sense the world.

Harvard psychiatry professor John Ratey cites the example of Buckminster Fuller, architect of the geodesic dome, who used to walk around with specially developed eyewear. Here was a man who felt overloaded by the strength of his visual perception. The glasses shut out all but a small part of his view, and left him able to walk around while thinking. Ratey suggests that many of the disorders we now label as autistic, or corresponding to Attention Deficit Hyperactive Disorder, may have their root causes in abnormalities, or rather simple differences in perception. I am reminded strongly here of the scene in the film *Rain Man*, where Raymond, the autistic man played by Dustin Hoffman, screams, as if in pain, when Tom Cruise attempts to give him a hug. Many autistic people are highly sensitive to touch, to noise, to quickly moving visual stimuli. In a real and observable way, their faculties seem too finely tuned to the sensory input of the world around them – rather like the fairy-tale princess who could sense a pea hidden underneath the tower of mattresses upon which she slept. Unsurprisingly, for many autistic people, the world out there is a bewildering, painful experience and they withdraw from it into a private reality, governed by their own rituals and routines.

A similar principle may be at work in the brains of people with the reading and writing disorder dyslexia. This is a widespread phenomenon, and not, as generations of teachers and parents once believed, related in any way to intelligence. Many dyslexic people have made sterling contributions to the fields of medicine, architecture, art and literature. Many more lead normal, intellectually fulfilled lives.

While most dyslexic people have normal hearing and visual capacities, many others report hearing and seeing things that people without dyslexia do not. Tests have indicated that dyslexic people have a more developed talent for hearing slower, deeper sounds, like vowels in speech, for example, or the bass 'riff' of a piece of music. But it seems that it is the relation between sight and perception that is most variable in cases of dyslexia.

There are two principal pathways leading from the eyes into the visual cortex, known as the geniculostriate pathway and the tectopulvinar pathway. The latter pathway seems to be what we use to orientate our eyes towards a particular element of our view. It provides the mechanism whereby I might find my pen amid the

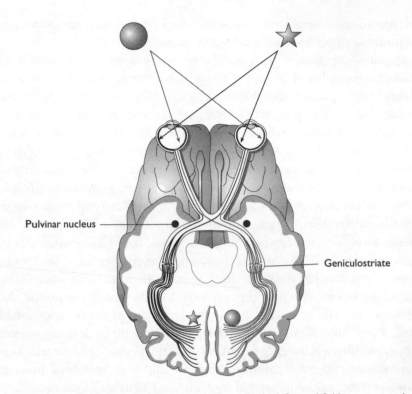

*The two visual pathways, showing that objects seen in the left visual field are processed
in the right hemisphere and objects seen in the right are processed in the left*

clutter of my desk, for example, or notice the brightly glowing lights
of a service station on a dull horizon. The pathway to the pulvinar
nucleus senses the interesting object and then the geniculostriate
pathway kicks in to help me see it.

Investigations into a phenomenon known as 'blindsight' have demonstrated the importance of the tectopulvinar pathway. Research into this
most peculiar aspect of the brain began with the Oxford psychologist
Larry Weiskrantz. In the 1970s, Weiskrantz was studying a patient who
had damage to an area of the visual cortex known as the right calcarine
fissure. The damage resulted in him being unable to see anything just to
the left of where he looked – he had a reduced field of vision.

Larry Weiskrantz sat his patient in front of a screen, on which
images were flashed only to the left half of his vision. He asked him to
reach out and touch the screen whenever something appeared. Oddly,
although this task might have been expected to be impossible, the
patient performed with great accuracy. Further tests revealed that he

was able to discriminate between horizontal, vertical and diagonal lines, and between the letters X and O. The subject was as astonished by his abilities as Weiskrantz himself – he maintained that he couldn't see anything, and swore he didn't know how he knew what was there.

Since then, advances in brain-scanning technology have enabled us to look inside the brains of blindsighted individuals as they do these seemingly impossible feats. Scans have shown that, while the bulk of the visual cortex does not light up, one small area – known as V5 – is activated in the presence of stimuli. This area corresponds to one end-point of the tectopulvinar pathway. It alerts us to whatever is new in our visual field, even if we are without the faculties that then enable us to 'see' it.

Some experts now believe that it's the other half of our visual mechanism, the geniculostriate pathway, that is faulty in people suffering from dyslexia. This pathway begins in an area of the thalamus that is subdivided into two regions – the first is a slow processing system that appears to deal with colour, and the second a faster system that provides information about movement and location. Many dyslexic people report that when they try to read, the words seem to move about on the page. Various studies have shown that dyslexic individuals process visual information more slowly than non-dyslexics. For instance, they have problems identifying the order of two sequentially flashed visual stimuli – like two numbers or words flashed one after another upon a screen – but they can perform the task perfectly well when the sequence is slowed down.

Research performed by Margaret Livingstone and Al Galaburda of Harvard Medical School showed that neurons in the fast layers of the thalamus, dealing with movement and location, were more disorganized in dyslexics.[12] This pattern would, presumably, result in the brain having a limited ability to clear out one image before it moved on to the next. And this might explain why the words seem to shimmer or move around on the page.

Paula Tallal of Rutgers University and Michael Merzenich of the University of California, San Francisco, used findings from research that Dr Merzenich had done in monkeys showing how well the brain can adapt to new sound stimuli.[13] They devised a CD-ROM game for dyslexic children called FastForward which is played fifteen hours each week. It trains their brains to register the quick changes between one sound and another in normal speech. After a four-week period, exercised brains showed a leap of as much as two years' worth of language ability.

In his book, John Ratey provides a fascinating glimpse of how such a minuscule difference of cellular organization could give rise to a whole facet of a person's character. One of his researchers reported to him her surprise on realizing that her mother had always been dyslexic, but had covered it up. She had also always been wary of crowds, or any busy, unfamiliar place. This aspect of her behaviour might have arisen from the same abnormality that created her dyslexia – being unable to process fast-moving information, being overwhelmed by it. Over time, she developed behavioural strategies to avoid being beleaguered – and these caused her shyness and lack of spirit of adventure.

Ratey suggests that even milder differences of personality might, in the final analysis, be the result of faulty processing at the sensory or motor level. The archetypal 'nerd', for instance, may really be someone who has withdrawn from a society they find hostile and bewildering. This is perhaps because they don't see people the way others do or because they cannot accurately judge when to chime in with an opinion. The underlying principle that follows is clear. Health professionals, teachers, court officials and others must stop labelling people as 'stupid', 'lazy' or 'bad' and consider the reasons why they might be the way they are. Such understanding is the hallmark of a healthy society and we are still a long way from that goal.

One key observation cautions against taking this theory too far. No two brains are alike in every way. So every single human brain, in that sense, could be said to have some 'abnormality' or other. If we notice that someone is shy and withdrawn, for example, and we then notice that the area of their auditory cortex responsible for processing language is smaller than other areas, we could say that they are withdrawn because they find communication with others difficult. Fine, as far as it goes, but we could also say that someone with an especially large language processing area was shy because they were overwhelmed by their extreme sensitivity to spoken sounds. No physician would have to look very far to find some curiosity in each and every human brain, which could then be seen as the cause of a disorder.

chapter**four**
Paying attention

You might be vaguely interested in learning how I got hooked on making television programmes. In the 1960s, when I was a registrar – a stripling, trainee obstetrician in a hospital in rural Essex – one patient elected to have her baby delivered using hypnosis as her sole pain relief. Pamela had had three babies delivered conventionally so she was a deal more experienced than her trainee doctor. She was convinced that the next labour might be more comfortable if she employed a hypnotist to attend and anaesthetize those parts that other painkillers did not easily reach.

It happened that at that time the BBC were making a programme on hypnotism – possibly one of the first programmes made about neuroscience. They heard of Pamela through her hypnotist, and got permission from the hospital to bring a lightweight crew to film her delivery. Pamela's due date was the Thursday before Easter, so learning by phone that she had been admitted, the crew battled to the countryside, hotfoot from Shepherd's Bush. In those days of good budgets – how TV funds have dwindled – a 'lightweight' crew included a cameraman with assistant, a soundman and assistant, an electrician and, of course, the producer and his assistant. They stood eagerly in the maternity wing, more expectant than any patient, and ready to shoot. None of them had seen a baby delivered, and only the blasé electrician had been in an operating theatre before, so they were trembling with excitement at the prospect in store. But Pamela was not in labour; she was reading the newspaper in a sitting room.

Crestfallen, they hung around all day awaiting the onset of labour. It seems incredible now that a media crew could be so naive as to believe that a pregnant woman delivered on her due date. By evening nothing had happened, but they decided to continue to wait as Pamela was having mild contractions. I took pity on them and suggested they came for a meal I offered to cook in my bachelor flat. Over the next few days, Pamela teetered on the verge of labour, the crew dithered about staying over the entire Easter weekend, and I became concerned about my patient because her blood pressure had risen – an unwelcome sign. By Easter Monday, the crew had camped four nights in my three-bedroom flat using every available space – it was not a pretty sight. That morning it became obvious to me that Pamela needed a Caesarean section. I phoned the consultant, who agreed and told me to get on with it. The BBC had invested a fearful amount in this adventure – massive overtime on a Bank Holiday weekend. The producer asked if I would ask Pamela if she was willing to have the Caesarean done under hypnosis. When I flatly refused he asked if they could at least film the operation (a Caesarean had never been previously shown on TV, even in black and white) and have the anaesthetist inject the drugs painlessly to induce sleep through a hypnotized arm beforehand.

I phoned my boss again. He was not impressed. I was well capable of doing a Caesarean section, he said, and he certainly did not intend to come in through the foul weather and spoil his Bank Holiday. If I wanted to let them film, he said, that was my affair. Sadly, I have always been a thespian and temptation proved too much. Pamela was wheeled into the anaesthetic room, the camera was switched on, the hypnotist pompously came in and, at great length, demonstrated to the cameras how good he was at making her right arm completely numb, and then went home.

Unhappily, it being a Bank Holiday weekend, we only had a locum anaesthetist, a pleasant foreign lady whose sole shortcoming was her extremely imperfect command of the English language and her consequent failure to understand why she, and her anaesthetic, were the focus of a BBC film crew's attention. Entering the anaesthetic room, she picked up a syringe full of prepared drugs and, without waiting, banged the lot into the patient's unhypnotized left arm. Pamela was wheeled into the theatre and there was that curious scurrying sound I associate with the media. It is the sound of an entire film crew scuttling behind their object of interest, desperate to keep quiet and not lose focus while adjusting lights, camera, microphone. I stood proudly at the operating table with the entire circus behind me, filming my every move. Unable to handle anything at all outside the operating field because of sterility, I cleaned the skin, draped the patient, opened the abdomen and incised the uterus without mishap. But as I was pulling the baby from the abdomen, I experienced the sensation that every surgeon, experienced or novice, deeply dreads because he cannot touch anything. It was the sensation of the pyjama cord around my theatre trousers inexorably loosening and then, with dread inevitability, the terrible sensation of my trousers inch by inch creeping down to my knees and then ankles. But not until the baby was safely handed to the waiting midwife did I recall the chaos in my flat and think, 'Did I remember to put clean knickers on this morning?'

In spite of all the distractions, at the key moments during that delivery I was using my attention, firing up specific parts of my brain. Attention directs our senses like a conductor, guiding them in different directions, disengaging them from one task and engaging them upon others. We all make use of a common mechanism within our brains to make sense of our sensations. Just imagine for a moment that you were able to see, hear and smell everything in your immediate surroundings all at once. The humming of your computer printer. The smell of your carpet. The car alarm outside and the dog barking. Your neighbour's stereo system turned up a bit loud. Somebody peering over your shoulder when you are trying to write. The unfolding events of the TV news in the adjoining room. A child's constant fidgeting. Imagine trying to think clearly for a moment in the midst of this sensory tsunami. Imagine trying to conduct a telephone conversation or look for your car keys in those surroundings. It ought to be well nigh impossible. So how do we manage? What within our brain enables us to choose what we are going to see, hear, smell? How can we tune into a conversation with someone else and ignore other sounds, find that missing set of keys amid the clutter of the office?

Paying attention unconsciously

In the 1940s, a group of American psychologists conducted some groundbreaking research into the factors that influence attention. The experimenters used a tachistoscope – basically a laboratory device to flash images for a usually short and very specific moment of time. The research team flashed words to a group of volunteers over varying periods of time and asked them to identify the words they had just seen. The words were of two types: neutral – including words like hammer, sheet, pin; and taboo – words with a high emotional content, like whore and penis.

At the very briefest duration – tiny fractions of a second – people were unable to identify what they had seen at all, registering only that they'd seen a burst of light. But as the time period became longer, something very interesting emerged. People took longer to recognize taboo words than the neutral words. The more socially unacceptable the word, the longer it took to register it.

This experiment was largely done to support the psychoanalytic, Freudian view that we employ certain unconscious 'defence mechanisms' in order to repress information that is upsetting us. But it is of interest here because this early research suggests that some agent inside our brains is making decisions about what we pay attention to, and what we choose to ignore. Psychologists sometimes call this the 'cocktail party effect' – based upon the observation that, even in environments that demand so much of our senses simultaneously, we are often able to follow conversations and at the same time respond if some-one on the other side of the room mentions our name.

In a later experiment, conducted by Drs Corteen and Wood in the 1970s, participants were conditioned to expect a small electric shock when they heard the name of a city. Their fear was measured by means of a sweat-sensitive pad placed on the skin. Possibly these hapless participants were offered financial sweeteners in recompense for their ordeal, but I doubt it. Neuroscientists and psychologists are sufficiently knowing about the human mind usually to be able to find a stream of willing research-fodder close at hand – possibly PhD students who refuse at their peril. Sometimes, of course, small cash sums, record vouchers, cans of beer and even humbugs have been used as a reward, but never in my experience for the most deserving – the PhD students.

Having tortured them in this way for some time, the experimenters then got the subjects to listen to two streams of words, one in each ear. They were instructed to repeat aloud the words they heard in one ear, but to ignore the words they heard in the other ear. Even when they were not paying conscious attention to it, the sound of a city name in the ignored ear provoked the same fear response. It became clear that we can pay attention to complex streams of information when we have sufficient motivation to, and that only some of this occurs at the conscious level. This is the cocktail party effect: we can hear our own names mentioned on the other side of a noisy room, even when deep in conversation, because the information has emotional significance.

Much more recently, Daniel Simons and Christopher F. Chabris at Harvard University asked subjects to watch a short film of some basketball players, one team in white and the other in black T-shirts.[14] They were asked to note down the number of passes that the white-shirted players made in the game. During the film, a woman entered the field of vision, and opened a dark umbrella. Of twenty-eight observers, only six noticed this event. The experimenters then expanded the experiment to include a person in a dark gorilla suit performing a nine-second routine in a stretch of footage that only lasted sixty-two seconds. Roughly half of the viewers failed to notice the gorilla.

I mention these experiments chiefly to demonstrate that paying attention is not the conscious, all-encompassing process we might consider it to be. We notice some things without knowing we notice them, while other things pass us by, even though we would consider ourselves to be on full alert. This highly selective aspect of human attention has given rise to considerable controversy over the years.

In the year 2000, during the Bush–Gore election campaign in the United States, the Republican Party was accused of using foul means to influence voters. The Democrats alleged that, during a Republican party political broadcast, the word 'RATS' appeared on the screen for exactly one-thirtieth of a second during a sequence in which other elements of the word 'DEMOCRATS' moved in and out of vision. They were saying, in effect, that their opponents had used a subliminal message to influence viewers. The Republicans defended themselves by maintaining that this was pure chance – even though the word 'RATS' was also in a larger typeface than 'DEMOC' and the ads had cost them a mere $2,576,000. This particular battle became forgotten amid the wider, and much more publicized, furore over the issue of the miscounted votes, favouring Bush.

This was not the first time that there had been a scandal over the use of this technique. In 1957, there was a massive outcry when James Vicary, a market researcher, announced that he had successfully inserted messages – for periods of time so brief that they escaped conscious detection – into a reel of cinema film. The messages, targeting no fewer than 45,699 patrons of a particular cinema in Fort Lee, New Jersey, were inserted during successive screenings of the film *Picnic*. The letters that were briefly flashed on screen (3/1000th of a second every five seconds) urged cinemagoers to 'Eat Popcorn' and 'Drink Coca-Cola'. Over a six-week period, Vicary boasted that this had resulted in a 58 per cent increase in food sales and an 18 per cent increase in drink sales. People in the 'Land of the Free' took great umbrage at the idea that it was possible for people to tamper with their thoughts without their consent. Their outrage was particularly strong in the tense milieu of the 1950s, in which it was suspected that all manner of unsavoury agencies, from aliens to communists, might be able to gain control over people's brains. When congressmen got involved in the protests – Representative Dawson said, 'Put to propaganda purposes [it] would be made to order for the establishment and maintenance of a totalitarian government' – Vicary's experiments were called to an abrupt halt. His team later announced that there hadn't been any subliminal messaging at all, and the whole affair had been an elaborate hoax. It remains unclear to this day what really occurred but it seems likely that Vicary was not exactly a reliable witness.

The modern view of subliminal manipulation of attention is a little less paranoid. So-called subliminal cuts are banned in advertising, both in the US and in the UK. But at the same time, experts on both sides of the Atlantic consider it to be of only very limited power to influence people's thoughts and actions. Some studies have shown that the influence of subliminal messages may last for as little as one-tenth of a second – which is probably not long enough to go out and buy some popcorn or vote for the Republicans.

It also seems that these messages only work when the circumstances are right. It is believed that subliminal messaging works – when it does – through a process called priming, the same mechanism we examined when looking at facial recognition. If a word like 'Coke' is flashed subliminally to my brain, then this message will have the effect of priming, or stimulating, other recognition units connected with my experience of Coke: quenching thirst, sweet taste, bubbles on the tongue, good with a shot of rum . . . But as priming has an effect on the brain for quite a long time afterwards, this liking for Coke may last – at least for longer than one-tenth of a second.

Arousal

What parts of the brain are we using when we pay attention? Neurologists have argued that, in fact, attention is not one process but four – arousal, orientation, reward and novelty detection, and executive organization – each with its own related set of brain regions.

Arousal is the faculty whereby our awareness increases. It is controlled by what we call the reticular activating system in the brainstem, the frontal lobes, the limbic system and sense organs. Information from the sense organs, or even from our own thoughts, can arouse us. The hippocampus, the seat of long-term memory, also communicates with the reticular activating system, comparing what we see in the present with the past.

The arousal system plays a big part in what we call the fight-or-flight response – that combination of brain and body activity that comes into action when we are startled by something. Imagine you are lying in bed, just drifting off to sleep. Suddenly you hear a loud crash outside. Immediately, you are fully awake, searching for the origin of the sound. Information from your auditory cortex is being hurriedly assessed and parcelled – some of these parcels travel to the amygdala, triggering the sensation of fear. The amygdala in turn communicates with the anterior cingulate in the frontal lobes, and then the hypothalamus and spinal cord.

The hypothalamus, Grand Vizier of the body's hormonal system, starts to fire up. Briefly, it suppresses bodily activity – heart rate is calm, blood pressure stays constant, breathing is quiet. This creates a bodily delay so that the upper cortex can work out what's going on outside our window. Then it swings into reverse – heart rate and blood pressure soar, the secretion of adrenaline heightens awareness and primes your muscles for action.

97

Meanwhile, the frontal lobes are at work, assessing the situation. If you determine that some neighbourhood cats have knocked a dustbin lid off, then your frontal lobes send a message to the amygdala to calm down. This sets a chain in action which concludes with the heart rate slowing down, and blood pressure and adrenaline levels dropping. What's happening here is that the lower, unconscious brain is calming down and handing control of the situation over to the higher brain. You begin to 'think' about what's happening rather than simply reacting to it.

If, on the other hand, you determine that someone is trying to kick your front door in, signals travel swiftly to the hypothalamus. This triggers the release of corticotropin releasing factor, or CRF, the brain's stress hormone, and of the neurotransmitters adrenaline and cortisol to prepare body and brain for swift action. It also talks to the pituitary gland, which secretes hormones affecting every major gland of the body. This rush of activity stimulates the amygdala and the brainstem – you become prepared to run or fight.

The intensity and speed of these processes differ from one individual to another. Calmer people will generally spend more time in the 'cool' mode, their lower brain activity dampened down as their higher brains gather and assess incoming information. More panicky types of people may do the opposite, immediately entering fight-or-flight mode, even if the information out there indicates that they do not need to.

Nowadays, I am not afraid of public speaking, but I can remember enough of my early days of stage fright to know that it is very real. In this instance, what's happening is a loop between the upper and lower brains. In our upper brains we see the expectant faces before us, feel our dry mouths and our shuddering limbs and conclude, 'Oh dear, I'm afraid.' This sends a message to the amygdala and thence to the whole nervous system, sending heart rate and blood pressure sky high, letting the stress hormones such as adrenaline flow. Our upper brain observes these fresh symptoms of impending disaster and says, 'Oh no – now I'm *really* terrified.' And it sends that message back to the amygdala – a vicious circle *ad infinitum*. People with stage fright who have taken beta-blocker drugs – which suppress the production of adrenaline – report that, while their brains still feel alert, and in some cases more than a little nervous, their bodies do not take up the baton, as it were, and thereby the cycle of panic thought–panic symptom–panic thought is broken. I have to say that for me, as for all public speakers I know, certain environments are more intimidating than others. I can relate from experience that standing to interrupt a minister in a debate in the House of Lords, speaking in front of the 24-carat-gold throne and with the Lord Chancellor on the Woolsack, knowing that there are real experts in the audience who are bound to have more knowledge than oneself, is pretty frightening. The pulse races, the mouth goes dry and breathing feels tight. Not surprising that more than one member has collapsed with a heart attack either during, or immediately after, making a speech in that formidable chamber.

Orientation

Once we are aroused, the orientation system allows us to fix our senses upon the item that has aroused us. This is essentially un-conscious – tiny babies turn their heads towards a novel sound. So do we adults, without thinking about it first. It has been shown that this apparently seamless procedure is made up of three components. First of all we use the posterior parietal cortex to disengage from whatever we were doing and pay attention to the new stimulus. If the stimulus

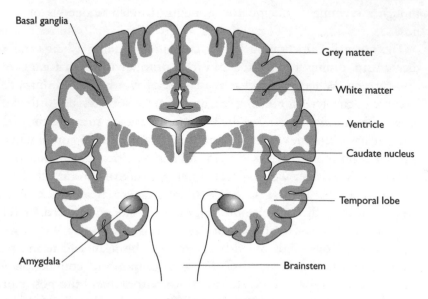

Brain in cross section

is visual, the frontal eye fields are engaged. Then our basal ganglia and parietal attention areas shift the focus of our attention onto the new stimulus. Thirdly, the lateral pulvinar – the area within the thalamus we discussed above in relation to dyslexia – acts as a filter, focusing our attention on the new stimulus and blocking out other information.

If the posterior parietal cortex should be damaged for any reason, a phenomenon known as Balint's Syndrome can arise, in which people are unable to pay attention to multiple objects. They are unable to shift their attention from one focus to another. Eric Courchesne at the University of California at San Diego has argued that a similar process may be at work in people with autism, leading to an inability to shift the focus of attention in response to social cues. John Ratey gives what may seem a rather surprising example of this in his book: if a mother points at a tree and says to her child, 'Look at the tree,' the child may be unable to detach its attention from her face and look at the object. This is surprising because, in general, autistic children have difficulty in attending to faces. But here, the child cannot take a cue from its mother's face or voice. The result is a difficulty in conducting social relationships – which is certainly one of the hallmarks of autism. People with that condition can also be curiously indiscriminating about where they direct their attention. An autistic child might, for example, remain fixated upon a bunch of keys, even though a seemingly enticing toy is being dangled under his or her nose.

The normally functioning brain has something like a hair-trigger mechanism, tuning it to notice and lock onto anything that is novel or surprising. When a subject is read a list of words: 'book', 'paper', 'volume', 'chapter', for example, and then a surprising word like 'treetop' is thrown in, an 'oddball' response can be measured in the brain. It has been known for a long time, from EEG measurements, that our brain activity shows a rapid surge in electrical potential about 300 milliseconds after we first report being aware of an oddball. This is known as the P300 response. Brian Strange, working in Ray Dolan's group at the Institute of Neurology, London, has used fMRI scanning to identify which part of the brain is activated.[15] When we experience various kinds of oddball stimuli – be it an odd noun, an odd font in which a noun is printed, or an emotional connection – the same parts of the cortex, the inferior prefrontal and the posterior part of the temporal cortex, show activity. Curious that anybody by the name of Strange should be working on oddballs. A number of researchers – such as Eric Halgren at the University of California at Los Angeles – have concluded that as the P300 surge occurs, there is a corresponding dampening down of activity in other areas of the brain. In other words, the peak stands out because it stands alone.

Research shows that it takes the brain 100–200 milliseconds to fire up in response to novel stimuli. Then comes the period of dampening down in other areas – then the P300 response. It's as if the brain is taking in everything, all the time, but mechanisms within it act to turn the 'contrast knob' up or down – focusing our attention on some features, shutting off our attention to others.

We can see how this would be a vital part of our memorizing procedure. If we were to record every aspect of every moment, our memory would swiftly become overloaded. Indeed the renowned Russian 'Memory Man' S.V. Shereshevski seemed to suffer from exactly this kind of filtering problem. Shereshevski could reproduce a table of fifty numbers in any order, vertically, horizontally or diagonally. And according to reliable reports he could recall these numbers months or even years later. When memorizing tables of numbers, Shereshevski could apparently see the table in his mind. Any mistakes he might make were invariably because a number was not properly legible, or because he had been distracted perhaps by a noise when he was studying the table. While he could remember the minutest details of a long story, he lacked an overarching awareness of its point or message.

It is interesting that the amygdala has a role here. It seems that the amygdala biases people to recall the gist, rather than the detail, of pictures with an emotional content. Normal people tend to remember the gist of an emotional story or image while people with a damaged amygdala don't show this switch.

Other brain structures seem to play a role in this filtering procedure. David LaBerge, working at the University of California, Irvine, performed a visual detection study on eight students. They were asked to look at a screen upon which a display of characters was flashed, and to search for a letter O among characters visually similar, such as C and G. With these letter displays flashing up for just one-fifth of a second, it was no easy task. The subjects had to keep the target letter O in mind, and also blank out the red herrings. LaBerge discovered that the harder the task, the more a specific region of the thalamus – the pulvinar again – had to work.[16]

The basal ganglia seem also to play a part in this process. Dick Passingham at University College, London, began his enquiries by asking human subjects to perform simple motor tasks like moving an arm while undergoing PET scans.[17] He then asked them to perform more complex tasks, such as rapping out a rhythm or tapping an intricate sequence on a keypad. His brain mapping studies showed that, when a task was new, there was a widespread and highly active network of neuronal activity. But as the sequence was mastered, became 'second nature' to the subjects, the circuits involved shrank back to the barest levels of activity. In other words, there was a visible difference between an activity that requires our conscious attention, and one that we have learnt to the point of it being automatic.

Passingham's studies were boosted by the arrival of cheaper, more repeatable fMRI technology. With this, he was able to see precisely which areas of the brain were involved in attending. He discovered that when subjects were having to think carefully about a task, most of their frontal cortex was active. The prefrontal areas leading to the brain's motor system were active, as were the cingulate and parts of the thalamus and parietal cortex. But crucially, once the task was mastered to the point where the subjects performed it without conscious attention, most of the higher cortex dropped out. It was now the lower rungs of the brain's motor system – the premotor cortex and the cerebellum, and the basal ganglia – that were doing the work.

It seems that, where attention is concerned, the basal ganglia act as an output filter in the same way as the thalamus acts as an input filter. Ann Graybiel, working at the Massachusetts Institute of Technology, studied what happened in the brain when a monkey learnt a simple association task – the sound of a click with a sip of juice. She found that, at first, as the monkey was still learning, the activity in the basal ganglia simply mirrored what was taking place elsewhere, in the higher cortex. But over time, a special class of basal ganglia neuron began to react on their own. They activated as the click sounded. In other words, as the skill was learnt, they took on the role that had been in the hands of the higher cortex. The task became an unthought habit. We can conclude that, just as the thalamus enables us to focus on particular aspects of what we experience, the basal ganglia enable us to focus on the appropriate actions – in both cases, freeing up the higher cortex for other tasks.

Reward and novelty detection

Once we are duly aroused and orientated towards the source of the arousal, our reward and novelty detection faculty comes into play. This depends upon the action of the mesolimbic pathway, a grouping of dopamine-containing neurons that controls the limbic system. When this is at work, we take note of new stimuli, and our reward system produces minute sensations of pleasure. It also tags the stimuli with an emotional value – pleasure, disgust, fear, etc. – which then stays with them in their transit into the memory. If the same stimulus recurs later, the memory of the emotions provides a response, which we use to devise a strategy to deal with the situation. So we know to avoid the cocktail party bore — the second we hear his loud, hectoring voice and see his pompous, overconfident body language, we remember similar situations in the past, and we know to make a bee-line for the kitchen.

A key region in this process is the nucleus accumbens – situated in the forebrain and connected to the amygdala and limbic system. It contains the highest store of dopamine in the whole brain and is also acutely sensitive to other neurotransmitters such as serotonin and endorphins. These 'pleasure chemicals' result in feelings of reward and satisfaction, and are thus very important motivators of action.

People with Attention Deficit Hyperactive Disorder are believed to have abnormalities in this region – in particular a low density of dopamine receptor sites. Unable to experience pleasure beyond a certain low threshold, they become predisposed to seek constant, immediate gratification, and ignore anything that might offer a more long-term reward. So, a child with the disorder would find it impossible to spend an afternoon practising his violin in order to win a competition. He'd be out of the door and into the nearest amusement arcade, but might not even arrive there. Monkeys with lesions in the region of the nucleus accumbens show similar traits – they would rather eat a peeled nut now than hoard unpeeled ones for the future. And Rudolph Cardinal, working in Cambridge, found that rats with a damaged nucleus accumbens showed similar tendencies to be impulsive.[18]

You may be puzzled that this disorder can be successfully treated with drugs like Dexedrine – which is a form of amphetamine known on the streets as 'speed'. It seems paradoxical to be giving anyone with attention and hyperactivity problems a compound that seems to accelerate everything – from pulse to thought processes. But such drugs have quite the opposite effect on people with ADHD. They act upon the synapses to increase the output of dopamine and block the action of certain enzymes that cause dopamine to be flushed away. Accordingly, the nucleus accumbens is able to maintain a more stable feeling of 'reward' and there is a reduced drive to go in search of excitement.

Executive organization

The final component of attention is the executive organization facility. This allows us to sustain our attention in the new direction, by blocking out irrelevant information. A key player in this process is the anterior cingulate gyrus (ACG), situated within the frontal lobes but sometimes considered a part of the limbic system. This acts as a filter for incoming data, prioritizing and throwing out what we do not need. The ACG shows increased activity whenever we concentrate on a task. It is a bizarre coincidence that we humans often scratch our head over roughly this area when we are thinking hard, almost as if we have some unconscious sense of where the activity is.

Mostly, the mechanism of attention involves using this four-step process to lock onto sensory information coming from the outside world. But it may not have escaped you that we also use it internally. Sometimes we pay attention to our own thoughts, for example, or to our own feelings. Sometimes we deliberately set a chain of thoughts in action, and keep the chain going, to the exclusion of other thoughts or incoming sensory stimuli. We might cope with the frustration of a traffic jam, for instance, by very meticulously working out exactly how we are going to spend our lottery jackpot, when it finally comes. We might work out how much paint we need to brighten up that spare room as we queue in the supermarket. The process of thinking requires attention.

When we think, our brains show activity in the very same areas that become active when we are actually doing something. If we imagine a colourful object visually, that part of the visual cortex is activated just as it would be if we were seeing it. And a different part of the visual cortex would respond if we imagined a moving object.

If we feel fear, an MRI scan will show activity in the amygdala. The same activity will be observable if we see a picture of a fearful face, or if we are asked to imagine being afraid. The same would be true for picking up an object, or travelling a familiar route. When we imagine something, we build on patterns built into our circuitry through previous imaginings, and previous instances of actually doing.

A crucial region in the thinking process is the dorsolateral pre-frontal cortex (DPC). Planning takes place in this area, as does decision-making. Areas within this region have more specific functions, rather like the different aisles of a supermarket – for example, there is an area that becomes active when we think about objects that we cannot see. Another area of the DPC sparks into life when we think about how many times we have done something before.

Intention, planning and initiating action are faculties particularly restricted in people with frontal lobe damage – as we will see later. This can result in them forming dozens of plans every day, yet failing to carry any of them out. The importance of the frontal lobes has been demonstrated by Chris Frith and his team at the Wellcome Department of Cognitive Neurology in London.[19] They asked normal subjects to perform a simple task – in this case, lifting a specified finger at a given auditory cue. The execution of this task caused activity in the auditory cortex and the motor cortex, as we might expect. But then Frith added an extra element to the task by asking the subjects to pick for themselves which finger they wished to lift. When they performed this, self-willed activity, a specific area within the frontal lobes – the prefrontal cortex, just behind the forehead – sprang into action.

So the 'will' is a brain faculty like any other – one that can be strengthened with use, or lost through damage. Neurologist Antonio Damasio described one patient who, after a stroke, had damage to the frontal lobes and lay for several months without speaking or moving. When she eventually recovered, she said that during her period of immobility she had not felt that she couldn't do anything, but that she hadn't wanted to.

As well as being the place where the will is generated, the frontal lobes play a role in the way we link our perceptions and our aware-ness of ourselves into a coherent experience. In other words, this is the area where we attach meaning to life. People suffering from depression show a low level of neuronal activity in this area – and correspondingly they often report that their lives seem devoid of meaning or purpose, fragmented and pointless. Conversely, the area is very active in people suffering from mania – for whom every outside stimulus and internal process seem linked in a sort of gloriously meaningful but deluded grand design.

In our exploration of the mechanisms of attention and intention, we have started to touch upon a question that, as yet, has no answer – though philosophers and scientists are set to fight it out for many years to come. This book is intended to be a journey through the mysteries of the human mind, and no enquiry into that subject would be complete without considering one of its most unique and perplexing faculties – the self.

Losing consciousness

A recent television series, in which ordinary people underwent rigorous SAS training, highlighted the deleterious effects of sleep deprivation on the workings of the mind. The subjects were forced to stand against a wall while listening to static 'white noise' and were shaken by guards whenever they showed signs of nodding off. This has been shown to be highly effective in 'breaking' the will of people before they face interrogation. The longer they go without sleep, the more disorientated they become. Their mental agility and memory become impaired. Such is their craving to enter this natural brain state that they will do or say anything to be allowed to curl up in a corner of their cell – even betray their comrades and their countries.

Sleep is an essential process. But, remarkably, its biological function is mysterious, in spite of a vast amount of research. It is not just humans that eventually crave sleep. All species that have been studied in detail appear to sleep, whether reptiles, birds or mammals. There seems no obvious evolutionary advantage in sleep as a sleeping animal is defenceless, cannot feed, cannot take care of its offspring, cannot avoid the risks of being eaten by a predator and cannot have sex and so procreate. The very fact that it is costly suggests that it must be a vital process. In some animals, for example whales and birds, it seems that just one hemisphere of the brain sleeps in turn. Rats chronically deprived of sleep will die within about two weeks – which is roughly how long they can last without food. But surprisingly, the cause of death is far from clear.

It is curious that humans vary so much in how much sleep they need. The average is around eight hours a night – but age has an impact on this figure. Newborn infants sleep most of the day, whereas the elderly may require only a few hours a night. For years I have required only about five hours' sleep a night, although after several days and nights with just five hours, I find I need a binge – a longer period of sleep. As I get older, I have found I need slightly more, not less, sleep and I also find that I feel I need more sleep if I have been on holiday or if I have regularly been sleeping longer on previous nights.

The stages of sleep

What exactly is sleep? It seems to be a set of four separate brain stages. We all know the difference between nodding off gently on the sofa to the news and that full-blown state of leaden unconsciousness that causes us to wake up hours later without having seemed to move in our beds. We also know that one is infinitely more refreshing than the other. It also seems more refreshing if we have been more or less horizontal – perhaps this is why sleeping in a first-class seat in an aircraft leaves one feeling better than sleeping half upright in a slightly reclining chair in tourist class.

When we are awake, our neurons are extremely active. Even neurons not being specifically used in a given task will fire off approximately one 'blip' of electrical current every second. We can measure this electrical activity with an EEG machine – the device that gives a pictorial representation of electrical activity in the brain, the brain waves. When we are awake, our brain waves are a series of short, tightly spaced teeth – like the serrated edges of a bread knife. These are so-called beta waves.

As we start to relax and close our eyes, there is a difference in the brain waves. The little 'peaks' of activity become slightly larger, and more spaced out, more regular. The 'Chinese firecracker' effect of alert wakefulness turns into a gentler, more rhythmic sequence of pulsed activity, like the hum of distant machinery. This is the shift from beta to alpha wave activity. When we are hypnotized, or when we are meditating, this is the wave activity going on inside our brain.

As sleep deepens – the first stage of actual sleep – we see theta wave formation. Theta waves are less regular, more like bad handwriting on the paper roll of the EEG machine. We can be easily aroused from this stage of sleep and may not even be aware that we were asleep. While this is going on, we may see vivid images before our eyes – sometimes a version of what we would see in the room we are in if we were awake. We may experience sudden jolts in our arms and legs – which can sometimes wake us up with the sensation that we have fallen to earth with a sharp bump.

As we enter the second stage of real sleep, breathing becomes more regular and we are less likely to be woken up by external intrusions. EEG scans still show theta wave activity, but there are occasional bursts of activity, known as 'sleep spindles', and larger spikes and dips, called 'k-complexes'. It may be that these little patches of activity represent the brain operating to shut out external stimuli, so that we can get on with the 'work' of sleeping.

In the remaining two stages of sleep, associated with delta wave activity, we become increasingly oblivious to our surroundings and are quite likely to feel startled and disorientated if we are woken suddenly. Delta waves are characterized by a 'high and low' pattern of regular peaks and troughs on the EEG machine – becoming more pronounced as we move from stage three to stage four of sleep. Interestingly, though, we can still take in information. Parents may snooze away, oblivious to traffic noise outside, but be instantly aroused if they hear the sound of their child crying.

During normal sleep, there are periods back and forth across this scale of brain-wave activity. After roughly ninety minutes of sleep, for instance, the cycle goes into reverse – going rapidly back to stages three and two – and then still further back to the beta-wave activity we see in the state of alert wakefulness. At this point, we enter rapid eye movement (REM) sleep – a term coined in 1953 by its discoverers, Nathaniel Kleitman and Eugene Aserinsky at the University of Chicago. Sleep researchers call this 'paradoxical sleep' – because of the contrast between our sleeping body and our seemingly alert mind. Some areas of the brain – including the brainstem – are more active during REM sleep than in our normal waking state.

Perchance to dream . . .

Around 80 per cent of people, if woken during REM sleep, will say that they have been dreaming. But if awoken during any non-REM stage of sleep, no more than half will claim to have been dreaming. And the nature of the dreams experienced is radically different. Non-REM dreams have a 'procedural' nature – for example, performing dull, day-to-day activities, like typing, or dialling numbers on the telephone. REM dreams, by contrast, are a more fantastical mixture of reality and the outright bizarre. They can involve intense emotions, illogical events and a suspension of the normal rules of time and space. Familiar people may turn into strangers, and vice versa.

Sophie Schwartz and Pierre Maquet at University College, London, noted a similarity between many of the aspects of REM dreaming and the symptoms of people with disordered brains.[20] For instance, the misidentification of faces and the disproportion of objects can be consequences of lesions to the temporal and frontal lobes. They are also very typical elements of REM-type dreams. Lewis Carroll's *Alice in Wonderland* gives a good account of the dreams associated with REM sleep. When people are scanned by PET and fMRI, they show similarities in their brain chemistry to what happens in some brain disorders.

There is increased activity in a region of the brainstem just above the spinal cord, called the pons, in REM sleep. Levels of the neurotransmitter acetylcholine increase sharply just before REM sleep, as if preparing for a burst of communicative activity. This then takes place, as the pons communicates not only with the spinal cord, but also with the thalamus and occipital lobes, site of the primary visual cortex. This is what seems to cause the rapid eye movements. There is also a heightening of activity in the amygdala, partnered with a corresponding dampening down within the dorsolateral prefrontal cortex. Since we know that this part of the cortex is responsible for rational thought, and the amygdala produces strong emotions, there could be some explanation for the powerful, yet irrational content of our dreams.

The sleep cycle repeats itself throughout the night (or whenever we are sleeping) – becoming shorter as we move towards the appointed hour of the alarm clock. As the cycle shortens, relatively more time is spent in REM sleep. We may pass through this cycle to the point of actually waking up several times a night, but if our brain is healthy and there is an absence of distracting stimuli, we will go back to sleep and not remember these intervals. People suffering from depression or anxiety, however, may experience trouble getting back to sleep after they have first woken up.

Disturbed sleep

Sleepwalking probably only occurs during non-REM sleep. Sleepwalking is close to wakefulness, and a number of brain functions are observable in sleepwalkers which wouldn't be seen in the deeper stages of sleep. Movement is the most obvious, but there is also goal-orientated action. Sleepwalkers always have a goal. Lady Macbeth spent the night washing her hands of the blood she had spilt. More prosaically the action might be to visit the toilet – something which had unpleasant consequences (for me) in the case of my sleepwalking climbing companion when I found that the foot of my sleeping bag was mysteriously damp in the morning. Sleepwalkers can even sometimes conduct limited conversations. In spite of old wives' tales, there is no evidence to suggest that it can be fatal to wake up a sleepwalker.

Various brain structures and neurotransmitters are involved in the sleeping-waking cycle. Humans tend to wake up in daylight and to bed when it is dark. This depends upon a particular part of hypothalamus, which responds to light – even in blind people individual neurons within it show a peak in firing activity once The hypothalamus also communicates with the pineal gland — it to secrete the hormone melatonin. Melatonin concentra lowest in daylight, and highest during the hours of darkness

Waking is partially controlled by areas in the brainstem locus coeruleus and the nearby raphe nuclei. These noradrenaline and serotonin to various parts of the brain alertness. They are most active when we are awake, and mostly inactive during REM sleep. The preoptic area cortex also seems to be involved in sleep. Neurons in brain are particularly active during non-REM sleep damage to this area often suffer from insomnia.

A few people – between 3 and 6 per cent of th get to sleep and stay asleep without any trou

predators. But it is also true that, unless we are very clever at hiding, we are even more vulnerable to predatory attack when asleep.

A third function of sleep is also likely: sleep acts as oil for the cogwheels of the brain. Earlier on, I mentioned the importance of REM sleep in memorizing and learning. It does indeed seem that the brain 'goes over' itself during sleep, reinforcing new firing patterns and etching them into memory. Numerous studies have shown that human and animal subjects master tasks more quickly and more thoroughly if sleep follows the learning procedure. It is also interesting to note that infants and small children – whose brains have the greatest amount of learning to do – need far more sleep than adults.

The meaning of dreams . . .

What place do our dreams have? Our ancient ancestors seemed to believe dreams were messages from another dimension, means by which spirits and gods could communicate with living humans. Jacob's dream in Genesis is of great symbolic importance. Near Beer-Sheba he lays his head on a stone pillow and dreams of the ladder ascending to heaven whereupon God is revealed and reiterates his promise to protect Jacob and the generations to follow. Where biblical dreams are not a form of divine communication they tend to reveal omens. Joseph, Jacob's favourite son, dreamed repeatedly. His dreams persuaded him of his own subsequent greatness (and his precocious attempts to boast to his brothers resulted in his being incarcerated). Later, when he had got out of the pit and then into and out of prison, he was able to forecast the fate of Pharaoh's unfortunate baker and his luckier butler, as well as the famine which eventually hit Egypt. In Roman times, soothsayers, of course, would have needed a fee to interpret dreams in this way.

Early psychoanalysts took this many steps further – merging the ancient belief that dreams 'told us something' with their scientific forays into the human psyche. Freud believed that dreams symbolically express the conflicts, desires and terrors of the individual unconscious mind. The dreams of each person would have their own, unique symbolic language, but it would be possible, through cross-referral, to assume that two different dreams could purport to the same hope or fear. Such a 'science' of interpretation is highly subjective and ultimately inconclusive. Freud's own powerful pre-occupation with the libido led him to see sexuality as the raging torrent from which all mental phenomena, dreams and otherwise, would spring.

A leading theoretician in this field is J. Allan Hobson of Harvard University. Hobson was the first person, in 1977, to note that REM sleep shares many properties with a state of wakefulness and that this may tell us something about the nature of our dreams. More specific-ally, he noted that neural stimulation proceeding from the pons activates brain mechanisms that would normally be processing visual information if we were awake. Finding no 'parade' to interpret, the sleeping brain effectively summons up its own – using both memory and emotional faculties – and these are our dreams. Meanwhile, the slumbering state of the frontal lobes ensures that dreams are signifi-cantly different to what we experience with our eyes open – our dreamed parade might thus be full of all sorts of mythical beasts and bizarre events. In short, Hobson's theory suggests that dreams are just an entertaining by-product of brainstem activity.

Antti Revonsuo, of Turku University in Finland, suggests an evolutionary explanation for dreams.[22] He argues that dreams allow us to rehearse behaviour that we may rely upon in daily life – particularly in life-threatening situations. Certain features do support this theory – notably the high level of activity in the amygdala during REM sleep. There is also the fact that fear dreams – in which we are falling, running, fighting, hiding, etc. – are the most commonly cited type of dream, and fear is central to the sensations experienced by SP suffer-ers (see above). On the other hand, these dreams may be rare, but more memorable. In fact, if we perform a repetitive activity for a long period of a day – typing, for instance, or operating a cash register – we will often report sensations of repeating this activity during non-REM sleep. This is backed up by studies of rats, whose brains show a certain pattern of neuronal firing after they have been trained to run through a maze. When they sleep, their brain activity repeats the original firing pattern. Neither can Dr Revonsuo's explanation, com-pelling though it is, account or provide any rationale for the simply bizarre content of our dreams. Perhaps, as Dr Hobson suggested, this is just a by-product of the fact that the rational part of our brains goes to sleep, even if other parts do not.

Another interesting theory is that dreaming helps the human

memory to clear itself of what is not needed. The neurotransmitter acetylcholine is produced by the pons in increased quantity just prior to REM sleep. We know from James Bower's work that this neurotransmitter may play a role in 'cleaning up' memories, preserving the relevant and junking the extraneous. And Allan Hobson has argued that the difference between waking and sleeping can be reduced to a difference in the balance of one type of neurotransmitter over another. In waking, the neural activity is dominated by amines, like serotonin and noradrenaline. In deep sleep, there is a balance between aminergic neurotransmitter systems and cholinergic systems, which would include acetylcholine. Hobson has suggested that a range of brain states are dependent upon the balance between these two systems in the brain – including meditation, day dreaming, REM dreaming, psychosis, depression and mania.

In 1983, Francis Crick, the Nobel Prize winner for his discovery of the structure of DNA, and Graeme Mitchison adopted the controversial stance of saying that 'we dream in order to forget'. Since the human brain takes in 100 billion billion bits of information in a lifetime, but can only store 100 thousand billion bits at any one time, there must be some procedure whereby memories are dumped. Their argument that dreams are the brain's waste-paper basket seems quite compelling. But this does not account for the fact that the act of dreaming itself produces memories, some of which stay with us.

When I was reading around the subject to write this book, I came across an account by Carl Jung of a dream experience he had in 1913: 'Before me was the entrance to a dark cave, before which stood a dwarf with leathery skin . . . I squeezed past him through the narrow entrance . . . waded knee deep through icy water to the other end of the cave, where I saw a glowing red crystal.'[23] More than one commentator has noted that Jung's dreams sound incredibly close to what we might see in fantasy novels by people such as Tolkien, and horror films like *Alien*. My first thought on reading such novels was that they didn't seem real. Which then made me think about that idea more closely. If they were dreams, then of course they wouldn't be real. What I actually meant was that Jung's dreams didn't sound like anything I'd ever dreamed, or would be ever likely to. And of course they wouldn't, because my brain isn't Jung's brain. Dreams are very personal and peculiar to the dreamer – which is one of the reasons why listening to someone else describing their dreams can be a boring experience. I cannot imagine what it must be like to be a psychoanalyst. And just as my brain creates my own very personal dreams, so it is responsible for many of the defining aspects of my identity. And I have heard of one architect who dreams of cement every night!

Where am I in all of this?

Think about yourself for a moment. What does that mean, exactly? Do you have a visual image of your body – now or in the past? Do you think in terms of situations you have been in, things you have done? Do you envisage some bodiless 'I AM' sitting just behind your eyeballs?

The sense of self is a crucial concept. If we define mind as the experience of having a human brain, then it follows that some conscious 'I' is experiencing that experience. So what are its attributes? Can we find it inside the brain? Can it be switched off?

Many tribal societies believe in not one, but a plurality of souls. And philosophers sometimes similarly distinguish between three levels of the self. There is the minimal self – which means the conscious experience of self in the here and now, reacting to but distinct from the immediate environment. Insects, birds, most animals can be said to have this form of self, and this alone. We have it too, but in addition to others. I am no touch typist so my minimal self at the moment is experiencing the touch of the plastic keys as my right forefinger prods away at my computer, the sensation of the chair under me and behind my back, the warmth of the room, the birdsong and the roar of traffic outside. I am also worrying about a crucial lecture I have to give tomorrow. And I am also experiencing levels of tiredness and hunger. Maybe it's time for a break . . .

We also have an objectified self. This is the capacity to serve as the object of one's own attention. For instance, I can ask myself – what sort of a mood am I in today? And further to that, we have a symbolic (sometimes called narrative) self. This is the capacity to form mental representations of ourselves through language. It is in evidence when I talk about how I have changed since I was twenty-one, for example. It provides an awareness of myself as existing over time.

It has been argued that this third level of the self is a relatively recent evolutionary development, an adaptation that helped us survive.[24] We are able to process personal and environmental information more successfully and this heightens our chance of continued existence and, hence, of reproducing our genes. Thus the symbolic self could include the capacity to reflect and to be introspective, to make long-term plans, to have a sense of one's own mortality, to develop moral arguments and even form governments.

The ability to think of yourself and your actions in the abstract enables reflection, and thus forward planning. For instance, if I were a wolf, and did not possess this level of self-awareness, I would hunt in a pack, the rules of which were determined by the relative killing and reproductive powers of its members. The strongest leads, has rights to the greatest share of the kill and reproduces the most.

But as a conscious human, it is possible there are more cooperative strategies that allow for a greater equality and greater specialization of roles, and hence a greater overall chance of survival. I can conclude, for instance, that I do not want to die and want to do as much as I can to avoid it. I can conclude that my neighbour, Ug, is a ruthless killer of bison but that I am better at seeing and tracking prey. I can suggest a transaction to him – I find the prey, he kills it and we share the spoils equally. Instead of only one of us surviving and passing on our genes, two can survive this way. And we can coopt others into our scheme, people who are nimble and agile tree-climbers and flint-knappers, ensuring a greater number of more efficient hunting expeditions, to the extent where we can even acquire a surplus of food that allows some people to stay at home getting better and better at making weapons or building shelters. It all begins from an awareness of myself.

But this still does not say precisely what the self is. The sociologist George Herbert distinguished between the self that knows (I) and the self that is known (me). The two have separate functions. The I-self does the thinking, the feeling, the acting. The me-self performs more objectified tasks – planning, choosing, exercising control. It's this second, me-self that we mean when we talk about self-awareness.

Myself and others

Babies develop a me-self some time between eighteen months and two years of age. A classic experiment to prove this self-awareness involves painting a red dot on a baby's nose and then placing him or her in front of a mirror. Babies who are self-aware understand that the dot resides on their nose and will thus touch it with their finger. They may even cry because they think they have a blemish; I have seen some chuckle and keep rubbing it. But babies who have not yet developed this sense, or who have some impairment, will reach out and touch the mirror. Studies performed on chimpanzees in the 1960s seemed to show that they too may have this degree of me-self awareness, though, if they do – and it is somewhat controversial – they develop it substantially later than human infants, at around six years of age. Other animals such as dogs, which are undoubtedly intelligent, do not understand what they are looking at. I did this experiment with a spaniel recently who grew very excited at seeing 'another dog', and who soon was looking behind the mirror to search for his new friend.

The next stage is to understand a self as existing over time. Beyond the age of two, most babies can identify themselves in photographs, even if not taken recently. By the age of three, a child understands that its shadow is created by its body. I think I can recall when this happened to me, when I would deliberately try to tread on my younger sister's shadow to assert my authority over her. But children also acquire notions such as shame, guilt and embarrassment. These ideas depend on a deepened awareness of self, and on self as something that others can evaluate. Accordingly, the children have to have developed an ability to understand others as separate and distinct from themselves.

At this stage, at about four years of age, something we call 'Theory of Mind' develops. A famous test of the Theory of Mind is the so-called Sally-Anne experiment. In this task the subject watches two girls play with a marble, a basket and a box. Sally puts the marble in the basket, and goes out of the room. While Sally is away, 'naughty' Anne puts the marble into the box. Sally returns to the room, and the watching child is asked where Sally will look for the marble. Children who have developed a Theory of Mind will correctly select the basket. They understand the state of knowledge that exists in another's mind, rather than relying solely on what they themselves know. Research has shown that children with autism show marked difficulty developing a Theory of Mind and will say that Sally will look in the box, where the marble actually is.[25]

A sense of self also allows us to misrepresent information, to deceive others for our own personal advantage, in a word, to lie. In one classic experiment, small children were given a set of stickers and asked to pick a favourite. They were then told that they would be visited by two puppets, who would ask them which sticker was their favourite. The first puppet, they were advised, would be a friendly sort who, after asking his question, would pick another sticker for himself. But the second puppet was a mean character who would almost certainly grab the child's favourite. Children up to the age of three were unable to deceive the mean puppet, thereby losing their favoured sticker. But from the age of four onwards, they were able to lie with ease, while still being truthful to the nice puppet.[26]

Some years ago, when making the film *The Human Body*, I watched four- and five-year-old children through a one-way mirror. They had been led singly into a room full of nice toys but with one irresistible toy – such as a wonderful painted engine. The adult bringing the child into the room told them they could play with whatever they wanted, only they must not even touch the really special toy. Once the adult left, for even just a few minutes, nearly all the children succumbed to temptation. And on the adult's return, when asked directly, nearly all the five-year-old children swore really touchingly that they didn't handle the forbidden toy, though one little boy paused and then burst into tears. Apparently, the more intelligent children tended to lie best in this experiment. And the ability to deceive represents an understanding of other people's state of mind – and how they can be manipulated. Four-year-olds are too young generally to lie like this.

As much as self-awareness may give us the capacity for deceit, it is also a vital prerequisite of self-policing. Only when we are aware of ourselves can we measure our own behaviour against that of every-one else. We have already looked at the role of the frontal lobes in regulating the impulses and drives of the lower brain. Unsurprisingly, the frontal lobes develop slowly in the human, only reaching maturity when we hit the age of twenty, or possibly (according to recent research) even later. A sense of self and the ability to self-regulate develops in tandem with the neuronal networks of the brain.

The role of the frontal lobes in self-awareness can be clearly seen in those who have suffered damage to that area. They often have difficulty, for instance, in remembering where they learnt specific information, even though they know the information perfectly. It is as if they are unable to conceive of themselves as an objectified self – someone who exists in time as well as space. Similarly, they tend to show a low degree of self-interest – they can identify disorders and abnormalities in other people, but not themselves. And quite often they do not show much interest in their appearance.

A classic example of the relationship between the frontal lobes and self-awareness comes from the neurologist Donald Stuss at the Rotman Research Institute in Toronto. He treated a highly intelligent man who had a tumour removed from his frontal lobes. The patient retained all his intelligence and knowledge afterwards, but was highly unproductive at work. Despite his poor performance, he was unable to recognize that he had a problem and was mystified by the attitudes of his boss and work colleagues. Stuss asked the patient to perform a role-play exercise, in which he, the patient, played the part of his boss. With this 'hat' on, the patient was able to swiftly and clearly identify the problems at work. But when asked to then evaluate himself from his own subjective viewpoint, the patient said he could not agree with any of the recommendations he had just made. He was unable to be objective in this way.[27]

Problems with understanding the self, and its relation to others, also seem to be related to the traffic between the two halves of the brain. David J. Turk, Michael Gazzaniga and others, of the Center for Cognitive Neuroscience at Dartmouth College, New Hampshire, showed photos of faces to J.W., a subject whose corpus callosum (see Chapter 2), the bridge joining the two halves of the brain, had been severed during surgery for epilepsy. Using computer-assisted manipulation techniques, the faces were morphed to form a sequence – one extreme of which was J.W.'s own face, and the other a picture of one of the researchers (in fact, it was the face of Michael Gazzaniga, whose face is well-known to J.W. and whose research features frequently in this book). The sequence was shown to J.W.'s left and right hemispheres, and he was asked to state the identity of the faces as they were shown to him.

J.W.'s right hemisphere was biased towards identifying faces it saw as 'others' and, conversely, his left hemisphere tended to identify faces as 'self'. The same thing happened when he looked at morphed sequences featuring his own face and that of two US presidents. These results suggest that two separate brain systems are used to formulate our understanding of ourselves and others. When there is a smooth flow of neuronal traffic between the left and right hemispheres, our brains can create a harmonious view of the world, as a person composed of a self among other people.

So the self appears to be created by an interplay between specific parts of the brain. However, our enquiry into this most philosophical element of the mind does not end here. This is because self-awareness is itself a product of an underlying state, that of consciousness.

Consciousness: a tool like any other

Consciousness has always proved extraordinarily difficult to define. One possible approach is to try to confine ourselves to the five observable properties of consciousness. Let us first examine the property of *sentience*. Sentience refers to the unique perspective that we each have about our own experiences. As we discussed earlier, there is no objective colour green, merely a route by which it is recognized in most people's brains. And differences in wiring create differences in perception – so I can never truly convey to you what the colour green means to me, nor can you to me.

Secondly, there is the property of *variable access*. When I am conscious of seeing the colour green, I am also relying upon mental processes of which I am unconscious. I see green, but I do not see or in any way sense the neuronal activity inside my brain. I can learn a list of the properties of serotonin and I can repeat it to you, but I cannot consciously sense the way my neurons and neurotransmitters store and retrieve this information. So we can talk about processes that are conscious and unconscious.

Next there is the property of *unified experience*. Consciousness, we can say, is like a movie, made up of the individual camera-shots that form our sensory and cognitive activity. It is the process that unifies our sensory and cognitive activities into a continuous experience.

Fourthly, there is *self-objectivity*. I am not just an experiencing I but an experienced Me, who can report on my mental experiences. As cognitive neuroscientist Steven Pinker puts it, 'I can not only feel pain and see red, but think to myself, "Hey, here I am, Steve Pinker, feeling pain and seeing red!"'[28]

Last, there is what we call *intentionality*. Intentionality implies a difference between what our sensory faculties tell us and what we do with the information, how we interpret it. For instance, I am always struck, when first arriving in a foreign country, by the unique smell. I do not necessarily know its components – it may be the tobaccos smoked, the food eaten, the trees that grow, the fuel used – but it always strikes me for the first few hours in any new country. Should I return to that country, I am still aware of the difference, but it is a *different difference* to the one I first perceived. And if I stay in the country for more than a few hours, my perception of the smell changes once again, to one that is barely observable. Clearly nothing has happened to either the molecules creating the smell or to my sensory apparatus. The difference lies in the way I treat the incoming information.

So we have arrived at some useful definitions of consciousness. But can we, with the techniques we have used to discover the brain activity underlying sensory perception, or attention and self-willed actions, subject consciousness to a scientific study? Can we find the brain units involved in consciousness and see them in action? The answer is yes, but there are some surprises.

Half a second later

Think of a blue elephant. And now you've done that, here is a second exercise. Don't think about a green elephant.

How did the second exercise go? I assume it went less well, since in order to think about *not* thinking about a green elephant, you first had to think of one! But let me ask another question. How long did it take you to do each of these little exercises? A nanosecond? Half a minute? Or do you think it took no time at all? It just happened.

We talk, especially in an enquiry into consciousness, about the present, the 'here and now'. Furthermore, we tend to assume that what takes place in the brain is instantaneous; that there is no point asking how long it takes me to think of a chair or to react to a flashing light because it is instant, it just happens.

But your brain does indeed take time over all its processes. You are just not aware of it. Experiments conducted back in the 1840s by Wilhelm Wundt at the University of Heidelberg showed that when two stimuli – noises, for instance, or flashing lights – occur within a short time of each other, the human brain tends to fuse them into one. The same thing happens with touch – if your arm is touched at four points in rapid succession (and I am talking of a maximum time lag of one-tenth of a second, so it's not one you can try out at home), you will perceive this as a single object trailing down your arm. This is, of course, the feature of the brain that makes movies and TV possible – we don't see twenty-four frames a second flashing across the screen, but experience them as a harmonious whole. Consciousness is not an instantaneous experience – it takes time to build itself, and the brain covers up for its own time lag.

Some 120 years later, Benjamin Libet at the University of Southern California became interested in this time lag.[29] He experimented on people undergoing stereotactic neurosurgery for intractable pain. Having first given a local anaesthetic to the scalp, he sent a pulse of electrical current into various parts of their body, such as the skin or the cortex, asking them to report on their sensations. Using EEG to measure the responses, he noticed that it took a surprisingly long time of pulsing before people reported that they felt anything. His conclusion was that it took around 500 milliseconds before consciousness caught up with the sensory reaction to the electrical current and manufactured it into a reportable experience.

Meanwhile, a German scientist called Hans Kornhuber was doing his own work on the consciousness of self-willed activity. He, like Libet, noticed that there was a time lag – a period of mounting neurological action inside the motor cortex – before people make a voluntary action. Libet took this research a stage further in an attempt to isolate the moment at which subjects first decided to make a movement. The volunteers reported that they first became aware of an intention to act about 200 milliseconds before they then produced the act – in this case, lifting a finger when they chose to do so, or in response to a buzzer. But the EEG data showed that, although they reported their first awareness of intention at 200 milliseconds, there was a stirring of motor activity even earlier – at 500 milliseconds. In a nutshell – the decision to take action occurs first subconsciously and takes around 300 milliseconds to transfer into consciousness.

Although the raw material of these experiments – buzzers and lifting fingers – might not be quite so appealing to readers as, say, human sexual behaviour, or the brain processes involved in dreaming, Libet's findings are quite shocking in their way. For they imply that we are not entirely conscious of the workings of our own brain. By the time we know that we want to do something, another part of ourselves has known it for roughly a third of a second. The purpose of this seems to be economy – by having two levels of processing, one conscious, one unconscious, we keep our higher brains free for the tasks that are the most demanding or unique.

Some years ago, a while after he had retired from first-class cricket, I happened to meet Tony Greig, the England ex-captain and all-rounder, in the green room of a television studio. How was it, I asked, that any batsman could face a fast bowler and repeatedly score runs when he might be consistently bowling at around 90 miles per hour? How could he face the four great West Indian bowlers – Holding, Roberts, Holder and Daniel – in the 1976 series, hour after hour, without being decapitated? Given that the distance between the stumps is only 22 yards, the ball leaves the bowler's hand and arrives at the bat in well under half a second. Allowing for the body's natural reaction time it seemed that it ought to be highly unlikely that any batsman, no matter how good, could consistently make high scores, particularly if the ball was moving erratically off the ground or swinging through the air. Greig thought for a brief moment and then told me that he didn't feel he could explain how he had personally done it but he thought that all good batsmen must anticipate what the bowler was about to attempt.

It seems that research done with sportsmen supports Libet's work. In the 1980s, Peter MacLeod at the Applied Psychology Unit in Cambridge studied world-class batsmen to see how they prepared themselves for balls that only take 440 milliseconds to leave the bowler's hand and arrive at the bat. MacLeod's results showed that the batsmen did not react immediately to variations in the speed and trajectory of an incoming ball. They modified their swing at a point 200 milliseconds before it hit. This is almost certainly faster than you or I could do it in a pub with one of those reaction-time machines, pressing the red button – even before the first drink.

More research with both cricketers and tennis players indicates that top-class performers are particularly skilled at anticipation. The best players make the earliest and most accurate predictions about what is about to happen. Tests were performed, for instance, on professional and novice tennis players, involving film footage of a person serving the ball. A hundred and twenty milliseconds into the flight of the ball, the film was stopped, and novices and professional players could predict accurately at this stage whether the ball was going to arrive on the forehand, backhand or right in the middle. But the professional players could do the same some 40 milliseconds *before* the ball had left the server's hand. Similar studies of batsmen have shown that they are making appropriate preparatory movements 100 milliseconds before the ball leaves the bowler's hand. Significantly, few of the subjects when questioned could accurately self-report on what they were doing. They were taking in information, forming plans of action based upon it and acting on their plans up to one-tenth of second before something happened, but they were not aware of it. This kind of analysis is now being taken up at Sheffield Hallam University, where I am currently university Chancellor. There they have a particularly well-equipped sports science centre with sophisticated motion-analysis equipment which helps break down exactly what happens and how sportsmen react. They hope that this approach may also lead to improved performance in people who are training to play sport at the highest level.

So the research suggests that, either way, our consciousness is never exactly 'in the moment' but always occurring a significant degree of time before or after it. But what areas of the brain are involved in creating this extraordinary pre-awareness? Michael Posner at the University of Oregon investigated this by asking volunteers to look at a screen upon which were flashed lists of words printed in different colours. Their task was to report on the colour of the word, not the word. A cinch when the word is, say, 'pill', in yellow type. But when the word itself is 'yellow' and the colour blue, the task becomes harder and requires more conscious effort. In such instances, the anterior cingulate was highly active. Whenever the brain is being mindful of what we are doing or experiencing, the anterior cingulate plays a part. As well as fulfilling other functions, we might call it the brain's concentration centre.

But rather than assume that this structure is the site of consciousness, we would do better to look at the other areas with which it works. Jeffrey Gray at London's Institute of Psychiatry did just that. He noted that the hippocampus, site of our long-term memory, has a particularly strong connection with the anterior cingulate, through a thick knot of fibres called the cingulum. Gray suggested a sequence from this physical connection: the cingulate would ask the hippocampus to expect a certain outcome, and the hippocampus would then report back on what had just happened and what was different or new about it by comparing it to its amassed memories of everything that had ever happened. The interaction between the two would create a sort of arc of consciousness – concentration combined with significance. A flowchart of further activity can then proceed from this point: how do we respond – with action or inaction? If with action, then what action?

In that sense, we can see consciousness as simply the high point of the brain's evolution. At some distant time in our pasts, we were only able to adapt to our environment over progressive generations. Then we became able to learn certain reflexes over a lifetime. Later on, like chimps, we could respond by trial and error to novel events in our environment. The simple reflexes grew fatter, heavier, more enmeshed, because, as we know, the more a pattern of firing occurs within the brain, the more deeply established it becomes. To be the best at the business of survival, we had to perfect the ability to respond instantly (or within a few hundred milliseconds at least) to changes in our environment. Was consciousness what we developed to do this, a tool that allowed for an immediate adaptation of our plastic brains to the needs of each moment?

The term homeostasis is widely used in medicine. Homeostasis is how different parts of the body achieve a steady state, despite changes around the body. There are many examples of homeostatic systems and the brain is one such organ which could be said to operate homeostatically. It 'seeks' to maintain a state of constancy in spite of the ever-changing landscape outside to which it responds. We can compare it simplistically to the heating and air-conditioning system of a large building – when the air temperature outside is cold, the system detects the low temperature, the thermostat kicks in, and the furnace responds by giving out heat. When the weather is hot, the system gives us cold air until a comfortable level is reached. To perform the same self-regulating function, the brain makes ceaseless adaptations within, changing levels of neurotransmitters and hormones, for example, or growing and pruning back synaptic connections. Consciousness is thus an ultimate refinement of a homeostatic system, enabling adaptations, tiny and massive, that are geared to each and every moment.

I am always aware, when venturing into such territory, that it can seem far removed from the day-to-day experience of having a mind. That tends to be the result of analysing something so much a feature of our existence that we rarely consider it. However, it is also clear that there is a lot more to us humans than simply being aware and paying attention. To be human is to be able to escape from the moment, as much as respond to it – to dream, to create, to remember, to feel. In the following chapters, therefore, we shall be looking at some of the more remarkable aspects of the human mind – beginning with emotions.

chapter**five**

The emotional mind

A famous accident over 150 years ago in a minor railway cutting near a tiny village in New England, USA, was eventually to have a huge influence on our knowledge and understanding of the working of the brain. Some might observe that had it had just a bit more influence, at least one Nobel Prize would not have been won for the wrong reason just over one hundred years later, and many thousands of lives may possibly have not been irretrievably ruined as a result of one of the biggest scandals in the history of medicine.

On a sunny afternoon on 13 September 1848, a gang of men were preparing the ground before laying railway track in a wooded cutting about three-quarters of a mile from Cavendish (population 1,300), Vermont. Their foreman, Phineas P. Gage, an able, hard-working and universally popular man, was in charge and they were making excellent progress. The gang was using explosives to level the shale rock on the floor of the forest. There are no totally reliable eyewitness accounts of what happened, but it seems that their meticulous foreman was uncharacteristically careless. All day they had been drilling holes in the rock, partially filling them with dynamite, inserting a fuse and then pouring a large amount of sand into the hole over the top. A tamping iron, 3 feet 7 inches long, which Gage had designed, was used to compact the mixture before triggering the fuse. But on one occasion that afternoon, Phineas Gage rammed the tamping iron into a hole without checking that his assistant had first poured in the protective sand. The resulting explosion drove the tamping iron out of the hole with huge force and it pierced Phineas Gage's left cheek. Although it weighed nearly seven kilos, it went straight through his face, removed his left eye from behind by piercing the base of the eye socket, and shot out through the top of his skull, leaving a massive hole extending back to almost the middle of his head. The bone loss in the cranium and the broken bone around the hole left a gap big enough for a man to insert a fist.

The force of this solid iron thunderbolt threw Gage several yards distant onto his back. The tamping iron lodged in the ground some sixty feet behind him. It isn't clear whether Gage lost consciousness, but he lay there twitching, apparently mortally wounded, until Christopher Goodrich came from the township with his oxcart and deposited him at Joseph Adam's inn in the centre of town. Clearly he was expected to die because Thomas Winslow, the neighbourhood cabinetmaker who lived just across the street (and who doubled as an undertaker in his spare time), came over to measure him for his coffin.

The story becomes a little confused about who first treated Gage for his terrible injuries. It appears that a Dr Edward Williams from Proctorsville, Vermont, was the first physician to examine him; by this time Gage was certainly fully conscious and able to speak because he is reported as saying: 'Doctor, here is business enough for you.' But the local general practitioner, Dr John Harlow, is given the credit for nursing him back to health, suturing the wounds and using clean dressings and a liberal supply of antiseptics. Remarkably, there seems to have been no infection and some weeks later his patient was well enough to return to his family in Lebanon, New Hampshire, to rehabilitate. Dr Harlow gets credit for the quality of his care but also for, importantly as it turned out, publishing the case later. He wrote it up for the *Boston Medical and Surgical Journal*: 'Passage of an iron rod through the head', where it appeared at the end of that year. What was remarkable to Harlow was that, at first, Gage appeared to recover unharmed and intact. He walked and talked normally, had normal sensation, and moved all his limbs without restraint.

It has been said that the story of Phineas Gage, and the insight that his injuries give into the workings of the brain, has resulted in his being mentioned or written about in no fewer than 60 per cent of all books on neuroscience. Because after this injury, Phineas was, in the words of one of his colleagues, 'no longer Gage'. He now had a totally different temperament and character. Whereas before he was patient and amenable, now he was irascible and fitful. Before the accident he was well organized and sociable, getting on well with everybody with whom he came into contact; now he was aggressive, demanding and irreverent. He showed no deference to anybody, made shocking sexual suggestions, and was obstinate, erratic, impetuous and unreliable. Indeed, though he wanted his job back as a foreman, he was undoubtedly unemployable in such a responsible capacity, particularly as it involved work with explosives. He became a bit of a drifter and took a variety of jobs as a coachman, ostler and cleaner. There being less and less chance of employment locally, it seems he spent several years in Chile caring for horses. At some point he ended up exhibiting himself at Barnum's Circus in New York. Over the next ten years, his health deteriorated, and he died, a chronic epileptic, in 1860. In 1867, his body was exhumed, some kind of post-mortem done and Dr Harlow, who had continued his keen interest in Phineas Gage's plight, gave his skull – together with the famous tamping iron – to Harvard's Medical School as an exhibit. They can now be seen in the Countway Library of Medicine, Harvard.

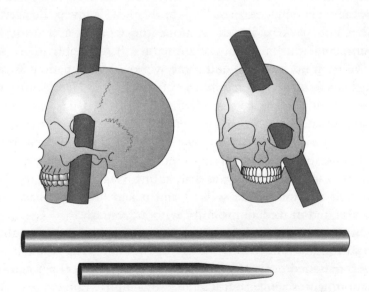

Phineas Gage and the famous tamping iron

Professor Moniz and the 'white cut'

Almost a hundred years after Gage had his world-famous accident, a doctor in Portugal was coolly and deliberately trying to reproduce a very similar injury in severely disturbed, mentally ill patients. Admittedly, he was attempting this in a much more controlled fashion. Professor Egas Moniz was then at the University of Lisbon, working as Professor of Neurology. Moniz's proper name was Antonio Caetano de Abreu Freire, but his godfather named him after the hero of the Portuguese resistance who fought against the Moors. His christening set the tone of what might be thought a rather macho existence. He became a Portuguese member of Parliament at the age of twenty-nine and Ambassador to Spain during the latter part of the first world war before becoming Minister for Foreign Affairs. In consequence, he became one of the signatories to the Treaty of Versailles at the end of the war, but had to resign from politics in 1919 after he was challenged to a duel as a result of a political disagreement.

By the time Moniz was ready to return to full-time medicine in Lisbon, he had already written a book on sexual function and the pathological aspects of sex life, two on hypnotism and its history, and, in 1917, a book on neurological injuries in war. The next few years in Lisbon were a stunning success personally and he gained a large international reputation as a neurologist as he developed new methods for looking at the human brain, while also continuing experimental work on animals. Until Moniz's day, the conventional way of examining the structure of the brain in an intact patient was using X-rays, with the risks that repeated exposure might bring the patient – although, of course, it was only much later that people began to be much more concerned at the risks of diagnostic radiation. That is, incidentally, a relatively recent concern. When I was a child of ten, it was normal practice in the more fashionable shoe shops to have your new shoes fitted under an X-ray machine. It seems incredible that the first X-ray I saw was my own foot in my local shoe shop, with the bones of my toes wiggling in the eerie greenish light of what was undoubtedly a powerful source of highly risky gamma radiation.

But the problem in Moniz's day was not a perceived risk of radiation; it was the fact that doctors could only obtain a very poor-quality image from X-rays of the nervous system. While my toes and other bones stick out well and cast a strong X-ray shadow, soft tissues such as brain, for example, hardly leave any image at all. A major problem was to find better ways of diagnosing such disease as tumours inside the brain. One method which somewhat improved the outline of the brain was to increase the contrast of the picture by injecting air into the head. But this technique, so-called air encephalography, still gave a blurry, unspecific image, was not without hazard and often left patients with crippling headaches for some time afterwards. Moniz began injecting human corpses. He used, among other compounds, sodium iodide in solution, and injected this into the cerebral arteries. Iodine salts are relatively opaque to X-rays, and so this way he was able to map the position of the arteries inside the brain. And when the location of the various arteries was abnormal this suggested displacement from their normal position by a tumour, for example.

One cannot help but suspect that the international acclaim and adulation that Moniz was accorded after his important studies on cerebral angiography were published led him a step too far. He started to experiment with psychosurgery. Moniz set out to try to treat what then (and even now) were very difficult and distressing conditions, such as severe paranoid states, extreme depression and schizophrenia. By the 1930s he had come across earlier research performed on the brains of monkeys and chimps. These particular animals, hitherto aggressive and anxious, became friendly and passive after certain areas at the front of their brains were cut away. Moniz, working in his mental hospital in Lisbon, started to think about trying this out on humans who showed somewhat similar symptoms. He was pleased with the results.

Prefrontal leucotomy, or lobotomy, was first performed on a human patient on 12 November 1935. Together with his assistant, Dr Lima, Moniz drilled a number of holes in a paranoid female patient's skull under local anaesthetic. He then injected pure alcohol into the area of the brain connecting the frontal lobes to the rest of the central nervous system in the expectation of pickling the nerve fibres. Immediately after the operation, the woman was less agitated and much calmer. As it turned out, other patients in this asylum were rather more fortunate because the Medical Director – either out of professional jealousy or because of genuine concerns about the ethics of Moniz's approach – refused to allow any more of the patients for whom he was ultimately responsible to undergo this surgery.

Moniz cast his net further afield, and there is a strong suspicion that he reported his clinical results with some considerable spin. He, together with Lima, now conducted twenty operations on patients from various places. Some suffered from schizophrenia, others from psychotic depression. Moniz admitted that many of the patients were somewhat sluggish after the surgery, but understated the extent of the negative effects of his work. Apart from being apathetic, they suffered incontinence, nausea and disorientation. Moniz appears to have committed the cardinal sin of not evaluating the state of his patients at long-term follow-up, and also disregarding the very negative symptoms that most of them would have reported – had they been able. But Moniz was now borne along by enthusiasm. Because Moniz felt that alcohol did not have a strong enough effect, he replaced this approach with a special knife, called a leucotome. A few blind strokes with this knife quickly inserted into the brain, and the famous 'white cut' was developed. Psychosis, particularly when patients were un-controllable or dangerous, was a common and untreatable disease and so there was extraordinary interest in any therapy that might make these very ill patients more tractable.

Dr Freeman's 'improvements'

One neurologist who developed this interest was Walter Freeman from George Washington University. He saw an opportunity in the 'white cut' revolution and was soon prepared to try it for himself on human subjects. His first patient, Mrs Hammatt, was a highly agitated and depressed woman from Kansas and she and her family were faced with her internment in a mental institution, or the knife. In those days internment in a lunatic asylum was virtual death; they chose the knife.

But just before being laid on the operating table, Mrs Hammatt became very agitated. She realized that in order to have the surgery, the doctors needed to have her head shaved. To calm her down, Freeman promised her this would not be done and that the curls of which she was so proud would not be harmed. Six cuts in the skull and several blunt cuts in the brain later, Freeman reported 'she no longer cared'.

A week after surgery, Mrs Hammatt became unable to speak

properly. She constantly mumbled repeated incoherent syllables and could not recall simple facts like the days of the week, or the current date. Writing was completely impossible for her. But gradually she seemed to get better, her speech returned and she was eventually discharged home, apparently free of the symptoms of extreme anxiety that had previously plagued her. In his autobiography, Freeman wrote of his first lobotomized patient that, after the operation, 'She survived five years, according to Mr Hammatt the happiest days of her life . . . She could go to the theatre and really enjoy the play without thinking what her back hair looked like or whether her shoes pinched.'

Dr Freeman, together with his assistant from George Washington University, Dr Watts, now recklessly embarked on an indiscriminate career in psychosurgery. Within a relatively short time, he was able to describe a series of 623 surgical operations, of which he reported 52 per cent of the results as 'good', 32 per cent as 'fair' and 13 per cent as 'poor'. Eighteen of the patients died. The documentation of what constituted a 'good' case was dubious and inadequate, and many of the nurses who cared for these patients afterwards recognized that they were frequently unable to use the toilet, often made sexual advances to nurses, sat unmoving for hours and showed apathy, dullness, loss of memory and delusions.

By now, Freeman and Watts were operating on a variety of disorders diagnosed as psychiatric, including drunks found in downtown Washington. Once they had established their lucrative private practices in offices there, Freeman started to experiment with a variety of 'improvements', the precise details of which he even kept from his closest colleague and accomplice Dr Watts. He also commenced a campaign of pure self-advertisement. He set up stalls at medical conventions and conferences, and used the press to make claims about his ability to treat what had previously been thought beyond treatment. Over subsequent years he set out to improve his surgical approach, to make it swifter and simpler. He travelled the USA, operating on a variety of often poorly diagnosed patients in some twenty-three states.

Among his improvements was the so-called 'transorbital technique', often done as an 'office procedure' with the patient being sent home in a taxi afterwards. His son, who sometimes used to assist him, described his method of anaesthesia, which was to stun the patient with a large electric shock. An assistant held the patient down on the operating table and, once the convulsions had subsided, Walter Freeman lifted an eyelid of the patient – the transorbital approach is graphically described by a bystander: '. . . lifting the eyelid, he inserted an ice-pick-like instrument through a tear duct. A few taps with a surgical hammer [sometimes Freeman is reported as flamboyantly using a carpenter's mallet when he was showing off his prowess] breached the bone. Freeman took position behind the patient's head, pushed the leucotome about an inch and a half in the frontal lobe of the patient's brain, and moved the tip back and forth. Then he repeated the process with the other eye socket.' One professor of neurology is recorded as fainting when he watched Freeman demonstrating his work.

There is a chilling, slightly blurry photograph of Freeman taken in about 1945. An apparently unconscious woman wearing striped pyjamas is lying on a metal operating table. Two nurses are holding her arms; another appears to be leaning on her legs. Freeman is facing the camera, demonstrating his surgical skills. Wearing a white, sleeveless smock, Freeman with bare, gloveless hands (without surgical gown, hat or mask) is tapping home his knife into the patient's brain through an eye socket. Closely surrounding this operating table are eight other men, mostly wearing respectable outdoor clothes, business suits and ties. Nobody is wearing anything vaguely resembling surgical dress, a mask or even a theatre gown, despite the fact that infection in the brain is one of the most deadly.

The wrong Nobel Prize

Once Egas Moniz, and then Freeman, had published their results, there was widespread international enthusiasm. Moniz's work was initially applauded everywhere; he became a commander of the Légion d'Honneur, gaining a number of honorary doctorates and being appointed as an honorary member of many national medical and scientific academies. The Nobel Prize for Physiology and Medicine was awarded in 1949 because, in the words of the Nobel citation, 'It occurred to Moniz that psychic morbid states accompanied by affective tension might be relieved by destroying the frontal lobes or their connections to other parts of the brain . . .' I wrote at the beginning of this chapter that a Nobel Prize was won for the wrong reason – because while there was little justification for the acclaim given to psychosurgery, the earlier work that Moniz had done on cerebral radiology was truly groundbreaking and influences many of the techniques still in wide use today, over seventy-five years later.

I think it very likely that Freeman was consumed by thoughts of the fame increasingly heaped on Moniz. He persisted with largely unaudited series of treatments and in doing so fell foul of many from the medical establishment. But the criticism was mostly due to other considerations – it was partly because of his advertising, partly because he was not a qualified surgeon but doing operations, and perhaps because a number of his patients died suddenly, sometimes of brain haemorrhage. Freeman may have been regarded with notoriety by the more serious members of the medical profession, but the plaudits from among the less discriminating and informed members of the profession, the press and the public were considerable. It brought him many prominent patients from the upper rungs of society, among them the Hollywood actress Frances Farmer, and John F. Kennedy's sister Rosemary Kennedy, who was crippled by the procedure, requiring constant care for the next sixty years.

But severe psychiatric disorders were, and still are, extremely common, and drug treatments for violent, disturbed patients were then very limited. Largactyl, the famous tranquillizer, was yet to be invented and barbiturates had only a very crude effect. The fate of the troublesome Randall P. McMurphy, hero of Ken Kesey's *One Flew Over the Cuckoo's Nest*, was a fate handed out to thousands of people throughout Europe and the USA as enthusiasm for the full-frontal lobotomy spread through the medical community. The problem was that while people lost their aggressive and destructive tendencies after the operation, so did they – like poor Phineas Gage – also lose vital elements of their personalities. They might have lost their capacity to become angry, for instance, but so had they lost their capacity to feel joy, or sympathy, or enthusiasm. They might have ceased to present a problem to those around them, but they had also ceased, in some cases, to be fully functioning humans. Moniz, and those others following him, had removed their soul. It was such drastic measures as the lobotomy that led the radical 1960s psychiatrist R.D. Laing to conclude that society merely condemned as mentally ill those people it wished to contain and silence.

Understanding other people

There is a rare disorder of the brain, Urbach-Wiethe disease, which can result in calcification in the amygdala. Ralph Adolphs described a patient who had impaired perception of fear after such bilateral amygdala damage in 1994.[30] The patient suffered no impairment of intelligence or motor function – but she found it difficult to recognize emotions in people's faces and voices. Fear and anger were impossible for her to detect. Fear and anger may be understood as concepts, but patients with amygdala damage may not spot them or react to them as they appear in their daily context.

This may appear to be merely interesting for the observer and frustrating for the sufferer. But the role of the amygdala is crucial for survival. It's one thing not to be able to read people's faces in a modern context. But it is quite another not to feel fear as a massive truck is bearing down upon us. During the filming of *The Human Mind* I stood wearing breathing apparatus in a flimsy iron cage in the sea off Cape Town while a two-ton, 18-foot-long great white shark bore down on me, rattling my cage and showing its rows of four-inch teeth. No matter how much my cerebral cortex was telling me I could keep calm and that I was not going to get hurt, the alarm bells in my amygdala were ringing unbearably.

In an age when survival was more precarious and humans bonded together in groups in order to ensure the best chances, group communication was vital. Among bushmen and other hunter-gatherers, the most severe sanction for breaking the rules of the group is to be excluded from the group – punishment that meant death in harsh environments. We can see the traces of this in the custom of 'shunning' – a terrible curse for the ancient Israelites, prevalent in the Welsh valleys until the early decades of the last century and still practised among Romany traveller groups. Perhaps this is still why they use the black ball at the Garrick Club in London. Group communication, at its most basic, entails an ability to read and express emotion. If another member of the group is angry, for instance, or fearful, then it pays to be able to interpret that and modify our behaviour accordingly. Monkeys released into the wild after having their amygdalae removed do not survive very long. They neglect their young, and prove unable to pick up signals of approaching danger from other members of the group.

If asked to describe 'emotion' I might be tempted to see it as a set of feelings – fear, anger, sadness, joy, etc. But looking at the above evidence, it seems less about feelings than a set of survival mechanisms that helps us to avoid danger and direct ourselves towards whatever is most beneficial. According to Joseph LeDoux, a prominent researcher into human emotions – and author of *The Emotional Brain* and *Synaptic Self* [31,32] – the emotional process is a body–brain interaction, the bulk of which remains buried below conscious view. The conscious 'felt' element is merely the tip of the iceberg, or as LeDoux puts it, 'the icing on the cake'.

There is a sad instance mentioned by Antonio Damasio.[33] A patient of his, after an operation to remove a brain tumour, became indecisive and irresponsible. Unable to make correct choices, he threw himself into one doomed venture after another. Dr Damasio's tests suggest that the patient was unable to 'feel'. Shown pictures of horrific scenes, he said he recognized that they were horrible, but he didn't feel it. In his daily life, he was unable to pick up the cues from others that help normal people to make choices. In the case of this particular man, the problem seemed to be caused by damage to the connections between his frontal 'conscious' cortex and his limbic system.

In the opinion of many scientists, emotions would seem to be rather like colours – more complex ones are made up of a combination of a limited set of more basic primaries. The primary emotions, most brain scientists agree, are fear, anger, sadness and joy. Others add disgust and surprise, and some say contempt as well. So the more complex emotion of guilt might be said to be composed of fear and sadness. Other scientists argue that emotions like surprise, disgust and guilt exist alone. And some interesting results from brain surgery patients would tend to back up this more complex, categorized view of emotions. When certain parts of their brain have been stimulated, they have been able to report some very specific and subtle emotional experiences, such as the shame one feels on making a social faux pas.

How does it work?

Information from the body itself plays some part in feeling emotions. There is documented evidence of spinal injury patients, paralysed from the neck down, who report some emotional blunting with a detachment similar to Damasio's patient. Damasio argues that one reason for their limited and incomplete detachment is that they still get direct brain stimuli from the cranial nerves – which directly connect the face, for example, with the brain. Perhaps a 'gut reaction' is not such a meaningless cliché after all.

Normally what happens is that an emotional stimulus – say, the sight of an angry face – passes from our visual cortex to the limbic system. At this stage, the information on that electrochemical email might read something like: 'Human face seen, now, at five feet – eyes flashing and teeth bared.' As part of a loop between the amygdala and the hypothalamus, signals are sent on to the body. The 'email' from the hypothalamus might say: 'Close threat, how are you going to deal with it?' But the hypothalamus also sends signals to the pituitary, the master gland of the whole body. Secretions from there, informed by the hypothalamus, rapidly direct heart rate, blood pressure, levels of tension in the muscles, alertness. This level of alertness is fed back into the hypothalamus – an email that might say, 'We are on alert, ready to fight, check with HQ' – and thence onwards to the higher cortex. The higher cortex takes the bodily information received and concludes, 'This means anger. So let's start responding.' We would then have what we consciously call an emotional feeling.

But without the body acting as a vital part of this loop of communication, the information we receive in our higher cortex is patchy. Think of a teletext page when there is poor TV reception – letters and numbers mixed up together, whole areas blank. If I was suffering from a spinal injury, my hypothalamus – not itself 'knowing' about the spinal injury – would send its information down to the body nonetheless. It would then 'check' to see what was happening, and receive the information that nothing was happening down there – constant heart rate, no muscular movement, etc. It would 'conclude' that, after all, things were in a state of calm. The higher cortex, processing this information, would hence register less.

We started out by highlighting the importance of the amygdala in all of this. So what is its precise role? It seems that it acts as a 'tagging' system for information coming in directly through the senses, a process that also involves consultation with the memory banks of the hippocampus. It can operate entirely outside of consciousness – as we might see if we heard a loud bang in the night and immediately hid under the sheets, even before we had assessed the reasons for the noise.

Essentially, the amygdala may assign an emotional value to information – i.e., this is good, this is bad, this is disgusting, this is frightening – which allows us to then assess the world and react to it accordingly. Dopamine plays an important role in its functioning. The effects of this neurotransmitter are relayed to the amygdala, and there are changes in its supply in response to pleasurable or painful stimuli. Disorders in the way the amygdala 'tags' information could be responsible for many mental conditions. The amygdala of phobic people, for instance, may tag more information as 'scary' or 'disgusting'. A happy or just normally functioning person might look at a tree in winter and see it as a beautiful structure, or not be moved by it at all. A depressed person might look it at the same tree and see only its dead, lifeless condition. Their amygdala is tagging all incoming information in the same way – as sad or horrible.

Some people are able to feel emotion, but are unable to express it. This condition is known as alexithymia. In their case, the disruption lies not between body and brain, but between the higher cortex where emotion is consciously processed and the regions of the brain that control facial expression and speech. Imagine trying to convince your lover to marry you using a flat voice without any guise of sincerity in your eyes. Imagine trying to lead your troops into battle. Clearly, we use our emotional faculties not just to read other people, but to influence them.

In expressing our own internal emotional states to others, and in reading their internal states, body language is very important. As a medical student in the 1960s I remember being taught by one of Britain's really great clinicians, Dr Bomford, the importance of good emotional contact with a patient. Shake hands at the start of a consultation, make eye contact, lean forward towards the patient, do not cross your arms or fiddle with your pen, do not answer the telephone or turn to engage another person in conversation. Sit close to them if they are lying or sitting, and try to keep your head at their level. Show interest in what they are saying. Surprisingly, this teaching was much before its time. A fellow consultant in the same hospital, an excellent chest physician technically, was much more typical of doctors after the war. His ward rounds were like a military inspection. Standing erect at the foot of the bed – never moving to get close to the supine patient – he would address each male patient by his surname. 'Ah, Watson, how are we this week?' Without really hearing the answer, there would be a brief, muttered conversation with the registrar and the ward sister, a long glance at the record and temperature charts, and terse recommendations to the staff for investigations. Meantime, the patient, particularly if male, would be lying rigidly to attention in bed. 'Jolly good, Watson, old fellow, splendid progress' – and on to the next patient. And this consultant, whom I cannot name, was absolute kindness, but never understood the devastating emotional effect he had during his weekly rounds. We students picked up the pieces by a second round after he had left.

Gestures, how we stand or sit, the use of our hands are all very important in conveying deference, indifference, trustworthiness. Tony Blair, our Prime Minister, for example, like many good politicians has a particular habit of opening out his hands as he speaks. It tells his audience that he is trying to be open and trying to gain trust. In his case I have no doubt that it is genuine, but many politicians use these gestures in a false way – and quite often, our emotional intelligence is capable of discerning this. This, perhaps, is the success of Rory Bremner, who is brilliant at imitating Tony Blair. He makes the gestures just slightly differently and they take on a different meaning to the beholder. But more importantly, Rory Bremner uses his face. When we communicate emotion, facial expression is by far the most important mechanism.

'Smile and the whole world smiles with you'

We humans have some 7,000 different facial expressions in our repertoire. And they tend to mean the same things wherever you are in the world. (This is not the case for gestures performed with the body – the Greeks, for instance, shake their heads to mean 'yes', and older people might take considerable offence at a thumbs-up sign.) There are experts who make a living out of facial analysis; organizations like the FBI take their work seriously. But for now a simple example may suffice. We use two muscles (the left and right zygomaticus) to produce a polite smile – the sort I might keep on my face at a cocktail party, for example. A genuine smile, on the other hand, such as I might produce when I see my wife after having finally freed myself of the cocktail party, uses four muscles – two extra around the eyes, the left and right orbicularis occuli. When this smile fades, it fades in a more even pattern than my false smile and more slowly. I do not consciously produce this. Facial expressions are a vital part of our emotional vocabulary, and while it is possible to become conscious of them, they largely take place in the region of unthought, habitual action.

Paul Ekman of the University of California at San Francisco pointed out that certain facial expressions are universal in humans, irrespective of their cultural background. These facial expressions do not substantially vary and are recognizable by other members of our species whether on the north-east coast of the USA, in South America, Japan, China or New Guinea. Ekman defined six such basic facial expressions: anger, disgust, sadness, fear, surprise and happiness. He described how we have automatic reactions that unfold within microseconds when we see these facial signals in others.

When we see disgust, for instance, a particular part of the amygdala works to identify it in the face of the person at whom we are looking. Another part of the brain will be working to pick up cues in their voice. It seems that the left side may read voice information, while the right responds to facial information, consistent with the fact that in 95 per cent of people, the language centre of the brain is in the left hemisphere. One of the problems, though, in studying these and other human facial states is that there are wide ranges of intensity in these emotions, such as happiness. I regret to emphasize that I support a North London football club, but the season is much on my mind as I write this chapter. I might feel happy if Arsenal won a match early in the championship season, but I would be ecstatic if it was at the end of the season and Manchester United had just lost. Picking up a pound coin lost in the football ground would give me a very different intensity of feeling from being informed that I had just won the million-pound Premium Bond draw. Cognitive neuroscientists sometimes try to get around this problem by measuring the degree of our arousal in response to a particular emotion. Another strategy is to attempt to measure the depth of a given emotion by assessing the actions it induces. Thus happiness may induce in us a tendency to engage with a situation; fear or disgust, conversely, depending on the depth of feeling, may lead us to turn away, shun contact or withdraw.

We humans are deeply social creatures and when we see an

emotion in another person we tend to experience it ourselves. For instance, as I showed earlier, it makes evolutionary sense for us, if we see someone eating a piece of food and registering disgust, not to go and repeat their mistake. As far as we know, the amygdala responds to four basic emotions: disgust, sadness, happiness and fear. It is uncertain whether a specific part of the amygdala is activated with each emotion – probably not. It may just tell the cortical brain, 'Hey, watch out – there's an emotional response needed.' So 'smile and the whole world smiles with you' doesn't always work. As an ad hoc experiment, I asked one of the producers of *The Human Mind* programme to try to smile at everyone when going out to fetch some milk. A few people did indeed smile back but one person asked him, quite aggressively: 'Who are you smiling at? Shall I wipe it off your face?' But even that response is quite telling. The individual in question did just what we are supposed to do when registering emotions coming off another person – he looked to see what the other's face was communicating about the environment. Finding nothing in the congested streets of White City that could possibly produce a smile, he concluded that the information was faulty and therefore coming from a faulty source, hence his threat. Admittedly, this response could have been due to the fact that Queens Park Rangers, the football club down the road, had just lost to Vauxhall Motors after a penalty shootout in a replay at home in the FA Cup. Expressions might be common to everyone, but the understanding of them differs from one individual to another. If your experience of smiles has been that people are mocking you, or are about to do something unpleasant, you won't be happy to see a smile. You may be afraid and defensive.

Dr Ulf Dimberg, of the University of Uppsala, Finland, has recently published a study in which volunteers were asked to respond to images of happy, sad or neutral faces. He discovered that when the volunteers mirrored the facial expressions they saw, the action was smooth and effortless. When, in contrast, they were asked to provide the opposite of the expression they were looking at – for example, to frown at a smiling face – their muscles continued to try to produce a smile. In other words, we are hard-wired to 'copy' our fellow humans.[34] In fact, as we shall see later, there are various neurons within the brain that appear to fire only in response to the actions of other humans. The presence of these so-called 'mirror neurons' would tend to confirm the notion that modern man evolved living in groups, and that imitating our fellow group members was a valuable strategy to survive.

It follows that the expressions we generate produce feelings within ourselves, as well as communicating our feelings to others. If I make a scowling face, the neurons in charge of that expression communicate to my higher cortex that a) I am frowning and b) there must be some reason why I am frowning. This goes to the amygdala, triggering, shall we say, a mixture of fear and low-level anger, which eventually gets back to my facial muscles with the message: something worrying here, get frowning! So my frown intensifies, and this new information goes to the amygdala and so on. A feedback loop may thus be set up – rather like our brief analysis of stage fright earlier. Cognitive Behavioural Therapy (CBT) takes its practice from a belief in this loop. CBT gets people to identify the triggers that make them sad, fearful or angry, for example, and to consciously substitute another emotion in their place. By doing this over and over again, the practice becomes habitual. The frown is replaced by a smile, and the amygdala reads this information as 'happy' and tells us to smile more.

Beyond a joke

A curious incident happened on the morning of 30 January 1962. It was business as usual in the girls' school in the Boboka province of Tanganyika; now, of course, Tanzania. The school hummed quietly with the activities of learning – the teachers' voices, the shuffling of feet, the usual whispering at the back of the class. And then it all went crazy. A particularly banal remark by one teacher set a couple of girls laughing. The teacher, realizing her faux pas, joined in for a moment or two. Like all the best teachers, she understood that getting irate can sometimes make a situation worse. The rest of her class joined in. After a few minutes, the teacher started to call for quiet. It was time to be getting back to the lesson. But it was useless. The girls were rolling in the aisles, tears streaming down their cheeks. Neighbouring classrooms, separated only by flimsy clapboard partitions, began to be affected too – teachers and girls alike, of all ages, became gripped with an epidemic of laughter.

Nearly all of us can remember similar incidents at school, probably equally banal, which gave an uncontrollable fit of the giggles. That combination of being young and being in a situation in which one is supposed to be behaving sensibly can be quite deadly – there is, I think, a case for this reaction being more pronounced among females.

On this occasion in Tanganyika, the situation became more serious. The laughing continued all day. The girls went home to their neighbouring villages, taking their laughter with them – and setting off their parents. Over the next fortnight, the laughter spread to villages throughout the province. Eventually, it was no longer any joke. The Red Cross was called in, because people were beginning to suffer from exhaustion, dehydration and malnutrition. The army was called in and forced the school to close.[35]

This story is, in a way, nothing more than a demonstration of the maxim that laughter is infectious. The sight and sound of our fellow humans having a good laugh makes us want to laugh, too. But why should that be so? Is this a mere trick of nature, or does it have some purpose? Laughter is a display of emotion – and some work has suggested the amygdala is partly responsible, although the orbitofrontal cortex has also been pinpointed by some recent research work. I recently saw footage of the remarkable 'Giggling Guru' – Doctor Madan Kataria, in Mumbai, India, who uses daily group laughter as a therapeutic tool for a range of physical and mental ailments. Like everyone in the room watching the footage with me, I was overcome by laughter at the glorious sight of these people laughing – indeed I am smiling now as I recall it. At the time of viewing, I felt a sense of great happiness for some moments afterwards. Perhaps now we can see why the Tanganyikan laughter epidemic became so hard to control. The sight of laughter in others makes us laugh. Our brain interprets this laughter as a sign of happiness – bringing on more laughter. Before we know it, we are stuck in the loop.

Laughter functions primarily as a social lubricant – and many scientists believe the smile, and its extension into a full-blown guffaw, is essentially a means of showing others that we are not a threat to them, and a means of promoting group bonding. Other primates exhibit forms of behaviour physiologically similar to the human laugh. Chimpanzees, for instance, will open their mouths wide, expose their teeth and make loud, repetitive vocalizations in situations that tend to evoke human laughter, such as rough-and-tumble play, or when they are being tickled. Even dogs and rats make noises of a certain pattern when playing. These are different to the noises they make during other interactions more related to survival and reproduction. So laughter may be a form of social activity in both animals and humans. This view is supported by the observation that, in humans, laughter is up to thirty times more likely to occur in a group than when we are alone.

It also seems that human laughter produces a phenomenon called *allomimesis* – in which the behaviour of individuals synchronizes, and results in them all reporting the same physiological and emotional sensations. Karl Grammer and Petra Weixler of Austria's Ludwig-Boltzmann Institute of Urban Ethology tested the allomimetic effects of laughter by secretly filming pairs of male and female strangers. Subsequent to the filming, the subjects were asked to complete a questionnaire, which required them to rate the experience they had just undergone, such as the pleasantness of the situation, their perceived risk of rejection by, and their interest in, their partner. The researchers discovered a pattern whereby if the participants were interested in one another, the frequency and emphasis of the male's body movements directly mirrored the amplitude and frequency of the female's laughter. In turn, the more mirroring there was between their body movements and the female's laughter, the more the males rated the experience as pleasurable. In other words, laughter gets us 'on the same wavelength' and thereby promotes bonding. This may help explain how the Tanganyikan laughter epidemic managed to spread so far.

We have yet to isolate the genes possibly responsible for a sense of humour, although we have already seen that there seems to be a link between a dominant left brain and a tendency to experience a more constant, positive outlook on life. However, the fact that laughter is a global phenomenon and that it depends on specific brain regions suggests that, in the past, there was an evolutionary advantage in being able to share a joke. Perhaps the logic is that laughter can defuse violence, promote group bonding and therefore assist in the business of survival. This is something that hostages kept by gangs in various lawless parts of the world seem to believe and report after being freed successfully.

The areas of the brain involved in laughter are at least three-fold: the frontal lobes assess the situation and detect 'what's funny', the supplementary motor area produces the necessary facial and vocal movements and the nucleus accumbens gives rise to the attendant feelings of pleasure. The curious event in Tanganyika might well have arisen from a disturbance to one or more of these brain regions.

Diseases like encephalitis – common in that part of Africa – can have bizarre effects on the brain.

In 1998, neurosurgeons at the University of California, San Francisco, were operating on a sixteen-year-old patient with severe epilepsy. They noted that whenever they stimulated the supplementary motor area of the left side of the brain she erupted in laughter. Furthermore, because she was conscious throughout the procedure, they were able to ask the girl what she found so funny. Each time they stimulated the area, she laughed, and provided a different explanation for her laughter – she saw a picture of a horse as being inexplicably hilarious, and on another occasion told the surgeons that it was they themselves who were so funny.

It is interesting to note that the stimulated area was within the girl's left brain. This suggests that the left brain produced the emotion, while her right brain searched for reasons in the immediate environment. We can see a similar interplay at work when stroke patients are asked by neuroscientists to provide the punch line to jokes. For example: 'A horse walks into a bar and asks for a pint of bitter. The barman says . . .'

a) Why the long face?

b) Two pounds fifty, please.

c) Nothing – but he takes out a gun and shoots the horse.

Patients with right-brain damage tend to choose the most literal interpretation – which in this case would be punch line b) – while those with left-brain damage choose the most random, seemingly inexplicable outcome – which might be punch line c). Sometimes I wonder about neuroscientists and their sense of humour; possibly you, too, are reluctant to choose a).

The normally functioning brain depends upon both hemispheres working in tandem – left producing the emotion, and right producing the meaning – for humour to work. Just as we produce the most laughter in interaction with other humans, so must the separate components of the brain interact in order for laughter to take place.

Asperger's and autism

Not all of us possess this in-built capacity to interact flawlessly with our fellow men. Some people have great difficulty in reading the facial expressions of others and in working out their mental state by observing their gestures and expressions. It is a particular feature of the disorder found more commonly in males known as Asperger's Syndrome, a condition which is a type of autism and was first described by an Austrian doctor, Hans Asperger, in the 1940s. Simon Baron-Cohen at the University of Cambridge conducted a test in which Asperger's Syndrome sufferers and normal subjects were shown pictures of faces depicting ten simple emotions – such as fear or joy – and ten more complex ones – such as guilt. They were shown both whole faces and separate parts, eyes or mouth. People with Asperger's Syndrome were able to read the basic emotions just as well as their counterparts, whether they saw whole faces or just eyes and mouths. But when it came to the more complex emotions, they had more trouble. People without the syndrome performed just as well at these more complex identifications even when only shown separate facial parts. But for people with Asperger's Syndrome, telling a complex expression from the eyes alone – a key way we communicate how we really feel – proved impossible.

Simon Baron-Cohen has suggested that autism and associated conditions like Asperger's may be variants of the 'male' brain. He quotes Hans Asperger: 'The autistic personality is an extreme variation of male intelligence. Even within normal variation, we find typical sex differences in intelligence . . . in the autistic individual, the male pattern is exaggerated . . .' Baron-Cohen points out there is essentially a type of brain which is systematizing (which he calls a Type S brain) and a more 'female' brain which tends to be more empathizing (the Type E brain). Perhaps what is most important about this is that men and women tend to express their emotions differently – for example, women are more alert to facial signals and pick up social nuances in a very intuitive way. They are more likely to be accommodating and less rigid in their view. Men, on the other hand, tend to be more interested in analysing details. Just possibly this is part of the reason why there are more male chess grandmasters. Men may relish railway timetables, train spotting, aspects of computing or technical details of various kinds, which fascination many women find almost incomprehensible. Perhaps all this is inherited from an aspect of human evolutionary past when men were focusing on hunting and women were more concerned with the social cohesion of the group.

John Ratey of Harvard cites an example of an autistic patient who reported that, until she was forty, she hadn't known that people told each other how they feel about things with their eyes. It seems that the eyes – not for nothing dubbed the 'windows of the soul' – are a particularly important indicator of human emotional states. Some key evolutionary differences have made this function paramount. For instance, the sclera – or white of the eye – is bigger in humans than in all other primates, and the very fact that it is white, not pigmented, would seem to lend it an advantage in signalling messages to other humans. Research has indicated that there is a considerable degree of overlap between the brain systems we use to follow the direction of someone's gaze, and those we use to infer the mental states of others.[36] It has also been argued that domesticated dogs, having lived so long with humans, have evolved with an ability to follow and read the gaze of their human owners – a trait not found in wild animals such as wolves. I find it interesting that a study, recently published in *Science*, suggests that this is a trick at which dogs perform better than most primates. Dogs can follow these signals of a man's intentions more efficiently than chimpanzees.

The raging mind

Anger, and its expression in violent, aggressive behaviour, is also a key part of our emotional make-up. In both Western and Eastern cultures, we set great store by the facility to control and even deny our emotions – particularly anger and grief. We could say that we attach a hierarchy of value judgements to what are only chains of chemical activity. Why, for instance, should anger be frowned upon, but joy not? Probably because, certainly in the modern age, anger is more threatening and is likely to cause more social disruption. Much psychotherapy involves getting patients to acknowledge how they really feel and stop judging their emotions, as a way of ultimately preventing them from bubbling up out of conscious control. The phrase 'own your anger' might be a psychobabble cliché of the 1980s, but it expresses an underlying truth – some of our emotions are destructive, and only by acknowledging them and understanding their origins can we hope to submit them to conscious control.

In our evolutionary past, anger must surely have played an important role; indeed, in some human situations it still does. Shows of aggression, particularly between males in the animal world, serve to warn off predators. Within the basic survival group, males engage in combat to gain preferential rights to females and to any food supplies that might be going. We can see the descendants of this at work today in any crowded urban pub on a Saturday night: young males competing in various ways in order to attract females, a process that often spills over into aggression and then violence. If you have managed to grit your teeth and watch programmes like *Ibiza Reps Uncut* on Sky television, or even *I'm a Celebrity, Get Me Out of Here*, you will have seen that these elements are only just below the surface of modern behaviour. Games that rely on strength and physical prowess, such as football or boxing, represent a stylized version of the violent combative instinct, and the response of some of the more vocal spectators demonstrates that such impulses are alive.

I admit to being very edgy at airport check-in queues. At times, I have to exert considerable self-control not to show belligerent behaviour to perfectly innocent members of the airport ground staff. But nearly all of us feel aggressive sometimes. The recently coined terms 'road rage', 'trolley rage' and 'air rage' are merely labels for an essential trait that comes out in everyone when we feel frustrated by the traffic jam, when others gain what seems to be an unfair advantage over us in the supermarket queue, or when we are too closely confined with other humans in the sardine-tin conditions of a long economy-class flight. A psychoanalyst might even argue that the gloating over such relatively small-scale events in the media enables us to cope with our own rage. We are able to see it as something 'out there', not within us – thank heaven it's them doing it, and thank heaven they are in court for it, not us.

So what's happening when we lose our temper? The frontal lobe area of the brain plays a big part. People with damage to their frontal lobes – such as, of course, Phineas Gage – often have difficulty in controlling their anger. MRI scans of people with antisocial personality disorder, characterized often by aggressive, destructive behaviour, also show low activity in the frontal lobe region.

In normal individuals, the frontal lobes act as the policemen of the emotional mind – in particular, the area called the ventromedial cortex. They receive information from the lower cortex pertaining to urges, impulses and responses, but they inhibit it, and form careful plans of action to address it. For instance, if I feel hunger as I walk through a restaurant to the table I have been allotted by the waiter, I do not grab a few chips from the other diners' tables as I pass by. My frontal lobes are effectively saying to my lower brain: 'I see that there is hunger. But we wait. I won't cause a scene.'

In the autumn of 2001, teams from the Toyota Motor Corporation and Sony unveiled a new car with the 'pod' concept. It effectively performs the function of the frontal lobes for its drivers – thereby, hopefully, reducing accidents and dangerous driving. The car uses sensors within the steering wheel to measure perspiration and pulse – both of which increase when we are stressed or angry – and then puts strategies in place to correct our behaviour. When the onboard computer of this car registers an increase in stress levels, or when drivers go too fast or too close to other vehicles, an alert message is flashed on the dashboard and calming music comes out of the speakers. The prototype car – known as Pod – can even convey the driver's mood to other motorists or pedestrians using lights attached to the front and rear bumpers. In other words, somewhat like functioning frontal lobes, the Pod car can attempt to override the possible dangers caused by an angry or stressed person at the wheel. It sounds like an infuriating motorcar.

But, of course, some degree of anger is not only inevitable, but a healthy feature of development. Children, particularly teenagers, go through a period when mood swings and flashes of temper are frequent. As we have seen, research has shown that the frontal lobes take a long time to develop, not reaching maturity until we are in our early twenties. Recent studies have even shown that while the frontal lobes go through a rapid spurt of growth up to about the age of ten or eleven, they may actually be in reverse during puberty. It seems that an economic decision is made to put certain wiring circuits on hold so that more energy and attention can be given to the crucial purpose of creating a human adult ready for survival and reproduction. Suddenly parents have a neurological explanation for why a teenager, if asked to do the washing up, might storm off in a foul temper, while their ten-year-old sibling might comply sweetly.

In the BBC television series accompanying this book, we followed the very courageous efforts made by a man to address his anger problem. We saw, in essence, that triggers for anger created a loop between his amygdala, his body and his memory. Something that 'set him off', like another motorist cutting him up in traffic, created bodily symptoms of rage – quickened heart rate, tensed muscles. His memory fed in instances where he had been angry before – in a sense, he experienced everything he'd ever been angry about, and its associated physical state. We saw that his frontal lobes were less active during this process. He was in effect hearing the 'noise' of his angry body and his angry memories, without the calming, judgement-forming faculties of the frontal lobes.

Talking formed a major part of his cure. Verbalizing angry feelings not only provides a window of time in which we do not act and do something we might later regret, it also rallies the sleeping frontal lobes into wakefulness. As we saw in the last chapter, the act of analysing one's own internal state requires activity in the medial frontal cortex. The act of putting that analysis into words calls upon further cognitive functions. The frontal lobes are kicked into life, the powerful feelings are interpreted and inhibited.

The important role of serotonin in the function of the ventro-medial cortex of the frontal lobes has been documented for some time. Monkeys with high levels of this neurotransmitter are more co-operative and less aggressive. And it is of interest that people who are not depressed but who take the antidepressant drug Seroxat, which boosts levels of serotonin in the synapses, tend to show more cooperative behaviour and lower hostility to other people. Serotonin has also been found to play an important role in anxiety. A US National Institute of Mental Health study found key genetic differences in some individuals leading to decreased serotonin production. Around 70 per cent of the people who had this genetic feature also reported higher levels of anxiety on statistically evaluated tests.

Could such a genetic mutation have occurred by accident? Might it have had some positive benefit to our ancestors in the past? One perplexing thing about evolution is that a strength is also often a weakness. Humans have the most complex brain of any species. But its complexity means that, while our brain is maturing, human off-spring are dependent upon their parents for a substantial time – which strains the business of survival. A tendency to low serotonin and corresponding aggression might be a similar 'double-edged sword' – one which could have helped our ancestors to see off threats and secure food in a harsh, competitive environment, but which is less helpful in more stable, settled times.

To return for a moment to monkeys and their serotonin levels.

One species of particular interest is the vervet. Vervets are small, weighing perhaps 5 kilos, feeding mainly on grasses. They are found in many parts of Africa and have been studied not least because of their very well developed social hierarchy. Females in the same tribe form a hierarchy, with the daughters inheriting their rank from their mothers – somewhat reminiscent of some of my colleagues in the House of Lords from the Scottish peerage, or the Daughters of the American Revolution. With the latter, however, any woman is eligible for membership who is no less than eighteen years of age and can prove lineal, bloodline descent from an ancestor who aided in achieving American independence. Vervets have the advantage they do not need to provide documentation for each statement of birth, marriage and death. High-ranking vervets take priority when it comes to the best food resources and the dominant males get the best sex. Colleagues in the Lords queue. One study of vervet monkeys who had reached the top of their hierarchy shows that they had higher levels of serotonin in their brain. I do not have any comparable bio-chemical data on the English Peerage and I know of no studies regarding Daughters of the American Revolution. However, one study does appear to show that American college fraternity officers at the top of their hierarchy have higher serotonin levels.[37]

Hoping

I think that personally I'm a bit of a casual optimist. My life has been spent in the belief that things will turn out satisfactorily in the end. A happy state of mind but not one, I think, that spurs a person on to the highest achievements. Many of my most successful friends are what I regard as pragmatic pessimists – prepared to take a dim view of things, unless surprised by the way they turn out. I think this is a personality trait that leads these friends to interpret information in a certain way, information that others might treat differently. They tend to say that the way they see things is the way things truly are. But of course, this belief is found in both optimists and pessimists – both groups believe the other to be looking at life in the 'wrong', rather than just a 'different', way. All this is hardly surprising, for as we have seen, the way our brain receives incoming information informs and modifies its very architecture. It takes a leap of understanding, even of faith, for anyone to consider that 'green' only means their version of green, not some universal state. Likewise for states of emotion – the physical structure of our brains and our very identities are bound together.

When assessing the importance of brain structure, one unresolved issue is the difference between the left and right sides of the brain. Measuring differences between the left and right brain is difficult and much of the work is controversial. But at the University of Wisconsin, Richard Davidson showed that abnormally low activity in the left prefrontal cortex seems to be associated with depression. Happiness to a large extent, it appears, is associated with more activity on the left side. Feelings of sadness also appear to be associated with more activation on the right. And people with a pessimistic view-point, or those undergoing a period of depression, show increased right-brain activity and, conversely, decreased left-brain activity. In Wisconsin they have been following very young children and this fundamental 'left-brain optimist versus right-brain pessimist' distinction would appear to be established not long after birth.

Another important part of the stage in the brain's theatre of sadness and joy is the hypothalamus, and within it, dopamine, which is prob-ably a leading actor. A 1950s experiment by James Olds and Peter Milner from Montreal observed rats after an electrode had been implanted into their hypothalamus. When the rats pressed against a bar, the electrode inside the hypothalamus received a small electrical stimulus. They seemed to enjoy the process so much that they would press the bar up to 4,000 times an hour, and preferred to do that than eat food.

This process can be reversed if rats are given a drug that blocks the action of dopamine. One typical compound is the anti-psychotic drug Haloperidol. This drug alleviates acute agitated states in psychiatric patients and is also used as a premedication before surgery – it helps people feel relaxed and comfortable. But the rat taking Haloperidol no longer receives pleasurable sensations, and it loses interest in press-ing the bar. People given this and similar drugs to combat symptoms of psychosis – like hallucinations and delusional thinking – often report anhedonia, an inability to feel joy and, most commonly, an important symptom of depression. Dr Tonmoy Sharma at the Maudsley Hospital, London, gives a graphic description of anhedonia. 'Many people who go into mild depression can be cheered by "tea and sympathy". But in severe depression, anhedonia becomes a serious problem. It's worse than not being able to get any joy from life.'

A team at the University of Texas headed by Helen Mayberg has identified a specific area – the tip of the cingulate gyrus – which shows abnormally low activity in people with treatment-resistant depression.[38] Antidepressants and therapy do not work for everyone so we need to know the underlying brain states. Given the complexity of the brain, and the protean nature of its extraordinary chemistry, it surprises me that the often seemingly blunderbuss therapy of giving antidepressive drugs in a relatively arbitrary way has been useful for so many people. But in years to come, I suspect people will look back at the therapies we currently offer for many disturbances of the human mind and compare these contemporary treatments with the medieval practice of seeking out witches and the barbarous treatment by cupping and blood-letting.

In our subjective world, differences of mood or attitude amount to little more than a view of life in general. I call myself a 'casual optimist' because, given the right information or circumstances, I can be happy, hopeful and joyful – but equally I can get depressed, feel that I am not achieving much and that my work is not highly regarded. But for some people, prolonged sadness takes root in the architecture of their brains, causing a predisposition that cannot even be treated by drugs. It was, to be fair, this aspect of severe depression and gross psychosis which spurred doctors like Egas Moniz and Walter Freeman on to go beyond the bounds of what we now would regard as acceptable medical practice.

Fear

Fear is arguably the most powerful emotion in our repertoire. Real fear results in massive changes in the body's systems which control blood flow, and indeed people can drop down dead from fear alone if the heart ceases its normal pulsation. The unique power of fear makes sense in evolutionary terms. Our ancestors developed all manner of impressive faculties like language and consciousness but they were by no means safe from predators or other perils. So fear assisted our survival. But if you are frightened, do you run like the wind, or freeze?

These are two competing motor responses, and animals may use either strategy, possibly because of a genetic predisposition. Also, their previous experience and the environment in which the fright occurs are important. Dr David Anderson's group in Caltech, Pasadena, have studied rodents.[39] Mice who displayed freezing behaviour after an initial fright had most neural activity in the lateral septum ventral and some parts of the hypothalamus, whereas mice who fled had more activity in cortex, amygdala and striatal motor areas, and different parts of the hypothalamus.

As we shall see, fear takes two routes in the brain. The first travels from the sensory input regions – our eyes and ears and noses – into the amygdala, hypothalamus and straight to the body, which immediately starts priming itself to escape. A second route has fear stimuli travelling more slowly to the frontal cortex, where they are assessed and subjected to reason. For instance, lying down in my tent in the jungle at night, I notice something apparently wriggling. I am immediately on full alert, thinking I have seen a snake. I am ready to bolt out of the tent. I look again. By now, information has travelled the second, slower route via my anterior temporal cortex and I can analyse the object as just a section of rope, which moves as my sleeping bag presses on it. My frontal cortex now 'points out' that there is no need to worry. I stop being afraid and my pulse and breathing return to normal, my blood sugar starts to fall, and normal blood flow returns to the organs that are not essential for a rapid escape.

Understanding the two routes of fear helps treatment of phobias. A key feature of such treatment is the gradual introduction of the source of their fear to phobic people. For instance, an arachnophobic is encouraged first to discuss spiders, then to look at pictures of them, see them in the flesh and finally even to handle them, starting with small ones. At each stage, they learn and reinforce that the object of their phobia is not dangerous. They are also asked to think about aspects of their phobia that are non-threatening – to think about the skill with which a spider builds its web, for instance, or the beauty of its construction. Inside the brain, related neurons are being teased and trained into a new direction. The quick fear route, which would have sent them into panic, is being superseded by the slower, higher-cortex route, which calls upon the new associations they have made. The message 'Not Dangerous' becomes ever more strongly imprinted in the new circuitry as it is tried out hundreds and hundreds of times, and the fear passes into the realm of reason.

While key areas like the amygdala and the cortex with its frontal lobes play a big part in all our emotions, a whole set of brain mechanisms and areas are called upon. A swift reaction to certain emotion-inducing stimuli is imprinted in the circuitry of our brains. However, a tiny baby, unless primed by a parent's fearful expression or voice, will not be afraid of a wriggling snake or of falling – until some of the connections are in place, it has not had a chance to learn such fearful responses. And so much else depends upon learning and memory.

To use the example of being startled in the night again, I may listen out for further sounds after being woken up by a loud crash, like the bark of a fox, and trawl through my memory to ask what that sound is. My memory will come up with a set of answers: 'Sounds like an animal – you've heard them before, barking dogs, mewling cats, etc.'; 'Sounds most like a fox – they're always hanging round your dustbins.' I draw upon my whole autobiographical self – upon things I learnt last week and things I learnt as a child. If my wife then asks me what the noise was, I call further upon my memory to say, 'A fox.' In that way, by comparing what I experience now with what I have experienced in the past, the contents of my memory, I can direct my response appropriately. In the next chapter, we will be looking at the way our brains develop, over time, to store memories about the world and ways of describing it.

It is interesting that a great percentage of our phobias are directed towards things that would, in our ancestral pasts, have posed a real threat: snakes, spiders, open spaces, people in crowds and heights, for example. Arguably, then, phobias are simply a primed survival response – but no longer appropriate to the conditions in which we now live. It seems that we are wired to avoid, or possibly wired to learn to avoid, the things that would have posed the greatest threat to us when we lived on the savannah. Psychologist Martin Seligman coined the term 'preparedness' to refer to this evolutionary aspect of human phobias.[40] He noted that there seem to be three types of stimulus at which we are primed to be afraid. First, anything that might be linked to disease – such as dirt in general, rotting flesh, maggots. Secondly, there are dangerous animals – for example, snakes and spiders. Thirdly, there is a category that Seligman called 'conspecifics' – that is, other humans who pose a threat. Under this heading we might class xenophobia – which is actually the fear of strangers, although the term is now more widely used to refer to a dislike of other nations or cultures.

Conditioning experiments by Arne Öhman of the Karolinska Institute have shown that we are indeed more predisposed to fear objects or animals in these broad categories. Tests have entailed teaching non-phobic participants to associate a given image with fear by administering an electric shock to them as they viewed it.[41] They can be conditioned to feel fear much more swiftly when exposed to images of snakes or angry human faces than when exposed to images of, say, a smiling face or the sun. Evolution seems very likely to have played its part – shaping our brains so that we are most likely to become afraid of the things that pose the greatest threat to our survival.

Changing the mood

I enjoy the pleasures of a decent white burgundy or a good red Chambertin, particularly after a stressful day. In doing so I entertain a form of behaviour that shares similarities with that of less fortunate people using needles and crack pipes on the street. There seems to be no human society that does not engage in some drug use, whether for ritual or purely recreational purposes. Many religions – including my own – sanction the use of certain drugs. In Judaism, wine has a celebratory value – its properties are well recognized by the psalmist: 'wine that gladdeneth the heart of man'. In Christianity it has important symbolic value and is a key part of the sacrament. And, of course, it induces feelings of sociability and relaxation, arguably providing better conditions for people to get together and reaffirm friendship and values. In many indigenous societies, substances obtained from cacti, coca leaves, mushrooms and many other plants are taken in order to induce hallucinations or trance-like experiences. Sometimes the users hope to be thus in touch with a higher power, or alternative reality. In the 1960s, Harvard University professor Timothy Leary purchased a massive amount of the synthetic hallucinogenic drug LSD to bring about radical social change through the mass altering of brain chemistry. His famous words – 'Turn on, tune in, drop out' – landed him with a thirty-year jail sentence. For centuries before this, writers and artists experimented with a variety of substances, summed up by Aldous Huxley as 'a chemical vacation from intolerable selfhood'. Many artists, perhaps with some justification, have believed drugs enhance their creativity. Among writers alone, the list is endless: for example, Baudelaire and Yeats, who experimented with hashish, Rimbaud with absinthe, Coleridge, De Quincey and Keats with opium, and Balzac who required caffeine.

Using certain substances to alter our brain is so widespread and longstanding that it is arguable that it is a basic human drive, just as is living in groups, or establishing social hierarchies. Could drug use at some time have held any evolutionary advantage? Even today, the business of daily life is demanding and drugs that can temporarily relieve us, by making us forget or perceive the world differently, have some benefit in reducing stress. Some drugs help with the business of survival. The leaves of the coca shrub – the source of the drug cocaine – are chewed in South America to keep hunger at bay and banish tiredness at altitude. I have tried coca myself when climbing at 16,000 feet or more in the Andes in attempts to banish my altitude headache. I have to say it didn't work. Alcohol also can possibly produce temporary benefits – making us more courageous and daring at times of battle or attack, or keeping out the cold.

Drugs have a social purpose. Drinking alone is considered to be the hallmark of an unhappy, perhaps addicted personality. Drinking in company is more enjoyable, certainly – we laugh more, relax more. The same may be also true for many other drugs – including cannabis and cocaine. So drug use could act as a sort of 'social glue' – making group bonding easier and longer-lasting. Even substances used in a more formal setting, like the peyote cactus or the sacred 'herb' smoked by the Rastafarians, are used for a social purpose – worship. Any practice that unites humans and keeps them united has a survival benefit.

What do drugs do when we take them? Put extremely simply, they inhibit certain brain areas, such as the responsible, rational frontal lobes, and excite others, such as pathways which carry neurotransmitters like dopamine and serotonin. Drug usage generally has three different effects on brain chemistry and hence on behaviour and perception. Stimulant drugs, such as cocaine and amphetamine, promote feelings of euphoria, well-being and sociability. They also tend to produce a feeling of energy and accelerated thought-patterns.

Depressant drugs, such as alcohol or tranquillizers, have the reverse effect – slowing down mental processes, enhancing relaxation. Psychedelic drugs, as well as promoting a range of mood changes, alter perception and sensation. Users might feel that time passes incredibly slowly or absurdly fast. Objects might seem out of proportion and hallucinations might take place. The experience of a drug is frequently affected by a person's basic mood or their tendency to depression or anxiety. The circumstances in which the drug is taken, the user's body weight and the number of times they have taken it before all modify the feelings produced. Genetic influences also play a part – many Asians, for example, cannot easily tolerate alcohol because they cannot metabolize it readily.

Over recent years, the use of cannabis has become so widespread that certain police authorities have experimented with 'decriminalization'. Press campaigns have argued that smoking cannabis is no more harmful than getting drunk, and might be less so – since it does not seem to result in a loss of inhibition, or increase in violence. In certain, much-publicized cases, judges have refused to prosecute people who have maintained that they use cannabis for the purpose of their religion or to relieve pain from arthritis or multiple sclerosis. Every weekend, young people from a range of social backgrounds take mind-altering drugs. There is not space within this book to cover the whole panoply of mind-altering substances known to man, or even the most commonly available ones on the London streets, so I shall restrict comment to five that are taken by mouth or smoked. They are frequently regarded as 'not serious': nicotine, alcohol, cannabis, Ecstasy and LSD.

Nicotine

One of the most enigmatic drugs of all is nicotine. It is one of the most abused of all drugs and the consequences of smoking tobacco are widely known and extensively ignored by millions of humans. Cigarette smoking is a major health hazard in the USA, where around one-quarter of the adult population smokes. Most smokers are of younger age, have lower income and often have a poorer education. What seems important is that regular smoking is nearly always started before people become adults. We should be more disturbed still that smoking among adolescents is on the rise and it is very common to see children – perhaps under twelve years old – smoking in the street in both Britain and the US. There is extensive research on the social aspects of smoking and it is clear that if it is started early in adolescence there is less chance of it being stopped later in life.

Nicotine has a very complex mixture of effects in the brain, both depressing and stimulating. It enhances some aspects of cognition – for instance, it appears to improve short-term memory. Much important research has been done in rodents where nicotine can be given (by infusion in solution) to particular parts of the brain involved in memory, such as the amygdala and the hippocampus. After such infusions, it has been widely confirmed that rats perform better at remembering the way through a maze. There is some evidence that people who smoke seem less likely to develop either Alzheimer's disease or Parkinson's disease. Tests in patients suffering from Alzheimer's, attention deficit disorder or schizophrenia confirm they had quicker reaction times and better memory after wearing a small nicotine patch on their skin. Studies like this, combined with animal studies that are helping to evaluate the underlying mechanism, may have therapeutic implications.

Another interesting effect, which is not fully understood, is that nicotine decreases sensitivity to pain. This is controversial and different studies have given conflicting results, possibly because researchers did not always take the sex of their subject into account. Animal studies are confusing because different species show different degrees of pain relief. Dr Jamner's group in the Department of Psychology and Social Behaviour in the University of California compared men and women – they gave electric shocks across the skin of thirty male and forty-four female smokers and non-smokers. During these experiments, the volunteers wore a skin patch that in some instances contained nicotine and in others a neutral substance. Needless to say, the volunteers did not know whether their particular skin patch contained nicotine or not. Men 'on nicotine' tolerated pain better – but there was no demonstrable effect in women. It is well known that nicotine also has a considerable effect on mood, but these researchers took this into account and concluded that the effects they reported were directly due to the pain-killing action of nicotine. Some of the same researchers have also done work on stress and nicotine. Smoking a cigarette increases the heart rate but, in tobacco users particularly, smoking has a calming effect. Is there a difference between men and women, which could be due to hormones? Women smokers, whether on the contraceptive pill or not, did not increase their heart rate or blood pressure under stress as much as non-smokers. There was, however, no detectable difference between men who smoked and those who did not.

Nicotine, and smoking cigarettes, has a considerable effect on brain regions associated with how alert we are, some compulsive repetitive behaviour, and how we perceive various sensations. Tobacco addicts show activation of these regions during craving and when shown cigarette packets, a lighter or even an ashtray. This pattern of regional brain activity is very similar to that found with most other addictive substances. It may seem strange that the relatively mild effects of smoking – somewhat improved cognition, alertness, relaxation, for example – can result in such a powerful reward that so many users are so 'hooked' on the drug. But this, of course, is why studies on addiction generally are so relevant. Trying to understand the precise mechanisms of how nicotine acts in the brain, though extremely important, is horrendously difficult. It seems that there are numerous (at least twelve) different receptors to which this powerful tobacco product can bind in human and animal neurons. These receptors all have different effects on function, acting in different ways with various neurotransmitters. And in turn, of course, these receptors are produced by different genes. Genetic influences on the effects of cigarette smoking may be important in unravelling the complex issues raised by this addiction.

Alcohol

Among other actions, alcohol has potent effects on areas of the brain-stem called the locus coeruleus and the raphe nuclei. These play an important role in both motor coordination and alertness, which unsurprisingly are two of the functions most impaired by having a drink or three. Substances like morphine have specific receptor sites within the brain – indeed our brain manufactures its own morphine in the form of endorphins, which are released in response to pain, stress and physical effort. Alcohol is different. It has no receptor sites of its own within the brain. Its molecules are electrically uncharged, which means that they are attracted to similarly uncharged regions within the brain — such as those that exist within the membranes of our neurons. As a result, alcohol has the potential to disrupt pretty much every brain function.

Alcohol also causes release of dopamine in the nucleus accumbens — the brain's reward system — which is why we perceive its initial effects as being pleasurable. This activity within our reward system also explains why alcohol use has what psychologists call a 'reinforcing effect'. In other words, we return to patterns of behaviour that give us pleasure. So however much you swear stoutly, as you gaze blankly into a fizzing glass of Alka–Seltzer, that you're never going to touch a drop again, science shows that you'll need will power.

Some of alcohol's effects may have less to do with its chemical actions on the brain and more to do with the very pervasive power of suggestion. Psychologists have performed tests on people who are receiving a dose of alcohol and others who believe they are but in fact are imbibing straight tonic water. They have found that believing you are drinking can in itself be sufficient to produce many of the symptoms of being drunk, such as sexual arousal and aggression.

Cannabis

In Britain, particularly among some younger people, cannabis is becoming almost as widely used as alcohol. Until the 1960s, when people like me began to travel to so-called 'hippie havens' like Morocco, India and the Far East, its use was largely confined to a small, rather sophisticated elite of musicians, painters and the like, and also to sailors in big ports. I remember my surprise at seeing the extent of its use in Afghanistan, when I arrived tattered, unkempt and malodorous in Kabul in 1963. But in 2003, a short walk through London's Camden Market attests to the different state of affairs now. The widespread availability of drug paraphernalia — papers, pipes, tins and fashion items bearing the distinctive saw-tooth design of the *Cannabis sativa* leaf — demonstrates the extent to which the use of this drug has become a 'normal' activity.

Cannabis is often presented as being a 'natural' and safe alternative to other drugs — but 'natural' doesn't equate to 'safe' or 'harmless'. Opium is 'natural' — it can be directly extracted from the heads of poppies. Cocaine comes from the leaves of a shrub. Many other sub-stances are also directly obtainable from plants, some of them very potent poisons – hemlock, muscarine and atropine, for example, all of which, incidentally, have been used in one society or another (with great danger to the users) for their mind-bending properties. We should not be seduced into believing that 'natural' always means 'good'. Everything we put into our bodies has an effect. Even drink-ing too much water direct from the purest mountain spring carries a risk – in excess, it can cause death.

Cannabis use as hemp, marijuana and hashish has a long pedigree. The earliest references to the drug come from Chinese texts dating back to 2737BC, indicating that it was used medicinally to treat rheumatism, bowel disorders and, bizarrely, absent-mindedness. Excavations of graves in Western Europe and the Middle East have indicated that ancient peoples may have sprinkled cannabis seeds onto hot stones – possibly as a treatment for pain, possibly for ritual pur-poses. Much more recently, writers like Baudelaire and his notorious Club des Hachichins (named after the hashishins, or assassins: trained killers in the pay of Arab sultans) took cannabis resin and reported transcendent experiences. (Alcohol has a medicinal history too. In the nineteenth century and early twentieth century, alcohol, usually in the form of brandy, was widely used on prescription in Britain for its medicinal value. We used to keep it on the ward at the London Hospital when I was a houseman there, and very useful it was to revive the physician after a difficult night-call.) Doctors only stopped giving tincture of cannabis for pain relief because it had such variable absorp-tion when given by mouth and because there were no standardized preparations of the plant extract. Added to which, pain-killing tablets of drugs like aspirin, paracetamol and codeine were more effective.

Cannabis contains over four hundred separate chemical com-pounds, sixty of which are believed to have a direct effect on the brain. The most potent is THC – tetrahydracannabinol. Research in the 1980s and 1990s has shown that there are specific receptor sites for THC, distributed throughout the brain. The areas most endowed with cannabinoid receptors are in the hippocampus, cerebellum, basal ganglia and hypothalamus. In these regions, THC acts to reduce the firing of neurons. So we have a general idea of how the drug can affect various faculties. For instance, one of the roles of the hypo-thalamus is in regulating appetite – cannabis users often report feelings of great hunger. Motor functions — carried out by the cerebellum and basal ganglia — are impaired by cannabis. According to figures published by the American National Institute on Drug Abuse, 6–11 per cent of fatal-accident victims have THC in their blood. The memory – in which the hippocampus plays a big role – is significantly impaired by cannabis use. Rats exposed to THC for eight months showed the sort of cell loss in the hippocampus that is equivalent to what we would normally expect in rats twice their age. Cannabis compounds release dopamine and this action, and the pleasurable effects of the drug, can be blocked by drugs that prevent opiates having a similar effect. One such drug is naloxone, which is used by anaesthetists to bring people round after an anaesthetic.

But we do not fully understand how THC acts on the brain to produce many of the pleasant effects of cannabis, such as heightened perception and relaxation. There are cannabinoid receptor sites within the cerebral cortex, and any disruption to normal chemistry here would result in changes to thought processes. Cannabis may also have specific effects on an area of the basal ganglia called the substantia nigra – which is responsible for the production of voluntary action. Many users do report feelings of lethargy and a lack of will to do anything, which might be a result of interference to this area. But that said, not every user is affected in the same way. The American comedian Lenny Bruce said he avoided cannabis because it made him highly excitable and overactive. Some people experience real anxiety, are paranoid and feel persecuted. Other users have visual and auditory hallucinations that are not always pleasant. It is still not entirely understood why this should happen in some cases and not others – other than by saying that some individuals seem to have predisposition, particularly if they have suffered from some form of mental illness in the past. We have always used the term 'not a happy drunk' to describe people for whom alcohol's effects are chiefly negative, so it should not be surprising that there are some unhappy cannabis smokers out there, too.

In 1998, a House of Lords Select Committee examined the use of cannabis for medical purposes.[42] The enquiry was because a number of patients, mostly suffering from nerve disorders such as disseminated sclerosis, were taking cannabis to relieve their symptoms of pain, nausea, visual problems and trembling. What they were risking was prosecution and a prison sentence, particularly if, with legal supplies impossible to obtain, they grew they own plants. The committee was broadly very sympathetic to their plight and recommended to the government that clinical trials of cannabis compounds should be commenced urgently – for if the drug were used for medical purposes, of course, decriminalization would have been needed. Within a mere six hours of publication of the report, a government minister rejected the findings of the committee totally – demonstrating, I think, poor judgement. This predictable knee-jerk reaction was produced by concerns about any form of drug taking in our society – except alcohol and cigarettes, which are, of course, responsible for far more deaths and disease in UK than any other environmental factor.

There is an amusing endnote to this enquiry. Every Select Committee calls a press conference when it launches a new report. On this occasion, just before the press conference, our parliamentary clerk, who ran the affairs of the committee brilliantly, pointed out that the press were bound to ask each of us on the committee whether we had taken cannabis. He suggested very tactfully that we should decide well in advance how we might respond to that question, clearly expecting that we would give an answer which might not be, how shall I say, too controversial. I admit that I was one of their lordships who had in the distant past some minor experience of the effects of this drug. As I was sitting there wondering what I might confess to, Lord Porter, the wonderful octogenarian – a brilliant academic from my university who won the Nobel Prize in 1967 for chemistry – leaned across to me and whispered, 'I've never ever taken cannabis.' And then, rather wistfully, 'What's it like?'

Ecstasy

Since the end of the 1980s, a synthetic drug called methyldioxymethamphetamine, or MDMA, has become popular among devotees of certain kinds of dance music. Known as Ecstasy, or simply 'E' and 'X' by its users, it rapidly gained a stronghold in youth culture. In January 2002, the *Observer* newspaper claimed that it had access to a police report in which it was stated that two million Ecstasy pills were taken in Britain every weekend. This is double the amount reported by the European drug monitoring centre in 1999.

The drug was first patented by the German pharmaceutical

company Merck in 1913, though never marketed. It is believed that Merck intended to develop it as an appetite suppressant, though for reasons now obscure the drug remained forgotten. Between 1977 and 1985, a few experimental therapists obtained permission to test it in psychotherapy sessions. The recipe for the drug was obtained, it seems, by underground chemists in the USA during the 1980s. As the drug's popularity increased, organized criminals took over its production and supply on a mass scale. Some estimates suggest that the bulk of the pills that come to Britain, and which now retail at between £10 and £20 a time, originate in Dutch laboratories, where they are produced for between 10 and 20 pence.

Ecstasy's chief effect on the brain seems to be in binding to serotonin receptors – which prevents the neurotransmitter from being reabsorbed. This means there is an increased quantity of serotonin remaining in the synapses. In turn, this leads to the short-term effects of positive mood and amiability, as well as increased energy. The action of increased serotonin on the hypothalamus and the brainstem also accounts for the loss of appetite and muscle spasms seen in users.

Ecstasy also increases levels of dopamine, as well as blocking its reabsorption. This explains two more of the drug's effects. First, many users find it pleasurable and want to take it again. And secondly their experience of the drug sometimes results in an exaggerated feeling of meaningfulness and significance. To quote the young Ecstasy-user in the *Observer* article: 'It's the best, most positive experience of my life. It's life-enhancing.' High levels of dopamine have been observed in people suffering from mania and psychotic delusions – states of mind not dissimilar to those attained by mystics and users of certain drugs. People report sensations of almost religious intensity – seeing reality 'as it really is', perceiving themselves and the world around them as some beautifully ordered design of interlinked phenomena.

Compared to the estimated numbers of regular users, the number of Ecstasy-related deaths is relatively low. The police reported sixty fatalities up to 2001. Quite rightly, much is made of these deaths in the media – they are made more poignant by the fact that most of the victims are young people at the threshold of adult life. Whether all the deaths are due directly to the drug is open to question. There are very obvious risks associated with swallowing any substance whose origins are not known. Manufactured by individuals who may not even have a chemistry textbook, merely some dubious information from the internet, Ecstasy is by no means a safe drug. The high profits involved mean that there is a great risk of unscrupulous behaviour on the part of the sellers. Police drug squads regularly seize tablets that actually turn out to be for dog worming or fish-tank oxygenating, and others that contain high levels of other, cheaper drug compounds.

There have been calls to downgrade Ecstasy as a serious drug, thus reducing the penalties for possession and supply. Advocates of the change argue that there is no proven link between Ecstasy and violence – as there is with alcohol. They also argue that it does not lead users into violent crime to finance a habit – unlike crack cocaine or heroin.

For myself, the most compelling evidence against downgrading the drug comes from neuroscience. Andy Parrott of the University of East London has studied the short- and long-term effects of Ecstasy on brain chemistry. He has found that as many as one in five first-time users experience some memory loss. Regular use also interferes with the brain's continuing ability to produce serotonin – resulting in sleeplessness and depression. Dr George Hatzidimitriou and colleagues at the National Institute of Mental Health in Bethesda have done some important work in monkeys.[43] They found that alterations to serotonin neurons lasted up to seven years after Ecstasy usage, and that nerve cells that were damaged frequently regenerated abnormally. A survey conducted by Britain's National Addiction Centre found that one in four regular users of the drug were likely to develop a serious psychiatric disorder. Although the chance of any member of the population developing psychiatric problems is high, this figure is still above the national average of one in five. There should be no talk of downgrading the drug until more is known about its harmful side effects.

LSD

Woodcuts dating back to the Middle Ages depict a phenomenon known as St Anthony's fire in which whole communities became seized by a sort of collective brain fever, dancing in the streets until they dropped from exhaustion. Such episodes were probably triggered by the ingestion of a substance called ergot – a fungus that grows on rye. Among other things, ergot causes the contraction of blood vessels – which can lead to brain disturbances and circulatory problems.

One of the most wonderful men I ever met was Professor J. Chassar Moir from Oxford, my old boss – a brilliant surgeon and a rounded, modest academic. He was responsible for synthesizing the active principle in ergot, to make ergometrine in the 1930s. This drug contracts the uterus and its blood vessels so effectively and safely that millions of lives have been saved around the world. Severe haemorrhage after giving birth is now almost a rarity. By the 1940s, a Swiss pharmaceutical company was researching the possible therapeutic properties of ergot. Subsequently ergot was in some of the first effective treatments for migraine – some of which are still in use today. While attempting to isolate certain further constituents of ergot, a chemist called Albert Hoffmann inadvertently spilt some on his skin. His account of what next occurred has entered legend.

Forty minutes later, Hoffmann experienced dizziness, visual distortions and paralysis. He became so worried that he asked one of his lab staff to help him get home. The journey was undertaken by bicycle because of wartime fuel shortages, and by the time Hoffmann arrived at his house, he was undergoing a terrifying set of sensations. 'Familiar objects and pieces of furniture assumed grotesque, threatening forms. The lady next door [who brought Hoffmann some milk to drink] . . . was no longer Mrs R., but rather a malevolent, insidious witch with a coloured mask.' Hoffmann says that more terrifying than his distorted perception of the outer world was his sense of a radical change in himself. 'Every attempt to put an end to the disintegration of the outer world and the dissolution of my ego, seemed to be a wasted effort. A demon had invaded me. I was taken to another world, another place, another time.'[44]

It seems hard to believe, from Hoffmann's haunted and haunting account, that this drug, lysergic acid diethylamide, could ever become at all popular. It sounds like the very worst sort of nightmare. But in the 1960s, drug use did not have the stigma attached to it that it has now. Drug-related crime was much less common, and Western society was coming out of a long post-war period of restraint and rationing. Young people had a bit more money and more time and there was a feeling of freedom in the air.

A research chemist called John Beresford, intrigued by Hoffmann's account, purchased an amount of the drug from the Swiss pharmaceutical company. Via Beresford, a Harvard University lecturer called Timothy Leary – who was then researching the effects of hallucinogenic mushrooms – tried some on a sugar cube. So impressed was Leary by his experiences that he ended up ordering another hundred grams. Throughout the 1960s, a time of wild optimism in many quarters, LSD was taken widely by devotees of the 'beatnik' culture. Many saw their experiences while under the influence as being equivalent to the mystic states described by Eastern philosophers and religious figures. For a time it was even used experimentally in psychiatric hospitals for depression and schizophrenia.

Now I come up hard against a familiar problem, a recurrent theme throughout this book. St Augustine put it rather beautifully when he wrote, 'I cannot grasp all that I am.' I have only my brain to interpret my brain. And I can only convey my experiences using the terms of my own experiences. I have not taken LSD, and rely on the accounts of other individuals who have – whose own accounts, of course, can only convey what it was like for them. In the 1960s, there was a famous televised attempt to convey an acid-trip, using two grey-suited, well-spoken presenters, very much of the BBC school. The episode is hilarious for its upright, very correct approach to the material. As the drug takes hold of the presenter, he stiffly reports distortions to space and time, rather as if he were reading a serious news item. At one stage in the planning for the TV series *The Human Body*, it was suggested that I might like to do this experiment. In the end, we decided that to do so might seem irresponsible. Admittedly, the amounts of LSD – about 80–100 micrograms – now taken in the common street form of the drug are tiny compared to what Hoffmann and Leary took. Nonetheless, the effects of the drug can be very potent at even this low level.

LSD users report a range of mental phenomena. Visual and spatial distortions are most common – objects appear to have an aura, or to leave a trace when they move. Sometimes they are frozen in space, even when moving. Things may seem out of proportion – a friend spent an evening sitting in an armchair chuckling at the enormous size of his hands. Users also report swift and inexplicable mood changes – feelings of great happiness bubbling up for no apparent reason, sometimes to be replaced by foreboding, sadness, even terror. The drug is slow-acting, reaching its peak some four to five hours after ingestion – a factor that can be dangerous when people, thinking the drug isn't working, decide to take more. At the peak of its effectivity, people can experience a range of unusual sensations – such as of being weightless, or pinned to the ground.

There is a wealth of literature on the subject of the LSD experience – such as Aldous Huxley's *Doors of Perception*. Some acid users seem to have undergone what we might call a merging of self and other – such that they no longer experience themselves as being separate from the world outside. This in turn has many similarities to the states of mind that mystics have written about for centuries. On the other hand, plenty of people seem to take LSD and do little more than sit round feeling generally 'odd'.

Little is currently known about the effects of LSD on brain chemistry. Structurally, the drug is similar to serotonin itself – in the same way that the hallucinogenic drug mescaline, from the magic mushroom, resembles the neurotransmitter norepinephrine. If such drugs are administered to rats, there is a shutting down of neuronal activity in the raphe nuclei. This is interesting, because this is a brain area associated with waking and sleeping (see above). During REM sleep, when we have some of our most fantastical and vivid dream experiences, the raphe nuclei is similarly inactive. So, arguably, LSD acts to bring on a state of wakeful dreaming in our brains.

The locus coeruleus, the brainstem area next to the raphe nuclei, goes into overdrive in the presence of hallucinogenic drugs like LSD. When this area is stimulated in rats, they become excessively aware – easily startled by the tiniest of stimuli. So we could argue that LSD has a two-fold action – making us super-tuned to the sensory input of our environments, but also making our brains interpret this information in a dream-like fashion.

Degrees of addiction

LSD is not considered to be addictive – indeed, people seem to build a tolerance to it very quickly, such that they need to wait a few weeks between doses if they want to experience the same effects with a similar dose. Drugs like heroin and alcohol, on the other hand, are considered to have strong addictive properties. If long-term users are unable to find a supply of their chosen drug, they experience physical withdrawal symptoms. It is not thought that cocaine, Ecstasy or cannabis have these addictive properties, yet people do report becoming dependent upon them in just the same way. Crack cocaine is especially notorious for inducing powerful cravings.

So how can this be so, if our bodies do not create a need for the substance in question? The answer returns us to the brain's reward system – to the importance of dopamine in areas like the nucleus accumbens, and to the power of conditioning. Cocaine use results directly in an increase of dopamine in the nucleus accumbens – in other words, the drug taps deep into our personal reward structures. We also know that rats will self-administer any substance that has the same action upon their nucleus accumbens. This includes cannabis and Ecstasy. Whenever we indulge in any form of pleasurable behaviour, we are creating a neuronal pathway between our reward centres and any associated memories of the experience. The link between the two is so strong that heroin and cocaine addicts can report powerful cravings for the drug simply on being reintroduced to features of the environment in which they used to take it. For instance, the sight of mirrors and silver foil, teaspoons and needles, or even the streets where the drug was bought, can lead to real physiological changes which are associated with withdrawal, such as raised heartbeat and blood pressure. When ex-cocaine addicts were shown items of drug paraphernalia in one study, brain scans revealed activity in the prefrontal cortex and the anterior cingulate, areas associated with motivation. Their brains were gearing them up to go in search of the drug, thanks to the tiniest of clues from the environment.

So it is easy to see why so many people, having kicked a habit, start to use drugs again – especially when they find themselves back in the same environment. In 1971, epidemiologist Lee Robins studied 898 US soldiers in Vietnam. Half made heavy use of narcotics, such as opium, heroin and morphine. Around 225 reported symptoms compatible with addiction to these drugs. Robins did a follow-up study of these soldiers after they had returned to the United States, and found that 95 per cent of the addicts had stopped using drugs. This suggests that, for these soldiers, all the cues or triggers that caused them to want drugs were associated with Vietnam. Once they were away from these cues, their need for the drugs went away.

Broadly speaking, virtually all drugs acting on the brain that change perception not only have harmful side effects at the time, but can cause permanent damage. The irreparable harm may be partly because the constant reinforcement of connections changes the working of the mind permanently. Alcohol can be regarded as a paradigm. We may think that alcohol use is relatively trivial, and being tipsy a bit of a joke. Let us leave aside the lost working days caused by alcohol use. It is by far the most widely abused drug and one that has huge negative effects on the health services in nearly every country. In Britain over 15 per cent of people attending accident and emergency units have alcohol-related injuries. Around 25 per cent of men admitted as emergencies to hospital are there because of alcohol abuse; over 5,000 people a year die in England and Wales as a direct result of its effects. Drink costs the NHS around three billion pounds a year, resulting in more than 28,000 hospital admissions.

Apart from its effects on other major organs like the heart and liver, alcohol can bring about a most profound change in the brain. It may appear to be a stimulant, but it is mostly a central nervous system depressant. It interferes with the neurotransmitter GABA, and frontal cortical control is progressively lost. The details are not pleasant. Although initially there may be a feeling of happiness and well-being, alcohol produces loss of emotional control, violent behaviour, inability to coordinate movement, nausea, confusion, stupor (when the individual is barely rousable) and coma. Alcoholic coma is not a minor problem – it results in death in about 1 in 20 cases. Once people who use alcohol heavily are habituated to this drug after five or so years, blackouts, nightmares and hallucinations are common if drinking stops. Withdrawal also produces uncontrolled trembling of the limbs, delirium and epileptic attacks that do not always respond to anti-epileptic drugs. Prolonged use of alcohol results in brain degeneration, particularly of the cerebellum with loss of Purkinje cells, and nutritional disorders with visual disturbance, loss of memory and impaired intellect. While this is not by any means a complete list of the horrors, dementia caused by loss of cortical neurons, nerve damage and palsy are also well documented. Finally, it should be mentioned that in my own field of medicine, alcohol abuse has a profound effect on the baby in the uterus – including causing abnormalities of head and face development, and of brain function. Alcohol can have an effect every bit as severe as repeated sporting trauma from boxing, or, of course, a major head injury.

Perhaps, before finishing, we could do worse than return briefly to poor Phineas Gage for him to have the final word. Once Dr Harlow had had his skull dug up years after his death, it was kept carefully in Harvard. Recently, Hannah and Antonio Damasio published an interesting reappraisal of the injuries Gage sustained.[45] Having photographed the skull inside and out and taken rigorous measurements of it, then compared these with the measurements of the tamping iron, they started to assess the clues. Careful assessment of the bone lost from the cranium, a missing molar tooth and a small chip on the left facial bone gave useful information. With the help of three-dimensional modelling of the brain and appropriate computing, they and their colleagues built up seven possible trajectories for the rod as it passed through the brain. Because there had been no infection, this excluded any trajectory piercing the fluid-filled ventricles of the brain, thus eliminating two possible pathways.

Finally, by a process of elimination, careful deduction and knowing basic clinical information such as the fact that Gage had intact speech after the event (and, therefore, Broca's area must have remained intact) a complete picture was built up. Detailed knowledge of the configuration of a modern brain was obviously important. Using this remarkable forensic process, the Damasios were able to give a reliable best estimate of the precise path the rod must have taken. Their results clearly showed that critical damage had occurred to the prefrontal cortex in its ventromedial region. This is the area which at least in part controls emotional processing, social cognition and behaviour. But the areas to the side, which process other aspects of cognition such as language, arithmetical ability and our perception of personal space, would have been undamaged. Interesting, too, that the damaged region has a high concentration of serotonin receptors. Work in monkeys has shown that low serotonin levels are found consistently in monkeys that are aggressive and socially un-cooperative. So perhaps, after all, like some of those patients undergoing prefrontal lobotomy, Phineas Gage had lost his soul through no fault of his own – beyond a brief moment of, until then, uncharacteristic carelessness.

chapter**six**
The learning mind

Holy Roman Emperor Frederick II (1194–1250) had a reputation as an amateur scholar. He filled his court with the famous astrologers and savants of the day. He wrote a book on the taming of falcons, and so insistent was he on the correct use of language that he once had the thumbs removed from one unfortunate scribe who spelt his name wrong – *Fredericus* instead of *Fridericus*. He was particularly fond of personally conducting experiments, which usually involved a strong element of cruelty. There are detailed accounts of Frederick written by Salimbene of Parma, an Italian Franciscan friar who died in 1287. Salimbene certainly recognized the Emperor's excesses but seems to have admired him. According to him, Frederick once selected two men, fed them handsomely upon a range of delicacies, and then ordered one of the men to go to sleep, and the other to go out hunting. The next morning, he had them both disembowelled in front of him, expecting to see that the man who slept had spent more time digesting. The court physician decreed that the man who slept had indeed digested his food better — but he may have made this up as everyone who worked for Frederick II was afraid of saying anything to challenge him. In another bizarre experiment, the Emperor had two convicts sealed up in an airtight room. Frederick observed the room closely from outside, hoping to see the moment at which the men's souls left their bodies and escaped.

But Frederick II is better known for his interest in languages. He was inspired by an account in Herodotus of the Greek scholar

Psammetichus, who wished to discover whether the Egyptians or the Phrygians – ancestors of the Greeks – had been the original race on earth. To this end Psammetichus seized two newborn children from their parents and had them brought up in complete isolation, with guardians who never spoke to them. According to Herodotus, the first word one of the children spoke was 'becos' – which meant 'bread' in the Phrygian tongue, and which thereby established to the delighted Greeks that they were the true inheritors of the earth. Frederick, unsatisfied by this account, decided to replicate the experiment. To make absolutely certain that his human guinea pigs would be exposed to no human language at all, he ensured that their caregivers were all deaf and dumb. The results displeased him considerably. Frederick had expected them to speak Hebrew – the first language, as he thought. But these children acquired neither Hebrew, nor for that matter Latin or Greek. Raised in these highly restricted conditions, they seemed to be lacking in intelligence, and unable to learn.

In Chapter 2, we dipped briefly into why Frederick's tinkerings were doomed to fail. The brain is a highly plastic organ – its neural connections group and regroup themselves according to the information that goes in. Functions like speech and language that are unexercised, particularly when we are very young, do not develop properly and their neurons become taken over by other faculties.

The brain in the womb

The brain goes through frenzied development in the womb – adding as many as 250,000 neurons a minute. And it grows after birth, reaching 80 per cent of the adult weight by the time the baby is two years old. At the same time, there is the sweeping, ruthless pruning process called apoptosis, which tailors the brain according to the needs imposed upon it by the environment. Apoptosis, a word coined by Hippocrates, is derived from the Greek meaning 'falling leaves', and is nowadays taken to describe the process of cell death. This process is present in all organs, particularly during early development; the most striking example of it that I can recall is the development of the hand. In the womb, our hands start off as paddles, but early on the webbing between the fingers dies away by apoptosis to leave separate fingers. All of us will be familiar with the growth of the tadpole, losing its tail and in the process developing into a frog.

And in the womb, the brain begins to develop after the first fortnight following conception. The first structure forms at around sixteen days – the neural plate. Over the next five days, this elliptical structure widens and flattens to resemble a circle with a groove cut into the top. The groove then closes over, so that what we have is a tube within a tube. The front end of this neural tube goes on to create the human brain, and its back end turns into the spinal cord. From around this point until birth, the brain will massively increase in weight – dividing and multiplying in just the fashion cells can be seen to do under a microscope. First the front end of the neural tube splits into three sections: the forebrain, midbrain and hindbrain. At seven weeks' gestation, each of these three structures divides again.

The early years

By birth, some faculties of the brain are present, but not yet fully connected. Much of the most active areas in newborns are related to survival at its most basic – breathing, feeding, sensation and movement. At the same time, other connections are present at birth that will not persist into childhood and adulthood. For instance, there are connections between the auditory and visual cortices which indicate that infants – if they could only tell us – are probably synaesthetes in their early years, hearing colours and seeing sounds. In most people, apoptosis prunes this faculty away before the hippocampus matures, ensuring that we cannot remember having it.

We tested the memory of some of our research team. One colleague could recall being terrified of a grandfather clock when lifted up to see it, at what must have been somewhere between two and three years old. Another recalled the shock of a goose entering the house and making a great racket – this can't have been after she was three years old, because she knows when her family moved from the countryside to the town. Significantly – although this is only a straw poll conducted over mid-morning coffees – these memories are clustered around a similar age. My own first memory – and I very much doubt that I am making this up – goes back to when I was around one year old. I remember being incredibly angry with my parents when I was left in a pram in a garden, in Crich in Derbyshire, on a summer holiday during the war. We only stayed in that vegetarian guesthouse twice – once when I was around twelve or thirteen months old and again when I was four – and I remember that garden very well, particularly the second time because my father gave me a balsawood aircraft to fly, which broke against the hedge on its first sortie. As I have never seen photographs of the garden, I think it likely that my memory is genuine and not reinforced by what I have seen subsequently, as so often happens with memories of early childhood.

As the hippocampus, site of the brain's long-term memory, does not reach maturity until we are three years old, it is very likely that most 'early memories' are false. People who say they can remember being in the womb, or being born, are probably mistaken. The human brain is like a complex building. It takes a long time for its various rooms and walkways to be constructed and furnished. It's a process so drawn out that, as we have already seen, some parts of our brain do not reach maturity until we are in our late teens, even in our twenties.

It is hard to say to what extent newborns experience the range of emotions that adults do. To the untrained ear, the crying of a baby sounds like an undifferentiated racket. But experienced mothers and nursing professionals feel they can often distinguish differences. A one-month-old baby can communicate varying messages, such as hunger, discomfort and fear, in specific ways. Many mothers report that the specific sound of their baby crying can induce a powerful bodily sensation in themselves. The American psychologist Jaak Panksepp suggests we all experience something similar when we listen to certain pieces of music and feel a shiver up the spine. Music most likely to trigger the 'tingle factor' (as one BBC Radio 4 programme called it) in listeners very often contains unexpected shifts of harmony or long build-ups to the completion of a certain musical phrase. Panksepp noted that the cries of human and animal infants, when separated from their mothers, follow the same pattern. I am not convinced by this description but it does seem that some mothers experience a drop in body temperature on hearing such cries, which is corrected when they are reunited with their infants. So even very small babies are able to express key messages in order to survive.

Other faculties seem to be present from day one of a newborn's life, or soon thereafter. Alan Slater at Exeter University examines babies when they are just one or two days old. His research indicates that, even at this stage, babies show a preference for looking at more attractive, symmetrical human faces. Like adults, they also show an instinctive interest in whatever is the most novel or unusual feature in their environment. In this respect, I remember with great fondness the late Dr David Baum, latterly Professor of Paediatrics at Oxford and more recently in Bristol, and first President of the Royal College of Paediatrics. When we were both in training at Hammersmith Hospital, David, who was then interested in the welfare of very small babies, invented the Baum nose. He would enter the neonatal unit wearing a large bow tie and a huge red clown's nose. Leaning over a newborn's cot he would very solemnly and very slowly move his head from side to side and then suddenly turn on a light inside the nose from a switch concealed in his pocket. If the baby moved its head from side to side to peer at his nose, David Baum would declare that this baby had an intact nervous system and was unlikely to be brain-damaged.

Throughout the first year of life, brain activity increases in the parietal, temporal and visual cortex, as well as in the basal ganglia and cerebellum. A full account of early brain development is beyond the scope of this book but we can see the effects of this growth spurt as the baby develops hand–eye coordination and spatial awareness. At this stage, one of the tireless favourites is 'peek-a-boo'. The baby's dawning understanding of the space it occupies becomes a source of fascination. The teddy bear has momentarily disappeared. Surely things can't just disappear? Or can they? As the bear remains hidden, a note of uncertainty and then anxiety creeps in. Perhaps, after all, the newly formed theory is wrong, and bears can disappear? Suddenly the stuffed toy is jumped back into view, and the baby laughs with a mixture of relief and joy. Through very simple games like this, babies learn to test out their theories and possibly to cope with acceptable levels of concern and anxiety.

Indeed, babies and young children test their theories on the world around them like tiny scientists. Peter Willatts at the University of Dundee performed a problem-solving experiment with six- to nine-month-old babies. A toy was placed out of reach on a tablecloth, behind a foam block, and then covered with a cloth. To get the toy, the babies had to devise and execute a three-step plan: pull the tablecloth to bring the whole assembly nearer, move the block out of the way and then lift the cloth. The six-month-old babies were incapable of doing any of this. The seven- and eight-month-olds could manage one or two steps of the sequence. It was not until the babies reached between nine and ten months that they could follow the whole sequence through. Dr Willatts, comparing his results to studies performed on the maturing infant brain, concluded that the planning and sequencing of action was only possible once the prefrontal cortex had reached a certain level of maturity.

Breastfeeding is best for early brain development and intelligence might be affected by whether or not a baby has been breastfed. Some mothers, for various reasons, either cannot or will not breastfeed. The standard formula milk bought over the counter is not an ideal substitute for it does not have the optimal ingredients for best nutrition. Dr Willatts considered that this might have implications for a child's subsequent learning ability when commencing school, so he compared children who as small babies had had bottle milk plus a special fat supplement he had researched, with those who had had standard formula milk. The particular fats he considers important are long-chain polyunsaturated fatty acids, present in breastmilk.

It turns out that babies who had had his supplement for the first four months were sharper and faster five or six years later. Six-year-olds who had been fed supplemented milk were not only more mentally alert and had a higher IQ, they were also better at solving problems – for example analysing and matching up photographs given to them under experimental conditions. So the moral is clear – breast is best.

The frontal lobes are the last area in the growing brain to become active – starting their journey at around seven months and continuing steadily until about two years. By the age of one, these fledgling frontal lobes are beginning to exercise control over the drives of the lower brain. Babies of this age can make a choice if offered one toy or another. Until this stage, most babies' attention can be diverted by any stimulus. But once the frontal lobes begin to grow, their little owner starts to develop his or her own priorities – fixating upon the fragile antique porcelain china, for example, rather than the slightly moth-eaten teddy bear being frantically waved in front of them.

Language begins to develop at eighteen months – although as we shall see later, even newborn brains are tailoring themselves to the communication-related elements of their environment. Wernicke's area – a banana-shaped sweep of neurons situated close to the ear in the left hemisphere – deals with language comprehension. It matures much faster than Broca's area, a smaller cone of material in the frontal lobe, which deals with language production. You can address quite complex instructions to two-year-olds, and they will understand you, without having the ability to respond. The shortfall between the two faculties might explain why children at this age – the so-called 'terrible twos' – can become so angry and frustrated. What I find interesting is that the ability to speak develops at quite a variable age. In the case of my own children, one refused to speak until fairly late (around two years old), one spoke at not much more than a year and one at around eighteen months. This in no way seems to be related to their ability or intelligence. It may be that some babies, being more or less contented with their environment, have a varying urge to communicate verbally.

The frontal lobes develop alongside the language areas, giving rise to the onset of self-consciousness. Children begin to understand themselves as separate entities, and to realize that other people have their own internal states. Language development both helps and is helped by this awareness: we use language to describe our own states, and to receive information about that of others. And it is only through being able to see yourself as a doing-I and a done-to-me that you can start to form basic subject-object-verb sentences. For instance: I (subject) hit (doing verb) the truck (object).

Although the two-year-old brain is very close in shape and weight to an adult brain, other faculties take years to fully develop – growing, shrinking back and growing anew in the meantime. For instance, an area called the reticular formation, a group of neurons that begins in the brainstem and projects up into the cerebral cortex and basal ganglia, plays an important part in maintaining attention. This only becomes fully developed at puberty – one reason why smaller children have a shorter attention span.

Puberty

Much of human communication is non-verbal. Our ability to read the facial expressions of others develops in yo-yo fashion – increasing at certain ages, shrinking back at others. Puberty seems to put the whole process on hold. This was shown in a study by Robert McGivern at San Diego State University.[46] His research team took a pool of volunteers, half of whom were pubescent and half of whom had not yet reached puberty. Black and white images of faces were flashed up on a computer monitor to each group for a very brief period – just one-eighth of a second. The volunteers were shown angry, happy, sad and neutral images, and were asked to say what kind of face they had seen while their reaction times were tested.

The results showed that the younger children, both boys and girls, were better at reading facial expressions than teenagers. And brain scans showed that a particular area of the prefrontal cortex was smaller in the teenagers than it was in the children. One explanation may be that the transition to adulthood, in brain and body, calls for a massive internal effort. As we might have to draft in an army of architects, builders, carpenters, painters and electricians to renovate a house, the developing teenage body and brain need to employ a raft of resources. Some of these come from outside – which is why teenagers have the ability to get through a week's worth of food shopping in a few hours. But other changes have to come from within, which means some economies have to be made. Certain brain areas shrink back to allow others the maximum resources – neuronal material, neuro-transmitters, glucose – as they develop.

For some faculties to be acquired, others have to be lost, at least temporarily. In turn, we can begin to see the reasons behind some of the most perplexing and frustrating aspects of teenage behaviour. Of course there is a risk involved when the brain deliberately sheds some of its faculties. In fact, we see this kind of trade-off throughout nature: testosterone, for instance, gives us strength, but may also shorten life-span. There is a quid pro quo in the growing brain. A reduced ability to read facial expressions may not seem particularly serious. But con-sider how important this is in sensing danger.

Teenagers – even those not driving – are the group most at risk from road traffic accidents. Being permanently plugged into personal CDs and MP3 players to escape the chiding voices of their parents might provide a partial explanation. But MRI studies also indicate that the brain of a teenager may not have a fully developed capacity to assess threats. Deborah Yurgelun-Todd of McLean Hospital in the United States, in a study which admittedly leaves a number of im-portant questions unanswered, flashed forty faces showing fearful expressions to adolescents aged between eleven and seventeen.[47] Younger teenagers reacted with fuller activity in the amygdala but less in the frontal lobes, while older females showed greater activation in the frontal lobes. Further studies indicated that adult brains showed stronger frontal lobe activity than that seen in older teenagers. Does this increase as we get older? I rather think it does. While I know of no data, it seems to me that we are much less likely to take risks as we age. When I think back to the rock faces I climbed in my teens and early twenties without really thinking twice, I am now horrified – I would simply be too scared to climb these again. And this probably applies to all kinds of decision-making in the way we conduct our professional lives.

We see a general change in behaviour with this shift in brain activity. When I was a boy, teachers and other figures in authority asked the perennial question: 'Why did you just do that?' to kids who had recently executed some inexplicably stupid or dangerous stunt, such as shinning the school flagpole or setting light to someone's hair. There came the perennial reply: 'I dunno.' A feeble excuse on which brain science possibly sheds some light. The brain of a child or teenager predisposes them to be more impulsive, less able to think clearly about the causes and effects of their actions. As brain activity shifts, in later adolescence, towards the more rational regions of the upper cortex, we start to see that set of attributes we call 'maturity'. A calmer outlook follows with more stable moods. There is a decreased propensity to take risks, and a heightened ability to think things through before starting on a course of action. These are attributes handed to us by our frontal lobes.

Professor Andrew Newberg at the University of Pennsylvania performed brain scans on eight Tibetan Buddhist meditators to see what happens to the brain when it enters a trance-like state through meditation.[48] Because a meditative state would be difficult to achieve in a noisy environment (for example, using MRI), Professor Newberg employed SPECT scanning, a technique similar to PET scans, which uses radioisotopes to measure brain blood flow. The Buddhists were seated in a darkened quiet room and, so as not to disturb them, injection of the isotopes was through long tubing from an adjacent room. To complete the experience, to make it as 'natural' an environment as possible, the meditators burnt incense sticks in the scan room. Newberg's research shows first that meditation causes a shutdown in the posterior parietal lobe, the area responsible for giving us a sense of self in terms of our place in time and space. People report that, during meditation, they experience a merging of the boundaries between themselves and the world around them, as well as losing track of the passage of time. Secondly, there is heightened activity in the frontal and prefrontal lobes. The more this increases, the more parietal lobe action reduces. Thirdly, this pattern of activity continues in practised meditators, even when they are not meditating. This once again provides a sterling example of how regular performance physically alters the chemistry of the brain. Newberg has suggested that teaching teenagers to practise meditation might exercise and strengthen the frontal lobes, giving them enhanced control over their feelings and behaviour. I do not intend to get into the power of prayer here, but certainly it should follow that this may be one way in which prayer exerts such a profound effect on many religious people.

It is useful to note here that Deborah Yurgelun-Todd's experiments with fear-processing in adolescents showed the pattern differing from one culture to another. In Western society, the increasing trend is for a longer and longer period of dependency upon parents, and a corresponding abdication of adult responsibilities. In the Britain of today, the scarcity of jobs and the rising costs of housing mean that young people are choosing to remain in education and to stay at home with their parents until a later age. Arguably the introduction of tuition fees here, and the resultant crippling debts hanging round the necks of new graduates, will merely lengthen the period of dependency upon parental support. But in many countries of the world, puberty goes hand-in-hand with adult responsibilities – providing income, for instance, and rearing one's own family. Accordingly, we may see earlier maturation of the frontal lobes as the brain of such teenagers responds to the pressures placed upon them.

Sex differences

By the time we are teenagers, the orientation towards sex and gender has fully matured in the brain. Male foetuses produce a surge of testosterone, which in turn informs the development of their brains, producing male-typical characteristics and behaviour. This surge in hormones appears to inform many of the differences we see in later life – such as girls' superiority at speech, and boys' at spatial and systemizing tasks like building with bricks.

When puberty sets in, we see three principal differences between the male and female brain. First, a region within the hypothalamus known as the medial preoptic area is two and a half times larger in men than in women. This region contains more cells responsive to male hormones than any other part of the brain. Experiments in monkeys show that when this area is stimulated, male monkeys become interested in any female around them, providing she is on heat. Also, if this area is removed or damaged, they lose interest in sex.

Secondly, the bridge that connects the left and right hemispheres – the corpus callosum – is thicker in women than in men. As I have already noted, this might explain why women (and males inclining towards the more female-typical end of the continuum) are better at communicating and more able to express emotions and understand the feelings of other people. These appear to be tasks that call for a shunting of information between the 'feeling' right brain and the 'analytical, vocal' left.

The results of this suggest that women's brains might be wired more efficiently for the task of social interaction. Studies by Professors Ruth Campbell and David Skuse at University College, London, have indicated that the root cause of this might be the female X chromosome.[49] Girls born with Turner's syndrome lack one of the paired X chromosomes and sometimes experience problems with social behaviour in later life. They may, for example, find it hard to read body language, and they can have difficulties in following the direction of another person's gaze. Work at the University of New York, Buffalo State School of Medicine and Biological Sciences has also indicated that the male and female brain may process information from human faces in different ways. Pre-pubescent boys use more of the right brain and girls more of the left, suggesting that girls are innately better at detecting more subtle nuances of facial expression – making them into better communicators.

The third difference between the male and female brain does not become apparent until we are much older. As the ageing process takes its toll – most visibly upon our reproductive systems, and upon the eyes, skin and teeth – there is a slight decrease in the size of our brain. Males tend to have a slightly bigger brain than females but they tend to lose brain tissue sooner. The loss is not great in either sex but a greater percentage of tissue loss in men occurs in the frontal and temporal lobes – areas concerned with thinking and processing emotions. Hence our archetypal image of the grumpy, fussy old man. Women's tissue loss occurs more in the hippocampus and parietal areas. Accordingly, they tend to be more forgetful in old age, and worse at locating objects.

The brain's growth to adulthood and beyond looks less like a flower emerging from a bud, and more like the action of a glacier, carving out the contours and idiosyncrasies of the landscape along its inexorable march – a bulge here, a cavity there, a strength in one area and a loss in others. Disorders, in a general sense, seem to emerge when the process is either too pronounced or incomplete. For example, it has been suggested that synthaesthesia might emerge as a result of inadequate cell death, though I am unaware of any real evidence for this. Perhaps left-handedness might have the same origins. And there is evidence that autism might emerge out of the brain 'trying' too hard to establish gender identity.

Simon Baron-Cohen's research in Cambridge has already been mentioned. Autism is more prevalent in males – and he feels that this disorder is an extreme form of male-typical brain chemistry. Male autists tend to have high levels of testosterone and develop male sexual characteristics earlier than their counterparts. Cooperation and sharing in play situations, understanding other people's emotional state and an early predisposition to be interested in human stimuli (to be interested in a person, say, rather than a clock) are traits more evident in girls than in boys. This difference is most clearly pronounced in autistic boys. The same goes for communication skills: girls score higher at detecting emotions from people's eyes, and autistic boys score worst of all.

Boys as we have already seen – whether autistic or not – show a general tendency towards what we call 'systemizing'. In play, they show a preference for toy vehicles, construction systems and weapons – objects with a definite purpose, which can be controlled according to a set of unchanging rules. Later on, boy-typical hobbies like stamp collecting or train spotting express a degree of preference for the classification of items over interaction with people. In adult life, this tendency shows through in the predominance of males in professions like maths and science, engineering and construction – disciplines that are more concerned with 'how things work'.

Anyone who has ever shared the business of driving and map reading with a spouse knows that there are also crucial differences in the way men and women understand spatial location. When boys and girls are asked to draw a map of a journey they have done once, the boys' maps tend to be more accurate. They centre upon the route taken from A to B, while girls' maps are more concerned with significant landmarks along the way. I became particularly aware of this once when attending a conference in which a female colleague and I were both staying in the nether regions of a large, meandering hotel complex. We became quite lost – and I remember trying to mentally retrace my steps in terms of various turnings left and right, without any success. My colleague, in contrast, got us back safely, because she remembered that our corridor was graced with a particularly bad imitation of a Matisse.

There are many people with degrees of autism who are entirely integrated into society – they hold down jobs, they have relationships and families of their own. But for some, the effort of doing this is exhausting, because they have learnt how to cope with other people by systemizing – in effect, they have developed impressively vast lists of the things people do. These lists work 90 per cent of the time but, of course, humans are not entirely predictable, so a constant updating is needed. For that reason, some autistic people shy away from environments or professions that call upon them to interact with other people. At the same time, they can excel in the manipulation of predictable systems. They can demonstrate what Baron-Cohen calls 'islets of ability' – brilliance at chess, or drawing, or at memorizing and classification – which seem essentially male, as distinct from female, abilities. Maths and engineering are professions in which people with varying degrees of autism can flourish, though, of course, this is not the same as saying that everyone who does well in these professions has some degree of autism.

But using Baron-Cohen's theories as a guide, we could begin to make some interesting, brain-based conclusions about other groups of people. The shy, anorak-wearing hobbyist, uncomfortable in social relationships and happiest at home with his neatly ordered collections and routines, is certainly an extreme archetype of the male personality. But it is present to a greater or lesser degree in most of us – the hero of Nick Hornby's *High Fidelity* and his companions at the record shop were really just passionate systemizers of music and albums.

They had the advantage that the object of their obsession is widely appreciated by the general population – whereas people who apply the same enthusiasm to steam engines, stamps or vintage wines are likely to be labelled, and sometimes cruelly dismissed, as 'nerds' or 'geeks'. The evidence suggests that such traits, and the extent to which they are present, boil down just to a surge in chemicals at a crucial time in our brain's development. As Baron-Cohen himself points out, by understanding the states underlying such differences in personality, hopefully we might in time learn to be a bit more tolerant.

There's an analogy to be drawn between the way each person's personal brain geography shapes their identity, and the way physical geography and climate affect the cultures and outlooks of whole nations. Countries with harsh desert environments and a corresponding scarcity of resources like water and food often have a tradition of showing hospitality to strangers. For a Bedouin, to turn away a visitor without feeding and watering him and offering him a bed for the night would be unthinkable. This acts as a form of insurance – the Bedouin gives, knowing that were he in the same situation, he would be sure to receive. The nature of the terrain shapes the behaviour of the people within it. In cooler, more abundant countries, there is less risk to human life, and therefore less need for such a tradition. In the same way, each of us is dependent for so many of the little quirks and idiosyncrasies of our identity upon the geography of our neurons.

That note brings me to a more contentious issue of brain and behaviour. For a long time, scientists and others have debated the issue of homosexuality, and whether it stems from bodily differences or from one's early experiences. An autopsy study performed on the brains of male homosexuals by neuroscientist Simon LeVay in 1991 showed that an area of the anterior hypothalamus was twice as large in heterosexual men as gay men – twice as large, in fact, as it was in heterosexual women.[50] LeVay came in for some heavy criticism, some of it from gay rights groups, who felt that the association of homosexuality with a variant of brain architecture could result in heightened discrimination. Not discouraged, LeVay, who is himself gay, went on to report that the corpus callosum – thicker, as you will recall, in women than in men – is often thicker in homosexual than in heterosexual men. And a further study done under the auspices of the National Institute of Mental Health has suggested that there may be a specific gene, passed down the maternal line, which influences sexual orientation in men.

Some people might at this point say: 'Is that it then? We know the answer, just like that?' But it is not so simple. A genetic or brain-based predisposition to homosexuality might not necessarily result in an adult who is orientated towards their own sex. The psychologist Daryl Bem pointed out in 1996 that biological differences merely produce a *tendency* towards certain social experiences. He coined the phrase 'the exotic becomes the erotic' to mean that sometimes we deal with the awkward feelings associated with being different from others by turning them into pleasurable feelings. And as we now understand, experiences can in turn feed back into the plastic brain, to reinforce and heighten original differences. So possibly a child with certain traits of homosexual-type brain chemistry might or might not go on to become homosexual, depending upon how his family and other children behaved towards him, and depending upon the extent to which his brain adapted to his perceptions of difference.

Now you're talking: the development of language

One fascinating and intricate way in which our plastic brain works is in the acquisition of language. What do we mean by language, and why is it there? We have already looked at the nature and purpose of emotions. Emotions may be defined as a means by which we communicate our own internal state and those of others to our higher brain. Frowning, for instance, is a way of telling both yourself and the people looking at you that you are angry. So is language just a more abstract tool for the same thing?

The short answer to that is yes. Chimps use language in exactly this way – in the wild they have a set of some thirty-six sounds. Other animals have greater or lesser vocabularies. But for all animals, except ourselves, one sound means one thing. They do not combine sounds into strings, or sentences, to create different messages. Human communication is crucially different. We use combinations of sounds called phonemes (such as 'da' or 'ba') to create an endless variety of potential meanings. In other words, for animals a sound is intimately linked to its meaning – a certain type of bark means 'danger', another type is used by mothers looking for their young. For humans, there is no innate connection between a sound and its meaning. The phoneme 'da', for instance, could be Tyneside dialect for 'dad', or Russian for 'yes', or it could be combined in German with the phoneme 'zu' to mean 'to it', or it could be combined with yet more phonemes, 'sta', and 'rd' and 'ly', to make 'dastardly' in English. A phoneme has no inherent meaning in human communication – it is just a building block of a word. You could not expect to tell the design of a vast Roman mosaic from looking at one tile. In the same way, a phoneme is the smallest unit of a wider pattern, but unlike a mosaic, in which tiles eventually conjoin to form a set image, human language can use phonemes to convey an infinite variety of meanings.

There are some unique elements of human physiology that make this use of sounds possible. Our vocal tract has evolved to have a very sharp right-angled bend and a larynx lower than that seen in other primates. This refinement creates a larger space in which the tongue can move along two axes and create two resonant cavities at the same time. By being able to filter and shape the sounds emerging from the throat, these cavities allow for a variety of contrasting sounds – like vowels and consonants – to be made in rapid time.

This refinement is at the expense of other faculties. Most primates have their larynx much higher up the vocal tract, allowing them to breathe and drink at the same time. By contrast, every bit of food and drink we swallow must pass over the trachea, or windpipe. It takes time for this feature to develop in humans – human infants are born with the ability to breathe and drink simultaneously and this remains for their first three months or so. But as the capacity to use language develops, this ability is lost. The better we become at talking, the more we are at risk of choking.

If language involved a change and a risk, it must have had some clear evolutionary benefit for us. So why do we need language, and how it did it come about? There are two main arguments. The first suggests that language, like consciousness itself, was merely the crowning glory of millions of years of selective breeding. The Darwinian view is that we continually select for adaptations that make us better at surviving and reproduction; this argument suggests that language was the ultimate survival device. With words, we could communicate sophisticated messages necessary for survival within ever bigger and more complex social groups. It would enable us to hunt more effectively and protect members of the group.

The second view suggests that language was merely a by-product of a wider expansion in other skills. Specifically, those skills would have been the production and use of tools. The argument is that to see a need for a tool, identify how to make it, make it and then use it implies the capacity for sequenced thought. There is evidence that the regions of the brain that control sequenced hand movement and speech rely upon the same mechanisms. This school of thought argues that we became predisposed to develop language as our brains developed through tool use. Language, like making and using a tool, is a sequence.

Furthermore, the basic unit of language, the sentence, conveys meaning via a three-step sequence: subject (I), verb (make), object (it). The words in brackets might give some clue as to my next point. The very process by which one would manufacture a tool implies some awareness of a key concept – a self, separate from others and capable of doing. So I, Ug, a caveman, am not the same as this piece of stone, nor this bison which I wish to kill, and by doing something to this piece of stone, I can kill this bison. Such strings of reasoning, it is argued, lay at the heart of our development of language.

Many theorists have seen language as the driving force behind a range of further innovations. By enabling accurate communication, for instance, we could argue that language enabled us to live in ever more complex groups – culminating, for example, in Nineveh, according to the account in the Book of Jonah 'a great city . . . three days' journey across'. Through its capacity to combine sounds to convey an infinite variety of meanings, we could say that language 'freed us from the moment', enabled us to think in the abstract, to create art, to invent, to dream.

Language also allows for the establishment of codes of action and morals, and for the 'how we got here' accounts, such as the story of the creation in Genesis or the moral codex of Hammurabi. These can then be passed accurately from one generation down to the next. In this way, the human group establishes and confirms its own identity – a process which leads us from being simple hunting and child-rearing packs into being tribes and eventually nation states. By enabling an analysis of our own internal states and those of others, language also allowed for social change. The anthropologist Jack Goody suggests that a further mutation of language, writing, enabled people to critically review their own history and the history of their groups or tribes, thus facilitating dissent and revolution and progress.

It is difficult to understand why writing seems to be so recent in human history. If we mean by writing a device for expressing linguistic elements by a series of man-made visible marks, writing is not much older than 5,000 or 6,000 years. But we know that humans from 30,000 or 40,000 years ago drew pictures, and there is recent archaeological evidence that primitive stylized engraving on bone might go back 75,000 years or more. So why did it take so long to develop written words? Is it because, until man started to build towns and lay down roots in one place, there was no pressure to use engraving for distant communication? Whatever the answer to this question, some people believe that the emergence of language shaped the architecture of our brain, and even suggest that the fundamental differences of left and right brain emerged as a consequence.

When a modern human hears someone say a sentence, a complex flurry of actions occurs inside the brain. First, it has to recognize that what it is hearing is language, as opposed to, say, the noise of a babbling brook, or a pneumatic drill. The evidence suggests that we have a hard-wired predisposition to do this, but our brain depends on the right sort of environmental stimuli to get this process up and running.

Many of us will admit to feelings of jealousy towards small children who, after only a few weeks in a new country, are able to chatter away like the natives. This is because of the plasticity of the brain's language circuits – a plasticity that exists only during a certain time frame. Patricia Kuhl, of the University of Washington at Seattle, has done work with newborns which indicates that we are all born with an innate ability to detect the difference between spoken language and other sounds, whether they are generated by humans or not.[51] We also seem, as I mentioned earlier on, predisposed to recognize the unique pattern of phonemes that make up our mother tongue.

But by the time we reach the age of a year, we can no longer recognize the phonemes and speech patterns of languages to which we have not been exposed. The circuitry inside our brain has undergone a growth and pruning process, such that it can only recognize the phonemes of the languages we hear on a daily basis – and usually that is whatever language our mother speaks. We dismiss all other sounds as non-language. Interestingly, this 'window of opportunity' for language may also apply to certain other faculties. A study led by Olivier Pascalis of the University of Sheffield has indicated that, during the same six-month period, we are able to recognize different human and monkey faces. But after that point we can only differentiate between human faces.

Hard-wired grammar

In the early stages, acquiring language is as much about what goes in as about what's happening inside the brain. George Hollich at Johns Hopkins University has suggested that the way mothers in particular and adults in general speak to babies enforces the process by which they learn the specific phonemes of their own language.[52] Phrases like 'Oozat ickle pwitty babba den?' are examples of 'Motherese', a simplified but exaggeratedly rhythmic form of speech common to all human groups, which helps the baby to learn.

Dr Hollich believes that infants understand much more than we think. 'If you consider the almost infinite number of words, as well as the potential mappings between words and meanings, learning a language ought to be impossible,' says Hollich. It has often been thought that children learn language step–by-step from one word to the next. The research at Purdue indicates that infants may be learning words and grammar simultaneously. For example, in one study, babies are shown a series of short animated sequences on a screen, such as an apple repeatedly colliding with a flower. Then another screen will show the apple in one corner and the flower in the other. A voice asks, 'What hit the flower?'

Of course, these babies can't talk yet, so the length of time they stare at a given image indicates their comprehension. If the baby looks longer at the apple it suggests the question is understood. If the baby looks at the flower, it suggests they can identify the word 'flower' but don't fully understand the question. By fifteen months, children look directly at the apple. This is surprising because most experts predict that infants should look at the object specifically mentioned in the question. Infants will do this, but only if the question is, 'Where is the flower?'

The position in which mothers instinctively hold their babies may also help language acquisition. About 80 per cent of mothers hold their babies on their left side, regardless of whether they themselves are left- or right-handed. So sounds tend to enter the baby's left ear – and thus will tend to be processed in the right hemisphere. The right hemisphere is not, in most humans, where our language faculties sit, but it does develop earlier than the left side. It also is better at interpreting the rhythmic and melodic sounds that parents use when talking to infants. The theory is that this establishes a loop of non-verbal communication between mother and child, as sounds from the newborn will enter the mother's left ear first, and travel to her own right hemisphere.

When babies start to make babbling sounds, they use the left, language side of their brains, and correspondingly make more movements with the right side of their mouths. The babbling of a six-monther born to French-speaking parents will sound different to that of one born to Japanese parents – because by this stage, babies only babble with the set of phonemes specific to their native tongue. Even deaf babies, born to parents who communicate with them via sign language, will make hand movements identical to the babbling of normal babies – suggesting that the seemingly nonsensical speech of infants is in fact a crucial rehearsal for the full-blown use of language.

The first two years are the most vital for language acquisition. The University of Chicago psychologist Janellen Huttenlocher has shown that the frequency with which parents speak to children up to the age of two has major consequences for their language use throughout the rest of their lives.[53] The more language they hear, the greater will be their vocabulary – regardless of whether they understand the words they are hearing. It is another classic example of the 'use it or lose it' principle – brains that get exercise grow ever stronger. So it is not surprising the experiments of Frederick II didn't work.

However, the plasticity of the brain is very important. As we have seen, in 95 per cent of people the left brain has assumed the responsibility for language by the time we are five years old – but evidence suggests that the right side can take over if problems occur at a sufficiently plastic stage. Children who have had the left side of their brain removed can still produce and comprehend speech – although they may have problems in using complex grammar or the future tense. As is the case in so many areas, the extent of the recovery depends upon the age at which the damage occurs. A young child can 'catch up' after the damage caused by a brain injury. His 65-year-old grandfather, on the other hand, might never regain the ability to speak after a left-brain stroke.

Which of these figures is most evoked by the word 'kiki' and which by 'bouba'? See what Professor Ramachandran suggests the great majority of people decide on page 65.

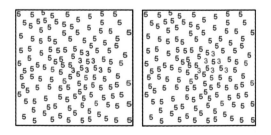

The numbers in the two boxes above are laid out identically. To most of us the mass of 5s and 3s is a jumble and it takes a few moments to identify the 3s. A person with synaesthesia, seeing 3 as red and 5 as blue, will immediately pick out the triangle of 3s on the right (see page 66).

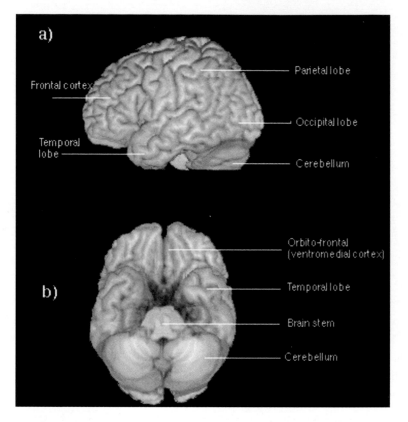

Images from MRI scans of the outside cortex of the brain:
a) the surface of the left hemisphere; b) the brain from underneath
showing both hemispheres.

An artificially coloured scan of the right hemisphere seen
from inside (medial view).

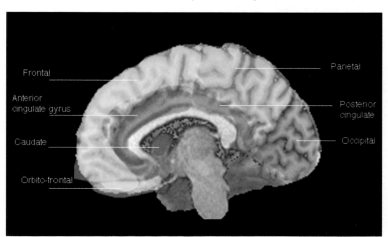

We thought that Imperial College physicists would be more introverted than Butlin's Redcoats, who relish being photographed. Introverts salivate more than extroverts (page 229), and our physicists had no difficulty licking sufficient gummed tape to seal these fruit boxes.

Building a bridge above a precipice 2000 feet up was a television metaphor for the initiation of a synapse: a) The first contact with the neuron on the other side is tentative – a grappling iron is thrown. b) I prepare to cross the synapse, hoping we've got a secure connection. c) This isn't quite as much fun as it looks. d) As more lines are brought across, our synapse becomes secure. e) Planks are laid between the ropes. f) The synapse is now so well used that our cameraman, the redoubtable Chris Hartley, can cross repeatedly and film an image.

OPPOSITE

Nick Murphy and I debate who goes into the shark cage first, as a two-ton great white hovers expectantly. Scan (a) shows a cross-section of the brain in the region of the alarm centre, the amygdala. Compare this with scan (b), which shows activity that is likely to be happening in the amygdala, and in the temporal cortex, during my frightening experience.

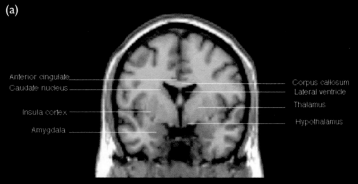

(a)

Anterior cingulate
Caudate nucleus

Insula cortex

Amygdala

Corpus callosum
Lateral ventricle

Thalamus

Hypothalamus

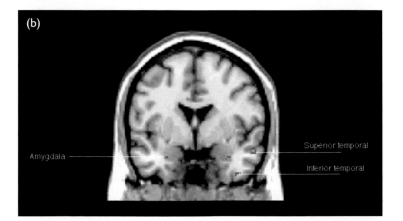

(b)

Amygdala

Superior temporal

Inferior temporal

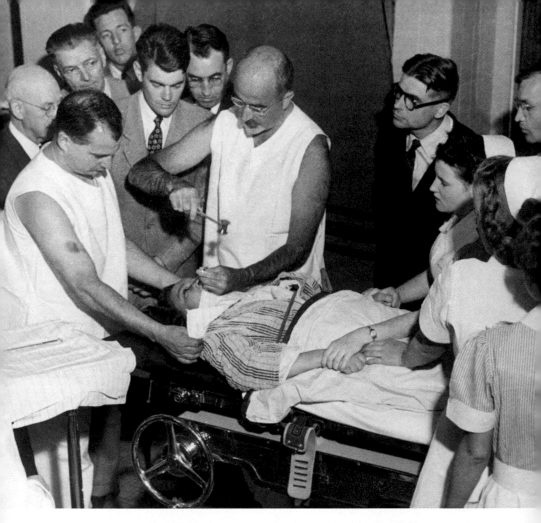

Dr Walter Freeman performing a lobotomy in 1949, in
which an ice pick is inserted under the upper eyelid of
the patient to cut the connections in the front part
of the brain. © Bettmann/CORBIS

OPPOSITE
De Kelder cave in South Africa, inhabited by man for
millions of years. Primitive man used flints as knives for
well over a million years, and certainly used sticks as tools
or weapons, but our hominid ancestors only relatively
recently — perhaps 100,000 years ago — thought to put
the two together to make something much more
formidable: an axe, or a spear.

Richard Wiseman, ace psychologist and member of the
Magic Circle, is able to gauge by reading vocal clues, body
language and my facial changes whether I am lying about
what I did last night — an increasingly useful skill
in criminal investigations (see page 302).

A huge proportion of our brain is used when socializing.
In fact, social interaction is one of the most taxing parts of
human existence. This piece of filming, a party scene that took
three days to make, was on screen for around 40 seconds.
Television is a voracious beast.

The evidence from stroke patients reveals just how compartmen-talized a process our use of language is – many areas are involved, each with specific purposes. For instance, if stroke damage affects Broca's area of the left brain, then people are unable to speak, but they don't lose their ability to understand what is said to them.

So what specific structures of the brain are involved when we produce and comprehend language? The business of distinguishing speech from non-speech noise occurs as an interaction between the thalamus and the auditory cortex. It proceeds from there into the main language processing areas. These are chiefly on the left side in most people, and sit surrounding the auditory cortex. As we saw ear-lier, two of the most crucial centres – Broca's and Wernicke's areas, dealing with language production and comprehension respectively – were first identified around 150 years ago. Thanks to increasingly sophisticated developments in brain-imaging technology, we now know that other areas play an important role – notably the Silvian fissure, the grooved part of the brain dividing the temporal and frontal lobes.

Further to the ability to detect the sound units of our own language is the ability to distinguish between one phoneme and another. There is a tiny part of the left brain that lights up only when we hear consonants – if this is not functioning normally, people show diffi-culties in distinguishing words that depend upon consonants for their meaning. For instance, we need to distinguish between 'p' and 'b' sounds to understand the difference between the words 'pat' and 'bat'.

Once we can distinguish one phoneme from another, we then begin to learn how to combine them into larger units, called morphemes, to convey meanings. A morpheme can be a whole word, like 'cup', or just a part of a word, like the suffixes '-s' and '-ly' in English. 'S' can make a noun plural – for instance, book/books. Or added to a noun, it can denote possession – as in 'the cat's basket'. Added to an adjective, like 'quick', the suffix '-ly' turns it into an adverb, to qualify an action, as in 'he walks quickly'. So morphemes have two functions – they can stand as words, and therefore convey ideas in their own right. And they can modify the meanings of other words.

The system of rules by which we combine words into phrases, and phrases into whole sentences, is called syntax. The English language has an 'analytic' syntax, meaning it relies on the order of words to signify changes in meaning. For instance, 'John kisses Mary' conveys a different meaning to 'Mary kisses John'. To show who's doing the action, and who has it done to them, we English speakers put the subject – the kissing person – first, followed by the verb, and then finally the object. In other languages, such as Hebrew, Latin or German, 'synthetic' syntax is used – meaning that changes tend to be made to the words themselves, such as adding extra morphemes to the front or the end of a word to denote whether it is the subject or the object of a sentence.

In the growing child, this ability to combine phonemes into morphemes and morphemes into sentences is one that develops in tandem with vocabulary. The first form of language we use is mimicry – babbling as a rehearsal of the sounds and patterns of our mother tongue. This gives way to the acquisition of real words – generally occurring at about the age of one. As vocabulary increases, babies will naturally start to combine words into rudimentary sentences at around the eighteen-month mark. And although these sentences may be grammatically incorrect, there is a slowly emerging logic – which suggests that a process far deeper than mere mimicry is going on inside their brain.

Linguists are particularly interested in the mistakes children tend to make at the age of three or four – errors which increase in frequency as their ability to convey complex meanings grows, and which also, interestingly enough, they wouldn't make at an earlier age. For instance, children, having learnt that the suffix 'ed' conveys the past tense, will apply the rule to all verbs they come across – so they might say 'I runned' or 'I holded', whereas at the age of two they might have correctly used 'ran' and 'held', because at this stage they were purely imitating their elders. Or, having learnt that the suffix 's' makes nouns plural, they might say 'mouses' or 'mans', instead of 'mice' and 'men'. So children move quickly beyond a simple imitation of their parents' speech. An in-built ability to learn the rules of speech is switched on when the vocabulary becomes big enough to need such rules. Children may apply them rather enthusiastically in the early stages – in the same way as it is hard to prise a child off their bicycle when they have just learnt to ride unaided. This is a crucial defining feature of human language – that we apply a set of rules to a set of sounds in order to create an infinite variety of meanings. Chimps taught to communicate via sign language never develop this capacity.

Ever since the groundbreaking 1950s work of linguist Noam Chomsky, the scientific community has accepted that this ability – a universal language acquisition device – is built into human brains from birth. So in a sense, Frederick II was not entirely wrong. His mistake was in believing that a specific tongue – like Hebrew or Latin – pre-exists within the brain, like the operating software that comes with a new computer. But the capacity to acquire and use a language – any language – does exist. What the meddling emperor failed to understand was that this 'program' has to be activated by exposure to sounds.

To date, we have not isolated any specific site in the brain responsible for this piece of software. Studies of certain injured patients suggest that damage to the more frontal regions of the brain's language centres – such as Broca's area – is associated with difficulties in grammar and syntax. We also know that patients with damage to Wernicke's area can preserve an ability to construct grammatical sentences, while talking incomprehensible gibberish. The effect would be not entirely unlike the stories created by the wonderful comic 'Professor' Stanley Unwin, who died last year. Here he is telling a very famous children's legend which you might recognize:

Once in a long far awow, in the Germanic land, there was a great city called Grubbelsberg or something like that, with an Obermeister-Bergelmasty who was in charge. Now there they had a surfeit or rat-suffery, where all they used to creep and out and gnaw sniff and gribble into the early mord (and the late evage) there, biting the bits of the table, also the tea-clothers; and when people were asleep in their beds, so these rats would gnaw into the sheebs and also the whiskers of those who was dangly hoaver.

There was a great suffery. Not only this: the larder, foodage, all the fine things of the world was not enjoying by the peopload themselves on account of these rats doing a sniffy most (and the chew-chew and stuffle down their ratty grebes); because these were the fattest raps and also over-producey in this great lovely city which was otherwise ... tsk tsk.

From *The Pidey Pipeload of Hamling*

Stanley Unwin claimed that his fascination with nonsense language was learnt from his mother who, when she tripped up one day, told her small son that she had 'falloloped over and grazed her knee clapper'.

197

Broca's area might be the brain's grammar centre, but scientists are by no means agreed on this. It may even be the case that there is no specific unit at all – merely a pattern of neural firing, taking place in a range of different regions of the brain. The problem is made more difficult by the fact that, where language use is concerned, no two brains are quite alike. Researchers have been able to pinpoint sites within the brain that control features of language as narrow as the names of fabrics, vegetables and gemstones. But the size and location of these areas differs in everyone – unsurprisingly when you remember that our brains are shaped by what we do and what happens to us in our daily lives. So we would expect to see some clear differences in the naming centres of, say, a market gardener and a Hatton Garden diamond dealer. And if this is true of the brain's naming sites, the same may also be true for grammar.

Alfonso Caramazza, psychologist from Harvard, suggests there are independent brain systems for grammar, meaning and word form, each with their own locations and components within the brain. There is evidence for this from studies of brain-injured patients – for example, victims of strokes that have affected one part of the brain. Some can name objects, but not supply any of the associations that go with them. For instance, they might be able to look at a picture of a church and name it 'church', but not be able to say what they thought it was there for, who used it, what went on inside, etc. Similarly, other people could look at the same picture and be able to tell you that it was used for worshipping God, people went inside and thought and prayed and sang, that the insides smelt of wood, wax and incense. But they would be unable to come up with the word 'church'.

I mentioned my puzzlement at the late development of writing during Palaeolithic times. It may be relevant that there are separate sites for reading and writing in our brain. One argument to explain this is that the brain's plasticity leads it to coopt neurons that might have been used for other purposes at earlier points in our evolution. They still could be coopted elsewhere if we do not activate them by learning to read and write. A rather cheap example of this process would be that my handwriting used to be fairly neat (even though I am medically qualified) but has become appreciably worse since computers replaced the pen and paper.

As is so often the case, the evidence that these skills sit in a specific corner of the brain comes from examining the brain in its disordered, rather than its healthy state. For instance, there are people who can write, but not read, and others who can read, but not write. Brain scans performed upon people with high verbal IQs show that they have activity in the superior temporal gyrus when reading, and in the middle temporal gyrus when naming objects. Conversely, people with low verbal IQs have the opposite arrangement. As we saw in our brief foray into the issue of dyslexia, people with this disability seem to have particular problems with the fast processing of both visual and auditory information.

So, to recap, the ability to acquire and use language is hard-wired into the human brain. When an infant makes its first sounds, it is making use of a distinct facility, one very different from the laborious way we, as adults or teenagers, must pore over text books and vocabulary lists as we struggle with a new language. This is why, even after years of practice, we never quite acquire the same level of fluency in a second or third language. Translators and interpreters, experts in their field, always translate from the second or third language back into their mother tongue, because this is the language in which they have the greatest degree of fluency. We develop our first language and we learn others. The learning of a second or third language involves the same parts of the brain we used when we uttered our first words. But because it is a learning process, it also calls on other brain areas, the same ones we use when we first begin typing on a computer keyboard, for instance, or learning the route from home to our place of work. These facilities of the human mind would be classed as memory, which is our next subject.

A rooted sorrow

Canst thou not minister to a mind diseased,
Pluck from the memory a rooted sorrow,
Raze out the written troubles of the brain
Macbeth, Act V Scene 3

Shakespeare was here unwittingly glancing upon some of the hot topics of brain research. When we think about memory, some key questions immediately emerge. The guilt-ridden Macbeth is talking here about the memory of the terrible deeds he has committed. We all shudder, sometimes, as we remember acts in which we would rather not have played a part or words we would rather not have uttered. Other memories, of course, can evoke quite a different reaction from our emotional palette – joy, sadness, anger and fear. But there is another class of memory that seems to have no clear emotional element – the memory we dip into to recall a name, for instance, or how to change a tyre. So do these two types of memory occupy different areas of the brain? What processes are involved when an event enters our memory, and when a piece of learning becomes 'second nature'? And if they are so rooted in the architecture and the chemistry of our brain, how is it that we can forget things over time? Why is it that my ninety-year-old mother can recall playing tennis and losing in Brook Green, Hammersmith, as a schoolgirl but not what she ate for lunch yesterday? And what is a 'memory' anyway – does it occupy a bit of shelf space inside the brain until it is recalled, or is it the act of retrieval itself that makes a memory?

It is a modern cliché that all of us over a certain age remember what we were doing when President Kennedy was assassinated. Over time, other world events have surpassed that tragic event in magnitude. But clichés often contain an element of truth. A brief trawl through your more personal memory banks will prove the point further – the memories associated with your most intense emotions are likely to be those you recall best.

All I think I am saying here is that certain memories stand out because they are unusual in comparison to the unremarkable routines of daily life. Studies have shown that the human mind selects novel stimuli – if you note how often and for how long an infant gazes at an object, you will see that it looks more frequently and for longer times at unfamiliar objects. This selectivity also works within our memories. You have probably driven to work more times than you have sat an exam, for instance, which is why you can recall the latter better than the former. If you were to remember every journey into work, your brain would quickly become clogged with detail, like Shereshevski, the hapless Russian 'Memory Man'.

But what is interesting about our memory of key traumatic events – whether we saw them unfolding on the news, or whether they occurred to us personally – is how much detail seems to enter the record. When we talk about September 11, it is significant that we remember *what we were doing* when we heard the news – a detail not relevant to the unfolding events in New York. We can often recall a host of other elements – how we learnt the news, what we were wearing that day, the weather outside. We call this the 'flashbulb memory': the ability of the brain, during intense experiences, to capture a moment in vivid and exceptional detail.

Memory and emotion

The anthropologist Victor Turner argued that the rituals and ceremonies conducted in tribal societies make great use of the inter-action between emotion and memory. Initiation rites, for example, are performed to ensure that young boys entering manhood learn the particular mythology and customs of the social group, and their own rights and responsibilities as adult males. Like all adolescent males everywhere, they might be more interested in other concerns, prob-ably of the female variety.

This, in Turner's view, is why rituals came into play. In ritual, the familiar becomes unfamiliar. People behave in a strange manner, they move in odd, stylized ways, they might wear face paint, masks, peculiar clothes. Songs are sung and words uttered that are never used in daily life. Different foods are eaten. Those undergoing the ritual are assaulted by strange sights, frightening and bizarre symbols. Their senses are sometimes rendered exceptionally keen through ordeals of starvation, pain and sleeplessness. We can see this to a lesser degree in the rituals still prevalent in the Western world. A wedding involves certain restrictions – such as the belief that the groom must not see the wedding dress, or glimpse his bride-to-be on the night before the nuptials. During the ceremony, we behave in certain, restricted ways. We put on our best clothes, mothers are expected to cry, the bride and groom undergo the 'ordeal' of the marriage vows. The ceremony is made meaningful because it is different from daily life. Indeed in the Hebrew language, one aspect of the word holy or sacred – *qadosh* – has an association with the meaning 'separate', or 'set apart'.

In our pasts, and in some tribal societies today, the 'set-apartness' of the rituals is more pronounced, more extreme. And Turner's theory was that such a battery of remarkable, fear- and wonder-inducing experiences served to ensure that the learning process was thorough and unforgettable. In other words, the deliberate oddness of the ritual tagged it with strong emotions in the minds of those undergoing it. And in turn, that meant that knowledge being communicated through the ritual became deeply etched in the memory.

Turner's interest in ritual may be related to the fact that his mother was an actress, and he grew up in a family where the theatre was a feature of daily life. Some of his theories on the importance of the unusual in learning are replicated in the techniques of some dramatists. The Marxist playwright Bertolt Brecht used the same concept in his *Verfremdungstechnik*, or alienation technique. Brecht, in accordance with his communist ideals, believed that the theatre's role was to teach. And that people learnt better, took the messages home and did not forget them if they witnessed something unusual. Brecht sought to do this by subverting the normal conventions of theatre – he kept the audience very close to the actors and it was often possible to see the stagehands moving furniture. Instead of enjoying some cosy bit of entertainment, the audience became 'alienated' from the play on the stage, not wrapped up in it. A clear example of this is seen in his musical play written with Kurt Weill, *The Rise and Fall of the City of Mahagonny*. At first it seems just like another boring night at the theatre, then suddenly a ten-ton truck roars onto the stage; the actors jump off the back of the lorry and start to build a set. I have never forgotten the production I saw aged seventeen; the novelty-detection system of the viewer's brain tags such an unusual experience with a higher than ordinary level of emotion. Thus a distinct memory is formed.

How is a memory is formed inside the brain? The formation of all memories – tinged with high emotion or otherwise – takes place via a process called long-term potentiation (LTP). It seems memories are formed at the instant they happen. The first stage lasts less than a second. When a neuron receives an intense signal due to incoming information, its interior floods with calcium. This alters the balance inside the neuron, priming it to fire much more vigorously and for longer if the same pattern of input comes its way again. The calcium also encourages the neuron to make growth changes, developing new connections to other neurons.

The dendrites – where information is received by a neuron – swell in response to the calcium flood, maximizing the number of synapses with which the neuron can communicate. The swelling goes down after six hours or so, but as this occurs, the growth of new dendrites will be cementing the pattern for as much as two days after the event. Meanwhile, regular pulses of chemical activity will pass down the circuit, keeping the original experience alive and preserving its memory in the circuitry of the brain.

The LTP process can be seen all over the brain – frustrating news for those who might hope that there is a specific place where memories are formed and stored. But we can nevertheless talk about certain regions as being particularly significant for the human memory. The hippocampus is particularly endowed with LTP-responsive cells. Its location, at the back end of the sensory processing trail inside the brain, suggests that its purpose is to capture and preserve incoming information. Furthermore, the hippocampus seems to be particularly sensitive to acetylcholine, a neurotransmitter that plays a role in suppressing prior activity in order to divert and focus attention. It has been argued by the neurobiologist James Bower, formerly at the California Institute of Technology, that acetylcholine 'cleans up' each memory, suppressing the irrelevant information and preserving what is most salient.[54] It may be that when the LTP activity is particularly intense – for instance, following on from an intense emotional experience – the acetylcholine clean-up job can only be partial. That is why we can remember certain events with 'flashbulb' detail – preserving the most seemingly irrelevant information.

So we can now understand why certain events enter the memory as vivid snapshots, and others more dully or seemingly not at all. A novel and intense experience, like witnessing or playing a part in an accident, triggers a correspondingly fervent sequence of action in the brain. But an experience we undergo every day is treated with greater selectivity. When the clean-up procedure goes to work within the hippocampus, only what is most novel enters the record. If nothing about my Tuesday mid-morning coffee break is remotely noteworthy, I may not, over time, be able to recall anything about it that distinguishes it from any other mid-morning coffee break.

Hippocampus and amygdala: their role in memory

We know much about the role of the hippocampus in preserving memory from studies of people with damage to that area. In one

famous case nearly fifty years ago, a man with severe epilepsy underwent brain surgery. The surgical procedure resulted in the removal of
roughly two-thirds of his hippocampal tissue. Ever since then, this
unfortunate man has been unable to lay down any new memories. It
is hard to conceive what this must be like. One analogy is said to be
that of the goldfish that never becomes bored of swimming around in
a small bowl because its memory span, we are told, is no longer than
seven seconds.* In normally functioning humans, our consciousness is
a stream – each moment is connected to the one preceding it and to
those that follow. With a damaged hippocampus, each and every
moment might appear anew. Our surroundings would appear
permanently strange, the people around us as eternal strangers. We
would be unable to formulate and execute plans of action at even the
simplest level because we would forget what our objectives were. As
I write this, a team at the University of Southern California, led by
Theodore Berger, are attempting to create the world's first artificial
hippocampus – using information derived from millions of cross-
sections of rat brains, programmed onto a silicon chip. One day,
future generations may just possibly possess the technology to replace
the damaged tissue of human brains with similar devices – ensuring
that the loss of faculties like memory can be overcome.

The amygdala also plays a role in memory. Here the brain 'tags'
incoming information with an emotional value. The frontal cortex
uses this tag to devise and direct the appropriate plans of action. If the
amygdala decides to tag the job interview we are facing as 'serious', for
instance, we behave in a serious manner and keep jokes to a bare
minimum – if we want to be employed. But information from the
amygdala also loops back into the hippocampus. So, when it comes to
recalling the interview, we also recall the emotions associated with it.
The more intense the emotions, or the more novel they are in the context of our everyday lives, the deeper they are etched into the memory.

The emotional content of a memory helps us to learn important
messages. In our evolutionary past, this would have had an added
survival benefit – directing us away from harm and towards safety,
without the loftier realms of the brain's thinking, higher cortex
becoming involved and slowing things down. Neuroscientist Joseph
LeDoux calls this the 'quick and dirty route'. When, for instance, we

---

*There is some evidence that fish have a much longer memory than just a few seconds.

see a snake – or a long, wriggling thing like a snake – the amygdala's direct connection to the processing centre in the thalamus results in an almost instantaneous perception of fear. A conscious awareness of what we have seen comes later on. LeDoux argues that human brains have evolved with this early, emotional hair-trigger because it would have been vital to us in the past. Predators like snakes strike extremely quickly. There's no benefit whatsoever in us standing round, hand on hip, fingers on lips, with our brain pondering what we might have seen. We need some mechanism that gets us out of harm's way, and fast. Thanks to the mechanism, we can go on to live another day – to survive and reproduce.

So the amygdala adds emotional colour to our memories. But does this mean that our memories are sitting, like little cans of film, in the archive of the hippocampus? Some people believe that this seahorse-shaped nubbin of brain tissue is less like a storage unit and more of a superefficient assembly line, which constructs memories as and when they are required. Antonio Damasio has argued that when we retrieve a memory, parcels of information come together from separate regions all over the brain. These so-called 'convergence zones' are situated next to or near the neurons that were involved in registering the initial event. Damasio has identified various regions that act as convergence zones for the uniting of sensory information about people, perceptions and emotions. The hippocampus, under this theory, would simply be the structure that brings the process together and filters out what is not required.

Damasio's view suggests that our brain does not store whole sequences of events, like reels of film, but breaks them up into their smallest constituent elements. So my memory of my first snowball fight is actually composed of little experience units, like 'wellington boots', 'cold hands', 'wet bottom', 'broken window' – which are all stored separately from each other, next to the neurons that first felt the cold, or saw the broken window. They can be used, alongside other units, to make up an endless combination of other memories – in the same way as we use combinations of sounds to make words. So the 'cold hands' unit might also go into my memories of skiing trips, 'wet bottom' might go into memories of my children when they were small. The hippocampus straddles these separate units of experience, splicing them together like a tape-editing machine to form different memories.

Episodic and procedural memory

If I suffered damage to my hippocampus, then I might expect to lose my memory of that first, ill-fated snowball fight. But what else would I forget? Interestingly, the man who had much of his hippocampus removed did not forget 'everything'. He could remember his life as young man before the operation, and skills he learnt during that time. He could also master new skills, such as new tunes on the piano, or writing while watching his efforts in a mirror.

This is because, in the exercise of learnt skills, he was using 'procedural memory'. In patients with Alzheimer's, we can often observe the same phenomenon – they may have suffered severe damage to their hippocampal tissue and be in a state of permanent bewilderment, but at the same time, certain 'islets of ability' endure, enabling them to perform quite complex actions which they learnt in the past. Clearly, memory does not just capture events and experiences, but also skills and sequences of action.

This distinction has led some neuroscientists to discriminate between 'episodic' and 'semantic' types of memory. Episodic memory equates to what we have described above, as our memories of events and episodes. Semantic memory is the sum total of what we have learnt, distinct from how or where we learnt it, or any of the emotions associated. It seems that the hippocampus is chiefly important for episodic memory. In a case described by Endel Tulving and Gene Schachter, a patient with severe hippocampal damage was unable to recall any significant event of his own past, but his semantic memory remained intact. He could describe with accuracy and detail the route he used to walk to school, and the details of changing a tyre, even though he could not recall anything that had ever happened at school, or any time he might have changed a tyre.

This is one of the reasons why, in the murder-mystery tale, the culprit feigning amnesia is so wont to be sniffed out by the investigating Poirot, Morse or Lord Peter Wimsey. People faking amnesia tend not to understand – having been denied access to this book – the difference between episodic and procedural memory, and thus will fake a general blotting-out of personal, autobiographical memories and learnt skills. So, for instance, they might pretend to have forgotten their names and also how to make a cup of tea – when in a genuine case, only the former would be beyond recall. They also fail to understand that in genuine cases of amnesia, the memory loss is fragmentary, and there is a continuous 'bubbling up' of little remembered details over time.

Amnesia and the case of the crime writer

Someone who became well acquainted with amnesia – to her great personal disadvantage – was the British detective writer Agatha Christie. On 3 December 1926, she disappeared from her home in Berkshire, leaving her car abandoned off-road in rural Surrey. For eleven days she remained missing, causing intense speculation in the press and a search involving police officers from three forces. Finally, on the evening of 14 December, her husband Archie – who had been having an affair, and was under suspicion of having murdered Agatha – identified a woman staying at a hotel in Harrogate as his wife.

Agatha Christie refused to speak to the press about her disappearance. Archie himself told them it had been due to an attack of amnesia. Throughout the rest of her life, the crime novelist maintained a strict silence on the subject. The press decided that the whole saga had been an elaborate stunt, designed to gain publicity for her next book. Agatha Christie, who had formerly not been shy of publicity, lived thereafter as a recluse. So what was the truth behind her disappearance? Was it, as her husband told the newspapers shortly after she went missing, that she was researching the phenomenon for a book? Was she simply trying to drum up media interest, or trying to seek revenge on her unfaithful spouse? Or did she genuinely experience a loss of memory?

One interesting indicator of the truth is that Christie signed her name in the Harrogate hotel register as a Miss Teresa Neele. The woman with whom her husband had been conducting an affair was called Nancy Neele. Some conspiracy theorists have suggested that Christie chose the name Teresa as an anagram of the word 'teaser'. Others have quite reasonably suggested that her motives might have been two-fold: a bit of publicity for the book, and one in the eye for her spouse. But Christie's subsequent withdrawal from public life might suggest that her plight was more genuine. It could be argued that she withdrew into obscurity because she was ashamed that her stunt had gone so awry. But it could equally be said that she was hurt, quite honestly offended that, instead of treating her amnesiac episode with sympathy, public opinion dismissed her as an attention-seeker.

Incidents of genuine amnesia can often involve a patchy retention of significant details. For instance, in one case, a preacher by the name of A. Bourne went missing, and was later found to be prophesying hell fire and damnation under the name of A. Brown. In another case, a doctor prompted an amnesiac woman to use a highly practised motor skill – to dial a random telephone number – and when she did so, she found herself speaking to her mother. So Agatha Christie's choice of pseudonym – a name similar to that of her husband's lover – may not have been a conscious trick, but a fragment of the truth bubbling up through her forgetfulness. Possibly it was the extreme stress surrounding the disintegration of her marriage – her husband married the real Ms Neele three weeks after divorcing Christie – which led to the bout of amnesia in the first place, and the choice of moniker was an unconscious way of signalling this.

As the case of Preacher Bourne/Brown indicates, amnesia does not result in total loss of memory. People may forget elements of their identity but not the skills they have learnt. So our memory for things we have learnt is separate and distinct from our autobiographical memories. Accordingly, there's a different type of activity within the brain as we master new skills – like riding a bike, or playing a musical instrument.

Second nature: the chemistry of procedural memory

Martha Curtis was a musical child prodigy who began playing the violin at the age of nine. She had suffered from epilepsy all her life, and as she grew, experienced seizures more and more frequently. In spite of extensive drug treatment, Martha had as many as four attacks of unconsciousness a month, sometimes collapsing on stage in front of an audience. In 1991 at the Cleveland Clinic, she had the first of three major operations. Eventually she had nearly 50 per cent of her right temporal lobe removed, a huge gamble for a musician because it is this area that is believed to be active when playing a musical instrument. To the astonishment and gratification of her surgeons, Martha's violin-playing was unaffected by the three operations. In fact she seemed to be able to master and learn pieces that she had hitherto considered too complex. Her doctors at the Cleveland Clinic concluded that, since she had been suffering from epilepsy from a very young age, Martha's brain had compensated for her faulty right temporal lobe. Being plastic at that age, it had coopted other brain areas into use, so that when Martha learnt and practised her violin-playing, the right temporal lobe was effectively bypassed.

Although Martha is clearly exceptional, every brain has a built-in element of plasticity. It adapts itself to the input. And we can see this process at work most clearly when we look at how we learn a skill. Many of us will be able to remember, with effort, the painful process of trial and error by which we first learnt to ride a bicycle, or how to drive a car. But very few of us remember this when we perform it as a matter of routine in later life. At a certain point, after repeated practice, we seem to be able to ride or drive without thinking particularly hard about what we are doing. We do it 'automatically'; it has become 'second nature'. Occasionally lorry drivers say they are unable to recall the route by which they arrived at their final destination. Driving from one city to another has become so familiar that they seem scarcely conscious of doing it.

Inside the brain, we can see a corresponding shift from the higher cortical areas of processing to the lower rungs of motor and balance as we learn and master a skill. When it is new to us, we are consciously thinking about it – remembering what to do at stage A and stage B, monitoring our progress. But over time, we start to think about it less and less, to the point where we are barely conscious. Once the procedural memory is stored in this lower level, it becomes permanent. This is why we don't forget how to swim or ride a bike, even though it has been a number of years between attempts. I find this with the physical skill of skiing. It was horrendously difficult to learn, but now comes totally naturally once a year, after a few seconds of hesitant starting. I do notice, however, that with age I have become more cautious in which slopes I tackle.

The reason for this shift from the higher conscious levels of the brain to the lower, unconscious regions is one of economy. The ever-plastic, ever-adapting brain sends procedural memories down to the basement as soon as it can, in order that it can be freed up for new tasks. If it did not, there would be a limit to what we could learn in a lifetime. And there isn't. There are limits to other elements of the equation that determine what we learn and what we don't – for instance, the degree to which a certain skill is important to us, the degree of motivation. But the human mind has the potential to continue to learn.

In the mid–1980s, some interesting experiments were done at Washington University in St Louis. Researchers made PET scans of volunteers as they read aloud a list of nouns. In a second experiment, they were asked not only to read the nouns, but to come up with a corresponding verb – for instance, to pair 'chair' with 'sit'. By comparing the PET scans, the research team, led by Marcus Raichle of the Mallinckrodt Institute of Radiology and Michael Posner of the University of Oregon, was able to isolate the area of the brain that was involved in thinking of the right verb to say.

But then the researchers noticed something new. When volunteers had been through the list a few times, the map of brain activity looked radically different. The overall pattern was one of markedly lower intensity. But paradoxically, when a word-association task was new, an area, the insula cortex, was dormant. It became active only when the task had been practised a few times. What was even more odd about it was that for years neurologists thought the insula cortex was purely involved in somatic and visceral sensation from, for example, the bowel, and taste perception – playing no part in the production or comprehension of language.

What the researchers had seen was a new task becoming a habit. The first time one of their subjects had to find an associated verb for a hitherto unseen noun, there was a raft of activity across the brain – from the cingulate cortex at the front to the cerebellum at the back. But as the skill became practised, there was a marked shrinkage of neuronal activity. The brain effectively turned down its own dimmer switch, so that it was using only the minimum areas and energy.

These results confirmed something that Richard Haier at the University of Southern California, Irvine, had also found. His work with PET scanners had shown that there was no link between the level of activity inside the brain and a person's IQ. A 'busy' brain was not, in his findings, a clever brain at all – in fact, it was rather the opposite. It seemed that a clever brain was one that could shrink back to the barest levels of energy consumption in the swiftest time – thereby freeing up its circuitry for other purposes. It's not what you know, but how quickly you can master it.

This brings me to another important aspect of memory. Because, if we can see a gradual shifting of information from the upper to the lower cortex as we commit things to memory, this implies that we are endowed with two different sorts of memory. We call this the distinction between the short and the long term.

We are all aware of this distinction in our daily lives. I might say that my knowledge of French, or of Freud, such as it is, resides in my long-term memory. My knowledge of the sentence I have just devised in my head and am now typing, on the other hand, resides in my short-term memory. The very construction of those labels expresses the chief difference between the two faculties – one holds information for a long time; the other empties itself more rapidly. Back in the 1950s, psychologist George A. Miller published a paper entitled 'The magical number seven, plus or minus two'. Within it, Miller put forward his thesis that the short-term memory of humans seems to be able to hold onto roughly seven units of information – such as words, names or numbers. And this idea is still largely accepted. The short-term memory of the average human is too small to encompass a London telephone number – one reason why there is always outrage when BT announces the arrival of yet another digit.

But the example I use above raises a question, because there are some strings of numbers I use most days – phone numbers of friends and colleagues, my PIN number for my credit card account – just as there are skills I call upon every day, such as typing or driving, which I can execute with the bare minimum of conscious effort. I don't have to keep them in the limited space of my short-term memory – regular use has ensured that they are stored in my long-term site.

So how, and why, does information transfer from one type of memory to the other? As we saw above, factors like the novelty of the incoming information and the intensity of the emotions attached to it help determine how indelibly a memory is stored. So does the frequency with which the information is encountered. I can reel off sums like 'seven times seven equals forty-nine' in an instant, not because I am actually doing the maths inside my brain but because I am revisiting a little pattern of words stored in my long-term memory, etched there after my having spent hours reciting multiplication tables, dirge-like, at school. The process of long-term potentiation has ensured that, whatever else I might fail to remember from my classes, some elementary maths will remain stuck inside my brain.

The shift from short to long term

Recent research conducted with mice and flies suggests that short-term memory uses proteins that are already present in the synapses. But in order to shift this information into the long-term memory, new proteins have to be manufactured. The creation of these proteins is controlled by a further protein called CREB. CREB would seem to be involved in many of the situations where the brain has to 'get used to' new conditions – for instance, in adjusting the body clock, or in developing a tolerance to drugs. Memory disorders are extremely common: we lose some memory with age, and the ravages of Alzheimer's disease are increasingly significant in our society. So a better understanding of the molecules involved in memory formation is of enormous importance. Many scientists, and some pharmaceutical companies, have an increasing interest in enhancing learning and memory with drugs, and so studies on CREB are a key area of research.

CREB is present in the nervous system or brain of many animals, from shellfish to humans. The fact that it has been present throughout evolution underlines its potential importance. In Los Angeles, Dr Alcino Silva has been working with mice.[55] They were placed in a chamber where they were given a small shock to the foot. Their memory was assessed later by putting the mice back in the same chamber and measuring the time they remained motionless, presumably in fear of receiving more shocks. Dr Silva then compared their response with that of mice born with a modified gene that blocked the action of CREB when they were given an oestrogen, tamoxifen.

When tamoxifen was administered to these mice before they entered the chamber, the length of time they remained motionless was unaffected two hours after shock training but was considerably shortened when measured twenty-four hours after training. This suggests that CREB-associated genes do not play a role in the creation of short-term memories but that they help in forming long-term memory, created after about a day and which can stay in the brain perhaps for ever.

Dr Leslie Ungerleider, at the American National Institute of Mental Health, used MRI to see what happened inside the brain of people as they attempted to 'hold on' to a remembered image of a face over increasingly long time periods.[56] When the delay was short, there was marked activity in the prefrontal cortex and temporal lobe.

But as the delay grew longer, the temporal lobe firing shrank, leaving only the prefrontal cortex at work. In other words, Ungerleider has pinpointed what may be the site of the short-term memory – somewhere within the frontal lobes. Ungerleider's studies built upon earlier work performed with monkeys. Using electrodes or radioactive pellets to 'knock out' the hippocampus or the prefrontal lobes, the researchers were able to note the distinct roles of these areas in long- and short-term memory. A monkey with a damaged hippocampus can hold a memory for about ten seconds, but no longer. It also loses its memory if there is any distraction during this period. But a monkey with a damaged prefrontal cortex had no working memory at all. In the English language, we talk of certain ideas or information as being at the 'front of our minds', and indeed the neurological evidence does suggest that this is where the brain activity is happening.

So we recruit different areas of our brains to help us remember information in the short and long term. And a variety of factors can determine whether the information gets shunted downwards for permanent storage, or whether it remains with us for only a few hours. Michael Merzenich of the University of California at San Francisco showed that motivation plays an important part in determining how deeply a memory is implanted. He studied the brains of monkeys as they learnt to associate a certain pattern of spinning wheels with a reward of food. He discovered that when a reward was entailed, many more neurons were coopted into the learning task. The same is surely the case for human learning. One of the reasons why my classmates still remember their multiplication tables is because we were all motivated to win the weekly prize.

Studies have also shown that our recall can be quite strongly influenced by the setting in which we learn things. Alan Baddeley, of the University of Bristol, asked volunteers to learn lists of unfamiliar words while weighted down with scuba equipment at the bottom of a swimming pool. He discovered that their recall of these words was more accurate when they were tested in the same circumstances. It's possible that we could all exploit this most curious aspect of our memories – and we don't necessarily need a load of diving equipment and a swimming pool. If you sniff a powerful aroma, like lavender oil, as you learn some fact, you may be able to recall it more efficiently if you sniff the same substance again when you are tested.

Sleeping on it

The ability of our brain to store information in the long term may also be affected by what we do after the event. A joint Belgian and Canadian study headed by Pierre Maquet demonstrated that when we are trained to do a certain activity, our brain continues to repeat the related pattern of neuronal activity during rapid eye movement (REM) sleep. REM sleep is the time when people dream. The work of Avi Karni and Dov Sagi at the Weizmann Institute in Israel has further shown that REM sleep improves the learning of a task.[57] They measured the length of time it took four subjects to learn how to recognize an embedded patch of stripes within a pattern, and tested them both before and after REM sleep. If they were woken before or during REM sleep, they failed to master the task. In other experiments conducted with rats, they found that interrupting REM sleep completely thwarted the learning of a new task, yet interrupting non-REM sleep just as frequently did not. So a good night's sleep, like emotion, acts as a kind of cement for our memories.

Dr Allan Hobson's group at Harvard have recently done some interesting work that shows the potential of the 'power nap'. Apparently, even a nap improves learning. Sara Mednick and Robert Stickgold, with colleagues at Harvard, have demonstrated that midday snoozing isn't such a bad thing.[58] It reverses the morning irritation, boredom and frustration with mental tasks that we all often feel, while a 20 per cent overnight improvement in learning a motor skill is largely traceable to a late stage of sleep that early risers miss. Overall, their studies suggest that the brain uses a night's sleep to consolidate the memories of actions and skills learnt during the day. In one experiment, subjects were asked to report the horizontal or vertical orientation of three diagonal bars against a background of horizontal bars in the lower left corner of a computer screen. Their scores on the task worsened over four daily sessions. A thirty-minute nap after the second session prevented any further deterioration, and a nap lasting one hour boosted performance in the third and fourth sessions to morning levels. The researchers wondered whether this effect was due to 'burnout' of brain visual circuits involved in the task. So they engaged a fresh set of neural circuitry by switching the location of the task to the lower right corner of the computer screen for just the fourth practice session. Subjects experienced no burnout and performed about as well as they did in the first session – or after a short nap.

How might a nap help? Recordings of brain and ocular electrical activity monitored while napping revealed that longer one-hour naps contained more than four times as much deep or slow-wave sleep and rapid eye movement (REM) sleep as the half-hour naps. Since a nap hardly allows enough time for the early morning REM sleep effect to develop, it would appear that a slow-wave sleep effect is the best antidote to burnout. The researchers suggest that neural networks involved in this task are refreshed by 'mechanisms of cortical plasticity' operating during slow-wave sleep. So when the boss catches you with your feet up – with the commodity markets going haywire – you tell him or her that you are merely restoring the plasticity of your brain.

Macbeth is obsessed by sleep but the power nap might not have been ideal. Having killed Duncan and the servants while they, and everybody else, were sleeping, he longed for prolonged sleep to provide relief from the state of mental torture into which he'd flung himself. His decline, from a war hero into a paranoid coward, indicates how powerful the human mind can be, and how dangerously it can distort our view of reality. As I shall explain below, the memory is far from exempt from this. We can remember, without knowing that we are remembering. And conversely, our memories can make us think we remember things that never happened.

The buried past: unconscious and false memories

In an experiment conducted by American psychotherapists in the early 1970s, a group of strangers were placed in a room and asked to pair off. Without speaking and without thinking too deeply, their task was to find a partner who reminded them of some close member of their family, or alternatively some missing element in their family. The newly formed couples were then told to speak, to compare notes as it were, about their backgrounds. They were then told to double up once again, teaming up with other couples who they felt shared the common attributes they had just identified.

These people formed units that replicated their experiences of being within their family group. They might discover, for example, that all four of them came from families where there had been difficulties in expressing anger, or love. Or they all had come from families shaken by bereavement, divorce or abuse. Even those who hung back and were reluctant to form either initial pairs or eventual foursomes had more than just this trait of reticence in common. When they did form foursomes eventually, they discovered that each had been through early and significant experiences of rejection – been abandoned, adopted, or brought up in orphanages or foster homes. What the therapists may have been seeing was the action of unconscious memory.

The work of social psychologist Robert Zajonc has indicated that our reactions to people differ depending upon whether we have seen them before, even if we do not consciously know that we have seen them. In one fascinating experiment – in chicks, not humans – he measured pecking rates (a form of mutual recognition) in chicks who had been housed together for just sixteen hours when they were one day old.[59] The chicks had been treated with a dye colour so those chicks who were strangers to each other and those who had been companions could detect each other. The chicks could discriminate between a stranger and a previous companion within one minute of meeting. It seemed that the opportunity to peck during the initial housing together was a prerequisite in producing social discrimination. In a famous human experiment, volunteers were shown a quick-moving display of faces. Secondly, they were shown another display – containing some of the faces they had seen before and some new ones – and asked to rate their attractiveness. Although the first assembly of faces was shown so fast it would have been impossible to register them consciously, these people consistently rated the twice-viewed faces as being more attractive. Later they were exposed very briefly to a view of a particular person. They were then asked to join forces with a couple, unaware that one of the couple was the person they had glimpsed momentarily. This couple were engaged in a staged dispute and the subjects were asked with which member of the couple they agreed. The subjects consistently sided with the people they had seen before.

For a long time neurologists have thought that we can be guided by unconscious memories. People with Korsakoff's syndrome, the result of brain damage caused by long-term alcoholism, suffer from amnesia; they are unable to form or retrieve any new conscious memories, so that patients cannot remember recent past events. There is evidence that their recent experiences are not totally forgotten – they are unconsciously stored and this storage may influence their behaviour without them understanding why. In 1911, the Swiss psychologist Edouard Claparède rather unkindly hid a small pin in his hand so that when he shook hands with a woman patient with Korsakoff's disorder, he pricked her palm. When reintroduced to Claparède a few days later, the patient had no conscious recollection of having met him before but refused, nevertheless, to shake his hand, feeling that something bad might happen, although she could not explain what or why.

Years later, Antonio Damasio was treating a patient with significant damage to his hippocampus. To test whether the man could still learn new information, Damasio developed a test in which the patient was exposed to social meetings with three different people. It was known as the 'good guy/bad guy' experiment because the situations were of three types. The first was pleasant and rewarding. The second, 'control' experience was neutral. And the third experience was rather nasty – in that the poor individual found himself stuck in a room with an abrupt, unfriendly experimenter, who subjected him to an array of mindlessly enervating psychological tests.

After the five days over which these experiences took place, Damasio then showed his patient a set of photographs of different faces – which included the three different experimenters. The patient was asked questions like, 'Who, out of these photographs, would you approach if you needed help?' and 'Who do you think is your friend?' Despite claiming that he did not recognize any of the faces he was shown, the patient consistently picked the 'good guy' as a friend, as someone he would approach for help. Damasio concluded that, in spite of the obvious damage to the learning and memory structures of his brain, the patient was still able to form and access quite a different type of 'memory' – unconscious 'memories' with an emotional content. In other words, as we have seen in other contexts, we can learn with our emotions.

Brain scientists in one corner, psychoanalysts in the other

Psychoanalysis – sometimes seen as the arch-enemy of brain science – rests upon exactly this view of the workings of our memory. It argues that we consciously remember only a small portion of our past, just as we are consciously aware of only a small portion of what is going on inside our brain. Psychoanalysts believe that our actions and thought-processes are governed strongly by unconscious processes. By delving into them, by being encouraged to verbalize them, we bring them into the realms of our conscious control.

Memory has been one of the traditional battlegrounds between the psychoanalysts and the brain scientists – the extremists of the former believing that experience and environment are everything and that the only cure is through talking, and the extremists of the latter maintaining that the root of every disorder lies in brain chemistry, which could be altered through surgery and drugs. The growing understanding of the interplay between the plastic brain and the environment to which it adapts itself has not yet resulted in any long-lasting truce between the two disciplines. But in some instances, recent findings in neurological science concur with things Freud proposed over a hundred years ago.

Both Freud and Jung believed that traumatic experiences create a splitting effect within the mind – the result being that people are plunged into destructive internal conflicts between different aspects of themselves. An example might be the fate of Wilhelm Reich, a psychoanalyst who some considered a natural successor to Freud. He died in prison in the USA in the 1950s, having been hounded by the American government for supposed communist sympathies. Reich had a number of extremely strange ideas, among which was his conviction that aliens were trying to contact the earth; he may have been nearer the mark with his view that the government had mounted a conspiracy against him. Freudians would point out that Reich experienced an early trauma – having caught his mother having sex with his tutor. The young Reich informed his father, and his mother committed suicide. So, in later life, it is proposed there was a 'splitting' of Reich's psyche into good and bad aspects. What he envisaged, in the form of invading spaceships and conspiring government agents, was actually his own guilt at his actions as a boy. All this seems fanciful. Perhaps Reich had good conscious reason to feel the way he did, particularly as various letters about Reich's 'activities', signed by J. Edgar Hoover to his secret agents, are still in existence.

Curiously, research conducted at McLean Hospital in Massachusetts has indicated that the corpus callosum – the bridge between the two halves of the brain – might be smaller in children who have been subjected to abuse or neglect at an early age. In later life this may possibly lead to reduced 'traffic' between the two hemi-spheres. Such people might find themselves supposedly less able to verbalize their feelings or memories, or achieve a balance between the left-brain 'thinking' and right-brain 'feeling' parts of their person-alities. In other words, what we would see is an individual of more disparate parts, which might even seem to be in conflict with one another – rather as Freud suggested.

Memory – and in particular the memory of trauma – is one arena in which scientists and psychotherapists seem destined to slug it out for a long time to come. The debate has become especially con-tentious since a number of people undergoing therapy 'recalled' years of buried memories, including recollections of traumatic abuse. In some high-profile cases, families torn apart by abuse allegations have sought compensation from the therapists concerned. There is even a group called the False Memory Syndrome Foundation, which offers support to families who have suffered in this way. But some evidence from brain science suggests that the two phenomena might be equally possible: first, that it is possible for people to repress or 'bury' traumatic memories, and secondly, that people can have memories that are quite false.

It is clear that human memory is highly selective and subjective. Last year, Tessa Livingstone, the producer of the BBC's *Child of Our Time*, and I filmed our own experiments into false memory. We tried to deliberately create false memories from childhood. We asked a number of adults if they could remember when they were in a hot-air balloon when a child. Not surprisingly, none could – after all, balloon travel is a bit of a luxury that few of us have ever experienced, including our subjects. Using family snapshots, we then made a collage photograph of people in the basket of a hot-air balloon, past-ing in childhood snapshots of our subjects when they were children. We used Photoshop, the computer program, to do this. Many of the 'photos' we created were very crude – and to our eyes, obvious forgeries. When we then showed these photos to our adults, most looked rather doubtful and still could not recollect their 'aerial journey'. Nevertheless, within a few days a surprising number of these adults telephoned or returned to tell us to say that, on reflection, they did remember the trip, sometimes quite well. One woman even recalled that shortly after the ascent she felt so frightened that she asked to be landed on earth so that she could be let out of the basket.

We have seen already that the degree of emotion associated with an event can determine how well it is remembered. But in traumatic memories, the reverse seems to happen. People who have been through deeply traumatic experiences seem to remember only fragments, or to have blanked the whole thing out. One explanation could be that the overload of the amygdala during the original event is repeated whenever a recall of the event is triggered. This produces emotions so intense that the person involved has difficulty in consciously processing the memory, and even more difficulty in verbalizing what they are remembering. A further argument is that the stress hormone cortisol may interfere with the process of long-term potentiation.

Whatever the mechanism, the younger a person is when they experience a traumatic event, the greater the chance that they will bury some or all of the memory. But what about people who have undergone repeated trauma – such as abuse victims, or the survivors of concentration camps and 'ethnic cleansing'? All the evidence would suggest that the human mind certainly buries isolated, stand-alone events of high emotional stress, but if such experiences were repeated, then they ought to remain within the grasp of our memories. Yet the incidence of memory loss is just as high in these cases.

One answer to this may be that someone who is repeatedly traumatized becomes adept at repressing the painful memory. This presumably would offer some psychological protection. The work of Chris Brewin at University College, London offers an alternative spin on this notion.[60] His work indicates that some people who suffer persistent memories of traumatic incidents may often have a less efficient interplay between the short- and the long-term memory. Possibly, people with a more efficient mechanism are better able to suppress their traumatic long-term memories in order to get on with their daily lives.

There's another false memory experiment you can try on yourself. Read the following list of words out loud: sour, candy, sugar, bitter, good, taste, tooth, nice, pea, chocolate, cake, heart, tart. Now put this book down for a moment and try to write down as many of the words as possible. A version of this experiment was first used by memory researchers Henry Roediger and Kathleen McDermott in 1995. They wanted to see how easy it would be to induce a false memory in normal healthy subjects. So let's look now at the list you made. If it includes the word 'sweet', then you have experienced a false memory. But it is easy to see how the conditions were favourable to you coming up with this word – because all the words in the list were related to it.

Stranger still, our brain seems to know a false memory from a true one, even if we don't realize it. Daniel Schachter at Harvard performed PET scans on volunteers as they looked at lists of words, some of which they had seen before, others of which were new to them. As they looked at each list, the subjects were asked to say whether they had seen certain of them before. Lists that the subjects had seen before activated the hippocampus and the language centres of the brain. But lists that the subjects thought they had seen, but in fact had not, also activated the orbitofrontal cortex. This area would seem to be a sort of anomaly detection system – pointing out when something is 'not quite right'. Studies at the University of California, Berkeley, have shown that people with damage to the orbitofrontal cortex may lack an ability to regulate their own behaviour – telling inappropriate jokes, acting overly familiar with strangers and using crude language.

One factor that influences how accurately we remember things is consistency. Studies have shown that we revise our memories in order to make them fit in with what we later know. Michael Conway of the University of Durham asked a group of student volunteers to take a 'study-skills' course that claimed to boost learning and recall. Compared to students who had not undertaken the course, they showed no improvement – indeed, their final exam performance was slightly worse. But all the students reported that the study-skills course had been helpful to them. There is an explanation for this. At the outset of the course, the students were asked to rate their studying skills. They were also asked to do so at the end of the course, and to recall how they had originally rated themselves. In describing their earlier performance, the students recalled themselves as significantly worse than they had actually been. In other words, they had revised their memories to be consistent with the view that, since taking the course, they had become better at studying.

Losing it: ageing and memory

Parents and teachers will know something of the scorn young people sometimes show whenever their elders have a lapse of memory. As we advance through life, we may become annoyed at ourselves as it becomes increasingly hard to remember to post a letter or where we put our car keys. Many people begin to worry quite seriously at this stage, seeing this forgetfulness not just as a sign of ageing, but as a possible indication of Alzheimer's disease. In actual fact, the patterns of memory loss are different.

For most of us, the problem is not that the memory has been wiped clean, but that we experience difficulty in retrieving it. Given the right cues, or even equipped with our own method of remembering, we can come up with the right answer. Research has indicated that older people can perform just as well as younger counterparts in memory and cognitive tests, but they respond better to comfortable conditions and a relaxed schedule. Given the pressures of time and stresses in the environment, their ability becomes impaired.

Learning 'how to remember' can also be particularly effective for older people. Making strange or unfamiliar associations can help to nudge memories into the light. For instance, I have difficulty remembering my car numberplate, LD52ZIR. I recall it by associating 'LD' with a Lethal Dose, which is just over 50 per cent of a rare chemical compound, ZIR. Incidentally, my rare chemical 'ZIR' does not exist.

We filmed Andi Bell, who is the reigning World Memory Champion, for the television series accompanying this book. Andi uses a combination of the association technique described above and another trick called the 'Method of Loci' to perform his memory feats. On the day we filmed him, he memorized the entire order of ten decks of cards in twenty minutes. On the face of it, this seems an impossible feat. He then explained to us exactly what he was doing.

First, he was marrying each card to a particular pictorial image in his mind's eye. For instance, the three of clubs was associated with

Mickey Mouse, because of its resemblance to the cartoon character's prominent black ears. The use of imagery helps with recall because it adds an additional trigger-facility – a little 'hook', if you like, that enables us to fish the memory out with greater ease. Studies have shown two further things: that a new memory linked to an older, familiar one has greater ease of recall. Secondly, the more bizarre the association between the old memory and the new one, the better the likelihood of recall. As we know, the human brain is attracted to the unusual and the novel.

The second stage of Andi Bell's memorizing process is to attach each of the pictorial images to points along a memorized route. This is what we mean by the Method of Loci – which is thought to have been devised by Simonides in 500BC. Invited to give a speech at the dinner party of a Greek grandee, Simonides temporarily left the building – perhaps, like most public speakers from time to time, he forgot his notes – or possibly he just wanted to get away from the banal conversation. While he was outside, the building fell down, killing all the guests and crushing them so badly that identification was impossible. Simonides proved invaluable to the concerned relatives because he was able to remember where each guest had been sitting around the dining table. Impressed by his own powers, he devised a technique whereby he visualized a room he knew well in great detail, and then placed items he wished to remember within certain locations around that room.

Andi Bell uses the streets of London as his particular 'memory room', and he spends a lot of time pounding the highways and byways of the capital, carefully memorizing features and landmarks along the route. His method not only gives him another trigger-device, but also ensures that he gets things in the right order.

The World Memory Championship, held each year in Britain, involves the competitors learning lists of thousands of words and random numbers, and quoting at length from novels and poems. Dr Eleanor Maguire of University College, London, decided to test the lead competitors to see how their brains differed from those of ordinary folk. She and her colleagues took the eight finalists in the Memory Championship, and two other volunteers who had been studied before and found to have an unusual ability to remember things. Dr Maguire's team then compared this group of memory champions with ten other people whose education and job were comparable.

This control group did not profess to having an especially good memory but were regarded as average. All had at least two to three hours of intelligence tests and other mental assessments, as well as MRI and fMRI scans. Maguire found that there were no physical differences in the brains of these memory champs, but they all used the techniques similar to those I have described. 'Although more research is needed, it may be that we all have the potential and neural capacity to improve our memories,' says Eleanor Maguire. So a better memory may be a question of practice using the special techniques I have described.

A research study in 1968 by Ross and Lawrence showed that undergraduates taught to use the Method of Loci were able to recall 38 out of 40 items on a list. Twenty-four hours later, they could still recall 34 items. Other studies have suggested that the Method of Loci can increase recall by between two and seven times.

I thought it might be interesting to put Andi Bell's methods to the test. With the camera crew filming, I tried to learn a list of thirty unrelated words in four minutes, by a combination of what I call marriage and burial. That is, I first 'married' each word to an image, and then I 'buried' it in a specific place within an imagined familiar location – my house in London. As I moved in my mind along a specific route around my house, I married and buried more of the words. For instance (words to be learnt in capitals):

WASHing an APPLE in the garden

A JET flying round MADLY in the hall

In the dining room an ACTRESS is smeared in MARMALADE

They tested me a few hours later, and I showed 70 per cent recall. This did not seem a satisfactory result to me so I tried to develop my own strategies. I was then able to recall another list of thirty random words in the right order after just three minutes of attempting to memorize them. Using the rhythm they made in my mind and associating them musically, I had 100 per cent recall. So there may be different methods we can use to enhance our minds and different techniques may help different subjects.

As I stated earlier, memory problems are not a sure-fire indicator of senile dementia. In fact, the statistics indicate that no more than 10–15 per cent of the population will develop Alzheimer's disease. And its effects on the memory are different and unmistakable. People with normal age-related memory loss tend to experience an increase in those 'tip of the tongue' memory moments, where they know they know something, but cannot quite recall it – usually because it is not an item they need to recall every day. People with Alzheimer's disease, in contrast, forget the names and functions of objects they encounter in their daily lives.

Exercise the brain

It was once believed that we are born with a finite number of neurons, and that from birth this declines. Nowadays it is understood that the actual volume of tissue lost due to ageing is very small. What does suffer significant loss is the basal forebrain, the area that supplies acetylcholine to the hippocampus. It is argued that this affects the plasticity of the brain, making it increasingly hard for the brain of an older person to adapt to changing circumstances. A key protein, called PP1, in mice – which seems to have a role in deleting memories – has recently been identified.[61] By blocking its action, researchers found that they could boost the learning and memory capacities of mice. The American National Institute on Aging (NIA) has also indicated that hormones play a role in age-related memory loss. Older men with higher levels of testosterone perform better at visual and verbal recall. A similar process seems to be at work for their wives – postmenopausal women who received oestrogen replacement therapy were able to maintain their verbal memory and proved better at learning new facts. This is particularly interesting because oestrogens, as we saw with the CREB-deficient mice, may play a part in the action of this protein.

Randy Buckner and his team at Washington University, St Louis, have shown that there are two basic types of age-related memory deficiency – so-called 'under-recruitment' and 'non-selective recruitment'.[62] When there is 'under-recruitment', older people are less able to use the specific areas of the brain that usually aid memory. 'Non-selective recruitment' is when older subjects tend to recruit parts of their brain that are not useful in tasks that require memory processing.

In an important scanning study in 2002, Dr Buckner compared activity in the brain of people in their twenties with healthy adults aged seventy to eighty. Each was asked to memorize a series of words while being scanned by fMRI. Their brain blood flow was measured in three specific areas of the frontal cortex. In the first study, the younger and older adults were shown words and asked to try to remember them for later. Dr Buckner says, 'As previous studies had shown, we confirmed that the older adults did not recruit the critical frontal regions as much as the younger adults.' The older people also showed non-selective recruitment of parts of the cortex that would not aid memory processing.

Dr Buckner then tried to see if the problem could be resolved by helping the older people with a trick that would recruit the appropriate frontal cortex. This time he gave them a list of words and asked them to put them in categories – such as whether the word represented something 'concrete or 'abstract'. When they did that, the older adults showed increased activity in the appropriate frontal regions, and their memory performance improved. This approach helps under-recruitment, but not, it seems, non-selective recruitment.

The increased blood flow they identified reflects greater activity in regions of the brain that are used during the tasks. Of the three areas of the frontal cortex Dr Buckner and colleagues imaged, two were in the left hemisphere and one on the right. The left hemisphere is generally dominant in language processing, so contains regions that you would expect to show increased activity while memorizing words; conversely, the right hemisphere should remain inactive. The third area the researchers studied was the prefrontal cortex, highly concerned with memorizing verbal material.

Aids to memory (such as putting words in categories) had no effect on non-selective recruitment in the older people. The young men and women used the left frontal area when they memorized words; that, it seems to Dr Buckner, streamlines their information processing. But older people used both left and right sides, even when they used strategies to improve their memories. What is most encouraging about these studies is that these healthy old people still had parts of their brain they could recruit to solve tasks – the frontal cortex on the 'wrong side' had not atrophied or degenerated, it was just 'under-recruited'. So the reduction in processing capacity of the brain with ageing is not completely irreversible. It is likely that rehabilitation therapy to improve cognition might be helpful to keep healthy older people living an active, independent life.

The next important area for this research is to see what happens in unhealthy older people – those with conditions like Alzheimer's disease. Currently, it is unclear whether there are cognitive tricks that could possibly be used by older people which might result in better retention of memory and slowing down the processes of brain deterioration.

A older study, undertaken in 1993 by Richard Mohs and team at Yale School of Medicine, showed that people with more education showed less age-related memory loss.[63] Years of schooling equip people with a sort of 'memory toolkit'. It gives them better methods to learn and recall data. Efficient learners are on the lookout for patterns and make increased use of tricks like categorization.

But there is no reason to suspect that you are doomed to lose your memory because you left school at the first opportunity. Even a daily walk to the shops can do the brain some good – research has shown that when adults aged sixty to seventy-five perform a gentle walking programme, their memory, judgement and planning abilities improve compared to adults who do other forms of exercise. And what does your brain think of your morning jog? At Nihon Fukushi University in Aichi, Japan, researchers studied seven healthy students who jogged a prescribed course for thirty minutes a day, three times a week, for twelve weeks. These students were tested for specific aspects of mental ability on three occasions during the three-month period. For comparison, seven sedentary non–jogging students did similar tests. After the twelfth week of the study, the joggers scored nearly 30 per cent better than the couch potatoes. There are a number of other studies that suggest that regular physical exercise enhances memory. Studies using MRI scanning might help to evaluate any brain changes due to exercise, though it seems that in general, physical exercise increases brain blood flow quite substantially. The evidence would suggest that this is valuable in older people, too. It is never too late to start exercising your brain.

chapter seven

A question of character

When Philip Larkin returns to his old Oxford college, he learns that his room-mate from the past now has a son who is old enough to be an undergraduate himself. This is quite an unwelcome surprise and it leads to poignant consideration of his own existence – what is it that has made the lives of two close friends, contemporaries at the most formative stage of their life, end up travelling down such divergent paths? Larkin, a solitary, never married and never had children. The theme of needing human company, but also feeling suffocated by it, runs through his poetry.

So what made Larkin tread his path? To some extent, our lives' journeys are dependent upon chance. The right job offer here, the sudden illness or little windfall there. In Larkin's case, he always maintained that he fell into librarianship because the War Ministry wrote him a stern letter, shortly after he had left university, asking him what he intended to do with himself. Exempted from military service because of his poor eyesight and fearing a life of dull oblivion in the civil service, he responded to the first advert he saw of a job that seemed bearable. It just happened to be a sub-librarian's post in Wellington, Shropshire. But is that really all there is to the matter?

> . . . Where do these
> Innate assumptions come from? Not from what
> We think truest, or most want to do:

Those warp tight-shut, like doors. They're more a style
Our lives bring with them: habit for a while,
Suddenly they harden into all we've got.

'Dockery and Son', 1963, Philip Larkin, *Collected Poems*
(Faber and Faber 1988)

Our personality is the driving force behind the experiences we undergo and the evidence suggests that chance may play only a small role. Some brain and psychological research strongly points to the fact that many of the key elements of our personality are present from birth, identifiable in the way our brain responds to the world. And they are certainly firmly, and largely irrevocably, established by the time we are of university age. I am convinced that this is the case with my own younger siblings, and certainly with my own children. The artistic child drew exquisite drawings and showed a visual sense of the colour of the world from the age of three. My most patient off-spring stood in his drenched cot aged one when a burst pipe flooded his room at night; when we opened the door in the morning there was a small, cold, waterlogged figure, in a totally sodden Babygro with hair plastered around his head, standing in a puddle of cold water – not crying, but simply waiting to be rescued. And the performer, well, he danced in the streets when he heard buskers, strutted even harder when he noticed people watching and was positively flamboyant to attract their attention if he thought they'd stopped watching. And each from his or her first year of life showed a different aspect of reasoning and sociability – aspects which to my mind are clearly identifiable today. So, in other words, Philip Larkin didn't have quite as much choice about becoming a librarian and a poet as he thought – his brain probably made him do it.

The licking test

For the BBC television series of *The Human Mind*, we undertook a little test in London's main fruit market, Spitalfields. After getting our victims to fill in a simple personality questionnaire, we asked two groups of people – a platoon of student physicists at Imperial College, and a troupe of Butlin's hospitality staff – to compete in licking yards of two-inch-wide gummed tape. This was the competition between the White Coats and the Redcoats. You will not be surprised to learn that Imperial College physicists tend to be serious introverts. They spent most of the time in the market looking as if they would rather be in a darkened room. The Butlin's Redcoats, on the other hand, looked as if they had momentarily come in off the beach, and were clearly extremely extroverted. As you can see from the photograph in the plate section, the physicists found it well-nigh impossible even to smile at their predicament, while the Redcoats were grinning from ear to ear and competing with each other to get on camera. Various psychological studies under controlled conditions have shown that introverts produce much more saliva than extroverts. So, after a quick splash of lemon juice on each contestant's tongue, we expected our physics students to be able to lick far more packing tape to encircle boxes full of oranges than the lively Butlin's group – even though, being extrovert, the Redcoats were certainly trying and competing much harder.

The British psychologist Hans Eysenck was among the first to categorize personality traits. He defined what he felt were a number of specific, different human personality types, and believed that these types could be linked to specific biological traits. The degree to which a person showed extroversion or introversion, he maintained, was linked to levels of arousal in the brain. In others words – guess what – our brain chemistry influences who we are.

It is worthwhile making a pit-stop here to briefly discuss what I mean by terms like 'personality' and 'extrovert'. 'Personality' in my definition is typified by the characteristics, emotional responses, thoughts and types of behaviour that are constant over time and circumstances in a particular individual. Eysenck devised a scale of personality upon which there were three extremities: Extroversion (E), Neuroticism (N) and Psychoticism (P). Character traits associated with type E might be, for instance, sociability and risk-taking. Traits associated with N might be guilt and excessive concerns about health. P types might be more likely to be aggressive and impulsive. Psychologists, over time, have improved on Eysenck's model – most notably Drs McCrae and Costa with their 'Big Five' scale of personality type.[64] These are:

OPENNESS TO EXPERIENCE   imaginative *vs* down to earth
variety *vs* routine
independent *vs* conforming

CONSCIENTIOUSNESS	organized *vs* disorganized careful *vs* careless self-disciplined *vs* weak-willed
EXTROVERSION	social *vs* retiring fun-loving *vs* sober affectionate *vs* reserved
AGREEABLENESS	soft-hearted *vs* ruthless trusting *vs* suspicious helpful *vs* uncooperative
NEUROTICISM	worried *vs* calm insecure *vs* secure self-pitying *vs* self-satisfied[65]

Eysenck asserted that people with an extrovert personality are continually in search of cortical arousal. They are more ready to go to parties to meet new people, they seek out new experiences such as adventure sports or foreign travel and, like our Redcoats, are likely to seek occupations that engage or entertain other people. They enjoy and value close bonds with others, being warm and affectionate. They also tend to be dominant socially, enjoying leadership, and are frequently assertive. Extroverts are much more ready to be exhibitionists, and have a sense of potency in accomplishing goals – they are more likely to become inmates of the Big Brother house. Introvert people, by contrast, prefer to stay alone, or in small groups of familiar people and in familiar surroundings. They are much less likely to act on impulse and generally take a cool, sober look at life. Like our Imperial College physicists, they may be most happy in a deserted basement laboratory on a sunny Bank Holiday weekend. Eysenck argued that introverts already have a predisposition to be highly aroused. Introverts don't seek out additional arousal and if, for example, human company is thrust upon them, they experience what is to them an unpleasant level of arousal overload.

The theory is that their extrovert counterparts are chronically underaroused. They have to go rooting out experiences that will provide the 'reward' of arousal; they are quite frequently in pursuit of a 'fix'. Philip Larkin, then, was on this reckoning an introvert with an inbuilt 'desire' to avoid cortical arousal. Poems like his 'Vers de Société' (1971) beginning with the lines:

My wife and I have asked a crowd of craps
To come and waste their time and ours

suggest that he viewed social occasions as a form of torture.

Hence our Spitalfields lemon test. The introverts salivated more because they were more sensitive to arousal. An extrovert, with his chronically low levels of cortical arousal, would need to seek out more than a drop of lemon juice to get his brain's reward centres going. Accordingly, when we filmed the test, we found that the introverts were able to lick at least 10 per cent more packing tape than the extroverts, and sometimes considerably more.

The motivation factor

Other scientists since Eysenck have attempted to add a degree of refinement to this scheme. For Professor Jeffrey Gray, who occupied the professorial chair in London previously held by Eysenck, the degree of cortical arousal is just one factor. Gray suggested there are two opposing systems within the human personality. The *behavioural approach system* (BAS) consists of those brain structures – such as the hypothalamus and amygdala – that lead us to approach certain stimuli in search of a reward. For instance, we might approach attractive people at a party in pursuit of flirtation, flattery, acceptance and sex.

Opposite it is the *behavioural inhibition system* (BIS), linked to the frontal lobes, which is sensitive to punishment and therefore controls and suppresses behaviour that might lead to danger or pain. So the BIS makes us stop at home to check our bank balance and tax liability while the BAS inclines us to the spending spree or an evening in the pub with our friends when we should be working for an exam. In this model, the extrovert is simply someone whose BAS is stronger than their BIS. Introverts, in contrast, have a stronger BIS than a BAS, and hence they flinch from experiences, for fear of a possible negative outcome.

This idea is supported by some work with PET scans which has shown that frontal lobe activity seems slightly greater in many people with introvert characteristics – in other words, their brain predisposes them to be more in control of their behaviour.[66] Dr Debra L. Johnson's study at the University of Iowa showed that introverts appeared to have heightened activity in both the frontal lobes and the anterior thalamus – an interplay possibly crucial for problem-solving and making plans. Extroverts, on the other hand, seem to show more activity in the anterior cingulate cortex, temporal lobes and posterior thalamus – structures involved in sensory processing. Perhaps this could help explain these differences in personality.

The 'social' element of this equation is interesting, because it suggests that we all treat other humans at some level as 'raw data', to be avoided or sought out depending on our degree of extroversion or introversion. A study by Turhan Canli and John Gabrieli at New York University looked at the response of the amygdala of introverts and extroverts when they were shown happy and sad faces.[67] Extroverts showed increased activity in the amygdala when they were shown happy faces, but both types responded with equal intensity to sad faces. Extroverts, in their search for reward and/or arousal, possibly understand that they will get more of the desired result from a happy person. Perhaps we also need to ask why, if – as Gray's idea suggests – extroverts seek reward rather than thinking of possible consequences, they are not equally excited by the sight of any human face, happy or sad, regardless of the possible consequences of contact with its owner? Perhaps the extrovert brain is more discriminating because of its increased need for arousal.

Dopamine's influence

Sensitivity to dopamine – the neurotransmitter involved in the brain's internal reward system – seems to play a part in determining whether we are extroverts or introverts. Extroverts seem particularly sensitive to the action of dopamine, especially in the nucleus accumbens area of the brain. As mentioned in Chapter 2, people who exhibit thrill-seeking behaviour (something that often comes with the extrovert personality) can have a mutation of a gene which results in dopamine being prevented from bonding to neurons. However, it remains highly controversial whether this dopamine gene is seriously altered in people who are outgoing and risk–taking extroverts.

To use a metaphor, dopamine is the currency that is fed into the slots of the nucleus accumbens – the fruit machine – in order to obtain the jackpot: the feelings of pleasure. Only, the theory goes, with extroverts, there is less money to play with and accordingly less stimulation. Consistently under-rewarded by their environment, they are compelled to go in constant search of ever-increasing sources of stimulation. So they engage in more social activities, more novel and unusual situations and sometimes more cocaine or gambling.

It has been suggested that people who exhibit criminal behaviour are more likely to have the mutation that prevents dopamine bonding. This is controversial but the notion ties in with our general understanding of reward centres in the brain. Extroverts certainly show a tendency to think about the rewards rather than the possible negative consequences of their actions. Nonetheless, it is a long way from finding a genetic link. Whatever the truth about the genetic background, professionals working in the courts and prison systems note that many of the offenders they deal with on a daily basis are not so much 'bad' as unable to see a link between what they do and what happens to them. The explanation 'I didn't know I'd get caught' is trotted out more often than we might think. It may be worth pausing to consider that activities such as scuba diving, bungee jumping and sky diving are excellent ways for the executive thrill-seeker to get his dopamine fix at the weekends. But they are options unavailable to people on lower incomes. Perhaps we should not be entirely surprised then that joy riding, petty theft and drug abuse are crimes more typically associated with people from poorer backgrounds. They might be less the strategies for personal gain or revenge on society and more the negative consequences of the dopamine-deficient brain's hungry quest for arousal.

Testosterone's influence

Testosterone is another substance that has powerful effects upon our character. For instance, girls born to mothers who have high levels of testosterone exhibit more male-typical 'tomboyish' behavioural traits like tree climbing, and a liking for competitive games. This is because testosterone is linked to increased levels of curiosity and aggression. A key difference might be whether you view the prospect of a white-water rafting trip as exciting or terrifying. If it's the former, then you may have high levels of testosterone.

A famous French experiment involved injecting one group of cows with testosterone and comparing their behaviour to that of un-injected beasts.[68] Cows in general are relatively timid animals and most breeds are not particularly adventurous. They often show various signs of fear if made to enter unfamiliar areas. They hover around the entrance, staying immobile and hugging the walls. All this is quite familiar – I show these traits myself at most parties. When cows are faced with novel objects, frightened animals delay rather longer before they approach them. They also spend less time studying unfamiliar objects. Fearful cows tend to feed less, become unsettled more easily and run further distances from a possible threat. So we can measure the anxiety levels of individual animals by analysing these reactions.

The French scientists confirmed that, with a good dose of testosterone, heifers on steroids entered unfamiliar fields or pens faster, spent less time in the doorway, kept their heads high indicating they did not feel threatened, and hugged the walls of a barn less. They fed for longer, were more ready to explore a maze and were less frightened by humans. In another experiment, the researchers looked at two different breeds of cow.[69] Heren cows, which are bred for their fighting ability and have naturally high levels of the hormone, were significantly less fearful and more ready to explore their environment than were Brune des Alpes cows, a dairy breed. Brune des Alpes cows have average blood levels of testosterone – that is, lower than the Heren cows – and in this research were more easily stressed.

It is inaccurate to think of testosterone as 'the male hormone'. It is produced by the testis in large quantities, but it is a hormone important for the function of the ovary, too. And androgens, the 'parent' hormones that give rise to testosterone, are produced by two small glands next to the kidneys, the adrenals, in both men and women. But excess testosterone produces characteristics in the body, brain and behaviour that we might call 'male-typical'. At the purely physical level, these would include a low degree of facial fat, resulting in a pronounced jaw and prominent cheekbones, a deep voice, large hands and greater upper-body muscle strength. At the psychological level, we also see heightened curiosity and sex drive, aggression and competitive behaviour.

Rather than seeing the profound differences between the two sexes as two opposing sides of a coin, we are better off considering the gender 'divide' as being more a continuous line of varying states, a spectrum. A tendency towards one or other end of this continuum has little to do with sexual orientation. No one has yet found any definite link between heterosexuality or homosexuality and increased or decreased testosterone levels. Yet differences in personality may still be linked to the levels of certain chemicals sloshing around inside our brains and bodies at some point during our past development or present activity.

It seems that differences in hormone levels can clearly hold sway over whole aspects of our character and the lives we lead – influencing the jobs we do, our choice of partner and our hobbies. But not all movie stuntmen have high testosterone, and not all librarians have it in short supply. The functions of testosterone are many and the effects various. I have already pointed out that older men with high levels of the hormone tend to show better visual and verbal recall. The various studies that have been done give inconsistent and variable results, but Daryl O'Connor at the University of Manchester was able to improve the verbal fluency of a group of men by giving them weekly injections of testosterone.[70] After just four weeks, they showed a 20 per cent improvement, but they also performed worse with a spatial task, which involved putting a peg into a specific place on a board. So while testosterone turned them into chatterboxes it isn't terribly clear whether they were better at washing up and ironing – and certainly not better with a clothesline. Personally, I find this experiment slightly surprising – not least because in my experience it is extremely hard to find men who are prepared to have injections at all, let alone with a substance that might shrink their testicles. But apparently the research was originally geared to trying to find a male contraceptive hormone – it may surprise you that giving men testosterone also tends to reduce testicular activity and to lower sperm count. This is because if testosterone is injected into a man it interferes with the natural stimulus to the hypothalamus – a feedback mechanism. The hypothalamus detects the testosterone and is 'fooled' into believing that this hormone is coming from the testes. Therefore it reduces its activity and stops stimulating the pituitary. In turn, the pituitary gland reduces its output, which normally stimulates the testes or ovaries. Without adequate pituitary stimulation, the testes tend to reduce activity and to shrink.

The Winnie-the-Pooh test

We can find brain-based evidence for other traits of personality besides extroversion and introversion. Research indicates that people with a tendency to be happy show increased left-brain activity, and their sad counterparts have heightened activity in the right. This link can also be seen in the cases of people who have suffered damage to one or other hemisphere. People with damaged right brains can be prone to bursts of laughter and euphoria, whereas people with damaged left brains may be given to crying or feelings of despair. And if a sequence of happy and sad video clips is shown to normal, well-adjusted people, you may observe the varying action of the left and right brain. Generally, unpleasant sights are a bit more likely to increase right-brain activity, and pleasant ones left-brain activity. It has even been suggested that people with more active left brains are better able to cope with the physical effects of stress.

This aspect of the brain's wiring may influence the way people think. Therapists maintain that anxious people tend to link their problems together into an overarching schema of doom. When the red reminder bill plops onto the doormat, they do not just register it as a problem to be solved. They also feel heightened regret that they have not been promoted, concern about their recent row with a close friend, worried that they've gained a little weight recently. They tend to link each separate islet of concern into a wider context which reinforces their sense of guilt and feelings of inadequacy. 'I am all wrong', such a person might conclude, 'because of this red reminder bill and this and this and this.' As we have seen, the right brain may possibly be better at grasping the bigger picture and may form wide conclusions from a disparate array of information. A therapist's rationale, based on evidence or not, might be to try to train the individual concerned to use a 'more left brain' approach. To learn to treat each problem as a separate entity, rather than thinking about the sum total of all the problems.

Philip Larkin showed a tendency that might be thought a 'right-brained' view of life. He once said that sadness was to him 'what daffodils were to Wordsworth', and that he believed 'most people are unhappy'.[71] Most of us would agree that such an outlook leads to a rather painful passage through life, but many creative people – including Larkin himself – would also argue that it is precisely this disposition that enables them to cut through the trivia of daily life and shed light on the reality beyond, however uncomfortable that may be. As Montherlant once wrote, 'happiness writes white' – meaning that only bland statements proceed from a state of joy.

To go from the subdued to the sublime, it should be obvious that if all the categories outlined by Eysenck and modified by McCrae and Costa are accurate, they should pass the Winnie-the-Pooh test. Either that or, heaven forbid, A.A. Milne, generous benefactor of the Garrick Club in London, got it all wrong. So – on these definitions – we have Tigger, sociable, fun-loving, wanting to try new things, affectionate and clearly an *extrovert*, with Owl, retiring, sober, distant and reserved, an *introvert*.

On the *openness to experience* scale, Rabbit is down to earth, routine, conforming, while Roo is independent, loves variety and shows the start of imagination. On the *conscientiousness* scale, Kanga is the most organized, careful and self-disciplined; Tigger on the other hand (who, of course, is also an extrovert par excellence) is the least conscientious – disorganized, careless and self-willed. It does not take much intelligence to see who I would elect to the *agreeableness* slot. Pooh is soft-hearted, trusting and helpful; probably there is no animal in the Hundred Acre Wood who is ruthless, suspicious and un-cooperative – after all, Owl, who is perhaps closest, does give Eeyore's tail back without a fight.* And the *neurotic* – well, as it happens, the most intelligent animal, the introverted Eeyore, of course, is worried, insecure and self-pitying. Presumably Christopher Robin himself would be the calm, secure and self-satisfied one – but he does not really count as he is away so often. That really leaves only Piglet, but Piglet is still very young indeed – hardly yet self-aware. One may hope that with Pooh's influence he may, in time, emulate him – a triumph of environment over genetics.

---

*There is a point about Owl here. You will recall that, outside his house, he has a notice that reads 'PLEZ CNOKE IF AN ANSR IS NOT REQUID'. Believe it or not, there is a very similar notice on an important house in London – the Speaker's House in the House of Commons – which says: 'PLEASE DO NOT RING IF ANSWER IS REQUIRED'. I leave you to work that out.

But of course, while we think of people as types – and hence A.A. Milne's delightful analysis – we have all these attributes in varying degrees. All of us will score somewhere along each scale. Moreover, the degree to which we score will change to some extent, depending on the environment around and within us and our mood at the time.

Left-brainers and right-brainers

A simple search on the internet can furnish you with a list of hundreds of famous personalities, fictional and otherwise, long-dead and living, who suffer from a seemingly gloomy view of life. The same does not seem to be true of the pathological optimist. Arguably, fictional characters who always look on the bright side start to grate on us after a while, seeming not only bland but even stupid and irritating.

A good example would be the main character in Eleanor H. Porter's children's book *Pollyanna*. Nowadays we use the term 'a Pollyanna' somewhat pejoratively to imply that someone with irrepressible cheerfulness might also be a bit naive and simple. From a psychological point of view, perhaps we are just jealous of people with that peculiar state of mind. What is remarkable about men like Philip Larkin, Winston Churchill and Tennyson is that they achieved greatness while apparently struggling against a state of mind (and brain) that told them to give up, that often affirmed everything was pointless, that frequently filled them with despair and dread.

Pollyanna, as you might recall, is a story about a little girl. I do not know whether I find the story more irritating than the character of the little girl, but Pollyanna always saw the good side of people, and her positive personality meant that eventually things always turned out for the best. *Pollyanna*, a moral fable of a certain American type, was published in 1913 and, for reasons I find totally mystifying, received immediate praise and success. The story is that the orphaned Pollyanna arrives in Beldingsville to live with her remote but dutiful spinster aunt. In spite of the lukewarm reception she experiences, everyone with whom she comes into contact is enlivened by her cheerful and infectious optimism. The miserable, the isolated, the sick and the awful – all are entranced by this little girl's enthusiasm and zest for life. But Pollyanna is then hit by a motorcar in the street (pretty advanced for 1913) and she loses consciousness as a result of her head injury. As she gets better she finds that she has lost the use of her legs, and learns that she will never walk again by overhearing a conversation between her aunt and a visiting medical specialist. A bit of a specialist myself, I can say that this is not the only fallible medical opinion ever given. She eventually does find a way to regain her past happiness – but I really won't expect you to read the book. Basically, Pollyanna appears to devise a sort of homegrown version of Cognitive Behavioural Therapy, called the 'glad game'. She employs this mental strategy in order to try to find something, in every situation, no matter how sad, that could make her happy.

I do not know what the cynical, child-hating Philip Larkin might have written about *Pollyanna* – I would be bemused if he ever read it. But a study in 1988 suggested that Pollyanna-type thinking, as well as being delusional, is a good strategy for mental health. Shelley E. Taylor of the University of California, Los Angeles, noted that people with the most robust mental health also appeared to demonstrate three types of illusory thinking.[72] They rated themselves in an unrealistically positive light relative to other people. They believed themselves to have more control over their lives than they actually do. And they had an unrealistically positive expectation of the outcome of events. By contrast, people with poor mental health showed a correspondingly more accurate and realistic attitude.[73]

This suggests that mentally healthy people maintain their illusions by actively filtering out information that would challenge their unrealistic views. There is an obvious difference between a mental illness like depression and a tendency to view things in a negative light. But presumably a tendency to be negative could lead to clinical depression. This stuff warns against any oversimple notion of a world divided into happy left-brainers and gloomy right-brainers. In light of Dr Taylor's findings, a happy brain seems to be one whose owner acts rather like an unprofessional scientist who is determined to prove his hypothesis regardless of the data to hand. He skips gaily over the fine details, ignoring an inconsistency here, placing undue emphasis there.

There is, of course, a limit to this talk of character. Namely, that we categorize and ascribe personalities and attributes to people on a superficial understanding of them and fail to understand the complexity of the human brain. It is summed up best for me by the approach of a man who I think had an extraordinary grasp of what it is to be human. I suppose the long tussle with the insanity of his wife, and the sadness and guilt which that caused him to feel, resulted in his constantly writing about the human mind – and the close relationship he saw between sanity and insanity. There is no doubt that Luigi Pirandello was one of the most significant playwrights of the twentieth century. One of his most important contributions was to take a long hard look at character in the context of how it is portrayed on stage – he turns the drama on itself, often a feature of good art in many different media.

His trilogy of plays about the theatre is extraordinary. The first of these, *Six Characters in Search of an Author*, is a masterpiece. It is Pirandello's definitive statement about the inconsistency of the theatre. In it, he points to the fact that when we watch an actor on stage, he is acting and not real. So his central theme (to which he returned repeatedly in his writing) is the conflict between reality and illusion. We see the actor, we may empathize with him, but, of course, he is pretending to be someone he is not, in a situation that he has not experienced in precisely the same way as the character he is playing. And, of course, this is exactly the paradox we experience when we judge another person in real life – we are effectively using our brain to judge theirs.

In *Six Characters*, we, the audience, start by entering an auditorium; the curtain is already open. A rehearsal is in progress on stage – incidentally, and ironically, another play of Pirandello's, *The Rules of the Game*. There are tedious arguments between the Actors and the Director about how to interpret what the author intended. The Leading Actor is protesting about having to wear a cook's hat. The Director replies, 'Yes, my dear fellow, you have to wear a hat and you have to beat eggs on stage *and* you have to represent the shell of the eggs you're beating – now, get on with it.' In the midst of this trivia about the nature of being an actor, Pirandello delivers a stunning *coup de théâtre*. Out of the gloom from the back of the theatre, six Characters, all dressed in black, slowly but dramatically make their way through the auditorium, and sombrely mount the stage uninvited. The Director protests he cannot be interrupted – he and the Actors are trying to portray real life and cannot be disturbed in rehearsal. The lead character, the Father, pleads, 'But let us be your drama.' The story that the Father is going to tell about what happened to him, his wife, his stepdaughter and three children, he promises, is much more real than any play could ever be. Unfortunately, he says, their author stopped writing about them and they are therefore held in suspended animation throughout time with their tragedy 'unresolved'.

In spite of himself the Director is fascinated. He and the Actors watch the Characters and see them act out their story. It soon transpires that the Father, an introverted, remote figure who loves his children but is estranged from his family, has visited a brothel. The Mother is left short of money and her daughter, the Stepdaughter, is working in this same brothel as a 'novice' (possibly a virgin, we do not find out) prostitute. The Father, during his visit, does not recognize his stepdaughter and he attempts to take her clothes off to seduce her. At this point in the play within a play, the Director stops the action. He protests they cannot portray such lurid action in a theatre even in the enlightened times in which they live – 1916. So, using the identical dialogue, the Actors then act out their interpretation of the short scene they have just witnessed. But instead of being poignant, it is now close to prurient. The Director, dissatisfied, takes over the role of the Father and acts out yet another version of this clandestine meeting between the Father and the Stepdaughter – and turns it close to farce. The Characters protest vehemently that this is not at all as it happened. As the drama proceeds, we, the audience, are thrown further into recognizing that what is being portrayed on stage cannot be portrayed accurately. It isn't real life. It is drama transformed into melodrama by actors, and a parody even more remote when done by the Director. And we, the audience, each perceive it differently again. And this is the essence of perceptions of personality – we are using our human mind to understand another person's mind. We cannot be objective. There is a key speech by the Father in which Pirandello sums up an indelible insight into personality and human consciousness.

> My drama lies entirely in this one thing. In my being conscious that each of us believes himself to be a single person. But each of us is many people, many people – according to all the possibilities of being that are within us. For with some people we are one person, and with others we are somebody entirely different. But we always have the illusion of being one and the same person with everyone we meet. But it's not true. It's not true. And we find this out very clearly when we are, by some terrible chance, caught in the middle of doing something we shouldn't be doing. And we are left

dangling, suspended in mid-air. And then we see that every part of us was not involved in what we were doing and it would be a dreadful injustice for people to judge us by this one act, as we are held there, as if we were suspended throughout eternity with one's personality summed up in a single, uninterrupted action. Now do you see the treachery of this young girl? She caught me in an unrecognizable situation, doing something I shouldn't have been doing, with her . . .

Victor Meldrew, the archetypal grouchy old man of the BBC1 comedy series *One Foot in the Grave*, was a great hit with audiences – not least because he tapped into a phenomenon of which we all have some experience. A psychoanalyst might say that we enjoyed watching Meldrew, not because he reminded us all of the moody men we knew, but because he spoke to the 'grumpy man' inside all of us. To see him 'out there', on the TV screen, the object of laughter and ridicule as his grouchy tendencies reached increasingly bizarre heights of excess, was in some way fundamentally reassuring to us. The laughter of the audience was the laughter of relief, a great unconscious cry of 'Thank heaven, it's not me.'

In the mood . . . for shopping

It's worth briefly considering what we mean by the word 'mood'. To do so, it is helpful to compare it to other classifications of behaviour, such as disposition, or emotions. We could say that disposition, like personality, is something that is constant, and observable over time. So Eeyore, for example, would be said to have a gloomy disposition – whatever happens to him, this aspect of him remains the same.

Moods, on the other hand, are transient. They are related to specific times, situations and triggers. So a piece of music might put me in a good mood. This might spill over, so that I continued to be in a good mood for a few hours afterwards. But then the feelings would fade and my more constant disposition would take over again. Emotions also fade and change over time, but they are a more conscious, communicative form of behaviour. Fear and joy exist to show both myself and others that there's something out there to be feared or glad about. I can also, providing that my frontal lobes are sufficiently well developed, show a degree of control over my emotions. I can stop myself feeling angry. I can suppress my joy if someone close to me has had some bad news. Moods are more shadowy. It is hard to consciously alter one's mood, and at the same time it is possible to have one's mood changed without being aware how it is happening, or even that anything is going on.

For decades now, supermarkets have used very subtle techniques to influence the mood of shoppers, and the science of 'retail atmospherics' even has its own 'learned' journals and publications. But why should it really matter what sort of a mood we're in? If I want some herrings and a packet of hooks, and the shop has herrings and hooks, I will buy them, won't I?

Retail atmospherics takes a rather different view. Its proponents base their theories on one indisputable fact of human behaviour. When we are in a positive mood, we are open to new experiences. When we are in a negative mood, we avoid them. If you translate this wisdom into the setting of your local supermarket, then a good mood will make you want to stay in the store longer, maybe have a snack at the cafeteria, explore different areas of the store, take a risk by buying new products. A good mood also makes us spend money because, in the Freudian interpretation, we seek a 'pay-off' to any pleasurable experience. Just as satisfactory sex ends with an orgasm, we seek some ultimate climax to a pleasant shopping experience. So we spend money. Other psychologists think the process is more about reciprocity – that is, having been given a pleasant experience by the supermarket, we want to say thank you, and so we buy things.

It would take nothing short of a tranquillizer dart to make me want to thank Mr Kwik-Save as I pick my way down crowded aisle 33 towards the peanut butter – especially when it turns out to be the wrong brand or, in my case, not kosher. But research has shown that there are a number of ways in which the retail environment can be manipulated to put customers in a better mood. Perhaps it even works on me.

Some of the more obvious tactics are music – personally, a xylophone rendition of 'Mr Sandman' never quite does the trick for me, however – and smell. But studies have also shown that the layout and general condition of the store have a powerful effect. A team at the University of Göttingen tested this in 1997 using two IKEA stores. The first store had been newly decorated. Its layout had been specially designed for ease of access and manoeuvrability. New goods were artistically displayed in unusual and interesting ways – for instance, a new armchair was suspended from the ceiling with a spotlight trained upon it. Products were arranged in a manner that was intended to be inspiring to the customers. For example, chairs were displayed, not stacked up boringly in the 'chair department', but included within whole suggested décor schemes for different rooms.

The second store was the complete opposite. It was shabby and in need of a good coat of paint. Its aisles were cramped and narrow, the layout confusing. Goods were just stacked up and arranged purely functionally, with no concern for aesthetic appeal. The Göttingen team found that customers in the first store spent longer over their shopping. They spent more money, they showed greater willingness to have a snack in the cafeteria and they made more spontaneous purchases – that is, they walked out with more than they intended to buy. The latter is a phenomenon that certainly affects me – despite my general lack of enthusiasm for the shopping experience.

I have to say that I have behaved extremely badly in a large IKEA store in London. (And to be fair to IKEA, things appear to have greatly improved there in recent years.) Perhaps the worst, but most popular, time to visit is a Monday Bank Holiday. Many years ago, on a tight budget, I went with my wife and two children to get a set of bookshelves. The atmosphere in this part of the store was lovely, the assistants helpful, and soon we were going back to get a bigger trolley, and then a bigger one still. Eventually we had a massive trolley, piled high with all sorts of 'assemble yourself and don't worry about abrasions' furniture. The trolley had a mind of its own and kept careering into displays and into small defenceless children. Anxious mothers stared wide-eyed in terror as they saw this juggernaut trundling towards them. If I dragged it behind me so I could see innocent bystanders over my shoulder, packages fell off the back and my diminutive offspring were left whimpering in the aisle, holding their feet. Increasingly slowly, we made our way to the check-out area, crowded and dark, with mysterious boxes piled in a chaotic fashion some twelve feet high on either side of a long gloomy corridor. Eventually we came to a complete halt, reminiscent of a pile-up after a crash following an Aston Villa match just beyond the nearest exit on the M1. There we encountered gaunt, haggard people, some with apparently starving children (judging from their pitiful cries), who had given up all hope of ever seeing their nearest and dearest again. No music played here in the silent, shadowy dark. I am ashamed to say that, with hardly a glance at each other, my wife and I wordlessly abandoned the trolley and slunk away.

For the *Human Mind* television programme we tried the effects of mood-manipulation for ourselves. Two identical twins were our unwitting victims. In the morning, one twin was submitted to various situations that should induce a positive, happy mood, and the other twin to experiences to induce a negative mood. The negative-mood twin went to a quiet room in a gym near a shopping centre. First, she was made to read and sign a serious-looking consent form. Then she read a series of statements from a laptop screen. She was told to imagine saying to a friend things designed to make someone feel bad, such as, 'I sometimes feel so guilty about the hurt I have caused my parents.' While reading it, she listened to some sad music – Barber's Adagio for Strings. After being left alone for a while, she was taken to the shopping centre and sent shopping for thirty minutes. Later, the other twin went through the same basic procedure, except that this time the statements were designed to induce a positive mood, such as, 'I feel I can do just about anything.' She also had the joy of listening to lively music. Thereafter, she was similarly given half an hour to go shopping.

The mood induction worked impressively. The sad twin bought less, looked at fewer items and went into fewer shops. She also felt less satisfaction with what she bought and did not really like the trainers she'd purchased. After just twenty minutes of shopping, she became distressed and didn't want to continue. Eventually she was taken back down and given the positive mood induction procedure to put her back in good spirits. Meantime our happy twin appeared more enthusiastic and more energetic. She bought lots of items, and went into several different shops, looking at lots of different products. She even bought a couple of gifts for her sister – it turns out, of course, that we are all likely to be more generous when we are in a positive mood. The twins were reunited and both were sent home happy after we had explained how we had manipulated them.

The eyes have it

This little demonstration shows that 'mood', unlike something hard-wired like extroversion or introversion, is a changeable commodity.

It can be influenced by a few subtle events, yet it has quite concrete effects on the choices we make in our lives. We do not even have to be aware of the events, in order for our mood – and resultant behaviour – to be altered. I regularly come out of the supermarket with more goods than I intended to buy. Some police stations have experimented by putting pink in the clink – coloured lightbulbs in the cells – which is thought to have a calming effect on distressed and violent prisoners. What is presumably happening here is an interplay between the sensory cortex and the limbic system – one that does not have to enter the conscious realm of the frontal lobes in order for it to have an effect on our behaviour.

But while the mood of anybody can be preyed on unsuspectingly by the subliminal trickery of the supermarket or the constabulary, some people show more marked tendencies with their moods. That is what is meant by the observation that personality is something that remains constant over time and regardless of circumstances. Some people are irritable, whatever happens to them. David H. Zald of Vanderbilt University undertook PET scans of eighty-nine subjects.[74] The team specified that they wanted only right-handed volunteers for the test – remember that a right-hander has a dominant left brain.

The subjects were given a questionnaire, which asked about the extent to which they had experienced unpleasant moods during the previous month. In the PET scans, Dr Zald and his team found that people who reported a tendency towards bad moods showed increased activity in the ventromedial prefrontal cortex. This little area – just behind the right eye in right-handed people – is understood to play a part in mood regulation. Studies in animals have indicated that the ventromedial prefrontal cortex has some role in controlling heart rate, breathing, stomach acidity levels and sweating – bodily functions that are also implicated in mood. It is not yet known whether heightened activity in this region is the consequence of bad moods, or the cause of them. But the next time you find yourself in a rotten temper, maybe you should try rubbing your right eye.

No, this is not a serious medical recommendation. But it is peculiar that some healthcare professionals seem to have helped people cope with high levels of anxiety by teaching them a simple eye-movement technique. EMDR (eye movement desensitization and processing) is a method first tried by Dr Francine Shapiro from Palo Alto, California. She noticed that, following her distressing cancer diagnosis, her feelings of anxiety were alleviated when she rapidly moved her eyes from side to side. Dr John Spector at Watford General Hospital now teaches the technique to people who have recently experienced extremely traumatic situations. The underlying theory is that negative, anxious, distressing feelings are situated within the right brain, and these feelings, if too powerful, cannot be processed or verbalized because those skills lie instead within the left brain. If EMDR works, its protagonists claim that it does so by stimulating right-to-left brain communication, ensuring that the person doesn't become overwhelmed by their state of anxiety. Apparently, brain monitoring has shown that there seems to be a normalization of brain-wave patterns after only three sessions, with right-hemisphere activity dampening down and left-hemisphere activity gearing up.

Brain chemistry and depression

So many features of personality depend upon underlying brain states. Techniques such as Cognitive Behavioural Therapy and even just regular practice at trying to put oneself in happy situations can effect a partial rewiring job within the brain, replacing old, undesirable patterns of thought and behaviour with newer, more helpful ones. Even something as simple as a regular laugh-in with friends seems to be able to set up a loop of positive feedback – so that by pretending to be happy, we can actually become more happy.

But though we have the ability to bring certain aspects of our mood and behaviour under conscious control, we do not undergo dramatic character change as a result. Even if I became noticeably more cheerful, people would not suspect that I had undergone a personality transplant. But there can be circumstances in which people do undergo rapid changes in personality. Depression, schizophrenia, bipolar disorder and strokes can all have very powerful effects on personality, leaving the sufferers, and their families and friends, feeling very much as if they have become 'someone else' – rather like Phineas Gage after his accident.

A relative of a depressed patient once described her to me, very aptly, as 'looking like herself, but as if she'd had all the air let out of her'. Depressed people can often seem to be lacking in buoyancy in this way – listless, weary, unconfident. What can be even more distressing is the speed at which someone can enter this state, from seeming to be perfectly well.

It is worthwhile to make another pause here to explain some terms in greater depth. Earlier on I discussed certain personality types, and considered the brain chemistry that might have shaped them. But we enter more murky territory when we begin to talk about depression as an illness. If Philip Larkin had taken a course of antidepressants, would he have turned into the life and soul of the party? The answer, obviously, is no.

Psychiatrists talk of two principal types of depression. Reactive depression occurs in response to distressing circumstances, such as job loss, infertility or bereavement. Endogenous depression (meaning 'arising from within'), on the other hand, can occur without any triggers. But in both cases, the condition induces a recognizable change in the mood, thoughts and habits of the sufferer. These changes include disturbed sleeping patterns, loss of appetite and sex drive, poor concentration, persistent or recurrent negative thoughts, feelings of loss, hopelessness and guilt. Depression also has a beginning and an end. Except in rare instances of a condition called persistent anhedonia, an untreated case of depression will alleviate itself in time. So depression is quite evidently a different beast from the more generalized negative or gloomy disposition. But it, too, is created by alterations in brain chemistry.

Wayne Drevets of the US National Institutes of Health is a key figure in establishing the neurobiology of depression and has emphasized how valuable brain scans have become in understanding what may be going wrong. Michael Posner at the University of Oregon has suggested that there are four areas of overactivity in the brains of depressed people. The prefrontal, outside edge of the frontal lobe, which enables long-term memories to remain within conscious access; the upper middle part of the thalamus – known to stimulate the amygdala; the amygdala itself – centre of emotions; and the anterior cingulate cortex – the area of the brain that becomes active when we concentrate on things. Posner suggests a scheme of action something like this. My overactive amygdala sends 'sad' feelings up towards my prefrontal lobe. This then consciously looks for a reason to attach to the emotion. It asks, 'Why do I feel sad?' and then rummages in the long-term memory to find some possible cause – for example, a bereavement. This business becomes hard after a while – other things arrive to claim my attention – but the feelings of sadness do not go away, and nor does the troublesome urge to look for a reason. So then my anterior cingulate cortex kicks in to shut out any other claims on my consciousness and ensure that my attention is focused on the sad feelings and my suggested reason for them. Small wonder I can't just 'snap out of it'.

Possibly our poet, Philip Larkin, in addition to having a negative-inclined outlook on life, might have suffered from a recurrent form of depression. His poem 'Aubade' (1977) describes his abject state of mind on waking every morning in the early dawn light to contemplate the certainty of his eventual death. This phenomenon, of waking early and having difficulty getting to sleep, accompanied by persistent negative thoughts, is a well-documented symptom of endogenous depression.

Larkin also stated in an interview with the *Observer* that his parents were 'rather awkward people . . . not very good at being happy. And these things rub off.'[75] His words possibly indicate an awareness that he might have inherited this tendency, though, of course, his rather depressive trait might have equally been produced by his childhood environment. But genetic variants can lead to low levels of serotonin in the brain and this, it has been shown, can be the cause of behavioural traits such as aggression and anxiety. And these are aspects of behaviour seen in some depressed patients.

Genes again

What about the genes which play a part in influencing our moods and attitudes to life? Some recent research, conducted by Dr Mary-Anne Enoch at the American National Institute of Alcohol Abuse and Alcoholism, has suggested that women may have a brain more likely to be hard-wired to experience greater levels of anxiety.[76] It is known that women in general have lower levels of an enzyme called COMT, which some scientists believe is responsible for regulating mood. The NIAAA study has linked lower levels of COMT to a mutation of a certain gene (called Val 158 Met) – and women with this mutation score particularly high on questionnaires designed to assess their levels of anxiety. Interestingly, the same results are not seen in men.

However, the findings of this study are somewhat controversial, in that scientists are by no means in agreement as to the functions of COMT. The current evidence suggests that it affects dopamine regulation in the prefrontal cortex, and changes in the COMT gene may increase susceptibility to schizophrenia and other severe disturbances.

There is some powerful evidence that depression may pass from one generation to the next. Serious depression possibly affects as many as two million Britons each year and perhaps ten million Americans. Some people are repeatedly thrown into the darkness of despair and for a proportion of families this is a recurring nightmare. An important study by neurologist Wayne Drevets and colleagues at Washington University School of Medicine has found that the brains of people with a family history of depression often show a characteristic abnormality.[77] An area called the subgenual medial prefrontal cortex, part of the forebrain the size and shape of your finger located behind the eyes and between the brain's two hemispheres, is consistently smaller. The post-mortem studies he has done – studies that would probably be condemned in Britain since the government's unsupportive attitude to the storage of brain tissues after post-mortem – have shown a most important finding. Although the brain of depressed people is smaller in this region, it has roughly the same number of neurons. The loss of bulk is because the supporting cells, the glial scaffold, is reduced. It would seem that the glial cells are not just acting as a glue but have a more important role. It is known that these cells store sugar as an energy source and they may also be important for the maintenance of adequate serotonin. Depression that occurs in association with this loss of cells may be associated with reduced levels of this neurotransmitter. Whatever the precise mechanism, these findings of cell loss are quite different from those in individuals with a single attack of depression. This is one reason for considering a possible genetic cause, running in families. But depression may run in families for another reason. As we know, the plastic brain responds to its surroundings – so a child surrounded by depressed adults may develop the brain of a depressed person itself.

A contender for a 'depressive' gene may have recently been identified. In February 2003, an American firm called Myriad Genetics, Inc. announced that it had found a single gene, known as DEP-1, which seems to be linked to depression. This firm has a strong commercial interest in offering people screening for possible cancer genes, but it is broadening its net. It is believed that the DEP-1 gene has no effect on serotonin or noradrenaline, usual suspects in disorders of brain chemistry (along with dopamine and acetylcholine). Rather, it seems to operate within an entirely novel pathway, which is still under investigation. Myriad Genetics have done their research on four hundred Mormon families in the Salt Lake City, Utah, area. Mormons are wonderful subjects for genetic research, because they are fascinated by genealogy and most keep excellent detailed family records that stretch back many generations. They also tend to have large families – many do not use contraception – and marriage is mostly to a small population – other Mormons. So any genetic tendency for a particular trait or disease carried by these people is likely to be more obvious and more common. It will almost certainly be a number of years before this research leads to any new antidepressant products becoming available on the market. But it is interesting that the founder of the Mormon Church, Brigham Young, believed that he held the answer to mankind's problems. In the case of depression, he might just have been right.

But how could a tendency towards depression have managed to enter our genes? It is hard to understand how such a condition could have any evolutionary advantage. Randolph Nesse, at the University of Michigan, has written extensively on this subject and argues that presumably at a former point in our history reactions associated with depression might have helped us to survive.[78] When dogs wish to avoid danger, such as conflict with other dogs, one strategy they adopt is to render themselves slower, smaller and seemingly lifeless. They flatten themselves to the ground, mute their responses and stay submissively still. Possibly depression in humans is a remnant of this inhibitory survival response. Depression often occurs as a by-product of high stress – enforcing a slowing-down of body and brain. Could it perhaps have also been the means by which the body and brain could repair and recover?

Depression can possibly also be considered as a faulty sub-set of emotion – a method by which we unconsciously signal to others that we are very much 'not okay', effectively asking for help. A study at Ohio State University has shown that men who are abusive and aggressive are actually less likely to display symptoms of depression or anxiety, even though they will freely report high levels of stress in their lives. Perhaps violent acts become the only means by which such men can signal their distress and seek help.

There are many other reasons for a sudden change of personality. It can happen as a result of a brain tumour, or after a left- or right-brain stroke. In *Mapping the Mind*, Rita Carter quotes the example of a High Court judge who, after a right-brain stroke, became a great crowd-pleaser. His courtroom rang with the sound of laughter, and defendants and lawyers grew increasingly aghast as they saw stiff penalties being handed out willy-nilly for minor offences, and serious criminals sometimes allowed to walk free. Eventually the judge was required to retire, a state of affairs about which, as Rita Carter notes, he was also blithely content.

We saw in the previous chapter how brain injury can result in a personality change. Phineas Gage became a different person. Another interesting example is the case of Unity Mitford, who it is said was a changed person – prone to fits of anger and depression – following a gunshot wound to the head. Unity Mitford was a notorious aristocratic socialite, sister of the brilliant novelist Nancy. As the daughter of Lord Redesdale, the second Baron, she had a privileged existence, being educated at home by her mother. Her parents certainly held right-wing political views and supported the British fascists. In 1936 another daughter, Diana, married the leader of the British Union of Fascists, Oswald Mosley. Both Diana and Unity travelled to Nazi Germany and Unity was flattered to meet Adolf Hitler, as well as many of his immediate governing circle, Himmler, Goering and Goebbels. Hitler apparently told the German press that Unity was 'a perfect specimen of Aryan womanhood', and some people consider that Unity was, in some way, in love with Hitler. When Britain declared war in 1939, Unity was still in Germany, with her world collapsing; she tried to kill herself with a shot to the head. Six months after the war was declared she was repatriated to Britain in an injured state on a special train, hired by her father. But some papers, which came to light just recently in the Public Record Office, imply that when she arrived back to Britain in January 1940, she was carried off this train on a stretcher but with no outward signs of any injury.

Guy Liddell, one of Britain's wartime spymasters and in charge of B Division of the Security Service (MI5), was involved with investigating espionage and conducting counterespionage operations. He was insistent that Unity be searched on arrival on her private train.

He later minuted: 'We had no evidence to support the press allegations that she was in a serious state of health and it might well be that she was brought in on a stretcher in order to avoid publicity and unpleasantness to her family.' The Home Secretary, it is said, stopped the search. The reasons for this intervention have never been satisfactorily explained. The present Lord Redesdale, Unity's cousin, and a friend and colleague of mine in the House of Lords, has been quoted as saying: 'I love conspiracy theories but it goes a little far to suggest Unity was faking it. But people did wonder how she was up on her feet so soon after shooting herself in the head.'

Sabotage of the self

In all our explorations of the human mind, one observation seems to keep cropping up. Our mental faculties are the pinnacle of a process of selective evolution, millions of years old. Our neurons compete for space and fuel, in the same way as our ancestors competed with one another for food and mating rights. Under this view, disparate mental phenomena such as consciousness, dreaming and even depression could be seen to have had an evolutionary purpose. The phenomena came into being, so the argument goes, in order to assist our survival. Their desirability in modern times depends upon their continuing ability to serve this purpose over changing circumstances – which is why traits like a depressive tendency and aggression are more likely to be labelled now as 'problems' than as strategies.

This is quite a compelling view, but it leaves a great swathe of human behaviour unexplained. Because every day, we humans do, say and think things that are not remotely helpful to our survival. We engage in practices that seem to be quite the opposite, in fact. And we could do no better than to look at the examples provided by our greatest writer for elucidation.

What is it about William Shakespeare that makes him such a genius? There is little doubt that the key to understanding his greatness is that he, more than any other writer in English, understood the workings of the human mind. From time to time, other writers from this and other countries, such as Chaucer, Montaigne and Dostoevsky, are cited as men who came closest to this aspect of Shakespeare's gift, but I suspect there is no one who so consistently portrays the full range of human consciousness. Whether we look at Lear, Prospero, Timon, Falstaff, Macbeth, Coriolanus, Richard II, Iago or Hamlet, we connect with those people at a very deep level, we know and understand them intimately, we empathize with them; we may not like them – indeed we may hate them – yet we laugh or cry with them, we fear for them, all because of the playwright's intuition. In Elizabethan and Jacobean times the English theatre flourished in a golden age, but none of Shakespeare's near contemporaries, I think, has this extraordinary understanding and the involvement with the breadth and range of the human mind. Christopher Marlowe was perhaps his closest competitor. On occasion, Marlowe may have written verse that was nearly as good but his 'leading men', Tamburlaine, Faustus and Barabas, the Maltese Jew, are exaggerated, mostly two-dimensional creatures in whom it is extremely hard to believe and who, consequently, only occasionally come to life. Ben Jonson was undoubtedly a gifted writer, but who has ever actually met a Sir Epicure Mammon (except very briefly at the Garrick Club) or thought like him? The characters of Subtle, the alchemist, and Volpone are convincing, but only at times; even at his best, Jonson's plays are largely peopled with caricatures rather than characters. This is good for farce or entertainment, but not so good for really changing the way we think about ourselves. The understanding of so many inner selves is what gives Shakespeare his towering reputation for intellect. And this understanding was a gift which augmented and stimulated the writings of others – as has been said of Shakespeare, he was 'not only witty in himself but the cause of wit in other men'.[79] And perhaps most remarkable is the fact that we do not know who Shakespeare really was. In spite of his brilliance in telling us about personality, we do not know him. We know virtually nothing about his own beliefs, beyond a few superficial likes and dislikes that creep out from the plays. Was he religious? Did he believe in God? What were his politics? Even his sexuality remains somewhat mysterious.

Many people consider that the single greatest play in the English language is *The Tragical History of Hamlet, Prince of Denmark*. This is because, within the context of this superb melodrama of revenge, Hamlet, the man, has a universal aspect to his character – he steps out of the play and exists almost independently. As an independent character, he succeeds where Pirandello's Father fails. *Hamlet* is the deepest look into the inner workings of the mind, a light shone into the psychic universe of the human brain. Though Shakespeare seems to have written sixteen plays after *Hamlet*, this is the drama that finds him at his apogee – all his writing is condensed in it, whether humorous, ironic, tragic or historical. And the poetry is among the finest he wrote, which is why, of course, so many phrases and quotations from it have crept into our language – so much so that we do not always recognize their origin when we read or hear them. What I find surprising and compelling about the play is that, every time I see it, and I've seen it more times than I can remember, it has me sitting on the edge of my seat. I know perfectly what happens in the duel at the end, but I still need to experience it because Hamlet himself transcends the play. Many essays, books, pamphlets and critiques have been written about this incontrovertibly great play – possibly more has been written about *Hamlet* than has been written about any other work written in the English language. Jan Kott, the Polish theatre director and critic, once remarked that the bibliography of *Hamlet* would fill two volumes of the Warsaw telephone directory. So it is with diffidence that I add my own inadequate understanding to so many previous analyses of *Hamlet*, and the way I believe it holds a unique, accurate mirror to human personality.

The man Hamlet

Hamlet has been described as a man who could not make up his mind, as a man eaten up with anger, who thought too much and was paralysed by his uncertainty, as a man who was self-absorbed and consumed by his troubles, as a man who was too good for his environment and times, as exhibiting a 'split apprehension of women and an attempt to salvage purity from an initial conviction of general debasement'. We have seen *Hamlet* interpreted as swashbuckling adventure, as a play about espionage, about vengeance, about the Oedipus complex, about subversion, or about totalitarian politics in a fascist state. Most of these are surely very short of the mark; others may be condemned as travesties.

The key to my thinking about Hamlet is this. It is inescapable that Hamlet repeatedly unnecessarily exposes himself to danger, and to unhappiness. And Hamlet is constantly wrestling with paradoxes within himself. The first puzzling thing about Hamlet is that he gets a clear commission when he meets his father's ghost on the battlements who spells out for him the nature of his death by murder. Whether the ghost is real, or whether this is Hamlet's own conscience or consciousness speaking, is open to interpretation (it is said, incidentally, that Shakespeare played the part of the ghost himself in the first production). But the position is clear: the ghost is telling the truth – indeed, Shakespeare's ghosts never lie. Hamlet is given instructions – he is to avenge his father's death but on no account to harm his mother, Gertrude:

> But howsoever thou pursueth this act,
> Taint not thy mind, nor let thy soul contrive,
> Against thy mother aught; leave her to heaven,

Yet this commission from his father (or his conscience) is met by his omission. He doesn't kill the King (until too late, at the end of the play when his own death is already encompassed), and, in spite of the ghost's instructions, he harms his mother hugely – for example, by what he says to her in the bedroom scene. Hamlet is certainly no coward, he is quite convinced of the truth of what the ghost says, he is a popular man of action, he has opportunity to kill the King, yet he fails to do what he has agreed. His indecision is, on a conscious level, motiveless.

A second paradox is that Hamlet is a 'good' man yet his conscience reverses the normal rule – it expressly asks him to do something that is forbidden, to commit a murder. True, there is a conflict about killing the King while "a is a-praying'. But if Hamlet has religious scruples, there seem none in executing the Ghost's command. And Hamlet could quite easily save himself from a conflict here. There would be no need for him to do the killing himself – he is clearly popular with his Danish subjects, he is the rightful heir to the throne and he can prove – in fact does prove – the case against Claudius. Yet his proof is private, only for his own 'satisfaction' and never intended as a cause for revolution or persuasion of others around him of the justice of his case. Indeed, he never argues the justice of his case, even to his closest friend, Horatio.

But the third set of paradoxes is the most revealing. The number of times that Hamlet consciously and deliberately puts himself at risk is striking. The play-within-a-play, 'Murder of Gonzago', memorably retitled 'The Mousetrap' by Hamlet when watched by Claudius, is a crystal example. Hamlet knows, and shows he knows, exactly what Claudius has done. He is certain that his father has been murdered, how the murder was done, where it was committed, and that the murderer has seduced his mother. Certainly, he has no need to observe the King's reaction to the play: 'the play's the thing, wherein I'll catch the conscience of the King'. His declared purpose is to study the King's facial reactions, yet earlier he admits the inscrutability of the King's smile: 'That one may smile, and smile, and be a villain'. The only possible outcome of this night at the theatre is to put Hamlet's own life in jeopardy. Hamlet increases his danger by visiting his mother's boudoir – no useful purpose can be served. He recognizes he is likely to be spied upon, and the killing of Polonius by stabbing him through the arras curtain compromises him further. He exclaims when seeing Polonius's dead body: 'Thou wretched, rash, intruding fool, farewell; I took thee for thy better' – implying he thought it was the King. Yet only a few minutes earlier, in the immediately preceding scene, he rejects the chance to dispatch Claudius when he has the ideal opportunity. Yet anybody else alive behind the arras poses no threat to him. His treatment of Ophelia is inexplicable; it can only serve to make himself unhappy – and he knows that he is being overheard, so the tone of his conversation with her is most injurious to his own interests. Equally paradoxical is Hamlet's trip to England with his treacherous 'friends' Rosencrantz and Guildenstern, with letters that he knows contain instructions for his own death:

> There's letters sealed: and my two schoolfellows,
> Whom I will trust as I will adders fang'd;
> They bear the mandate; they must sweep my way
> And marshal me to knavery.

Indeed, in being 'marshalled to knavery' he has already agreed with himself to kill Rosencrantz and Guildenstern (even though he has not done the easier and more appropriate task – kill the King, the fount of the knavery). Above all, Hamlet agrees to fight a duel with furious Laertes, valiant and skilled a fighter though Ophelia's brother is. This is the man whose father Hamlet has assassinated, and whose beloved sister he has made mad. Hamlet knows clearly that foul play is likely

– indeed, Horatio warns against the fight and offers to make excuses for Hamlet so that he need not turn up for the fatal duel. In switching foils during the fight, yet again Hamlet shows his suspicions. He knows intuitively the foil is poisoned, and when he sees the King warn the Queen not to drink, he makes no overt move to prevent her from taking poison. So though Hamlet avows he is against suicide and murder at the start of the play, by the end of it his actions have produced eight deaths (including his own) to no conscious advantage – the stage is littered with bodies.

So what is going through Hamlet's mind?

The portrayal of Hamlet demonstrates how profound was Shakespeare's insight into this particular aspect of personality, as into so many other facets of human psychology. Everything the Prince of Denmark does is geared to cause his own self-damage. The self-damage is at an unconscious level; the most likely interpretation therefore is that Hamlet is gaining a psychic reward. He achieves unconscious pleasure from his actions and his predicament. In this respect he exhibits an extremely common trait. This kind of behaviour, attempts at self-destruction or self-damage, frequently occurs among some individuals who though not in the slightest bit mad exhibit neurotic behaviour. Some psychoanalysts refer to this as psychic masochism.

Hamlet's behaviour, although neurotic, is certainly not, in my view, abnormal. Sigmund Freud (and we shall come to him in a moment, because he also attempted to analyse this play) would assert it is. To me, his behaviour is that of a perfectly normal individual who shows a common character trait and his reactions reflect only a rather more extreme version of how many of us might react in a similar situation.

Hamlet's reactions are merely towards one end of a common spectrum of self-damaging behaviour. His behaviour is near the end of the spectrum, because of the intense stress and disorientation of his position. But nearly all of us react in similar neurotic ways from time to time, only the reaction is less because our circumstances are not generally as extreme. Have you ever lost your temper when there was no conceivable advantage to you? Have you ever gained brief satisfaction by verbally attacking someone you love, only to feel deep remorse afterwards? Have you ever shown aggression to a colleague or friend when it might have been far better to have been temperate or forgiving?

Occasionally, our attempts at self-damage produce catastrophe, as happened in Hamlet's case. One most celebrated catastrophe of this kind in real life was that of Oscar Wilde. He should never have pursued his libel case; he knew his defence was far from secure. All Wilde's reliable friends advised him against this action in court, and the inevitable public exposure. The result was ruin, the absolute disgrace from which he never recovered. In Carson, the counsel for the Marquess of Queensberry, he was up against a contemporary from his days at Trinity College. Wilde knew that Carson and he were poles apart – Carson had always been a conservative, rigid, ambitious man with no time for the views of men like Wilde, who was soft, liberal, affectionate, more intelligent and more gifted. Wilde's replies in the witness box to a man quite prepared to destroy him eloquently point to his inability to avoid continuing with his downhill career of self-damage:

CARSON: May I take it that you think 'The Priest and the Acolyte' was not immoral?

WILDE: It was worse; it was badly written.

CARSON: I take it, that no matter how immoral a book may be, if it is well written, it is, in your opinion, a good book?

WILDE: Yes, if it were well written so as to produce a sense of beauty, which is the highest sense of which a human being can be capable; if it were badly written, it would produce a sense of disgust.

CARSON: A perverted novel might be a good book?

WILDE: I don't know what you mean by a 'perverted' novel.

CARSON: Then I will suggest *Dorian Gray* as open to the interpretation of being such a novel?

WILDE: That could only be to brutes and illiterates. The views of Philistines on art are incalculably stupid.

This highly articulate man, so capable of dissembling when he wants and manipulating the emotions of others, cannot resist a cheap victory. 'It was worse; it was badly written'; 'The views of Philistines on art are incalculably stupid'. A brief, cheap *frisson*, bought so expensively.

I wonder whether this 'reward activity' has some similarities with other risk-taking behaviour, or with behaviour that seeks pleasure from something which gives us a feeling of insecurity, horror or danger. Is this why *Alien* is one of the most popular films ever? Or why Mary Shelley's not particularly brilliant novel *Frankenstein* is one of the most universally known books and a bestseller for the last 150 years? We humans enjoy jeopardy. We get 'pleasure' from it.

Defence mechanisms

All of this is, of course, not so far from Sigmund Freud. Modern theorists working in the field of human behaviour frequently treat this nineteenth-century Austrian with a degree of scepticism – and with good reason. For instance, Freud placed too much emphasis on the sex drive, or libido, in the formation of the self. Others point out that his understanding was too heavily rooted in the very specific cultural background of nineteenth-century Viennese bourgeois society to be of much use to people in other places and eras. And a major problem with Freud, like my interpretation of Hamlet, is that his views were often assertions incapable of proof, and not subjected to statistical evaluation. Some critics would view his work as little different from phrenology.

Nonetheless, Freud's observations provided a bedrock for seeing various elements of human behaviour as survival strategies – helpful or otherwise. Studying cases of hysterical paralysis and fainting – which chiefly affected affluent young Viennese women with no out-let for their sexual or emotional energies – Freud was the first to coin the term 'defence'. In essence he argued that feelings were the same as other observable forces in the physical world, like magnetism or pressure. Energy, as we know from our early physics lessons, never goes away – it merely converts into different forms. Freud seems to have believed the same was true of emotional energy. That which was denied expression did not go away, it merely built up and found other, less obvious and often less helpful forms of expression. Perhaps the most helpful analogy is that of a fast-flowing stream. If for some reason the stream is dammed up, then it bursts its banks, flooding the surrounding terrain.

In cases of paralysis and fainting, Freud argued that, in order to avoid being overloaded by overwhelmingly powerful feelings, people unconsciously 'cut out'. They became ill in a manner that baffled the best physicians, because there was no physical cause for their disorder.

What 'afflicted' them was, in fact, a survival strategy or defence mechanism. And in spite of the disruption this bout of fainting or paralysis caused to their lives, in spite of their consciously expressed hatred of the symptoms affecting them, this strategy nonetheless provided a form of unconscious gratification. By 'cutting out' – through paralysis or loss of consciousness – they obtained some temporary relief from their emotional distress. The focus of their concern, and the concern of everyone around them, became the 'illness' – not the underlying feelings which were too uncomfortable to look at. In addition, they were fussed over and treated as invalids – a way of ensuring they received the love and attention they might have been lacking in their daily lives. So in this way, we see how an apparently inexplicable, disruptive and unhelpful strategy can serve a clear purpose.

Other analysts, such as Melanie Klein, and Freud's daughter Anna, have taken Freud's theory further, and argued that there are as many as ten 'defence mechanisms' in human behaviour – all of which have a common purpose of avoiding powerful and uncomfortable feelings. They also have in common the fact that they can cause as much trouble or more than they seek to avoid.

For instance, people employing the technique of *projection* take their uncomfortable feelings and project them onto others. A glance at the tabloid press will show how universal this particular trait is – asylum seekers, Islamic fundamentalists, warmongers and Michael Jackson all serve a particular purpose in being figures of hatred. By hating them, and by seeing them as forces of evil in the world, rather than as flawed human beings like ourselves, we can cope with our own powerful feelings of hatred – towards ourselves, and even towards people we also love, like our parents and children. We could argue that the lavish detail given in some newspapers to accounts of rape, torture, murder and sexual misdemeanour is a further example of projection. It recognizes impulses that exist within all humans, but by holding up certain individuals as scapegoats and roundly condemning them, it provides a means by which we can deal with these impulses.

Another strategy, one which might apply to the doomed Prince of Denmark, is that of *displacement*. Displacement occurs when we deflect feelings from their rightful object onto another. A classic example of this is the office hierarchy in which the boss, angry with his wife, rips into his undermanager, who proceeds to be nasty to his PA, who then goes home and kicks the cat. But sometimes we attack ourselves rather than the people we are angry with. And so we return to the Prince of Denmark. We could argue that Hamlet is actually furious with his father for dying, and with his mother for remarrying. But he knows that he should love and respect his parents, not be angry with them. The discrepancy between what Hamlet feels and what he knows he ought and ought not to feel gives rise to a great weight of uncomfortable feeling. So, unconsciously, Hamlet 'displaces' it by undertaking forms of action that attack himself. In his various ill-fated strategies, we have a clear demonstration of the way a defence mechanism can paradoxically do the very opposite of what it was meant to achieve. Perhaps the most appropriate metaphor might be of a rusty, ill-fitting suit of armour, which protects us from arrows, but cuts and chafes us when we wear it.

The psychoanalytic and the neurological interpretation of human behaviour are traditionally at odds with one another. For instance, a psychoanalyst might say that an agoraphobic – someone afraid of leaving the house – was actually afraid of what they might do if they left the house, or was trying to control the behaviour of their loved ones. A neurologist would instead pinpoint an overactive amygdala and an underactive frontal lobe. But it is faintly possible that the two disciplines are not that far apart. Psychoanalysts argue that the story of the human psyche is a story of conflict between the 'id', the impulsive, unthinking emotional element, and the 'ego' – which is the rational, thinking, society-conforming part of the self. It has been suggested that this sounds curiously like the struggle between the frontal lobes and the limbic system! Some people have proposed that this may be 'in the genes'; in the rare disorder Angelman syndrome, babies are born without any expression from certain genes on one maternal chromosome – chromosome number 15. The result is mental retardation, speech difficulties, changes in the EEG with epilepsy, and jerky, awkward movements. In its polar opposite, Prader-Willi syndrome, where babies are born lacking expression of the equivalent genes on paternal chromosome 15, the symptoms in later life include mental retardation, placidity, obesity and an underdeveloped sex drive. It has been argued, fancifully in my view, that the father's genes might be responsible for those regions of the brain that correspond to the 'id', while we inherit our ego-systems, including the rationalizing component of the frontal lobes, from our mothers.[80] Our personality, in this view, is nothing less than a competitive battle between male and female genes inside our developing brain.

Whatever you make of this theory, it seems clear that our brain can sometimes hinder us as much as it can help. This may become even more clear as I go on to discuss, in the following chapter, the ways in which our brain is wired to help us interact with one another.

chapter**eight**

The loving mind

In July of 1852, a 41-year-old wealthy and handsome Irish landlord named John Rutter Carden attended a dinner party given by the Bagwells of East Cork, another influential family in his social circle. At this sedate affair, he was introduced to Eleanor Arbuthnot, the attractive young daughter of some neighbours. Eighteen-year-old Eleanor was not exactly swept away with Carden's charms – but from the moment he laid eyes on her, he was in love.

Carden and Eleanor's family moved in the same milieu of landed folk who hunted, dined and weekended together on a regular basis. There were endless opportunities for the two to meet. Carden, whose love for Eleanor seemed to grow stronger at every meeting, approached her mother and formally requested her daughter's hand in marriage. Her mother, a redoubtable widow, did not have a low opinion of Carden, but she felt that her daughter was too young to consider matrimony, and she also knew that her suitor's feelings were not in the slightest bit reciprocated. Her daughter seemed mystified and embarrassed by all the attention. As gently as she could, she advised Carden to drop the matter and find a bride elsewhere. He shouldn't have had any trouble – his name had been linked in the past with numerous women.

But Carden was a tenacious individual. When he came of age he inherited the run-down Barmane Castle. The estate had been neglected by his military family; its Irish tenants had long paid no rent and were not about to pay now. The castle was energetically rebuilt by Carden to withstand the assaults from the tenantry that followed, and the castle was successfully defended in floor-by-floor combat. He thus acquired a formidable reputation as a ruthlessly efficient rent-collector on this Tipperary estate – fending off assorted rebellions by his tenants and earning himself the nickname 'Woodcock' for his famous ability to avoid bullets. Like this bird, he was hard to hit. On one occasion, he dodged the rifle-fire of two disgruntled tenants, captured the culprits and marched them straight to the local police station. They were subsequently hanged. Later, he aimed a swivel-mounted cannon at a mob of protesters from the battlements of his castle, dispersing them swiftly. The tenants agreed that 'Woodcock' Carden was a reasonable landlord; they just did not expect to pay rent. Clearly, he was not the kind of man to give up easily.

For two years, Carden pursued Eleanor at every opportunity. He wrote her notes, declaring his undying passion in the flowery terminology of the medieval troubadours. He developed the notion that she was equally in love with him but that she was prevented from showing it by her family because they opposed the match. He followed the girl from Inverness to Paris, remaining a spectral and irritating presence at balls and parties, staring mutely at the object of his obsession from across crowded rooms and halls. When she was at home, he kept a lonely vigil outside her house. When she dined in restaurants, he sat at a table nearby, occasionally approaching her, but just as often worshipping her from afar. Nothing would dissuade him from his romantic cause – not gentle pleading, nor threats, nor public disapproval.

Matters reached a head in July 1854. On Sunday 2 July, Eleanor, her sister and mother went to church in their carriage. Woodcock Carden was lying in wait for their return – with three hired hench-men. They overpowered the coachman and seized the horses. Carden, armed with a bottle of chloroform, attempted to drag Eleanor away. In his disturbed mind, this was not abduction – since Eleanor wanted to be with him. But for a girl who wanted to be carried off, she certainly made a great fuss about it. She screamed and fought him. Her governess, a Mrs Lyndon, attacked Carden with her fists until his face was unrecognizable. Nonetheless, his passion was so great that he succeeded temporarily in kidnapping the un-fortunate girl. The authorities gave chase, and Carden – who had regularly dined and hunted with the influential lawgivers of the area – suffered the ignominy of arrest.

Carden was committed for trial at Clonmel – charged with attempted kidnapping, actual abduction and felonious assault. But popular support for him ran very high. Indeed songs were written about him. The Irish gentry — fans of his ruthless methods of dealing with tenants – backed him to the hilt. Women – those who had not experienced his stalking at first hand, at least – considered him a romantic figure. The press presented him as a passionate Celt, whose love had been cruelly spurned by a frigid English girl unworthy of it. It is a measure of his popular appeal that, although the charge then carried a possible penalty of transportation to Australia, Carden received only two years' hard labour.

He served the full sentence. Offered an early release if he promised to stay away from Eleanor and never make any contact with her again, Carden refused – saying that he would far rather die in the Crimea. He was still in love with her. What's more, he knew that she still loved him. When Carden heard news that a servant had been dismissed from Eleanor's household, he was convinced that this was because she had been caught smuggling out love notes from his beloved.

Two years in jail did nothing to change Carden's point of view. Upon gaining his freedom, he made formal applications to the Lord Lieutenant of Ireland, and to the ancestral head of Eleanor's family – Viscount Gough of Loughcooter. They refused to intercede on his behalf. Still convinced that she would one day escape the tyranny of her family, Carden turned Barmane Castle into a paradisiacal playground for Eleanor – installing a Turkish bath and furnishing the place in the height of mid-nineteenth-century fashion. Until his death in 1866, Carden remained in love with Eleanor – following her forlornly as she travelled around Ireland and Europe. His was a life shaped by a single, overpowering obsession. We might add that poor Eleanor's life was considerably shaped by it too. Despite her good looks and sizeable inheritance, she never married, and devoted her time to the education of her nephews and nieces.

Stalkers

If he were to seek help for his unfortunate condition nowadays, 'Woodcock' Carden might be told that he was suffering from 'erotomania'. Stalkers – people who obsessively pursue and harass others, sometimes for years – display this type of behaviour. Stalking often includes an element of delusional belief – such as thinking, without any grounds, that the object of the stalker's obsession is equally 'in love' with them. In Woodcock's case, he thought that young Eleanor wanted to be with him and was being held prisoner by her family. He skewed all incoming information to fit this faulty hypothesis – as in his notion that the maid had been sacked because Eleanor had asked her to smuggle out a *billet doux* to him.

Nowadays, particularly in big cities, it seems increasingly possible for people to live their existence alienated from the world. Sometimes only the media provide a minimal contact with society outside, and that contact falls short of reality. It is not surprising that the objects of erotomaniac obsession, then, are often public figures – such as actors, pop stars and politicians – whom the 'stalker' has never even met. John Hinckley Jr, who shot President Reagan, suffered from a mistaken belief that his actions would impress the actress Jodie Foster. According to some accounts, Hinckley watched the film *Taxi Driver*, in which Foster starred, several times a day. It is, incidentally, quite an unspoken problem for my own profession – a surprising number of doctors, mostly men, are persecuted in this way and usually their family suffers as well.

Erotomaniacs, or stalkers, are a risk to themselves and a risk to the people they pursue. They generally have quite a shaky sense of personal identity, they are given to sudden, violent outbursts, and they are very sensitive to real or imagined rejection. Some stalkers are prone to having brief, turbulent love affairs and often have quite frequent periods of intense depression. Erotomaniacs may have eating disorders, are prone to drug abuse and often show other self-destructive tendencies. Very little solid work has been done to understand the underlying causes but erotomania is possibly the result of a problem with brain chemistry. The evidence is poor, but in some cases erotomania is preceded by an injury to the brain, or by epilepsy – suggesting that it has a neurological origin, perhaps within the temporal lobes. Another view is that it is a variety of Obsessive Compulsive Disorder (OCD). Certainly a key feature of OCDs is what psychiatrists call 'intrusive thinking' – in other words, the sensation of being unable to stop having certain thoughts. In the case of erotomanic people, of course, the thoughts are centred around the person with whom they believe they are in love.

Brain scans of people with OCD have revealed a peculiarity of the neural circuits which pass from the basal ganglia, through to the anterior cingulate gyrus and orbitofrontal cortex. To quickly refresh the geography: the basal ganglia are believed to play a role in the planning and timing of actions, the anterior cingulate gyrus is the area that becomes activated when we are concentrating on something, and the orbitofrontal cortex, among other things, plays a part in guiding behaviour sensibly (remember Phineas Gage?). In OCD, we see a sort of 'vicious circle' – in which the basal ganglia tell people to act, the anterior cingulate ensures that they become fixated upon acting, the orbitofrontal cortex tells them that whatever they are doing is wrong, and this final part of the circuit sends them back to square one. This explains why people with OCDs may find themselves 'imprisoned' by the need to wash their hands hundreds of times a day, or unable to leave the house without checking, again and again, that they have switched the lights off, locked the doors, etc. As with so many disorders of the brain, OCD is really just a malfunction of a sensible system, devised to ensure that we carry out our plans with efficiency.

Is love embedded in our brain structure?

The tale of John Rutter Carden also highlights another point – that there is a fine line between the states of mind we class as 'sane' and 'insane'. At one level, his is no more than an extreme tale of un- requited love – something that many of us may have experienced to some extent at some point in our lives. Even when love is reciprocal, in the first flush at least, most people experience an element of obsessive thinking. Song lines like 'You are always on my mind' and 'I've got you under my skin' express this classic feature of attraction. When we are first in love, we think of our lovers many times a day, to the exclusion of other people, other concerns. Without this facet of human cognition, Vodafone and Orange would never find it worth running a text message service. So if love itself is more than an idea, could it be the result of a specific state of brain chemistry? If that is so, can we observe it and can we measure it? Would it have been worthwhile for Andrew Marvell to have put his coy mistress into an fMRI scanner?

To be human is to be involved in relationships with other humans, and love is an aspect of ourselves which seems deeply etched within the structure of our brain. We are created from a relationship, however transient, between two humans. Possibly more than any other mammal we are raised most typically in family units comprising two or more humans. We enter and become part of further networks of human relations – schools, workplaces, army battalions, cricket clubs and informal groups of like-minded friends. The human being is a social animal – and there is no human society known to anthropologists in which the norm is for people to live their lives in solitude. From vast cities to small nomadic bands of Kalahari bush people, the human existence is one conducted alongside others. The instinct to be a part of a group has evolved since we were vulnerable hominids, incapable of hunting successfully on our own or protecting ourselves from predators.

But most of us also need a bit of 'space' and solitude – although the length of time we are prepared to spend in our own company differs from one person to another. In general, though, it doesn't take very long before our more basic need for company takes over and we begin to feel uncomfortable alone. This trait was studied by Stanley Schachter in 1959. Dr Schachter from Columbia University was one of those larger-than-life individuals, interested in everything, provocative, entertaining and sometimes highly controversial. His interests were wide – how people communicate and work in a group, the effect of being the oldest or youngest child in a family, the causes of obesity, nicotine addiction, the power of suggestion, and the interpretation of pauses in human speech, for example 'ums' and 'ahs'. His arch announcement about the power of 'bubba psychology' ('bubba' is Yiddish for grandmother) was typical. Any grandmother, he stated, could out-predict an economist – and therefore the stock market – because a bubba understands that people are not coldly rational about investing their money. 'Bubba psychology' hit the headlines and became argot for a time in *The Wall Street Journal*.

Solitary confinement is one of the most extreme human punishments. Being a solitary castaway, or a prisoner of war or terrorism, can be agonizing and devastating – as Schachter pointed out, the hermit-like isolation can lead a person to withdraw so much that they become akin to a schizophrenic. So the role of the religious hermit seems almost totally 'unnatural'. Schachter wrote of isolation for religious purposes:

> The solitary [hermit] begins to see himself as he really is. The meanness, the crookedness of natural character begins to stand out in a strong light; those wounds to disobedience or conscience in the past have left festering, now give forth their poisoned nature. There may be terrible uprisings of lower nature, and more formidable yet, resistance of self-will to the straight-jacket into which he will thrust it. Here you get the reason for what look like eccentricities of asceticism, its bread-and-water fasts, scourges and the rest, even to midnight immersions practiced by Celtic solitaries. It is Master Soul, the rider, whipping Brother Ass, the body, into obedience . . .

Schachter conducted one experiment on isolation rather like an extreme version of the TV show *Big Brother*. Schachter found five male volunteers prepared to live alone. The men were given very basic, separate accommodation – a bed, chair, table and toilet. Their rooms had no windows; they had no access to books, newspapers, radio or television. One man lasted twenty minutes before declaring that he wished to leave. Three of the volunteers managed two days in the room. Even the fifth man, a resourceful individual who racked up a total of eight days alone, eventually began to feel extremely anxious. Regrettably, unlike the winning *Big Brother* contestants, this man did not receive £50,000 and a period of C-list celebrity status – although his efforts somewhat advanced our understanding of the human mind. Humans need some form of contact with others, and they begin to experience anxiety when they are socially isolated. Even activities like watching TV or reading a newspaper can serve to maintain an illusion of contact with the outside world – without it, we are lost.

Schachter's studies did not stop there. Like so many of these classical researchers, he would not have obtained ethical approval for this study now. He felt that if social isolation makes people anxious, then people who are anxious might experience an increased drive to mix with other people to reduce their anxiety. In one experiment he recruited a number of women undergraduates, mostly psychology students. When the subjects arrived for the experiment for which they had blindly volunteered, they were greeted by a researcher in a white lab coat in a laboratory surrounded by coils of wire, transformers and electrodes. The experimenter introduced himself as

Dr Gregor Zilstein of the Department of Neurology and Psychiatry and told the volunteers that the proposed experiment required them to receive an electric shock. To make some subjects more afraid than others, the experimenter used two different descriptions of the shock they would shortly experience. To the group he did not want to make fearful, he offered reassurance. He stated that they would feel no more than a tickle or a tingle. To those in whom he wanted to induce severe anxiety, he said that the shocks would hurt, but that they would be helping humanity because of the value of the research. 'Of course,' he said, 'these shocks will be quite painful but they will cause no permanent damage.' Before the shocks were administered, these students were asked to complete a questionnaire about their feelings about participating. They were asked, 'How do you feel about being shocked?', to which they replied by choosing from a five-point scale, ranging from, 'I dislike the idea very much' to 'I enjoy the idea very much'.

The poor students were then told that there would be a ten-minute delay while he prepared the electrical apparatus. He pointed out that he could not set up the devices with everyone hanging around, watching. So the subjects were given a choice. They could wait in one of the small adjacent rooms, just big enough for one person but where they could relax looking at magazines in a comfortable chair. As an alternative, they were offered an uncomfortable classroom nearby where there was room for everyone and plenty of hard seats. The students also filled out a form indicating their preferences on a score of five points from, 'I very much prefer being alone' to 'I very much prefer being together with others'. Over 60 per cent of the women expecting a nasty shock chose to spend the waiting period with other people. The great majority of women expecting a mild shock preferred to wait in comfortable isolation. Schachter concluded that, just as solitude makes humans anxious, so anxiety motivates us to want to be with other humans.

Of course, no shock of any kind was administered. But the ethics of such an experiment would now be regarded as extremely dubious. Needless to say, one problem is the impossibility of getting properly informed consent. Also the researcher is causing quite severe distress by making some volunteers fearful. He is also effectively threatening the self-esteem of those who found themselves troubled by participating.

Fitting in with the group

Most of us – unless we are enviably accomplished – will have had some experience of what it meant at some time in our lives not to fit in and to lose self-esteem. I used to wait in vain as the team captains at school picked everyone but me. (I am convinced to this day that I was good enough to be a Second to my Boy Scout Patrol Leader.) And those excruciating Saturday–night hops, spent in the local youth club where everybody had a smarter pullover and a better haircut. All of us will remember the levels of discomfort and anxiety that this failure to fit in produces.

But my hugging the bookshelves at a party is hardly human evolution in action; it is probably some form of mildly phobic behaviour, maybe induced by being repeatedly rejected as a member of my classmates' tiddlywinks team. Social exclusion tends to happen for three other main reasons – because we break, or don't seem to know, the 'rules' of behaviour; because we are incompetent or clumsy; and because we are unattractive. Each of these factors is a threat to the survival of the group. Someone who doesn't know the rules, or who knows them and still breaks them, threatens the cohesion of the group. Someone who is incompetent is a drain on resources – they'll eat the food, but be useless on the hunt, for example. Someone who is unattractive – and more on this later – may have inferior genes or bring illness to the group. Faced with social exclusion, we experience anxiety, and anxiety, as we know, then makes us wish to belong. In evolutionary terms, this anxiety would motivate humans to try harder to win the group's approval.

Perhaps in one sense the human brain has evolved into a highly 'social' organ itself. From the moment of conception, the brain develops by dividing itself into ever increasing complexity. Neurons develop by forming connections with one another, and by passing communications along those connections. Neurons are fed and nourished by communication with their neighbours – the seldom visited neural network is the network that tends to die away, which is why we can lose skills and faculties that we do not practise. And the brain depends upon the input of the external environment in order to develop. As we have seen in earlier chapters, we need contact with other humans to learn language and to process emotions. A brain that grows without sight, sound or touch of other humans is severely compromised indeed. It has been argued with good reason that the size and complexity of the human brain is partly determined by our living in large and intricate social groups. Studies of humans and our near–relations in the animal kingdom have shown a relationship between the size of the cortex and the complex nature of the social group.

So the human brain is a brain geared to interaction with others. There may even be neurons within the amygdala that are only activated in response to displays of emotion by other humans. It seems that in monkeys there are certain nerve cells in their frontal lobes that fire when the monkey undertakes specific tasks with its hand – such as picking up food and putting it in its mouth. What is so intriguing is that these particular neurons also fire when the monkey being tested sees another monkey doing the same thing. These neurons have been called 'mirror neurons' and Professor Ramachandran argues that 'with knowledge of these neurons, you have the basis for understanding a host of very enigmatic aspects of the human mind: "mind reading" empathy, imitation learning, and even the evolution of language.' There is now good evidence that similar neurons exist in other primates, particularly humans. Professor Rizzolati from Parma, the scientist who first described mirror neurons, and his team used fMRI and reported that there may be mirror neurons in a region of the temporal lobes called the superior temporal sulcus.[81]

Mirror neurons, if they truly exist in humans, appear to depend upon the input of human-generated information. For instance, these areas of the brain appear to be activated only when we watch another human performing a task, not when we watch a robot performing it. They seem to be activated only when watching goal-oriented behaviour – such as shelling a nut – and not when watching mimicry or purposeless action. However, as few people yet have attempted to record electrical activity from single neurons in humans, it is difficult to prove that they do fire in the way I am speculating. Indeed, it would be intriguing to find out whether, if they truly exist, they fire in response to watching a monkey undertaking human-like actions. And if this were the case, it would argue the basis for our empathy with them.

The human brain is also wired to be able to identify and dis-criminate between other humans – even when the information provided is minimal. If you were shown a film clip of me walking round in complete darkness, with only little points of light indicating key areas of my body, you would be able to identify what you saw as the figure of a male human, walking. You might even, if you knew me, be able to identify me as Robert Winston. Studies have shown that, whatever the level of visibility, humans are able to identify others by the way they move.

An impressive array of brain systems are involved in the simplest of interactions between people. Take the example of going to a party. We use our ability to recognize faces, our memory to acknowledge the person who actually invited us, and we recall other people to whom we might wish to talk. We use our amygdala to judge by their emotions what sort of a mood they are in, and our frontal lobes to direct our behaviour towards them accordingly. We use our attention and skill at focusing to concentrate and conduct a conversation amidst the hubbub of cocktail party chatter. We use our motor skills to know how close to stand to other people, and to balance a plate of snacks on our knees as we sip a drink. And our nose is telling us meantime what an appallingly unpleasant Beaujolais it is we're drinking – you might even be casting furtive looks to see into which plant pot you can pour it.

If just one simple faculty within this system happens to be working awry, then the social consequences can be disastrous. Perhaps we have trouble recognizing faces, causing us to seem aloof and rude. Perhaps we find it hard to switch attention between one focus and another, causing us to seem slow or boring. Perhaps we have difficulty recognizing other people's states of mind, causing us to seem insensitive or selfish. Perhaps we rush up to other people and conduct conversations just inches from the end of their noses – causing us to seem overbearing or plain disturbed. Maybe we miss the flowerpot and soak the elegant Qum carpet. The outcome for all five is that we end up being excluded from the group.

A cocktail party might seem a trivial example. Admittedly, the human race would probably just about continue if these gatherings were outlawed tomorrow. But the skills we call upon in such a situation are essential to our survival. Without a social brain, how could we meet suitable partners, fall in love and raise children? How could we identify people potentially of benefit to us, or others who might wish us harm? Without an ability to interpret and 'enter into' the emotional states of other people, how could we develop morality, or exercise compassion and forgiveness? These skills are central to being human, and they depend upon brain activity that is largely outside our conscious control.

It must be love

In evolution, the choice of mate depends upon the ability of one animal to recognize qualities in another of its species that would lend potential offspring an advantage in the business of survival. An aggressive 'alpha male' chimpanzee is likely to be better at hunting food and at defending his partner and offspring from predators or other males. So, female chimpanzees prefer to breed with alpha males. Not only would they be useful to have around while the female is saddled with the responsibilities of caring for her brood, but the alpha male's 'successful' attributes would be passed, through the genes, to her offspring.

We can see Darwin throughout nature and the principle is at work with humans. Society might have evolved to the extent that attributes like big muscles and an aggressive personality no longer lend an evolutionary advantage. But nonetheless, human females look for other indicators of 'alpha male' qualities. As Henry Kissinger, perhaps no great whiz in the looks department, has famously pointed out, 'power is an aphrodisiac'. Signals like a smart suit, a costly watch, a flashy car or a brilliant mind communicate that the male in question can amply provide for the female and her offspring, and pass on his survival advantages to the next generation. So these things become included in what we see as 'attractive'. Similarly, men still value attributes in a woman that communicate her superior ability to pro- duce and care for healthy offspring – hence the timeless appeal of the 'hourglass' female figure, with its childbearing hips and ample breasts.

Of course, it is clear that in many respects to be human is to transcend the limitations of our evolutionary past. We do not, for the greater part, evaluate potential love matches and partners on the basis of looks or wage-earning abilities alone. We are motivated by characteristics like kindness and sense of humour, and by common goals and experiences. The temptation is to argue that such aspects might convey little or no evolutionary purpose at all. But that gentle musician and actor-comedian Dudley Moore, a rather short gentleman with small eyes and a prominent nose, once said he 'laughed women into bed'. Humour is attractive. Scan the 'lonely hearts' column of any newspaper or magazine and you will see time and again the term GSOH – good sense of humour. A man who can make people laugh is probably also a man with higher intelligence, a clear survival advantage. He is also a man with a level of social ability – one that could be used for security and gain. A kind man might be of little use in the hunting ground, but what about playing an active part in raising children? These examples show that, however much the world we live in may change, we are still flesh-and-blood machines orientated towards survival and reproduction. So the science of attraction and arousal is one of the most fascinating areas of brain research.

Hey, good looking

The evidence suggests that, whether we live in mud-huts or Manhattan loftspaces, attraction works on the same principles as it did in our evolutionary past. Various studies have indicated that what both men and women rate as attractive, handsome, beautiful, sexually arousing, etc., is symmetry. A Canadian study in 1999 showed that the more symmetrical men's bodies were, the greater the likelihood they were to have a range of sexual encounters. Newborn babies also show an increased preference for symmetrical faces, and this continues throughout our development. The Darwinian thinking is that a symmetrical face is not merely more pleasant to look at, but is also an indicator of physical health and strength – and this is why we un-consciously regard it as more attractive.

A good deal of what I feel is 'soft' research in this area has been done on orgasm. Much of it probably should be taken with more than just a grain of salt. But for what it is worth, a study by the aptly named Randy Thornhill at New Mexico University suggests regular orgasms are up to 40 per cent more common in the female partners of men with symmetrical bodies. Given that orgasm is pleasurable and that failing to achieve orgasm may carry some perceived stigma, how do we know that Randy's subjects were telling the truth? Or did he stand by the bedside with a clip board? But if orgasm does have an evolutionary purpose, perhaps it increases fertility. A University of Cardiff study by Dr Jacky Boivin, announced at the British

Association for the Advancement of Science in 1998, claimed that, when a woman experiences orgasm, or at least a heightened degree of pleasure in the sexual encounter, she retains more of her partner's sperm, thereby increasing her chances of conception. Women in their mid-thirties were asked to rate their last sexual encounter in terms of the degree of pleasure it had given them and were tested within three hours of having had sex. Of those women who had given the experience a low score, nearly half had a post-coital sperm count of zero. Of the high scores, only one in ten had a low post-coital sperm count. But I remain very dubious about these findings – post-coital tests of the number of sperms left in the cervix are notoriously in-accurate and unreliable.

But we are on more solid ground with the notion that humans seem to be hard-wired to be attracted to those partners whose bodies and faces most accentuate the characteristics of the opposite sex. So the ideal woman, in every society and culture, has smooth skin, large eyes, plump lips and a relatively unpronounced jaw, attributes which most identify her as a woman. In addition, factors like youth and body shape indicate the woman's ability to carry out the role of childbirth.

In early adolescence, as their ability to conceive and bear children is switched on, women begin to store fat around the lower regions of their bodies. Studies at the University of Texas, by Devendra Singh, show that this pattern of fat distribution has a powerful effect on the way males rate female attractiveness. By measuring the distribution of fat, and asking male volunteers to rate a range of female shapes, Singh's team came up with the finding that the ideal waist-to-hip ratio is one of 0.7, regardless of the weight of the woman. Researchers have compared Miss America winners over a number of years – and found the same ratio. It is thought that this ratio repre-sents the optimal condition for childbearing – and it alters as women go past the menopause. Production of female hormones decreases at this stage and the way fat is distributed across a woman's body starts to become closer to that seen in men.

Women equally are attracted towards men with the greatest distri-bution of 'male' sexual characteristics. Men are on average taller than women, and height lent us a survival advantage in terms of fending off predators and in collecting food. So taller men are more likely to be rated as attractive by the opposite sex, and are therefore more likely to reproduce. A research study performed in Liverpool and

Poland studied this factor in a group of 3,000 men. They found that men who married and had children were on average 3 centimetres taller than men with no children. The unmarried men were also markedly shorter than the married men.

The higher presence of testosterone in men gives their body a whole set of differences from the female form: for example, a 'harder', bony facial look, with prominent jaw and cheekbones, and minimal facial fat. Female faces, or feminine-looking male faces, remain more childlike, with features less pronounced, large lips and more facial fat in the cheek area. Theoretically, men with more 'masculine' faces should be men who offer the greatest evolutionary advantage, because testosterone offers survival advantages – increased courage, aggression and sex drive. A handsome face, so the theory goes, tops a healthy body. The craze for the ragged, emaciated look of 'heroin chic' runs contrary to good biological sense.

Bizarre as it may seem, a simple difference in facial characteristics can mean the difference between a lifetime of success and one of failure. Researchers have found, for instance, that the facial dominance – grooved, growly and meanly masculine-looking – of graduates from a military academy tends to predict their final rank at the end of their careers. It has also been shown that more feminine-faced men show an increased likelihood to be found 'not guilty' in certain criminal proceedings, or to be handed lighter sentences. But it is in the arena of sexual attraction that the face plays the most important part.

What women want

A study at St Andrew's University by Ian Penton-Voak showed pictures of male faces to women at the peak of their conception cycle.[82] When asked to select the type of man with whom they would be most likely to have a casual fling, the women chose the most macho-looking faces – think George Clooney – over more gentle, feminine or less conventionally handsome types of faces, such as Leonardo DiCaprio or Willem Dafoe. In other words, when they were most able to conceive, they chose men who seemed the most likely to offer their offspring a genetic advantage.

In a refinement of this first study, Penton-Voak's team asked women to state how highly attractive they rated themselves, and also asked them to select male faces with whom they would be most likely to have a long-term relationship. This is where I have to admit that I glossed over certain facts earlier on. Because in some respects, women's biology leads them to want two, sometimes contradictory, things out of the men with whom they mate. Their evolutionary programming should be telling them to have sex with men who most demonstrate good health and strong male characteristics. But they also seek men who will stick around and help to look after the children. Unfortunately, the closer a male is to the ideal masculine type, the more likely he is to have high levels of testosterone. Accordingly, he is likely to have a strong sex drive and to seek out sex with a range of partners. In other words, the 'good genes guy' won't be the sort of guy who wants to stay in at night with the Ball and Chain and the kids. And also, his similarity to the 'ideal type' means that other women will be more responsive to his advances.

In accordance with this, both women and men associate macho, high-testosterone looks with the 'wham, bam, thank you, ma'am' approach, and not with sticking around to help raise children. In another St Andrew's study, which involved a vast number of participants, images were shown of two male faces - one masculine and one feminine. They were presented alongside two dating adverts and the subjects had to say which face went with which advert. The only real difference in the two adverts was that one man obviously seeking a short-term fling, while the other was interested a long-term relationship. The participants - both male and female overwhelmingly linked the macho face to the advert seeking a fling.

So we see a trade-off in the way women select males purposes of sex and reproduction. Women who are in temporary sexual fulfilment will have no qualms about sex most outright macho men - because they are not concerned whether he will stick around and help. Women who want to make choices. While they lose in the 'good genes' department they gain in the 'nurturing partner' department. Their occur at an unconscious level, but they are also after more open to conscious scrutiny, such as their sense

The conventional wisdom would be that the most testosterone males would be the worst choice relationship, because of their propensity to go to make babies with other females. But studies show that women who rated themselves as attractive still plumped for the macho males to have babes with. Does this suggest that such women are less concerned about a man's 'stick-around' qualities because they feel able to provide for their own offspring, and simply want males to provide good genetic material? Women who rated themselves as less attractive showed a heightened preference for non-macho-type males – suggesting that they are more attracted to signs of sticking around, rather than those of 'top-quality' genes. The 'more attractive' women's choice in picking the macho guys might also be because they rated themselves as being sufficiently able to get other men to help raising the children or persuade the father to stay put.

But, of course, we do not base our choices on looks alone. In an earlier series for BBC Television, *Human Instinct*, women were asked to sniff men's T-shirts and then match them to faces. The experiment tends to confirm that we are more attracted to people with a genetic make-up different to ourselves – thereby ensuring that our offspring get the best possible inheritance. It is now thought that what may influence women in the 'sniff test' of mate selection is immunity to different diseases and infections. In other words, the ideal breeding partner is one who is immune to different types of disease than those to which we are immune ourselves. The resultant offspring would then be immune to the maximum possible range of threats to its survival.

When it comes to the question of genes, most of us prefer a mixture of the familiar and the exotic. We all tend to seek sex with people to whom we are not related. All of us carry some defective genes; if our chosen partner carries similarly defective DNA, it could mean disaster for our children. Statistically, most of us carry at least twenty to thirty variations in our genes that could cause a hereditary disorder. The results of marriage within the same group are well illus-trated by diseases like Tay-Sachs. Tay-Sachs Syndrome is a serious disease. The brain neurons become swollen with fat and these babies develop blindness, paralysis and dementia. These children die within the first few years of childhood. The disease mutation is very commonly carried in the DNA of Ashkenazi Jewish people – about 1 in 35 will carry a mutation that could cause the disease in a child if they marry another carrier. Ashkenazi Jews had ancestors originating from Eastern Europe or Russia and they have always tended to have children with people from the same origins, not least because they had little choice in the matter, and, of course, because of religious observance and social custom. But the consequences have been the increased risks associated with inbreeding.

So, however much we may be programmed to seek 'outside' genes, there is also a human preference for what is familiar and similar. Sigmund Freud is perhaps most famous for arguing that small boys and girls have an unconscious wish to sleep with their mothers and fathers, and an accompanying fear of punishment from the other parent. More recent research into human behaviour indicates that his theories may contain a grain of truth. Photo-imaging techniques have now made it possible to morph and merge photographs with great degrees of subtlety. After modifying photographs, one study showed that volunteers were more attracted to faces that resembled their parent of the opposite sex.

Hawaii is an ethnic melting pot. There, Polynesian, Oriental, Indian and European people live in roughly equal numbers. Studies there have shown that children born of mixed relationships tend to marry into the ethnic group to which the opposing sex parent belonged. Boys, in a sense, look for the genetic model presented by their mothers, and girls go for that presented by their fathers. Other studies have shown that factors like parental eye-colour and age affect our choices of mate. However, the likelihood is that these things influence us, not because we are seeking to mate with people who carry the same genes, but simply because our sexual identity is formed at a very young age. In its malleable plastic state, the human brain becomes stamped with the image of the ideal mate. These images would naturally bear more than a passing resemblance to our own parents, if we were raised by them. I have not come across studies that examine adopted children, but – if these observations are correct – one would expect that people adopted as babies would have similar tendencies.

What men want

Men are arguably less 'choosy' when it comes to mate-selection, and are more ready to have sex, regardless of the partner. I have previously written about the study in which an attractive female stranger approached men on a university campus and suggested they go to bed. Three-quarters of the men responded positively. In contrast, when a similar approach was made to women by a male stranger, none of the women agreed.[83]

This difference has nothing to do with morality – although we may consciously provide that as the explanation. It boils down to biology. A woman has to bear a child for nine months, and nurture her offspring. This means she is less able to find food for herself and her baby, and is more vulnerable to attack from predators. Accordingly, she has to make very careful choices about the men with whom she mates – evaluating, as I pointed out earlier, their good genes versus their stick-around qualities. She can also only reproduce relatively few times within her lifespan. By contrast, each male has the potential to create millions of offspring, with the only necessary investment being the length of time it takes him from the initial approach to ejaculation.

But men are not just more interested in sex and less in relationships – although there is a tendency within our culture to assume this. Lord Byron summed up this attitude most neatly when he wrote: 'Love of man's life is a thing apart, 'tis woman's whole existence.' Are men really wired to reproduce all over the place, while women need commitment?

An American study conducted by M.J. Montgomery and G.T. Sorrell in the 1990s showed that adolescent boys fall in love earlier and more often than girls.[84] It also asked the subjects to answer the following question: 'If you met someone who had all the characteristics you desired, but you were not in love with him or her, would you marry them?' The cynical male might assume that more of the girls would have said no than the boys. But the reverse was true. Almost two-thirds of the boys said no, they wouldn't marry someone if they were not in love. This compared to just one-third of the girls.

These results tie in neatly with a study conducted by the American sociologist William Kephart. Kephart questioned 1,000 college students about their experiences of being in love, and the age when this occurred. He noted that, while girls initially fell in love more often and began to do so at a younger age than boys, there was a distinct pattern relating to sexual maturity. By the age of twenty, girls reported fewer and fewer cases of infatuation, whereas in boys the number continued to increase. Kephart argued that these results indicated a clear pragmatism on the part of women. As they become physically able to bear children, they are less inclined to be persuaded by romantic notions of love, and more geared towards rational decisions about long-term relationships. As the Montgomery and Sorrell study indicated, women are more likely to marry without love being part of the equation.

So, however far we think we have come from our evolutionary past, our brain and body tell a very different story. Everything we know about the science of attraction, and the Darwinian forces at play behind it, begs one question – is there really any such thing as love? Fortunately, the answer is yes.

The thrill is gone

William Proxmire, who retired in 1989, was a Democrat senator for Wisconsin known for his high personal standards of integrity, dedication and, especially, frugality. Proxmire started his career in counterintelligence during the second world war and later entered politics, standing unsuccessfully for the Wisconsin State governorship three times. Finally he was elected to the Senate to fill the vacancy created by the death of the now infamous Joe McCarthy. William Proxmire spent his political life as the Senate icon campaigning mercilessly against wasteful government spending. Over the years he took credit for saving millions of dollars of public money. His campaigning in the US caused programmes targeted by central government to be curtailed, modified or cancelled. He is remembered in this context for his successful fight against American plans to finance a supersonic transport plane. But he is best known for his Golden Fleece awards. These awards put government officials on notice 'to prevent fleecing of taxpayers'. He announced his first award in 1975; this was an attempt to galvanize public opinion against the decision of the National Science Foundation to finance an $84,000 study about why people fall in love.

William Proxmire, the old conservative, said in defending his position that people 'want to leave some things in life a mystery . . . and right at the top of the list of things we don't want to know is why a man falls in love with a woman, and vice versa'. But I do not believe we scientists should be blamed for offending the senator, or anyone else. It is sometimes said that scientific knowledge overturns the mysteries of life and thus makes the world a poorer place. But these studies are genuinely important. Although some of man's greatest attributes, like heroism and altruism, may be reduced to what seems a genetic equation, the study of psychology has a huge value for all societies. So what if consciousness and language are portrayed as a set of electrical waves in the brain? Does it matter if some scientific evidence strongly supports the view that laughter, affection and even the transcendent nature of a religious experience may have their roots in the interplay of neuronal activity? This is no indication that scientists should halt their endeavours. Science will never reach a point where it can explain and interpret the whole mystery of human existence – and nor should it aim to. The journey counts more than any intended goal. Understanding the neurological and psychological basis of love adds an important dimension to what will always be an enduring mystery.

Senator Proxmire was not the only person to protest about love and sex. Doris Autkrystof in her *Amedeo Modigliani: The Poetry of Seeing*[85] describes how, on Monday 3 December 1917, a group of guests gathered in the gallery of Berthe Weill's, the Paris art dealer, for the debut of Amedeo Modigliani's only solo exhibition. But it was bad luck that the local gendarmerie was located exactly opposite the gallery. There were a number of large paintings of provocatively posed naked women hung in the gallery itself and, to attract the huge crowd that entered, one of Modigliani's big nude canvases was prominently displayed in the window. Berthe Weill was hauled in to see the Commissioner of Police, who ordered her to 'take down all that filth' because the naked women were, outrageously, displaying pubic hair. The public scandal that followed, and the police activity, closed the exhibition. But love can be what makes another human paint an extraordinary series of obsessive masterpieces.

Amedeo Modigliani's paintings of Jeanne Hébuterne started when they met in 1917. One is in the Courtauld Collection in London, another in the Guggenheim in New York, and several others are in private hands. They are testimony to a great and poignant story of love. Some of the many paintings of Jeanne are breathtaking, and in some, Jeanne's delicate, fragile beauty stands fresh after ninety years have passed. The thirty-three-year-old Modigliani met Jeanne Hébuterne when she was an art student of just nineteen. Modigliani had suffered with repeated chest infections since he was a teenager. In some ways their story is a little resonant with that of *La Bohème*, but in reverse. Besotted and passionate immediately, they lived together in Montmartre. Their public love – and the violence between them – became a Paris legend. The poet and critic, André Salmon, described what he saw on one occasion:

> He was dragging her along by an arm, gripping her frail wrist, tugging at one or another of her long braids of hair, and only letting go of her for a moment to send her crashing against the railings of the Luxembourg. He was like a madman, crazy with savage hatred.

Some of Amedeo Modigliani's many pictures of Jeanne show exquisite tenderness, but others seem distant and indistinct, and a few make her look disinterested and passive, even blurred. I find it interesting that he painted her in outdoor clothes, in formal clothes, in a nightdress, pregnant, wearing a large hat – but as far as I know, he never painted *her* naked. Because of the Great War, by a year later, in early 1918, conditions in Paris had become so difficult that Modigliani travelled to join the many other artists in their haunts in the south of France. Jeanne went with him and soon became pregnant, but shortly afterwards she and Modigliani had a stormy separation. Jeanne's parents were Catholic and her mother strongly disapproved of the Jewish Modigliani. But their love proved overwhelming and they were gloriously reunited before their daughter was born. It seems that on the way to register the child Modigliani got totally drunk, and the baby remained officially fatherless until she was adopted by Amedeo's family in Livorno, in Italy. By 1919, Jeanne was pregnant again and they moved into their first proper home together in Paris, the only environment Modigliani really liked. And now he was financially more secure and becoming a real success; at an exhibition in London, the writer Arnold Bennett bought one of the paintings and said that it 'reminded him of his own heroines'. But his chronic alcoholism had always been a problem. That, combined with his poor diet, was getting the worst of him and his health now rapidly deteriorated. Days after New Year in 1920 his neighbour and friend for fifteen years, the painter Ortiz de Zarate, hearing strange noises upstairs and not having seen the couple around, suspected there might be something wrong. He went up to call in and was greeted by a shocking sight. Modigliani was writhing around and delirious, their apartment was in a state of chaos. The bed was strewn with empty bottles, and sardine cans were dripping their oil onto the filthy sheets. Beside him on the disordered bed sat a motionless Jeanne, heavily pregnant. Extraordinarily, she had listlessly not bothered to call for help, or for a doctor. When medical help came it was already too late. It was obvious that Modigliani had acute cerebral tuberculosis and was dying. He remained in a coma and finally expired on 24 January 1920. Montmartre produced an enormous funeral, attended by what seemed its entire population. Hardly a distinguished artist, writer or poet of the time was not present. Just two days later, Jeanne, aged twenty-two, threw herself out of a fifth-floor window, killing both herself and her unborn child.

It seems unbelievable, but Jeanne's family refused to allow them to be buried together. It was only years later that, in recognition of the love they shared, her body was finally released from its solitary grave and she was reburied with Amedeo.

This tale, so often repeated in various ways, illustrates a point. It is possible to analyse much of what goes on in the brain when love is in the air, but we will surely never stop being fascinated by the many forms love takes, nor by the heights of achievement and destruction to which it may drive us. For those of us temporarily more interested in the mechanics of the business, scientists have identified three separate and distinct categories of the love experience – lust, attraction and attachment. Anthropologist Helen Fisher, of Rutgers University, has argued that each of these stages had a different evolutionary purpose. Lust evolved to get us looking for mates, attraction to help us focus our attentions on an ideal partner and attachment to stay with them and raise our offspring.

Some mechanisms for a deadly sin

An MRI scan of the loving brain reveals that each of these stages has its own separate set of brain activities. When we are in lust, the airborne chemicals, pheromones, are particularly active. As we have seen, in the animal kingdom pheromones may act to indicate when a potential mate is on heat and ready for fertile intercourse. In humans, the actions of these chemicals on the brain may be more subtle, but still seem to be important.

The chemical androstenol (which, ladies, is said to smell faintly of sandalwood) is found in male sweat and can increase women's social interactions with men. Incidentally, it can – for those seriously interested – be bought on the worldwide web for around $30. Dr Andrew Scholey and colleagues at the University of Northumbria exposed both men and women to this type of pheromone. When asked to rate the attractiveness of another person, based only on a character sketch, women gave a higher score when in the presence of the pheromone even though they could not always consciously perceive it. In one controlled study he and his colleagues investigated the effects of exposure to male axillary secretions.[86] Thirty-two female undergraduates, of whom half were on the pill, gave a rating of attractiveness to male character sketches and photographs of male faces. They were tested on two separate study days, corresponding to different phases of their menstrual cycle, while exposed to male axillary pheromones and, unknowing, under a control condition without a pheromone. Pheromone exposure increased the enthusiasm of the women's ratings of vignette characters and faces. Use of the contraceptive pill or menstrual cycle phase had equivocal effects on the response of these young women to the vignettes but not to ratings of photographs.

Similar findings were reported in a study at the University of Vienna, conducted by Karl Grammer. His team asked men to rate photographs of various women by how attractive they found them. They then asked the men to repeat the task, but this time after having smelt female pheromones known as copulins. The effect of the copulins was to make the men far less discriminating – such that they gave higher scores to women they had previously not fancied.[87]

Studies at the University of Chicago have shown that a pheromone with an undetectable odour, with the improbable name of Delta 4-16 androstadien 3-one, has a significant effect on glucose usage in the brain. Undetectable steroids like this can have differing effects on women and men. A woman's temperature may rise, while a male experiences a fall in temperature – but these measurements tend to vary depending on the person taking the readings and how sexually active this observer is.

We are a long way from understanding the full nature and extent of pheromonal action upon the brain. As humans, we are driven to seek shortcuts, and as a result, the newspapers will always be full of advertisements proclaiming the 'scientifically proven' benefits of various so-called pheromone sprays and aftershaves. Various studies have indicated that it is possible to synthesize pheromones, and that these ersatz hormones can have powerful effects on behaviour. In one American study, seventeen young men were given an aftershave that, unknown to them, contained a lab-manufactured pheromone. Of the group, 41 per cent reported a noticeable increase in their sexual activity.[88] I am tempted to say that the scientist who can finally patent a powerful but harmless pheromone scent will find themselves sitting on a goldmine. But, as with the use of subliminal advertising, any device that allows one human to alter another's behaviour without their consent, particularly in the arena of sexual relations, is highly dubious.

Like the pheromones that lead to it, love itself can be a dangerous thing. Novelists, poets and songwriters have long made a link between the properties of love and the experience of being addicted to drugs. And it seems that there is much scientific truth in this. A study by Larry Young at Emory University in Atlanta, Georgia, examined rodent sexual behaviour and the related activity in an area of the brain called the ventral pallidum.[89] The pallidum is an area particularly involved in reward and addiction. Young has suggested that the reward and pleasure systems of the brain exist primarily to ensure that we are interested in sex, and therefore reproduce.

The prairie vole, a shy, grey-furred little creature not unlike an English fieldmouse, has proved to be of particular interest to people involved in the research of sexual behaviour. This is because prairie voles are monogamous. They mate for life and, rather sweetly, they normally opt to remain celibate if a partner should die before them. Male voles also show an active concern in the rearing of the young. Studies have shown that these family-loving prairie voles have high levels of a particular receptor in the ventral pallidum. A study at Emory University bred the related prairie vole genes into mice – who, in contrast, are normally sexually promiscuous creatures. The mice began to imitate the prairie voles in behaviour – settling down and remaining with a single partner. Studies of another promiscuous creature, the montane vole, have shown that they have significantly lower levels of this receptor in their ventral pallidum.

This work does not prove that monogamy may be genetically determined, but certainly suggests an influence. Monogamous creatures may get enough pleasure from being with one partner, while their more promiscuous counterparts have to seek repeated 'affairs' in order to achieve the same levels of satisfaction from their less enriched ventral pallida. This area is also activated when addicted rodents obtain a fix of drugs, or even when they enter areas of their cages associated with receiving the drug. The picture is somewhat reminiscent of what we learnt in the previous chapter about extro-version and thrill-seeking behaviour – in that the brains of people with these traits seem to be chronically 'unrewarded' by their activities, and thus they go in continual search of ever greater stimuli. Sexual promiscuity in humans may be a sub-type of this behaviour.

Rather unsurprisingly, this is an area of research that has suffered from lack of funding. It has been difficult for scientists to convince funding bodies that they should part with money to allow them to perform brain scans on copulating couples and cocaine snorters. And it was ever thus. Wilhelm Reich, favoured student of Freud and at one time a leading light in the field of sexual behaviour, was effec-tively drummed out of the academic community when it was discovered that he was performing research on people as they engaged in sexual intercourse. It should also be pointed out that the reason so much sexual research involves rodents and monkeys is because it is hard to find human volunteers. There can, after all, be few situations less erotic than sitting in an MRI scanner with a team of white-coated scientists looking on – even if they are behind a glass screen in an adjoining office watching on an oscilloscope monitor.

High levels of pheromone production might account for what psychologists refer to as the rope-bridge effect. In a famous experi-ment at the University of Vancouver, two groups of men were asked to walk across two very different bridges. One was a very unremark-able pedestrian footbridge – no more perilous than the various stone and iron affairs that traverse the Thames and which many of us happily cross without batting an eyelid every day. The other was like a special effect from an Indiana Jones film – a swaying rope-bridge which dangled over a menacing 230-feet drop (but, I write proudly, not as half as terrible as the one across the chasm, 2,000 feet up, in South Africa, as seen in the plate section of this book). As they reached safety on the other side, the two groups of men were approached by an attractive female who – rather unfairly, even if it was in the interests of science – flirted with them a little and gave them her phone number while handing them the inevitable questionnaire to fill out. The men who had crossed the dangerous rope-bridge included more sexual content in their questionnaire answers. And a considerable number of them rang up the researcher later on. An explanation for this would be that fear (and possibly relief from it?) causes arousal in both brain and body, including feelings which lead us to overrate the attractiveness of the opposite sex. And I thought that most people went bungee jumping just for the view.

The feeling of falling in love

Attraction can be defined as a form of focused attention and goal-orientated behaviour. Attraction is, of course, vital for the continuation of the species. For that reason, we experience actual pleasure when we see an attractive face. Analysis of the brain chemistry involved shows that some pleasure–and–reward regions of the brain – specifically the medial orbitofrontal cortex – are stimulated by the sight of attractive human faces. The level of stimulation is at its highest when the faces are looking directly at us, and when they are smiling. So, unromantic as it sounds, we humans are all wired to have a 'roving eye'.[90] Further to this, when we experience attraction to another person, our brains become fixated upon them. We ignore other people, we may even neglect our appearance, our work or our health. We have started to be in love. Tests taken at this stage indicate high levels of a chemical called phenylethylamine (PEA), structurally similar to amphetamines. This may account for the fact that some people describe this stage as a 'rush' of excitement, coinciding with other amphetamine-like symptoms such as increased heart rate, racing thoughts, loss of appetite, disturbed sleep and enlarged pupils. In the past, women sought to simulate some of the signs of attraction as part of their beauty routine. In medieval Italy, they put drops in their eyes extracted from the root of belladonna, which has the effect of dilating the pupils. It is no coincidence that 'belladonna' means 'beautiful woman'. In more modern times, studies have shown that increased pupil size has a powerful effect on both men and women. Show somebody two pictures of the same person, identical except that one of them has been artificially morphed to increase the size of the pupils, and the morphed picture will most often be identified as being more attractive.

The production of PEA is just one of the changes that take place inside our brain when we are in love. Thanks to modern technology, we can look inside the 'loving brain' and see exactly what is happening. Andreas Bartels and Semir Zeki of the Department of Cognitive Neurology at University College, London, undertook brain scans of seventeen subjects as they looked at pictures of their sweethearts, and then at pictures of friends who were the same sex as their beloved.[91] When the subjects were gazing upon their lovers, there was specific activity in the media insula and part of the anterior cingulate – areas we use to concentrate and block out other stimuli. There was activity in the caudate nucleus and the putamen, which are part of the brain's pleasure-and-reward circuitry.

As we've seen, feelings associated with love can also seem to have the quality of an obsession, or an episode of mental illness. People also show an increased propensity to think in irrational ways about the object of their affection – idealizing them and attributing qualities to them that they may not truly have. There is a grain of truth in the notion that falling in love is a little like a bout of madness. Donatella Marazziti of the University of Pisa argues that the evolutionary consequences of love are so important that there must be some long-established biological process regulating it. It is difficult to know how seriously to take statements like this – Darwinian pronouncements of this sort seem to be proliferating as more people attempt to sell their version of science, and they risk the work of others whose good science may not be taken seriously. But Dr Marazziti reports that she managed to find twenty subjects who had recently fallen in love in the six months before her study (possibly not too difficult in Tuscany) and she compared these people with twenty OCD patients not on drugs, and twenty normal controls. She measured the levels of the protein responsible for serotonin transport in circulating blood cells. Her findings suggest that subjects who were in the early romantic phase of a love relationship were similar to OCD patients in probably having reduced serotonin levels in the brain. Once the initial flush of being in love falls off, after twelve to eighteen months, Dr Marazziti notes that serotonin levels return to normal. Professor Sylvia Finzi at Pavia University, presumably one of her competitors, archly noted that the symptoms of being love 'were usually easily recognizable' and that: 'Reducing love to a game of molecules belittles it . . . No neurotransmitter will ever be able to keep love in a cage.'

There are all sorts of risks in taking research of this sort too seriously. First, all the subjects in love were female – what happens to males? Secondly, how do you define 'being in love'? Thirdly, is a group of twenty people enough for statistical significance? And, among other objections, does measuring the level of a related chemical transporter really reflect what is happening in the brain? I put these arguments, not because I disapprove of Dr Marazziti's work or wish in any way to undermine it. But reports on these kinds of psychological issues generally get massive attention in the press and the reports sometimes misrepresent the importance of really solid insights into brain function.

However intensely we may feel the first rush of attraction, we probably do not need scientists to tell us that it does not last for ever. This thought has not stopped research by Cindy Hazan of Cornell University, who has written extensively about attachment.[92] One long-term study, which has involved 5,000 subjects in thirty-seven different cultures, has shown that attraction lasts for between eighteen months and three years. The suggestion is that by four years any child produced is sufficiently biologically secure for a couple to break up and move on. According to this theory we humans are serial monogamists. As the *Sunday Times* – always keen to report on intellectually tough scientific issues – pointed out in August 1999:

> Hazan's findings offer a scientific explanation for many famous bust-ups, including that of the marriage of Prince Charles and Princess Diana, who fell out of love soon after the birth of their second son. Another celebrity cited as proving Hazan's theories is golfer Nick Faldo, 42, who dumped Brenna Cepelak, 24, bang on 30 months after their adulterous affair began.
>
> Gwyneth Paltrow, who recently won an Oscar for her role in the romantic comedy *Shakespeare in Love*, said of her failed three-year relationship with actor Brad Pitt: 'I was sure that Brad was the love of my life, and then suddenly one day I did not feel the same. Nothing happened, but doubt set in.'

As I understand it, Dr Hazan has identified dopamine, phenylethyl-amine and oxytocin as the chemicals that produce what Elvis Presley famously described as 'that loving feeling'. Whether or not she actually measured them in her subjects was far from clear to me in what she has published. She is reported as asserting, 'Like a drunk grows immune to a single glass of alcohol, the effect of these chemicals wears off, returning people to a relatively relaxed state of mind within two years.'

According to Helen Fisher of Rutgers University, who at least has used fMRI, levels of dopamine and PEA also reach a peak during the earlier phases of love.[93] It is not clear why levels of these chemicals drop after this period, but it might be that the brain develops a kind of 'tolerance' to producing its own 'drugs', and eventually stops making them at higher levels than normal. This could explain why some people, sensing that – in the words of the old song – 'the thrill is gone', continually go off in search of new love affairs. Mistakenly, they believe that one day they will find the continuously stimulating partner – the ideal who will ensure them an everlasting supply of PEA.

Chocolate manufacturers have recognized the value of the publicity surrounding research into the neurotransmitters associated with love. Chocolate, as it is sold for the consumer market, is an extraordinarily complex compound and contains various chemicals, among which are small amounts of PEA. The 'health benefits' of consuming products from the plant *Theobroma cacao* (translated as the 'food of the gods') have relied on the information that chocolate, especially rich, dark chocolate, contains catechins, which may give protection against heart disease, cancer and numerous other diseases.

Chocolate manufacturers and those reliant on this industry are very ready to point out that eating chocolate boosts one's appetite, but does not cause weight gain – though how this works is a mystery to me – and that sugar in chocolate has a calming effect and reduces stress. It is also stated quite frequently that chocolate has analgesic properties – but I will continue to take paracetamol. There is some evidence that serotonin and endorphin levels are altered in the brain after eating chocolate. But for me, certainly, and a number of other people I know, the caffeine, phenylethylamine and theobromine elements in chocolate seem quite frequently to start a migraine attack. This probably happens as a result of the release of the neurotransmitter norepinephrine, which alters cerebral blood flow. So, far from being a case of 'chocolate is the food of love, play on', it might be more, 'Not tonight, dear, I've a headache.'

Accentuate the positive

The final phase of love is attachment. It is said that once PEA levels start to drop off, this is what humans are left with – attachment. It would seem to have a clear evolutionary purpose, because our children spend so much time being dependent upon their parents. Attachment is associated with raised levels of oxytocin and vasopressin in the brain – which have the effect of inducing bonding and reducing aggression. Bonding works for parents, but is also a powerful psychological force between them and their offspring. And oxytocin induces smooth muscle contractions (the muscles over which we do not have conscious control) and heightens nerve sensitivity. Its presence therefore enhances the pleasurable qualities of sex, and so it is not surprising that in both women and men, levels of the chemical rise dramatically from the first kiss to the post-coital cuddle. It continues to act throughout the reproductive cycle. It has a powerful effect on uterine contractions, and during labour and delivery when oxytocin levels are at their highest it is crucial for the birth of a baby. Because the release of oxytocin allows the milk ducts in the breast to contract, it enables breastfeeding. Solid research shows that blocking the production of oxytocin in rats prevents bonding between mothers and their young.

Reduced oxytocin levels may be just one of the factors involved in mothers who experience problems bonding with their new babies. This could even be why mothers who have had difficulty with their labour due to weak contractions, and those not having a labour at all (but are delivered by Caesarean section), occasionally feel emotionally removed from their new infant. I do not know of any good work to prove this, however, and admittedly there are likely to be many other factors which impair the relationship between mother and child after a difficult delivery. A University of Washington study showed that the act of childbirth itself normally triggers a certain neural pathway. Mice born surgically were found to have mothers who were significantly less maternal towards them. But if the mothers were given injections of the neurotransmitter norepinephrine during the surgery, their nurturing skills increased.

The hormone oxytocin also seems to play a role in the memories we form to aid our social interaction. Jennifer Ferguson at Emory University has rapidly made a name for herself in this field. In a series of interesting publications she and her colleagues have shown that mice bred so that they are missing the oxytocin gene do not develop social memory. These male mice were repeatedly introduced, along with other, normal mice, to a female who was unable to conceive. The normal mice, after repeated pairings, began to spend less and less time exploring the female. But the mice without oxytocin showed the same level of interest in her, no matter how many times they were introduced. But in spite of their lack of social airs and graces, these modified mice were perfectly capable of remembering other things – like finding their way through a maze, locating and remembering where a food was by its smell, and being able to seek out – wait for it – chocolate. The evidence suggests that oxytocin helps the brain to 'remember' socially important information and that the amygdala is a key in this process.[94]

Oxytocin seems also to have a role in maintaining feelings of comfort and well-being in close relationships. Dr Rebecca Turner at the University of California in San Francisco tested the idea that oxytocin is released in response to intense emotional states.[95] She asked twenty-six women between the ages of twenty-three and thirty-five (who were not lactating) to remember and re-examine a past event that caused them to feel a positive emotion about somebody, such as love or infatuation, or a negative emotion, such as a break-up. Because the well-being induced by massage may change oxytocin secretion, the respondents were also given a Swedish massage of their neck and shoulders for fifteen minutes. Blood was taken before, during and after the parts of the experiment and their levels of oxytocin measured. It is not surprising to me that the results did not show a great deal – measurements of oxytocin like this are likely to be a very crude reflection of what is happening in the brain. Nevertheless, the relaxation massage was associated with a rise of oxytocin and past negative emotion seemed to cause oxytocin levels to fall slightly; positive emotions had no demonstrable effect. There was marked variability between subjects. Some women who showed substantial fluctuations seemed to have more secure relationships.

The evidence suggests that male-brain activity is just as important in the process of bonding and attachment. High levels of vasopressin are found in prairie voles and hamsters whose female partners have just given birth – and they exhibit correspondingly high levels of aggression in response to any threats towards their young. But while it increases aggression towards the outside world, vasopressin also stimulates father–child bonding. Hamsters – who do not traditionally play the role of 'doting dad' – when injected with additional vasopressin spent more time around their pups. A study at the University of Amherst, Massachusetts, has shown that an interaction between vasopressin and testosterone in male voles ensures they remain aggressive towards outsiders but are friendly and nurturing towards their own offspring. In the human male, testosterone and hormones like oxytocin or vasopressin have contradictory effects. The story goes – and the older I get, the less I believe it – that, in most men, testosterone production decreases with age. As a result, the oxytocin and vasopressin in the male brain may become the dominant chemicals. So some behavioural experts conclude that older men become less interested in seeking sexual activity with a range of partners, and more geared towards a single, stable relationship.

So the evidence suggests that, over time, the first mad fever of love becomes replaced by a more solid partnership, one more ideally suited to the raising of children. But some research has suggested that the most long-lived relationships are those that preserve a degree of the earlier, less rational phase. Dr Ellen Berscheid, Regents Professor of Psychology at the University of Minnesota, was the first to identify the 'pink-lens effect', whereby couples in love idealize their partners and make overoptimistic judgements about them. We think, for instance, that our lovers are 'brilliant' and 'wonderful'; we overestimate their intelligence, their honesty, their generosity and their looks. As we saw above, this effect has been shown to decrease over time. In general we would expect that, as a relationship progresses, we become more realistic about our partner's strengths and weaknesses – we 'love them for what they are', rather than some idealized, rose-tinted view we may have picked up in the initial frenzy of attraction.

But a study at the University of New York, Buffalo, has also shown that the greater the intensity of the pink-lens effect, the greater the likelihood of the couples staying together. Another, more long-term study at the University of Texas, Austin, followed 168 couples who married in 1981. Once again, the couples who idealized one another the most at the outset were also those whose relationships were the most long-lived. So – here is the absolutely obvious solution to life's most complicated problem – it takes a degree of irrationality to make a happy marriage. But, certainly, an ability to 'accentuate the positive and eliminate the negative' is a great asset for any married couple – as I suspect it is in any human partnership or friendship.

Damned lies and statistics

Why, if the human brain is such a finely tuned device making continual choices based on our need to survive and reproduce, do we repeatedly make mistakes? How do people end up in abusive, damaging relationships? Why do certain people gain advantages by cheating and lying, and how is it that we are unable to spot them?

In evolutionary terms, there is much to be lost by making a wrong decision about another human being. A cheater, for instance, might employ the strategy of pretending to gather food for the group, but secretly keep the greater share for themselves. If, over time, cheaters develop strategies that successfully mask their dishonesty from other members of the group, these abilities would tend to enter the gene pool – ensuring that every group has a convincing liar within it who pays lip-service to the community but really only looks out for themselves. In times of scarcity, people like this would be dangerous to the survival of the group.

This is thought to be one reason why the human brain has developed a specific mechanism for assessing the mental states of other people. Work at the Institute of Neurology at University College, London, by Joel Winston in Ray Dolan's[96] group has pinpointed the importance of the superior temporal sulcus (STS) region of the temporal lobes in making such judgements. The STS becomes activated when we are observing the movements and gestures of other humans but it is also active when we view static images of the human face and judge their trustworthiness. Perhaps we use the STS to work out what people are thinking as much as what they are doing. Various studies using fMRI and PET scans performed while people are attempting to infer the mental states of others also show a 'loop' of activity, encompassing the medial prefrontal cortex, lateral inferior frontal cortex and the temporo-parietal junction. We have evolved a complex mechanism to ensure that we know what our fellow humans are about to do.

As already discussed, people with autism show a specific inability to 'read' other people in this way. And there is evidence to suggest that this aspect of autism is related to a particular abnormality within the brain. Uta Frith, of the Institute of Cognitive Neuroscience at University College, London, has conducted a number of important studies.[97] One involved taking PET scans of subjects' brains as they watched a sequence of moving shapes on a screen. The subjects – ten of whom had autism, ten of whom did not – were shown three sequences. In the first, the shapes moved in a random fashion; in the second, they moved in a goal–orientated fashion, chasing and 'fighting' one another. In the third sequence, the shapes' movements were more subtle, and were designed to elicit descriptions from the viewers that involved attributing mental states to the shapes – for instance, coaxing, teasing, tricking. In other words, in this third set of movements, the subjects were being asked to identify certain human traits of behaviour.

The study made a number of interesting findings. It became clear that the autistic people were much less accurate or consistent when it came to the third collection of shapes. Secondly, PET scans revealed that a common network of brain regions was active in both groups when they watched the third sequence. This network – composed of the superior temporal sulcus and medial prefrontal cortex – is one area where our brain assesses information about the intention of others. Crucially, in the autistic participants, a specific site – known as the extrastriate cortex – was highly active, but, unlike in the brains of the non–autistic participants, not in tandem with the brain regions around it. The researchers have argued that autistic people's inability to 'read' others may stem from this bottleneck in the brain's processing system – one bit of it is working fine, but it cannot communicate with the rest, like an axle which spins without turning the wheels.

In our evolutionary past, we needed to know who we could rely on. As the old saying 'blood is thicker than water' suggests, family members are more likely to be trustworthy. And psychological studies have shown that we are, in fact, more inclined to trust people whose facial characteristics resemble our own. At McMaster University in Canada, psychologist Dr Lisa DeBruine asked participants to play a simple trust game, in which they could not see their partners. The game involved asking them to choose between two options: dividing a small sum of money between themselves and their partners, or opting to trust their partner to divide fairly a far larger sum of money. In other words, the game tested how trusting people were.

Before each game, the participants were shown computer-morphed facial images which – they were told – were pictures of the people they would be playing against. The pictures were manipulated in order to resemble either the participants' own faces, or the faces of an unknown person. The results showed that when the participants believed they were playing against people whose faces resembled their own, they were more likely to trust their partners. This makes some evolutionary sense; people who resembled us were likely to be blood relatives and therefore more likely to behave unselfishly towards us. If your chief evolutionary objective is passing on your genes to the next generation, then assisting your relatives – however distant – gives at least some of your genes an elevated chance of being passed down the generations. Unfortunately, the business of living in increasingly large cities requires us to trust a circle of others much greater than the sum total of our blood relations. So it will be a long way to go before our brain will allow us to achieve the perfectly harmonious, cooperative society.

Lying to ourselves

It seems that, as far as assessing the behaviour of other, unrelated humans goes, our brain has predisposed us to be pretty cynical. A particularly interesting study at Cornell University, now known as the 'holier-than-thou' experiment, has shown how accurate we are at judging others' behaviour, and how poorly we judge ourselves.[98] In one test, people were asked to say how much of their fee for participating in an experiment they would give to charity. One group of participants said they would give half of their five-dollar remuneration, but in practice gave an average of $1.80. Moreover, after meeting each other, they tended to estimate that they themselves would be more generous than the other participants in the study. A total of $19.89 was raised from this study; had participants given what they had promised, the charities would have received $31.72. These people were generally accurate in predicting how selfishly others would behave. But they were also consistently overoptimistic about their own levels of altruism. Perhaps this indicates how important cooperation is to the group. We depend upon the input of others in order to survive and this may explain why our ability for detecting selfish behaviour is more sensitive.

The need to behave in a manner most beneficial to group survival seems to have resulted in the evolution of mechanisms that signal to others when we are lying. We can see what's going on inside a lying brain – Daniel Langleben at the University of Pennsylvania has shown a pattern of increased blood flow to the anterior cingulate gyrus, which as we know becomes active when we need to concentrate on something.[99] But other brain regions are also important. A team led by Tatia M.C. Lee at the University of Texas at San Antonio recorded fMRI scans of participants who were told to do deliberately badly on a memory task.[100] The results indicated a complex loop of activity, involving areas of the prefrontal cortex and the parietal lobes. To lie effectively, it seems the brain has to first come up with the truthful response, then use further mechanisms to suppress it, produce a fresh, false response and monitor its own performance. Small wonder that we find it hard to lie continually.

We can spot liars from the way they smile. One of the first great neurologists to make detailed studies of the human face was the remarkable eccentric but phenomenal doctor Guillaume Benjamin Duchenne. He has been something of an icon to me ever since I became interested in the terrible disease to which he gave his name, Duchenne muscular dystrophy. This fatal disease, affecting only boys but carried by girls, was one of the first genetic disorders my scientific group and I attempted to detect in the human embryo in 1990.

Duchenne was something of a late starter – and as somebody who did not publish his first scientific paper until the age of thirty-two (very late indeed, these days), I empathize with that – as I do with the fact that he was, by all accounts, a remarkably undistinguished medical student. When he left provincial Boulogne for Paris, he was ridiculed for his coarse accent and had difficulty scraping a living. His father, like those before him, was a seafarer and Duchenne seemed to haunt the Paris teaching hospitals as an unpaid attachment; he was described as a lonely, mariner-like figure. But Duchenne had a most important quality for good scientific research – he kept immaculate records of what he saw. Moreover, he was persistent and would follow patients from hospital to hospital to gain insight into their con-dition. Over time, his neurological diagnostic skills came to be praised and he developed a particular interest in muscle diseases. This led to his attempts to stimulate muscles with electricity to try to preserve their function in wasting diseases like dystrophy, which included experiments to stimulate the facial muscles. His immaculate note-keeping, combined with his interest in photography, have left us an extraordinary resource, the record of his work dating back to 1860.

The Pinocchio factor

Duchenne eventually became internationally recognized for all kinds of research on brain function and for the identification of a number of important degenerative diseases. But relevant here is that he studied the mechanism of facial expression during emotion and recorded it in his atlas of photographs. This book is recognized to this day as being an enormous contribution to medical photography. Charles Darwin used a number of his photographs in his book, *The Expression of the Emotions in Man and Animals*. From Duchenne's pioneering work, we now know that we use four major facial muscles in the production of a real smile, but only two in a false, 'social' smile.

With the advantages lent to us by brain-scanning technology, we can confirm the mechanism of the false, social smile. The smile I fix to my face for a cocktail party (*Rictus ginantonicus*) – originates in the left brain. This communicates with the right brainstem, ordering the right lower facial muscles to respond. Simultaneously, the left hemisphere sends a command across the corpus callosum to the right hemisphere. The right hemisphere in turn causes the movement of the left lower facial muscles. An involuntary smile, which shows true feelings, on the other hand, will be betrayed by movement in the muscles around the eyes.

So an analysis of a simple human smile can tell us a great deal about a person's intentions. But facial expressions are not the only means by which a liar can be spotted. Liars also touch their noses more frequently when they are practising their devilish art. This 'Pinocchio effect' is thought to be because increased blood flow causes erectile tissue within the nose to swell, thereby making the hairs inside our nostrils stand up.

Dr Richard Wiseman at the University of Hertfordshire has conducted some of the key research into lying, and shown that true emotions tend to be registered on the face as fleeting 'micro-expressions' which last no longer than a quarter of a second. Wiseman, who began his working life as a stage magician and as a member of the famed Magic Circle, can certainly be said to know a fair bit about the business of deception. He has developed a list of some of the most glaring indicators of a fib. I spent a long session with him recently, which was filmed for television. I gave him two accounts of how I had spent successive evenings. One was strictly truthful, and one a fabrication. There was no way he could know beforehand which account was true. I pride myself at being quite a good liar – my children take pleasure in shaming their father by recounting how I used to cheat them from the age of six. I regret to say, I cannot bear to lose, even at Scrabble. One evening, I told Dr Wiseman, I had given a named lecture, received a gold medal, been publicly critical to a government official and had dinner with various members of the medical establishment afterwards. The following evening, I recounted how I had turned up slightly late for a dinner in Parliament, where I had heard a speech given by a notable football team manager about how his team had deservedly won the Premier League Championship. Moreover, I said, this appalling Scot had dared to suggest the club I support was 'rubbish'.

The TV producer and his team recording this farrago of nonsense were horrified because they thought they had wasted a valuable day's filming. There was no way, they felt, that Richard Wiseman would untangle my stories because I had sounded very plausible. But Dr Wiseman does not need a lie detector – indeed, he points out that these are useless. Moreover, he knows nothing about football, but this did not matter to him. He was looking for the involuntary signs we give out that reveal we are not telling the truth. These might include moving the head a lot when talking, repeated touching of the face, too much (or too little) eye contact, sweating and dilated pupils, remembering too few or too many details, delivering abrupt answers to questions and leaving long gaps, or no gaps at all, before answering questions. Repetitious 'ums' and 'ahs', too, are a bit of a giveaway. Building up a complete picture, together with voice quality, Wiseman has been invariably accurate with his assessments – as indeed he was in assessing which of my two stories was a fabrication. Dr Wiseman's research shows that even when a listener is blindfolded, the detection of a liar is mostly made with high accuracy by the blindfolded person. Voice quality changes. His research has led to the development of a software package called 'Verdicator', which checks for lying cues within the human voice. That, together with his records of how liars behave, means that you would not want to meet Dr Wiseman if you had just been arrested for robbing a bank.

Another big name in lying research is Paul Ekman of the University of California. Ekman has built a 3,000-item-strong database of universal human facial expressions – certain combinations or 'Action Units' which are used solely when we are telling lies. Ekman's Facial Action Coding System is now consulted by groups as disparate as the FBI and Hollywood animation studios. He maintains that everyone has a specific set of facial 'giveaway clues' – what poker players would call a 'tell'. When Mrs Thatcher publicly denied that she ordered the sinking of the *General Belgrano*, for instance, her eyelids engaged in a brief but rapid flutter. When Kim Philby denied being the 'third man' who tipped off Burgess and McLean that their cover as double agents had been blown, his right inner eyebrow gave a quick involuntary flicker.

TV footage of former US President Bill Clinton has, unsurprisingly, also undergone some quite thorough investigation by those interested in the science of lying. Alan R. Hirsch of the Smell and Taste Treatment Research Foundation in Chicago noted a range of changes in Clinton's body language when he publicly denied having sex with Monica Lewinsky. He compared this public interview with the one Clinton gave when he was sworn in as President. During the interview about Monica Lewinsky, Bill Clinton showed a 250 per cent increase in hand-to-face touching, and a 355 per cent increase in drinking and swallowing. Meantime his stuttering rate increased by 1,400 per cent, and other errors in speech by 1,700 per cent. While all this sounds impressive, there is a real problem of analysis. No matter how careful the investigators are, there is a huge difference between an interview given in highly favourable circumstances like a presidential inauguration, and one when a man in President Clinton's position is faced with an extremely hostile interviewer, in a situation which threatens both his public position and his private life.

But if our brain is built with this amazing equipment to assess the mental state of others, and if lying gives off obvious clues, how do liars get away with it? It may be more interesting to rephrase the question, and ask why do they get away with it? Could there be some evolutionary benefit in not detecting lies?

It is worth noting that, like my camera crew, we humans are not that good at spotting a *practised* liar, particularly one that knows how to obfuscate. One technology to improve the average person's ability to spot a fraud depends on being able to slow down and freeze video footage. In Dr Wiseman's studies, when he slowed video footage down to one frame per second, two-thirds of his 120 volunteers were able to spot the liars, which indicates that while we may all have the 'knack', we just can't use it much in daily life. Other studies have shown that ordinary individuals score only marginally worse than skilled professionals, like police officers and psychiatrists, in detecting liars. So why aren't we better at it?

One obvious answer is this. Just as we have evolved sophisticated brain technology to detect and signal lies, the liars themselves have been one step ahead of the game. In other words, cheats have evolved their own, increasingly sophisticated mechanisms for avoiding detection. And if you are a liar, the most deadly weapon of all is the ability to persuade even yourself that you are telling the truth.

Another possibility could be that the consequences for group survival in exposing cheats might be worse than the consequences of their cheating. For instance, given the example of the 'hunting cheat' above, perhaps it would be better for the overall survival of the community to have someone who contributed *something* to the group, rather than casting them out and thus being denied any contribution from them. We can see how accusations of lying, or socially harmful behaviour, have significant negative repercussions for any society. They do not merely result in one person or group of people being excluded, but create wider rifts and faction fighting in those who remain. Such damage could compromise the survival chances of a human group, particularly in harsh conditions.

We do not need to look at our ancestral past on the savannah to see that lies – or rather the facility to tell them and not be detected – are vital to smooth human relations. Take the example of a wife who asks her husband if he likes her new haircut. His actual feeling may be that he does not, or perhaps does not at that particular moment, but he will say, 'Yes, lovely, dear' because he knows this is better for his wife's self-esteem and for the continued functioning of their marriage. Likewise, it helps that his wife is able to believe what she most wants to hear, rather than root out an unflattering truth.

Similarly, when a father first glimpses his newborn child, his partner and everyone else around will almost certainly reel off a list of imagined similarities, such as, 'He's got your eyes', 'She's got your chin'. In fact, research has shown that very few facial characteristics of either parent are detectable in the faces of newborn infants. But it is in the interests of the family group for a father to believe that the child is his, thus ensuring that he sticks around to provide resources. Neither the mother nor the father believes a lie is being told – but if fathers did not have this capacity to 'gloss over' an obvious untruth, the social consequences could be disastrous. In a host of social situations, a 'white lie' goes undetected, because detecting it might simply do more harm than good. So does that mean that we are fundamentally without a sense of right and wrong? Not a bit of it – as I shall go on to explain.

The moral mind

We have seen that, in order to live alongside other people, our brains have had to evolve sophisticated technology for detecting and assessing the behaviour of others. We have also seen, time and time again, that the driving force behind so much of our mental make-up is the old evolutionary need to reproduce and survive. But we humans have the ability to move beyond the simple requirements of food, shelter and sex. Unlike most other animals – or what we know of them to date, at least – we are not bound by the immediate needs imposed upon us by our personal drives and the environment in which we find ourselves. Faculties such as the sense of self, and language, have given us the ability to move beyond the moment – to consider ideas in the abstract, to formulate plans, envisage improvements to the way we live our lives, and communicate them to one another, to create art, to have ideas.

A key area in which these for the most part uniquely human faculties play a part is in the development of attitudes such as morality, forgiveness and compassion. I have little doubt that, at one base level, morality is likely to be a hangover from our evolutionary past. The group requires rules in order to function safely, and sanctions in order to make people obey them. Commandments such as 'Thou shalt not steal' and 'Thou shalt not kill' are present in virtually every form of human society – probably because intra-group theft and murder would have been dangerous to group survival. I put stress on the term intra-group, because the same rules do not universally apply to other tribes or nations. In spite of the Ten Commandments, the ancient

306

Israelites were not above killing Canaanites, or rustling their cattle, even though their treatment of the stranger, the foreigner, the captive and the slave was morally far advanced compared to the treatment the nations around them seemed to enforce on other peoples.

As I noted earlier, rule-breakers are rewarded with social exclusion. And this applies whether the rule concerns itself with the appropriate shirt to wear to a cocktail party, or not chatting up other men's wives. We use rules to ensure that our groups 'work' efficiently. And this drive to cooperate would seem to have a neurological basis inside our brains. In a study conducted by James K. Rilling at Emory University in Atlanta, Georgia, volunteers were asked to play a game called the 'Prisoner's Dilemma', in which players have to decide when to trust one another. MRI scans performed when the volunteers were cooperating together revealed a specific pattern of brain activity in the regions linked to pleasure and reward, like the caudate nucleus and nucleus accumbens. In other words, we may be hard-wired to receive pleasure from cooperation.

But human morality goes way beyond the simple survival needs of the group. What about, for instance, the principle that suggests we give up our seat on a crowded bus to an elderly woman? In evolutionary terms, there might be no conceivable value in helping the elderly. They are weak, they cannot hunt or bear children or defend us from predators. They are a drain on resources. Yet we accord them compassion and respect. Archaeological evidence suggests that 40,000 years ago our Palaeolithic ancestors – for whom survival must have been a far dicier business than it is for us – fed and looked after the elderly and the infirm.

What value could there be, for example, in forgiveness? The strictly deterministic, evolutionist point of view would suggest that we need to punish people who break our rules in order to prevent them, or others, from doing it again. So how could we have evolved codes of action that encourage us to forgive, to turn the other cheek?

From an anthropological point of view, one answer might be that these values only emerge as society becomes increasingly complex. In a simple society, there is relatively little specialization of roles. The men hunt, kill, make tools and build shelters. The women give birth, nurture children and prepare food. But as human groups become larger, we see an increased specialization. Larger groups allow for increasing amounts of food to be brought into the camp, so that there is a surplus to reward those who have not participated in the actual act of finding and killing it. These individuals can specialize in other tasks which benefit group survival, like making tools, or pottery. As time goes on, specialization increases, such that people become adept at tasks less directly related to the business of hunting and killing enemies. Classes of individuals like farmers, bakers, scribes and builders enter the ranks – all contributing something to the group, all receiving something in return for their contribution. More specialization means more surplus, more surplus means that survival becomes easier and easier – which in turn means that we can afford to show compassion to the weak and the elderly.

Not everyone would accept this view of the evolution of morality. It has been noted, for instance, that the ability to acquire a surplus of produce, through techniques like farming, was the driving force in creating social divisions, rather than social harmony. A man who has surplus can pay others to perform tasks for him; he can also acquire possessions like larger houses, clothing, pottery and jewellery, which serve to accentuate his superiority to others. We start to see a class system, divided along the lines of power and wealth – quite the opposite of a compassionate society.

It might be of interest to take a look at the examples below.

You are watching a view from a footbridge over a railway. You can see a runaway railway carriage, heading towards a forked junction. There is a lever in your hand, which you can pull to determine the direction of the railway carriage after it hits the fork. If you move the lever forwards, the carriage will kill one person. If you move the lever backwards, it will kill five people. Which way do you pull the lever?

Now you are standing on another footbridge. This time you can only prevent the railway carriage from killing five people by pushing the person standing next to you off the bridge and into its path. Do you do it?

Did you answer 'forwards' to the first example, and 'no' to the second? If so, don't start worrying whether this demonstrates something bad about your moral character; this is how most people would answer both the hypothetical questions.

But in coming up with your two answers, you were probably using two different systems of your brain's 'moral network'. Joshua D.

Greene at the Center for the Study of Mind, Brain and Behavior at Princeton achieved considerable publicity in the popular press with this study. He gave sixty dilemmas to volunteers, and undertook fMRI scans of their brains as they weighed up the options.[101] The second of my examples involves a strong emotional content – because it requires us to imagine ourselves actively pushing another person to their death, regardless of the maths involved. Other dilemmas were like the first type, or had no moral component at all. Greene discovered that, in considering the 'emotional-type' dilemmas, there was significantly higher activity in three brain areas associated with processing emotions – the medial frontal gyrus, posterior cingulate gyrus and the superior temporal sulcus (STS). This latter region of the brain is thought to be the centre of our 'mentalizing' capacities – in other words, the skills we use to guess the mental states of other people. Brain scans of psychopaths often show lower levels of activity in the STS.

In contrast, the non-emotional type of judgements, as in the first example, showed more brain activity in areas like the dorsolateral prefrontal cortex and parietal lobes. These play a role in working memory. This pattern suggests that, when we have to deal with a dilemma with a strong emotional content, we put reality on hold for a moment and dip into our brain's little toolkit of social skills in order to decide how to act. There isn't some 'Organ of Morality' inside the brain as phrenologists might once have hoped, but instead there is a complex interplay between areas that control abstract thought and social behaviour. This implies, but does not prove, that morality evolved as a consequence of us living in increasingly complex social groups.

In another joint study, involving teams from the Universities of Sheffield and Manchester, brain scans were taken as volunteers read and made judgements on a number of social scenarios. The scenarios were designed to invite the reader to make a judgement invoking empathy or forgiveness. For example, an empathy-inducing scenario might be – *Your boss is not himself today. What do you think might be wrong?* A forgiveness-inducing scenario might be – *A young man in your street, whom you know to have recently lost his job, is visited by the police. What has happened?* The researchers found that very specific brain areas were active in the two types of scenario: one set of brain regions for empathy, and another for forgiveness.

We also know that humans mirror the action of others in order to understand their emotional states. Our amygdala registers the pattern associated with sadness when we see a sad face, and it meets anger with anger and fear with fear. In other words, the architecture of our brains predisposes us to interpret other people by feeling what they do, by putting ourselves in their shoes. It could be that concepts like compassion, empathy and forgiveness are just further refinements of this basic function – the add-on extras of the social brain.

In an earlier chapter I looked at the possibility that language was merely a further specialization of the brain areas that became enlarged as our ancestors made and used tools. It could be that the moral brain came as a later development along the same evolutionary river. The ability to conceive of oneself as a doing-I and a done-to-me, of a distinction between self and others, was central to the development of grammar and to the ability to build complex toolkits. It could be argued that the ability to verbalize these understandings also predisposed us to become moral. Your brain needs a level of abstraction to come up with a moral supposition such as 'I wouldn't like this if it was done to me' – one only possible with the fluidity lent to us by language.

chapter nine

The amazing mind: intelligence, creativity and intuition

Hermann and Pauline were worried about their sixteen-year-old son. He had always been a difficult boy — when he was born he seemed to have an overly large, misshapen head which, despite the doctor's assurances, never shrank down to an entirely normal shape. When his grandmother first saw him, she cried, 'Fat! Much too fat!' – and throughout his childhood, the boy was a heavy-set, rather lumpen figure, disinclined to running about or joining in the games of his peers. He did not learn to speak until he was nearly three, and was prone to bouts of terrifying anger. In one of these fits, he struck his violin teacher with a chair – and the teacher fled, never to return.

At school he was by no means unpopular, although – a little surprisingly for a Jewish boy in Central Europe – he struggled with foreign languages and teachers were exasperated by his ponderous way of thinking for a long time before answering questions, and even more by his habit of quietly talking to himself under his breath. The boy seemed happiest on his own, building card-houses of immense size and intricacy.

In 1894, when their son was only fifteen, Hermann and Pauline moved to Milan, to pursue business opportunities in the family's electrical engineering firm. Their son, to Pauline's regret, stayed behind in Munich to continue his education, lodging with family friends. The letters he wrote to his parents were sporadic, typically teenage – desultory and grudging in tone, reporting that he was doing extremely well at geometry, but telling little else of his life or his feelings. Then one day, he showed up in Italy. He and his form teacher hated one another, the boy reported. The teacher had said the school would be a better place if he weren't in it. His pupil quite agreed. So he had gone to see the family's old doctor and persuaded him to write a note – claiming that a decline in the boy's physical health necessitated him leaving school and going to live with his parents.

Not surprisingly, Hermann and Pauline were annoyed and distressed at this move on their son's part. He had lied for his own advantage and he had dared to quit school, a mere fifteen-year-old boy, without consulting them. But pleading and threats did nothing to change his mind. He had decided what he was going to do. He was going to prepare himself for the entrance exams for a highly prized place at the famous Zurich Polytechnical School. At the age of just sixteen, and without the benefit of specialized tuition, it seemed like a long shot. But impressed by their son's determination – and possibly also feeling a little guilty at having left him behind in Germany – his parents backed him.

Unfortunately, things turned out as they had feared. Their son did well in the mathematical and scientific papers of the entrance exam, but poorly in languages and history. The school suggested he needed at least another year of secondary education. Sighing at their son's stubbornness, Hermann and Pauline agreed that he should enrol for another year at a renowned Swiss school. But what was to say that he would cope any better there? How long would it be before he showed up in Milan again, citing personal antagonisms as the cause of his departure, and stubbornly insisting on some new and equally improbable plan of action?

In many respects, this little historical tale is no different from a drama played out between parents and children all over the world. The business of raising children is never easy, but some never seem to be happy from day one. They are difficult, at home and at school. They are wilful and impulsive, stubborn and argumentative. In the end, the only thing their loving parents can do is stand back and let them follow their own paths. Some of them do well – others, because of their indecision, or their stubbornness, their lack of social skills or their refusal to 'play the game', will always find life tough.

Need Hermann and Pauline Einstein have been so worried? Their son, Albert, did finally gain entrance to the Zurich Polytechnic

School. And, of course, he went on to become part of history. The most renowned scientist of the twentieth century – the originator of the Theory of General Relativity, which radically altered the way we think about time and space. He is acknowledged as the possessor of an extraordinary intelligence, a genius, to rank alongside Mozart, Newton and Leonardo da Vinci, and countless others whose work has shaped our history.

But as we have seen, Einstein's childhood and adolescence were fairly unremarkable. His story, up until the point at which he gained admittance to the Zurich Polytechnic, was quite a familiar one of awkwardness and various tussles with authority. So what was different about Albert Einstein – what enabled him to turn from a difficult boy into a world-famous genius? Could it be that there was some quality, some aspect within his brain, which made him into a man of such extraordinary intelligence?

The contents of a Costa Cider jar

In 1955, Einstein died of an aneurysm. Not always a modest man, he had already made arrangements for his body to be cremated but his brain to be preserved for scientific research. Within seven hours of his death, the pathologist at Princeton, Dr Thomas S. Harvey, was dissecting his brain. Harvey preserved the unremarkable-looking object in formalin and then cut it into 240 blocks, each roughly the size of a sugar cube. Sections were cut from these blocks, and they were examined under a microscope. Neurologists all over the country eagerly awaited the results of Harvey's work. But his findings, when they came, were greeted with sighs of disappointment. Harvey said he could find nothing whatsoever that was remarkable or unusual about the structure of Einstein's brain. It was like any other damned brain, and it held no clue as the incredible powers of its former owner.

So for a long time the brain lay pickled in a jar, but forgotten. In the mid-1970s, a journalist, Steven Levy, attempted to find the whereabouts of this treasured organ. Einstein's brain turned out to be still with Dr Harvey, now living in Wichita, Kansas. It was in two mason jars in a cardboard box that was marked with the words 'Costa Cider'.

Dr Marian C. Diamond was one of the first scientists to get hold of bits of Einstein's brain for detailed study. When the brain pieces arrived in her laboratory in Berkeley, California, they were now in a jar marked 'mayonnaise'. In 1985 she published a paper which gave news which was unimpressive if not frankly disappointing – Einstein's brain cells were no more and no less than those of any other average ageing man. Dr Diamond had compared the number of neurons with the number of glial cells in many areas of the brain and it was entirely average. Only in Brodmann's area 39 of the parietal cortex was there a difference. If you have ever hit the side of the head with your hand after saying something really silly, you now know you've got the right spot. And here there were actually fewer neurons in proportion – the ratio of neurons to glial cells was considerably less than average.[102] But like his ideas, Einstein's brain continued on its travel. In the 1990s, Dr Sandra F. Witelson and colleagues at McMaster University in Ontario, Canada, were given a unique opportunity. They painstakingly measured the size and shape of Einstein's 'organ of the mind' and in June 1999 the *Lancet* published their study.[103] The external surface of Einstein's brain was compared to those of the brains of thirty-five men of similar age. Each brain hemisphere was wider than average, even though the overall brain size was quite unremarkable. But Einstein's brain had an unusual pattern of both right and left parietal lobes, an area that is thought to be important for mathematical abilities and spatial reasoning. His brain also had a much shorter lateral groove, the parietal operculum, that was partially missing – and the parietal lobes themselves were 15 per cent wider than was seen in nearly all other brains.

Dr Witelson reports a similar structural variation in the brain of the famous mathematician Gauss, and the rather less well-known physicist Siljestrom. She tentatively concludes that she might have found the site of a specific kind of intelligence. But obviously the skills of the likes of Einstein and Gauss only provide evidence of one brand of intelligence. We do not only acknowledge some mathematicians and physicists to be geniuses. Clearly, the worlds of writers, musicians and artists, social theorists, actors and directors have contributed their fair share. And we also speak of high intelligence without any mention of genius. Among any ordinary collection of humans, there seem to be people who are 'brighter' than others. So what do we really mean by intelligence? Is a bright person someone who knows a lot, or just someone who has the capacity or the motivation to learn a lot?

Or might it rest in entirely different abilities — such as the power to discriminate between useful and useless information in the swiftest time? But was Einstein's brain truly unusual? How do we account for intelligence – is it related to a specific feature of the brain, such as the findings from Einstein's autopsy might just suggest, or to our experiences and environment? Did Einstein's brain just develop in this way because of something in the environment? If the latter is the case, then perhaps we all have the capacity to be intelligent.

The measures of intelligence

In January 2003, a twelve-year-old boy from the Midlands won the finals of a television show called *Britain's Brainiest Kid*. When interviewed, he said that he'd been initially inspired by taking a test on the website of Mensa – a global organization for people whose IQ scores place them in the top 2 per cent of the population. He also said his interest had been sparked by watching an episode of the US cartoon show *The Simpsons*, in which child prodigy Lisa Simpson decided to join a high-IQ society not dissimilar to Mensa.

Little Lisa Simpson provides an interesting starting point for our journey down the lanes of human intelligence. For she is, undoubtedly, what we might call a child genius. She follows in the tradition of Mozart, who mastered the harpsichord at the age of three, was composing symphonies by the time he was six and spent his adolescence as the musical darling of the European aristocracy. Lisa Simpson does not enjoy quite the same benefits. Ignored by her beer-guzzling father Homer, teased mercilessly by her demonic brother Bart, patronized and belittled by teachers at school, Lisa's life is closer to what many gifted youngsters experience in reality – a hard time. It's not surprising that the parents of many of these child geniuses decide to educate their offspring at home, for better or for worse.

But, cartoon or not, it is notable that Lisa's background is that of blue-collar Middle America. Her surroundings are comfortable, not affluent. She attends a state school. Her parents are, for the most part, loving and kind, but far from being intellectuals – like Einstein's parents, in fact. Any skills Lisa has would seem to come from something innate inside her brain. And this returns us to one of the key themes of this enquiry.

We have seen much of the brain's adaptive, plastic ability to rewire itself continually – within limits – according to the environment in which it is put to work. So how, then, do we explain intelligence? Are child-geniuses merely the product of highly pressurized parenting, or do they possess some innate quality just itching to be teased into life? If this is the case, do we all have the capacity to free the genius inside ourselves – becoming more efficient at solving problems, more swift to remember, more creative? The short answer is yes, we do. While our chances of becoming Pulitzer-winning novelists or Nobel-winning scientists might be fairly slim, we all have the capacity to boost our intelligence.

But before we can explore the secrets of intelligence, it is necessary to explain what the term really means. This is not easy, as there are many different definitions to consider. Nonetheless, all theories come to an agreement on two things: first, that humans have a range of different abilities, and secondly, that intelligence can be equated with how high or low a person scores on a particular ability scale. The earliest definitions of intelligence came in the late nineteenth century from the French theorist Alfred Binet, now thought of as the 'father of IQ'. Binet had been commissioned by the French government to identify children with special educational needs – and to do this, he developed a test that measured children's verbal, memory and mathematical skills.

Over time, Binet's scales of intelligence developed into two further concepts: mental age – which claims to indicate how far behind or ahead a child or adult is relative to others of similar age; and Intelligence Quotient (IQ) – calculated by dividing the mental age by the chronological age and multiplying it by 100. Needless to say, there is a problem with this means of 'measuring' intelligence. It rests on the assumption that tests of verbal and reasoning ability are the best markers of what makes someone 'clever'. This might be true in our particular time and culture – but what of other times and cultures where abstract puzzles were or are far from the norm?

IQ also ignores interpersonal skills – such as understanding other people's state of mind or knowing how to put people at ease – at which some people can be highly skilled, without having any ability at solving puzzles. A third problem with IQ tests is that they involve a skill, in the end, like any other. A student who has been doing dozens of dummy-runs before taking an IQ test will be familiar with the types of questions asked and perform higher than someone who has sat down to complete one for the first time. I remember as a small boy in the 1940s how important IQ was considered by my parents and by everybody else. Children like me practised IQ tests and, over time, certainly our scores improved, frequently enabling my middle-class suburban contemporaries and myself to get into particular schools. But were we, hot-housed small boys and girls, really more intelligent?

Intelligence, rather than being some specific ability – like being able to run fast over a defined distance – is a modular facility of the brain. In other words, there are different kinds of intelligence in all of us. Simon Baron-Cohen at Cambridge University has shown that many autistic people, for example, show high levels of intelligence in fields that involve 'closed systems' with predictable rules, such as mathematics or imitative drawing. But at the same time, they may have significant impairment in their social relationships.

It has been suggested, building on this idea of intelligence as a set of abilities, that we can think of two distinct varieties. Raymond Cattell has argued that *fluid intelligence* is our ability to see, interpret and manipulate relations between things – regardless of experience or practice.[104] A test of your fluid intelligence might be:

NOW is to NEVER
as
CLOSE is to a) FAR b) SELDOM c) NOWHERE d) WIDELY.

Crystallized intelligence, meanwhile, is the knowledge we acquire through experience. It has been defined as 'the extent to which a person has absorbed the content of culture' or 'the store of knowledge or information that a given society has accumulated over time'. Someone who uses crystallized intelligence is someone who puts his acquired knowledge into practice. A doctor who learns which of his patients likes to be greeted with a smile and a joke and which prefers to get straight down to business is using his crystallized intelligence. One who treats all patients the same is not.

These views of intelligence seem plausible – but are they really separate entities? Various studies suggest, for instance, that people with high fluid intelligence are more likely to employ crystallized intelligence. And conversely, how likely is it that someone who cannot see the connections between things is able to learn from experience? Another problem with this view of intelligence is that, once again, it relies for measurement on standard problem-solving tests. All manner of factors can influence a person's score when they are asked to sit down and complete a paper in exam conditions.

The intelligence of the footballer

In the 1980s, Howard Gardner, the distinguished American psychologist, challenged the traditional IQ model of intelligence.[105] He attempted to demonstrate that this was not an adequate measure of a person's intellectual abilities on its own. He proposed not two, but seven different arenas of intelligence – musical, verbal, mathematical/logical, spatial, kinaesthetic (bodily control), intrapersonal (self-understanding) and interpersonal (understanding of others). The clear strength of this idea is in recognizing that people can display high intelligence in one or more of these arenas yet deficiency in others. However, it is difficult to support his argument fully. Paul Gascoigne, that remarkable English footballer who at his peak was one of the most mesmerizing players, clearly had outstanding kinaesthetic skills. The horrendous injuries to his knees, and the various operations that followed, were so serious that had you or I suffered them, we might never have walked normally again. All Arsenal supporters will remember with regret but admiration his astonishing curved free kick to score the winning goal against Arsenal in the Wembley FA Cup Semi-Final in 1991. And few can forget the irony of his reckless – dare one say, unintelligent – tackle in the subsequent Cup Final that damaged his leg so badly that he put his whole career in jeopardy. But in Gascoigne's case, such was his muscular development, his mental determination for fitness, the ability of his brain to help him understand where his knee was in space, and his ability to read instantaneously where other players would place the ball, that he was back playing international football. But it is doubtful whether his ability and body control could be seen as intelligence, gifted though he was. David Beckham, the England captain, has outstanding spatial judgement and physical agility. Yet he would be the first to admit that he is not the most eloquent of men, even though at the same time he has an admirable knack of putting other people at their ease and being highly and delightfully socially aware.

One advantage of Gardner's view of intelligence is that it does match much of what we know about the workings of the brain. Just as we saw that 'memory' could be fractionated into different forms that depend on different brain areas, we depend on different neural sub-systems for different arenas of our intelligence. It also implies that, with use and practice, we can make improvements. So, if intelligence is a set of skill arenas, would we be wasting our time if we tried to determine what an intelligent brain looked like, or what factors might cause it to be so? This has been a hot topic for research for many years. It builds upon a finding, way back at the start of the twentieth century, that most humans perform at consistent levels at a whole variety of cognitive tasks. In other words, that there seems to be some sort of general intelligence. Scientists have dubbed this *Spearman's g*.

The g-type

G can be measured by tests which fall into four rough categories: perceptual organization, working memory, processing speed and verbal comprehension. If we take processing speed, for example – it has been shown that people with faster 'inspection times' perform better on mental tests. The inspection time is how long it takes to register an image. If an image is flashed on a screen for 0.25 of a second, most people will have no difficulty in naming or describing it. But as the time gets shorter and shorter, only more intelligent people are still able to register what they see. Reaction times are also a measure of mental ability – if told to hit a button when they see a certain configuration of lights flashing, people will generally take a third of a second to register the correct cue (this is known as the decision time), and one-sixth of a second to move their hands (the movement time). It is thought that shorter decision times may be markers of higher intelligence.

More recently, intelligence researchers have suggested that an ability to overcome distraction might be a true marker of intelligence. Jeremy Gray at Washington University in St Louis, Missouri tested forty-eight subjects for g-type intelligence.[106] Using fMRI, the researchers measured brain activity as the participants performed a challenging mental problem. They had to keep a list of three words or faces actively in mind. Every few seconds, they had to add another word or face to their list, and drop the oldest item. But before they forgot the old item completely, they had to indicate whether the new item they were adding matched the oldest item they were dropping.

So for example, I might have the words FISH, CHAIR, BLUE in my mind. Then a new word would be given to me: ORANGE. I would say that this didn't match my oldest word: FISH, before dropping it. I'd then have CHAIR, BLUE, ORANGE in my mind. And so on to the next word: SEAT. And this does match the oldest word in my sequence. So I would confirm this before updating my new list: BLUE, ORANGE, SEAT.

The volunteers' brain activity was monitored as they got stuck in to this fiddly task. To complicate things more, the researchers threw in extra distractions – showing them items that did not match the oldest in their lists, but which did match one nearby in the ongoing sequence. Not surprisingly, the volunteers found these 'lure' items particularly confusing.

The study found that participants with higher g-scores were better able to respond correctly and swiftly, despite the interference from the 'lure' items. They appeared to do so by engaging several key brain regions more strongly, including the prefrontal and parietal cortex. The exercise seems complex, but the skill it was testing is similar to something we all call upon in daily situations. Imagine, for instance, trying to drive a car while conversing with someone in the back seat, or copying down a telephone number in the midst of a noisy party. Gray's study indicates we are able to concentrate better on a task in the midst of distractions the more intelligent we are.

So does this also mean that there is a specific site within the brain that houses our intelligence? PET scans have been performed on volunteers' brains as they act out simple and complex versions of three tasks – verbal, spatial and motor. Researchers discovered that the more complex the task, the greater the activity observable in the lateral frontal cortex – alongside the specific brain areas related to the problem. The results suggest that the frontal lobes might house a 'pool' of general intelligence, recruited in problem solving to assist more specific areas of the brain.

Intelligence born or made?

What creates individual differences in intelligence has been a question over which psychologists have argued for more than a century. And scientists are still attempting to tease out what part of our intelligence is due to 'clever genes' and what role our environment plays. It is known, as with Einstein for example, that there are structural differences in some intelligent brains. And people with a bigger brain, for instance, do seem to score higher in IQ tests most often – but overall, men do not score higher than women, even though the male brain is larger on average. Paul Thompson of the University of California, Los Angeles, has also performed scans on the brains of identical and non-identical twins, and suggested that intelligence might be related to the ratio of grey to white matter inside the brain.[107] His findings are powerful support for the notion that intelligence is, to an extent, genetically determined.

Thompson discovered that identical twins – who share the same genes – had exactly the same ratio of grey to white matter in their brains, and this corresponded to identical IQ scores. Non-identical twins, on the other hand, had varying amounts of grey and white matter in their brains, and they also scored differently in IQ tests. Furthermore, the more grey matter there was in the brain, the higher the IQ score tended to be. His MRI scans focused particularly on the two areas of grey matter controlling reading comprehension and speaking (Wernicke's area and Broca's area); these were highly similar in size in identical twins. Although these areas were similar in non-identical twins, the differences were greater than with identical twins, and fewer than in two unrelated individuals. This would suggest that our genes play a part in determining how much grey matter we have in our brains, and how correspondingly intelligent we are – at least if this is measured in terms of IQ. This is supported by the fact that identical twins who have been separated at birth tend to show as many similarities in intelligence as those who have been raised together.

But if we are born with intelligence, does that mean we are stuck with what we've got, or is it a faculty that can grow or shrink with age? Some considerable energy has gone into researching the relationship between intelligence and ageing. We have seen in earlier chapters that some degree of cognitive decline is inevitable in the ageing brain, although the evidence also suggests that we humans can do much to lessen its impact. Professor Ian Deary of Edinburgh University was interested in seeing whether intelligence was a faculty that changed over time. In this endeavour, he was aided greatly by the fact that every Scottish eleven-year-old sat a series of mental tests as part of a 1932 survey. Using his best detective skills in 1998, Deary tracked down a number of 77-year-olds who had taken part in these original tests. He discovered that most adults scored higher in their dotage than they had at the age of eleven – suggesting that intelligence improves with experience. He also discovered that those who scored in the higher ranges back in 1932 continued to show signs of higher intelligence in later life – indicating, happily, that we generally move forwards rather than backwards. He also found that change in thinking ability in these elderly people was related to a particular genetic background, further evidence of a genetic predisposition for intelligence.[108]

The 1932 records were also used in a study of intelligence and longevity performed by Professor Deary with Edinburgh University's Professor Lawrence Whalley.[109] He found that Scots who performed highest in the 1932 tests were also the most likely still to be alive in 1997. This might have something to do with the fact that an ability to use long-term planning is a key marker of intelligence. Arguably, people with lower intelligence might be more motivated by short-term gain, and would be thus more likely to engage in potentially harmful, but more immediately pleasurable activities. This could include a whole range of potentially life-shortening types of behaviour, such as risk-taking or the use of tobacco and alcohol. I personally find this research quite compelling. When I look around at the eighty- and ninety-year-old peers in the House of Lords who gained a peerage by appointment (perhaps through the law or another profession, presumably because in most cases they were particularly able), I am struck again and again how high intelligence seems to be a preservative. Many of these old men, though sometimes quite infirm, are extraordinarily articulate and many muster the best argument in debate. If ever there was evidence for not having an arbitrary retirement age, this must surely be it.

Professor Whalley's findings fit quite neatly with research recently conducted by Professor Merrill Elias of the University of Boston's Statistics and Consulting Unit. He has been evaluating the relationship between IQ and obesity. Men with a Body Mass Index of 30-plus (this would correspond to a man of 5 feet 8 inches in height weighing 14 stone), scored an average 23 per cent lower on IQ tests. The association in women is less convincing. It is not entirely clear why the connection only applied in men, nor whether a low IQ leads to obesity, or the other way round. Perhaps people with a lower IQ might be more likely to choose foodstuffs that are less healthy. People with a lower IQ might, for instance, end up in lower-income jobs, and therefore be inclined towards cheaper foods that are high in fat and sugar content.

Another long-term study of intelligence was undertaken by K. Warner Schaie in Seattle between 1956 and 1991, which involved testing adults every seven years.[110] Schaie's study used the model of fluid versus crystallized intelligence we discussed above. It found that there was a steady decline in inductive reasoning, spatial orientation, perceptual speed and verbal memory. But there was far less age-related decline in verbal or numerical fluency. The study also looked at outside factors that favoured the maintenance of mental abilities. The people who showed the least decline in their faculties had no cardiovascular or chronic disease, their personalities were flexible in mid-life and they lived with partners who also showed high levels of mental ability.

Boosting the intelligence of mice

So whatever your genetic inheritance, your way of life and environment can play a big part in determining your intelligence, and how well it lasts. Claire Rampon, of Princeton University, has shown how environmental factors can trigger the activity of intelligence-related brain systems.[111] Dr Rampon put groups of genetically similar mice into 'enriched' environments: basically a large box, with a floor covered with bedding material and items such as toys, birdhouses, small castles with multiple floors, a running wheel, paper tunnels – really all the sorts of things mice like to have available in their spare time. They were in this environment for three hours, six hours, two days or two weeks. She subsequently used gene probes to analyse 11,000 different genes in their brain, and to compare how well those genes were expressing (i.e. working) with littermate control animals kept in a standard environment. Even three hours made a difference. Dr Rampon discovered that the mice in the learning environment showed increased gene activity in over 150 genes associated with brain function, particularly those probably involved in neuron formation and structure, synapse function and brain plasticity and death of cells in the brain. What was particularly interesting was that some of these genes are known to be associated with learning and memory, and others are linked to age-related memory deficits such as Alzheimer's.

One of Dr Rampon's colleagues is Dr Joe Tsien from Princeton. His remarkable announcement from Princeton in 1999 caused a media sensation. His team had genetically modified mice to make them 'smarter'.[112] Dr Tsien found that adding a single gene to mice significantly boosted their ability to negotiate a maze and to learn from objects and sounds around them. Moreover, they could memorize better. (The mice were called Doogie after Doogie Howser MD, a precocious character on American TV.)

First, the team tested the ability of the genetically modified animals to recognize an object. They put the mice into a box where they explored two objects for five minutes. Several days later, one object was replaced with a new one, and the mice went back into the box. Genetically modified mice remembered the old object and devoted their time to exploring the new one. Unenhanced mice spent an equal amount of time exploring both objects, indicating that the old object was no longer familiar. Gene-modified mice remembered objects four to five times longer than the normal controls.

Emotional memory was assessed by giving the mice a mild shock to their feet when they were put in another cage. At varying intervals later, the transgenic mice had more pronounced fear of the cage than the control mice. This was the case with a conditioned reflex – when the mice were taught to associate an audible tone with a shock, thus employing a different pathway in the brain. Spatial learning was measured by getting the mice to swim in a pool of water that had a hidden platform onto which they could climb to get out of the water. This is a very standard test, widely used in psychological testing. The transgenic mice found the platform after an average of three sessions, the control mice after six.

The gene Dr Tsien used, NR2B, helps control the brain's ability to associate one event with another by influencing the NMDA receptor, a receptor for the glutamate neurotransmitter. Dr Tsien not only gave mice extra copies of the NR2B gene, but he ensured that their activity increased as the mice aged, counteracting the decline of the natural gene. And as they got older, the brains of the mice retained physical features that usually characterize juvenile animals; in particular, they had a high level of plasticity and the ability to form long-term connections between neurons. These results could be of major interest to researchers trying to understand and treat human disorders that involve the loss of learning and memory. Clearly there is a commercial interest here: the NR2B gene – or what it is responsible for producing – could be a target for the pharmaceutical industry. There are, of course, extraordinary ethical and social issues raised by this discovery. Should genetic technology, if it was safe, be used to modify or enhance mental and cognitive attributes in people?

Boosting the intelligence of humans

Leaving aside the many ethical issues, safety is undoubtedly one key problem. Genetic modification is fraught with dangers to any off-spring. The balance of genes and how they express in the brain would be altered at the peril of any human guinea-pig. So, while we are a long way from making superhumans by meddling with their genes, can we humans benefit by environmental changes? Obviously, the answer to this question must be yes, otherwise why would parents waste their money by sending their child to Eton or Cheltenham Ladies' College? But could a regime of brain-exercise for all of us or a simple change of lifestyle and eating habits give our grey cells a crucial kick-start? Encouragingly, some studies have suggested that activities as seemingly non-cerebral as chewing gum give you a mental workout. A University of Northumbria project tested volunteers for their ability to recall a series of words and pictures which they learnt after having chewed gum for three minutes. The gum chewers performed better – possibly because the act of chewing causes a surge of insulin in the body, and the hippocampus, seat of our long-term memory, is packed with insulin-responsive cells.

Three million people play bingo in the UK every year and you might think this is a mindless activity. Many people even bring their knitting to keep them occupied during the game, and some, such as a maiden aunt of mine, play the cards upside down to make it a bit harder. But anybody who has ever attended a bingo hall will have been amazed at the ability of certain old ladies to simultaneously listen to the numbers called, conduct a conversation, drink a port and lemon and play several game cards at once. Bingo is an activity that calls for high levels of attention, focus and efficient working memory. The players have to be able to check numbers off quickly and need rapid hand–eye coordination. And a recent PhD thesis submitted by Julie Winstone of the University of Southampton showed that experienced bingo players are helping to keep their brains in tip-top condition. She tested 112 women aged between eighteen and forty, and sixty and eighty-two, for faculties like speed processing, memory recall and scanning the environment for data. The study showed that the bingo players, old and young alike, scored significantly higher. Interestingly, in some areas of intelligence, the older bingo players were doing better than their younger counterparts.

Of course, some of the best examples for us to follow come from the redoubtable nuns of Mankato who keep their brains active well into old age by doing puzzles and participating in debates. We can all do the same for ourselves, but the thing to remember is that the brain adores a challenge. It is busy all the time, whether we are resting or working, but so much of that activity is routine. To build and strengthen new connections, the brain needs the challenge of fresh and unusual stimuli. So if you are doing the *Times* crossword in ten minutes flat (as my old history master at school used to do), you might not be giving your grey cells as much exercise as they deserve.

There's a lot of evidence to suggest that repetition is bad for brain health, and novelty is good. A study led by Robert Friedland, at the Case Western Reserve University School of Medicine, showed that people who had led mentally diverse and stimulating lives were less likely to develop Alzheimer's disease.[113] Arnold Scheibel of the University of California has conducted autopsies on elderly subjects and demonstrated that the neurons of those who had led more challenging and diverse lifestyles had a great density of receptor sites. So the message should be – make some changes while you can.

Laurence Katz, neurobiologist at Duke University Medical School, North Carolina, whose outstanding work on pheromones I've quoted before, suggests that unfamiliar challenges, however trivial or bizarre, are best for brain performance. So try brushing your teeth with the wrong hand. Make a cup of tea with your eyes shut. Read this paragraph backwards. It won't make you a genius, but it will give your brain a boost.

And when it comes to certain mental skills, training one part of the brain can be seen to have knock-on benefits elsewhere. But this effect has led to somewhat dubious research with equally questionable results. The Mozart Effect is a term coined by Alfred A. Tomatis some forty years ago. He alleged an increase in brain development in those children under the age of three who were made to listen to the music of Mozart. At Irvine, California, physicist Gordon Shaw and Frances Rauscher, a former concert cellist, studied the effects of listening to Mozart's Sonata for Two Pianos in D Major (K.448) on a number of college students. I blush in remembering that when I listened to it, aged nineteen, I fell asleep. However, Shaw and Rauscher found an enhancement of spatial-temporal reasoning, measured by the Stanford Binet IQ test. This effect was only brief and nobody else has been able to entirely duplicate their results as far as I am aware. Dr Rauscher has since moved on to study the effects of Mozart on rats. He claims that after he exposed rats in utero and then sixty days after birth to different types of auditory stimulation, animals that were exposed to the Mozart completed mazes faster and with fewer errors. Now he is removing their brains so he can slice them and see precisely what has changed as a result of this exposure to eighteenth-century German culture. He speculates that this intense exposure to the music is a type of enrichment that has similar effects on the spatial areas of the hippocampus of the brain.

In 1997, Drs Rauscher and Shaw announced that they had proved that piano and singing are superior to computer instruction in enhancing children's abstract reasoning skills. They looked at three groups of pre-school children: one received private piano/keyboard lessons and singing lessons, a second received private computer lessons, and a third group received no training. Those children who received piano/keyboard training performed 34 per cent higher on tests measuring spatial-temporal ability than the others. They claimed that these findings indicate that music stimulated higher brain functions required for mathematics, chess, science and engineering. Certainly, Drs Shaw and Rauscher have stimulated an industry. They have also created their own institute: the Music Intelligence Neural Development institute (MIND).

To be scrupulously fair to Dr Shaw and Dr Rauscher, they argue that they have been terribly misrepresented. What there is, apparently, is 'a pattern of neurons that fire in sequences, and there appear to be pre-existing sites in the brain that respond to specific frequencies'. This is not quite the same as showing that listening to Mozart increases intelligence in children. However, according to various press reports, Shaw has not waited for the hard evidence before he helps parents to achieve their desire of enhancing their children's intelligence. Gordon L. Shaw's book and CD *Keeping Mozart in Mind* are available on Amazon.com priced $52.95 (or $41.50 secondhand). Apparently, the Governors of Tennessee and Georgia have been so impressed by this research that they have started programmes giving a Mozart CD to every newborn.

One important influence on a child's intelligence is the happiness of its environment. Some very recent research at King's College in London by Dr Terrie Moffitt and Dr Karestan Koenen of Boston University involved testing the IQ of British twins. No fewer than 1,116 pairs of twins at the age of five helped this enquiry. The mothers of these children had quite often been in an abusive relationship – 476 of them had suffered domestic violence and in 151 cases the violence had been classed as 'serious'. When the mother had been in an abusive relationship, the average IQ score of the twins was eight points lower than in children with happy, unabused mothers. It made no difference whether the twins were identical or not, demonstrating that this effect was not likely to be genetically determined.

A healthy mind in a healthy body

There can be no doubt, however: if you want to keep your brain healthy, you should also play attention to your body. The Roman dictum *mens sana in corpore sano* would indicate that we have known for some centuries about the benefits of regular physical exercise for the brain. More recently, Dr Henriette van Praag, who studied opiate receptor function at Bar Ilan University in Israel, has worked on brain regeneration after injury and diseases at the Laboratory of Genetics at the Salk Institute at La Jolla, California. She examined the hippocampus – the site of the long-term memory – of mice who had access to a running wheel. Compared with mice deprived of exercise, the active mice had twice the number of cells in this region involved in memory.

And the same trends seem likely to be true for humans. Studies performed in the USA in the 1970s showed that children's reading scores were boosted considerably when they performed a short dance exercise every day for six months. A more recent educational study has shown that just five minutes of general jumping around at the start of the day results in improved concentration and more efficient learning of material. A simple explanation for this is that any physical activity raises our heart rate and increases blood flow to areas throughout the body, including the brain.

Different types of exercise can have varying effects on our mental health. A Harvard study in 1994 demonstrated that men who burn more than 2,500 calories a day in aerobic activity were 28 per cent less likely to suffer from depression. This might have something to do with endorphins – the natural opiates produced within the brain after physical activity. We've all of us experienced the warm, contented feeling that suffuses us after completing a physical chore, like digging the garden or climbing a steep hill. This may have less to do with our sense of achievement and more to do with the fact that our brains are flooded with endorphins. Sequenced movement activities like tai chi and hatha yoga have also been shown to have benefits for mental health – reducing stress levels and aggression.

Food for thought

Your brain is affected by what you put into your body as much as what you do with it. You may have been told as a child that eating oily fish, such as sardines, kippers, mackerel and herring, was good for your brain. And unfortunately for fish-haters, this is true. We saw in Chapter 6 how important fats are for the adequate development of a child's brain. And a particular type of long-chain fatty acid, found in breastmilk and oily fish, is vital for brain function. Norwegian and Danish research has shown that babies who were breastfed for less than three months were more likely to score below average for mental skills when they were five years old. It is interesting to note also that the lowest rates of dyslexia are found in Japan, where the diet includes a lot of fish.

When I was a small child it was wartime and, with rationing, many foods were in short supply. I remember I was forced to eat many repulsive foods. Reconstituted dried egg wasn't so appalling, but I found cheese completely repellent. I still remember meals at the age of two or three. I recall being seated on my nanny's knee in the kitchen being fed liquid cheese, while my parents were comfortably ensconced in the dining room. I still have a loathing – indeed almost a phobia – of all cheese to this day. No doubt the fat in it was good for brain development, but not nearly as good as the spoonfuls of cod-liver oil we were forced to eat. One swallow and a feeling of extreme nausea followed rapidly. But the Scandinavian research shows that my parents, together so many other wartime couples, were not so short of the mark and were being cruel to be kind. A child's brain contains a huge amount of fat, and fat intake is needed – especially during the first twelve months of life – for its adequate growth. And fish oils turn out to be remarkably good for brain development. Nowadays we can take them in more sophisticated ways – for example, in a pill capsule.

My family have always been convinced that fish helps make you brainy. My maternal great-grandfather was a rabbi and a rather bookish intellectual. He lived for much of his later life in Ramsgate, by the sea. In the belief that fish was really good for the brain, he eventually bought himself a large rod and spent many fruitless hours in often bitter weather on Ramsgate pier. My great-grandmother constantly teased him about his passion for fishing because he always came home wet but empty-handed. After one frustrating day spent in this useless activity this normally honest and highly moral man decided he would impress his family with his prowess. On the way home he guiltily slipped into the local fishmonger and furtively purchased two fish which the fishmonger quickly wrapped for him. On his return he proudly laid his prized catch on the kitchen table. The triumphant hunter-gatherer glanced round smugly at his expectant family. My grandmother, then a little girl, rushed to the table, picked up the fish and said, 'Oh, Dad, aren't you clever? Did you catch both these kippers?'

A recent experiment in Durham involved giving fish oil supplements to primary school children over a period of six months. Educational psychologist Madeleine Portwood selected a group of 120 children, aged six to eleven, who all showed evidence of learning difficulties, such as problems with coordination, reading, handwriting and spelling. Some of the results have been dramatic. After only three months of taking the supplements, one child's reading age improved by four years. For others, there has been a two-year leap in learning abilities.

Dr Portwood points out that, as a nation, we are not consuming nearly enough of the fatty acids so vital for healthy brain function. The government recommends eating one to two portions of fish like salmon or mackerel a week, but only around a third of us serve it up regularly. In addition, she believes some children are deficient in fatty acids, not because of their diet, but because their bodies fail to make proper use of the fatty acids they are getting. It seems that these substances help neurons to grow and to form connections with one another. They may also be important in the brain's construction of myelin, giving the white matter its colour. This is the fatty sheath that covers neurons and conducts electrochemical messages through them.

Numerous studies have confirmed the importance of long-chain fatty acids in brain function. Laura Steve and John Burgess of Purdue University in the USA have discovered that children with higher amounts of the acids in their blood show better overall academic achievement and are specifically better at mathematics. Meanwhile, work being performed at Oxford University has shown that fish oil supplements can be useful in controlling the symptoms of Attention Deficit Hyperactive Disorder. In a six-month study, children attending a school for learning disorders were divided into two groups. One group took supplements for the whole period of the study, while another group switched after three months from taking a placebo to taking supplements. The results showed that taking the supplements led to a reduction in cognitive problems, behavioural problems and anxiety. Bernard Gesch, also of Oxford University, is taking this knowledge into the British prison system, where he has found evidence of a poor diet, low in some minerals and selenium, and high in the wrong kinds of fats.[114] He has found that young offenders in an Aylesbury institution showed a 30 per cent drop in instances of aggression when given fish oil supplements with their daily diet.

And if you come out in a rash when you eat fish, maybe you should try ginseng. So far there have been claims for its effectiveness in treating acidity, back pain, cancer, Crohn's disease, depression, impotence, chronic hair loss, urinary difficulties, chronic diarrhoea, headache, high blood pressure, insomnia, rashes of various kinds, hot flushes, diabetes, and as an aphrodisiac. Now it seems it improves intelligence. Dr Scholey, of the Human Cognitive Neuroscience Unit, University of Northumbria, Newcastle[115] undertook three studies involving mathematical tasks of varying difficulty, when a number of young men and women were tested for speed of problem solving. They were given different amounts of ginseng in a randomized fashion and were not informed whether what they had ingested was a placebo or the real thing. Different doses of ginseng improved accuracy and slowed responses. The most striking result was achieved with 320 milligrams of a ginkgo-ginseng combination. But the question remains: why did it take over 2,000 years for the Chinese to find out its cognitive value from a British scientist?

Evidence from Papua New Guinea indicates that there's one substance we should steer clear of if we want to keep our intelligence in tip-top health. Back in the 1950s, doctors noticed that among a certain tribe, the Fore people, there was a high incidence of a condition known locally as kuru, or the 'laughing death'. This degenerative brain disease causes its sufferers widespread mental decline, with depression, memory loss and impaired reasoning – these are, perhaps, the nicer of its symptoms. In addition, kuru sufferers were gradually robbed of the ability to walk, talk and even eat. It wiped out at least 10 per cent of the population. Initially, the colonial authorities thought that, since it was confined to one specific tribe, kuru was a genetic condition. They sought to prevent its spread by confining the movements of the Fore people to their homeland.

But anthropologists noted that there was something specific about Fore culture that might have been playing a part in the spread of the disease. To put it plainly, Fore villagers honoured their dead by eating certain parts of their bodies. It was considered a noble and respected action on the widow's part to prepare her deceased husband's body for consumption by steaming it in bamboo tubes. Furthermore, it became clear that kuru was most predominant in the women and children of the tribe. This custom stemmed from the belief that certain body parts, if eaten, imparted specific qualities to the eaters. And eating the brain should have helped them to gain wisdom and intelligence. We now know, of course, that kuru is almost certainly a prion disease, a disease of a disordered protein in the brain, causing damage similar to Creutzfeldt-Jakob disease (CJD), or BSE in cattle.

Drink not always a demon

You are unlikely to be in any situation where eating human brains is a possibility. But you might be interested in the benefits of a more common practice: visiting the pub. I have already dealt with excessive alcohol consumption and the risks of it causing irreparable damage to brain tissue. But it seems that the occasional tipple can be beneficial to your mental functioning. Research by Monique Breteler at Holland's Erasmus University has shown that light to moderate drinkers may be less likely to develop degenerative changes in the brain and possibly Alzheimer's disease. A further study at Milan University, by Alberto Bertelli, suggests that wine might be the ideal drink for brain-boosters. A chemical called resveratrol – found in vines, grapes and various drinks produced by fermentation – increases the activity and effectiveness of the MAP-kinase enzyme by up to seven times. In human tissue studies, this enzyme stimulates the growth of connections between neural cells, which may be good news for general brain health. Currently, research at the University of Marburg is looking into ways to breed a resveratrol-heavy type of grapevine, having isolated the related genes. The stuff is most con-centrated in red wine – one fluid ounce of a good claret contains around 160 micrograms of resveratrol – so don't be surprised if you don't get the same results from a Chardonnay. My old boss, Professor Murdo Elder, a Scot, used to creep into my office after hours to rummage around the drawers to, I regret to say, steal (or rather borrow, perhaps) the odd bottle — I've always kept a good malt there, purely for medicinal purposes as it's not uncommon to find the occasional member of staff in a dangerous state of collapse at the end of the working day. Professor Elder was adamant that my contribution in this respect was the most important I made to the academic health of the department. And he was convinced that he wrote far better scientific papers after a glass of scotch. He knew nothing, I am sure, about the research on resveratrol but it might just be that whisky has other properties.

What is very clear is that all the evidence suggests that the brain and the body are intimately involved with one another. Brain health affects bodily health, and vice versa. Increasing evidence suggests that factors such as stress, depression and mental attitude can have a visible effect on the behaviour of our bodies. As we shall see next, the idea of 'mind over matter' is beginning to seem less like a cranky belief confined to paranormal investigators and more like a basic fact of human biology.

Mesmerizing . . .

We come now to a fascinating and rather sad individual. Not many of us have made such an impressive contribution to human history that our surname contributes a new verb, noun or adjective. One thinks of 'galvanize' from Galvani, and 'Faradism' from Michael Faraday. Hans Mesmer was brought up on Lake Constance and qualified as a doctor at the late age of thirty-two. At the age of forty he became interested in the effects of magnets on the body and believed that he had discovered an entirely new principle of healing involving 'animal magnetism'. This 'animal magnetism' that he used was different from physical magnetism in that he believed that he could 'magnetize' paper, glass, dogs and all manner of other substances. Of course, had he but known it, much of modern neuroscience is founded exactly on this principle. The MRI scanner aligns molecules by their magnetic field, and dogs certainly fit the rule — though they are not often studied.

He set up his plate first in Vienna and then in Paris. Rather like the handful of millionaire plastic surgeons used now by the rich and famous in Hollywood, Mesmer's practice on the Place Vendôme quickly became a honeypot for the Parisian bourgeoisie. He had established his reputation in the years before through being apparently able to treat physical maladies using only the lightest touch of his hands. His basic notion was that people could be cured by the use of a magnetic field. So many of the deserving poor flocked to him for treatment that he resorted to mass methods of healing. He designed a magnetic *baquet*, a wooden tub nearly two metres across and around 30 centimetres or so deep, filled with water and iron filings. In this tub were fixed iron rods that his patients could grasp. In order to extend his practice, he 'magnetized' a tree, so that patients could be healed by holding ropes hanging from its branches. These devices 'worked' by inducing a 'crisis', normally convulsions or swooning.

Mesmer seriously believed that there was hard science behind the practice of what we might now call faith healing or the laying on of hands. He believed – building on Isaac Newton's theory of a universal substance called the ether – that bodily disorders were the consequences of imbalances within the body's own magnetic fluids. Rather as we might even out a tube of toothpaste by squeezing it, these imbalances could be put right simply by touching, gentle palpations, or by passing the hands over the affected areas – a process which quite often resulted in the patients, as they were being 'cured', entering a trance-like state. There is an extraordinary cartoon of Mesmer from a French newspaper of around 1790. A fainting woman – clearly very well dressed – is collapsed in a chair and over her looms Mesmer, wearing a frock coat and making 'magnetic passes' which look sexually explicit. And Mesmer is wearing a huge head of an ass, with very long ears. He looks a little like Bottom in *A Midsummer Night's Dream* and presumably the implication is the same – that a cuckold is in the making.

For Mesmer, often regarded as the father of hypnosis, these trance-states were of minor interest, a mere side effect of his awe-inspiring treatment. So captivated was the public imagination by Mesmer's treatment that he began – not unlike some latter-day American evangelist preacher – to treat the 'sophisticated' people of Paris en masse, in stage shows carefully engineered with the use of elaborate costume, mirrors, lighting and music.

Some of the scientific community, instead of dismissing Mesmer as a side-show trickster, took his work very seriously. But possibly because he threatened its own lucrative treatments the medical establishment was very concerned about Mesmer. A Royal Commission into Mesmerism was set up which reported very critically. So Mesmer established a foundation – the Society of Honour – behind which he could hide. It consisted of a clinic, a teaching establishment and a register of qualified members who had received his training, and who paid for the privilege. From there he published his *Catechism on Animal Magnetism*. At one point the catechism asks in what way should one touch a sick person in order for him to experience the effects of magnetism.

First of all, one must place oneself opposite the patient, back to the north, bringing one's feet against the invalid's; then lay two thumbs lightly on the nerve plexes which are located in the pit of the stomach, and the fingers on the hypochondria [region below the ribs]. From time to time it is good to run one's fingers over the ribs, principally towards the spleen, and to change the position of the thumbs. After having continued this exercise for about a quarter of an hour, one performs in a different manner, corresponding to the condition of the patient. For example, if it is a disorder of the eyes, one lays the left hand on the right temple. One then opens the eyes of the patient and brings one's thumbs very close to them. Then the thumbs are run from the root of the nose [bridge] all around the socket.

Had his patients been put into a brain scanner after this therapy, it might well have been possible to prove an effect likely to be therapeutic. By 1791, Paris was in chaos. Being a foreigner, it was simplest for Mesmer to leave the revolutionary city. He retired at the age of fifty-four and settled eventually near Lake Constance. He had been fêted and famous in Paris, but now he was poor, obscure and forgotten. But he seems to have been contented enough with the quiet life, doing a little medicine, playing his glass harmonica, and remaining detached from the outside world until his death in 1815, at the age of eighty-five.

But Mesmer's rather fantastical *son et lumière* demonstrations created the bedrock for a new area of scientific consideration. The notion that physical symptoms could be alleviated by making suggestions to the brain spawned a century of scientific enquiry into the possible benefits of hypnosis. When Sigmund Freud began his forays into the unconscious mind towards the close of the nineteenth century, it was with a nod to the practices Mesmer had originated. Freud's earliest investigations centred upon the possibility that certain states of paralysis could be cured through inducing patients to relive traumatic experiences, which had become buried in the unconscious mind.

The brain *is* the body

However much scepticism we now feel towards the likes of Mesmer and Freud, medical professionals all over the world accept that there is a very powerful link between the physical body and states of mind. The placebo effect, which must have played a most important role in Mesmer's cures, is now firmly established as a healing entity. We also understand, for example, that some complaints can be purely psychosomatic – that is, arising from the mind. GPs now routinely look for symptoms of depression in those patients who repeatedly come to the surgery with aches and pains that remain resistant to any sort of treatment. In many cases, these patients are not time wasters or attention seekers. Nor are they are suffering from some well-hidden brain tumour or heart disease, but from a very elusive and disguised form of depression. It can, in many cases, be alleviated with antidepressant drugs.

Those inclined towards a more psychoanalytic view would say that people with this form of depression probably come from backgrounds where they were told to 'pull yourself together' and keep a 'stiff upper lip'. Becoming ill is therefore the only way that they can signal their emotional distress. But whatever perspective you take on this, when you have seen – as I have – people writhing in agony with a condition that has no bodily cause at all, you cannot possibly doubt the mind's power over the flesh.

Stress is perhaps the most classic, and common, example of the way a state of mind can affect the body. Consider the following scenario for a moment: You're in the office. The deadline is an hour away, and you've got a nagging headache. As each minute goes by, that pile in your In tray seems to grow ever more mountainous. Your phone keeps ringing. Each minute is punctuated by the little 'blip' sound telling you that more email has arrived in your computer. You spill your coffee, and when you go to fetch a cloth, you knock that carefully collated report onto the floor, sheets of paper flying everywhere. Your heartbeat soars, you come out in a sweat, your stomach churns and the headache intensifies. Your thoughts are muddled, panicky, incoherent. Stress, the demon of the modern urban lifestyle, is on the increase – and it can be a killer. High levels of daily stress are implicated in a raft of conditions from heart disease to cancer and even infertility.

Studies have shown that the ability to handle stress is vital to the functioning of our bodies. Robert Sapolsky of Stanford University has shown that rats raised in a 'gentle environment', which involved soft handling and regular touch and massage, produced increased amounts of serotonin, resulting in lower levels of aggression. As adults, they also had stronger immune systems and lived longer. But of course he is only demonstrating what all animal researchers and farmers know. Treat animals with courtesy, kindness and humanity and they will be healthier and much more gentle.

This phenomenon is equally true of humans. You may have noticed yourself that if you develop a cold or some other infection during a time of high stress in your life, it lingers longer and makes you feel worse. This is because substances such as cortisol and adreno-corticotrophin (ACTH), released when we undergo physical and mental stress, can compromise the body's ability to repair its own tissue and to fight infection. When a virus or bacteria enters the body, white blood cells divide and increase in number in order to fight the invasion. ACTH slows down the production of these white blood cells – thereby impairing our ability to stave off infection.

Dr Ronald Glaser of Ohio State University has demonstrated this effect by testing the blood of students before and after they sat examinations. The students emerging from the exams – in which we can assume they underwent a stressful experience – had significantly fewer white blood cells. Glaser also tested couples who were undergoing marital therapy. His results suggest that those couples who reported high levels of stress in their marriage had a less robust immune system.

We noted earlier that there seemed to be a link between high IQ and longevity. Research conducted at the University of California, Berkeley, has suggested that this could be related to the body's immune function. Dr Marian C. Diamond (who made the study of Einstein's nerve cells) noted that animals with damaged dorsolateral cortices – the area of the brain associated with complex cognitive functions – also had reduced levels of lymphocytes, which kill off viruses and neutralize toxins within the body. She proceeded to test this on humans by testing their blood before and after they had engaged in a one-and-a-half-hour session of contract bridge. Her results provided partial proof of the hypothesis – the bridge players had increased levels of CD4 T lymphocyte cells.

But why should this be? It is one thing to say that the brain can be tricked into suppressing or boosting the immune system, entirely another to suggest that group therapy or a tricky card game or falling in love can halt the progression of a disease. One explanation might be that the mind's ability to control the immune system is dependent upon attitude. For instance, our immune systems might not be impaired by stress per se, but affected by our personal attitude towards stress. Perhaps it matters just who is playing bridge, and with whom.

The field of psychoneuroimmunology is new, but one that is

gaining some acceptance within the scientific community. It might be said to have gained its first foothold when a scientist called Robert Ader, of the University of Rochester School of Medicine in New York, experimented by conditioning mice to feel sick after they had drunk sweetened water. He enforced this conditioning by giving the mice a drug immediately after consuming the sweet water, which made them vomit. After a few repetitions, the mice were sick whenever they drank the sweet water, without needing to ingest the vomiting drug. But Ader's curiosity was alerted by the fact that these conditioned mice started to die, becoming susceptible to infections that they would normally have fought. When he studied the side effects of the vomiting drug, he discovered that it also suppressed the immune system of the mice. But its effects were short-lived; they ought to have reversed after the mice stopped taking it. The fact the mice were dying suggested one thing – it was their brains that were causing the suppression of the immune system.

Since this experiment was conducted in 1975, numerous studies have proved that mental stress can impair the body's ability to fight infections. More importantly, we are beginning to see that this is a process that can be affected by our own attitude. Given the right mental equipment, we can make our immune systems work more efficiently. A neat example of this is provided by the 'sherbet test'. It is known that adrenaline – though this too is released under stress – has the ability to boost the body's immune system. If we are given a dose of sherbet along with a dose of adrenaline, we can immediately see the adrenaline's positive effects on the body's white blood cells. But, rather like Ader's mice, our minds then become conditioned with repeated doses. If, later on, we are given a dose of sherbet without an adrenaline chaser, the immune system continues to behave in its adrenaline-boosted manner. Conceivably, then, the brain has the power to heal the body.

Medical professionals are beginning to make use of this knowledge in the treatment of disease. Dr David Spiegel and his colleagues at Stanford University, California, followed eighty-six patients with advanced breast cancer and secondary deposits.[116] Fifty of these women had psychotherapy each week for ninety minutes – the idea being that this would simply help them to cope with a terrible diagnosis – and thirty-six had routine oncological care. After ten years, only three of the patients were alive, and death records were obtained for the other eighty–three. Women in the group treated with psychotherapy had an average life span of thirty-seven months after diagnosis; the women in the control group only nineteen months. These findings are not conclusive: one of the problems is that to some extent the groups may have been self-selecting – there may have been something different between the people taking up the offer of psychotherapy and those refusing it, and this could introduce bias. Nevertheless, these results have continued to attract a great deal of interest.

More recently, Dr Spiegel's findings have been somewhat corroborated by Fawzy I. Fawzy, MD, a professor of psychiatry at the UCLA School of Medicine. Dr Fawzy recruited sixty-eight people with malignant melanoma skin cancer and invited half to participate in a ninety-minute education and support group once a week for six weeks. Compared with melanoma patients who received standard medical care, those in the group showed less fatigue and depression, and better coping abilities. Six years after Dr Fawzy completed this study, he learnt of Dr Spiegel's research and tracked down his participants to see if those in his group showed a better survival rate than the others. Despite the brevity of his group sessions (just six weeks), they had: among the patients who received only standard care, ten had died. But among his group participants, there were only three deaths.[117] As this was a study where the patients were randomly allocated to one or other of the groups (and thus the researchers could not influence what treatment was chosen), the results seemed impressive, but recently Dr Fawzy went back to re-evaluate the outcome more than ten years after the initial treatments. Essentially the death rate was the same in both groups – so the effect of psychotherapy, if it exists at all, may be somewhat transient.[118]

Recently, Dr Christoffer Johansen's group from the Department of Psychosocial Cancer Research, Institute of Cancer Epidemiology in Copenhagen, made a thorough review of the world scientific literature in this field.[119] They identified forty-three randomized studies of the effect of psychosocial intervention in cancer patients. There were eight studies in which the survival of each individual patient was assessed; of these, four appeared to show some significant improvement. Of interest was the general effect of psychotherapy on anxiety and depression; this was also inconsistent. It was disappointing that psychotherapy and positive thinking only seemed to be consistent in helping a few patients with their general symptoms. As so often happens with subjects which are of wide interest and newsworthy, it was obvious that there had been much soft research and that enthusiastic stories of the benefits of positive mental attitudes in the press were based on quite flimsy evidence. Dr Johansen and colleagues drew some important conclusions. They commented that more large-scale studies with much sounder methods were needed and that, in the meantime, they felt that the question of whether psychosocial intervention among cancer patients had a beneficial effect was unresolved. In too many of the studies, a number of essentials were missing or incomplete; the failures of research method included inadequate randomization of patients allocated to different treatment groups, patients with different stages of disease being studied in each group, no assessment being made of psychological profile, and an absence of rigorous follow-up.

It goes without saying that stress is a broad term, used loosely. The stress of having a serious, possible fatal, disease like cancer is different from the stress we experience travelling to work and different again from that experienced performing sport. Studies show that the way we respond to stress depends on the type of stress, and whether we feel able to control it. Short-term controlled stress like a bungee jump can actually boost the production of the body's own infection-fighting cells. Similarly, long-term controlled stress − such as a demanding job − can result in increased production of relaxant chemicals such as endorphins and enkephalins. This might explain why, when engaged in a period of high stress, we often fall ill after the pressure has eased off, rather than during it. Many actors report that they fall prey to colds and influenza just after finishing a job. 'I'm just resting' may not just be a thespian's way of glossing over a period of unemployment after all.

And the reverse is also true: the most damaging kind of stress is the stress we feel we cannot control. In one experiment, rats were exposed to a series of shocks that could be stopped by pressing a metal bar. Another group also received shocks, but there was no mechanism by which they could escape them. Both groups were then injected with mitogens, substances which would normally stimulate the immune system. The rats experiencing stress they could not control had diminished production of lymphocytes. But the rats who were in control of their stress suffered no impairment to their immune function.

Similar experiments have been conducted with humans. In one

experiment, healthy volunteers were exposed to noises over which they had control, and other volunteers to those they did not. In each case the noise was more than 100 decibels. Those who had no control over the noises were obviously increasingly helpless and began to feel rising anxiety. More importantly, when compared with those who could have turned the noise down if they felt they did not want to continue with the experiment, those with no control showed marked impairment of their immune system after the experiment. Studies of the families of Alzheimer's sufferers, and people who have lost partners, also confirm that various types of uncontrollable stress cause most damage to the immune system.

So if this is the case, we should, by enabling people to reassert control, also help them to improve the response of their immune system. This is a possible reason why activities like group therapy and relaxation techniques may have a beneficial effect on the prognosis of disease. The more we feel we can control stress, the better placed our immune system may be to cope with its effects.

The genius inside

So we can, at least to some extent, boost both our brain and our body. But how does intelligence relate to that most elusive of human faculties – creativity? If we can make our brain stronger, can we also learn to unlock the secrets of creative genius, becoming better painters, composers, writers?

Before we can answer these questions, it is necessary to arrive at a definition of creativity and an understanding of the brain processes involved. Robert J. Sternberg, Yale University Professor of Psychology, suggests that creative thinking has a number of observable traits. First, there is an ability to switch between primary conscious and secondary unconscious thought processes. Secondly, and related to the first point, creative individuals show a low level of cortical activity. This could explain why children are more adept at thinking creatively than adults – because their frontal lobes are less developed. A child might, for instance, make an observation like 'those clouds look like mashed potato and that aeroplane looks like a sausage'. Adults generally refrain from making such statements if they don't want to seem odd. But those associations might be exactly what an artist or a poet uses in creating a painting or a poem. This brings us to Sternberg's third point. Creativity, he claims, is a right-brain activity – which entails making loose, or freeform associations between seemingly unrelated phenomena.[120] The right brain, it is maintained by some people, is better at grasping concepts in their entirety, at seeing the 'bigger picture' rather than the fine detail. This relies on a tendency to connect items into an overarching schema, rather than see them as individual and unconnected. Correspondingly, creative individuals are better at unfocused thought – at suggesting connections between ideas rather than in solving problems. One of the ways we can observe this is by using a device called the biofeedback machine – which shows users their EEG brain-wave patterns on a screen, and enables them to produce alterations in their internal brain states by concentrated effort. Creative individuals, asked to create a certain biofeedback pattern, are said to be markedly worse at this than their less creative counterparts.

Creative people seem sometimes to show a greater variability of response to external stimuli – factors like heart rate, galvanic skin response and cortical arousal increase more sharply in response to sensory input. We noted earlier on that this is also an observable trait in people of introvert-type personalities – so there might be some basis for assuming that creative people are likely to be more 'sensitive' to the world they experience. Arguably, this can explain why many artists, poets, novelists and the like tend to be introverts. They retreat from a world they find bewildering and potentially threatening to their sensitive sensory apparatus and seek solace in an 'inner world'. The fact that most creative people prefer solitude to do their work only reinforces their introversion.

Of course, if we took the arguments above to their natural conclusion, we might end up saying that all poets, composers, artists, etc., are right-brained introverts. And this is not the case at all – as anyone who has the slightest acquaintance with the life story of Ernest Hemingway can confirm. Certain activities, such as drawing and music for instance, may rely heavily on left-brain processes – which are arguably more developed in right-handed people. And novelists, playwrights, poets and the like also demonstrate a high degree of linguistic fluency – once again a left-brain activity. Guy Claxton, of the University of Bristol, suggests that the secret of creativity lies in an ability to switch modes. In other words, regardless of which side

343

of your brain is dominant, if you are creative, you are able to suppress the elements you normally rely upon and dip into your opposite hemisphere. So a painter wishing to convey, for example, what the sky looks like to a child would switch off his analytical left brain and dip into his right to make the analogy of clouds with mashed potato. Certain neurotransmitters like acetylcholine may help this process and this – a simple difference of our chemical inheritance – might explain why some individuals find it easier than others.

Creativity appeared to be an entirely natural process for Mozart, who claimed that his intricate musical compositions came to him whole, stimulated by playing billiards, without needing any editing or even posing any disruption to his daily routine. Beethoven made endless sketches of what he intended, often hastily put together, before building up the final score of his great works. For Haydn, on the other hand, composition was a formal experience. Before sitting down to write he would dress in his best clothes, try things out on the keyboard and prepare himself for the meticulous craft of his trade. Brahms rose at 5 a.m., brewed monumentally strong black coffee and then sat down to write. Occasionally he could be seen, a solitary figure, lips pursed, sitting in a corner of his favourite coffee house during the later mornings. For others, creativity seemed to be linked to specific disorders of the brain. The Russian composer Dmitri Shostakovich claims in his biography that he was able to hear music inside his head simply by tilting it to one side. This might have been because Shostakovich had a fragment of shrapnel embedded inside his skull from his activities in the first world war. When he tilted his head, this shell splinter prodded and stimulated his brain's auditory cortex.

While Johannes Brahms seems to have shunned company and imbibed caffeine to achieve inspiration, other creative people have sought more extreme methods to engage their creative brain systems – and to disengage their normally dominant rational brain. Samuel Taylor Coleridge, for instance, wrote his epic poem *Kubla Khan* under the influence of laudanum. Not exactly a genius, fellow opiate-devotee William Burroughs is said to have created the manuscript for *The Naked Lunch* (1959) in such a drug-suffused state that he could not recall having written it. And frankly to me it reads like it. The painter Francis Bacon deliberately did without sleep and food in order to enter a heightened state of creativity.

Others eschew drugs and deprivation in favour of the fluid 'right-brain' thought processes of the dream state. The Nobel-winning physicist Niels Bohr famously arrived at his understandings of atomic structure at a point when his daytime ponderings were getting him nowhere. Exhausted and frustrated, he fell asleep and had a dream that featured a racecourse in which the horses ran in lanes corresponding to the orbit of electrons. The chemist Friedrich Kekulé describes how he dreamed two important observations on structural chemistry. The first is his description of the basic linking of the carbon atom:

> During my stay in London [1854–56] I resided for a considerable time in Clapham Road in the neighbourhood of the Common … One fine summer evening I was returning by the last omnibus … I fell into a reverie, and lo, the atoms were gamboling before my eyes! Whenever, hitherto, these diminutive beings had appeared to me, they had always been in motion; but up to that time I had never been able to discern the nature of their motion. Now, however, I saw how, frequently, two smaller atoms united to form a pair; how a larger one embraced two smaller ones; how still larger ones kept hold of three or even four of the smaller; while the whole kept whirling in giddy dance. I saw how the larger ones formed a chain, dragging the smaller ones after them, but only at the ends of the chain … The cry of the conductor, 'Clapham Road', awakened me from my dreaming …

Hardly the usual famous man sitting on the Clapham omnibus. A second important vision appeared to Kekulé in 1862, and led him to understand the benzene ring, the foundation of so much modern organic chemistry:

> … I was sitting writing at my text book, but the work did not progress; my thoughts were elsewhere. I turned my chair to the fire and dozed. Again the atoms were gamboling before my eyes. This time the smaller groups kept modestly in the background. My mental eye, rendered more acute by repeated visions of this kind, could now distinguish larger structures, of manifold conformation: long rows, sometimes more closely fitted together; all turning and twisting in snakelike motion. But look! What was that? One of the snakes had seized hold of its own tail, and the form whirled mockingly before my eyes. As if by a flash of lightning I awoke; and this time also I spent the rest of the night in working out the consequences of the

hypothesis. Let us learn to dream, gentlemen, then perhaps we shall find the truth . . .

Bruce Miller at the University of California, San Francisco, is particularly interested in the ability of some autistic people to recall remarkable detail – like the British man Stephen Wiltshire, who was able from an early age to create fantastically detailed and accurate drawings, such as his remarkable rendition of the Victoria and Albert Museum. It seems that brain scans of these 'autist savants' revealed one common facet of brain architecture: they all had impaired function within the left anterior temporal lobe. Miller has argued that, because of this impaired left-brain function, savants have superior access to the creative resources of the right brain. Dr Allan Snyder, from Sydney, Australia, who has gained a great deal of attention in the press for his views, has taken these ideas a bit further in an attempt to see what happens if we can train a normal brain to shut down its analytical functions and draw more heavily on the right brain. He used a technique called Transcranial Magnetic Stimulation, which involves encircling the skull with a series of powerful magnets. TMS is an experimental treatment currently being tested as an alternative to electroconvulsive shock therapy in patients with depression. Although not yet part of mainstream medical treatment, he claims some encouraging signs of its efficacy. When applied to a normal brain, the strong magnetic fields from the TMS device act to inhibit or shut down certain regions of the brain. Snyder asked volunteers, while fitted with a TMS device, to undertake a battery of tests, including drawing, mathematical reasoning, memory and looking for errors in texts. His experiments showed an average 30 per cent improvement on the tests. Subjects reported becoming more alert, more attuned to the fine detail of the world around them. Their drawings reflected this heightened awareness. Snyder's experiments have yet to unearth a mathematical or artistic genius, and as far as I am aware have not appeared in the peer review literature, so caution in interpreting these results is needed.

Not so rare at all

We all pick up cues from our environment without necessarily being fully conscious of what we are doing. Perhaps you, like me, have found yourself in a dubious part of a town and suddenly felt alert to a possible danger. This is a skill we all use in our daily lives. Driving along a busy stretch of road, we can tell – without exactly knowing *how* we can tell – which pedestrian is likely to suddenly sprint in front of us. Walking alone down a darkened street, we can tell by the body movement of the person approaching us whether they are likely to pose a problem to our personal safety. We have an innate ability to sense what is going to happen. And when we analyse our thought processes later on, it becomes clear to us how we reached our conclusion. Body language, a person's manner and speed of walking, the direction and intensity of their gaze – all of these are very good indicators of someone else's intentions, fair or foul. But what is interesting is that, in so many circumstances, we act on the information received *before* we have a conscious awareness of why we are acting. Our brain knows before we know.

We looked at this phenomenon briefly when dealing with the faculties of perception and attention. It has been shown that top sportsmen have only marginally faster reaction times than the general population. What lends them a unique advantage is their ability to anticipate, to modify their behaviour according to incoming information, without consciousness getting in the way and slowing it down.

The crucial feature of this ability for athletes is that it remains 'buried' in the lower motor portions of the brain. When we practise something new, as we have seen, the cortex and the basal ganglia work in unison. But over time, the higher, 'thinking' regions of the brain drop out of the equation, freeing themselves up for new activities. The process becomes embedded in the motor regions of the brain. If consciousness for any reason re-enters the equation, there is a slowing down, and an attendant lack of fluidity in the execution of the task.

Perhaps this has happened to you – you for some reason find yourself thinking about an activity you have been performing effortlessly for years. Suddenly, you lose confidence. You make mistakes, reinforcing your lack of confidence. Merely by thinking about how you do something, you forget how to do it.

Many sportsmen live in terror of this phenomenon, which some call 'the yips'. The darts-player Eric Bristow found his playing abilities paralysed for ten years due to an attack of the yips. It is thought that stress may cause performers to suffer a loss of confidence. Accordingly they become more self-conscious, thereby putting a once-fluid skill under deliberate scrutiny. Thinking, in short, seems to be one of the worst things you can do. The golfer Severiano Ballesteros was once asked what was going through his mind just before he struck the million-dollar shot. To which he calmly replied, 'Nothing.'

Hardly surprisingly, one of the ways sportsmen ensure that a skill remains firmly embedded in their motor cortices is by regular practice. As we know, the neurons of the brain fire in the same pattern whether we are performing a task or whether we are just going through the motions in our heads. For that reason, many sports psychologists now teach visualization techniques to their charges. The regular exercise of the related neural pathways cements the ability within the lower, unconscious regions of the brain.

Sportsmen are not the only people who rely on the ability to know without knowing. Devotees of detective fiction will know all about the intuitive 'hunch', that innate precognitive sense that keeps the hero pursuing his quarry, even when his gun and his badge have been taken away and he's been threatened with a lifetime of directing traffic. The television series *Columbo*, starring Peter Falk, was far more concerned with the hunch effect than it was with the solving of a crime. Each episode began with the murder taking place in front of our eyes – the satisfaction for the viewers lay in watching Columbo prove that his intuition was correct.

Fiction aside, cognitive scientists are convinced that intuition – the ability to direct our behaviour according to unconscious cues – plays an important role in the way professionals such as hospital trauma teams, policemen and firemen do their jobs. Cognitive psychologist Gary Klein has made a study of people who have to make split-second decisions in the course of their daily lives.[121] His research has led him to conclude that we often disregard the power of the intuitive hunch or gut instinct, preferring to teach people to rely on lengthy, slower, and sometimes far less efficient codes of action.

Klein was led to this conclusion, in part, through his dealings with a fire commander who insisted that he had extra-sensory perception (ESP). The commander related one key event that had convinced him to believe in his paranormal abilities. He and his crew had encountered a fire at the back of a house. Standing in the living room, he and his men doused the fire – which seemed to be in the kitchen – with water. But the flames did not recede. At this point, the commander reported that he had the sense that something was very wrong. Without knowing why, he ordered everyone to get out of the house. Just seconds after they did, the floor where they were standing collapsed into a burning basement. Had he not had this hunch, he and his men might all have died.

Seen in retrospect, this commander issued an order because the fire he was tackling did not match his expectations. If it was solely centred at the back of the house, why did it not recede when doused with water? There were other indications that all was not as it should be – the levels of heat where the firemen were standing were far more intense than they should expect from a small kitchen fire, again more consistent with a fire burning down below. Hot fires also make a lot of noise, but this fire was eerily quiet – because the real blaze was happening below them, muffled by the floor.

Klein continued to interview legions of veteran firefighters, and began to observe something crucial about the way human intuition works. Over time, the firefighters developed a personal 'archive' of different fires, how it felt and smelt to be near them, and how they could be expected to behave. Each time they encounter a new fire, they delve into this archive to find associations that match, and which then tell them how to behave. In other words, intuition is not some paranormal ability to see the future, but a technique of learning what to look for in a given environment, and of doing so without the conscious brain getting in the way. The supposedly psychic fire commander merely knew what signs to look for when encountering a fire, and when he detected an anomaly, he knew that it meant trouble.

The same ability has been observed in neonatal intensive-care nurses, who often have to make split-second decisions to save the lives of newborns. When premature babies develop an infection, the results can be devastating – sickness spreads like wild fire throughout the tiny body, resulting in rapid death. For that reason, skilled nurses have to become intuitively adept at spotting the early signs of infection so that they can act in time to save the baby's life. When interviewed by one of Klein's research colleagues, such nurses would say that they didn't entirely know how they knew, they 'just did'. But pressed further, it seems that these experienced nurses had built up a working archive of extremely subtle clues. For instance, the complexion of a premature baby in the early stages of infection would fade rapidly from pink to greeny-grey. They might cry frequently, yet suddenly become listless and lethargic. Their feeding patterns would become abnormal, their abdomens distended. But interestingly, half of the symptoms used by the neonatal nurses were not mentioned in any of the medical literature. They based their decisions on knowledge they had acquired themselves, and they applied it almost without knowing they were doing so.

Many doctors have had some experience of an intuitive decision taken under extreme pressure. One dire emergency I remember as a young surgeon in a rural hospital was when I was called to casualty to see a semi-conscious unmarried woman of twenty-two. She looked close to death and had a low, almost unrecordable blood pressure. She had been picked up by ambulancemen and there was nobody with her from whom to find out how she came to be in this state. She was deadly pale, her abdomen felt doughy and mildly distended. The likely explanation seemed that she was bleeding internally. And as I watched, she slipped into unconsciousness. Speed was clearly critical – no time to wait for tests here. There aren't many conditions that can put a young woman's life in such jeopardy in this way; an ectopic pregnancy is probably the most common. So simply on the odds, it seemed likely that she had a pregnancy in a fallopian tube – such things can bleed catastrophically. There was no time to lose if I was right, but it's a big decision to rush a person to an operating theatre and open the abdomen without even allowing time to scrub up properly. But the anaesthetist was doubtful about giving her an anaesthetic with her blood pressure, as it was by now unrecordable. So I opened the abdomen while he was still arguing – again not an easy decision to come to even on the spur of the moment. A huge amount of clotted and unclotted blood poured out from the open abdomen – so at least that part of my diagnosis was correct. But on looking at the fallopian tubes, both were entirely normal and there was no sign of a bleeding pregnancy anywhere in her pelvis. At the back of my mind was the thought that, very rarely indeed, an ectopic pregnancy can implant in the abdomen on the bowel. But this degree of bleeding was extraordinary for the very rare possibility of a bowel implant. I'd never seen it, and not consciously heard of it – but in a flash came the thought that with this degree of bleeding the liver might be the even rarer culprit. The incision was extended, a rapid search made – and there was the ruptured eight-week pregnancy on the liver. The pregnancy was quickly grasped and removed, a heavy pack was hastily inserted around the bleeding site, and miraculously we could immediately start to feel her pulse, at first ever so faintly.

The extra sense

So human intuition would seem to be less of a mysterious 'sixth sense' than a super-efficient means of evaluating information from the five senses we do possess. Nevertheless, the search for this elusive faculty goes ever onwards. Some researchers believe the sixth sense is a forgotten 'homing' instinct – still active in our animal ancestors, but now dormant in ourselves.

The argument for a human sense of direction comes from the fact that there appears to be a mismatch within the allocation of our senses. Taste and smell could be said to act as a discrete pair – because they operate in the same way. Things to be tasted and smelt have first to be dissolved in water, usually the water in our mouths or nasal passages, and the actual processing of what they represent is done through chemical interaction. Meanwhile there is one difference between taste and smell – we have to put things in our mouths to taste them, but we can smell things at a distance.

We can draw the same parallels between hearing and touch. These operate through mechanical forces only – they both pick up meaning through motion. Touch, like taste, requires contact, whereas hearing, like smell, can be done at a distance.

Creating this set of parallels leaves sight on its own. We could argue that, like hearing and smell, it is a 'distant' sense – one not requiring contact for processing to take place. So could we be overlooking a natural contender for the sixth sense – one that works through contact? And if so what could it do?

Some scientists have pointed out that certain homing creatures, like butterflies and homing pigeons, find their way through space thanks to tiny magnetic-field-sensing materials inside their bodies. Pigeons find their way thanks to an in-built compass, a pod of magnetite crystals situated close to their skulls. Monarch butterflies are liberally doused with a fine, magnetically charged network of wing fibres. But we humans have no such faculty. If there is a sixth sense that equips some people to find their way more efficiently, it is very unevenly distributed throughout the human population, and seems to have no obvious markers in the body.

Others have suggested that the sixth sense may be more of a 'sense 5a', a refinement of the brain's olfactory powers. I have already mentioned the vomeronasal organ which contains receptors sensitive to chemicals that the nose itself seems unable to detect – like pheromones. A team led by Catherine Dulac at Harvard University has been able to isolate a gene in rats and mice that enables them to sense out pheromones.[122] Humans also have the gene, but with mutations that appear to render it useless. Yet, you will recall that humans can be influenced by pheromones, without being aware that they can detect them. This is thought to be one of the reasons why the menstrual cycles of women synchronize when they live in a communal situation. But if we haven't got the genes to detect pheromones, how is it that we can be influenced by them? Possibly, the human nose, though a crude device compared to the olfactory systems of many animals, is able to detect certain 'stronger' pheromones.

So there are interesting indications that we humans might, or indeed should, be endowed with a sixth sense of direction, or for detecting pheromones, but no concrete evidence that we are. That doesn't stop much extremely 'soft' research. From the days of Isaiah to the horoscope in your daily paper, we humans have been fascinated by the possibility that we can glimpse the future. Dean Radin, of the Boundary Institute in Los Altos, California, is currently engaged in a global study into ESP. Using online tests on his website *www.boundaryinstitute.org*, Radin has studied the results of over half a million trials, from 4,000 people in fifty-seven countries. His findings are certainly interesting, at least to the more gullible. On one particular test, where participants have to guess which of five cards conceals a picture image, top scorers get it right 48 per cent of the time over twenty-five trials. That may not seem terribly impressive – but the odds against that happening are, it is claimed, 2,669 to 1. A similarly small, apparently statistically significant result has erratically been shown when people attempt to influence the generation of random numbers with their thoughts.

I am extremely cynical about most of the stories of ESP, psychic ability and luck, as is the psychologist Dr Richard Wiseman. He describes how he conducted an experiment to see if there were individuals who could be genuinely regarded as lucky people.[123] Using the mechanism of a television show watched by around 13 million people, he asked the viewers to predict the winning numbers in the next UK National Lottery. During transmission, viewers who felt themselves to be unduly lucky or unlucky were requested to contact the TV show. Dr Wiseman expected just a few hundred to phone; an estimated million calls were received. With this huge number, only the first 1,000 callers could be sent a questionnaire. On the form they received, they were asked to state whether they classified themselves as naturally lucky or unlucky and whether they had psychic ability. The responses showed that, between them, these viewers intended to buy around a total of 2,000 tickets. When the researchers reviewed the data, they found that certain of the forty-nine possible numbers were frequently chosen by 'lucky' people, but avoided by 'unlucky' ones. Richard Wiseman states that his analysis showed the best shot seemed to be 1, 7, 17, 29, 37 and 44. After agonizing about the ethics of this, for the first and only time in his life, he says, he bought a ticket himself. Later that week, the draw was broadcast and the result was 2, 13, 19, 21, 32 and 45. Richard Wiseman had not managed a single number. Had the 'lucky' people done any better? Thirty-six of all the respondents had won money, four of them winning the princely sum of £58. The winnings were equally split between lucky and unlucky people. On average both unlucky and lucky people bought three tickets each, matched one number only and lost equal sums.

My cynicism about psychic ability might itself have something to do with the chemical make-up of my brain. Peter Brugger, of Zurich University Hospital in Switzerland, took twenty believers in the paranormal and twenty confirmed sceptics, and asked the two groups to try to make out faces in a sequence that included both discernible and scrambled faces and other objects. He then repeated the exercise with words – some of which were real words, others scrambled versions of words and others just sounds. Brugger found that the believers were far more likely to say they had seen faces and heard real words when they had not. In an attempt to understand what might be the crucial differences in brain states between these groups, Brugger gave l-dopa – synthesized dopamine – to both. As we know high levels of dopamine are implicated in schizophrenia and mania – both of which can include a tendency to see the world as inherently meaningful and replete with coincidences. Brugger found that, when given dopamine, the sceptics replicated the results of the believers. Meanwhile, the extra dopamine had no discernible effects on the

353

results of the believer. So perhaps we should talk less about the existence of the paranormal and more about people's differing capacities to believe in it.

Earlier on, in Chapter 3, I mentioned the findings of a Swiss neuro-surgeon who, when operating on a patient with epilepsy, seemed to have found a possible neurological basis for the so-called out-of-body experience. This sensation of being outside one's body is particularly central to the accounts of some people who have, or claim to have, experience of what it feels like to die on the operating table. The near-death experience is a controversial area for brain science. If everything that we call 'mind' is a product of the working human brain, how can it be that some attributes of 'mind' can seemingly endure when the brain is no longer working?

Scientists and surgeons alike have been interested in this question ever since general anaesthesia has been in use. From full-blown accounts of meetings with the Maker to more mundane incidences of reporting conversations between the surgical team, there is a wealth of evidence to suggest that some aspects of consciousness cannot be put to sleep easily.

In one study, done in the 1980s, patients 'listened' to informative audiotapes while unconscious, and then they were tested for general knowledge after the procedure. Their scores rose from 37 per cent to 62 per cent subsequent to the unconscious learning experience. A number of scientists now believe that it's quite possible for the brain to absorb information while it is functionally unconscious. However, it has also been noted that any 'learning' that takes place seems to dissipate within a few hours after regaining consciousness. Also it seems that the deeper the level of anaesthesia, the patchier the memories will be. This supports the view that rather than there being some sharp conscious/unconscious switch within the brain, there is actually a subtler spectrum of differing states – ranging from fully alert at one end to dead at the other. The closer we are to waking consciousness, the more likely we are to absorb information.

But of course there is a great difference between these poorly controlled experiments and the near-death experience. By its very definition, this latter state is one in which the brain is not deemed to be at all close to waking. Professor Bruce Greyson, of the Division of Personality Studies at the University of Virginia, has subjected the near-death experience to extensive study, and by analysing the accounts of hundreds of individuals, has come up with a list of common attributes.[124] Near-death experiences, for instance, include a sensation of accelerated thought processes. People undergo a change in emotional state – most commonly reporting feelings of peace and bliss. Furthermore, they report abnormal spatial experiences, such as being outside of their bodies. In addition, they commonly report paranormal sensations, transcending the normal boundaries of time and space – such that they can see into the future or the past, or witness events outside the range of their sensory apparatus. But the mere fact that most near-death experience accounts are similar is convincing evidence for some that they merely arise from the chemistry of the brain.

Dr Susan Blackmore, psychologist at the University of the West of England, offers the view that the near-death experience is merely a product of the potentially dying brain. For instance, the commonly reported sensation of being in a tunnel and proceeding towards a pinprick of bright light simply represents the random firing of neurons within the visual cortex. The feelings of peace and bliss are a product of endorphins, released in response to the massive physical trauma of bodily death.

Scientists studying the near-death experience admit that their endeavours are thwarted by one obvious factor. Like consciousness, death is not some instant process, but a smudgier continuum of several stages, between which the boundaries are blurred. So how can we tell where the near-death experience fits in – does it occur as the brain loses consciousness, and if so, at which precise point during this loss-process? Does it occur while the brain is effectively 'dead', or when the brain starts to work again? Sleep studies, as we have seen, indicate that every night we shuttle backwards and forwards across the continuum between being close to waking and being 'dead to the world'. It might be the same for the dying brain – at certain points along its journey to absolute oblivion, there might be moments where it becomes more and less alert. There might also be differences due to individual peculiarities of neural wiring. As we have seen repeatedly throughout this book, no two brains will ever be completely alike. This in turn could mean that in some individuals certain brain functions, like hearing and memory, remain 'switched on' at lower levels of consciousness.

To date, research into near-death experiences has come up with no hard and fast answers. For every neuroscientist who steadfastly claims there can be no consciousness without a brain that is at some level still alive, there will be others who wish to storm the fortress, for reasons both noble and vainglorious. For everyone who draws comfort from the notion that every corner of existence can be rendered meaningful by the laws of science, there are others who wish to believe in mystery, in another dimension for which man's 'three score years and ten' is but a shallow rehearsal. And such divisions are evidence of the most enduringly beautiful aspect of the human mind. We've all got one, but how very differently each of us puts it to use.

But when we talk about creativity, we are essentially referring to a very rare subset of human abilities. If we were to sit down and draw up a list of people who had become famous for their extraordinary abilities, it would comprise only a tiny percentage of the total population. The focus of this book is the brain that exists inside all of us, not the rare exceptions. And there is much evidence to suggest that every brain is endowed with a myriad of extraordinary abilities. Each of us, in our daily lives, has the ability to anticipate what is about to happen, to unconsciously pick up cues from our environment and direct our behaviour accordingly. From the sportsman who knows which way an incoming ball will hit his bat, to the tourist who senses he may have strayed into a bad neighbourhood, to the fireman who knows when to get out of a collapsing building, to the artist communicating with us through his painting or his music, or the scientist solving the problems of the human mind, we are all truly remarkable.

References

1 Fried, I., et al., 'Electric current stimulates laughter.' *Nature* (1998), **391**:650

2 Gur, R.C., et al., 'An fMRI study of sex differences in regional activation to a verbal and a spatial task.' *Brain and Language* (2000), **74**:157–70

3 Lane, R.D., et al., 'Neuroanatomical correlates of pleasant and unpleasant emotion.' *Neuropsychologia* (1997), **35**:1437–44

4 Blanke, O., Ortigue, S., Landis, T., Seeck, M., 'Stimulating illusory own-body perceptions.' *Nature* (2002), **419**:269–70

5 Franzini, Louis R., and Grossberg, John, *Eccentric and Bizarre Behaviours* (John Wiley & Sons, 1995)

6 Blackmore, S., 'Crossing the chasm of consciousness.' *Trends in Cognitive Science* (2002), **6**:276–7

7 Sampaio, E., Maris, S., Bach-y-Rita, P., 'Brain plasticity: "visual" acuity of blind persons via the tongue.' *Brain Research* (2001), **908**:204-7

8 Leamey, C., 'Development and plasticity of cortical areas and networks.' *Nature Reviews Neuroscience* (2002), **2**:251-62

9 McCoy, N., and Pitino, L., 'Pheromonal influences on sociosexual behavior in young women.' *Physiology and Behavior* (2002), **75**:367–75

10 Luo, M., Fee, M.S., Katz, L.C., 'Encoding pheromonal signals in the accessory olfactory bulb of behaving mice.' *Science* (2003), **299**:1196–201

11 Field, T., 'Preterm infant massage therapy studies: an American approach.' *Seminars in Neonatology* (2002), **7**:487–94

12 Livingstone, M.S., Rosen, G.D., Drislane, F.W., Galaburda, A.M., 'Physiological and anatomical evidence for a magnocellular defect in

developmental dyslexia.' *Proceedings of the National Academy of Sciences USA* (1991), **88**:7943–7

13   Tallal, P., Merzenich, M.M., Miller, S., Jenkins, W., 'Language learn-ing impairments: integrating basic science, technology, and remediation.' *Experimental Brain Research* (1998), **123**:210–19

14   Simons, D.J., and Chabris, C.F., 'Gorillas in our midst: sustained in-attentional blindness for dynamic events.' *Perception* (1999), **28**:1059–74

15   Strange, B.A., Henson, R.N., Friston, K.J., Dolan, R.J., 'Brain mechanisms for detecting perceptual, semantic, and emotional deviance.' *NeuroImage* (2000), **12**:425–33

16   LaBerge, D., and Buchsbaum, M.S., 'Positron emission tomographic measurements of pulvinar activity during an attention task.' *Journal of Neuroscience* (1990), **10**: 613–19

17   Ramnani, N., and Passingham, R.E., 'Changes in the human brain during rhythm learning.' *Journal of Cognitive Neuroscience* (2001), **13**:952–66

18   Cardinal, R.N., et al., 'Impulsive choice induced in rats by lesions of the nucleus accumbens core.' *Science* (2001), **292**:2499–501

19   Driver, J., and Frith, C., 'Shifting baselines in attention research.' *Nature Reviews Neuroscience* (2000), **1**:147–8

20   Schwartz, S., and Maquet, P., 'Sleep imaging and the neuro-psychological assessment of dreams.' *Trends in Cognitive Sciences* (2002), **6**:23–30

21   Benedetti, F., et al., 'Influence of a functional polymorphism within the promoter of the serotonin transporter gene on the effects of total sleep deprivation in bipolar depression.' *American Journal of Psychiatry* (1999), **156**:1450–2

22   Revonsuo, A., and Valli, K., 'The reinterpretation of dreams: an evolutionary hypothesis of the function of dreaming.' *Psykologia* (2002), **35**:472–84

23   Jung, C., *Memories, Dreams, Reflections* (Collins, 1962)

24   Sedikides, C., and Skowronski, J., 'The symbolic self in evolutionary context.' *Personality and Social Psychology Review* (1997), **1**:80–102

25   Baron-Cohen, S., 'The development of a theory of mind in autism: deviance and delay?' *Psychiatric Clinics of North America* (1991), **14**:33–51

26   Peskin, J., 'Ruse and representations: on children's ability to conceal information.' *Developmental Psychology* (1992), **28**:84–9

27   'Self-awareness and the frontal lobes: a neuropsychological perspective.' In Strauss, J., and Goethals, G.R., eds, *The Self: Inter-disciplinary Approaches* (Springer Verlag, 1991)

28   Pinker, S., *How the Mind Works* (W.W. Norton, New York, 1997)

29   Libet, B., et al., 'Responses of human somatosensory cortex to stimuli below threshold for conscious sensation.' *Science* (1967), **158**: 1597–600

30 Adolphs, R., Tranel, D., Damasio, H., Damasio, A., 'Impaired recognition of emotion in facial expressions following bilateral damage to the human amygdala.' *Nature* (1994), **372**:669–72

31 LeDoux, J.E., *The Emotional Brain* (Simon and Schuster, New York, 1996)

32 LeDoux, Joseph, *Synaptic Self: How Our Brains Become Who We Are* (Viking, New York, 2002)

33 Damasio, A., *Descartes Error: Emotion, Reason and the Human Brain* (Picador, 1995)

34 Dimberg, U., 'Unconscious facial reactions to emotional facial expressions.' *Psychological Science* (2000), **11**:86–9

35 Rankin, A.M., and Philip, P.J., *Central African Journal of Medicine* (1963), **9**:167–70

36 Calder, A.J., et al., 'Reading the mind from eye gaze.' *Neuropsychologia* (2002), **40**:1129–38

37 Hooper, J., and Teresi, D., *The 3-Pound Universe* (Dell Publishing Co. Inc., New York, 1986)

38 Mayberg, H.S., et al., 'Cingulate function in depression: a potential predictor of treatment response.' *NeuroReport* (1997), **8**:1057–61

39 Mongeau, R., Miller, G.A., Chiang, E., Anderson, D.J., 'Neural correlates of competing fear behaviors evoked by an innately aversive stimulus.' *Journal of Neuroscience* (2003), **23**:3855–68

40 Rachman, S., and Seligman, M.E., 'Unprepared phobias: "be prepared".' *Behaviour Research and Therapy* (1976), **14**:333–8

41 Öhman, A., and Soares, J.J., 'On the automatic nature of phobic fear: conditioned electrodermal responses to masked fear-relevant stimuli.' *Journal of Abnormal Psychology* (1993), **102**:121–32

42 Select Committee on Science and Technology, House of Lords, *Cannabis: the scientific and medical evidence*. Session 1997–8, 9th report. The Stationery Office: HL paper 15

43 Hatzidimitriou, G., et al., 'Altered serotonin innervation patterns in the forebrain of monkeys treated with MDMA seven years previously: factors influencing abnormal recovery.' *Journal of Neuroscience* (1999), **19**:5096–107

44 Hoffmann, A., *LSD – My Problem Child* (J.P. Tacher, 1983)

45 Damasio, H., et al., 'The return of Phineas Gage: clues about the brain from the skull of a famous patient.' *Science* (1994), **264**:1102–5

46 McGivern, R.F., et al., 'Cognitive efficiency on a match to sample task decreases at the onset of puberty in children.' *Brain Cognition* (2002), **50**:73–89

47 Killgore, W.D., Oki, M., Yurgelun-Todd, D.A., 'Sex-specific developmental changes in amygdala responses to affective faces.' *NeuroReport* (2001), **12**:427–33

48 Newberg, A., et al., 'The measurement of regional cerebral blood flow

during the complex cognitive task of meditation: a preliminary SPECT study.' *Psychiatry Research Neuroimaging* (2001), **106**:113–22

49   Lawrence, K., et al., 'Interpreting gaze in Turner syndrome: impaired sensitivity to intention and emotion, but preservation of social cueing.' *Neuropsychologia* (2003), **41**:894–905

50   LeVay, S., 'A difference in hypothalamic structure between hetero-sexual and homosexual men.' *Science* (1991), **253**:1034–7

51   Kuhl, P.K., 'A new view of language acquisition.' *Proceedings of the National Academy of Science USA* (2000), **97**:11850–7

52   Hollich, G.J., et al., 'Breaking the language barrier: an emergentist coalition model for the origins of word learning.' *Monographs of the Society for Research in Child Development* (2000), **65**:1–123

53   Huttenlocher, J., 'Language input and language growth.' *Preventive Medicine* (1998), **27**:195–9

54   Hasselmo, M.E., and Bower, J.M., 'Acetylcholine and memory.' *Trends in Neuroscience* (1993), **16**:218–22

55   Kida, S., et al., 'CREB required for the stability of new and reactivated fear memories.' *Nature Neuroscience* (1998), **5**:348–55

56   Ishai, A., Haxby, J.V., Ungerleider, L.G., 'Visual imagery of famous faces: effects of memory and attention revealed by f-MRI.' *NeuroImage* (2002), **17**:1729–41

57   Karni, A., Tanne, D., Rubenstein, B.S., Askenasy, J.J.M., Sagi, D., 'Dependence on REM sleep of overnight improvement of a perceptual skill.' *Science* (1994), **265**:679–82

58   Mednick, S., et al., 'The restorative effect of naps on perceptual deterioration.' *Nature Neuroscience* (2002), **5**:677–81

59   Zajonc, R.B., Wilson, W.R., Rajecki, D.W., 'Affiliation and social discrimination produced by brief exposure in day-old domestic chicks.' *Animal Behaviour* (1975), **23**:131–8

60   Brewin, C.R., and Beaton, A., 'Thought suppression, intelligence, and working memory capacity.' *Behaviour Research and Therapy* (2002), **40**:923–30

61   Genoux, D., et al., 'Protein phosphatase 1 is a molecular constraint on learning and memory.' *Nature* (2002), **418**:970–5

62   Logan, J.M., et al., 'Under-recruitment and nonselective recruitment: dissociable neural mechanisms associated with aging.' *Neuron* (2002), **33**:827–40

63   Inouye, S.K., et al., 'Cognitive performance in a high-functioning community-dwelling elderly population.' *Journal of Gerontology* (1993), **48**:146–51

64   Pervin, L.A, John, O.P., eds, 'A five-factor theory of personality.' *Handbook of Personality: Theory and Research* (Guilford Press, 1999)

65   Gazzaniga, M., and Heatherton, T., *Psychological Science* (W.W. Norton, 2003)

66 Johnson, D.L., et al., 'Cerebral blood flow and personality: a positron emission tomography study.' *American Journal of Psychiatry* (1999), **156**:252–7

67 Canli, T., et al., 'Amygdala response to happy faces as a function of extraversion.' *Science* (2002), **296**:2191

68 Boissy, A., and Boissou, M.F., 'Effects of androgen treatment on behavioural and physiological responses of heifers to fear-inducing situations.' *Hormones and Behaviour* (1984), **28**:66–83

69 Plusquellec, P., and Boissou, M.F., 'Behavioural characteristics of two dairy breeds of cows selected (Herens) or not (Brune des Alpes) for fighting and dominance ability.' *Applied Animal Behaviour Science* (2001), **72**:1–21

70 O'Connor, D.B., Archer, J., Hair, W.M., Fu, F.C., 'Activational effects of testosterone on cognitive function in men.' *Neuropsychologia* (2001), **39**:1385–94

71 Larkin, P., *Required Writing: Miscellaneous Pieces 1955–1982* (Faber & Faber, London, 1983)

72 Taylor, S.E., et al., 'Portrait of the self-enhancer: well adjusted and well liked or maladjusted and friendless?' *Journal of Personality and Social Psychology* (2003), **84**:165–76

73 Taylor, S.E., and Brown, J.D., 'Illusion and well-being: a social psychological perspective on mental health.' *Psychological Bulletin* (1988), **103**:193–210

74 Hagen, M.C., et al., 'Somatosensory processing in the human inferior prefrontal cortex.' *Journal of Neurophysiology* (1988), **88**:1400–6

75 Larkin, P., *Required Writing: Miscellaneous Pieces 1955–1982* (Faber & Faber, London, 1983)

76 Enoch, M-A., et al., 'Genetic origins of anxiety in women: a role for a functional catechol-O-methyltransferase polymorphism.' *Psychiatric Genetics* (2003), **13**:33–41

77 Bowley, M.P., Drevets, W.C., Ongur, D., Price, J.L., 'Low glial numbers in the amygdala in major depressive disorder.' *Biological Psychiatry* (2002), **52**:404–12

78 Nesse, R.M., 'Is depression an adaptation?' *Archives of General Psychiatry* (2000), **57**:14–20

79 Bloom, H., *Shakespeare: The Invention of the Human* (Fourth Estate, 1999)

80 Badcock, C., *PsychoDarwinism* (HarperCollins, 1994)

81 Iacoboni, M., et al., 'Reafferent copies of imitated actions in the right superior temporal cortex. *Proceedings of the National Academy of Science USA* (2001), **98**:13995–9

82 Penton-Voak, I.S., et al. (1999), 'Menstrual cycle alters face preference.' *Nature* (2000), **399**:741–2

83 Clark, R.D., and Hatfield, E., 'General differences in receptivity to sexual offers.' *Journal of Psychology and Human Sexuality* (1989), **2**:39–55

84 Montgomery, M.J., and Sorrell, G.T., 'Love and dating experience in early and middle adolescence: grade and gender comparisons.' *Journal of Adolescence* (1998), **21**:677–89

85 Autkrystof, Doris, *Amedeo Modigliani 1884–1920: The Poetry of Seeing (Basic Art)* (Taschen America Llc, 2000)

86 Thorne, F., et al., 'Effects of putative male pheromones on female ratings of male attractiveness: influence of oral contraceptives and the menstrual cycle.' *Neuroendocrinology Letters* (2002), **23**:291–7

87 Grammer, K., 'Androsterone: a male pheromone?' *Ethology and Sociobiology* (1995), **14**:201–7

88 Cutler, W.B., Friedmann, E., McCoy, N.L., 'Pheromonal influences on sociosexual behaviour in men.' *Archives of Sexual Behaviour* (1998), **27**:1–13

89 Young, L.J., Lim, M.M., Gingrich, B., Insel, T.R., 'Cellular mechanisms of social attachment.' *Hormones and Behavior* (2001), **40**:133–8

90 O'Doherty, J., et al., 'Beauty in a smile: the role of medial orbitofrontal cortex in facial attractiveness.' *Neuropsychologia* (2003), **41**:147–550

91 Bartels, A., and Zeki, S., 'The neural basis of romantic love.' *NeuroReport* (2000), **11**:3829–34

92 Kobak, R.R., and Hazan, C., 'Attachment in marriage: effects of security and accuracy of working models.' *Journal of Personality and Social Psychology* (1991), **60**:861–9

93 Fisher, H., et al., 'Review. The neural mechanisms of mate choice: a hypothesis.' *Neuroendocrinology Letters* (2002), **23** Suppl, 4:92–7

94 Ferguson, J.N., et al., 'Social amnesia in mice lacking the oxytocin gene.' *Nature Neuroscience* (2000), **25**:284–8

95 Turner, R.A., et al., 'Preliminary research on plasma oxytocin in normal cycling women: investigating emotion and interpersonal distress.' *Psychiatry* (1999), **62**:97–113

96 Winston, J.S., Strange, B.A., O'Doherty, J., Dolan, R.J., 'Automatic and intentional brain responses during evaluation of trustworthiness of faces.' *Nature Neuroscience* (2002), **5**:277–83

97 Castelli, F., Frith, C., Happe, F., Frith, U., 'Autism, Asperger syndrome and brain mechanisms for the attribution of mental states to animated shapes.' *Brain* (2002), **125**:1839–49

98 Epley, N., and Dunning, D., 'Feeling "holier than thou": are self-serving assessments produced by errors in self- or social prediction?' *Journal of Personality and Social Psychology* (2002), **79**:861–75

99 Langleben, D.D., et al., 'Brain activity during simulated deception: an event-related functional magnetic resonance study.' *NeuroImage* (2002), **15**:727–32

100 Lee, T.M., et al., 'Neural correlates of response inhibition for behavioral regulation in humans assessed by functional magnetic resonance imaging.' *Neuroscience Letters* (2001), **309**:109–12

101 Greene, J.D., et al., 'An fMRI investigation of emotional engagement in moral judgment.' *Science* (2001), **293**:2105–8

102 Diamond, M.C., et al., 'On the brain of a scientist: Albert Einstein.' *Experimental Neurology* (1985), **88**:198–204

103 Witelson, S.F., Kigar, D.L., Harvey, T., 'The exceptional brain of Albert Einstein.' *Lancet* (1999), **353**:2149–53

104 Cattell, R., *Abilities: Their Structure, Growth and Action* (Houghton Mifflin, Boston, 1971)

105 Gardner, H., *Frames of Mind: The Theory of Multiple Intelligences* (Basic Books, 1983)

106 Gray, J.R., Chabris, C.F., Braver, T.S., 'Neural mechanisms of general fluid intelligence.' *Nature Neuroscience* (2003), **6**:316–22

107 Thompson, P.M., et al., 'Genetic influences on brain structure.' *Nature Neuroscience* (2001), **4**:1253–8

108 Deary, I.J., et al., 'Cognitive change and the APOE epsilon 4 allele.' *Nature* (2002), **418**:932

109 Whalley, L.J., and Deary, I.J., 'Longitudinal cohort study of childhood IQ and survival up to age 76.' *British Medical Journal* (2001), **322**:819

110 Bosworth, H.B., and Schaie, K.W., 'Survival effects in cognitive function, cognitive style, and sociodemographic variables in the Seattle Longitudinal Study.' *Experimental Aging Research* (1999), **25**:121–39

111 Rampon, C., et al., 'Effects of environmental enrichment on gene expression in the brain.' *Proceedings of the National Academy of Science USA* (2000), **97**:12880–4

112 Tang, Y.P., et al., 'Genetic enhancement of learning and memory in mice.' *Nature* (1999), **401**:63–9

113 Fritsch, T., et al., 'Effects of educational attainment on the clinical expression of Alzheimer's disease: results from a research registry.' *American Journal of Alzheimer's Disease and Other Dementias* (2001), **16**:369–76

114 Eves, A., and Gesch, B., 'Food provision and the nutritional implications of food choices made by young adult males, in a young offenders' institution.' *Journal of Human Nutrition and Diet* (2003), **16**:167–79

115 Scholey, A.B., and Kennedy, D.O., 'Acute, dose-dependent cognitive effects of Ginkgo biloba, Panax ginseng and their combination in healthy young volunteers: differential interactions with cognitive demand.' *Human Psychopharmacology* (2002), **17**:35–44

116 Spiegel, D., et al., 'Effect of psychosocial treatment on survival of patients with metastatic breast cancer.' *Lancet* (1989), **ii**:888–91

117 Fawzy, F.I., et al., 'Malignant melanoma: effects of an early structured psychiatric intervention, coping, and affective state on recurrence and survival 6 years later.' *Archives of General Psychiatry* (1993), **50**:681–9

118 Fawzy, F.I., Canada, A.L., Fawzy, N.W., 'Malignant melanoma: effects of a brief, structured psychiatric intervention on survival and

recurrence at 10-year follow-up.' *Archives of General Psychiatry* (2003), **60**:100–3

119 Ross, L., et al., 'Mind and cancer: does psychosocial intervention improve survival and psychological well-being?' *European Journal of Cancer* (2002), **38**:1447–57

120 Sternberg, R.J., Kaufman, J.C., Pretz, J.E., *The Creativity Conundrum: A Propulsion Model of Creative Contributions* (Philadelphia, PA, 2002)

121 Klein, G., *Sources of Power: How People Make Decisions* (MIT Press, Boston, 1988)

122 Pantages, E., and Dulac, C., 'A novel family of candidate pheromone receptors in mammals.' *Neuron* (2000), **28**:835–45

123 Wiseman, R., *The Luck Factor: Change your luck – and change your life* (Century, London, 2003)

124 Greyson, B., 'Biological aspects of near-death experiences.' *Perspectives in Biology and Medicine* (1998), **42**:14–32

Glossary

ACTH – AdrenoCorticoTrophic Hormone is made in the pituitary gland; from there it enters the bloodstream, sending a message to the adrenal glands. The adrenals then produce various hormones in response, in particular cortisol.

Adrenal glands – These glands in the vicinity of the kidney are essentially a collection of cells specialized to produce the hormones cortisol, adrenaline and noradrenaline. These substances are important in the response to stress – fear, excitement, anxiety of various types, and in particular the classic fight-or-flight response to attack by a predator.

Alzheimer's disease – Dementia more common in advanced age, often with a genetic component, affecting about 20 per cent of people over eighty but occasionally much younger people. Usually involves wasting of brain substance and changes in the brain proteins. Loss of memory is a prominent symptom, as is impairment of language and comprehension. Psychiatric changes are frequent.

Amygdala – An almond-shaped structure in the medial temporal lobe involved in a range of emotional functions, including the detection of significant events in the environment, fear-conditioning and enhancing storage of emotional memories. Via the hypothalamus, it can prompt release of stress hormones such as adrenaline into the bloodstream, giving a fright response and disrupting the control of rational thought. It is part of the so-called limbic system.

Anterior cingulate cortex – A region towards the front of the inside surface of the hemispheres. All its functions are not completely understood but it helps decision-making when the brain receives sensory stimuli that conflict, and it processes attention, concentration and pain perception. It is involved in controlling the autonomic nervous system. Morphine-like drugs decrease the activity in this region.

Autism – A condition characterized by lack of social awareness and failure to understand the emotions of others. Autistic children may be isolated, socially inept and aloof, and have narrowly focused interests.

Autonomic nervous system – This controls involuntary functions such as heart activity, digestion, blood-vessel constriction and relaxation, and sexual activity such as erection. It has two systems that work in opposition:

Sympathetic – speeds the pulse, constricts and dilates blood vessels, relaxes the bronchial tubing in the lung, reduces digestion. It is most active when stimulated by stress in response to the adrenals.

Parasympathetic – slows the pulse, increases gut motility, stimulates sexual arousal, increases salivation and constricts the pupils. It prepares the body to rest.

Axons – These are the long fibres of nerve cells (neurons). They can be thought of as the wiring of the nervous system.

Basal ganglia – A group of centres (or nuclei) in the centre of each hemisphere just above the midbrain. They play an important part in planning and coordinating movement and position of the body. They exert their influence over the networks that link the motor cortex to other cortical areas.

Brainstem – The part of the brain connecting its two cerebral hemispheres to the spinal cord. It is divided into three areas: midbrain, pons and medulla oblongata. It is the oldest part of the brain, where most basic, involuntary functions (such as breathing and control of heart rate) are regulated.

Broca's area – The area of the frontal lobe cortex – usually the left inferior frontal gyrus – described by Paul Broca as controlling speech.

Central nervous system – This is the 'controlling' part of the nervous system. It is covered by membranes called meninges. The brain, spinal cord and optic nerves are all part of the central nervous system. It is connected to the peripheral nervous system, which is made up of afferent nerves that carry sensory impulses from all parts of the body to the brain, and efferent nerves that take motor impulses to the muscles.

Cerebellum – This structure lies above the brainstem and behind the pons, and regulates balance and coordination of movements.

Cerebrospinal fluid – The watery fluid surrounding the brain and spinal cord. It contains glucose and proteins. It is derived from the bloodstream and is filtered by a membrane in the hollow structures inside the brain, the ventricles.

Cerebrum – The great bulk of the brain, divided into the two hemispheres, right and left, which are connected by the corpus callosum.

Cognition – The higher functions of the brain, which are often specifically human. They include: comprehension and speech, memory, problem solving, attention, calculation, and visual and auditory perception.

Coordination – Ordered, organized working of muscle groups or individual muscles to produce controlled movements.

Corpus callosum – The thick band connecting the two cerebral hemispheres.

Cortex – The outer layer of the cerebrum, which is rich in neurons and in which 'thinking' occurs. It normally has a layer of neurons about 4mm thick. But the word 'cortex' can be applied to the outer layer of many organs, including the ovaries and adrenal glands.

Corticotropin – See ACTH.

Cortisol – Hormone released by the adrenal glands during stress, but which is also necessary for the normal function of almost every part of the body. It regulates blood pressure, the use of sugars and proteins and causes break-down of muscle protein into amino acids which can be used as an emergency energy source.

Dementia – Serious progressive loss of intellectual function, often associated with a disease such as Alzheimer's, but there are many different causes. There may frequently be a personality change, preventing a sufferer from engaging in any normal activity.

Dendrite – The thin part of a nerve cell that transports newly received impulses into the neuron.

Electroencephalography (EEG) – The commonly used technique that records the electrical activity in the brain, mostly from the cortex.

Epilepsy – An epileptic attack is a fit (or seizure), often with loss of consciousness, or occasionally changed consciousness, which may only be perceived by somebody who knows the person well. Severe attacks cause violent movements. It is due to an electrical storm arising from a focal point in the brain. Mild attacks in the temporal lobe may cause hallucinations or 'religious' experiences.

Evoked potentials – These are electrical signals recorded (usually on EEG) from the brain or scalp in response to a stimulus.

Frontal lobes – The largest lobes of the human cerebral cortex. The front part (anterior) is associated with learning, behaviour and personality. The back part (posterior) is the motor cortex controlling voluntary movements.

Glia – The cells of the brain making up most of its bulk. There are five times more glial cells than neurons. They are of various types, helping brain repair, brain nutrition, maintenance of cerebrospinal fluid and construction of the fatty myelin sheath of neurons.

Grey matter – The part of the brain, such as the cortex, where neurons are concentrated.

Hemisphere – Half of the brain's cortex (left or right), which is divided into four main lobes: frontal, temporal, parietal and occipital.

Hippocampus – Part of the temporal lobe immediately behind the amygdala, involved with memory and learning. It is part of the limbic system. The name means 'sea horse' – a reflection of its shape.

Hypothalamus – a collection of centres (nuclei) beneath the thalamus and part of the limbic system, which, through the pituitary gland, regulate hormones in the body and help maintain the body's internal state: for example, temperature control, food intake and heart activity.

Lateral geniculate nucleus – Part of the thalamus involved in processing visual stimuli and passing them to the cortex.

Limbic system – Structures forming around the border of the brainstem which are derived from a more primitive part of the cortex and are associated with learning, memory and emotional processing. The system includes the amygdala, the hypothalamus, part of the thalamus and the cingulate gyrus. Its utility as a concept is now hotly debated, because the range of functions it seems to undertake are done by independent sub-units of the system, and also by areas of the brain not originally thought part of the limbic system.

Magnetoencephalography (MEG) – Maps and localizes brain activity by recording magnetic fields produced by active neurons in response to stimulation. Magnetic fields are not distorted by passing through the scalp or skull, so it has advantages over EEG.

Medulla oblongata – Lower part of the brainstem which controls automatic functions and acts as a relay between the brain and the spinal cord.

Memory – Now considered as divided into a variety of types. Memory can be remote or episodic, such as long-time-past events from, say, childhood. Working memory allows you to recall events from a short time previously, such as whether the kettle is switched on. Prospective memory is the ability to remember a planned commitment. Procedural memory is associated with learnt motor skills and does not require intentional recollection – such as knowing how to ride a bike.

MRI/Magnetic Resonance Imaging – or nuclear magnetic resonance – is a method of imaging parts of the body using the magnetic properties of individual tissue types to build up a three-dimensional view. Functional magnetic resonance imaging (fMRI) allows the observer to see how the brain is metabolizing and can thus build up a picture showing what part of the brain is active during a given task.

Myelin – The fatty sheath that forms around axons and acts as a kind of insulator. Myelin greatly increases the speed at which nervous impulses can be sent.

Nerve fibres – These are axons that extend from the main body of the neuron and carry impulses to the nerve cell (afferent) or away from it (efferent).

Neuron – The individual nerve cell containing axons and dendrites and connecting with other neurons by synapses.

Neurotransmitters – Chemicals stored at the end of the axons in the synapses. When an electrical impulse reaches the synapse, neurotransmitters are released and cross the gap of the synapse. This initiates a message to the neighbouring neuron or cell, such as a muscle cell. There are around fifty different neurotransmitters, which may excite or inhibit transmission of an impulse. They include glutamate, GABA, acetylcholine, adrenaline and noradrenaline, dopamine, serotonin. Each of these transmitters has a different function.

Nucleus accumbens – Contains neurons that are part of the basal ganglia. It plays a role in regulating movement and complex motor activity. This structure is thought to be 'the reward centre of the brain' and an important neurotransmitter in its function is dopamine.

Optic nerve – The nerve that extends from the back of the eye – the retina – connecting it to the brain.

Paralysis – Inability to move a part of the body.

Peripheral nervous system – The nerves outside the central nervous system which run through the body to and from organs such as skin, muscles, joints.

PET – Positron Emission Tomography: a scanning technique using radioisotopes, such as radioactive oxygen, to identify blood flow or metabolically active brain areas.

Pituitary gland – The master gland at the base of the brain, connected to the hypothalamus, which controls other glands in the body, such as the adrenals, pancreas, thyroid, ovaries and testes.

Placebo – A sham or neutral treatment, often in practice a drug, which is inert and has no activity and therefore no intrinsic scientific value in improving or changing the medical condition. Because a person may expect to feel better after any treatment, placebo treatment may lead them to feel better and to have fewer symptoms from an ailment.

Pons – Part of the brainstem controlling respiration, and which is associated with arousal and sleep. It helps in control of the autonomic nervous system and is a relay centre between the cortex and cerebellum.

Proprioception – Awareness of position and movement in space.

Proteins – Compounds made up of amino acids that are responsible for all functions of cells. Proteins are produced as a result of the message produced by the DNA.

Pulvinar – Part of the thalamus involved in processing visual information.

Purkinje cell – A giant neuron with massively branching dendrites making many (perhaps up to 200,000) connections to other neurons. This cell is mostly found in the cerebellum.

Sensory cortex – Network of neurons (many of which are located in the parietal lobe) responsible for processing of sensations, including pain, smell, taste, temperature, vision, hearing, touch and proprioception.

Synapse – The gap connecting neurons to each other, controlled by the production of neurotransmitters. A typical neuron may have 10,000 such connections to other neurons.

Thalamus – The centre above the brainstem that acts as a relay station between cortex and sensory organs (e.g., retina, skin, inner ear) with the exception of some olfaction. It has many other functions, which include an influence on mood and some body movements.

Turner's syndrome – Loss of one of the paired X chromosomes in girls, occurring when the embryo is formed. It results in infertility, absent periods, short stature and cognitive changes.

Vagus nerve – The nerve which, among other functions, controls heart rate by carrying most of the parasympathetic signals from the brain to the body. When stimulated it slows the heart. It is a long nerve and is called a 'cranial nerve' because it is directly connected into the brain, in the region of the brainstem.

Ventricles – The four cavities in the brain containing cerebrospinal fluid.

White matter – The myelinated neuronal fibres and supporting glial cells making up much of the central nervous system.

Index